T0246438

Norway

LISA STENTVEDT

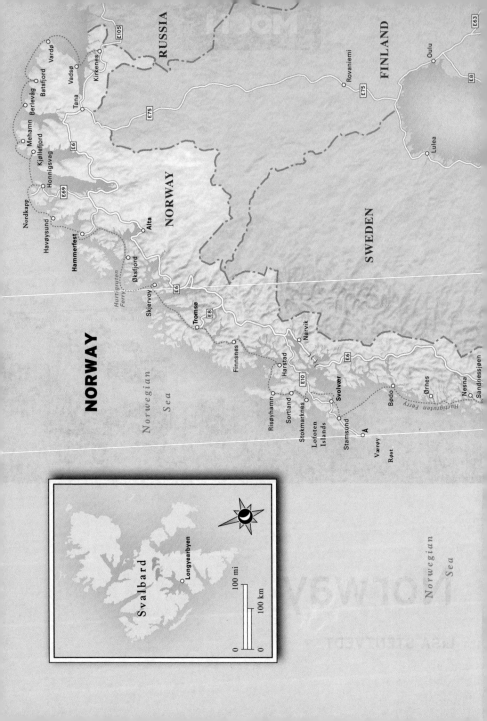

NORWAY

RUSSIA

FINLAND

SWEDEN

NORWAY

Norwegian Sea

Svalbard

Longyearbyen

Norwegian Sea

100 mi

100 km

© MOON.COM

E75 E12 E18

Turku

Mariehamn

E8

Vaasa

*Gulf of
Bothnia*

Baltic Sea

Visby **Visby**

STOCKHOLM

Uppsala

Gavle E18

Umea Nykoping

E4 Vasteras

Linkoping

Falun Orebro

E4 Jonkoping

Ostersund **SWEDEN** E4

Karlstad

E14 E18

E45 Gothenburg

Hamar E6 Moss E6

Trondheim OSLO Fredrikstad

Steinkjer Lillehammer Drammen Porsgrunn E18

Brønnøysund Molde Arendal **Kristiansand**

Rørvik E6 **NORWAY**

Kristiansund E16

E6 **Bergen** Flekkefjord

E39 E18 **Stavanger**

Ålesund Haugesund

Måløy Florø

Sognefjorden

Hurtigruten Ferry

DENMARK

*SEE
"CENTRAL AND
SOUTHERN NORWAY"
MAP*

North Sea

250 mi

250 km

0

0

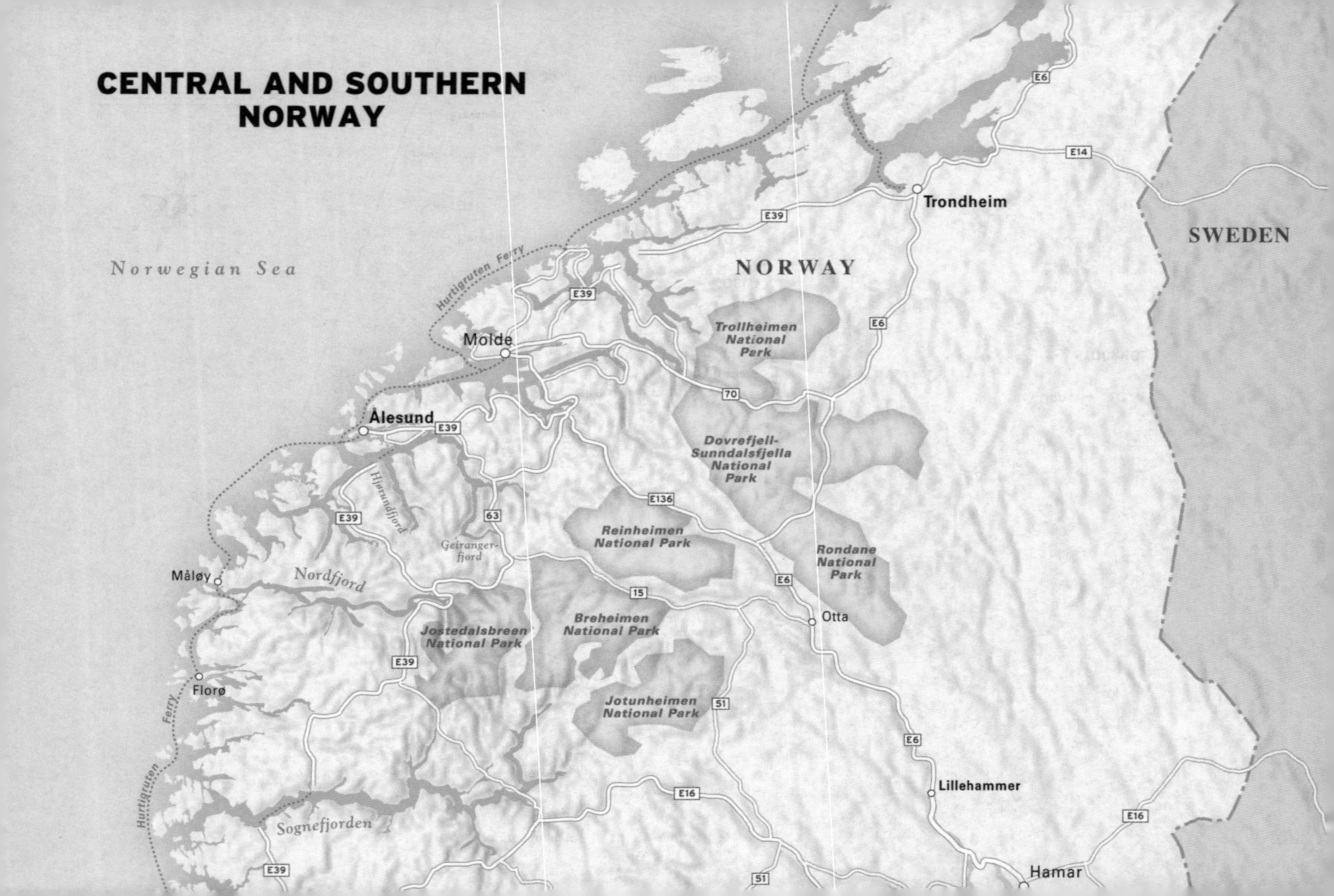

CENTRAL AND SOUTHERN NORWAY

SWEDEN

NORWAY

Norwegian Sea

Trondheim

Molde

Ålesund

Måløy

Florø

E6

E14

E39

E6

70

E136

E39

E39

E39

63

15

51

E6

E6

51

E16

E16

E39

E39

Hamar

Lillehammer

Otta

Trollheimen
National
Park

Dovrefjell-
Sunndalsfjella
National
Park

Rondane
National
Park

Reinheimen
National Park

Breheimen
National Park

Jotunheimen
National
Park

Jostedalsbreen
National Park

Geiranger-
fjord

Hjørundfjord

Nordfjord

Sognefjorden

Hurtigruten ferry

Ferry

Hurtigruten

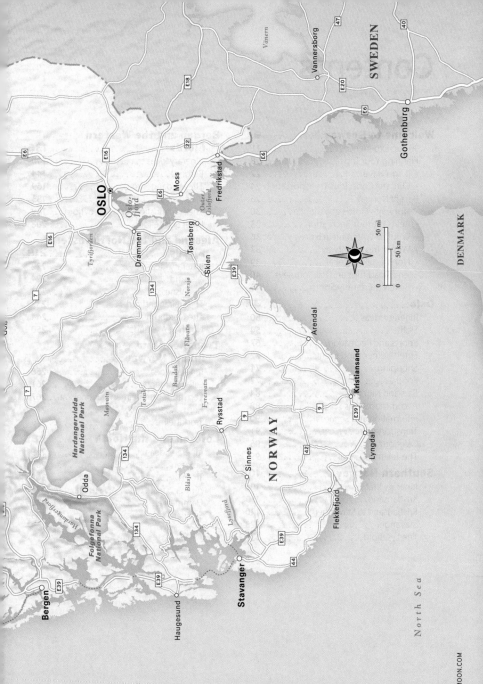

Contents

Borgund Stave Church

WELCOME TO

Norway

Majestic mountains, breathtaking fjords, the northern lights dancing across the dark winter sky, and the Viking era may come to mind. But no preconceived ideas can fully prepare you for a trip to Norway. In fact, visitors' most common reaction to the landscape is, "I've never seen anything like this."

Norwegian scenery is almost unreal, particularly the western fjords, where steep mountains tower above shocking blue waters, and tiny villages and abandoned farmhouses are scattered across valleys you'd think would be impossible to reach. This wondrous landscape will make you feel quite small, and truly inspired.

The natural beauty of Norway draws visitors to return again and again. Add the spectacular northern lights in the winter and the midnight sun in the summer, and you'll find that the country is a year-round destination, depending on what type of adventure you prefer.

Ease of access to nature also sets Norway apart. Even when you are in culturally rich cities such as Oslo or Bergen, you can head outside and simply start walking, and you will soon find yourself surrounded by forest or on a mountaintop. Sail through the UNESCO-listed Nærøyfjord on a fully accessible (and electric) vessel, start a hike right at your doorstep, or marvel at the serenity of waking up in a village with less than 200 inhabitants. Although Norway has become an increasingly popular destination for international travelers, there is something truly untouched and unspoiled about this stunning place.

Trolltunga

10 TOP
EXPERIENCES

1 Hiking **Pulpit Rock** (page 132) and **Trolltunga** (page 176), two of Norway's most famous hikes and photo ops.

2 Feeling time slow down in quaint fjord villages such as **Lofthus** (page 174),
Undredal (page 206), and **Geiranger** (page 237), picturesquely nestled along
the fjords and surrounded by mountains and waterfalls.

3 Road-tripping the **Lofoten Isles,** caught in the dramatic landscape of northern
Norway, where you can stop to join the Arctic Surfers, learn about Norwegian
fishing culture, and stay in a traditional rorbu (fisherman's cabin) (page 294).

4 Going on a fjord cruise through the UNESCO World Heritage-listed western fjords: the **Geirangerfjord** (page 240) and the **Nærøyfjord** (page 192).

5 Seeing the **northern lights** flickering over the snowy mountaintops of northern Norway, or through the transparent ceiling of a canvas dome (page 316).

6 Learning about Norway's Viking heritage at **Njardarheimr** (page 202).

7 Admiring the work of Gustav Vigeland in Oslo's Frogner Park, which includes the **Vigeland Sculpture Park** (Vigelandsparken), the largest sculpture park in the world created by one artist (page 63).

8 Strolling through Bergen, starting with picture-perfect **Bryggen,** the city's historic wharf (page 146).

9 Experiencing and learning about **Sami culture** through Sami-run companies and activities in Røros, Alta, and Tromsø (page 314).

10 Exploring the Gothic **Nidaros Cathedral** in Trondheim, where the kings and queens of Norway are crowned and Norway's patron saint, Olav, is buried (page 276).

Planning Your Trip

WHERE TO GO

Oslo

Most visitors to Norway will visit the capital by default, after flying into the Oslo Airport. Fortunately, the city has a lot to offer, from world-class museums to a thriving restaurant scene. Visit the neoclassical **Royal Palace,** meet the many sculptures of **Vigeland Sculpture Park,** see *The Scream* and more at the **Munch Museum,** learn about the Nobel legacy at the **Nobel Peace Center,** and enjoy cross-country skiing just outside the city near the **Holmenkollen Ski Arena.** Then pop into chic shops for Scandinavian design pieces and grab a drink in one of the city's sophisticated bars to get a feel for this beautiful Norwegian city. Those who choose to linger in the city can also take advantage of a number of day trips, to see glassblowing up close at the historic **Hadeland Glassverk,** visit some of the islands in the scenic Oslofjord, and beyond.

Southern Norway

The coastline southwest of Oslo is a popular summer destination among Norwegians, especially cute-as-a-button **Kristiansand.** You'll see locals arriving by boat at the city dock to grab dinner at one of the seafood restaurants along the boardwalk. Continuing west along the coast, there are a number of unique small towns and attractions, including **Lindesnes Lighthouse,** the southernmost point on the mainland of Norway. Situated on the southwestern corner of Norway, **Stavanger** is a beautiful city, rich in history. Take your time wandering the **Fargegaten,** an incredibly colorful street in the center of the city. The nearby **Lysefjord** is one of the biggest draws

Vigelandsparken

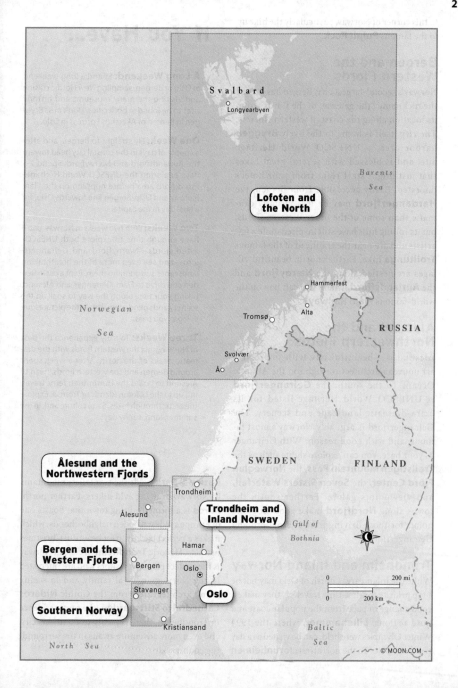

Svalbard
Longyearbyen

Barents
Sea

Lofoten and
the North

Hammerfest

Norwegian
Sea

Tromsø
Alta

RUSSIA

Svolvær

Å

SWEDEN   FINLAND

Ålesund and the
Northwestern Fjords

Trondheim

Ålesund

Trondheim and
Inland Norway

Gulf of
Bothnia

Hamar

Bergen and the
Western Fjords

Bergen

Oslo

Oslo

Stavanger

0   200 mi

Southern Norway

0   200 km

Kristiansand

North Sea

Baltic
Sea

© MOON.COM

22

to this corner of Norway, particularly the hike up to the famous **Pulpit Rock.**

Bergen and the Western Fjords

Norway's second-largest city, Bergen has earned the nickname "the gateway to the fjords" from its location along the coast of western Norway. The city itself is home to the lively **Bryggen** harbor area, a UNESCO World Heritage Site, and is blessed with several great hikes that just might start right from your hotel's doorstep. Easily accessible from Bergen, the **Hardangerfjord** may be less visually dramatic than some of the other Western fjords, but its rolling hills have still inspired quite a few artists and are near the trailhead of the famous **Trolltunga** hike. Farther north, beautiful villages are nestled along the **Nærøyfjord** and the **Aurlandsfjord,** where you can hop on the world-famous **Flåm Railway.**

Ålesund and the Northwestern Fjords

Ålesund is a beautiful city with impressive art nouveau architecture right on the Atlantic Ocean. To the south, the **Geirangerfjord** is UNESCO World Heritage-listed for its extra-dramatic landscape and scenery. The Geirangerfjord is arguably Norway's most famous, and with good reason: With Geiranger as your base, you can explore sights such as the **Trollstigen Mountain Pass,** the **Norwegian Fjord Center,** the **Seven Sisters Waterfall,** and viewpoints galore. Farther south, the towns along **Nordfjord** make good stopping points for those driving from Næroyfjord and Geirangerfjord.

Trondheim and Inland Norway

While the inland areas north of Oslo may not be a top priority for first-time travelers, they make a good change of pace from the popular coast and fjord regions. **Lillehammer,** where the 1994 Winter Olympics were held, can be visited as a day trip from Oslo. To the northwest, **Jotunheimen**

If You Have...

- **A Long Weekend:** Spend a long weekend in Oslo or Bergen, sampling New Nordic cuisine and visiting the many museums and historic sites to be found in both cities. Don't miss Bryggen in Bergen or Akershus Fortress in Oslo.

- **One Week:** Fly straight to Bergen, and after a couple of days in the coastal city head toward the Aurlandsfjord and Nærøyfjord. Spend 2-3 days exploring the UNESCO World Heritage-listed fjord area before hopping on the Flåm Railway and Oslo-Bergen line towards Oslo, for a final day in the capital.

- **Two Weeks:** With two weeks in Norway, you'll have enough time to explore both UNESCO-listed fjords—Næroyfjord and Geirangerfjord—and see even more of the breathtaking landscapes surrounding them. Rent a car in Bergen and drive to Flåm, Geiranger, and Ålesund, taking your time along the way to soak up the scenery and spend a few days in the picturesque villages you pass.

- **Three Weeks:** To truly experience the best of Norway, mix the western fjords with the dramatic peaks of the north. After a week spent around Bergen and the western fjords, head to Ålesund to board the Hurtigruten ferry, traveling up to the Lofoten islands or Tromsø. Explore the arctic through hikes, Sami culture and, in the summer, long, sunny days.

National Park holds the two tallest mountains in Norway, drawing avid hikers. Farther north, **Røros** is a former mining town that boasts one of Europe's oldest wooden neighborhoods, which makes a perfect backdrop for beautiful Christmas markets. Historic **Trondheim** in central Norway is the perfect place for visitors who are interested in the Norwegian royal family and in seeing grand architecture. From the Gothic **Nidaros Cathedral** to **Stiftsgården** (the royal residence in Trondheim), there is plenty to do in this city, and even more adventure awaits in the surrounding countryside.

Lofoten and the North

The beautiful Lofoten Isles offer one of the world's best road trips, with their dramatic scenery, breathtaking hikes, and impressive beaches. If you're heading farther north, **Tromsø** is the perfect place to experience northern Norway in all its glory—from dog-sledding to whale-watching—and a good jumping-off point for **northern lights** chasers. **Alta** is also a destination that is not to be missed, where you can learn about Sami culture and the arctic way of life.

WHEN TO GO

High Seasons

The high season for visiting most of Norway stretches from May to September, with June-August being the busiest months. However, in northern Norway, where winter tourism is the big focus, the high season is December-March. A general rule of thumb to keep in mind is that if you want to see the beauty of southern Norway (the fjords), you should aim to visit in the warmer months, while if you are after the northern lights and snow-covered landscapes, the winter months in northern Norway is your best bet.

Spring

Spring in Norway doesn't really kick in until April, with May being considered a part of the high season in the more tourist-dense areas. If you want to beat the crowds, but still catch Norway's scenery at its most beautiful, **late spring** is a great time to visit.

Summer

Summer is the main tourist season in Norway, and when the country is at its most beautiful. This is also when **fjords** and popular hikes are most accessible, with longer opening hours for most attractions, and fewer road closures due to snow. This is also the **busiest season,** and areas such as Oslo, Flåm, and Geiranger are bustling with visitors from all over the world. In the north, visitors can experience the **midnight sun,** when the sky stays light for 24 hours.

Trondheim

Fall

I always say that **September** is the best time of year to visit Norway, as the crowds are starting to die down, but opening hours are still at their peak (plus, it is a beautiful time of year). During the months of October and November it gets colder and the fall storms start swooping in, especially in the west and north of Norway.

Winter

In the south of Norway (Oslo, Bergen, the fjord region) winter is the low season, with very limited opening hours for most attractions, and not as much choice when it comes to public transportation. However, this is when northern Norway wakes up: Wintertime in the north is beautiful, and the chances of seeing whales or the **northern lights** are at their highest during this season.

BEFORE YOU GO

Passports and Visas

Norway is a part of the European Schengen Agreement, which allows passport-free travel between participating countries. So travelers (even citizens of non-Schengen countries) entering Norway from any other Schengen country may enter Norway without a passport. Your passport will be checked as you enter the Schengen area, so if Norway is your first stop, expect to show it upon arrival. When visiting Norway as a tourist you may stay in the country for 90 days. Travelers from the United States, Canada, the UK, and Australia do not need a visa to enter Norway. Travelers from South Africa need to apply for a tourist visa online in order to enter.

There are currently no vaccination requirements to visit Norway.

What to Pack

The absolute key to packing for Norway is layers, regardless of whether you are traveling in

Climate-Conscious Transportation

Norway is invested in the environment and sustainability, which will come as no surprise when you see the epic landscapes the Norwegians call home. So, sustainable and environmentally friendly ways to travel have become increasingly important and the country has passed a number of laws to minimize the impact of tourism. For example, the Norwegian Maritime Authority and the Norwegian tourism industry are currently working toward a goal of having zero emissions from cruise ships coming to the World Heritage fjords by 2026.

Even before then, it is possible for travelers to explore parts of Norway in a low-emission way. Here are a few of Norway's greener modes of getting around:

- **In Oslo and Bergen:** Oslo city buses, Bergen local buses, and the Bergen Light Rail Bybanen are all fully electric.
- **Flåm Railway:** This historic train has been run by electricity since 1944.
- *Future of the Fjords:* This award-winning ship is the world's first fully electric vessel made of carbon-fiber, and you can travel on it through the Aurlandsfjord and the UNESCO-listed Nærøyfjord.

the summer or the winter. Always assume that there may be sudden weather changes during your trip, and pack accordingly. You will want to be able to put on or remove as many layers as necessary. Wool is key for winter trips, and most Norwegians swear by a wool base layer under their outdoor clothing, whether they are hiking in the fall or skiing in the winter.

Electrical plugs in Norway are the same as the rest of Europe, with two round pins. Bring a plug adapter to charge your devices.

TRANSPORTATION

Most international flights to Norway will arrive in either Oslo or Bergen, the two largest cities. The smaller airports found around the country (Tromsø, Trondheim, Kristiansand, for example) all connect to those two. Most likely, unless you are traveling up north, you will arrive by air and then stay on the ground for the duration of your visit. Trains link Oslo with Bergen—on the highly recommended and scenic Oslo-Bergen railway—and with towns in eastern Norway up to Trondheim. The Aurlandsfjord and Nærøyfjord region can be visited without a car, but to visit most of the western fjords and the northern regions, you should rent a car or use regional and local buses.

taking the train from Flåm

BEST OF
Norway

Norway is a large country, and enjoying many of its attractions is dependent on the weather or time of year. It is practically impossible to cross off all bucket-list destinations and top experiences in one trip. The two-week itinerary below is best experienced in April-September, when the weather in southern Norway is most beautiful, hiking conditions are favorable, and opening hours are longer. However, at this time of year, it's usually too bright at night to see the northern lights.

In order to explore the north and the south in the same trip, you'll need to fly between the regions and rent a car at different points.

Southern Norway

If you only have 7 days in Norway, I recommend following the first 7 days of this itinerary without the add-on days, and flying home from Bergen on Day 7. This entire leg of the trip does not require a car.

If you have a little more time (around 10 days), you can either continue along the itinerary to Stavanger, Pulpit Rock, and the Lysefjord, or follow this itinerary until Day 5, then opt for the add-on days to go north toward Geiranger before heading to Bergen. You'll need a car for parts of this longer trip.

Days 1-2: The Best of Oslo
WHERE TO STAY: NEAR OSLO CENTRAL STATION

On the first day, start your morning with a self-guided walking tour of the main sights in Oslo's city center: the **Oslo Cathedral,** the Norwegian Parliament **Stortinget,** the **Royal Palace,** and **city hall.** Once you have passed city hall, head to the **Nobel Peace Center** before having lunch along the docks at **Aker Brygge.** Afterwards, head to **Akershus Fortress** to explore some of the city's military and medieval history.

The next morning, take the subway (T-banen)

to the Majorstua stop, and walk 5-10 minutes to **Vigelandsparken,** Vigeland Sculpture Park, the largest sculpture park in the world made by just one artist. If you have time afterwards, visit the **Vigeland Museum** to learn more about sculptor Gustav Vigeland.

Days 3-5: Scenic Train Rides, Fjords, and Views for Days
WHERE TO STAY: FLÅM

After breakfast, it's time to head out of the big city in the most scenic way. Get on the **Oslo-Bergen Line** (Bergensbana) for an epic train ride to **Myrdal.** The journey from Oslo to Myrdal takes 5 hours. There, change trains for the **Flåm Railway** to Flåm (1 hour), and enjoy the stunning landscape of the Flåm Valley along the way.

The next morning, head out on a **fjord cruise** through the **Aurlandsfjord** and the **Nærøyfjord.** The landscape of the latter is what put the Norwegian fjords on the UNESCO World Heritage List. After 1.5 hours of sailing, the cruise ends in Gudvangen, home to **Njardarheimr Viking Village.** Spend some time in the village, meeting Vikings and joining one of their guided tours. When you get hungry, have lunch in Gudvangen. After your day with the Vikings, get on the shuttle bus back to Flåm (20 minutes), and have dinner at the Viking-inspired brewpub **Ægir.**

Start your third day in the region by heading to the **Stegastein Viewpoint** in Aurland, for a bird's-eye view of the fjord landscape you sailed through yesterday. A round-trip tour leaves Flåm several times a day. Afterwards, put your hiking shoes on and head to **Brekkefossen** waterfall (2 hours round-trip). After your hike, make sure you have booked 1.5-2 hours in the **FjordSauna,** a floating sauna at the end of the Aurlandsfjord. It is the perfect way to soothe your muscles after a hike and gives you the chance to swim in the (cold) fjord, only to warm up inside the sauna seconds after.

Oslo Cathedral

Optional Days 1-2: North to Geiranger
WHERE TO STAY: GEIRANGER

Driving Distance and Time: 281 kilometers (175 mi), 6.5 hours

Rent a car in Flåm and drive north to the Geirangerfjord region. On the way, stop in Loen to ride the **Loen Skylift,** which offers views of Nordfjord. Have lunch at the restaurant at the top before continuing on to the village of Geiranger.

On the first full day visiting the Geirangerfjord, drive or hike up to **Westerås farm.** The trailhead for the hike up there (mainly Sherpa steps,

hiking around Geiranger

45 minutes) starts from just behind the Hotel Union. At the farm, refill your water bottle (there is a stream with a tap in the corner of the parking lot) and hike up to **Storseterfossen waterfall** (strenuous, about 1 hour each way), where you can walk behind the waterfall. Head back into Geiranger town to have lunch and explore the shops around the village.

Optional Day 3: Geirangerfjord
WHERE TO STAY: FLÅM
Driving Distance and Time: 260 kilometers (161 mi), 4.5 hours

Enjoy your last breakfast overlooking Geiranger before driving the 3-4 minutes down to the fjord and boarding the morning ferry from Geiranger to Hellesylt (with your car). Sail through the UNESCO World Heritage-listed **Geirangerfjord,** seeing the famous **Seven Sisters** and **Suitor** waterfalls along the way. From Hellesylt, drive back to Flåm. On the way, stop in **Fjærland,** on the north side of the Sognefjord, to walk the 5-minute trail from the road and see the **Bøyabreen** glacier. Return your rental car when you get back to Flåm.

Day 6: Bergen
WHERE TO STAY: BERGEN CITY CENTER
Get on an early morning bus to **Bergen** (about 3.5 hours), Norway's second-largest city. Spend

Stavanger's colorful Fargegaten street

the afternoon strolling around Bergen's famous **Bryggen** area, before heading up **Mount Fløyen** for some epic views of the city. Get there by hiking (approximately 40 minutes uphill) or by taking the **funicular.**

Day 7: Bergen to Stavanger
WHERE TO STAY: STAVANGER CITY CENTER
Driving Distance and Time: 207 kilometers (129 mi), 5 hours

Spend your morning in Bergen, exploring the **KODE Museums,** or if you are traveling with children, the **Bergen Aquarium**. Head to **Troldhaugen** to learn more about composer Edvard Grieg in his home. On selected days the site hosts lunch concerts, and it is worth staying for lunch if you visit on one of those days. Afterward, rent a car and spend the late afternoon and evening driving to **Stavanger.**

Day 8: Stavanger
WHERE TO STAY: PREIKESTOLEN BASECAMP
Driving Distance and Time: 39 kilometers (25 mi), 45 minutes

After breakfast, explore the beautiful **Stavanger Old Town** before heading over to **Fargegaten** for lunch. In the afternoon, visit one of Stavanger's museums, or the **Viking House** AR experience. In the evening, drive to **Preikestolen Basecamp** to spend the night, so you'll be ready for an early start the next day.

Day 9: Hiking Pulpit Rock
WHERE TO STAY: STAVANGER
Driving Distance and Time: 39 kilometers (25 mi), 45 minutes

Wake up early and pack a lunch from the breakfast at Preikestolen Basecamp. Start your hike up to **Pulpit Rock** as early as you can to avoid the crowds. The hike will take you around 2 hours each way. Spend some time and enjoy your lunch at the top of this impressive mountain plateau and overlooking the dramatic **Lysefjord** below. After you have made it back down to your car, drive back into Stavanger to stay the night before catching a flight home or up north the next day. Consider staying at an airport hotel if you have an early flight.

Northern Norway

A spring or summer trip to northern Norway centers on a road trip through the Lofoten isles. You will need a car for this leg of the trip.

Day 10: Lofoten
WHERE TO STAY: SVOLVÆR

Fly to Svolvær airport or Harstad-Narvik airport (stopovers are needed from Stavanger) and pick up a rental car for your **Lofoten road trip.** Spend the remainder of the day exploring Svolvær and the city's galleries.

Day 11: Svolvær to Vestvågøy
WHERE TO STAY: BALLSTAD

Driving Distance and Time: *78 kilometers (48 mi), 1 hour and 15 minutes*

On this day, make the drive from Svolvær to the island of Vestvågøy. On the way, make a stop in **Henningsvær** to get a feel of a real Norwegian fishing village, and visit some of the local galleries there. Make sure to visit the **Lofotr Viking Museum** Vestvågøy, before heading to **Ballstad** for the night.

Day 12: The End of the Road
WHERE TO STAY: REINE

Driving Distance and Time: *69 kilometers (43 miles), 1 hour and 25 minutes*

Drive from Ballstad to Moskenesøy island and the literal end of the road in **Å.** Explore the fisheries museum there, and be sure to try the Lofoten specialty torrfisk (stockfish, dried and salted cod) at some point. Heading back to **Reine** to spend the night in the traditional Norwegian fishermen's cabins there. On the way, stop to view the beaches at **Flakstadøy** and consider a detour to the beautiful village of **Nusfjord.**

Pulpit Rock

Day 13: North to Tromsø
WHERE TO STAY: TROMSØ CITY CENTER

Driving Distance and Time: *284 kilometers (176 mi), 4.5 hours*

Drive all the way back across the Lofoten isles to the Harstad-Narvik Airport to drop off your rental car and catch an afternoon flight to Tromsø (one stopover needed).

Day 14: Tromsø

After a lush hotel breakfast, head out to explore the city. Make sure to visit the **Perspective Museum** and to stroll along the Tromsø Island to the **Tromsø University Museum.** After lunch, consider a trip to **Polaria** before catching an evening flight back to Oslo. It is recommended to have 1 night in Oslo before flying out of Norway, to prevent any delays affecting your flight home.

Norway's Fjords at a Glance

Lysefjord

The Norwegian fjords are the country's main draw for visitors. A fjord is an inlet of water, carved thousands of years ago by glaciers during the several ice ages in northern Europe. The glacier would bulldoze its way through the mountainous landscape, creating narrow valleys that eventually extended below sea level. As the glacier melted and retracted, the ocean flowed in and filled these valleys, creating the water-filled fjords. While they are found all around the country, it is in western Norway (north of Bergen and south of Ålesund) where the most dramatic and spectacular fjords are located.

Today, the fjords are impressive sights, with dark blue water surrounded by massive mountains towering above. Norwegians have lived by the fjords for centuries, and it is believed that they settled in these (now) rural areas to benefit from their easy connection to the ocean. The Vikings especially appreciated the land around the fjords, because not only could they access the ocean through the fjord arms, but also they had a clear view of any enemy boats coming to their villages.

Fjord	Why Go	Access From	How Long to Stay	Where to Stay
Oslofjord page 95	Though it is not considered as dramatic as the fjords farther west, the Oslofjord makes for a nice day trip from Oslo.	Oslo (1.5 hours to Drøbak by ferry) One great spot to get a good view of the Oslofjord and bay is from the top of the Oslo Opera House.	1 day	Oslo
Lysefjord page 131	The number one reason to go is to hike the famous Pulpit Rock or Kjerag.	Stavanger (45 minutes by car or 3–5-hour boat excursions)	1 day per hike, or a day trip from Stavanger (by boat)	Stavanger, Preikestolen Basecamp (for Pulpit Rock), Lysebotn (for Kjerag)

Fjord	Why Go	Access From	How Long to Stay	Where to Stay
Hardangerfjord page 169	A landscape of rolling green hills connecting the fjords with the mountains above it and known for its local cider production, the Hardangerfjord is the perfect fjord to visit if you are based in Bergen and limited on time.	Bergen (1.5 hours by car or bus to the south side of the fjord) Voss (1.5 hours by car or bus to the north side of the fjord)	1-2 days	Norheimsund, Odda, Lofthus
Aurlandsfjord and Nærøyfjord page 189	The Nærøyfjord is perhaps the most spectacular fjord in Norway. Paired with the charming villages lining the Aurlandsfjord, and its proximity to a major city and airport (Bergen), the area is perfect for first-time visitors.	Bergen (3 hours by car or 5-hour boat tour)	2-3 days	Flåm, Aurland, Gudvangen, Undredal
Nordfjord page 244	Its location makes Nordfjord a natural stop along the way for those traveling between the Nærøyfjord and the Geirangerfjord. Stop here to reach a mountaintop without hiking, and to see the glacier arms Kjenndalsbreen and Briksdalsbreen.	Ålesund (2.5 hours by car)	1-2 days	Stryn, Loen, Olden
Geirangerfjord page 237	The Geirangerfjord is perhaps the most unspoiled fjord in Norway and can only be seen fully by boat. Be sure to take a fjord cruise, a RIB excursion, or kayak tour from the village of Geiranger.	Ålesund (2.5 hours by car or 5-hour fjord cruise)	1-2 days	Geiranger

Best Outdoor Recreation

Norway is a haven for outdoor enthusiasts, with natural wonders at your doorstep regardless of where you are. The accessibility of nature in Norway is perhaps what makes the country stand out most. You never have to walk far to find yourself surrounded by forest, mountains, or water.

Hiking

Hiking is the best way to experience nature in Norway and can almost be considered the national sport of the Norwegian population. On weekends you will always find Norwegians out hiking or walking in nature. You'll find a variety of hikes and walks across the country, suitable for most skill and fitness levels.

Pulpit Rock
LYSEFJORD, SOUTHERN NORWAY
8.2 kilometers (5 mi) round-trip, 4-5 hours, moderate
This spectacular rock formation offers views of the Lysefjord below, and the hike itself is surprisingly easy for such an epic view and end point.

Trolltunga
HARDANGERFJORD, BERGEN AND THE WESTERN FJORDS
20 kilometers (12.5 mi) round-trip, 7-10 hours, strenuous
Those wanting a strenuous, full-day hike are in for a treat with Trolltunga, or the Troll's Tongue. The rock stretches out over the water below like a tongue, giving you the perfect photo op.

Aurlandsdalen Valley
AURLANDSFJORD, BERGEN AND THE WESTERN FJORDS
20 kilometers (12.5 mi) one-way, 6-8 hours, strenuous
Aurlandsdalen has been nicknamed Norway's Grand Canyon. This mostly downhill full-day hike through the lush Aurland Valley takes you from mountain to fjord.

Reinebringen
REINE, LOFOTEN AND THE NORTH
2.7 kilometers (1.7 mi) one-way, 2.5 hours, strenuous
From the top of this mountain, you will get views of all the islands surrounding the town of Reine, and the jagged mountaintops of Lofoten.

Fløyen
BERGEN
3 kilometers (1.9 mi) one-way, 45 minutes, moderate
The seven mountains surrounding Bergen offer hikers of all fitness levels and abilities an opportunity to explore the great outdoors. The hike up to Fløyen is a relatively easy way to get a great view of the city. You can even reach it without hiking by riding the funicular.

Kayaking

With so many beautiful lakes and stunning fjords, kayaking is a great way to get close to nature and explore Norway. It is possible to find a kayak rental in most fjord destinations, or join a guided kayak tour.

Nærøyfjord
BERGEN AND THE WESTERN FJORDS
On a kayak trip through the Nærøyfjord from Flåm, you will glide past tiny fjord villages and remnants of Viking graves beneath mountains that make you feel tiny.

Lovatnet (Lake Loen)
ÅLESUND AND THE NORTHWESTERN FJORDS
The serene glacial lake Lovatnet (Lake Loen) is

1: view from Reinebringen overlooking Reine and Hamnøy, in the Lofoten islands 2: walking on Jostedalsbreen Glacier known for its distinct green color, a result of the glacier arm nearby that fills it with melted water. Kayakers shouldn't miss one of the most picturesque lakes in Norway.

Geirangerfjord
ÅLESUND AND THE NORTHWESTERN FJORDS
When visiting the village of Geiranger, consider joining a guided kayaking tour through the Geirangerfjord to get close to famous Seven Sisters and Suitor waterfalls, which can only be reached by boat.

Bicycling
With such a breathtaking landscape to explore, experiencing Norway on two wheels is special. There are several areas where travelers can (and should) rent a bicycle for a more active vacation.

Rallarvegen
BERGEN AND THE WESTERN FJORDS
The most famous cycling route in Norway is Rallarvegen, which goes from Finse (the Oslo-Bergen line stops there, and you can bring your bicycle on the train) all the way down to Flåm and the fjord through the lush Flåm Valley.

Trollstigen
ÅLESUND AND THE NORTHWESTERN FJORDS
One of the most dramatic roads in Norway is Trollstigen, which stretches between Geiranger and Åndalsnes. In the summer months, when the road is open, many cyclists (carefully) cycle up or down these hairpin turns.

Glacier Tours
In Norway you will find (mainland) Europe's largest glacier, the Jostedalsbreen glacier, in

1: hikers overlooking Aurlandsdalen
2: cycling in Norway 3: kayaking on the Nærøyfjord

addition to other smaller ones, such as Folgefonna glacier. Each of these has several glacier "tongues" stretching down from the top of the mountain where the majority of the glacier is found, and some of these tongues can be accessed on a tour. Glacier tours include walking on the ice, known as blue ice hiking, a technical activity that requires expert guides.

Folgefonni Breførarlag
FOLGEFONNA NATIONAL PARK, BERGEN AND THE WESTERN FJORDS
These glacier hiking specialists in Hardanger will take you on a blue ice hike across **Juklavassbreen,** one of the more accessible glacier arms of the Folgefonna Glacier.

Fjærland Guiding
INNER SOGNEFJORD, BERGEN AND THE WESTERN FJORDS
The village of Fjærland is located very close to the Jostedalsbreen Glacier, and from there you can join Fjærland Guiding on a tour across **Haugabreen,** the glacier's arms.

Olden Active
NORDFJORD, ÅLESUND AND THE NORTHWESTERN FJORDS
In Nordfjord you will find even more accessible arms of the Jostedalsbreen Glacier, which is the largest glacier in mainland Europe. From the town of Stryn, Olden Active will take you on a blue ice hike across **Tystigbreen** glacier.

3

Wildlife-Watching in Norway

Norway is not particularly known for its wildlife-watching, but there are some sought-after experiences. In the north, whale-watching tours are very popular, and on some of the islands along the coast of Norway visitors can spot puffins and other aquatic nesting birds.

WHALES

Whales frequent the northern coast of Norway and Svalbard in the winter months, and there are plenty of whale-watching tours running from destinations in the north. The whales that are most commonly found in this region are sperm whales, but you can also see killer whales, humpback whales, and even blue whales (from Svalbard). The season runs from October to March, with January being the best month for whale spotting.

Where to See Them

- In **Tromsø** there are plenty of whale-watching tours taking you from the city center and out to sea on half-day and full-day trips—some even come with a whale spotting guarantee (page 317).

- **Svalbard** is a haven for whale-watching tours, and perhaps the best place to go if you are hoping to see larger whales such as the blue whale (page 334).

PUFFINS

From April to August every year puffins gather along the Norwegian coast for nesting. The small black-and-white bird with the bright orange beak draws hikers from all over the country to the island of Runde, Røst in Lofoten, and even as far north as Svalbard.

Where to See Them

- Hiking across **Runde Island** to the lighthouse is a great way to spot the puffin, and other bird species such as sea sole, European shag, and razorbill (page 229).

POLAR BEARS

Polar bears might come to mind when you think about Norwegian animals. However, while these bears do live in Svalbard and can be seen occasionally on an excursion or boat tour, it is important to be aware that it is illegal in Norway to seek out polar bears. It is also illegal to facilitate tours that advertise or try to do this. So, you will not find tours that are set up to find or "chase" polar bears when you visit Norway.

Above: puffins

A Winter Trip to Norway

Northern Norway is absolutely stunning in the winter, and it's the perfect place to see the northern lights. In addition, the majority of the Indigenous Sami people live in this region, and you can learn about Sami culture through various experiences and activities. Make Tromsø your base for this truly unique trip.

Day 1: Welcome to Tromsø

After breakfast, walk to **Telegrafbukta** in the south of Tromsø island (20-30 minutes, easy walk) to visit the **Tromsø University Museum.** Spend some time exploring the exhibits, learning about the northern lights and the Indigenous Sami people. Walk back to the city center for lunch at **Smørtorget.** After lunch, head across the Tromsø bridge to **Fjellheisen cable car,** to head to the top of the mountain and enjoy epic views of the city. After marveling at the views, and perhaps a coffee in the café at the top, head back down and walk over to the **Arctic Cathedral,** one of the main sights of the city (5-10-minute walk from the base of Fjellheisen). Head back into the city center for dinner. Stay at one of the centrally located hotels near the docks, such as Scandic or Radisson (tours depart from right outside the lobby).

Day 2: Whale-Watching

It's time to leave Tromsø on a tour. If you are visiting during whale season (October-January), join a **whale-watching** expedition; you'll spend

8 hours at sea looking for these majestic animals. At night, head out on a **northern lights chase**—catching a glimpse of this phenomenon is a bucket-list item for many visitors.

Day 3: Heading North

Driving Distance and Time: 381 kilometers (237 mi), 6 hours

It's time to travel even farther north, into the land of arctic living. Rent a car in Tromsø and start your 6-hour drive to **Alta.** Along the way you will want to stop and look at the beautiful landscape, so allow extra time and make sure to drive safely. Drive straight to Glød Explorer to stay the night in one of the most unique accommodations in Norway: the **Aurora Canvas Dome.** These domes have glass ceilings; if you're lucky you'll see the northern lights dancing above.

Day 4: Local Life in Alta

Driving Distance and Time: 33 kilometers (20 mi), 40 minutes

Wake up and head to **Trasti & Trine** after breakfast (10-minute drive). You're in for a day of **dog sledding** through the nearby forests. First, you'll learn how to prepare your dog team for the adventure ahead, and then you'll get to try to drive the sled yourself. Afterwards, head to the **Alta Museum** to learn more about the UNESCO-listed rock art of Alta. At night, prepare for another unique sleeping experience, as you check into Alta's **Igloo hotel,** made entirely out of ice and snow (18-minute drive).

Day 5: Sami Culture

Driving Distance and Time: 22 kilometers (14 mi), 25 minutes

Wake up in the Igloo Hotel, and head straight inside to warm up in the sauna at Sorrisniva, which is open for igloo guests in the morning before breakfast. After a nice breakfast, head to **Sami Siida,** a Sami camp where you can learn about the life and history of the Sami in Alta. In the new main building of the camp there is a small gift shop and restaurant where you can grab lunch and do some shopping. Afterwards, head back to Sorrisniva to head out on the **Finnmarksvidda Mountain Plateau** on a guided **snowmobiling excursion.** Enjoy dinner at the fine dining restaurant **Maku,** and spend the night at the **Arctic Wilderness Lodge** overlooking the Alta River.

Day 6: Back to Tromsø

Driving Distance and Time: 381 kilometers (237 mi), 6 hours

It's time to drive back to Tromsø after breakfast. Opt for an early start to make the most of the daylight on the way. Stay in the city center, where you'll be close to most of the city's restaurants. Head back home the next day.

Alta's Igloo Hotel

Norway Like a Local

The Scandinavian concept of **hygge** has made its way across the world in recent years, and if you want to explore Norway like a local, embracing this term and concept is the way to go. In Norway, the Norwegian words "hygge" and "kos" are used interchangeably, meaning that warm, cozy feeling you experience when things are good and you are more than just comfortable—you are comfortable in good company, and everyone's worries are far away.

In Norway, we seek out hygge and kos wherever we can in our daily life. This can be by going on a walk with a friend you haven't seen in a long time to catch up, lighting the fire when the family all gets home from work and school on a cold night, or taking the time to enjoy an extra cup of coffee with a loved one in the morning.

Norwegians are also not averse to putting themselves through a little struggle in order to find the feeling of hygge, such as heading out on a very strenuous hike in order to enjoy the view with a **Kvikk Lunsj** (a Norwegian chocolate bar known as the "hiking chocolate") at the top, or braving the cold on a long ski trip, before heading inside to warm up in front of the fire with some **Gløgg** (a Norwegian version of mulled wine).

To experience hygge on your trip to Norway, there are some things you can do.

- Make sure always to bring a Kvikk Lunsj when **hiking** and enjoy it at the top or when you feel like a break is needed.

- Seek out experiences that may give you a little discomfort, but with a hefty reward, such as jumping in the cold fjord before warming up inside the **FjordSauna** in Flåm.

- Hike up **Aksla mountain** in Ålesund in the evening after dinner to catch the sunset over the ocean and outlier islands from the top.

- Brave the cold and sleep in the **ice hotel in Alta,** warmly wrapped up in reindeer pelts, lots of layers, and thermal sleeping bags.

- Most importantly: **slow down.** Norway is such a large country, and it is impossible to see it all in one trip. So, make sure to take the time to enjoy the moment in each destination you visit, and take in the scenery wherever you are. Don't rush to get anywhere, as regardless of where you end up going for your visit, it will be amazing.

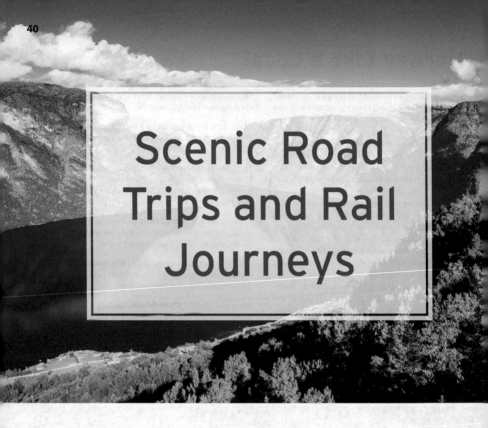

Scenic Road Trips and Rail Journeys

Everything about Norway is scenic, especially as you travel west or north from Oslo and the flat farmlands surrounding the capital. The farther you drive in either of those directions, the more spectacular the landscape gets, and so regardless of whether you follow the road trips outlined below, you will have a scenic drive.

The train journeys of Norway are the same. The farther north or west you go, the more dramatic the scenery. In addition, the engineering work it took to build these railroads becomes more impressive as well. The Oslo-Bergen Line and the Flåm Railway already come highly recommended as the most scenic rail journeys in Norway (and Europe), and so below you will find an alternative that leaves you a little closer to Ålesund and the northwestern fjords.

Each of these journeys is short enough to fold into a longer Norway trip.

The Best of the Sognefjord
3 DAYS / 508 KILOMETERS (316 MI)
START/END: BERGEN
Day 1
Start in Bergen and follow E39 north to the outer Sognefjord. The 3.5-hour drive to the fjord village

of **Balestrand** will have you following E39 north until you reach the Oppedal-Lavik ferry, after which you will head east along the fjord and Route 55. This route wraps along the northern side of the Sognefjord, and the drive just gets more scenic the farther into the fjord you go. End your drive in Balestrand, where you can stay at a family-run hotel overlooking the fjord and enjoy the views surrounding this small village.

Day 2

It's time to continue farther inland along the Sognefjord, and you will start the 4-hour drive by taking the Hella-Dragsvik ferry and getting on Route 13. A little later on, after you have passed through the larger town of Sogndal, you will follow Route 5 and cross the fjord back over to the south side of it on the Manheller-Fodnes ferry. During the ferry crossings, make sure to get out of your car, stretch your legs, and enjoy the view of the fjord landscape.

Borgund Stave Church

Once you get to Lærdal, where you can make a detour for the **Borgund Stave Church** if you'd like, it's time to drive over the **Snow Road,** a national tourist route between Lærdal and Aurland. Note that the Snow Road is only open during the summer months, and if you are doing this drive in the winter, you can get through the mountain via the Lærdal Tunnel and shave half an hour off of the drive.

On the way down the mountain on the Aurland side, make sure to stop at the **Stegastein Viewpoint,** which offers spectacular views of the fjord below. Continue on to **Flåm,** where you will spend the night.

Day 3

The drive back to Bergen along E16 will take you a little less than 3 hours, so feel free to spend the morning and early afternoon exploring Flåm and its main attractions: the scenic **Flåm Railway** and the fjord cruise through the **Nærøyfjord.** If you are interested in Vikings, you can stop in Gudvangen on the drive back to Bergen to visit the Viking village of **Njardarheimr.**

Traditional Norway from Oslo

2 DAYS / 629 KILOMETERS (390 MI)
START/END: OSLO

Day 1: Morning

It's time to leave the big city and drive southwest towards Drammen. Follow E18 until you reach

Drammen, before taking E134 toward Notodden. Stop at **Heddal Stave Church** there and take a little detour south along Route 360 to **Skien** for lunch. The drive out of the city and along the main highways isn't the most scenic but is necessary in order to get out of Oslo and into a more beautiful landscape. The drive time from Oslo to Heddal Stave Church is just short of 2 hours.

Day 1: Afternoon

After lunch, follow Route 36 and eventually Route 41 (with a brief stint along E134 after the town of Seljord) to **Dalen,** for a total drive time of just over 2.5 hours. For a faster, but slightly less scenic route, follow E134 all the way instead of taking off on Route 41. Spend the night at the historic fairytale hotel **Dalen Hotel,** surrounded by the landscape that has inspired many Norwegian painters and artists. On the drive here you will pass lakes, farms, and mountains, in addition to miles and miles of forest land, for an almost troll-like drive through the Norwegian landscape.

Day 2

It's time to drive back to Oslo. Head east along E134 and continue toward Skien and the eastern coast along Route 36 once you reach Seljord. At Skien, turn onto E18 and follow this highway north along the coast. Stop in the coastal town of

Tønsberg for lunch, and consider visiting the **Slottsfjell museum** while you are there. Even if you don't visit the museum, make sure to catch a glimpse of the Viking ship replica **The Oseberg Ship** in the harbor. The total drive time today is 4 hours.

Oslo to the Northwest by Train

6-HOUR TRAIN JOURNEY
START: OSLO
END: ÅNDALSNES

Morning

Take the SJ train from Oslo toward Trondheim in the morning. The 4.5-hour train journey to **Dombås** will first take you through the forests and farmlands of eastern Norway before it starts climbing up to this mountain station at 659 meters above sea level (2,162 feet). The terrain surrounding you gets increasingly dramatic as you near Dombås and leave eastern Norway behind. Make sure to buy some food on the train (unless you brought lunch with you), as the change at Dombås is a short one.

Afternoon

Then it's time to change trains and get on the scenic **Raumabanen Railway.** This 1-hour and 40-minute journey will take you from the mountains and all the way down to sea level at **Åndalsnes Station,** from where you can reach both Ålesund and Geiranger by bus or rental car. The 115-kilometer (71-mi) railway travels down the mountain past rivers and waterfalls, vast mountains, and widespread forests.

closeup of the replica Oseberg Ship in Tønsberg harbor

Best Kid-Friendly Spots

Families traveling with children will find that Viking history may spark the interest of younger travelers. Additionally, there are some animal-focused attractions in the major cities that will keep the young ones entertained.

OSLO AND SOUTHERN NORWAY

- **Kristiansand Dyrepark** is Norway's largest zoo, where kids can see and meet animals from all over the world. Perhaps the most unique section is the Nordic Wilderness, where you can see moose, wolverine, and wolves (page 113).

- Make sure to visit **Viking House** in Stavanger for a unique journey through the Norwegian Viking Age using AR technology (page 125).

- The **Vigeland Sculpture Park** in Oslo's Frogner Park is a fun place for children to explore, with statues of children, toddlers, and adults in various moods and stages of life (page 63).

BERGEN AND THE WESTERN FJORDS

- The **Bergen Aquarium** is a great place for the whole family to explore, with penguins, sea lions, and tropical and arctic species of fish (page 147).

- In Gudvangen, at the end of the Nærøyfjord, families with children should make sure to visit **Njardarheimr,** to experience reenactors living in a "real" Viking village (page 202).

- A fast-paced **FjordSafari** in a RIB boat is the ideal way for young travelers to explore the fjords, with more action and a more personalized guiding experience than the fjord cruises. FjordSafaris are available in the **Hardangerfjord** and the **Aurlandsfjord and Nærøyfjord** regions (pages 171 and 192).

LOFOTEN AND THE NORTH

- Families doing the Lofoten road trip should make sure to stop at the **Lofotr Viking Museum,** where kids can learn more about Norway's Viking history and how these warriors lived their lives (page 301).

- Don't miss spending a day with the reindeer at **Tromsø Arctic Reindeer,** where you can go reindeer sledding, learn about these fascinating animals, and try your hand at feeding them, before sitting around the fire to learn about Sami life and culture (page 313).

- Dog-loving families should head out on a **dog sledding** excursion in **Alta,** where you can not only meet and cuddle with your new four-legged friends, but also try your hand at sledding through the forests with them (page 324).

Above: Tromsø Arctic Reindeer

Oslo

Oslo is most travelers' gateway to Norway, and the country's only major city. Here, you'll find a notable nightlife scene, a calendar packed with cultural events, a sophisticated array of restaurants, world-class museums, and cosmopolitan shopping districts. With a growing population, the capital has seen a lot of changes in recent years, and each visit to Oslo will lead you to new discoveries.

Despite all of its charms, the city is often given short shrift by visitors, who head straight to the fjords and Norway's other natural wonders. But underestimating Oslo is a mistake. From award-winning cocktail bars, to the flagships of unique Norwegian fashion brands, to lively festivals drawing artists from around the world, the capital offers a mix of uniquely Norwegian charm and international flavor.

Highlights

Look for ★ to find recommended sights, activities, dining, and lodging.

★ **Akershus Fortress:** A guided tour of this fortress and the museums housed within provides insight into 700 years of Norwegian history (page 54).

★ **Oslo Opera House:** The first opera house in Norway is an impressive architectural sight, equally striking whether you're attending a performance or walking on the roof (page 57).

★ **Nobel Peace Center:** Learn about the impact Nobel Prize winners have had on the world through interactive exhibits (page 57).

★ **Royal Palace:** The seat of the royal family of Norway represents Oslo at its grandest, surrounded by beautiful parks (page 59).

★ **Vigelandsparken:** Within Oslo's Frogner Park, you'll find more than 200 sculptures by Gustav Vigeland; this is the largest sculpture park in the world dedicated to one artist (page 63).

★ **Hadeland Glassverk:** Founded in the 18th century, Hadeland Glassverk is still very much a working operation, filled with shops and activities for the whole family (page 66).

★ **Shopping for Norwegian Design:** The simple minimalism of Scandinavian design is very much the rule in Norway, and Oslo has the biggest concentration of shops (page 74).

★ **New Nordic Cuisine:** Oslo is a great place to experience this food movement rooted

in traditional Scandinavian cuisine, which has been growing in popularity in recent years (page 78).

★ **Heddal Stave Church:** Visit the largest remaining stave church in Norway, dating back to the 1200s (page 99).

Oslo

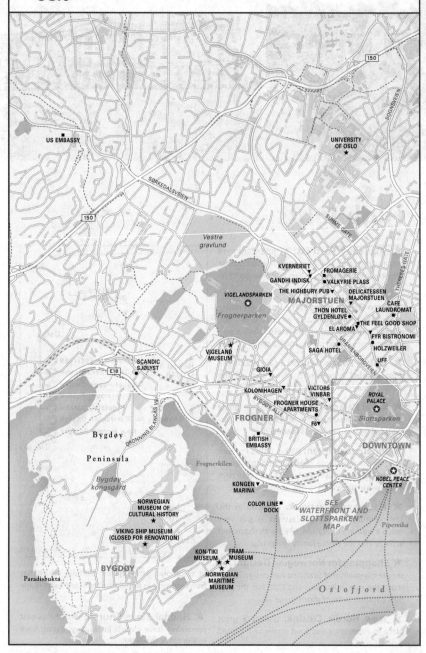

US EMBASSY

UNIVERSITY
OF OSLO

SØRKEDALSVEIEN

150

SUHMS GATE

THERESES GATE

Vestre
gravlund

KVERNERIET · FROMAGERIE
GANDHI INDISK · VALKYRIE PLASS
THE HIGHBURY PUB · DELICATESSEN
VIGELANDSPARKEN · MAJORSTUEN
Frognerparken · MAJORSTUEN
THON HOTEL · CAFE
GYLDENLØVE · LAUNDROMAT
EL AROMA · THE FEEL GOOD SHOP
· FYR BISTRONOMI
SAGA HOTEL · HOLZWEILER
VIGELAND · UFF
MUSEUM
GIOIA
SCANDIC
SJØLYST
E18
KOLONIHAGEN
BYGDØY ALLE
VICTORS
VINBAR
FROGNER HOUSE
APARTMENTS
ROYAL
PALACE
Slottsparken
FROGNER
F6

DRONNING BLANCAS VEI

BYGDØY VEI

URANIENBORGVEIEN

Bygdøy
BRITISH
EMBASSY
DOWNTOWN
Peninsula

Bygdøy
kongsgård
Frognerkilen
NOBEL PEACE
CENTER

NORWEGIAN
MUSEUM OF
CULTURAL HISTORY
KONGEN
MARINA
SEE
"WATERFRONT AND
SLOTTSPARKEN"
MAP
VIKING SHIP MUSEUM
(CLOSED FOR RENOVATION)
COLOR LINE
DOCK
Pipervika

Paradisbukta
KON-TIKI
MUSEUM
FRAM
MUSEUM
BYGDØY
NORWEGIAN
MARITIME
MUSEUM
Oslofjord

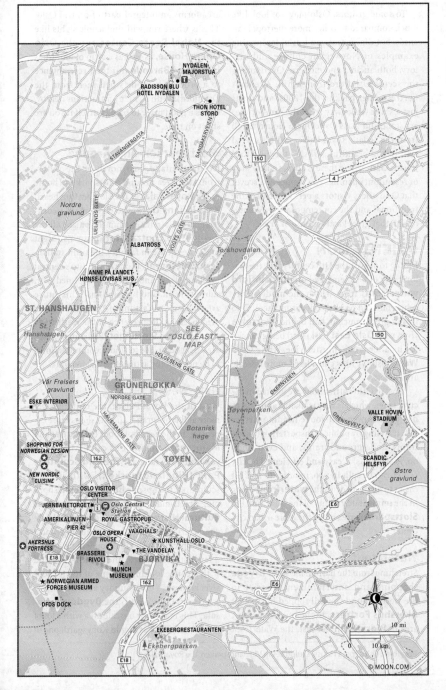

To some visitors, Oslo may not look like much compared to other more metropolitan cities, but dig in and you'll find fascinating examples of Norwegian culture and history, both ancient and modern. Overlooking the scenic Oslofjord from a hill, Akershus Fortress dates back to the 1200s, and it sits just a short walk away from the state-of-the-art stone and glass Oslo Opera House. Stroll from the sedate Royal Palace, with its regal stature and beautiful parks, to the busy Karl Johans Gate, where there is always a new shop or restaurant opening. You'll quickly discover that Oslo offers visitors a perfect blend of the traditional and the contemporary—a combination that gives locals a sense of pride.

ORIENTATION

Dating to at least the 11th century AD, the historic city of Oslo emerged on the **Oslofjord waterfront,** from which the modern city center fans out on each side. From there, Oslo is split pretty much in half by the **Akerselva** river, with **Oslo East** (Oslo Øst) being known for its alternative, hipster vibe, while **Oslo West** (Oslo Vest) is considered more upscale and classic.

Most of Oslo's attractions are located in the city center, which is very walkable and easy to navigate. However, if you're heading farther out, traveling by public transportation (buses, trams, underground trains, and even a hop on, hop off bus) is easy and efficient. The city center can be split in two, in order to make it easier to navigate, with the **waterfront** being in the immediate vicinity of the fjord, and the **Slottsparken** area being the more urban city center.

Waterfront

Stretching from the harborside **Aker Brygge** shopping and entertainment district in the west, around the hill topped by ancient **Akershus Fortress,** to the revitalized port area of **Bjørvika** in the east, the Waterfront area forms an integral part of central Oslo. This is where you will find iconic sights like the **Nobel Peace Center** and the **Oslo Opera House,** as well as a strip of buildings nicknamed **Barcode** (for their resemblance to a product barcode when seen from the Oslofjord). With so many attractions nearby, this is a good place to base yourself if you are short on time.

Slottsparken and Around

Heading inland, just north of the waterfront, the area around Slottsparken (home to the **Royal Palace**) is Oslo's beating heart. **Karl Johans Gate,** the city's main pedestrian street, stretches from the palace all the way to **Oslo Central Station** in a straight line. The square in front of the train station, **Jernbanetorget,** is one of the city's central meeting places and a transit hub, lined with subway, tram, and bus stations. This entire area is also Oslo's administrative center, as evidenced by the presence of the **Rådhuset** (City Hall) and **Stortinget** (Parliament). This area is a good place to find accommodations, to be near all the action and major sights.

Oslo West

West of the Royal Palace, the buildings get more and more grand, and the shops more expensive. In the neighborhoods of **Frogner** and **Majorstuen** (some locals call it Majorstua) you'll find the famous **Vigeland Sculpture Park (Vigelandsparken),** with its 200 sculptures, the upscale **Bogstadveien** shopping street, and the **Norwegian Museum of Cultural History.** These neighborhoods are characterized by large, bright buildings and a rather upscale, posh vibe. You will find quite a few embassies here, and walking around with a coffee looking at some of the (expensive) homes is a great Sunday activity.

Also in Oslo West is the **Bygdøy** peninsula. This is another upscale area with a lot of rich homes (such as Bygdø Kongsgård, one of

---

Previous: Oslo Opera House; sculptures in Vigelandsparken; the Royal Palace.

the royal family's homes), but it is mainly of interest to anyone with a love for museums. Here, you will find several museums worth visiting on your trip to Oslo, such as the **Kon-Tiki** and **FRAM** expedition museums.

Oslo East

On the eastern bank of the Akerselva, you'll find perhaps the most unique neighborhood in Oslo, **Grünerløkka.** This area is a popular hangout for locals, with cute boutiques, small cafés, and a hipster vibe that feels like a constant music festival. This is the best place in Oslo to grab a coffee and enjoy some people-watching. Oslo East is also home to the **Tøyen** neighborhood, where you'll find the **Botanical Garden** and **Natural History Museum.**

Outside Central Oslo

By following the Akerselva river north, you'll reach **Anne på Landet** (Hønse-Lovisas Hus), **Mathallen,** and **Kontrast** (all along the river, east of Grünerløkka). North of Grünerløkka you will reach the neighborhoods Torshov and Storo.

North of Oslo

North of the city center you will find the Holmenkollen ski jump arena and the **Norsk Teknisk Museum** science center. Both can be reached by public transport, but if you want to venture farther out of the city, consider a visit to **Hadeland Glassverk.** The glassworks village is a great day trip for the whole family.

PLANNING YOUR TIME

How long you stay in Oslo depends on the length of your entire trip. **Two days** is the perfect amount of time to get a good feel for the city, but if you're in Norway for a week or less, you can get by spending just one day to take in Oslo's main sights. The luxury of **three days** allows you to add a hike in Nordmarka, a forested area north of the city, or an excursion to Hadeland Glassverk or the historic city of Tønsberg.

The **high season** in Oslo, as with the rest of Norway, is from June to August, with the **shoulder season** (May and Sept.) becoming increasingly popular as well. However, the influx of travelers is somewhat balanced out by the fact that many locals flee the capital during their summer break to go abroad or to their cabins in southern Norway. Therefore, the city never feels overcrowded (though it is definitely busier during summer months).

the pedestrian Karl Johans Gate

Visiting Oslo in the **low season** (winter months) is a great way to avoid crowds completely, but in return, the city will feel slightly less alive. Opening hours are more limited, and locals tend to hibernate a little in the dark winter months, when the sun rises at about 9:30am and sets around 3pm.

Hours and Weekly Closures

Note that, as in the rest of Norway, most shops and stores are closed on Sundays, while many museums and attractions in Oslo are closed on Mondays, even during high season. So, if you only have one or two days to spend in Oslo, try to avoid those days.

On Fridays and Saturdays, you will find that many restaurants are open later than they are on weekdays, especially those that double as bars. However, Norwegians traditionally eat dinner quite early compared to other European countries, around 6pm-7pm when dining out. If you are dining out, make sure to double-check what time the last seating is, as it is easy to mistake the late opening hours for dining hours. If you are hoping for a 9pm reservation, this is often the last seating at the nicer restaurants.

Advance Reservations

Most activities in Oslo have high capacity and do not need to be booked in advance. However, some of the more limited offers—mainly **the summer tours of the Royal Palace**—need to be booked in advance. Additionally, it is wise to make dinner reservations a few days in advance in order to avoid having to wait.

Tourist Passes

The **Oslo Pass** is the official Oslo city card, available for purchase online (www.visitoslo.com) and at the Oslo Visitors Center, or you can download the app. Available as a 24-, 48- or 72-hour pass, it gives you free public transportation around the city as well as free and discounted entrance to several major attractions and museums, including Akershus Fortress, the Kon-Tiki Museum, and the Nobel Peace Center. (Please note that your Oslo Pass can only be used once per day per attraction/museum.)

Itinerary Ideas

DAY ONE

If you only have one day in Oslo and want to ensure you don't miss out on any main sights, this is the itinerary for you. Demonstrating just how walkable Oslo is, it only takes one hour in total to walk to all these sights without stopping.

1 Start your day by heading toward the **Royal Palace** and the surrounding park of Slottsparken, which makes for a beautiful morning stroll. If visiting in summer, prebook one of the interior palace tours.

2 Walk down the main pedestrian street of **Karl Johans Gate;** you'll pass the grand Nationaltheateret and the Norwegian Parliament buildings along the way.

3 Continue toward the **Oslo Cathedral** and pop inside to marvel at the baroque details and three-story altar.

4 For lunch, head to the **Royal Gastropub** in Østbanehallen. This food hall is set in the king's former waiting room from the late 1800s and early 1900s, when he primarily traveled to various parts of Norway by train.

5 Just a short walk from Østbanehallen you will find the stunning **Oslo Opera House.**

If you happen to get here in time for a tour (Sun.-Fri. 1pm, Sat. noon), consider joining; alternatively, enjoy an invigorating walk on the building's roof to take in the views of Oslofjord and the distinctive skyline known as the Barcode behind you.

6 From the Opera House, walk west along the water to **Akershus Fortress.** Spend some time walking around the grounds and visiting the Norwegian Armed Forces Museum.

7 From Akershus, head west toward Aker Brygge and the **Nobel Peace Center,** across the bay. Visit the center to learn more about the prestigious award, handed out in Oslo each year.

8 For dinner, there are several options in the upscale dockside neighborhood of Aker Brygge. Try **Entrecote by Trancher,** a Norwegian take on a steakhouse, serving carefully selected cuts of meat.

DAY TWO

1 On your second day in Oslo, head to the waterfront **National Museum.** This massive museum on the Aker Brygge waterfront opened in summer 2022 and is the largest art museum in the Nordics.

2 Head toward the **Rådhuset** (City Hall) and take in the monumental brick towers looming over the main entrance.

3 Keep walking toward the Nationaltheateret subway station, taking the train west one stop to Majorstuen. Grab lunch at **Kverneriet,** which serves great burgers and milkshakes right next to the station.

4 From Kverneriet, walk along the main road Kirkeveien toward the entrance of the famous, can't-miss sculpture park of **Vigelandsparken.**

5 After a stroll through the Vigeland Park, it's time to learn more about the Norwegian sculptor behind it, Gustav Vigeland. Leave the park at the southern gates, and head across the street to the **Vigeland Museum.**

6 After your museum visit, walk to tram stop Frogner Plass and get on tram #12 back to Majorstuen. Stroll down Bogstadveien, a lovely shopping street that is a little less crowded with tourists than Karl Johans Gate. To break up your browsing, consider stopping at **Delicatessen Majorstuen** for a glass of wine.

7 Grab dinner at **FYR Bistronomi,** a gastronomic bistro at the other end of Bogstadveien.

8 If you fancy some after-dinner drinks, stroll 10-15 minutes to **F6 cocktail bar** (named after its address, Frognerveien 6).

OSLO LIKE A LOCAL

1 If you're lucky enough to have a third day in Oslo, start your day slow by taking the subway to Nydalen subway station, serviced by lines 2, 4, and 5 (all of which go through the city center). Enjoy a lovely morning walk down Akerselva, stopping by **Tim Wendelboe** for a coffee on the way.

2 When you get to **Mathallen,** Oslo's main food hall, browse all the amazing offers by the vendors here. This is a great place to stop for lunch.

Itinerary Ideas

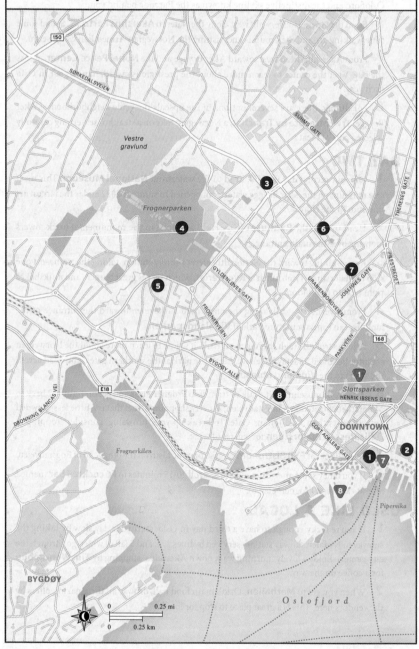

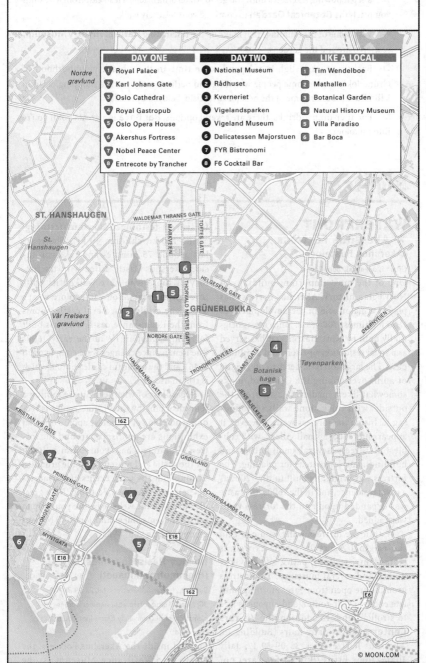

DAY ONE
1. Royal Palace
2. Karl Johans Gate
3. Oslo Cathedral
4. Royal Gastropub
5. Oslo Opera House
6. Akershus Fortress
7. Nobel Peace Center
8. Entrecote by Trancher

DAY TWO
1. National Museum
2. Rådhuset
3. Kverneriet
4. Vigelandsparken
5. Vigeland Museum
6. Delicatessen Majorstuen
7. FYR Bistronomi
8. F6 Cocktail Bar

LIKE A LOCAL
1. Tim Wendelboe
2. Mathallen
3. Botanical Garden
4. Natural History Museum
5. Villa Paradiso
6. Bar Boca

© MOON.COM

3 Keep following Akerselva until you get to Ankerbrua bridge. Head east from here until you reach the **Botanical Garden** to continue your leisurely walk.

4 Visit some of the buildings that make up the fascinating **Natural History Museum,** scattered around the gardens.

5 Backtrack west slightly to spend some time in the vibrant neighborhood of Grünerløkka. After some people-watching and perhaps some vintage shopping, head to **Villa Paradiso** for some of the best pizza in Oslo, beloved by locals.

6 For after-dinner drinks, there are several options; **Bar Boca** is a great spot if you're into mixology.

Sights

WATERFRONT
★ Akershus Fortress
(Akershus Festning)
Grounds open daily 6am-9pm

One of the most important buildings in Norwegian history, Akershus Fortress has played a major role in the development of Oslo for almost 700 years. Since it was originally built by King Håkon V, it has served as a royal residence, a prison, and a military base. The large fortress, perched on the top of a hill overlooking the Oslofjord, looks somewhat like a medieval castle from the outside, with thick stone walls surrounding it. Inside the fortress walls, however, it appears more like a small village, with cobblestone streets, several small houses and buildings, and lawn areas for relaxing. The fortress was originally built in the 1200s as a royal residence, and in the 1600s, the castle was expanded upon and the fortress walls were added.

Within the fortress walls, you can find the original Akershus Castle as well as restaurants, walking paths, scenic viewpoints, and several museums. The fortress grounds are open from early morning until late evening year-round, and anyone is free to stroll around. In addition, the **Visitors Center** arranges daily tours (Building 18, Akershus Fortress; tel. 23 09 39 17; daily 10am-4pm; https://kultur.forsvaret.no/ forsvarets-festninger/akershus-festning; adults 100 kr, children 40 kr). The tours last around 75 minutes and take you inside Akershus Castle, filled with the history of those who have walked its halls through the years. You can explore what's left of the original medieval castle, rooms from the Renaissance castle that was built for King Christian IV in the early 1600s (the Renaissance changes were completed in 1646), and the beautiful castle church, which is still in use.

Regardless of whether you are joining a tour, dropping by the visitors center is recommended to get the latest update on what exhibitions are on display around the fortress, and to purchase your entrance ticket for the castle and museums on the grounds. Throughout the year, events and concerts take place at Akershus Festning. It's a great idea to check the website before your trip to see what events and exhibitions will be happening during your visit.

Norway Resistance Museum
(Hjemmefrontmuseet)
Building 21, Akershus Fortress; tel. 23 09 31 38; https://kultur.forsvaret.no/museer/norges-hjemmefrontmuseum; daily 10am-4pm; adults 100 kr, children 40

Located inside the Akershus Fortress, the Norwegian Resistance Museum is one

Waterfront and Slottsparken

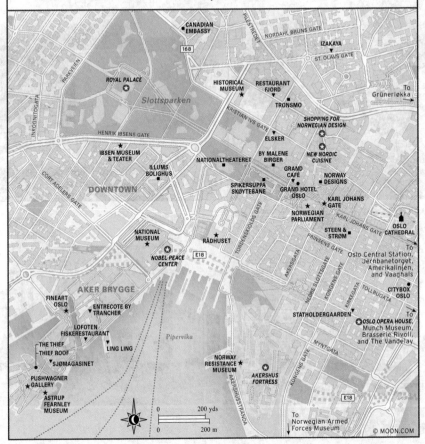

of the best places to learn about Norway under German occupation during World War II. The museum opened in 1970 with the purpose of educating visitors on how Norwegians stood their ground against the occupying forces, from the start of the occupation in 1940 until liberation in May 1945. The photographs, artifacts, documents, and other memorabilia on display from this dark period of Norwegian history portray what life was like in Norway during the time.

Norwegian Armed Forces Museum (Forsvarsmuseet)

Building 62, Akershus Fortress; tel. 23 09 35 82; https://kultur.forsvaret.no/museer/forsvarsmuseet; daily 10am-4pm; adults 100 kr, children 40 kr

Within Akershus Fortress, the Norwegian Armed Forces Museum (Forsvarsmuseet) has been in this location since 1860 and covers the development of the Norwegian military from the 1400s until today. It houses historic artifacts ranging from weapons to military uniforms worn through the years. Among the

permanent exhibitions well worth visiting are the INTOPS exhibit, focusing on international operations Norway has participated in, and the Swedish Union exhibition, which focuses on the period of union between Sweden and Norway (1814-1905) and the role of the military during that time.

★ Oslo Opera House
(Operahuset Oslo)

Kirsten Flaagstads plass 1; tel. 21 42 21 21; www.operaen. no

The Oslo Opera House opened in 2008, becoming the first opera house in Norway. The building itself is spectacular, and its central location ensures that visitors can see its unique architectural design. Depending on whom you ask, the building resembles a ship, a ski slope, or the zigzag hairpin turns found on mountainsides all over Norway. Regardless of their inspiration, Norwegian design and architectural company Snøhetta created a building worth seeing and went on to win several architectural awards for the project.

The highlight of the building's engaging, interactive design is that its sloping rooflines allow visitors to walk on top of the building. Despite the roof's seemingly gentle slope, the top is much higher up than it first appears, offering lovely views of the Oslofjord, and inland, the distinctive stretch of Oslo skyline known as the Barcode (the reasoning behind the name will be pretty self-evident when you see it).

The Opera House is home to the Norwegian Opera and Ballet, which stages several performances throughout the year—a lovely opportunity to get inside the opera house. Alternatively, you can join a guided tour (English tours Sun.-Fri. 1pm, Sat. noon; adults 120 kr, children 70 kr), to get an up-close look at what goes on behind the scenes of a performance, from the costuming department to the backstage hallways. Tours last about 50 minutes.

1: Akershus Fortress 2: Munch Museum 3: Nobel Peace Center 4: Oslo Opera House

Munch Museum (MUNCH)

Edvard Munchs plass 1; tel. 23 49 35 00; www. munchmuseet.no; Mon.-Tues. 10am-6pm, Wed.-Fri. 10am-9pm, Sat.-Sun. 10am-6pm; adults 160 kr, children under 15 free

Edvard Munch might just be the most famous artist to have come out of Norway, known worldwide for the painting that has become known as *The Scream (Skrik)*. But there is much more to the painter, and his story is one that Norwegians are proud to showcase at this museum. There are 13 floors of experiences and ways to explore Munch and his art. The fourth floor is where you will find the exhibition called Munch Uendelig (Endless Munch), home to the artist's most famous works, including not only *The Scream* but also *Madonna,* which shows the shirtless upper half of a woman that has at times been interpreted as the Virgin Mary.

MUNCH has a fun, secret exhibit for children, with additional stories of Munch and his art displayed through peeping holes in the walls—explained in a way that is more suitable (and fun) for younger visitors. On the 13th floor of the MUNCH building, the **Kranen Bar** is open Wednesday to Saturday from 3pm until 1am, and is a great place to sip cocktails while enjoying the view of the revitalized Bjørvika port area.

★ Nobel Peace Center
(Nobels Fredssenter)

Brynjulf Bulls Plass 1; tel. 48 30 10 00; www. nobelpeacecenter.org; Thurs.-Sun. 11am-5pm; adults 120 kr, children over 12 50 kr; under 12 free

Located just a stone's throw from the Rådhuset, this museum/center is dedicated to the Nobel Peace Prize, its winners throughout the decades, and the impact and legacy of their work. The exhibitions here are varied, inspirational, and interactive, and their aim is to inspire visitors to work toward a more peaceful world. The Nobel Peace Center is located in the former Vestbane (Western Rail) Train Station, and so from the outside the building looks grand and slightly old-fashioned. Inside,

Henrik Ibsen

Henrik Ibsen (1828-1906) was an influential Norwegian playwright and author who gained international popularity in the latter half of the 19th century. Ibsen was a prolific writer of drama, poems, and dramatic prose, and his plays are still being put on all around the world. Often referred to as "the father of realism"—a theatrical movement that aimed to make plays more closely resemble everyday life—Ibsen is sometimes mentioned in the same breath as William Shakespeare. His most notable works include *Peer Gynt* (1867), *A Doll's House* (1879), and *Hedda Gabler* (1890).

IBSEN MUSEUM & TEATER

Henrik Ibsens Gate 26; tel. 40 02 36 30; https://ibsenmuseet.no
The best place to learn more about Ibsen during your visit to Oslo is the Ibsen Museum & Teater, which houses not only Ibsen artifacts and collections, but also a theater where Ibsen plays are regularly performed. The core of the museum is Ibsen's actual apartment, which is furnished with original furniture and objects, offering an intimate glimpse of Ibsen's life.

GRAND CAFÉ

Karl Johans Gate 31; tel. 98 18 20 00; www.grandcafeoslo.no
If you want to really walk in the footsteps of Ibsen and other famous contemporaries, including sculptor Gustav Vigeland and explorer Roald Amundsen, a visit to Grand Café on Karl Johans Gate is an absolute must. Part of the Grand Hotel, and opened in 1874, this is where Ibsen would meet with like-minded artists to sit and talk until the early hours. If you visit MUNCH during your trip to Oslo, you can view Edvard Munch's painting *Henrik Ibsen på Grand Café*, which is an illustration—as its name suggests—of Henrik Ibsen during one of his visits to the café.

however, the space has been transformed to large, modern exhibition areas.

The Nobel Foundation is a private institution that was established in 1900 by the will of Alfred Nobel, and its main mission is to spread knowledge and encourage discussion about culture and natural sciences around the world. Nobel was a Swedish inventor, chemist, and philanthropist. He is mostly known for the invention of dynamite, but he actually held more than 350 patents during his lifetime. His will left over $260 million to the Nobel Foundation (in today's estimated value). All of the Nobel Prizes are handed out in Sweden, with the exception of the Nobel Peace Prize, which is handed out in Oslo each December—usually on the 10th, which is the anniversary of Alfred Nobel's death.

Nobel specified that the Peace Prize was to be handed out by a Norwegian committee, and though no one knows for sure, there are a couple theories why. At the time of Nobel's death (and when he wrote his will),

Norway and Sweden were in a union, and it seems that he felt it was only appropriate that Norway was allowed to hand out the most distinguished of the awards as a sign of good faith and friendship between the nations. In addition to this, Norway at the time was doing more work than Sweden to maintain peaceful international relations, for example with the Inter-Parliamentary Union, and had fewer military traditions than its union partner.

The Nobel Peace Prize aims to recognize those who have promoted and contributed to world peace in some way. Nobel wished for the Prize to be awarded to someone who had done "the most or the best work for fraternity between nations, for the abolition or reduction of standing armies, and for the holding and promotion of peace congresses." To be awarded the Peace Prize, a person needed only to fulfill one of the demands listed. The latter two demands (regarding standing armies and peace congresses) are quite clear and specific, while the first one (promoting "fraternity between nations") can be interpreted quite widely. Thus, the Nobel Peace Committee has been given quite free rein in their selection, and some winners have caused controversy through the years. Notable winners have included Nelson Mandela, Yasser Arafat, Henry Kissinger, Aung San Suu Kyi, Theodore Roosevelt, Barack Obama, and Malala Yousafzai.

If you are visiting on a Friday between May and October, make sure to drop by the Nobel Peace Center at noon, when they release a peace dove together with the staff's "good news of the week."

National Museum
(Nasjonalmuseet)

Brynjulf Bulls Plass 3; tel. 21 98 20 00; www.nasjonalmuseet.no; Tues.-Wed. 10am-8pm, Thurs. 10am-5pm, Fri. 10am-9pm, Sat.-Sun. 10am-5pm; 200 kr

After the closure of the former Nasjonalgalleriet and a long period of construction and planning, the new National Museum of Norway opened in 2022. The Museum, just next to Aker Brygge and the docks, is now the largest art museum in the Nordics and is home to artworks of every era, from ancient to modern. There are several floors of permanent and temporary exhibitions—more than 5,000 pieces—so it is advisable to check the website before your visit in order to plan your time wisely and decide what you'll want to see.

On the top floor you'll find the Light Hall, which is used for temporary exhibitions. This hall, the first of its kind, covers a space of 2,400 square meters (almost 19,000 sq ft), and within the walls of the hall are 9,000 energy-efficient LEDs that can be adjusted to set the mood for the current exhibition on display. The hall can be used as one large exhibit room, or divided into several smaller spaces. Within the large space, curators can display art hanging on the walls in a classic way, or construct brand-new types of exhibitions, such as rebuilding a small house under the high ceiling.

Astrup Fearnley Museum
(Astrup Fearnley Musseet)

Strandpromenaden 2; tel. 22 93 60 60; www.afmuseet. no; Tues.-Sun. 11am-5pm; adults 150 kr, children free

Founded in 1993, the Astrup Fearnley Museum is one of the leading modern art museums in the Nordics. Naturally, this is where you will find the extensive Astrup Fearnley Collection, one of Europe's most comprehensive bodies of international contemporary art, founded in 1995 when the Thomas Fearnley Foundation and the Nils Astrup Foundation merged. One of the most famous (and controversial) pieces in the collection is the porcelain sculpture of Michael Jackson and his pet chimpanzee Bubbles, which the museum purchased for $5.1 million in 2002. In addition, the museum has displayed works by artists such as Jeff Koons, Cai Guo-Qiang, and Cindy Sherman. The museum is located at the very tip of Aker Brygge, and from the café inside you can enjoy some lovely views of the Oslofjord.

SLOTTSPARKEN AND AROUND

The area around Slottsparken (the Royal Palace Park) stretches in a straight line from the Royal Palace to Oslo Central Station. The street in between is called **Karl Johans Gate** and has been considered an important vein of the city for centuries. It is the key shopping and pedestrian street of Oslo, and along the almost mile-long walk you will pass several important sights, such as the **University of Oslo,** with its three grand stone buildings facing the university square; **Nationaltheateret,** where famous actors and playwrights have been roaming the halls for centuries; and **Spikersuppa,** a large fountain that is transformed to a skating rink in the winter.

★ Royal Palace
(Slottet)

Slottsplassen 1; tel. 22 04 87 00; www.kongehuset.no; interior tours June-Aug.; tour adults 175 kr, children 125 kr

Oslo's Best Art Galleries

Home to several impressive museums, with MUNCH and the National Museum being the largest and most popular, Oslo has a vibrant artist culture. Below are several smaller galleries in the city that are worth exploring.

PUSHWAGNER GALLERY

Tjuvholmen allé 25; tel. 91 54 12 87

Pushwagner was one of the most important contemporary artists of Norway, and this gallery, located by the waterfront area of Oslo, is dedicated to some of his works. Pushwagner was born Terje Brofos in Oslo in 1940 and passed away in 2018. He painted works within the pop art style, and his works can be described as eclectic, psychedelic, and colorful.

KUNSTHALL OSLO

Rostockgata 2-4; tel. 21 69 69 39; https://kunsthalloslo.no

Kunsthall Oslo ("Art Hall Oslo") displays international and Norwegian modern art, with a large focus contemporary. Exhibitions rotate often, so you never quite know what you will see during your visit. The gallery is also home to a good independent art book store.

FINEART OSLO

Filipstad brygge 2; tel. 22 01 24 20; www.fineart.no

In a 2,000-square-meter (21,528-sq-ft) space, Fineart Oslo houses photography, graphic art, paintings, and drawings from all over Norway and beyond. One of their four rooms is dedicated to photography, and works by famous photographers such as Philippe Shangti, Norman Parkinson, and Patrick Demarchelie have been on display (and for sale) here.

The Norwegian Royal Palace is the official home of His Royal Highness King Harald V and Her Royal Highness Queen Sonja of Norway. Completed in 1849, it has a classic design with a large balcony and six massive pillars in front. With 173 rooms, there's space for the Norwegian Government to meet with the king each Friday in the Statsråd Hall.

Norway has had its own monarchy since the union with Sweden ended in 1905. The country operates as a Constitutional Monarchy, where King Harald V is, legally, the Head of State of Norway. However, the tasks performed by the king and other members of the royal family are mainly ceremonial. The actual power to run the country lies with the Norwegian Parliament and other elected bodies.

The Palace is only open to the public through guided **tours,** held in the summer months. The tour visits several important palace rooms, including the Statsråd Hall and the Grand Dining Room, where the royal family can host up to 220 dinner guests. It's recommended to book your ticket in advance, as they quickly sell out. Tickets are usually made available online during March each year.

The palace gardens, or **Slottsparken,** on the other hand, are always open to visitors. One of the first large parks in the capital, Slottsparken surrounds the Palace on all sides. The park area includes several sculptures; in 2016 Princess Ingrid Alexandra (who will one day become the first queen of Norway to inherit the throne through succession, not marriage) opened a sculpture park, with works by and for children; each piece was chosen to increase curiosity and playfulness.

The main parts of the park are open year-round, while the area right behind the palace, called Dronningparken (Queen's Park), is only open May 18-October 1.

Historical Museum

Frederiks gate 2; tel. 22 85 19 00; www.khm.uio.no/
english/visit-us/historical-museum; Tues.-Wed., Fri.-Sun.
11am-4pm, Thurs. 11am-8pm; adults 120 kr, children free

The historical museum is the place for a dive deep into the culture and history of Norway, as it is home to the largest cultural and historical collections in the country. Permanent exhibitions focus on the arctic, the Viking Age (793-1066), and more, and the collection includes the oldest skull in Norway. It's definitely worth a visit for history buffs.

Norwegian Parliament
(Stortinget)

Karl Johans Gate 22; tel. 23 31 31 80; www.stortinget.
no; via guided tour only, Mon.-Fri. June-Aug; free

The Norwegian Parliament sits tall and proud facing the Royal Palace across Studenterlunden Park. The paved walkway up to the main entrance is named Løvebakken, or the Lion's Hill, due to the two resting lion statues on the stone railing. The Parliament building opened in 1866; the word "Stortinget" refers to both the building and the parliament itself. During the summer holiday from late June to early August, it is possible to visit Stortinget as part of their summer tours, running Monday-Friday on a first-come, first-served basis. The schedule varies each year.

After the Coronavirus pandemic, a digital tour of the building was created and is now available on the Stortinget website. The tour not only takes you through the rooms of Stortinget, but also explains the history and significance of the building and the role of the Norwegian Parliament.

Rådhuset

Rådhusplassen 1; tel. 23 46 12 00; www.oslo.kommune.
no/radhuset/#gref; daily 9am-4pm; free

The Rådhuset, or Oslo City Hall is a commanding redbrick building that comes into view when you arrive in Oslo by sea. It's easy to spot its two massive, distinctive front towers. Opened in 1950, today it's open for anyone to visit. This is where the Nobel Peace Prize is handed out each year.

The clocks of the City Hall boast Norway's largest chimes, which play throughout the day from 7am to midnight, with songs that vary with each hour. At 7am Oslo is woken up by "Morning Mood" by Edvard Grieg, while later in the day you might hear themes from *Downton Abbey*, *Jurassic Park*, or *Top Gun*. In 2022, during the Russian invasion of Ukraine, the afternoon song selections included Ukranian folk songs, followed by "Give Peace a Chance" by John Lennon and "Heal the World" by Michael Jackson. The building and its grand, marble-clad, mosaic-trimmed interior are impressive, and it's worth dropping by around the top of the hour just to hear the tunes coming from the towers.

Oslo Cathedral
(Oslo Domkirke)

Karl Johans Gate 11; tel. 23 62 90 10; www.
oslodomkirke.no; Sat.-Thurs. 10am-4pm, Fri. 4pm-
11:30pm; free

The Oslo Cathedral is a beautiful baroque church dating back to 1697. This cross-shaped building in rust-colored brick once towered over the city, but now it blends in a little more as there are several multi-story buildings around it. The bell tower still manages to inspire awe, however, with its symmetrical windows, big clock, and several pointed spears around the bell itself. The clock is Norway's oldest that is still in use. This is still an active parish church, hosting weekly sermons and concerts. The original altar and pulpit, dating to 1699, are both still intact, and when the church is open, you are free to explore its beautiful interior. This space is inviting for anyone seeking some quiet amid the bustle of a busy city evening.

OSLO WEST

The Bygdøy Peninsula is a little farther west of Frogner and Majorstuen, and this is the walkable area where a lot of Oslo's major museums are located. The peninsula is also home

to several popular beaches, mainly on the west side of the island.

★ Vigelandsparken

Opposite Kirkeveien 19; open 24 hours; free

Vigeland Sculpture Park is perhaps the most popular attraction in Oslo, and with good reason. The sculpture park, part of **Frogner Park** (Frognerparken), is the largest in the world created by one artist, Gustav Vigeland. In addition to carving, sculpting, and casting more than 200 sculptures, Vigeland also designed the layout of the park himself.

Gustav Vigeland was born in Mandal in 1869 and lived most of his life in Oslo, until his death in 1943. He is best known for his stone sculptures, but he also made wood carvings. He had long dreamed of creating a massive monument of some sort, and finally got the approval to start his project in 1907. He envisioned a square tiled with stone, where the tiles would create a sort of labyrinth leading to a large central monument. This is exactly what you will find in the Vigeland Park. He worked on the project, with new ideas continuously being added, up until his death. The park was not fully completed, with all pieces installed, until around 1950.

The sculptures in the park display a range of human emotions and relationships; you'll find beautiful and whimsical depictions of everything from the frustrations of parenthood, to love between siblings, to vanity, grief, and anger. The largest of the sculptures, **Monolitten** (*The Monolith*) is both fascinating and slightly grotesque, as it displays human bodies twisted together into a large stone column. Fun fact: the entire *Monolith* was carved from the same piece of stone! Another popular, though much smaller, statue is called **Sinnataggen,** depicting an angry little boy throwing a tantrum.

Vigeland Park is particularly busy on Sundays, when locals and visitors alike head out to get some fresh air, enjoy a walk with friends, or lounge on the grass.

Vigeland Museum (Vigelandmuseet)

Nobels Gate 32; tel. 23 49 37 00; https://vigeland. museum.no; Tues.-Sun. noon-4pm; adults 100 kr children free

Next to the Vigeland Park, you can learn more about Gustav Vigeland and his life at this museum, which houses 1,600 additional sculptures as well as some of his drawings and wood carvings. Together with the Vigeland Sculpture Park, the museum is part of a comprehensive view of Vigeland's art. The museum also offers tours of Vigeland's apartment in Oslo, which has been kept intact with its original furnishings, so you can get a glimpse into his life in Oslo with his wife Ingerid. Check the website to find out if a tour will be held during your visit.

Norwegian Museum of Cultural History (Norsk Folkemuseum)

Museumsveien 10; tel. 22 12 37 00; www. norskfolkemuseum.no; daily 11am-4pm Oct.-Apr., daily 10am-5pm May-Sept.; adults 180 kr, children free

Norsk Folkemuseum is one of the many museums located on the Bygdøy peninsula in western Oslo. This open-air museum is packed with historic buildings and aims to teach visitors about the culture of Norway and its development from the 16th century until today. One of the main attractions is the **Gol Stave Church,** which dates back to around 1200.

Every day there is a varied program of events and tours around the museum, including a guided tour of the permanent exhibitions and displays, Norwegian fairy tales in front of the fireplace, traditional cooking classes, and more. There is a museum shop and a café on property, where you can enjoy lunch during your visit.

1: Royal Palace 2: Oslo Cathedral
3: Vigelandsparken

Viking Ship Museum
(Vikingshiphuset)

Huk Aveny 35; tel. 22 13 52 80; www.khm.uio.no/besok-oss/vikingskipshuset

The Viking Ship Museum is an important attraction for those interested in Norway's Viking heritage. The museum houses many artifacts from the Viking age, but perhaps most important are the original Viking ships that can be found here: The Oseberg, Gokstad, Tune, and Borre ships are all Viking ships that have been found in excavations around Norway.

The Viking Ship Museum is closed for renovations until 2026.

Fram Museum

Bygdøynesveien 36; tel. 23 28 29 50; www.frammuseum.no; daily 11am-5pm; adults 140 kr, children 50 kr

Another museum of Bygdøy, the Fram Museum, is dedicated to polar exploration and the expeditions of Norwegian explorers Fridtjof Nansen, Otto Sverdrup, and Roald Amundsen. These men lived in the late 1800s and early 1900s, and all set out to explore the world. Roald Amundsen is perhaps most famous for leading the first expedition to reach the South Pole, while Fridtjof Nansen was the lead on the first crossing of Greenland. Otto Sverdrup was a part of this expedition as well as others led by Nansen and Amundsen. The polar expedition ship *Fram* ("Forward" in Norwegian) is the main attraction. Known as the world's strongest wooden ship, it's quite an impressive sight. It is possible to go inside the ship on your visit to see the cabins, cargo hold, engine room, and lounges in the interior, allowing visitors to envision what it might have been like to be on one of the polar voyages.

Kon-Tiki Museum

Bygdøynesveien 36; tel. 23 08 67 67; www.kon-tiki.no; daily 11am-5pm; adults 140 kr, children 50 kr

The *Kon-Tiki* is another famous Norwegian ship, and this museum is perfect for those interested in the fascinating stories of Norwegian explorers. The *Kon-Tiki* is actually more of a raft than a traditional ship, and it has one large sail in the middle. This makes it even more impressive to think that it sailed more than 8,000 kilometers (4,970 mi) in 101 days. It belonged to explorer Thor Heyerdahl, a Norwegian archaeologist and adventurer. He built the boat to demonstrate his theory on how far it would have been possible for people to sail in the past, before they had the tools for ship-building we have today. A lot of visitors are surprised to learn of all the things Heyerdahl did, including overseeing important explorations to the Galapagos and Easter Island. Another fun fact that you'll learn more about at this museum is that he actually won an Academy Award for his documentary about his crossing of the Pacific Ocean onboard the *Kon-Tiki*. In the museum, you will get to see not only *Kon-Tiki* itself, but also his other vessel *Ra II* and several artifacts from Heyerdahl's many expeditions.

Norwegian Maritime Museum

Bygdøynesveien 36; tel. 22 12 37 00; www.marmuseum.no; daily 11am-4pm; adults 140 kr adults, children 50 kr

The Norwegian Maritime Museum invites you to explore the role of the ocean in Norwegian history, from stories of mythical monsters to the shipping and ferry routes that have covered the Norwegian coastline for centuries. There are interesting exhibits for all ages, but the museum is especially fun for the younger visitors; the museum even hosts "baby tours" on the last Wednesday of every month, designed for children younger than 2 years of age.

OSLO EAST
Botanical Garden

Sars' Gate/Monrads Gate; tel. 22 85 17 00; www.nhm.uio.no/utstillinger/botanisk-hage; daily 7am-5pm; free tour Sun. noon May-Aug.

An important green space for locals, but perhaps even more popular with tourists, the Botanical Garden is worth a visit for botany enthusiasts as well as those

Oslo East

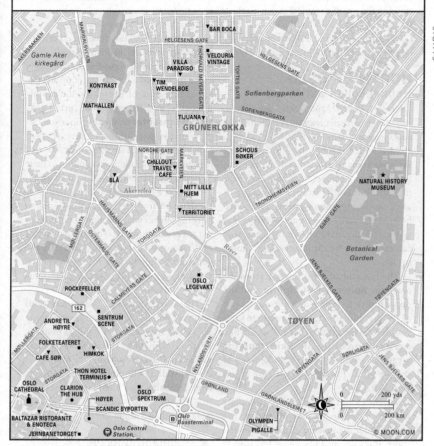

who just want a lovely stroll. The gardens contain more than 5,500 different plants from all over the world, grown in several different types of climates and environments. Don't miss the small garden **Dufthagen** (Scent Garden), filled with plants and flowers that give off very distinct odors and aromas. Another favorite is the **Victoria House,** built in the style of Victorian-era greenhouses. In the summer months (July-Aug.), join one of the free English tours of the gardens. Tours cannot be pre-booked, and are available on first-come, first-served basis.

Natural History Museum

Sars' Gate 1; tel. 22 85 17 00; www.nhm.uio.no; daily 10am-5pm June-Aug., Tues.-Fri. 11am-4pm, Sat.-Sun. 10am-5pm Sept.-May; adults 120 kr, children 60 kr

One of several buildings scattered in and around the Botanical Garden, the Natural History Museum is home to permanent exhibitions on geology, zoology, and the climate, in addition to temporary exhibitions that change regularly. In the building called **Klimahuset** (Climate House, opened in 2020), you'll find several environment-focused exhibits that make learning fun for adults and children alike; it is the first exhibition in the Nordics focused solely on climate. You can experience what it's like to stand in the eye of a tropical storm, peek at what the world would be like if it was 3°C (37°F) warmer, and learn about how you can help affect the climate in a positive way.

NORTH OF OSLO
Holmenkollen Ski Arena

Kongeveien 5; tel. 22 92 32 00; www.holmenkollen.com; daily 10am-4pm; museum adults 160 kr, children 80 kr, simulator adults 110 kr, children 55 kr

Holmenkollen is more than just a famous ski jump arena where national and international ski jump competitions have been held for years. It is also a place where locals go to work out (just try running to the top and see how out of breath you get!), and to enjoy great views of the city, and it offers an assortment of fun experiences for thrill-seekers, just north of Oslo.

The fun and adventurous activities include the **Kollensvevet Zipline,** and the opportunity to rappel down from the top of the ski jump tower. If you prefer to keep your feet on the ground, but still would like a taste of adrenaline, the **Ski Simulator** gives you a sense of what it's like to sit at the top of the tower before soaring off on your skis.

A visit to Holmenkollen isn't complete without a trip to the **Ski Museum,** the world's oldest museum dedicated to the sport. It opened in 1923, and offers insight into 4,000 years of skiing history. There are more than 2,500 pairs of skis on display, some having belonged to Norwegian royals and athletes. The oldest pair of skis in the museum date back to AD 600!

Holmenkollen is located almost 9 kilometers (5 mi) northwest of Central Oslo. Subway line 1, in the direction of Frognerseteren, services the nearest subway stop (helpfully named Holmenkollen). From Jernbanetorget, the travel time by subway is 26 minutes.

Norsk Teknisk Museum

Kjelsåsveien 143; tel. 22 79 60 00; www.tekniskmuseum. no; Tues., Wed., Fri. 9am-4pm, Thurs. 9am-9pm, Sat.-Sun. 10am-5pm; adults 165 kr, children 110 kr

This immersive and fun museum experience focuses on scientists' brilliant past discoveries, and looks ahead to possible developments in the future. From the history of oil and gas to the invention of electricity, the exhibitions at NTM will awaken your curiosity. At **Oslo Vitensenter** on the first floor you can try your own scientific experiments. In fact, Norsk Teknisk Museum offers over 100 "try-it-yourself" installations, in addition to their 25 permanent exhibitions—fun for all ages.

There is a daily program of activities at the museum, from testing out 3D printing to learning Morse code. The most popular event is a science show, which is usually put on two to three times a day; scientists entertain the audience by conducting fun experiments, some of which result in small explosions, smoke, and fire.

The museum is located 7 kilometers (4 mi) north of Central Oslo. The journey time using public transportation is around 25 minutes. By tram, take number 11 from Jernbanetorget to Kjelsåsalléen. From there, the museum is a short walk (5-10 minutes). Bus 54 leaves from Jernbanetorget and takes you straight to Kjelsås Stasjon, which is an even shorter walk (less than 5 minutes).

★ Hadeland Glassverk

Glassverkveien 9, 3520 Jevnaker; tel. 61 31 64 00; www. hadeland.com; Mon.-Fri. 11am-4pm, Sat.-Sun. 11am-5pm; free entry, fee for selected exhibitions

Around an hour north of Oslo you will find Hadeland Glassverk, a glassworks village that was founded in 1762, making it Norway's oldest continuously operating industrial business. Hadeland Glassverk is the glass supplier of the Norwegian royal family, and you won't find a Norwegian household that doesn't have a wine glass or a vase from Hadeland.

The glassworks village today is much more than a factory. In the cluster of old houses on the property you will find several restaurants, cafés, shops, galleries, and exhibitions. A highlight is the exhibition *Monet & Friends: Life, Light & Color,* in which the walls and floor of the gallery come alive with colors, art, music, and photographs, offering an immersive experience depicting the life and influence of Monet and his contemporaries.

There are 10 different shops around Hadeland Glassworks, each with a different concept and focus. Of course, you will find shops dedicated to the glass made there, with some collections being made exclusively for their outlets at Hadeland. Additionally, there is a large food hall with stands focusing on local food, drinks, and produce. If you love finding local goods and gifts on your travels, Hadeland is a great day trip from Oslo.

Hadeland is located around 70 kilometers (43 mi) north of Oslo. If you have a car, following main road E16 will get you there in around 1 hour and 15 minutes. Follow E18 toward Sandvika, and take E16 toward Hønefoss from there. Then, take Fv241 (also known as Hadelandsveien) until you reach your destination.

By public transport, you can reach Hadeland in 1 hour and 45 minutes. Take bus 200 to Hønefoss from Oslo Bus Terminal. Frøm Hønefoss, bus 113 takes you straight to Hadeland Glassverk (this is also the name of the stop).

Sports and Recreation

TOURS

Oslo is a very walkable city that is easily explored on your own, but joining a tour can help you get the lay of the land and more context on the city, especially on your first day.

Oslo Free Walking Tour
Jernbanetorget; daily 10am; free
Nordic Freedom Tours offers free walking tours of Oslo every day, starting from the big tiger statue at Jernbanetorget, in front of Oslo Central Station. There is usually one tour per day, but during school holidays and otherwise busy times there may be more available. Tipping is not expected but is happily received, as the local guides provide these tours for no salary. The tour lasts around 1.5 hours, and highlights include Aker Brygge, the City Hall, Stortinget, and the Oslo Stock Exchange.

FoodTours.eu
Karl Johans Gate 31 (meeting point); tel. 0045 50 123645; https://foodtours.eu; Tues.-Sat. 1pm; ages 12 and up 1,080 kr, children 11 and under 900 kr
If you want to immerse yourself in local Norwegian cuisine, a food tour might be the ideal way for you to explore Oslo. "Taste of Oslo" is a 4-hour experience including seven different food tastings and 3-4 kilometers (1.8-2.5 mi) of walking. All together, these tastings will make up the size of a meal, so it is recommended that you show up just a little hungry for the tour. Menus change based on the season and the venues visited; you can expect to sample and learn about Norwegian traditional dishes such as the heart-shaped waffle, and the Norwegian hot dog.

City Sightseeing Norway Hop-On Hop-Off Bus
Universitetsplassen (first stop); tel. 223 32 000; www.stromma.com/en-no/oslo; daily 10am-4pm every 30 minutes; 24-hour ticket 400 kr, 48-hour ticket 495 kr
For those less keen on walking, this traditional open-air, hop-on, hop-off bus tour starts near Nationaltheateret, in front of the old University buildings along Karl Johans Gate. It covers the main sights of Oslo on its round-trip, including the Royal Palace and the Vigeland Sculpture Park, with audio guides available in several languages. The complete round-trip, if you don't hop off, takes around 1 hour. You get a 24- or 48-hour ticket for the bus that lets you hop on and off at any of

the stops while your ticket is valid. This is a smart way to cover a lot of ground if you're short on time.

PARKS

On warm summer days, there is nothing the people of Oslo love more than finding a green area to gather with friends to sit on blankets, listen to music, catch up, and drink beer they brought with them. (Bear in mind that consuming alcohol in a public place that does not hold a liquor license is technically illegal—but law enforcement often turns a blind eye to smaller crowds gathered simply to enjoy the sun.)

Ekebergparken

Kongsveien 23; tel. 21 42 19 19; www.ekebergparken. com; daily; free

Located on the waterfront a few kilometers east of the Opera House, Ekebergparken is perhaps the most unique park in Oslo after Vigeland Park. It's also a sculpture park, opened in 2013, with sculptures ranging from modern pieces by contemporary artists to classical sculptures dating back to the 1880s. You'll recognize famous names such as Damien Hirst, Salvador Dali, and of course, Gustav Vigeland. Perhaps one of the most fascinating art installations is *Pathfinder #18700* by Fujiko Nakaya. This is a mist/fog installation, aimed to change the way you view the nature around you. At specific intervals throughout the day, the forest around the installation is filled with fog, leaving you with an almost eerie impression of the park.

There are several pathways and trails around the park, making it a pleasure to explore on foot. Trams 13 and 19 service the stop Ekebergparken, and this is the closest to the park.

Frognerparken

Kirkeveien; daily; free

Frogner Park is best known for housing the Vigeland Sculpture Park, but the area surrounding the famous sculptures should not be ignored. This is the largest park in central Oslo, with several different species of Norwegian trees, and Norway's largest collection of roses (14,000 roses of 150 different species), making a walk here on a blooming spring day ideal for a flower enthusiast.

Sofienbergparken

Sofienbergparken; daily; free

Sofienbergparken is one of the most popular parks in Oslo, especially among locals. Find it in the Grünerløkka neighborhood, east of the Akerselva. There is a dog park and children's playground, and public toilet facilities available, but perhaps most exciting about this park are the pay-per-minute barbecues. The cost of 30 minutes of barbecuing (pay by credit card) is the same as the price of a one-time-use barbecue at the grocery store, making this is a more environmentally friendly option, at no extra cost. For a truly local idea of an afternoon, bring some food to the park, fire up the barbecue, and enjoy your meal while people-watching from the lawn.

HIKING

Norwegians love to hike, and in Norway's capital city, you'll find an array of trails just a subway ride away. One of the most popular weekend escapes for Oslo residents is **Nordmarka**, north of the capital, with lots of hiking, camping, and recreational opportunities. The forested area is around 430 square kilometers (166 sq mi), with the highest peak, Svarttjernshøgda, some 719 meters (2,360 ft) above sea level. Most of the trails are well-marked, and there are signs set up around the area to indicate the direction of each hike. Drop by the Oslo Visitors Center for specific information on which route to choose and how to get there; it's possible to reach several trailheads in Nordmarka by subway and bus.

1: Hadeland Glassverk 2: view from Ekeberg Sculpture Park 3: one of the many cascades along Akerselva 4: Bakken Strand

Sognsvann

Distance: *3.7 kilometers (2.3 mi)*
Time: *45 minutes*
Trailhead: *Sognsvann subway station (at the end of line 5)*
Information and Maps: *www.visitoslo.com/en/product/?tlp=2982813&name=Sognsvann-lake*

Sognsvann is a lake just north of Oslo, located in the Nordmarka area, that's popular for walking, running, and cross-country skiing in the winter. This easy loop trail circumnavigates the lake and is accessible for travelers with disabilities, though it is made of gravel, so it is best attempted with a wheelchair meant for outdoor use. There is a kiosk by the lake that sells ice cream, drinks, and other snacks in summer. If you're visiting in the warming months, bring your swimwear and jump in the water after your walk.

To get to the trailhead, take subway line 5 to Sognsvann (in the direction of Sognsvann). The total travel time from Jernbanetorget is 19 minutes.

Grefsenkollen

Distance: *3.1 kilometers (1.9 mi)*
Time: *1.5 hours*
Trailhead: *Bus stop Grefsenkollveien (take bus 25)*
Information and Maps: *www.visitoslo.com/en/product/?tlp=3073403&name=Wanderung-nach-Grefsenkollen*

Grefsenkollen, a little bit east of Norsk Teknisk Museum and the Akerselva river, is a great option for anyone who's looking for an easy hike with great rewards. From Grefsenkollen you will get great views of the city and the fjord, and there is even a restaurant and café at the top. The top of Grefsenkollen is 379 meters (1,243 ft) above sea level. It is not quite a mountain, but more of a hilltop. The word "koll" (or "kollen") is what Norwegians call smaller mountains that do not quite resemble proper mountains such as those you will find in western Norway. Some locals opt to spend the night at Grefsenkollen in their hammocks, so they can wake up to the beautiful sight of the sunrise over Oslo.

To get to the trailhead, take bus 25 from Majorstuen to Grefsenkollveien. The journey time is 28 minutes.

CYCLING

Oslo is not only a very walkable city, but also bike-friendly. Because a lot of locals commute to work on bicycles, you will notice quite a few bicycle lanes along the main roads in the city. Most bike routes in Oslo extend from the city center toward the outer edges of the city to encourage more people to use bicycles as their mode of transportation. For visitors, however, walking is the easiest way to get around, particularly in central Oslo, because so many cycle paths lead out of the city center (and not around it). Many bike routes in Oslo are considered "green routes," meaning that you can cycle the entire route without really spending any time in traffic or on main roads. Simply put your helmet on and enjoy the ride through the greenery of Oslo.

The main thing to know about, if you are interested in cycling in Oslo, is the **Oslo Bysykkel** (city bike) scheme (tel. 91 58 97 00; www.oslobysykkel.no; daily; 59 kr for a day, 60-minute trips at a time). Like in many other European cities, the Bysykkel scheme allows you to pay a daily, weekly, monthly, or even yearly fee, in exchange for access to the city's communal bikes. There are 252 drop-off points around Oslo, and you can use the Bysykkel app to learn where there are bikes available. When you are done, simply park your bike at one of the drop-off points.

Nydalen-Majorstua

Distance: *4 kilometers (2.5 mi)*
Time: *20 minutes*
Trailhead: *Nydalen Underground Station*
Information and Maps: *www.bikemap.net/en/r/5521305/#10.93/59.9398/10.7397*

The bicycle paths and lanes between Nydalen and Majorstua station are collectively known as "the green route." This network takes you through lush parks and other green spaces filled with trees, grassy flats, and gravel pathways. More than half of this route is gravel, as it takes you past neighborhoods, playgrounds,

Oslo in Winter

While most people visit Oslo in the summer months, there is still plenty to do in the winter. Travelers heading up north to chase the northern lights might find themselves with a few days to spend in Oslo during the colder months, and they won't be disappointed. Cross-country skiing and sledding are just a subway ride away from the city center, and the Christmas market in December will get you in that holiday spirit. Oslo is particularly beautiful in the winter snow as well. The main thing to note when visiting during this season is that the days are a lot shorter, as the sun rises as late as 9:30am and sets around 3pm.

Locals know how to make good use of their daylight hours, and on the weekends, you'll find them all leaving the city center to go skiing. But the most important thing they do in winter is embrace the Scandinavian concept of "hygge," which loosely translates as "coziness." This includes bracing the cold to meet up with friends for a glass of wine or lighting the fire in your apartment to stay warm. Norwegians rarely complain about the cold, and simply dress for it without the drama. The best thing you can do to adopt this is to bring base layers of wool and warm shoes on your trip.

ICE SKATING ON SPIKERSUPPA SKØYTEBANE

Every winter, Spikersuppa (literal translation: "the Nail Soup"), a fountain located between the Royal Palace and Norwegian Parliament, is turned into a small, free ice-skating rink. It's a great place for beginners trying ice skating for the first time, and you can rent skates at a little hut nearby (tel. 90 66 33 65; 150 kr). It's especially beautiful during Christmas, when the holiday lights are up.

CROSS-COUNTRY SKIING

In the winter months, you'll find lots of Oslo residents crowding public transportation with skis and snowboards in tow, heading out to cross-country skiing routes. There are several places in Oslo where you can rent skis completely free of charge through an organization called **BUA** (www.bua.io) on a first-come, first-served basis (though they usually have enough for everyone). If that fails, you can rent skis from **SkiMore Oslo** (www.skimore.no).

One great route is to ski from the Sognsvann Underground Station to Ullevålseter (5.3 km/3.3 mi one-way). Subway line 5 takes you to Sognsvann (the end stop) in 19 minutes. This is what Norwegians call a lysløype, or lighted route, meaning the ski route is lit with lamps during the darker months, making it perfect for an after-work ski session. At Ullevålseter there's a small café serving coffee and snacks for those who want to take a break and warm up.

JUL I VINTERLAND

At Christmastime (Nov.-Dec.), the center of Oslo, from Spikersuppa to Karl Johans Gate, is turned into Santa's village. Jul i Vinterland (Christmas in Winterland; www.julivinterland.no) draws vendors from all over the country, selling Christmas presents, treats, and hot chocolate. There is a Ferris wheel, caroling, storytelling, and more happening around the area. And, of course, the little ones can meet Santa!

sporting fields, and forested areas. The park area behind Ullevål Hospital is particularly relaxing, and you might find yourself forgetting that you are in a major Norwegian city.

Akerselva

Distance: 8 kilometers (5 mi)
Time: 30 minutes

Trailhead: Kjelsås Station
Information and Maps: https://ridewithgps.com/routes/35010925

Akerselva is not only a lovely bike route, but also a great walk for those who prefer it. From Kjelsås, simply follow the river all the way down to central Oslo and the fjord. Along this route you will find several historic bridges, parks, old factories, cute cafés, and places to stop and rest. On a sunny day, many of the grassy areas around the river are busy with locals having a barbecue, playing frisbee, or just relaxing on the grass.

BEACHES AND SWIMMING

There are several great beaches along the Oslofjord, perfect for cooling down in the summer. Though you may not think of Norway as a beach destination, you'll find that some of these strands are very popular and get quite crowded during the summer holidays. Many of the beaches have cafés and ice cream huts open during the day, where you can grab a cold drink to cool off.

Katten
Mosseveien, bus stop Katten
This popular, sandy beach has bathroom facilities as well as a kiosk that is open in the summer. In addition to the sand beach, there are both grassy and rock slopes to relax on. Katten is located south along the Oslofjord, past Ekebergparken.

Katten is popular enough to have its own bus stop. From Jernbanetorget, take bus 83 toward Tårnåsen. Get off at Katten after a journey of 13 minutes. Once you get off the bus, cross under the road through a pedestrian tunnel; there are steps leading down to the

tunnel, but they have tracks for wheelchairs and strollers.

Paradisbukta
Bygdøy
Paradisbukta, on Bygdøy, is a lovely beach on a bay, with some rocky slopes. This bay originally belonged to the royal family as part of their lands, but was given to the municipality in 1929 after locals started using it. Right near the beach you will find Kongeskogen (King's Forest). There is a memorial to the victims of the 2004 tsunami in the Indian Ocean in Paradisbukta, and it's worth seeing if you visit the beach. To get there, take bus 30 from Jernbanetorget toward Bygdøy. Get off at stop Huk. The total journey takes 28 minutes, and from Huk, Paradisbukta is a 5- to 10-minute walk away.

Bakken Strand by Skinnerbukta
Malmøya
A hidden gem, this beach is a little less busy than Skinnerbukta, another beach nearby, just south of Ekebergparken in the Oslofjord. Malmøya is quite picturesque, and has a dock with a diving tower just off the water's edge. To get here, catch bus 85 toward Ulvøya and get off at Malmøya. The bus ride takes 16 minutes. From there Skinnerbukta and Bakken Beach is a 15-minute walk across the little island, and it is well worth it.

Entertainment and Events

THE ARTS

The well-known Opera House is not the only place to catch a show in Oslo. The city is filled with music and performance venues, with concert arenas such as **Valle Hovin stadium** (Innspurten 12; tel. 21 80 21 80; 900 kr), **Oslo Spektrum** (Sonja Henies Plass 2; tel. 22 05 29 00; https://oslospektrum.no; 1,000 kr), and **Telenor Arena** (John Strandruds vei 16; https://telenorarena.no; 1,000 kr) drawing big-name artists like Bruce Springsteen,

the Rolling Stones, and Madonna. In addition, you can enjoy acoustic performances and local artists at places like **Rockefeller** (Badstugata 2; tel. 22 20 32 32; www.rockefeller.no; 500 kr) and **Sentrum Scene** (Arbeidersamfunnets Plass 1; tel. 22 20 32 32; www.rockefeller.no).

Musicals and plays are staged mainly in Norwegian across the city, but traveling ensembles always perform in English. For example, Oslo Spektrum has hosted shows such as *Cats* and *Disney on Ice* in the past.

Oslo Opera House (Operahuset Oslo)

Kirsten Flaagstads plass 1; tel. 21 42 21 21; www.operaen. no; 500-1,200 kr

The Opera House is an attraction in and of itself, but this is also the main venue for ballet and opera performances in Oslo. Classical music concerts are also put on here, often with a focus on small, intimate ensembles (think acoustic performances with just a singer and a pianist). Events happen several nights a week, so you have a good chance of attending a performance during your visit.

Nationaltheateret

Johanne Dybwads Plass 1; tel. 22 00 14 00; www. nationaltheatret.no

This is Oslo's most important performance venue, and perhaps the most famous. The building itself is known as Norway's most beautiful theater, and there is a lot of history in the walls: The theater opened in 1899, and the first plays put on here were written by famed Norwegian playwrights like Henrik Ibsen, Bjørnstjerne Bjørnson, and Ludvig Holberg. This is a great place to see a classic play like *Hedda Gabler*. They also put on more child-friendly shows, like *The Little Prince* and *Hakkebakkeskogen* (based on a Norwegian children's book). The plays are mainly translated to Norwegian, and ticket prices range from 400-800 kr.

Folketeateret

Storgaten 21-23; tel. 21 09 65 00; www.folketeateret. no; 400-800 kr

Folketeateret was the former home of the Norwegian Opera, before they moved to their new opera house. The stage here is Norway's largest, housing up to 1,400 guests. Today, you'll find that Folketeateret is used as a musical stage: they have put on productions of *Chicago, Chess, Mamma Mia,* and *We Will Rock You* in the past. The performances are often translated to English from Norwegian, but make sure to check this before you book your ticket.

FESTIVALS AND EVENTS

Oslo is popular place to host a music festival, drawing major international names as well as lesser-known Scandinavian talents. Matstreif is one of the largest food festivals in Norway, and takes place in Oslo each year.

Spring
The 17th of May

The Palace and Karl Johans Gate; www.oslo.kommune. no/17-mai; May

Norway's Constitution Day is simply called 17 Mai, and regardless of where you are in Norway, if your visit coincides with this day, there will be festivities including a parade, a marching band, and games for children. That said, Oslo is perhaps the best place to be: The parade up Karl Johans Gate is massive, and the royal family looks on from the balcony of the palace above. You can see the parade from anywhere along Karl Johans Gate street, but of course most people want to stand as close to the palace as possible. In addition to the parade, you'll see people all over the city in their Bunad (the Norwegian national costume, which varies by region but mainly consists of a white shirt, decadent silver brooches and other jewelry, and a long dress with many different patterns and colors), waving flags and drinking champagne to celebrate. If you want to dine out in Oslo on the 17th of May, make your reservation weeks in advance, as everyone and their grandmother will be out celebrating.

Summer
Øyafestivalen

Tøyenparken; www.oyafestivalen.no; Aug.; day pass 1,300 kr

Traditionally a rock-focused festival, Øyafestivalen (known to locals as simply Øya) has expanded to many music genres and artists over the years. The festival lasts four days and is held in Tøyenparken, where attendees sit on the grassy slopes to enjoy the music; most people pack a picnic and bring a blanket

☆ The Best of Norwegian Design

In general, Norwegian design has a few typical characteristics: clean, traditional lines; minimalism and simplicity; and a color palette inspired by nature. In recent years, Nordic home goods, furniture, and style have become increasingly popular, and can be found in interior design magazines all over the world. Often incorporating light wood details, this decor style leaves lots of room for open space (Norwegians call it "clutter-free"). The same can be said for Norwegian clothing: Sleek, classic cuts, and simple details and colors are the hallmarks, and again words like "minimalistic" and "functional" apply. Most Norwegian brands have their flagship store in either Oslo or Bergen, and these are the best places to find their latest designs and see what's new from each brand. Norwegian brands to look for include **BRGN** (a brand creating stylish, waterproof rain clothes for city living) and **byTimo** (an Oslo-based brand designing vintage-inspired clothing).

Should you find yourself admiring the sleek spaces and classic, chic local style while in Oslo, there are plenty of places in the city to pick up a piece for your home or closet:

- **Høyer:** Find upscale fashion and home goods right off of Karl Johans Gate (page 75).

- **Illums Bolighus:** This is the go-to place for Scandinavian home goods (page 75).

- **Holzweiler:** This luxury brand is known for soft fabrics and clean designs (page 75).

to sit on. Tickets usually sell out months in advance, as this is one of the biggest happenings in Oslo.

Fall
by:Larm
Various locations; https://bylarm.no; Sept.; 1,350 kr

The perfect event for anyone wanting to explore and discover Scandinavian artists, especially those who are yet to be signed, by:Larm spreads across four days and several venues in Oslo. It was originally held in Trondheim in 1998, and moved from city to city for 10 years before settling permanently in Oslo. by:Larm has been a stepping stone into the industry for

artists such as Aurora, Nico & Vinz, Sigrid, and Kaizers Orchestra. Billie Eilish performed at the 2018 festival.

Matstreif
Youngstorget; www.innovasjonnorge.no/matstreif; every Sept.; free

Matstreif is a national food festival, where producers from all over Norway gather to display and sell their food. Offerings include popular Norwegian cheeses (from providers like Ostegården cheesery) and cider from Hardanger. In previous years, the food festival has been held at Rådhusplassen, in front of City Hall.

Shopping

SLOTTSPARKEN AND AROUND

In central Oslo you will find that most of the shopping stretches along Karl Johans Gate, in addition to several shopping centers in the area. From souvenir shops and fashion flagship stores (such as H&M) to electronics and

cosmetics (Lyko, Teknikmagasinet), the street has a large variety of stores. If you are looking for more unique shops, however, simply venture out into the side streets. Real estate on the main street has become quite expensive, and so it is home mainly to major brands and chain stores.

Steen & Strøm

*Kongensgate 23; https://steenogstromoslo.no; Mon.-Fri.
10am-7pm, Sat. 10am-6pm*

This is the only department store in Norway
and can be compared to Selfridges and
Debenhams of London, or Macy's and Saks
Fifth Avenue of New York. At this traditional
department store, you will find cosmetics,
clothing, shoes, and a large food court.

Høyer

*Jernbanetorget 6; tel. 22 17 03 00; www.hoyer.no;
Mon.-Fri. 10am-8pm, Sat. 10am-6pm*

Høyer is a luxury store that has curated a large
selection of Norwegian and Scandinavian
brands, and it is worth visiting if you want
to browse the best of Norwegian design, both
clothing and interior.

Illums Bolighus

*Haakon VIIsgate 10; tel. 22 01 55 10; www.
illumsbolighus.no; Mon.-Fri. 10am-7pm, Sat. 10am-6pm*

Illums Bolighus is a traditional store with
roots dating back to 1925, when they were
founded by appointment to the queen of
Denmark (a statement they proudly display on
every window of the store). Here you can shop
home goods and glassware from Scandinavian
brands in an open space that might remind
you of a department store.

By Malene Birger

*Karl Johans Gate 37-43; https://bmbpaleetoslo.no; tel.
22 41 33 14; Mon.-Fri. 10am-8pm, Sat. 10am-6pm*

This is the Norwegian flagship store of
By Malene Birger, the quick-growing
Scandinavian brand tailored to the modern
woman. Keywords such as bohemian, contemporary, and feminine describe the style, and
the pieces in the collections of this brand are
pricey, but are meant to be investment pieces.

Norway Designs

*Lille Grensen 7; tel. 23 11 45 10; www.norwaydesigns.no;
Mon.-Sat. 10am-6pm*

Just off of Karl Johans Gate you will find
Norway Designs, a store dedicated to supporting sustainable Norwegian craftmakers
and designers. Across a space of 500 square
meters (5,400 sq ft), the store has a large selection of Norwegian glassware, ceramics, home
goods, and clothes.

Tronsmo

*Universitetsgata 12; tel. 22 99 03 99; www.tronsmo.
no; Mon.-Wed. 9am-5pm, Thurs.-Fri. 9am-6pm, Sat.
10am-4pm*

Tronsmo is a bookstore that has stood its
ground through the years as chain book-
stores have taken over the market all across
Norway. The result is a charming, unpretentious store that doesn't listen to the large publishing houses when selecting their inventory.
As they say themselves, they are always looking for literarure that they think "deserves
attention." If you are looking for alternative
literature, such as critical pieces on globaliza-
tion and politics, or American beat literature,
this is the place to go.

OSLO WEST

In the area of Majorstuen and Frogner, you
will find that the stores get more exclusive
and expensive; this is where you will find
the flagship stores of the more luxurious
brands, such as HAY, Hestra, and Change
of Scandinavia. Oslo West's main shopping
street is **Bogstadveien** (www.bogstadveien.
no), which becomes **Hegdehaugsveien**
(the two streets are connected in a straight
line, and you could easily think they are the
same street); at the end of Bogstadveien, on
Valkyrie Plass, there is often a farmers market on Saturdays.

Holzweiler

*Oscars Gate 19; www.holzweiler.no; Mon.-Fri. 10am-
7pm, Sat. 10am-6pm*

Holzweiler is a well-known Norwegian fashion brand that started out selling thick, luxurious, soft scarves and is now a small clothing
empire, with everything from shoes to lounge-
wear (you will recognize their hoodies around
town from the small clothes hanger embroi-
dered on the chest). They often collabo-
rate with international designers on their

collections, and a visit to their flagship store is worth it to get a look into what they have been working on.

Uff

Hegdehaugsveien 24; 63 92 89 80; www.uffnorge.org; Mon.-Sat. 11am-6pm

Uff is a secondhand company that has been operating several vintage shops in Oslo since the 1980s. Their store in Hedgehaugsveien started as a pop-up but eventually became permanent. At Uff you can find vintage and secondhand items for a fraction of the original price; the Hegdehaugsveien location, where they send their more "preppy" styles, is at the end of Bogstadveien (Bogstadveien technically "becomes" Hegdehaugsveien at one point). You can also find Uff in Thorvald Meyers Gate 74 (Oslo East) and Prinsensgate 2b (central Oslo).

Eske Interiør

Sofies Gate 16; tel. 40 00 52 53; www.eskeinterior.no; Mon.-Fri. 11am-5pm, Sat. 11am-4pm

If you are looking for interior pieces and design for your home, look no further than Eske Interiør. This shop is known for its unique collection of interior design products, and they carry pieces from lesser known as well as famous brands and designers, such as Christina Lundsteen, House of Hackeny, and Tom Dixon.

The Feel Good Shop

Bogstadveien 8; https://thefeelgoodshop.no; Mon.-Sat. 11am-5pm

If you are looking for presents (for a friend or for yourself) with meaning, The Feel Good Shop has you covered. In this (alternative) store you will find crystals, jewelry, and essential oils for the home and your body, all designed with a purpose. From powerful crystals for use in meditation to aromatic incense for your home, the Feel Good Shop just wants to make you feel good.

Fromagerie

Valkyriegata 9; 22 60 19 95; www.fromagerie.no; Mon.-Fri. 10am-6pm, Sat. 10am-5pm

Fromagerie, at the end of Bogstadveien, is a cheese store selling a large selection of Norwegian, Scandinavian, and European cheeses. They have one of the largest selections and variations of cheese in Oslo, and those wanting to buy some Norwegian cheese to bring home are likely to find plenty of choices here.

OSLO EAST

The colorful neighborhoods of **Grønland** and **Grünerløkka** are the perfect places for vintage shopping and interior design finds. Most stores in this area are independent, and you are unlikely to find any well-known brand names here.

Velouria Vintage

Thorvald Meyers Gate 34; tel. 909 75 191; https://velouriavintage.no; Mon.-Fri. 11:30am-7pm, Sat. 11am-6pm, Sun. noon-6pm

This independent vintage store is a must for anyone hoping to find some treasures on their Oslo trip. Veluria Vintage sells secondhand shoes, bags, clothes, and other accessories dating back to the 1960s, '70s, and '80s, and each product is hand-selected.

Mitt Lille Hjem

Markveien 56c; www.mittlillehjem.no; Mon.-Sat. 11am-6pm, Sun. midnight-6pm

Mitt Lille Hjem, meaning "my little home," is a colorful little store in the Grünerløkka neighborhood. Every piece in this store is carefully selected, and you will find everything from home decor (such as scented candles and art) to clothes and furniture here. They also have a selection of really good coffee table books, such as *100 Years of Fashion* by Cally Blackman and *Dior in Bloom*, published by Flammarion.

Schous Bøker

Schous Plass 7A; tel. 46 12 00 54; www.schousboker.no;
Wed.-Sun. noon-5pm

This independent used bookstore offers a range of genres but specializes in children's books and modern classics. They also have a large selection of comics. The store has an old-school charm about it, and you'll find comfortable chairs and the opportunity to buy a coffee during your visit.

Food

The culinary scene in Oslo is varied and international, and you will find great restaurants featuring cuisines from all over the world. Try the city's best stone-oven baked pizza at **Villa Paradiso,** explore New Nordic cuisine at Michelin-starred restaurant **Kontrast,** or visit **Sabaki** for a teppanyaki meal. At any given time, there will be a new, hot restaurant to try, but some eateries have over time become staples of the city. Dine in historic surroundings at the **Akershus Fortress restaurant** or visit **Olympen,** the restaurant locals nicknamed "Lompa" decades ago, for example.

Perhaps unsurprising, given its famous coastline and pristine waters, Norway is the world's second-largest exporter of **seafood,** and you'll find restaurants all over the world proudly serving Norwegian salmon. Fittingly, seafood is a large part of Norwegian cuisine, served as fresh as possible, ideally almost straight from the sea. Naturally, Oslo offers a great selection of seafood restaurants, and you'll find that many other restaurants will have some variation of fish soup on the menu.

In addition to having a large variety of different cuisines, Oslo also offers some truly superb gourmet restaurants, including a handful of Michelin-starred establishments. Don't miss out on the industrial style at **Restaurant Kontrast** or **Statholdergaarden's** royal atmosphere; both are one-star Michelin restaurants.

Generally, it is not necessary to book a table at restaurants in Oslo, but there are some exceptions. In the summer months, and especially on weekends, it is smart to reserve a table in advance, to ensure you get to eat when (and where) you'd like. Some of the fancier and more expensive restaurants have a more strict seating window, and so a good rule of thumb is that the more expensive the restaurant is, the more necessary it is to book a table.

WATERFRONT
Local Cuisine
Ekebergrestauranten

Kongsveien 15; tel. 23 24 23 00; www.
ekebergrestauranten.com; Tues.-Sat. noon-9pm (last
seating), Sun. noon-8pm (last seating); 235-325 kr

Located near Ekebergparken, on the water east of the Opera House, Ekebergrestauranten offers Nordic cuisine in an elegant and modern environment with great views of Oslo and the fjord. Typical dishes here might be moules frites (mussels and fries), duck leg confit, and beef tournedos. It is located a nice, 30-minute hike from the city center, and the large restaurant and outdoor seating area are usually busy. Their outdoor patio is especially lovely in the summer.

Steakhouse
Entrecote by Trancher

Bryggetorget 10; tel. 22 44 44 60; https://trancher.no/
aker-brygge; Wed.-Sat. 5pm-10pm; 245-525 kr

If you are looking for a really great steak, this is the place. The staff are self-proclaimed experts on entrecote (a premium cut of beef), and rarely disappoint. The simple menu in this small restaurant has only one main course on it, but there are several delicious sides to add. Because the restaurant focuses all its attention and culinary skills on this piece of

☆ New Nordic 101

Norwegian and Scandinavian cuisine has long been characterized by traditional, meat-focused meals, usually with a side of potatoes and carrots (vegetables grown underground being the easiest to come by in colder climates). However, recent years have seen the emergence of a branch of Scandinavian cuisine named "New Nordic."

In short, New Nordic cuisine endeavors to preserve the traditions of Scandinavian cuisine while bringing in innovative approaches from modern chefs. The focus is still very much on simplicity and functionality—buzzwords when it comes to most things Nordic—and on making the most of local and seasonal produce. New Nordic restaurants serve traditional dishes like salmon, meatballs (kjøttkaker), and reindeer, but instead of the traditional sides of potatoes and carrots, you might find whipped cucumber, steamed asparagus, and crème fraîche mousse. Another tradition from Nordic cooking seen in New Nordic cuisine is the idea of making use of as much of an animal

plate at Ekebergrestauranten

as possible when cooking, also known as "nose-to-tail dining." Therefore, do not be surprised to find moose tongue or even bone marrow on the menu in some of the fancier restaurants serving New Nordic cuisine.

Oslo is one of the best places to try this emerging way of eating; below are a few places to start.

- **Ekebergrestauranten:** Enjoy Nordic dishes made with local, seasonal ingredients and an incredible view of Oslo (page 77).

- **Vaaghals:** Helmed by a roster of celebrity chefs, Vaaghals is one of the city's most famous places to try New Nordic cuisine (page 79).

- **Kontrast:** This Michelin-starred restaurant has a seasonal menu offering its take on modern Scandinavian cuisine (page 81).

meat, you will find that this is the best steak in Oslo, served in a low-key and warm atmosphere with wood accents.

Seafood
Lofoten Fiskerestaurant
Stranden 75; 22 83 08 08; www.lofoten-fiskerestaurant. no
Centrally located in Aker Brygge, Lofoten Fiskerestaurant serves seasonal dishes based on the latest catch. The view over the waterfront is absolutely lovely, and they pride themselves on serving "Norwegian dishes with international standards." The

atmosphere in this large restaurant is modern, and the restaurant feels rather upscale with its white tablecloths and classic table settings.

Sjømagasinet
Tjuvholmen Allé 14; tel. 23 89 77 77; www.sjomagasinet. no
Sjømagasinet is a modern restaurant specializing in grilled seafood dishes. Seasonality and sustainability are key here, along with a large wine selection to find the perfectly paired white wine to go with your fish. They create a bright and

elegant atmosphere in their large, open dining room.

French
Brasserie Rivoli

Operagata 3; tel. 21 42 05 90; www.rivoli.no; Tues.-Fri. 11:30am-11pm, Sat. 2:30pm-11pm; 275-395 kr

With a sleek, clean design and large windows that let in lots of natural light, Brasserie Rivoli is an informal, French-inspired restaurant with a Scandinavian twist. The menu features French and local classics from oysters and French cheeses to fresh Norwegian seafood dishes, and you won't be surprised to find that this restaurant was featured in the Michelin guide.

Asian
Ling Ling

Stranden 30; tel. 24 13 38 00; www.linglingoslo. no; Tues.-Fri. 4:30pm-midnight, Sat. 1pm-midnight; 255-495 kr

Ling Ling is Hakkasan's first restaurant in Scandinavia, serving a Cantonese menu where Hakkasan's popular dishes have been given a Norwegian flair. Of course, they use local ingredients and produce, and you can expect dishes such as plaice dumplings, grilled cod in ginger soy sauce, and a dim sum platter with Norwegian king crab dumplings. Ling Ling also has a large rooftop terrace that is a great place for a drink, offering views of Aker Brygge and the fjord.

Breakfast and Brunch
The Vandelay

Operagata 30; tel. 40 63 14 11; https://thevandelay.no; Wed.-Fri. 8am-11:30pm, Sat. 9am-11:30pm, Sun. 9am-5pm; 375-595 kr

The Vandelay has quickly become a beacon for breakfast and brunch in Oslo, though it's also a great place for dinner. The menu changes with each meal, so you can come back later the same day and try something completely new. The interior that awaits behind their signature pink door is a stylish and luxurious space, and while there is no official dress code, people tend to keep it smart casual here. This spot is known for its bacon cheeseburger, and for the Instagram-friendly design.

SLOTTSPARKEN AND AROUND

Østbanehallen is an indoor market-like collection of restaurants and food shops that are open year-round. It is located in the old railway hall (the name Østbanehallen means "The Eastern Rail Hall"). Restaurants include **Olivia** (Italian) and the historic **Royal Gastropub** (pub fare). You'll also find places to get sandwiches and lighter bites from cafés, such as **Steam Sandwich Bar** and **Flavours Café.** If you are leaving Oslo by train, drop by Østbanehallen to get your snacks and lunch for the trip, as it is conveniently located under the same roof as the train station Oslo S.

Local Cuisine
Vaaghals

Dronning Eufemias Gate 8; tel. 92 07 09 99; www. vaaghals.com; lunch Tues.-Fri. 11am-2:30pm, dinner Tues.-Sat. 5pm-11:30pm; 8-course tasting menu 815 kr

Vaaghals is a modern restaurant in the Barcode district with a lovely terrace and an open kitchen. The atmosphere in this intimate restaurant is modern and businesslike, with wooden tables and chairs, and no tablecloths. The restaurant is well-known among Norwegians, with celebrity chefs including Arne Brimi having fronted it throughout the years. Here you get to really sample New Nordic cuisine from a menu featuring gourmet twists on Scandinavian dishes, such as pan-fried hake (from Norway) with barley, artichoke, and a shellfish sauce.

StathoLdergaarden

Rådhusgata 11; tel. 22 41 88 00; www. statholdergaarden.no; Mon.-Sat. 6pm-midnight; 5 courses 1,475 kr

Stadholdergaarden is a grand and upscale gourmet restaurant known for its fancy dishes and tasting menu. The surroundings and atmosphere are quite regal, and you might feel as if you are dining in the Royal Palace. Statholdergaarden was awarded a Michelin star all the way back in 1998 and has proudly continued serving some of the best gourmet food in Norway ever since. The menu changes frequently, and you can expect dishes such as gnocchi with asparagus and a parsley butter sauce, veal with kale, carrot in a lemon sauce, and scallops with onion, beet, and a scallop foam.

Seafood
Restaurant Fjord
Kristian Augusts gate 11; tel. 22 98 21 50; www. restaurantfjord.no; Tues.-Sat. 5pm-9pm seating; 5-course menu 695 kr

Restaurant Fjord is modern and stylish, and slightly on the expensive side, serving locally sourced seafood in a variety of ways. They change their menu monthly to reflect the best available produce and fish, and the large, open restaurant gives off a luxurious yet intimate vibe.

Japanese
Izakaya
St. Olavs Gate 7; http://izakayaoslo.com; Mon.- Sat. 5pm-1am; 57-130 kr per plate (3-4 per person recommended)

Izakaya is where Norwegian and Japanese cuisines meet. Located in a basement, it has a homey, informal vibe. The dishes are small and made for sharing, so you can spend hours sampling different bites with friends. They also have several types of sake and shochu on their drink menu—perfect for those who simply want to try something new from the bar.

Sabaki
Karl Johans Gate 39; tel. 23 89 86 86; www.sabaki.no; Tues.-Fri. 11am-8pm, Sat. noon-7pm; 145-245 kr

If you are in the mood for Japanese food, Sabaki is your place, with classics like sushi, maki, and sashimi, along with a unique take on teppanyaki and robatayaki—food cooked on an open grill in the middle of the table. The restaurant is trendy and modern, and though it doesn't seat that many people, the layout makes it feel spacious.

Italian
Baltazar Ristorante & Enoteca
Dronningens gate 27; tel. 23 35 70 60; www.baltazar. no; Tues.-Sat. 11am-10pm; 195-295 kr

Right behind the Oslo Cathedral, you will find Baltazar in the courtyard. This intimate Italian restaurant has a special charm, and it is known for great pizza and a changing a la carte menu. They also have outdoor seating in the summer months, so this is a nice place to people-watch while enjoying a glass of wine from the extensive wine list. In addition to classic Italian dishes such as pizza and filletto di manzo (filet mignon), they have a three-course sharing menu that's 750 kr per person.

Pub Fare
★ Royal Gastropub
Østbanehallen, Jernbanetorget 1; tel. 21 08 22 72; www. royalgastropub.no; Mon.-Wed. 11am-11pm, Thurs.-Sat. 11am-12:30am, Sun. noon-11pm; 239-300 kr

Located inside Østbanehallen, the food court within the oldest part of Oslo Central Station, this restaurant is easy to bypass if you're not watching for it, but you'd be well-advised to stop for the amazing pub-style menu, large selection of beer, and the ability to say that you have enjoyed your dinner in royal surroundings. The Royal Gastropub is set in what was once the king of Norway's private waiting chambers when he traveled Norway by train, and the decor hints at that history. The space is separated into several sections, which gives each one an intimate feel.

OSLO WEST
Local Cuisine
Kolonihagen
Frognerveien 33; tel. 99 31 68 10; https:// kolonihagenfrogner.no; Tues.-Sat. 5pm-10pm (wine bar until 12:30am), Saturday brunch 1pm-4pm; 170-205 kr

Kolonihagen serves food based on the locally sourced produce they have available, so the menu changes regularly and can include anything from New Nordic cuisine to Asian dishes. Entrées can be served a la carte, but there is also a great 4- or 5-course menu that blends the available flavors perfectly, especially when paired with wines from their extensive selection. The atmosphere is friendly and unpretentious, even though the small backyard seating area is quite the Instagram spot.

FYR Bistronomi

Underhaugsveien 28; tel. 45 91 63 92; www.
fyrbistronomi.no; Mon.-Sat. 5pm-midnight; 155-215 kr
(small plates)

FYR is a gourmet restaurant with an open kitchen, so you can watch the chefs prepare your food in charming, intimate surroundings. The outdoor seating area is also a popular spot for lunch in the summer. Expect Nordic dishes with fresh, local ingredients, adjusted as the seasons change.

Kontrast

Maridalsveien 15a; tel. 21 60 01 01; www.restaurant-
kontrast.no; seatings Wed.-Sat. 6pm-8pm; tasting menu
2,300 kr

Restaurant Kontrast focuses on seasonal produce. Their New Nordic menu changes weekly, and sometimes even daily, as a result. Swedish chef Mikael Svensson worked in several Michelin restaurants around Europe before opening Kontrast in Oslo, and they received their first Michelin star in 2016. They only serve one tasting menu, and dishes that might appear include bone marrow, scallops, and baked kohlrabi. The atmosphere is cozy and intimate in this small restaurant.

Mexican
El Aroma

Bogstadveien 9; tel. 23 20 10 20; https://elaroma.no;
Mon.-Sun. noon-10pm; 150-250 kr

This restaurant is centrally located along the Bogstadveien shopping street, serving popular Mexican dishes such as enchiladas, burritos, and quesadillas. The atmosphere is unpretentious, perfect for couples as well as families. They make their guacamole and salsa fresh every day, and use fresh ingredients for all meals in season.

Tapas
Delicatessen Majorstuen

Vibes Gate 8; tel. 22 46 72 00; https://delicatessen.no;
Wed.-Sat. noon-10pm, Sun.-Tues. noon-9pm; 115-170 kr

When Delicatessen first opened in 1999, it was the first tapas bar in Norway. Today there are three locations, which have become the go-to places for locals who want tapas and a lovely glass of white wine. They serve a varied selection of Spanish tapas dishes in an informal and vibrant atmosphere.

Indian
Gandhi Indisk

Majorstuveien 36; tel. 22 60 42 00; Mon.-Sat. 3pm-
10pm; 189-259 kr

This popular restaurant in the capital serves traditional Indian food in a warm, inviting atmosphere in the basement of a former police station. It is one of Oslo's oldest Indian restaurants, having celebrated its 30th anniversary in 2022. The atmosphere here is warm, friendly, and welcoming, and feels intimate even when it is busy.

Pub Fare
Kverneriet

Kirkeveien 64B; tel. 90 60 03 33; www.kverneriet.com;
Mon. 4pm-9pm, Tues.-Wed. 4pm-10pm, Thurs.-Fri. 11am-
10pm, Sat. noon-10pm, Sun. noon-9pm; 169-239 kr

If you are looking for a great burger with fries and a milkshake, look no further than this spot a few meters from Bogstadveien and the Majorstuen subway stop. Kverneriet serves American food with a Scandinavian twist, though not in the diner-style restaurant you might expect from the menu: The atmosphere in this small restaurant is more reminiscent of a fancy bistro, and the dishes are carefully curated with the best ingredients Oslo has to offer. The fries are handmade, and don't miss out on the parmesan and parsley topping.

Ice Cream
Gioia

Eckersbergs Gate 41; tel. 45 28 91 18; www.gioia.is; Sat.-
Sun. 11am-5pm; 52-152 kr

For dessert or a snack on a hot day, drop by Gioia for some handmade Italian gelato. Gioia is Italian for joy, and that's exactly what you get here. They change up their gelato flavors monthly, depending on the ingredients they have access to each season. Expect classics like strawberry and vanilla, but the strawberry ice cream in the summer is made from wild Norwegian strawberries, and the vanilla is from Tahiti. There are only a few seats available inside, so the best option is to get your ice cream to go.

OSLO EAST
Local Cuisine
Olympen

Grønlandsleiret 15; tel. 24 10 19 99; www.olympen.no; Tues.-Fri. 11am-11pm, Sat. noon-11pm; 545 kr (3-course house menu)

Locals call it by its nickname, "Lompa." This restaurant/bar has been operating since 1892 and is truly a staple of the Oslo food scene. The menu is traditional, with classic Norwegian dishes such as trout and pan-fried common ling (a codfish). They pride themselves on serving healthy portions, so make sure to show up hungry. As with many other restaurants in Oslo, Olympen uses fresh, local ingredients. You'll find that the vibe here is rustic and charming, and the interior is old-fashioned, with lots of wood paneling and dark leather chairs.

Italian
★ Villa Paradiso

Olaf Ryes Plass 8; tel. 22 35 40 60; www.villaparadiso. no/restauranter/grunerlokka; Mon.-Wed. 11am-9pm, Thurs.-Sat. 11am-10pm, Sun. noon-9pm; 136-215 kr

Villa Paradiso has become the go-to for the best pizza in Oslo since their opening in 2004. They serve authentic Neapolitan pizza made using fresh ingredients and baked in a wood-fired oven. The atmosphere is rustic and very traditionally Italian. Their small dining area gets busy as this is a local favorite, and sometimes the room can feel a little loud. Make sure to book ahead in the high season, or prepare to wait for a table.

Food Court
Mathallen

Vulkan 5; tel. 40 00 12 09; https://mathallenoslo.no; Tues.-Sat. 10am-8pm, Sun. 11am-6pm; 50-400 kr

Mathallen means "the food court," and that is just what this is, a great place to shop for delicacies to bring home or grab lunch. There are more than 40 bars, restaurants, and shops inside, and among the eateries worth trying you will find **Breddos Tacos** (Mexican) and **Helt Villt** (Villt means wild game). **Hitchhiker** uses fresh ingredients and produce to create international street food-inspired dishes, and is highly recommended.

Coffee and Light Bites
Tim Wendelboe

Grüners Gate 1; tel. 40 00 40 62; https://timwendelboe. no; Mon.-Fri. 8:30am-6pm, Sat.-Sun. 11am-5pm; coffee 49 kr

Coffee lovers shouldn't miss a visit to Tim Wendelboe. Coffee beans from all over the world are sent here to be roasted, and they always have a selection to choose from. There are only a couple of tables inside, so this is not the place to hang out. Grab your coffee to go and head out to explore the neighborhood.

Chillout Travel Cafe

Markveien 55; tel. 22 35 42 00; https://chillout.no/ pages/chillout-grunerlokka; Mon.-Fri. 10am-7pm, Sat. 10am-6pm, Sun. noon-6pm; 49-129 kr

To meet fellow travelers and like-minded people, head to Chillout for a coffee and to browse travel books and souvenirs. The café serves coffees from across the globe and freshly made pastries and sandwiches, and gives off a very youthful and European vibe.

1: Mathallen food court 2: the outdoor seating at ГYR Bistronomi 3: coffee from Tim Wendelboe 4: Hønse-Lovisas Hus

OUTSIDE CENTRAL OSLO

Coffee and Light Bites

Anne På Landet - Hønse-Lovisas Hus

Sandakerveien 2; www.annepaalandet.no; daily 11am-5pm; 49-139 kr

Set in a picturesque, historic little house right by the Akerselva river, Anne På Landet is a café serving great coffee and light lunch. On the lawn outside there are several tables and chairs making this a good spot for a snack while strolling down the Akerselva. Don't miss out on the classic heart-shaped Norwegian waffles.

Bars and Nightlife

The nightlife in Oslo is not as varied as the food scene, and you'll notice that there is no clear "party area" like in many other European cities. Instead, you will find bars, nightclubs, and pubs scattered around the city, with most of them being within walking distance of Central Oslo.

Because Norwegians usually go out late (often not until midnight if they are going clubbing), you'll find that many cocktail bars and pubs are busier earlier in the evening and quiet down between the hours of 9pm and midnight. Norwegians do not have a specific drink of choice and tend to match the drink with the occasion. If you are meeting friends at a bar, a cocktail or glass of wine is often preferred, while a trip to the pub deserves a beer.

You'll find that on the first Friday after the 11th/12th of the month, lots of places get busy with large groups from 4pm until late. This is because Norwegians love the concept of "Lønningspils" (payday beer). Those working in the public sector get paid around the 12th each month, and so the first Friday after payday, colleagues will gather around a watering hole near their job for a few beers.

Pier 42, the cocktail bar at the Amerikalinjen hotel

Going Out the Norwegian Way

When it comes to going out in Norway, many visitors find themselves questioning whether "going out" is even the right term. Because alcohol in Norway is expensive (a full night out can easily set you back 1,000 kr or more), it's not very common to go out to a bar or pub until late: The majority of the night is spent at home. Norwegians will gather at someone's house or apartment (usually whoever lives closest to the city center) to drink, listen to music, play drinking games, and just chat.

This is called a **vorspiel** (deriving from the German word for foreplay—in English, perhaps better translated as pre-drinks or pre-gaming). This usually lasts until midnight or sometimes even later, when Norwegians finally emerge to enjoy the final hours of the night.

The majority of bars and nightclubs in Norway stop serving alcohol at 2am, so those who want to keep the party going at this time will usually head back to the apartment where they started the evening (or to another one) for the after-party, called **nachspiel** (also deriving from German, meaning after-play).

So, if you have found yourself a table at a local bar and wonder why it is so quiet at 9:30pm on a Friday night, just give it a couple of hours and the locals will start flocking in. Or, do as the Norwegians do: Grab some drinks to enjoy at your accommodations, and head out around midnight, when things get hopping.

WATERFRONT
Rooftop Bar
Thief Roof

Landgangen 1; tel. 24 00 40 00; https://thethief.com/the-roof; Apr.-Sept.; cocktails 149 kr

The rooftop of the luxurious Thief Hotel (open only in summer) is a great place to grab a cold drink on a warm day. It's equally fun on colder nights, when they cover the roof and add a bunch of heating lamps to keep you warm (it's very typically Norwegian to insist on sitting outside despite the cold). This is one of the few rooftop bars in Oslo, and the atmosphere on this large terrace is stylish and upscale.

SLOTTSPARKEN AND AROUND

Behind Oslo Cathedral to the north is an area with a trio of good bars: Himkok, Andre Til Høyre, and Cafe Sør.

Cocktail Bars
Himkok

Storgata 27; tel. 22 42 22 02; www.himkok.no; Mon.-Sat. 5pm-3am; cocktails 136 kr

Himkok was already considered a must-visit in Oslo before it was named number 30 on the World's 50 Best Bars list in 2020 by 50 Best. The bar has its own micro-distillery, just one of the things that puts its cocktails on the map. You could spend hours sampling the different cocktails, as well as a large selection of craft ciders from all over the world. The bar is quite large, and the interior is almost industrial with an elegant atmosphere.

Andre Til Høyre

Youngs Gate 19; www.andretilhoyre.no; Tues.-Wed. 5pm-midnight, Thurs. 5pm-2am, Fri.-Sat. 4pm-3am; cocktails 165 kr

The name of this chic cocktail bar translates to "the second on the right," and it is designed to look like you've just entered someone's apartment. The name is somewhat a mystery, but one can assume it has to do with directions given to get there. Explore three rooms, each with a very different interior, with the overall goal of making you feel like you're in someone's home enjoying your drink.

★ Pier 42

Jernbanetorget 2; tel. 21 40 59 00; https:// amerikalinjen.com/no/restauranter-i-oslo-sentrum/pier-42/; Mon.-Sat. 4pm-11:30pm; cocktails 195 kr

Located inside the Amerikalinjen hotel,

Pier 42 cocktail bar takes you on a journey from Norway to New York, in the footsteps of the Norwegians who emigrated on the Norway America Line. Their concept is all about contrasts, reflected in their impressive cocktail menu. They have developed cocktails inspired by comparisons between Oslo and New York, for example the Calvin Klein and Holzweiler (named after famous design brands from both cities), or Cross-Country Skiing and American Football. The bar itself is named after Pier 42 in New York, where the ships crossing from Norway would dock, and the surroundings are luxurious and stylish, with gold details and green velour sofas facing large windows looking out onto the street.

Pub
Cafe Sør

Torggata 11; www.cafesor.no; Sun.-Thurs. noon-1:30am, Fri.-Sat. noon-3:30am; cocktails 139 kr

Café Sør is a relaxed, cozy place to grab a glass of wine during the day, and by night it's a busy bar where you can mingle with locals. During the day, they serve light meals to go with their drinks, while in the evening they often host live bands and DJs. The atmosphere in this large bar is informal and rustic, with exposed brick details, and the interior can remind you of a living room from the 90s.

Nightclub
Elsker

Kristian IVs Gate 12; tel. 45 25 60 42; www.facebook. com/ElskerOslo; Wed.-Thurs. 6pm-1:30am, Fri.-Sat. 6pm-3:30am

Meaning "lover," this is an LGBTQ+ institution in Oslo. The large bar and nightclub has several dance floors, each playing a different style of music, and is always a good time. On weekends there are live DJs, and they routinely put on drag shows, trivia contests, and other fun events in the evenings. Everyone is welcome here, but it is first and foremost a place for everyone in the LGBTQ+ community to feel at home.

OSLO WEST
Cocktail Bar
F6

Frognerveien 6; tel. 22 55 55 65; www.f6.no; Tues. 4pm-1am, Wed.-Sat. 4pm-3am; cocktails 150-175 kr

Named for the bar's address, Frognerveien 6, this intimate cocktail bar is a quiet getaway from the busy plaza outside, serving a selection of classic cocktails as well as their own concoctions. Their Nordic Mule and Nordic Spritzer are both variations of popular cocktails with a Norwegian twist. The atmosphere is warm and relaxed, and the exposed-brick walls and dark interior make it feel intimate.

Wine Bar
Victors Vinbar

Skovveien 15; tel. 90 95 79 77; https://victorsno. wordpress.com; Tues.-Thurs. 3pm-11pm, Fri.-Sat. 3pm-midnight; 109-199 kr per glass

Victors Vinbar is a family run wine bar with a relaxed atmosphere and a cozy outdoor seating area. The colorful interior gives off Mediterranean vibes, with large tapestries of Italian seaside towns covering the walls. The outdoor seats are popular in the summer, and are first come first serve.

Pub
The Highbury Pub

Bogstadveien 50; tel. 22 46 17 71; https://highbury.no; Mon.-Tues. 3pm-midnight, Wed.-Thurs. 3pm-1am, Fri.-Sat. 1pm-1am, Sun. 2pm-midnight

If you are looking for a traditional English pub, or just somewhere to catch the game, the Highbury is your spot. This informal pub has both indoor and outdoor seating and is located right in the middle of Bogstadveien shopping street, making it a great place to grab a drink to take a break from browsing. The decor is dark and rustic, with carpeted floors and low lighting.

Beach Club
Kongen Marina

Frognerstranda 4; tel. 22 55 40 55; www.kongenmarina. no; daily 10:30am-11:30pm

Not just a bar, Kongen Marina is the closest

thing Oslo has to a beach club. Located right on the water, it's a chill spot to watch the boats dock and depart throughout the day. The vibe gets increasingly playful as the night goes on, and in the evening this will remind you more of a beach club in the south of France than a bar in Oslo West.

OSLO EAST
Cocktail Bars
Tijuana
Thorvald Meyers Gate 61; tel. 96 00 81 78; https:// tijuana.no; Mon.-Sat. 2:30pm-3:30am, Sun. noon-3:30am; cocktails 129-139 kr
For Mexican vibes in a fun atmosphere, Tijuana is the place to go. This self-proclaimed rum house naturally serves a selection of rum-infused cocktails, but also shakes up a mean margarita. It's a fun place to go for a nightcap or for a drink during the day. They also serve Mexican food in the daytime (289 kr for a taco tasting menu).

Bar Boca
Thorvald Meyers Gate 30; Mon.-Fri. 4pm-11pm, Sat.-Sun. 3pm-11pm
With over 20 years of experience in creating cocktails, Bar Boca has become a staple at Grünerløkka. This intimate bar can get busy in the evenings, so arrive early to get a table. The interior gives off 1950s vibes, with wood paneling and overhead bookshelves.

Pigalle
Grønlandsleiret 15; tel. 24 10 19 99; www.olympen.no/ pigalle; Thurs. 7pm-1am, Fri.-Sat. 7pm-2:30am
Pigalle has an art deco interior and a 1920s theme that will make any fan of *The Great Gatsby* smile. The bar itself dates back to the '60s, and through the years there has been a go-go bar and a concert venue on the premises. In its original days, there were stationary

telephones on each table at Pigalle, so you could call the other tables to speak to other visitors. In the late hours, the vibe changes from cocktail bar to nightclub.

Wine Bar
Territoriet
Markveien 58; www.territoriet.no; Mon.-Thurs. 4pm-12:30am, Fri. 3pm-12:30am, Sat.-Sun. noon-3am; glass of wine 150-1,400 kr
This intimate wine bar proudly serves a selection over 400 different wines, and most of them are available by the glass. The exposed brick and low-lit interior perfectly enhances a warm and relaxed atmosphere.

Live Music
Blå
Brenneriveien 9C; www.blaaoslo.no; Tues.-Fri. 4pm-midnight, Sat.-Sun. noon-midnight
This is an intimate venue that hosts national and international acts, and DJs. If you are a music lover, and want to discover a new band or artist, check out the lineup during your visit and enjoy a musical experience in a laid-back atmosphere. Expect to see mainly jazz, indie, and rock artists performing here.

OUTSIDE CENTRAL OSLO
Pub
Albatross
Torshovgata 5; Mon.-Thurs. 4pm-1am, Fri. 2pm-1am, Sat.-Sun. 4pm-1am
Bar Albatros was started by three of the bartenders from Bar Boca, and here you will find a low-key atmosphere complemented by a selection of vinyl albums on display behind the bar. Their concept is that "there is no concept," so you can expect everything from natural wines to cocktails here.

Accommodations

Most accommodation options in Oslo are found in the downtown area around Karl Johans Gate. The farther away from the fjord you travel, the fewer lodging options there are. This is with good reason, as staying near the Royal Palace or Jernbanetorget puts most of Oslo's sights within walking distance. Oslo is a very walkable city, especially when you stay in this area.

Chain hotels dominate the selection of hotels in Oslo, and this is true for a lot of places in Norway. **Scandic, Thon,** and **Clarion** are the three major players, each with its own style. At Thon hotels, you can expect to see bright colors and interiors that stand out, and some of their city hotels have a complimentary evening buffet included in their rate. The Clarion chain, with hotels such as **The Hub** and **The Thief,** try to make their hotels less "chain-y," but you still know to expect a great level of service and a playful atmosphere in their hotels. Scandic is perhaps the most traditional of the three, with a clean, classic decorating style that sometimes can remind you of a conference hotel. Regardless, all three can be considered stamps of quality and service, so don't judge the chain hotels prematurely.

Of course, there is also a (small) selection of more unique boutique hotels available in the capital. Amerikalinjen, Grand Hotel, and Saga Hotel are all fine examples. These options stand out, not only because you won't find their interior and branding anywhere else in the capital, but also because they all have a story to tell. **Grand Hotel** is the old-est hotel in Oslo (it opened in 1874), and **Amerikalinjen** shares an important part of Norwegian history with its guests, as it retells the story of Norwegian immigrants to the US.

Hotel prices in Oslo usually range from 1,800 to 2,500 kr for a double room in the high season, and it is generally difficult to stay there on a budget. However, some providers keep their prices down by offering fewer amenities. **Citybox,** for example, is a chain of hotels with basic rooms and (almost) staff-less service, where you can stay a night for less than 1,000 kr.

WATERFRONT
Over 3,000 kr
The Thief

Landgangen 1; tel. 24 00 40 00; https://thethief.com; 3,200 kr

It's perhaps the most expensive hotel in Oslo, but you get what you pay for at this luxurious property. The Thief is named for its location on the docks of Oslo, where thieves were previously executed. The interior is grand and luxurious, and all guests at The Thief gain free entry to the Astrup Fernley Museum right next door. (The museum has also equipped the hotel with its art.) If you are not staying here, a visit to the rooftop bar, The Thief Roof, is worth it for the view alone.

SLOTTSPARKEN AND AROUND
Under 1,500 kr
Citybox Oslo

Prinsens Gate 6; tel. 21 42 04 80; https://citybox.no/oslo; 899 kr

Citybox offers simple, modern rooms and comfy beds at a fair price. Is a great stay for anyone who does not need anything more than the basic amenities during their stay. At Citybox, you are in charge of your own check-in, checkout, and payment—something that allows the hotel to keep their prices so low.

Thon Hotel Terminus

Stenersgata 10; tel. 22 05 60 00; www.thonhotels.no/hoteller/norge/oslo/thon-hotel-terminus; 1,345 kr

Centrally located just north of Oslo Central Station and newly refurbished, Terminus has a colorful atmosphere with fun and lively decor both in the rooms and around the hotel. The rooms contain all basic amenities, the lavish breakfast is often locally sourced, and sustainability is a priority throughout the hotel.

1,500-3,000 kr
Scandic Byporten
Jernbanetorget 6; tel. 23 15 55 00; www.scandichotels. no/hotell/norge/oslo/scandic-byporten; 1,580 kr
The rooms at Byporten are welcoming and modern, and have everything you need for the night; some rooms have a mini-fridge. One of the best things about this hotel is the breakfast overlooking the busy Jernbanetorget (the square in front of the central station). The meal is great, but the people-watching is better.

Clarion the Hub
Biskop Gunnerusgate 3; tel. 23 10 80 00; www. nordicchoicehotels.no/hotell/norge/oslo/clarion-hotel- the-hub; 2,300 kr
This large hotel is located just across from Oslo Central Station to the north, offering a modern and elegant atmosphere with stylish, clean rooms in the heart of the city. They have two bars and a restaurant on property, but perhaps most impressive is their dedication to the environment. On their roof you will find a 200-square-meter (2,100-sq-ft) garden called GrowHub, where they grow the herbs and vegetables used in their restaurant and breakfast buffet.

Grand Hotel Oslo
Karl Johans Gate 31; tel. 23 21 20 00; https://grand. no; 2,590 kr
An institution in Oslo, the Grand has been at its location along Karl Johans Gate since 1874. The hotel boasts old-school luxury, and the staff and service are truly top-notch: In 2014, the Rolling Stones stayed there for 10 days without anyone finding out until their last day, when Mick Jagger himself posted about it on Instagram. Other famous guests who have walked the halls of the Grand include Henrik Ibsen, Barack Obama, Oprah Winfrey, and Justin Bieber.

★ Amerikalinjen
Jernbanetorget 2; tel. 21 405 900; https://amerikalinjen. com; 2,800 kr
Located in the former headquarters of the Norwegian America Line, this hotel pays homage to its history in every decorative detail, taking you back to the century between 1820 and 1920 when hundreds of thousands of Norwegians booked their passage across the Atlantic by boat. The rooms are spacious and luxurious, decorated with artifacts from the crossings, with elegant marble features in the bathrooms. The small library, accessible to guests, is a great place to relax and people-watch after a busy day, as the majestic building overlooks Jernbanetorget outside. In addition to their cocktail bar, Pier 42, and the Atlas restaurant (where breakfast for hotel guests is served), their jazz club, Gustav, brings New York to Oslo.

OSLO WEST
Under 1,500 kr
Frogner House Apartments
Various; tel. 93 01 00 09; https://frognerhouse.no; 1,100 kr
Frogner House has a large selection of self-service apartments of various sizes around western Oslo across several buildings, most of them within walking distance of one another. They are ideal for anyone wanting to cook for themselves while visiting Norway, or for a longer stay in the city.

Thon Hotel Gyldenløve
Bogstadveien 20; tel. 23 33 23 00; www.thonhotels.no/ hoteller/norge/oslo/thon-hotel-gyldenlove; 1,395 kr
This hotel was refurbished in 2018 and displays an interesting blend of colorful modernism and traditional style, with bright orange rococo furniture, fun wallpaper, and dark wood details. The rooms are vibrant, and the breakfast is impressive and (mainly) locally sourced. With their central location on Bogstadveien, this is a great place to stay for anyone looking to hit the shops during their stay.

Scandic Sjølyst

Sjølyst Plass 5; tel. 23 15 51 00; www.scandichotels.no/ hotell/norge/oslo/scandic-sjolyst; 1,400 kr

This newly renovated hotel is located in one of Oslo West's more high-end neighborhoods, near Bygdøy and all of its museums and within walking distance of Frognerparken, home to the Vigeland Sculpture Park. The rooms are bright and simply furnished, as is their restaurant, Skabos Hage.

1,500-3,000 kr

Saga Hotel

Eilert Sundts Gate 39; tel. 22 55 44 90; https:// sagahoteloslo.no; 1,545 kr

This hotel is located just behind the Royal Palace, and on the outside it has kept its grand, traditional architecture. On the inside, however, it has had a modern overhaul. Each room at this charming hotel is equipped with a Nespresso machine and minibar, and the new design makes this a nice place to relax after a day of exploring Oslo.

OUTSIDE CENTRAL OSLO

Under 1,500 kr

Thon Hotel Storo

Vitaminveien 23; tel. 23 40 02 00; www.thonhotels.no/ hoteller/norge/oslo/thon-hotel-storo/; 1,200 kr

The first thing you will notice when entering this hotel is the large, colorful mural behind the reception desk. This sets the tone for the rest of the hotel, the latest addition to Oslo's Thon hotel family. Storo is an up-and-coming area with lots of shops, bars, restaurants, and a cinema nearby.

Radisson Blu Hotel Nydalen

Nydalsveien 33; tel. 23 26 30 00; www.radissonhotels. com/en-us/hotels/radisson-blu-oslo-nydalen; 1,200 kr

This stylish hotel is filled with cool art pieces and sculptures. Each of the modern rooms here has a minibar and work desk, and the hotel restaurant, N33, offers an a la carte menu that can also be ordered as room service.

Scandic Helsfyr

Innspurten 7; tel. 22 92 22 00; www.scandichotels.no/ hotell/norge/oslo/scandic-helsfyr; 1,300 kr

This is the largest of the Scandic hotels in Norway, with 450 rooms in total. Yet Scandic Helsfyr has retained a homey feeling, and mixed with modern lines and furnishings, this is a popular hotel for conferences. The hotel is located a short walk from the Helsfyr subway station, so you are never far from the busy city center, and the concert arena Valle Hovin is within walking distance.

Information and Services

VISITOR INFORMATION

You'll find the **Oslo Visitors Center** (Jernbanetorget 1; tel. 23 10 62 00; www. visitoslo.com/en/tourist-information-centre; Mon.-Sat. 9am-6pm, Sun. 9am-4pm), the city's only official tourism office, immediately on your left as you enter Østbanehallen. Here you can gather brochures and find information on things to do in the capital, as well as get assistance with planning your trip.

HEALTH AND SAFETY

Oslo is generally a safe city, with minor risks compared to other major cities. However, vigilance is always advised, especially when walking alone at night. There are some instances of pickpocketing around the main shopping areas.

There are many pharmacies across the city, with one in every shopping center. They follow regular store opening hours, and are closed on Sundays, with the exception of **Vitus Apotek Jernbanetorget** (Jernbanetorget 4B; tel. 23 35 81 00), which is open 24/7.

Legevakt is the Norwegian word for urgent care, and **Oslo Legevakt**'s location in Storgata (Storgata 40; tel. 116117 or 23 48 72 00) is open 24 hours. There is often a bit of a wait time, so make sure to call ahead if you can. Regardless, Legevakta should be your first stop in case of emergency. For urgent dental care, **Oslo Tannlegevakt** (Schweigaards gate 6, 3rd floor; tel. 23 43 00 60) is open evenings and weekends, when traditional dentists are closed. Note that dental care in Norway is very expensive, so if you are able to postpone your dentist trip until you get home, this might be advised.

FOREIGN CONSULATES

You will find that most embassies and consulates to Norway are located in Oslo, usually in the area around and behind the Royal Palace. If you are a US citizen in need of a new passport (and to report a lost or stolen one) or need to report an emergency or crime, the US Embassy hotline deals with this. For non-emergencies, you must make an appointment online.

- **US Embassy:** Morgedalsveien 36; tel. 21 30 85 40; no.usembassy.gov

- **British Embassy:** Thomas Heftyes Gate 8; tel. 23 13 27 00; www.gov.uk/world/organisations/british-embassy-oslo

- **Canadian Embassy:** Wergelandsveien 7, 4th floor; tel. 22 99 53 00; www.canadainternational.gc.ca/norway-norvege

LAUNDRY AND LUGGAGE STORAGE

Most hotels offer a laundry service for guests and have a quick turnaround time. Laundromats are not very common in Norway, as most homes are equipped with a washing machine (and usually a dryer). That said, **café Laundromat** (Underhaugsveien 2; tel. 21 38 36 29; www.laundromat.no/wash) is both a café and a laundromat, mainly catering to students (and people whose laundry machines have broken).

For **luggage storage,** the lockers at Oslo Central Station are self-serviced and are available during the opening hours of the train station (Mon.-Sun. 4:30am-1am). (You can leave your luggage in the lockers overnight, but you will not be able to access them while the station is closed.) You pay at machines using cash or credit card (Visa and Mastercard) and get assigned a locker in the size you paid for. Prices range from 60 to 100 kr per day.

Transportation

GETTING THERE
Air
Oslo Airport Gardermoen
OSL; Edvard Munchs veg; tel. 64 81 20 00; https://avinor.no/flyplass/oslo
Gardermoen (OSL) is Norway's main international airport, as well as its main domestic hub. To get from Gardermoen to the city center, the airport express train **FlyToget** takes you directly to Oslo Central Station in 20 minutes. The cost of Flytoget is 220 kr per adult. Alternatively, **regional trains** also service the airport train station, a more affordable (but slightly longer) journey. These usually take a little over 30 minutes, and a one-way ticket costs 114 kr. You can book tickets through Vy or the Ruter app.

Train
Oslo Central Station (Oslo S)
Jernbanetorget 1; tel. 81 50 08 88; https://oslo-s.no
Oslo Central Station (Oslo Sentralstasjon, Oslo S for short) is the main train station for Oslo. Most trains to the rest of Norway connect here. You can also reach Oslo S from Stockholm and Gothenburg in Sweden. From Oslo you can get on Bergensbanen (the Oslo-Bergen line), which is one of the most popular

train routes in Norway due to its scenic views along the way.

Vy (tel. 61 05 19 10; www.vy.no), formerly NSB, is Norway's main railway company. Downloading the Vy app will allow you to keep your tickets in one place; you can also use it to check for updates, delays, and potential service disruptions on your phone.

Bus
Oslo Bussterminal

Schweigaards Gate; tel. 23 00 24 00; https://oslobussterminal.no

The main bus station for Oslo is simply called Oslo Bus Terminal. From here, all international bus routes depart (such as to Sweden and Germany). In addition, coaches to southern, northern, and western Norway all originate at Oslo Bussterminal. The bus terminal is located in downtown Oslo, a short walk from Jernbanetorget and Karl Johans Gate.

Nettbuss was the largest bus company in Norway before merging with **Vy** (tel. 40 70 50 70; www.vybuss.no). Via the Vy network you can reach most major cities and destinations in Norway, in addition to Swedish cities like Gothenburg and Stockholm. On their long-haul routes to and from Sweden, some of the buses are double-deckers; the upper level is more luxurious with wider seats, extra leg room, and power outlets at each seat. **Nor-Way Bus Express** (tel. 22 31 31 50; www.nor-way.no) connects Oslo with towns and cities all across Norway, such as Stavanger, Bergen, Trysil, and Kristiansand. Line 192 is particularly beautiful and takes you around the south coast of Norway from Stavanger via Arendal and Kristiansand.

Boat

There are two companies operating short cruises to Oslo from other destinations in Europe. There used to be more routes, but the passenger numbers have decreased in recent years, as international travel by plane has become more accessible. A cruise to Oslo is an event in itself, with all the amenities this mode of transport entails: bars, restaurants, clubs, live entertainment, and shops (many Norwegians take advantage of duty-free shopping to purchase cheaper alcohol and other goods that are highly taxed in Norway). Both of the below cruises take cars on board, convenient for those who plan to drive on their Norway trip.

The **DFDS** (tel. 44 871 522 9966; www.dfdsseaways.co.uk; runs daily, overnight cruises to Copenhagen, Denmark; 1,400 kr for a one-way cabin) and **Color Line** (tel. 22 94 42 00; www.colorline.no; runs daily, overnight cruises to Kiel, Germany; 2,500 kr for a one-way cabin) docks are not located in the same place along the waterfront of Oslo. Color Line picks up passengers heading to Kiel from their terminal at Filipstadkaia (Filipstadveien 25), and the DFDS cruise departs from across the bay past Akershus Fortress (Akershusstranda 31).

GETTING AROUND

Getting around Oslo is surprisingly easy, as the city has a great public transit system, across the subway (called the T-bane), buses, and trams (trikk). All belong to the same network, so by downloading the **Ruter Reise** app (www.ruter.no), you can check schedules and find optimal travel routes across the whole city. The logo for Ruter is a hashtag (#), and you will see it around the city indicating tram and bus stops, and where there are steps or walkways down to the subway. Tickets can be purchased on the Ruter app as well; a 24-hour pass costs 117 kr for an adult. A one-time ticket costs 39 kr, so if you are planning to make more than three trips in a day, the 24-hour pass will be more cost-efficient. This lets you travel on the tram, buses, and subway in Oslo.

As simple and efficient as the transit system is, odds are you may not even need to use it during your time in the city, as most of the sights are concentrated in the very walkable city center.

A Scenic Tram Ride

For sightseeing that won't cost you more than the price of a tram ticket, get on **tram 19** at Majorstuen in Oslo West. This route takes you all the way down **Bogstadveien,** around the back of **Slottsparken** (the Palace Park) before stopping at Jernbanetorget, at the end of **Karl Johans Gate.** From there, you'll start climbing the hills up to **Ekebergparken** and beyond. As the tram line goes higher, the view of the city behind you (and below you) gets more and more spectacular. Tram 19 ends at Ljabru. The total travel time from Majorstuen to the end stop is 34 minutes. It is possible to walk back, but I recommend getting the tram the opposite direction. If you would like to walk, get off at Jomfrubråten and walk through the park on your way back to central Oslo. This will take you around 45 minutes.

one of Oslo's trams

T-Bane

The Oslo subway system has five different routes crisscrossing the city, all meeting in the middle, such that each of the five metro lines serves the Majorstuen, Nationaltheatret, Stortinget, Jernbanetorget (Oslo Central Station), Grønland, and Tøyen stations. So if you are staying in the city center, near any of those, you will be able to catch the metro in any direction you like. A subway ticket costs 117 kr for a 24-hour pass, and 39 kr for a one-way ticket. These are valid on all modes of public transportation in Oslo.

The subway system in Oslo is trust-based, meaning that you do not have to show or scan your ticket anywhere to get on the subway. However, several times a week there are checks, where staff from Ruter, either in uniform or civilian clothes, will ask to see tickets for everyone on board.

Bus

Bus stops are well-distributed throughout the city, getting you even closer to destinations where the metro is not sufficient. Tickets must be purchased on the Ruter app in advance, and cost 117 kr for a 24-hour pass, and 39 kr for a one-way fare, the same as a ticket for all public transportation in Oslo.

Tram

Oslo's signature light blue trams run on six lines throughout the city. As a rule, trams leave every 10 minutes or so, with the exception of evenings and weekends, when the tram runs more slowly. Between 2022 and 2024, all trams in Oslo are being replaced so that they will all be completely wheelchair-accessible. To travel with the tram, the ticket system is the same as for all other public transport within the city: purchase your ticket on the Ruter app in advance, and show it only when there is a ticket check on board.

Greater Oslo

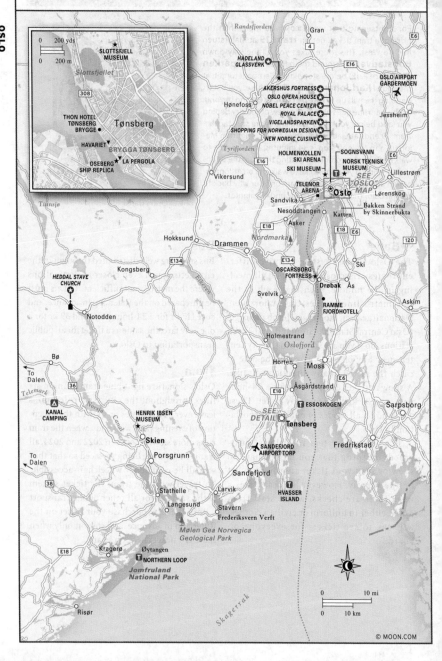

0 200 yds
0 200 m

SLOTTSFJELL
MUSEUM

Slottsfjellet

308

THON HOTEL
TØNSBERG
BRYGGE

Tønsberg

HAVARIET

BRYGGA TØNSBERG

OSEBERG LA PERGOLA
SHIP REPLICA

Randsfjorden   Gran
                                E6
                      4
HADELAND   E16
GLASSVERK
                              OSLO AIRPORT
                              GARDERMOEN
AKERSHUS FORTRESS
OSLO OPERA HOUSE
Hønefoss   NOBEL PEACE CENTER
ROYAL PALACE   Jessheim
VIGELANDSPARKEN
SHOPPING FOR NORWEGIAN DESIGN   4
NEW NORDIC CUISINE
Tyrifjorden
HOLMENKOLLEN   SOGNSVANN
SKI ARENA   NORSK TEKNISK   E6
SKI MUSEUM   MUSEUM   Lillestrøm
E16   SEE
Vikersund   "OSLO"
TELENOR   MAP   Lørenskog
ARENA   Oslo
Tjimsjø   Sandvika   Bakken Strand
Nesoddtangen   by Skinnerbukta
Asker   Katten
E18 E6
Hokksund   Nordmarka   120
Drammen
E134
E134
Kongsberg E134   OSCARSBORG   Ski
FORTRESS
Svelvik   Drøbak Ås
HEDDAL STAVE
CHURCH   RAMME   Askim
FJORDHOTELL
Notodden
Holmestrand   Oslofjord
Bø
Horten   Moss
To
Dalen   E6
36   Åsgårdstrand
Telemark   E18
Canal   ESSOSKOGEN   Sarpsborg
HENRIK IBSEN   SEE
KANAL   MUSEUM   DETAIL   Tønsberg
CAMPING
Skien   Fredrikstad
To   Porsgrunn   SANDEFJORD
Dalen   AIRPORT TORP
38   Sandefjord
Stathelle   Larvik
Langesund   HVASSER
Stavern   ISLAND
Frederiksvern Verft
Mølen Gea Norvegica
Geological Park
E18   Kragerø   Øytangen
NORTHERN LOOP
Jomfruland
National Park
Risør   Skagerrak

0   10 mi
0   10 km

© MOON.COM

Oslofjord

The Oslofjord stretches 80 kilometers (50 mi) south from Oslo to the Skagerrak Strait, and is not what most people imagine when thinking of Norwegian fjords: That is, if you are hoping for the dramatic scenery of steep mountains, dark blue waters, and epic viewpoints, you won't find it here. That said, the Oslofjord still has much to offer, with the fishing town Drøbak and former Viking stronghold of Tønsberg, mainly frequented by Norwegian tourists, worthy of visiting. A day trip to either of these locations might just be the perfect way to spend a warm summer day.

DRØBAK

This quiet fishing town is a popular day trip by boat for Oslo locals, giving visitors the laid-back feel of southern Norway without requiring them to travel too far from the capital. The main sight in Drøbak is actually offshore on the island of Oscarsborg, which you'll pass on your way to the town if you're arriving by ferry. Long a point of defense for Oslo, the Oscarsborg Fortress also served an important role in World War II. In town, you'll also find a popular aquarium as well as some historic buildings.

Sights
Oscarsborg Fortress
(Oscarsborg Festning)

Husvikveien; tel. 64 90 41 61; www.forsvarsbygg.no/ no/festningene/finn-din-festning/oscarsborg-festning; daily; free

This island fortress was once the winter harbor for the capital back before the 20th century when the inner Oslofjord used to freeze over, and it has always played an important part in protecting the city. The fortress is a massive, rounded stone wall shaped like a half moon when seen from the top, and the walls are thick enough to house a hotel and several museums. The fort you see today

dates mostly to the 1800s, and played its most important role during World War II, when the German warship *Blücher* was famously sunk by the torpedo battery in the early hours of April 9, 1940.

The fortress itself is open to visitors 24/7 and entry is free. Inside, there are several museum exhibits with their own specific opening hours. The **Fortress Museum** (Mon.-Sun. 10am-5pm) shows the military history of the fortress, with a focus on the events of April 9, 1940. The **Coastal Artillery Museum** (Mon.-Sun. 10am-5pm in summer) displays the history of the Norwegian Kystartilleriet. In addition, staff give guided tours of the fortress. The tours cost 100 kr per person and are held daily in the summer season, and upon request in the winter. Tours are held outdoors and last 1.5 hours.

To reach Oscarsborg, travel by ferry from Drøbak. There are several ferries daily, and the crossing takes around 10 minutes. The ferry leaves from Sundbrygga in Drøbak. Tickets costs 110 kr (adult round-trip) and can be purchased from the ticket machine on the dock.

Drøbak Aquarium

Havnegata 4; tel. 91 10 84 20; https://drobakakvarium. no; daily 10am-6:30pm Apr.-Aug., daily 10am-4pm Sept.-Mar.; adults 70 kr, children 50 kr

Since 1995, the Drøbak Aquarium has been showing visitors the wildlife found in and around the Oslofjord up close. Some of the animals even have names: You can meet Hugo the catfish and Morgan the eel. Other wildlife found here (and in the fjord) include scallops and colorful echinoderms, including starfish. They have 14 aquariums, two large tanks, and a touch pool, which allows visitors to touch some of the aquatic wildlife—especially fun for children.

Vestfold Coastal Paths

Surrounding Tønsberg, the 980-kilometer (600-mi) Vestfold archipelago and shoreline make up the western coast of the Oslofjord. This area is scattered with great, clearly marked hikes and pathways to explore; all are relatively easy. Below are a few standouts.

ESSOSKOGEN

Distance: 5.8 kilometers (3.5 mi)
Time: 1.5 hours, loop
Difficulty: Easy
Trailhead: Near Essoveien 100
Information and Maps: https://ut.no/tur/116020/kart
Leaving from Tønsberg, this walk takes you past beaches along the coast and through the forested area of Essokogen (the Esso forest). The pathways through the forest are well-kept, and this is an easy hike for all ages.

HVASSER ISLAND

Distance: 9.2 kilometers (6 mi)
Time: 2 hours, loop
Difficulty: Easy
Trailhead: Fynsletta Parkering, Fynveien, Hvasser
Information and Maps: https://ut.no/tur/1112154705/kart
Another popular coastal path is found on Hvasser island, a 30-minute drive from Tønsberg. Walk-

Food and Accommodations

Telegrafen

Storgata 10; tel. 91 52 53 59; https://telegrafendrobak. no; Mon.-Thurs. 4pm-11pm, Fri.-Sat. 4pm-2am, Sun. 1pm-11pm; tapas 50-199 kr

Telegrafen serves authentic, homemade Spanish tapas, with a large selection of dishes to share in addition to a wine bar with a good selection of Spanish wines. The name Telegrafen means "The Telegraph," as the building functioned as the local telegraph station from 1915 to 1984.

Kumlegaarden

Niels Carlsens Gate 11; tel. 64 93 89 90; www. kumlegaarden.no; Mon.-Wed. 11:30am-8pm, Tues.-Sat. 11:30am-9pm, Sun. 1pm-8pm; 325-498 kr

This restaurant takes up two of the oldest buildings in Drøbak and serves traditional Norwegian meals in a historic atmosphere. It's decorated in an old-fashioned Norwegian style that will make you feel as if you have traveled back in time. On the menu you will

find dishes like kjøttkaker (Norwegian meatballs) and komle (Norwegian potato dumplings, which the restaurant is named after).

Ramme Fjordhotell

Rammeveien 100; tel. 64 98 32 01; www.classicnorway. no/hotell/ramme-fjordhotell; 2,600 kr

The 42 rooms at this unique hotel are meticulously furnished with classic Norwegian style, but the hotel's most remarkable feature is the opportunity it offers to rent the former cabin of Edvard Munch, located right on the water. The hotel further plays up the Munch connection with some rooms named after his paintings, many of which he painted in the area.

Getting There

If you are considering a day trip to Drøbak, taking public transit is recommended. That way you can enjoy an ice-cold beer on the docks with the locals without having to worry about a designated driver.

ing around the entire island, following the coastal path, makes for a lovely Sunday walk. The trail loops around the island, and the trailhead is at the parking lot. The hike itself is easy, following pathways and trails around the windswept island. In some places you can overlook the ocean and archipelago off the coast. At Tjønneberget (along the trail) there is a Tourist Cabin where you can buy waffles and coffee on the weekends from Easter until September.

STAVERN COASTAL PATH

Distance: 35 kilometers (22 mi)
Time: 9-11 hours
Difficulty: Moderate- strenuous (due to length)
Trailhead: Stavern
Information and Maps: www.visitvestfold.com/en/articles/the-coastal-path-in-stavern
Perhaps the most popular of the Vesfold coastal paths is this longer walk over relatively flat and easy terrain. You'll enjoy not only beautiful views of the archipelago and Skagerak ocean but also interesting sights and activities along the way, including **Fredriksvern Verft** (tel. 93 88 03 33; www.forsvarsbygg.no/no/festningene/finn-din-festning/fredriksvern-verft; daily; free), a fortress complex from the 1700s, and the UNESCO-protected **Mølen Gea Norvegica Geological Park** (Hyttesone I 239; www.geoparken.no).

To hike this trail and get back by public transportation, bus 01 (www.vkt.no) takes you from Tønsberg to Stavern in 1 hour and 50 minutes (59 kr). From Helgeroa, the trail's endpoint, bus 206 takes you back to Stavern in 20 minutes (43 kr). Check the schedules before your walk, to ensure you have a ride back.

Ferry
The most enjoyable and scenic way to reach Drøbak from Oslo is by ferry. Public ferry B21, operated by Ruter (www.ruter.no), leaves Aker Brygge twice daily in the high season (June-Aug.), and on weekends only in April, May, and September. The journey takes around 1.5 hours and costs 114 kr one way.

Bus
From Oslo Bussterminal bus route 500, also operated by Ruter, leaves for Drøbak every half hour. The journey takes around 45 minutes, and the price is 64 kr per adult.

Car
Drøbak is located 39 kilometers (24 mi) south of Oslo. The drive here, along the main coastal road, the E6, takes around 40 minutes. There is plenty of parking in town; download the EasyPark app to find parking spaces and prices, and to start your parking session. Parking costs 34 kr per hour, for a maximum

of 4 or 5 hours (depending on where you park). On some days, the first two hours are free.

TØNSBERG
Among the oldest cities in Norway, Tønsberg is a beautiful town on the Oslofjord dating back to at least the 800s. International travelers may recognize the city as an important setting for Marvel's *Thor* movies. Tønsberg made an appearance in the movies for good reason, as the city has strong ties to the Viking Age. This is a popular destination for Norwegians, who enjoy this picturesque seaside town in the summer by having a beer outside at one of the many restaurants along the dock. Visitors with an interest in the Viking Age might opt for a day or two in Tønsberg to explore the city's sites and history and enjoy one of the nearby hikes along the Vestfold coast.

Sights
Brygga Tønsberg
www.bryggaitonsberg.no

Tønsberg's brygga, or dockside area, has been an important part of the city and its trade for more than 1,000 years. Some of the buildings along the dock date back to the 1800s, and in the summer you'll find lots of people here soaking up the sunshine, visiting the bars and restaurants, and watching boats sail in and out of the harbor. This district serves as the "main street" of Tønsberg, and you may find comedians and musicians performing at some of the bars.

Slottsfjell Museum

Farmannsveien 30; tel. 33 31 29 19; https://vestfoldmuseene.no/slottsfjellsmuseet; Tues.-Sun. 11am-4pm; adults 100 kr, children 70 kr (free Tues.)

Sitting at the foot of Slottsfjell, the mountain—more like a large hill—that looms over Tønsberg to the north, you'll find the Slottsfjell Museum. Slottsfjell literally translates to castle mountain, and the origin of the name will quickly become clear as you explore the ruins of an old castle and fortress that cover the mountain. The museum showcases some of Tønsberg's long history, including a collection of Viking artifacts found over the years. A highlight is the *Klåstad*, the only Viking ship on display outside of Oslo. You can also learn more about the history of the (more famous) *Oseberg* ship in town here, as it was found in the area as well, by visiting the **Oseberg Ship Replica** (Saga Oseberg, Ollebukta 3; tel. 91 58 35 85; https://sagaoseberg.no).

Tønsberg was founded during the Viking Age and is mentioned in the Snorre saga to have existed before the battle of Hafrsfjord in year 872. This is the earliest mention we have of it, and the town's role at the time would have been as a marketplace. The *Oseberg* ship, which was uncovered just outside the city, is dated to year 834. During the Middle Ages, Tønsberg became an important town, with churches, convents, and a fortress (the ruins of Tunsberghus fortress date back to the 1300s). A large number of Viking graves, as well as royal graves, can be found in the area. This shows that Tønsberg was likely the seat of the royals in the Viking Age and Middle Ages.

Since then, Tønsberg has been an important town (and eventually city) for traders, fishermen, and sailors. It was one of Norway's three Hansa towns from 1250 to 1530, and later an important trading port for the English and Dutch. Many whalers also had Tønsberg as their base. Today, Tønsberg is a lively summer town with a bustling dock area, popular among Norwegians on holiday.

Food and Accommodations
Havariet

Nedre Langgate 30E; tel. 33 35 83 90; www.havariet.no; Mon.-Sat. 11am-1am, Sun. noon-1am; 159-415 kr

Havariet has been serving traditional meals on the Tønsberg docks for over 30 years. They are open all day, and you'll find that it is a popular place for a late breakfast (served until 2pm). The menu is international, with a particular focus on seafood. Their dishes include fish soup and steamed scallops and halibut, as well as poke bowls and sashimi.

La Pergola

Conradis Gate 4; tel. 33 33 30 23; www.lapergola.no; Tues.-Sat. noon-10pm; 189-415 kr

This charming Italian restaurant right by the docks has a cozy and welcoming atmosphere. In addition to serving traditional Italian dishes like pasta and pizza (made fresh in their stone oven), there's a selection of barbecue dishes as well. For lunch, they have a separate menu with a "one price fits all" approach, with all dishes priced at 179 kr.

Thon Hotel Tønsberg Brygge

Nedre Langgate 40; tel. 33 34 49 00; www.thonhotels.no/hoteller/norge/tonsberg/thon-hotel-tonsberg-brygge; 1,400 kr

Also located right by the docks, this hotel keeps you close to all the action in Tønsberg. This modern, stylish hotel has inviting rooms with fun and colorful details; expect bright colors and funky wallpapers. The lobby bar is open until midnight.

Getting There

Tønsberg is 103 kilometers (64 mi) south of Oslo, and the drive along main road E18 takes about 1 hour and 15 minutes.

Reaching Tønsberg by bus is surprisingly difficult (it takes 2.5 hours, including a bus change in Sandefjord), but trains run regularly. There is a regional train (R11) leaving Oslo every hour, stopping at Tønsberg. The train journey is a little faster than the drive (1 hour and 11 minutes), and a one-way adult ticket starts at 249 kr. If you are planning a day trip, the last train leaving Tønsberg for Oslo leaves between 10pm and 11pm. The train station is located a 5-minute walk north of the docks, in the city center (Jernbanegaten 2).

The Telemark Canal

Telemark is a region and former county southwest of Oslo. It stretches from Kragerø in the south (on the coast) all the way to the Hardangervidda mountain plateau in the north. The main attraction here is the man-made Telemark Canal, an important mode of transportation for goods and trade, completed more than 100 years ago. Along the Telemark Canal you can explore the varying landscapes of this part of Norway, from the rolling hills and archipelago of the coastline to the forested and mountainous areas of inner Norway.

In addition to its very "traditional" Norwegian scenery of old mountain farms and never-ending forests and mountains, Telemark is home to Norway's largest remaining stave church: the Heddal Stave Church. Travelers come here from all over the world, and it is a great place to learn more about the history of Norwegian stave churches. The area is home to several historic hotels, and travelers who are after a unique place to stay during their trip to Norway will favor Telemark.

★ HEDDAL STAVE CHURCH

Heddalsvegen 412, Heddal; tel. 92 20 44 35; www. heddalstavkirke.no; daily 10am-4pm; adults 90 kr, children 30 kr

Heddal Stave Church

What is a Stave Church?

Stave churches, with their distinctive look, are unique to Norway today. Although there were hundreds (even thousands) of them across Scandinavia in the Middle Ages, only a few are left—all but one of them in Norway.

HISTORY

A stave church is a church built using a specific method, where "staver" (posts) bear the weight of the construction as a sort of frame. The name comes from the Norwegian word "stav" (which descends from the Old Norse "stafr"), which describes the posts supporting the church. This building technique was prominent in Scandinavia in the Middle Ages, and it is believed that at one point there were more than 1,000 stave churches in Norway. Today, there are only 28 stave churches in Norway left from the Middle Ages. In addition to this, there is one stave church in Sweden and one in Poland (which was actually moved there from Norway).

The churches were Christian and were important to daily life in the Middle Ages. The church served as a natural gathering spot for the community, and people would travel from nearby villages to attend services. Today, some of the stave churches in Norway are still in use, such as Heddal Stave Church and Undredal Stave Church in Undredal, western Norway.

APPEARANCE

Usually, a stave church can be recognized by its dark timber look, an attribute of the tar used for preservation. The Heddal, Gol, and Borgund Stave Churches (located in Lærdal, along the Sognefjord in western Norway) are considered typical examples of the style. But since "stave" only describes the type of structure, there are stave churches that look more like traditional churches, and even some that are painted in different colors, such as the small, white Undredal Stave Church. The interior designs of the churches vary but the inside is generally not as dark as the exterior, since tar is not used for the inside of the churches.

VISITING TODAY

Quite an effort has been devoted to the preservation of these churches, as they need to be maintained in the same way they were back in the day—using tar. Therefore, when visiting a Stave Church, you will find that there are splashes and drops of tar on the ground around the church, and on hot days you can even see it melting off. One concern we are faced with is that only a limited amount of people know the correct way to preserve the churches using this technique, so it is vital for their knowledge to be passed on to the younger generations.

Most stave churches that are preserved can be visited today. Several of them also have visitors centers where you can find more information about that specific church and its history.

The massive, brown wooden stave church at Heddal is a beautiful building and the epitome of what you imagine a stave church to look like. With dark wooden features, this 29-meter (95-ft) tall building can be seen from a distance as you approach.

The church is still in use today as the main church of the local Agder and Telemark parish. Yet, it is also set up for visitors who want to come and learn more about its interesting history. Heddal Stave Church dates back to the 1200s, and both the interior and exterior of the church take visitors back to the Norwegian Middle Ages. Inside, you will find traces of the church's 800-year history, with furniture and artifacts that have been kept through the centuries.

Getting There

From Oslo, the church is a little less than a 2-hour drive (117 km/73 mi). Follow E18 southwest out of Oslo, toward Drammen. From there, take E134 toward Notodden.

By public transportation, getting to the church will take you a little less than 3 hours.

From Oslo bus station, take the express bus run by **Vy** (www.vy.no) toward Notodden, getting off at Notodden Bus Station. There, change to local bus 185 or 6 (tel. 81 50 01 70; www.farte.no). Get off at either Svintrud or Heddal Barneskole. From either stop, the church is around a 5-minute walk.

SKIEN

The main "port" of Telemark and the Telemark canal is Skien. This city has around 50,000 inhabitants and is perhaps known best for being the birthplace of Norwegian author Henrik Ibsen. It is a good base for exploring the Telemark Canal and area surrounding it. In addition to being able to see the canal and one of its locks from the city center, you can visit this area's many shops and restaurants.

Sights
Telemarkskanalen

www.telemarkskanalen.no

The Telemark Canal is human-made and stretches all the way from the coast to the interior of Norway. Along the way, it covers 105 kilometers (65 mi) and ascends or descends up to 72 meters (236 ft) through an impressive system of sluser (locks). It was completed in 1892, and by then 500 men had spent 5 years blasting the canal through the mountainous terrain of Telemark. It contains 18 locks, and when joining a cruise on the canal you will travel through several of them.

The Telemark Canal was an important addition to the trade of Norway, as it connected the interior of Norway with the ocean. Through the canal, timber, stone, and passengers could be transported to the ocean towns along the coast much more easily than before. Today, the Telemark Canal is a popular tourist attraction, and a sail along the canal will take you through the beautiful scenery of this part of Norway.

In the center of Skien you will find **Skien Sluse,** one of the first locks in the canal. It was completed in 1861, and from time to time you can see it in use during the summer months.

Henrik Ibsen Museum

Venstøphøgda 74; tel. 95 54 45 00; www. telemarkmuseum.no/henrik-ibsen-museum; Tues.-Sat. 11am-5pm May-Aug.; adults 100 kr, children 40

Not a lot of people know that Henrik Ibsen spent his childhood in the center of Skien. When he was 7 years old, his family moved to a summer farm just outside of the city. Ibsen's childhood home has been made into a museum where you can learn more about the famous writer's life and accomplishments. Here you can gain insight into his childhood and upbringing. The museum contains furniture and other items that once belonged to the Ibsen family, and there is a small shop for anyone who feels like picking up an Ibsen play or two during their visit.

Sports and Recreation
Telemark Canal River Cruises

Hjellebrygga (Nedre Hjellegate 21); tel. 40 92 00 00; www.booktelemark.no/en/half-day-trip-morning-skien-lunde-skien; daily morning and afternoon trips May-Aug., Tues., Thurs., and Sat. in Sept.; adults 1,025 kr adult, children 375 kr

This trip covers the eastern part of the Telemark Canal, starting and ending in Skien. It departs either in the early morning or in the afternoon and is ideal for those with just one day to explore Telemark. During this trip you sail one way from Skien to Lunde, and from there, there is a 1-hour bus transfer back to town. Along this journey you will enjoy the changing landscapes along the canal as you travel into the country on board one of the veteran ships, the *Victoria* or *Henrik Ibsen*. It is also possible to do this trip the opposite way, starting by bus in Skien and taking the boat from Lunde to Skien. The entire trip lasts approximately 7 hours including the bus transfer.

Kanal Camping

Sluseveien 21, Lunde; tel. 91 57 54 21; www. kanalcamping.no; kayak 370 kr/day, canoe 320 kr/day

Kanal Camping has kayak and canoe rentals to suit all skill levels, from experienced

Dalen and the Western Telemark Canal

cruising the Telemark Canal

From Skien, the Telemark Canal stretches inland to destinations such as Lunde and Dalen. A beautiful, lush area, Dalen is perhaps the epitome of traditional Norwegian landscapes. While it's a bit of a detour from Skien and the more central areas of the Telemark Canal, Dalen is the perfect area to include in your trip if you want to slow down and immerse yourself in breathtaking scenery. Spend a night at the historic Dalen Hotel, to really breathe in the fresh air and take in the surroundings.

FULL-DAY CANAL CRUISE

Lastein Pier; tel. 40 92 00 00; www.booktelemark.no/en/day-trip-western-parts-canal; daily departures at 7:40am or 8:30am, returning by 6pm or 6:35pm late May- early Sept.; adults 1,170 kr adults, children 375 kr
This trip covers the western part of the Telemark Canal and departs and ends in Dalen. The excursion includes traveling on two different boats, the MS *Victoria* and the MS *Henrik Ibsen*; about halfway you disembark (at Kjeldal lock) and wait for the other boat as it comes back down the canal. Both of these ships are considered veterans of the Telemark Canal, and along the way you will get to see the beautiful lakes of the canal that can almost resemble fjords.

DALEN KAJAK & CANOE RENTAL

Aasmund Nordgards veg 6; tel. 92 81 70 12; www.dalenbb.com/kajak-canoe; 400 kr/day
Come here to rent kayaks or canoes by the day.

DALEN HOTEL

Hotellvegen 33; tel. 35 07 90 00; www.dalenhotel.no; mid-Apr.-mid-Oct.; 4,500 kr
If you want to stay overnight in the region, the Swiss-style Dalen Hotel is known by many Norwegians (and tourists) as the "fairy-tale hotel," due to its distinctive yellow exterior with green trim. The hotel dates back to 1894 and can be found just a short walk from the banks of the Telemark Canal. Their 49 rooms are all decorated with a historic twist, transporting you back in time. The on-site restaurant, Restaurant Bandak, serves a French-inspired menu with Norwegian produce and ingredients, and offers several set menus for guests (895 kr for three courses).

GETTING THERE

From Oslo, it will take you around 3.5 hours to reach Dalen along E134 (213 km/133 mi). This route will not take you through Skien, but it does go past Heddal Stave Church, and it is worth making a stop there. The drive from Skien will take you a little over 2 hours, traveling via Bø along Route 36 and eventually E134 (132 km/82 mi).

to beginner. They are located in Lunde, a 45-minute drive from Skien along the canal.

Food and Accommodations
Jacob & Gabriel
Arkaden, Bruene 1; tel. 35 70 72 91; https:// jacoboggabriel.no/spise; Tues.-Thurs. 5pm-11pm, Fri. 5pm-midnight, Sat. noon-midnight; 165-295 kr
Jacob & Gabriel is the newest restaurant in town, serving a menu consisting of seafood, locally sourced beef, and pasta. They have an à la carte menu, but the best value is perhaps their three-course set menu (595 kr). The interior is homey and rustic, with bare brick walls and earth-colored details. The atmosphere is lively and welcoming.

Brasseriet Madame Blom
Kongensgate 6; tel. 35 90 58 00; www.thonhotels.no/ hoteller/norge/skien/thon-hotel-hoyers/brasseriet-madame-blom; Mon.-Fri. 6pm-9pm; 250-395 kr
Brasseriet Madame Blom is a decadent restaurant with gold details and beautiful chandeliers. In spite of the grand setting, the atmosphere is friendly and informal. The menu is small but well thought out, and you can expect dishes such as steamed halibut and sous vide beef tenderloin.

Thon Hotel Høyers
Kongensgate 6; tel. 35 90 58 00; www.thonhotels.no/ hoteller/norge/skien/thon-hotel-hoyers/; 1,600 kr
Old meets new at Thon Hotel Høyers. The hotel has been in business for more than 160 years, and though it is today part of the Thon chain, it has kept its historic charm. Now, the colorful details of the Thon chain are combined with the classic beauty of the original hotel. The result is stylish and modern rooms, with lime-colored details and rose-covered wallpaper. The lobby still has some of its old-school style, with beautiful chandeliers and Chesterfield chairs. The hotel has 107 rooms in total.

Getting There and Around
Skien can be easily reached by car or bus from Oslo (or Kristiansand in the south). Traveling along the canal is best done by boat, and getting around the area with public buses is also possible (www.farte.no).

Train
Reach Skein by taking the train to Bø from Oslo, Stavanger, or Kristiansand. From Bø, Skien is a 1-hour drive or bus ride (www.farte.no).

Bus
From Oslo, the Haukeliekspressen bus (www.nor-way.no; around 500 kr) takes you to Seljord in less than 3 hours; then you can change to the Telemarksekspressen bus (www.nor-way.no; around 300 kr). The latter takes you from Seljord to Skien. From Bergen, take line 930 (www.skyss.no; 149 kr) to Seljestad to connect with Haukeliekspressen. Haukeliekspressen has four daily departures. The Telemarksekspressen bus has up to 10 daily departures.

Car
From both Oslo and Kristiansand, Skien is around a 2-hour drive along Route E18.

Air
Travel by air to Sandefjord (Torp), a 45-minute drive from Skien. There is a shuttle bus from the airport to the Torp train station, which connects with all train stations along the coast, including Skien.

Sandefjord Airport Torp
Torpveien 130; tel. 33 42 70 00; www.torp.no
Sandefjord is an alternative airport to Oslo Gardermoen, with both domestic and European routes available. Inland you can reach it by connecting in Oslo, Bergen, or Trondheim, while international destinations include Amsterdam, London, and Vienna.

JOMFRULAND NATIONAL PARK
https://jomfrulandnasjonalpark.no
Jomfruland is a marine national park along the east coast of Norway. It covers the

archipelago outside of Kragerø and a stretch of land that is 27 kilometers (17 mi) long. Most of this marine national park (98 percent) is an underwater area of nearly 12,140 hectares (30,000 acres). The main island of Jomfruland is just over 7 kilometers long (4.4 mi) and 1 kilometer wide (1.6 mi).

The archipelago, its long stone beaches, and the wildlife that lives there are all part of the national park. It is a great place for bird-watching, hiking, and relaxing. This is a relatively small national park. Therefore, you only need to spend a few hours here, looking out over the archipelago or swimming at the beach.

Beaches

Øytangen

The northern tip of the island

Øytangen is a long, public beach on the northernmost tip of the Jomfruland island. This is a shallow sandy beach that is ideal for families. There are no facilities here, as with most public beaches in Norway. If you have snorkeling gear with you, you can see hermit crabs and flounder below the surface.

Bird-Watching

Up to 92 species of birds have been found to lay their eggs on the island. Around 40-50 of these come back yearly during the main bird-watching season, which is from March to November. During these months, the bird-watching tower on the northern tip of the island is staffed by Norway's Ornithology Society on a voluntary basis. Among the birds you can see on the island are nightingale, rosefinch, barred warbler, and the red-backed shrike. The bird-watching station regularly posts photos and information about sightings on their Facebook page (www.facebook.com/Fuglestasjon), so it

is good to check there before you visit the island.

Hiking

Northern Loop

Distance: *7 kilometers (4.4 mi)*
Time: *1.5 hours, loop*
Difficulty: *Easy*
Trailhead: *The dock at Jomfruland*
Information and Services: *https://ut.no/ turforslag/118147/rundtur-jomfruland-nord*

The whole island of Jomfruland is small and walkable, so you can hike pretty much anywhere you'd like when exploring the island. This loop starts at the dock where you get off the ferry from the mainland and takes you in a loop around the northern half of the island. It is a relatively easy walk, passing farmlands and rocky beaches, and taking you through forested areas. Of course, there are plenty of ocean views, with the vast archipelago stretching both inland and out toward the sea.

Getting There and Around

You can reach the park by ferry from Kragerø 3-5 times a day (www.fjordbat.no; tel. 40 00 58 58; around 40 minutes; 62 kr per person). Note that if there are really strong winds, it is not possible for the boat to dock in Jomfruland.

To reach Kragerø, follow E18 from Oslo toward Kristiansand. The 201-kilometer (125-mi) drive will take you around 2.5 hours. From Kristiansand, the drive will take you around 1 hour and 45 minutes (137 km/85 mi).

Once you are in the national park, you can get around on foot, or by renting a bicycle by the Tårnbrygga dock, where the ferry comes in (Sykkelknut Bicycle Rental; Tårnbryggeveien 1-3; tel. 92 42 69 69; www. facebook.com/sykkelknut; daily May-Sept.; 50 kr per hour).

Southern Norway

If you want to holiday like the Norwegians, southern Norway is the place to go. In the summertime, Norwegians migrate from Oslo and the cities in eastern Norway to their cabins and holiday homes along the southern coast. Here, you will find beautiful beaches and an archipelago unlike anywhere else in the country, and the weather tends to be much more temperate in the summer season.

The cities of Stavanger and Kristiansand are the two major draws of the south, but there are plenty of quaint towns and idyllic destinations along the southern coast as well. The two modern cities have lots to offer travelers, from the bucket list-worthy Pulpit Rock hike outside of Stavanger to the popular tourist attraction Kristiansand Dyrepark (a zoo and amusement park). Telemark is a perfect region to explore for

Highlights

Look for ★ to find recommended sights, activities, dining, and lodging.

★ **Gimle Gård:** This stately home in central Kristiansand has been preserved in the exact same way the last owners left it (page 111).

★ **Kristiansand Dyrepark:** Meet Nordic animals and catch shows based on popular Norwegian children's stories in this large amusement park (page 113).

★ **Baneheia:** The lovely city park of Kristiansand offers lots of trails for visitors who want to hike near the city (page 114).

★ **American Festival in Vanse:** Vanse in Lista is a town with a strong American influence, and every year they put on a massive American festival (page 121).

★ **Fargegaten:** Translating to "the color street," this street in the center of Stavanger is known for its very colorful buildings (page 123).

★ **Pulpit Rock:** One of the most famous hikes in Norway, this massive mountain plateau offers incredible views of the Lysefjord below (page 132).

Fargegaten

Pulpit Rock

Stavanger

Setesdal Vesthei Ryfylkeheiane landskapsvernområde

Gimle Gård

Baneheia

American Festival in Vanse

Kristiansand

Kristiansand Dyrepark

0   20 mi

0   20 km

© MOON.COM

Southern Norway

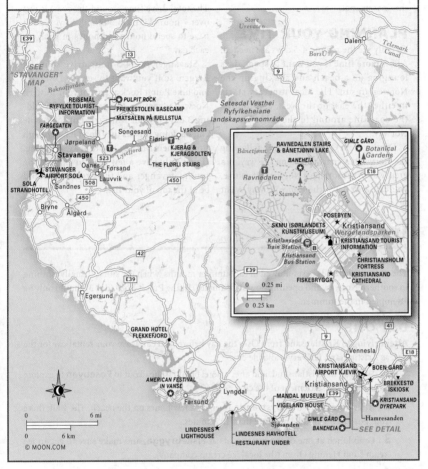

those who want to see a more traditional side of Norway, with Heddal Stave Church being a main attraction.

The drive between the cities of Stavanger and Kristiansand is a lovely road trip for those who want to take their time along the coastline, stopping to sightsee along the way. Lindesnes Lighthouse is the southernmost lighthouse in Norway, and it includes

an outdoor museum with several interesting exhibitions. Additionally, along the drive you will come across the town of Vanse, which has strong ties to the United States (and a yearly American Festival).

Southern Norway is mainly a summer destination, and the towns and cities truly come alive in the summer months. The scenery is not as mountainous and dramatic here as in

Previous: Stavanger at night; Gimle Gård; Pulpit Rock.

the northwest part of Norway, but if you want a relaxing trip with lots of sun and ice cream, this is your spot.

PLANNING YOUR TIME

To truly see the region, 4-5 days are needed. Allow more time if you want to spend days lounging on a beach and soaking up the Norwegian sun. The ideal itinerary starts in either the east or the west, and follows the coastline around to the other side of Norway.

Driving from Oslo to Stavanger, following the Norwegian coastline along the way, is a great way to see southern Norway. Of course, you can also drive the opposite way. Visit Kristiansand, Norway's "summer city," and stop to see cute coastal towns, such as Mandal. The total drive time around the coast is just over 7 hours (551 km/342 mi), so you don't have to spend hours and hours in your car each day.

Stavanger is a 4-5-hour drive south of Bergen, so if you want to see the Lysefjord and hike Pulpit Rock as part of your western Norway adventure, this can be done by adding 3 days to your itinerary. Lots of people end up doing this, as they don't have enough time in their Norway trip to see everything. If you only have a few days to explore the south, Stavanger and the Lysefjord should be at the top of your list.

Itinerary Ideas

The itinerary below is best followed in the summer months, when the sun is (usually) shining in southern Norway, and opening hours are ample. Hiking Pulpit Rock (day 3) should only be attempted in the summer.

DAY ONE

After driving to Kristiansand from Oslo the day before, you can leave your rental car for the day, as Kristiansand is a very walkable city.

1 Wake up in Kristiansand, and after a hotel breakfast head out to **Posebyen** to explore the old wooden settlement of the city.

2 After a stroll, head to **Bystranda** to enjoy a few hours on the beach. The walk there from Posebyen will take no more than 10 minutes.

3 Grab lunch at one of the restaurants at **Fiskebrygga,** and make sure to get an ice cream from Hennig Olsen (the local ice cream company).

4 After lunch, walk along the water toward **Christiansholm Fortress** and learn more about the history of the city here.

5 From there, walk 5 minutes toward the **Kristiansand Cathedral** and explore the inside of this beautiful church.

6 After your cultural afternoon, head down Markens and enjoy dinner at **Hos Naboen.**

7 After dinner, the rooftop at **Radisson Blu Caledonien** is the only rooftop bar in town, offering great views of the city. Head there for drinks before you are off to bed.

Itinerary Ideas

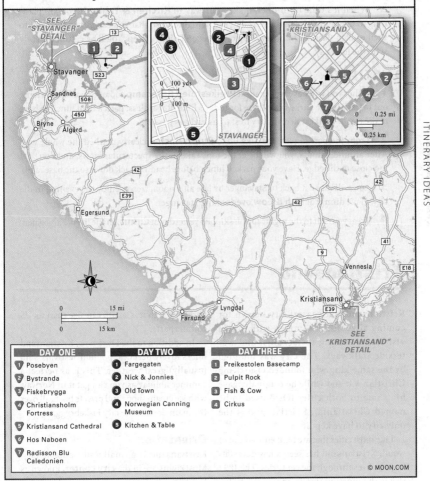

DAY ONE	DAY TWO	DAY THREE
1 Posebyen	1 Fargegaten	1 Preikestolen Basecamp
2 Bystranda	2 Nick & Jonnies	2 Pulpit Rock
3 Fiskebrygga	3 Old Town	3 Fish & Cow
4 Christiansholm Fortress	4 Norwegian Canning Museum	4 Cirkus
5 Kristiansand Cathedral	5 Kitchen & Table	
6 Hos Naboen		
7 Radisson Blu Caledonien		

© MOON.COM

DAY TWO

1 From Kristiansand, it's time to head to Stavanger! Get an early start after breakfast. The drive from Kristiansand is 3.5 hours. After checking into your hotel, head to **Fargegaten** to have a look at this fun, colorful street in the middle of the city center.

2 Enjoy a nice lunch at **Nick & Jonnies,** right in the middle of Fargegaten.

3 After lunch, walk over to gamlebyen, the Stavanger **Old Town.** The walk here is no more than 10 minutes. Stroll along the old wooden buildings here, and make sure to take some photos.

4 The **Norwegian Canning Museum** is right in the middle of Old Town. Visit for an hour of (surprisingly) interesting canning history.

5 When it's time for dinner, make your way to **Kitchen & Table.** If you are planning to hike Pulpit Rock the next day, skip a nightcap, so that you can either drive out to Preikestolen Basecamp this evening or get a good night's sleep. You'll be getting an early start the next day.

DAY THREE

1 Either you will have woken up at **Preikestolen Basecamp** today, or you'll be driving out to park in the parking lot there for today's hike. Regardless, pack a light lunch to have at the top of Preikestolen and try to start as early as possible.

2 From the parking lot, the hike up to **Pulpit Rock** is clearly marked the whole way. After around 2 hours, you will be at the top! Take in the spectacular views, and don't get too close to the edge. Have your packed lunch before heading back down to the basecamp.

3 You will make it back to Stavanger by late afternoon, free to enjoy the evening in the city. Have dinner at **Fish & Cow** overlooking Stavanger.

4 Treat yourself to the nightcap you skipped yesterday at **Cirkus,** in the lively Fargegaten.

Kristiansand

Kristiansand is a coastal city known for coming alive in the summer, with lots of visitors, charming restaurants, and waterside walkways. The city was founded by the same king who founded Oslo, King Christian VI, and while he originally gave his name to both cities (Oslo used to be named Christiania), Kristiansand is the only city to have kept it.

Like most cities that are built entirely out of wood, Kristiansand has seen a few devastating city fires through the centuries. The 1892 fire is the most infamous one, as it left 350 houses ruined in its wake. As a result, the city council demanded new buildings in the city center to be built using brick, and since then, Kristiansand has not been victim to another major fire.

The city is a particularly popular destination for families, with Kristiansand Dyrepark being the major draw. This is the largest amusement park in Norway, with a zoo, several carousels and rides, and themed "lands" similar to those found in American theme parks, though it is smaller in size than its US counterparts.

In addition to the Dyrepark, Kristiansand offers lovely beaches, popular festivals, and (usually) great weather. This is as perfect a summer holiday as you can get it in Norway, with ice cream shops and private boats all over the main dock of the city Fiskebrygga.

Orientation

Kristiansand is a small and walkable city. Most sights are in the **city center,** known as Kvadraturen, due to its perfectly angled streets ("kvadrat" means "square" in Norwegian). Kvadraturen surrounds Markens (the pedestrianized street) and Fiskebrygga (the city dock) on the south side of the river.

Just south of this area you will find a large island, Odderøya, and north of the river is where Gimle Gård, the Natural History Museum, and the Botanical Gardens are located. Though these are not in the city center, they are not too far away to reach on foot.

Kristiansand Dyrepark and Sørlandssenteret

are both located outside of the city center to the northeast.

SIGHTS
City Center
Posebyen

Posebyen; open 24/7; free

Posebyen is a neighborhood in Kristiansand consisting of old, white wooden houses. This is actually the oldest part of the city, and the only neighborhood that survived the last major city fire in 1892. Today, a stroll around the area will give you a glimpse into what life was like in Kristiansand back in the day, and you'll find many blue plaques noting houses of historical significance, such as the former post office from 1695 (Kronprinsensgate 45) and Berntsens Hus (Kronprinsensgate 59) from 1855, one of the best preserved houses in Posebyen. A peculiar thing you might notice about the buildings is that most of the corners facing the street are rounded, not squared. This was to prevent fires from spreading across the street to the next square of houses.

Kristiansand Cathedral

Gyldenløves Gate 9; tel. 38 19 69 00; www. kristiansanddomkirke.no; Mon.-Fri. 10am-5pm summer, Sat.-Sun. services; free

The cathedral in Kristiansand is one of the largest churches in the country. It was built in 1883-1884 in the Gothic style. The large, gray church towers over the square by the Wergelandsparken park, in the center of the city. The current cathedral is actually the fourth church built in that spot, as the previous ones were destroyed in fires.

SKMU (Sørlandets Kunstmuseum)

Skippergata 24B; 38 07 49 00; www.skmu.no; Thurs.-Sun. 11am-5pm; adults 120 kr, children under 16 free

Sørlandets Kunstmuseum (Southern Norway's Art Museum) houses a large permanent collection as well as temporary displays. The heart of the museum is the Tangen Collection, the world's largest collection of Nordic modern art.

Christiansholm Fortress

Østre Strandgate 52B; open 24/7 in summer; free

When the city of Kristiansand was founded in 1641, the fortress Christiansholm was planned as a measure to protect the city from invaders coming by sea. It was completed in 1672. Today, the large round fortress, surrounded by thick stone walls, is open to the public. From the walls, you can see across the harbor and waters outside of Kristiansand. The military history society of **Christiansand Artillerie Compagnie** (www.cac-krs.no) puts on reenactments and tours sporadically through the summer season.

Fiskebrygga

Gravane 6; daily; free

Fiskebrygga (the fishing dock) in Kristiansand opened in 1936 and has been a main center of the city ever since. The harbor is a charming little dock area, complete with waterways and public parking spaces for visiting (small) boats and a cute bridge connecting the two sides of the harbor. Grabbing some ice cream from the Hennig Olsen stand here is a must, and there are lots of restaurants lining the wooden houses along the docks. The area gets very crowded in the summer but is worth seeing.

Greater Kristiansand
★ Gimle Gård

Gimleveien 23; tel. 38 10 26 80; www.vestagdermuseet. no/gimlegard/apningstider; grounds open 24/7, main house tours every hour 10am-4pm June 25-Aug. 17; adults 100 kr, children 50 kr, gardens free

Gimle Gård is a stately former home, and perhaps one of the most beautiful ones in southern Norway. It was built in the late 1700s as a summer house for a rich trader and merchant named Bernt Holm and stayed in his family for five generations. The final family member who lived there, Ottilie Arenfeldt Omdal, died in 1982; he gifted the house to the municipality. The house is surrounded by a beautiful English garden and the Botanical Gardens of Kristiansand. The gardens can be accessed all day, free of charge.

In the summer season there are guided

tours of the house every hour during opening hours. Tour guides will explain the history of the house and the generations of the family who lived there, all the way up until the last owner left it in 1982. The tour takes you through both the new and the old kitchen, and tells the story of how the house was taken over by the German army during the occupation. You'll also get to see the bedroom where a king once stayed and hear the tale of an (alleged) horse that was ridden through the ballroom.

Botanical Gardens

Gimleveien 27; tel. 38 05 86 20; www.uia.no/naturmuseum-og-botanisk-hage; open 24/7; free

The Botanical Gardens of Kristiansand make up the large green area surrounding Gimle Gård. Here, you will find almost 2,000 different plants and flower species to explore. This is a great park for a stroll, or to sit on the grass and take in the variety of the plants. This is also where you will find Norway's largest collection of cacti.

★ Kristiansand Dyrepark

Kardemomme By; tel. 97 05 97 00; www.dyreparken.no; open 24/7; adults 519 kr, children under 13 489 kr

Dyreparken offers fun for all ages, with a variety of "lands" to explore. Their zoo has both exotic and Nordic animals, with the Nordic area perhaps being the most interesting for visitors. Here, you can see moose, wolf, wolverine, and lynx. In total there are 117 different species across the zoo.

The eight themed lands across Dyreparken have perhaps become more popular than the zoo, focusing either on the animals you can see (Africa, the Jungle, Nordic Wilderness, Kutoppen Farm, and Asia) or family entertainment (Hakkebakkeskogen, Kardemomme By and Kjuttaviga/Captain Sabertooth's World).

Kaptein Sabeltann (Captain Sabertooth) is a famous children's character in Norway, and for the past 30 years every single Norwegian child has grown up hearing about this feared pirate ("the most dangerous pirate on the seven seas" is one of the ways he is described). In Dyreparken, you can visit Kaptein Sabeltann's world, and walk around a "real" pirate village. In the summer evenings there are live shows, with actual pirate ships sailing around the bay. Shows usually sell out months in advance.

Also inspired by a famous Norwegian children's tale is the land called Kardemomme By (Cardamom Town). This exotic town is home to a variety of fun characters, such as the three thieves Kasper, Jesper, and Jonathan (and their pet lion), the old man Tobias (who predicts the weather from his tower in the middle of town), and the grumpy Tante Sofie (Aunt Sophie). Visiting Cardamom Town on any given day, you will see various performances of actors throughout town, making it a fun and immersive experience for children.

One day is enough to visit Dyreparken. Note that the evening Captain Sabertooth show is only available in Norwegian. Even if you cannot follow the words, however, the show is both visually impressive (with full-size pirate ship battles happening in front of your eyes and actors flying above the crowd), and the music is spectacular.

There are food concessions in the park, including several quick-service and sit-down restaurants.

To get to Dyreparken from Kristiansand, simply follow E18 north-east for 10 kilometers (6 mi). The total drive time is just 10 minutes, and Dyreparken has plenty of parking spaces for visitors (100 kr per day). Bus M1 (www.akt.no) also stops at Dyreparken and can take you there from the city center in 15 minutes.

BEACHES

Bystranda

City center

Bystranda, meaning "the city beach," is a beautiful white sand beach located right in the middle of Kristiansand. It gets very busy

---

1: inside Gimle Gård **2:** Fiskebrygga **3:** pirate ship at Kristiansand Dyrepark

Summering the Norwegian Way

Norwegians love their cabins. In fact, there are almost 500,000 cabins in Norway, with 2.5 million Norwegians having access to one (whether they own one or go with friends and family). "Cabin culture" is a large part of the Norwegian philosophy of hygge, and there is nothing as cozy and relaxing as spending time in your cabin. When you think of a cabin, you might picture a timber structure in the mountains, with skis next to the door. This is the case for many cabins, but there is another type of cabin that you will typically find along the southern archipelago.

Norwegians spend their summers in these coastal cabins. In the archipelago outside of Kristiansand, these cabins are built on islands with no road connection, so more often than not, there will be a small boat tied up outside. Norwegians will stock up on all the food (and alcohol) they need for a week (or more), take the boat over to their tiny island, and spend their holiday there. The only exception might be when they take the boat to a larger town to find a bar or an ice cream kiosk on the dock.

There are plenty of cabins and small houses available for rent on Airbnb (www.airbnb.com) for those wanting a truly Norwegian holiday. Prices vary throughout the season, but a small cabin with 4-5 beds will usually set you back 2,000-5,000 kr per night.

in the summer months, but is the perfect place for those who do not have a car or don't want to travel too far to go to the beach.

Hamresanden

Hamresandveien 15

Hamresanden has been called one of Norway's best beaches. It stretches for 3 kilometers (1.8 mi) of white sand. To get there, take bus 35 or 36 (tel. 38 03 83 00; www.akt. no) from the center of town toward Kjevik-Tveit. After about 20 minutes, you will reach the stop called Hamresanden. There are public toilets and a small kiosk selling waffles and ice cream on the beach in the summer.

SPORTS AND RECREATION
Parks
Wergelandsparken

Gyldenløves Gate 14; open 24/7; free

Wergelandsparken is the most central park in Kristiansand, located right in front of the Kristiansand Cathedral. The park was founded by Oscar Wergeland, brother of Henrik Wergeland (one of Norway's most famous poets and writers), in 1860. In the middle of a park there is a statue of Wergeland, made by another famous Norwegian: Gustav

Vigeland (the sculptor behind the Vigeland Park in Oslo).

Ravnedalen

Ravnedalen; open 24/7; free

Ravnedalen is a lush, green valley and park in Kristiansand. There is an outdoor stage where there are concerts in the summer (see displays in the park for what's on). There is also a small café, Café Generalen, open daily during the summer months.

★ Baneheia

https://ut.no/sted/144855401/baneheia-rundt-stampene

Baneheia is an outdoor area overlooking Kristiansand with several trails, ponds, and walkways to follow. The walk up to Baneheia is 3 kilometers (1.8 mi) and will take you around 30 minutes to get there from the city center. If you start at Markens, simply take a left at Kirkegata and walk all the way to the end of the street, past Wergelandsparken. There you will see the edge of Baneheia and can follow the footpaths from the end of Fritz Jensens Gate (the street that meets Kirkegata).

There are a few viewpoints where you can look out at the city and ocean beyond, in addition to floating docks and a beach where you can swim in the ponds. There are three main ponds; the swimming dock is located in the biggest one, known as 3. Stampe

Hiking
Ravnedalen Stairs and Bånetjønn Lake

Distance: 2.6 kilometers (1.6 mi)
Time: 1 hour
Difficulty: Easy
Trailhead: The Café in Ravnedalen
Information and Services: https://ut.no/turforslag/1112396/ravnedalen-og-rundt-banetjnn

This is a lovely trail that includes some steep steps and an easy loop around a small lake in Ravnedalen. Start by taking the trail to the left from the café, and head up the old stone steps to get some great views of Kristiansand. Head back down the steps (the same way as you came), walk to the end of the valley, and follow the small river up to the Bånetjonn Lake. There, you will find a nice trail that loops around the lake.

Watersports
Aquarama

Tangen 8; tel. 38 60 20 20; www.aquarama.no; open 24/7; adults 215 kr, children 175 kr

Right by Bystranda is Aquarama, a large indoor and outdoor water park and swimming pool. On a rainy day, this is a popular place for locals and visitors alike to have fun. Aquarama has five water slides, a climbing course above a pool, a wave pool, and more.

Odderøya Museumshavn

Nodeviga 38; tel. 90 77 44 46; www.vestagdermuseet.no/odderoya; 11am-5pm June 25-Aug. 14; 175 kr/hour

At Odderøya, the half island in the center of the city, you can rent stand-up paddleboards in the summer. Nodeviga is a quiet bay between the island and the city center, where the conditions for SUP are ideal. You can also paddle farther away, and enjoy the view of Christiansholm Fortress from the water.

ENTERTAINMENT AND EVENTS
Performing Arts
Kilden Performing Arts Center

Sjølystveien 2; tel. 90 58 11 11; www.kilden.com; ticket office Mon.-Fri. 11am-3pm

Kilden opened in 2012 as Kristiansand's new main house for concerts and shows. It is home to the Kristiansand Philharmonic, the Kristiansand Opera, and the Kristiansand Theatre. Every year, more than 850 performances are hosted here, including stand-up comedy and concerts, as well as ballets and operas.

Festivals and Events
Sommerbris

Odderøya; www.sommerbris.com; June

Sommerbris is another popular outdoor festival, set on Odderøya. This festival focuses more on Norwegian artists than Palmesus does (see below), with artists such as Hellbillies, Gabrielle, and Di Derre performing on their main stage.

Palmesus

Bystranda; www.palmesus.com; first weekend of July

Palmesus is perhaps the most famous festival in Kristiansand, selling out months in advance. This beach festival takes place on Bystranda every July and will make you forget you are in a (usually) cold country. Artists who have appeared in the past include David Guetta, Matoma, Macklemore, and The Chainsmokers. The music styles at this festival usually encompass club, DJ, pop, and hip-hop.

Sørlandets Matfestival

Tresse; www.sorlandetsmatfestival.no; second weekend of July

The Southern Norway Food Festival takes place every year in July, with street food vendors and local producers displaying their foods in the city center for a weekend. There are also activities for adults and children happening throughout the festival, such as the chili competition, where they find out who will be named southern Norway's "Chili Master."

Måkeskrik

Odderøya; www.maakeskrik.no; July

The Måkeskrik festival at Odderøya leans toward the heavier side of music—think hard rock, metal, and heavy metal. Mainstream artists occasionally join the lineup, but most bands who play at this festival fall within hard-rocking genres of music. Past performers include Motorpsycho, Kvelertak, and Blood Command.

SHOPPING

Markens

Markens Gate; www.kvadraturen.no; Mon.-Fri. 10am-6pm, Sat. 10am-5pm

Markens is the main shopping street of Kristiansand. It is lined with cozy cafés and restaurants, and all of the city's shopping is within walking distance. For travel gear and souvenirs, head to **Reisemagasinet** in Tordenskioldsgate 17. **Kollektivet** (Markensgate 31) is a must-visit for anyone looking for unique and sustainable clothing and decor. This is a collective of local artists and designers where they all sell their plastic-free, zero-waste designs and products.

Sørlandssenteret

Barstølveien 35; tel. 38 04 91 00; www.sorlandssenteret.no; Mon.-Fri. 10am-9pm, Sat. 10am-7pm

Located near the Dyrepark, Sørlandssenteret is the largest shopping center in the Nordics and offers a wide variety of shops and restaurants. You will find Scandinavian chain stores such as H&M and Monki here, as well as more upscale brand stores such as Alexander McQueen, Balmain, and Armani. In total they have over 150 restaurants and shops carrying everything from clothing and beauty products to decor and home goods.

FOOD

City Center

Hos Naboen

Markens Gate 19A; tel. 45 22 68 88; www.hosnaboen.no; Mon.-Sat. 10:30am-11pm, Sun. 11:30am-9pm; 169-299 kr

"Hos Naboen" translates to "at the neighbor's," and that's exactly the type of atmosphere they are going for: that friendly visit next-door. This warm and welcoming restaurant serves a selection of international and Norwegian dishes, and you will find grilled salmon, tenderloin of deer, and club sandwich on the menu.

Bønder i Byen

Rådhusgata 16; tel. 91 14 72 47; www.bønderibyen.com; Mon.-Sat. 11am-late; 275-335 kr

The concept at Bønder i Byen (which means "Farmers in Town") is a cross between urban and rural. Here, they use produce and traditions from rural Norway (the farms) and create more urban and modern dishes—their own twist on New Nordic cuisine. The restaurant is rustic and informal, and on the menu you can find dishes such as veal tenderloin, homemade meat chops, and chicken confit.

Hos Moi

Nodeviga 2; tel. 38 17 83 00; www.hosmoi.no; Mon.-Sat. noon-11:30pm; 255-425 kr

Right on the docks of Fiskebrygga you will find Hos Moi, a seafood restaurant with an extensive wine list. The restaurant is modern and Nordic, with birch details and light tables. The large windows overlook the wharf, and the atmosphere is formal yet lively. On the menu you will find lots of fresh seafood, from oysters and scallops to turbot and the catch of the day.

Le Monde

Markens Gate 15; tel. 38 34 04 24; www.lemondetapas.no; Mon.-Thurs. noon-late, Sun. 2pm-late; 39-1,290 kr (small plates)

Le Monde serves authentic Spanish tapas right in the middle of Kristiansand. The dishes are small and meant to be shared and enjoyed together. On the menu of this lively restaurant, you will find Spanish classics such as chorizo and Iberian ham, but they also have a small menu of larger dishes served during lunch hours, including a chicken sandwich and mushroom pasta.

Hennig Olsen Ice Cream

Hennig Olsen is the oldest ice cream producer in Norway and Scandinavia, with roots dating back to 1924. They hail from Hannevika, just outside of Kristiansand, and you will find that many southerners are quite proud of their ice cream heritage. Whatever you do during your trip, do not get into an argument with a local about what is the best ice cream in Norway, because you will find yourself being dragged down to Fiskebrygga to the ice cream bar so they can prove you wrong.

The small ice cream parlor at Fiskebrygga serves only Hennig Olsen ice cream, in a variety of flavors, as do most restaurants and cafés in the city and region.

BRYGGA ISBAR
Gravane 20; daily 11am-9pm; 42-72 kr
The ice cream bar on the docks of Kristiansand usually has a long line, but it is worth the wait. They have a large selection of ice cream flavors, as well as toppings and sauces—for you to truly make your own ice cream. Make sure to try at least two different flavors if it's your first time trying Hennig Olsen ice cream. The bar is small, and does not have any seating; most people get an ice cream and find a spot in the sun on the docks.

Happy Donuts
Østre Strandgate 67; tel. 91 92 24 62; Mon.-Sat. 10am-8pm, Sun. noon-8pm; 25-54 kr per donut
Happy Donuts is a colorful little kiosk selling a large selection of donuts. The concept opened in Kristiansand in late 2020 and has since opened branches in other Norwegian cities thanks to its quick rise in popularity. It is not uncommon to see a line outside their (small) shop, but the donuts are worth the wait. From chocolate-filled donuts covered with Oreo to vanilla-filled ones with a Kinder Egg topping, there are almost too many options. There are no seats inside, so grab your favorite donuts and head on over to the park, Bystranda, just a short walk away to enjoy them.

Greater Kristiansand
Café Generalen
Ravnedalsveien 34; tel. 38 09 07 91; www. cafegeneralen.no; Mon.-Sat. noon-9pm, Sun. noon-6pm May-Aug.; 145-295 kr
Cafe Generalen is located in Ravnedalen park and proudly serves dishes from recipes dating back 100 years. The large outdoor seating area

overlooks a small pond and the park, making this is a great lunch spot after a walk or hike in Ravnedalen or Baneheia. On the menu you will find several types of hamburgers, homemade soups, and waffles.

★ Brekkestø Iskiosk
Brekkestø 48; tel. 48 18 80 43; daily noon-6pm June-Aug.; 45 kr for one (huge) scoop of ice cream
Brekkestø is located in the archipelago outside of Kristiansand and is a popular destination for those visiting their cabins in the area. Most visitors arrive by boat, but it is also reachable by car (30-minute drive). At Brekkestø, they serve the biggest ice cream in Norway, at a surprisingly reasonable rate. The bowls are absolutely massive, and you'll want to get one of their ice creams for the photo alone. The ice cream is (of course) from Hennig Olsen, the pride of southern Norway.

Brekkestø is a charming little coastal village, with just the ice cream shop and small grocery store and several lovely white wooden houses. Those who have the time should spend a little while walking around there with their ice cream.

ACCOMMODATIONS
City Center
Scandic Bystranda

Østre Strandgate 74; tel. 21 61 50 00; www.
scandichotels.no/hotell/norge/kristiansand/scandic-
kristiansand-bystranda; 3,000 kr

Scandic Bystranda faces the Bystranda city beach, and its central location makes it ideal for those wanting to explore Kristiansand on foot. Their award-winning hotel breakfast is worth staying there, and guests can enjoy working out at the nearby SATS (Norway's largest gym chain) for free. The 229 rooms are welcoming and have a very relaxed feel, with dark green or rust-colored walls and deep brown details.

Radisson Blu Caledonien

Vestre Strandgate 7; tel. 38 11 21 00; www.
radissonhotels.com/no-no/hoteller/radisson-blu-
kristiansand-caledonien; 3,200 kr

The tallest building in town, the Radisson Blu Caledonien also boasts the only rooftop bar in Kristiansand. The hotel is newly refurbished, and each of the 147 rooms is in tune with the usual modern feel of Radisson hotels. Their rooms are quiet and comfortable, with pastel details and soft beds.

Near Kristiansand Dyrepark
★ Abra Havn Pirate Village

Kardemomme By; tel. 97 05 97 00; www.dyreparken.
no/abra-havn; 2,500 kr

Abra Havn is located in Kristiansand Dyrepark and is the ideal location for families with pirate-loving children who want to stay in the middle of all the action of Dyreparken. Resembling a pirate village, Abra Havn consists of 171 different-sized apartments across a private harbor, just a 6-7-minute walk to the entrance of Dyreparken. Each apartment is uniquely decorated, but with an overall pirate theme. There are events happening throughout the day for guests staying in Abra Havn, such as the 8am "wake up call," when King Sabertooth's pirate ship sails into the harbor with music and laughter to wake you up for a new day of shenanigans.

Greater Kristiansand
Boen Gård

Dønnestadveien 341; tel. 38 99 18 13; www.boengaard.
no; 4,600 kr

Just a 20-minute drive from Kristiansand you will find charming Boen Gård. They have just 18 rooms, with 14 of them being based in two of their historic buildings. The remaining four

ice cream in southern Norway

are in the former servant's wing of the main house. This old farm, with a main house dating back to 1814, combines new and old with its renovated rooms featuring original wood walls and vintage photos.

INFORMATION AND SERVICES

Kristiansand Tourist Information

Rådhusgata 18; tel. 38 07 50 00; www.visitkrs.no

The tourist information center is located inside the city hall and is the place to pick up maps and information.

GETTING THERE AND AROUND

As one of the larger cities in southern Norway, Kristiansand is relatively easy to reach by most modes of transportation.

Train

The **train station** of Kristiansand is found in the center of the city, with daily trains (www.vy.no) to Oslo (4.5 hours) and Stavanger (3 hours; from 400 kr).

Bus

There are several bus routes servicing the distance between Oslo, Stavanger, and Kristiansand. From Oslo, there are several daily departures with **Vy Buss** (www.vybuss.no), taking you to Kristiansand in a little over 4 hours. From Stavanger, **Nor-way** (www.nor-way.no) has two daily departures, getting you to Kristiansand in 3 hours and 45 minutes.

The **main bus station** in Kristiansand is located right by the train station (Vestre Strandgate 43), on the southwest side of Kvadraturen.

There is not a large amount of in-city bus transportation, as the majority of the sights in the city are within walking distance. Local buses in Kristiansand are operated by **Agder Kollektivtrafikk** (tel. 38 03 83 00; www.akt.no; 35 kr for a single ticket within the city) and can take you to Kristiansand Dyrepark (bus M1) and the area around the Botanical gardens (bus 19).

Air

Kristiansand Airport Kjevik

Kristiansand Lufthavn; tel. 67 03 04 00; https://avinor.no/en/airport/kristiansand-airport

The small airport in Kristiansand, Kjevik, is located just 16 kilometers (10 mi) from the city and has daily domestic departures between Kristiansand and cities like Oslo, Bergen, and Trondheim. Local bus 35 toward Tveit stops at the airport and takes you into the city center in 30 minutes (www.akt.no).

Car

Kristiansand is within easy reach of anyone with a car. From Oslo, follow E18 south for 319 kilometers (198 mi). This journey takes around 4 hours, and there are several service stations along the way. From Stavanger, E39 in the southeast direction takes you to Kristiansand in 3.5 hours (234 km/145 mi). Between Kristiansand and Stavanger there are several interesting sights worth stopping to see.

Kristiansand to Stavanger

The drive from Kristiansand to Stavanger doesn't take longer than 3.5 hours, but you should set aside some extra time to stop along the coast. There are a few places of interest that are worth making the trip for, whether you are driving between the two cities or based in either of them. Enroute between Kristiansand and Stavanger you can explore the quaint coastal town of Mandal, visit the southernmost point in Norway, and dine at an underwater restaurant.

MANDAL

The charming seaside town of Mandal is known for its picturesque beach, popular dockside restaurants, and cute wooden houses.

Sights
Mandal Museum

Store Elvegate 5; www.vestagdermuseet.no/mandal; 11am-5pm June 20-Aug. 15; 100 kr

Norway's southernmost city (with 11,000 inhabitants) is also the birthplace of many famous Norwegians: Adolph Tidemand (painter), Amaldus Nielsen (painter), and Gustav Vigeland (sculptor). Mandal Museum is dedicated to showing you the works and lives of these artists.

Vigeland House

Grensegata 3A; tel. 48 85 48 29; www. vestagdermuseet.no/mandal; daily 11am-5pm June 20-Aug. 15

Part of the Mandal Museum is the childhood home of sculptor Gustav Vigeland. Here, you will get to see several of his works, as well as learn about the childhood and upbringing experienced by Gustav and his (lesser known) brother, artist Emanuel Vigeland. Access to Vigeland House is included with your ticket

to Mandal Museum, so after browsing around the museum's main building, head on over to Vigeland House for a guided tour.

Beach
Sjøsanden

Grønviksveien 8

Sjøsanden is a large, white sandy beach in the center of Mandal, and some say it's one of the best beaches in Norway. It is located a short stroll from the city center, so it is easily accessible. It is 800 meters long (2,625 ft), and there is usually plenty of space to set up camp for the day. There is a walkway along the beach and free parking available for visitors. As with most beaches in Norway, there are no toilets or changing facilities.

Food
Kastellet

Kastellgata 12E; tel. 38 60 08 20; www.kastellet.no; Mon.-Tues. 11am-4pm, Wed.-Sat. 11am-9pm; 180-339 kr

This popular restaurant is located along the waterfront in the city center, just a short walk from Sjøsanden beach. This makes it a great place to grab lunch for those stopping in Mandal for the day. The modern interior is welcoming and informal, and their outdoor seating gets quite busy and lively in the summer. They focus on Nordic and European cuisine, with a mix of Norwegian dishes such as oven-baked halibut and salmon, and more southern dishes such as Spanish tapas and serrano ham sandwiches.

Getting There

Mandal is a 50-minute drive from Kristiansand (45 km/28 mi) along main road E39. Vy Route 190 (www.vybuss.no; from 99 kr) will get you to Marnarkrysset stop, which is just a 4-minute drive by local bus to the city center (Route 200; www.akt.no; 35 kr).

☆ American Festival in Vanse

www.americanfestival.no; June

Every summer, usually in the last weekend of June, the small town of Vanse in Lista comes alive with the American Festival. The municipality of Lista has a long history of inhabitants emigrating to the US and has strong ties to America (with street names such as Route 8 and Brooklyn Square).

The festival is mainly a local experience and attracts Norwegians who have family ties to the US, as well as visiting Americans with Norwegian heritage. During this 4-day festival there is a street parade of American cars, lots of stands where you can buy food and souvenirs, and several concerts. Past performers have included Kjell Elvis (a Norwegian Elvis impersonator) and Nashville singer/songwriter Kinsey Rose. An assortment of American-style foods is usually available, from hamburgers to deep-fried items.

Vanse is a little more than an hour's drive from Kristiansand, along E39 for most of the way (and then Route 43 into town). The total driving distance is 101 kilometers (63 mi). The driving distance from Stavanger is 167 kilometers (104 mi), and this drive will take you 2.5 hours—also along E39.

LINDESNES

Sights

Lindesnes Lighthouse

Lindesnesveien 1139; tel. 38 25 54 20; https://lindesnesfyr.no; daily 10am-5pm; adults 80 kr, children 25 kr

Lindesnes Lighthouse is a living museum as well as a working lighthouse serving the southernmost point on Norway's mainland. The outdoor area surrounding the museum consists of several small buildings, built to withstand the intense weather found along the coast, housing exhibitions related to the lighthouse and life there. The current lighthouse dates back to 1915, and from the 15-meter (49 ft) tower you can look across the ocean. Amongst the permanent exhibitions is one dedicated to MS *Palatia*, a ship that was tragically sunk outside of Lindesnes during the war, with almost 1,000 war prisoners from the Soviet Union on board.

Restaurant Under

Båly; www.under.no; seating 6pm-8pm; set menu 2,500 kr, wine pairing 1,650 kr

Under is a unique fine dining restaurant, literally placed at the tip of the land in Lindesnes and lowered into the ocean. It is the first ever undersea restaurant in Europe and serves dishes inspired by the sea outside its windows. The atmosphere in this small restaurant is intimate and muted, as if you were dining on the bottom of the ocean. From the large glass window, you can see across the ocean floor, and gaze at the fish and life that swim around there. The set menu changes often, and the dishes are created to showcase the variety of species found nearby. You can expect anything from crab and scallops to cod.

Accommodations

Lindesnes Havhotell

Båly; tel. 38 60 08 00; www.havhotellet.no; 1,750 kr

As Under is located a little "off the beaten path," staying in Lindesnes is ideal for those opting for a wine pairing. This modern hotel is located a 3-minute walk from the restaurant, with a nautical and Nordic style throughout. They have 77 rooms, 9 of which are accessible.

Grand Hotel Flekkefjord

Anders Beers Gate 9; tel. 38 32 53 00; https://grand-hotell.no; 1,900 kr

About an hour northwest of Lindesnes, Grand Hotel Flekkefjord is located between Kristiansand and Stavanger, making it a good place to base yourself if you are exploring the coast between the two cities. This historic hotel dates back to 1897, and

its 29 rooms are all spacious and decadently decorated. You can expect ornate wallpapers and draped curtains in each room, with deep red or royal blue details. The hotel has been refurbished, so modern comfort meets old-fashioned style here.

Getting There

From Stavanger, Lindesnes is a 3-hour drive along E39, covering a distance of 128 kilometers (80 mi). The drive from Kristiansand will take you about 1.5 hours, also along E39 (110 km/68 mi).

Stavanger

Stavanger, Norway's fourth-largest city, is situated on the southwest coast of Norway. This small but vibrant city is known for its picturesque old town of white wooden houses and cobbled streets, its important role in the development of the Norwegian oil industry, and its proximity to the Lysefjord and the famous Pulpit Rock. These are just a few reasons people visit Stavanger; there is a lot to explore here.

The Lysefjord and Pulpit Rock are located a short distance outside the city, so most travelers opt for a night or two in Stavanger before heading there.

Orientation

Stavanger is a walkable city with a small city center that includes the popular street **Fargegaten** and most attractions in the city. Just west of the city center is the **Old Town,** which is a sight in and of itself as well as a neighborhood. Sights in the Old Town include the Norwegian Canning Museum and the Viking House.

SIGHTS
City Center
Stavanger Cathedral
Haakon VIIs gate 2; tel. 51 84 04 00; https:// domkirkenogpetri.no; Mon.-Sat. 11am-4pm, Sun. service 11am

The cathedral in Stavanger is the only Norwegian cathedral that has kept its original architecture from the Middle Ages, and

the only one that has been in continuous use since the 1300s. The Anglo-Norman church was built in 1125, most likely by English carpenters and workers. The cathedral is large and gray, with two massive stone towers on each side of the facade, and intricate carved details around the large windows. The massive stone structure is the oldest standing cathedral in Norway, and was built in a Gothic style.

★ Fargegaten
Øvre Holmegate

Fargegaten is a nickname given to Øvre Holmegate, due to the bright colors each building along the street is painted in (Fargegaten means "the color street"). The houses along the street are pastel purple, bright pink, yellow, and blue, and it is impossible to walk through it without smiling at its charm. Artist Craig Flannagan planned the color scheme, and in 2005 the street was closed for vehicles. Along this pedestrian street you will find cafés, bars, and concept stores.

Norwegian Petroleum Museum
Kjeringholmen 1A; tel. 51 93 93 00; www.norskolje. museum.no; daily 10am-7pm June-Aug., Mon.-Sat. 10am-4pm and Sun. 10am-6pm Sept.-May; adults 150 kr, children under 16 75 kr

Along the harbor of Stavanger, you will find the Norwegian Petroleum Museum. The building itself is worth seeing, as it is shaped like an oil rig. Inside, you can learn the history of the Norwegian oil industry and its importance to Norway's culture

---

1: sunset along the southern coast 2: Lindesnes Lighthouse 3: Restaurant Under

Stavanger

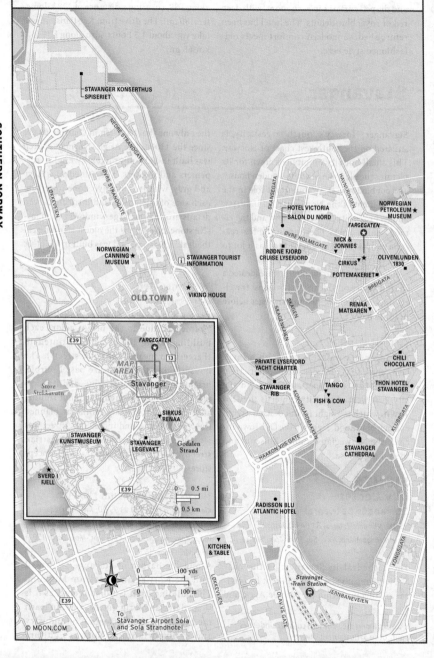

STAVANGER KONSERTHUS
SPISERIET

NEDRE STRANDGATE

ØVRE STRANDGATE

LØKKEVEIEN

SKANSEGATA

HAMNERINGEN

HOTEL VICTORIA
SALON DU NORD

NORWEGIAN
PETROLEUM
MUSEUM ★

FARGEGATEN

ØVRE HOLMEGATE

NICK &
JONNIES

NORWEGIAN
CANNING
MUSEUM ★

i STAVANGER TOURIST
INFORMATION

RØDNE FJORD
CRUISE LYSEFJORD

CIRKUS ★

OLIVENLUNDEN
1830

OLD TOWN

★ VIKING HOUSE

POTTEMAKERIET

BREIGATA

SKAGEN

RENAA
MATBAREN

SKAGENKAIEN

E39

FARGEGATEN

13

MAP
AREA

Stavanger

Store
Stokkavatn

PRIVATE LYSEFJORD
YACHT CHARTER

CHILI
CHOCOLATE

KONGSGÅRDBAKKEN

THON HOTEL
STAVANGER

SIRKUS
RENAA

STAVANGER
RIB

TANGO
FISH & COW

KLUBBGATA

STAVANGER
KUNSTMUSEUM

STAVANGER
LEGEVAKT

Godalen
Strand

SVERD I
FJELL

E39

0   0.5 mi

0   0.5 km

STAVANGER
CATHEDRAL

HAAKON VIIs GATE

RADISSON BLU
ATLANTIC HOTEL

KONGSGATA

KITCHEN
& TABLE

LØKKEVEIEN

Stavanger
Train Station

0   100 yds

0   100 m

E39

OLAV Vs GATE

JERNBANEVEIEN

© MOON.COM

To Stavanger Airport Sola
and Sola Strandhotel

and economy. You can also explore exhibits dedicated to how oil is collected and used, and the technology involved in these processes.

Old Town
(Gamlebyen)
Øvre Strandgate

Stavanger's Old Town is one of the top sights in the city, with its 173 wooden houses charmingly located by the city harbor. Most of the houses are white, small, and slightly crooked from the test of time. There are lots of ornate gardens around the neighborhoods, and spring and summer are especially beautiful times to visit. The picturesque buildings have mostly been restored and date back to the late 1700s and 1800s.

Viking House
Strandkaien 44; tel. 41 24 67 16; www.vikinghouse.no; daily according to the cruise schedule (advance booking recommended); 175 kr

At Viking House you can learn about the history and culture of the Viking Age through the use of virtual reality technology. This is a truly immersive experience right on the edge of the Old Town, where you will start by boarding a Viking ship and joining a "live" adventure set in the Viking Age. You will travel back in time (through the use of VR) and learn about Harald Hårfagre and the Battle of Hafrsfjord (872). The 25-minute experience needs to be booked for a specific time slot.

Norwegian Canning Museum
Andasmauet 15; tel. 45 87 38 46; https://iddismuseum. no; Sat.-Mon. 11am-4pm, Tues.-Wed. 11am-3pm, Thurs. 11am-7pm, Fri. 11am-3pm; adults 100 kr, children under 18 free

In Stavanger Old Town you will find the Norwegian Canning Museum, a peculiar museum dedicated to the canning industry of Stavanger. Exhibitions teach visitors about what working life was like for those in the industry, and about the printing presses used to print on the cans. On Sundays in summer there are guided tours of the museum included in the ticket price.

Greater Stavanger
Stavanger Kunstmuseum
Henrik Ibsens Gate 55; tel. 51 84 27 00; www. stavangerkunstmuseum.no; Sat.-Mon. 11am-4pm, Tues.-Wed. 11am-3pm, Thurs. 11am-7pm; adults 100 kr, children under 18 free

The Stavanger Museum of Art dates back to 1865, and through the years they have established an impressive collection of art in various genres, including works from Norwegian artists such as Kitty Kielland, Olaf Lange, Christiane Schreiber, and Hans Gude. In 1915, the collection contained 45 pieces of artwork, and today they house around 3,000 pieces. Their exhibitions are varied, from classical and nationalistic pieces to art nouveau and contemporary works. In the summer months there are guided tours held several times a week. The tour schedule varies, so check the website before your visit.

Sverd i Fjell
Møllebukta

The monument Sverd i Fjell is found in Hafrsfjord, outside of the city. Created by Fritz Røed and unveiled in 1983, the monument consists of three massive Viking swords standing in the ground and stands in memory of the battle of Hafrsfjord, a well-known Norwegian battle between a group of Viking kings. Some tales say that the battle laid the foundation for Harald Hårfagre to unite the country as one, and it is believed that Harald Hårfagre united Norway not far from this point in 872.

FJORD TOURS

Most people visiting Stavanger want to know how to travel to and see the Lysefjord. The start of the fjord is located a 45-minute drive from the city, so most travelers make a separate overnight trip there if they are planning on doing one of the hikes along the fjord. However, there are some day tours that operate out of Stavanger.

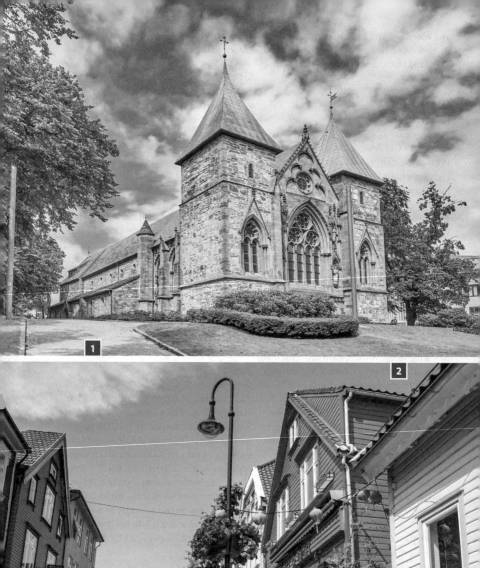

Rødne Fjord Cruise Lysefjord
Strandkaien; tel. 51 89 52 70; https://rodne.no; 610 kr

Rødne Fjord Cruise takes you from the center of Stavanger and into the Lysefjord. During their fjord cruise you will get to see the spectacular Pulpit Rock from below, as well as learn more about life along the fjord and other sights found in the Lysefjord. The excursion lasts 3-3.5 hours, and there are daily departures from June to September. In the low season there are departures on weekends.

Stavanger Rib
Strandkaien 37; tel. 40 08 68 86; https://stavangerrib.no

For a more fast-paced way to explore the Lysefjord, the FjordSafari offered by Stavanger Rib takes you on a RIB (Rigid Inflatable Boat) into the fjord. The experience lasts around 2 hours, and you will be equipped with a thick bodysuit to keep warm during the speedy parts of the adventure.

Private Lysefjord Yacht Charter
Strandkaien; tel. 93 49 77 07; https://privatecruise.no

If you prefer to explore the Lysefjord and scenery around Stavanger on your own, there are private yacht cruises offered as well. This is ideal for groups of friends and larger families that want the privacy of their own boat. Prices vary depending on the size of the yacht and length of experience, but the regular cruise lasts 3-4 hours, and the extended Lysefjord cruise lasts 6-7 hours.

BEACHES
Greater Stavanger
Godalen Strand
Øvre Sandvikveien 26

Godalen Beach is a popular beach in Stavanger, with a playground for children and diving board on the dock. In the summer there is a kiosk selling ice cream and snacks.

Solastranden
Axel Lunds Veg 23

Solastranden has been named one of Norway's most beautiful beaches. This picturesque white sand beach is popular for swimming, kite surfing, and SUP. Find it in Sola, an 18-minute drive south of Stavanger. The beach is a 20-minute drive south of Stavanger (16 km/10 mi) along E39 and Route 509.

ENTERTAINMENT AND EVENTS
Performing Arts
Stavanger Konserthus
Sandvigå 1; tel. 51 53 70 00; www.stavanger-konserthus.no

The main concert hall in Stavanger, Stavanger Konserthus is found right on the bay Sandvigå in the city center. There are mainly music concerts put on here throughout the year, but the venue does also host plays and operas, and from time to time stand-up comedy shows. Prices vary, depending on the show.

Festivals and Events
Mablis Music Festival
Våland; www.mablisfestivalen.no; June

Mablis is a weekend festival that happens every June, drawing big-name Norwegian artists and their fans to two stages. They partner with local restaurants, which put up stalls offering an impressive selection of food from restaurants such as Sirkus Renaa and The Shack. Past performers have included Gabrielle, Emilie Nicolas, and Kjartan Lauritzen.

Utopia Music Festival
Bjergstedparken; www.utopiafest.no; Aug.

Utopia is Stavanger's "city festival," as it takes place in a park in the middle of the city. The lineup for this two-day festival includes pop, rock, hip-hop, and rap music from Norway and beyond. Past artists who have appeared include DJ Snake, Alan Walker, and Astrid S.

1: Stavanger Cathedral **2:** colorful Fargegaten

What's Brewing Beer Festival

Tou, Kvitsøygata 25; www.whatsbrewing.no; Oct.

What's Brewing is a whimsical beer festival taking place in the fall, ideal for beer lovers. Included in your ticket is a beer tasting glass, and then you purchase tokens for beer at the festival. Prepare to sample beer from microbreweries all over Norway.

SHOPPING
City Center
Chili Chocolate

Søregata 27; tel. 40 45 32 87; www.chilichocolate.no; Mon.-Fri. 10am-7pm, Sat. 10am-6pm

Chili Chocolate is a small chocolate factory making local treats. Founded by two friends in 2016, they create high-quality chocolate using French Valrhona as their supplier. To spice up their creations, they also use local ingredients such as syrup from Jæren and blueberries from Melsheia.

Olivenlunden 1830

Breigata 25; tel. 92 04 34 81; www.olivenlunden1830. no; Mon.-Fri. 10am-7pm, Sat. 10am-6pm

Olivenlunden 1830 was founded in 2001 by two Norwegian friends, who discovered an olive oil store in Paris in the late '90s. This inspired their mission to make the Mediterranean diet more common in Scandinavia, and ever since, olive oil and balsamic vinegar have become staples on many Norwegian tables. At their store in Breigata you can browse a large selection of Mediterranean goods, perfect for those who love to cook.

Pottemakeriet

Breigata 14; tel. 99 26 62 86; www.pottemakeriet.no; Mon.-Fri. 10am-5pm, Sat. 10am-3pm

Pottemakeriet is not just a store where you can by local ceramics and home decor, but also it's the ceramics workshop of Sonya Molohon. Watch her work and ask questions about the products you find in this charming store. Everything is handmade and unique here, and you can spend a lot of time browsing the displays looking for the perfect gift or souvenir.

FOOD
City Center
Nick & Jonnies

Øvre Holmegate 20; tel. 51 86 41 58; www. gaffelogkaraffel.no; Wed.-Fri. 6pm-late, Sat. 4pm-late, kitchen closes 9pm; 89-295 kr

Nick & Jonnies is a stylish and informal restaurant, with dark wood details, brown leather sofas, and an open bar and kitchen facing the guest area. This makes for a fun and informal atmosphere, and the international menu here consists mainly of smaller dishes meant to share, such as Korean fried chicken, Chinese spiced duck leg, and garlic confit flatbread.

Fish & Cow

Skagen 3; tel. 51 50 50 50; www.fishandcow.no; Mon.-Fri. 4pm-midnight, Sat. noon-1am, kitchen closes 9:30pm; 245-325 kr

Fish & Cow offers views over Torget, the center of Stavanger city. This friendly and informal restaurant is therefore a great place for people-watching. The modern brasserie serves a selection of Norwegian and international dishes, such as beef tartar, grilled entrecote, and dry-aged pork loin.

Kitchen & Table

Arne Rettedals Gate 14; tel. 51 50 25 00; https:// kitchenandtable.se/stavanger; Mon.-Sat. 6pm-9:30pm; 245-425 kr

Kitchen & Table, headed by chef Marcus Samuelsson, offers dishes usually found in Manhattan restaurants but prepared using Norwegian and Scandinavian ingredients. The menu in this stylish and formal restaurant changes with the season, and dishes may include veal tenderloin, creamy paprika gnocchi, and a classic cheeseburger.

Renaa Matbaren

Steinkargata 10; tel. 51 55 11 11; www.restaurantrenaa. no/matbaren; Tues.-Fri. 4pm-10pm, Sat. 11am-10pm; 230-480 kr

Renaa Matbaren is an informal bistro with light wooden benches, tables, and no fluff. Cutlery and glasses are placed in a little wooden box by your seat, and there is no fancy table setting or cloth. Their motto is "uncomplicated food, made to nourish," and that's exactly what you get. The atmosphere is relaxed, and on the menu, you can expect French dishes such as bluefin tuna tartar and scallop quenelle.

Tango

Skagen 3, 3rd floor; tel. 51 50 12 30; www.tango-bk.no; Tues.-Sat. 6pm-midnight (last seating 9pm); six courses 1,490 Kr

Tango is a small Michelin-recommended restaurant seating only 30 people at a time in the heart of Stavanger. The restaurant serves a varied menu focused on high-quality, local ingredients, and there is a strong focus on seasonal produce. The atmosphere is intimate and homey, and you can choose between a 6- or 8-course set menu featuring dishes such as crayfish, scallops, and souffles.

Old Town
Spiseriet

Sandvigå 1; tel. 40 00 13 24; https://spiseriet.no; Tues.-Sat. 11am-11pm (kitchen closes 10pm), Sun. 1pm-6pm (last seating 4pm); 145-165 kr (small plates)

A short walk north of Old Town, Spiseriet is located inside the Stavanger Concert Hall, offering great views of the fjord and mountains outside. This modern, bright, and spacious restaurant serves dishes from both sea and land, all local of course. Dishes found here include mackerel from Sirevåg, fresh oysters, and steaks from Vikeså.

Greater Stavanger
Sirkus Renaa

Lagårdsveien 61; tel. 48 89 55 46; www.sirkusrenaa. no; breakfast and lunch daily 8am-4pm, pizzeria Mon. 8am-5pm, Tue.-Fri. 8am-10pm, Sat. 9am-10pm, Sun. 9am-5pm; 150-280 kr

Sirkus Renaa truly is a circus of options: a bakery, pizzeria, ice cream parlor, and café. Their philosophy is rooted in "thinking globally, eating locally," and they use only local ingredients and produce. The pizzeria at Sirkus Renaa uses a wood-fired oven, serving authentic Neapolitan pizza from 4pm on weekdays

and almost all day on weekends. For breakfast, their bakery serves freshly made sandwiches and wraps. Afterward, their ice cream factory makes Italian gelato using local ingredients, fresh berries, and cream from Røros.

BARS AND NIGHTLIFE
City Center
Cirkus

Øvre Holmegate 23; tel. 61 40 93 03; 122-165 kr

In the middle of the colorful Fargegaten you will find Cirkus. As the name suggests, this is a circus-themed, colorful bar. Inside you'll find dark paneling, mismatched low chairs and couches, and a friendly, lively vibe. They usually have several local beers on tap, in addition to a variety of international brews.

Salon du Nord

Skansegata 1; tel. 51 86 70 00; www.salondunord.no

This upscale, stylish cocktail bar is inside the Hotel Victoria. The vibe is almost speakeasy-like, and they are truly trying to blend the old and the new. Their signature cocktails are worth trying, each inspired by the Hotel Victoria itself, such as the Royal Visit (a vodka-based cocktail inspired by the visit of the King of Siam in 1907).

ACCOMMODATIONS
City Center
Radisson Blu Atlantic Hotel

Olav Vs Gate 3; tel. 51 76 10 00; www.radissonhotels. com/no-no/hoteller/radisson-blu-stavanger-atlantic; 1,500 kr

The Radisson in Stavanger is a modern hotel within walking distance of most of the city's attractions. Their 364 rooms are spacious and simple, with neutral colors and little detail. Many rooms face the fjord; make sure to request it when you make your reservation if you want a guaranteed fjord view.

Thon Hotel Stavanger

Klubbgata 5; tel. 51 59 95 00; www.thonhotels.no/ hoteller/norge/stavanger/thon-hotel-stavanger; 1,900 kr

In the city center you will find the colorful

Thon Hotel Stavanger, a modern hotel with 148 rooms and recognizable Thon details: lots of colors, bright wallpapers, and pink or lime-green details in the rooms. They serve an evening buffet Monday through Thursday from 6pm to 9pm, which is ideal for those who are too tired to eat out. The hotel also has an exclusive lounge for hotel guests, with newspapers and coffee available all day.

Hotel Victoria
Skansegata 1; tel. 51 86 70 00; www.hotel-victoria.no; 2,400 kr
Hotel Victoria mixes the classic with the contemporary; this 120-year-old hotel has been completely refurbished to provide modern elegance in 107 individually designed rooms. The decor features luxurious green wallpaper and light beige details. Their classic and superior rooms are somewhat small, but deluxe rooms offer extra space.

Greater Stavanger
★ **Sola Strandhotel**
Axel Lunds Veg 27; tel. 51 94 30 00; www.solastrandhotel.no; 2,200 kr
Twenty minutes from Stavanger you will find Sola Strandhotel, located right on the popular Sola beach. This hotel appeals to those who want a weekend getaway, and the hotel is perhaps best known for its relaxing beach views and spa. This property offers 135 bright and welcoming rooms with a white and beige color scheme.

INFORMATION AND SERVICES
The **Stavanger Tourist Information** (Strandkaien 61; www.regionstavanger.no; Mon.-Fri. 9am-4pm) can help you with maps and information relating to the city.

Stamps and **mail services** can be found in most grocery stores, as Norway has moved its post offices into services called "post i butikk" (post in store).

The **emergency room** is Stavanger Legevakt (Armauer Hansens Vei 30; 116117; open 24/7). You must call in advance to notify

them of your arrival, and to ensure they have the capacity to see you. If you are in urgent need of an ambulance, call 113.

GETTING THERE
Train
Reach Stavanger by daily trains from Oslo in 7.5-8.5 hours (500-1000 kr, depending on availability). The earlier you book, the cheaper your ticket, and Vy (www.vy.no) makes tickets available for booking up to 3 months in advance. The train station in Stavanger is located just south of the city park, within walking distance of most centrally located hotels and sights (Jernbaneveien 3).

Bus
Stavanger can be reached by bus from Oslo, Bergen, and Kristiansand. From Oslo, Vy (www.vybuss.no) travels to Stavanger in 8 hours and 20 minutes, with three daily departures. From Kristiansand, Vy has five daily departures traveling to Stavanger in 3 hours and 45 minutes. Those traveling from Bergen will find that there are lots of daily departures available from Nor-way (www.nor-way.no). Their fastest departures are specifically highlighted on their website, and the travel time is just 4.5 hours. The buses stop at the **Stavanger Byterminal** (Jernbaneveien 3), which is the main bus station in the city.

Car
The scenic route from Oslo to Stavanger travels via Kristiansand and around the southern coast of Norway. The route, which follows E18, covers 552 kilometers (343 mi) and will take you 7.5 hours if you drive it all in one go. But make sure to stop along the way to enjoy some of the sights found in Kristiansand and along the coast.

Alternatively, follow E134 and Route 450 inland through the country. This route is 110 kilometers shorter (442 km/274 mi) but actually takes up to 8 hours, because the roads are more narrow and winding. This route will allow you to make a stop at both Heddal Stave Church and Dalen in Telemark along the way.

Air
Stavanger Airport Sola
Flyplassvegen 320; tel. 67 03 10 00; https://avinor.no/en/airport/stavanger-airport

Stavanger Airport Sola is a small international airport with daily flights to all major cities in Norway, run by SAS, Norwegian, and Widerøe. The airport bus (www.flybussen.no; 158 kr) takes you from the airport to the city center in 20-30 minutes, and departs every 20 minutes.

GETTING AROUND

Stavanger has a small city center, and so getting around is best done on foot. The walk from Fargegata to the Old Town will take you about 10 minutes, and so most of the sights in the city can be explored in a day on foot.

Public Transit

The public transportation system in Stavanger consists of city buses and is operated by **Kolumbus** (tel. 51 19 99 00; www.kolumbus. no). The main bus station **Byterminalen** (Jernbaneveien 3) is a location worth noting, as most buses stop here. Download the app Kolumbus Billett to purchase your tickets. A one-way ticket costs 41 kr, and a 24-hour ticket costs 60 kr. The app Kolumbus Sanntid lets you plan your trip and check the schedule for all the bus stops around the city.

Taxi
Stavanger Taxi (tel. 51 90 90 90; www.stavanger-taxi.no) can get you anywhere around the city and region when needed. They have a clever online booking service for those who do not want to make international phone calls. If you want to head out to the Solastranden beach, but don't have a car available, opting for a taxi is your best bet.

Car
It is not necessary to rent a car to explore Stavanger, but you might want to consider one to see the Lysefjord. There are only a couple of car rentals available in the city center, with **Hertz** (Olav Vs Gate 13; tel. 51 53 82 02; www.hertz.no) being the most central. However, there are several more companies in the arrivals hall at the airport, including **Avis** (tel. 97 47 40 00; www.avis.no), **Europcar** (tel. 51 65 10 90; www.europcar.no), and **Sixt** (tel. 94 83 70 07; www.sixt.no).

The Lysefjord

The Lysefjord is a 42-kilometer (26-mi) long fjord, best known for the popular hike to Pulpit Rock, which overlooks the fjord. At its deepest, the fjord is 422 meters deep (1,384 ft). Along the fjord there are several famous hikes in addition to Pulpit Rock, such as Kjerag and the Flørli Stairs. Therefore, this destination outside of Stavanger is a haven for outdoor enthusiasts and those seeking spectacular fjord views.

The start of the fjord is at Oanes and Forsand, 46 kilometers (28 mi) from Stavanger. From there, the fjord stretches northeast all the way to Lysebotn, where it ends. Traveling by boat is the easiest way to get from one destination to another along the fjord, and some spots are not even reachable by car (such as Flørli). Bear in mind that transportation around the Lysefjord is not the easiest, and you will be dependent on ferry departure times to cross the fjord. Therefore, expect to spend at least one night in the Lysefjord area (either on the Pulpit Rock side or the Lysebotn side of the fjord) if you are planning on hiking. The fjord itself can be seen in a day trip from Stavanger.

The stops along the Lysefjord (from start to end) are Lauvvik, Oanes, Forsand, Songesand, Flørli, and Lysebotn. Scheduled car ferries service these stops through the summer. Most of these are not considered destinations themselves, as the sight here is the fjord. Therefore,

Lysefjord Experiences

Most travelers to Stavanger are interested in visiting the Lysefjord. The start of the fjord is located a 45-minute drive from the city, and there are three main ways to see the fjord: by hiking, traveling through the fjord by car ferry from start to end, or by taking a tour directly from Stavanger. There is no road going along the fjord, so it is not possible to see it by car.

HIKING

Along the Lysefjord there are three popular hikes offering spectacular views of the fjord below. These are Pulpit Rock, Kjerag and Kjeragbolten, and the Flørli stairs. Each of these will give you breathtaking views of the fjord landscape (page 132).

CAR FERRY

Seeing the Lysefjord up close is best done by boat, and this requires no physical activity. **Rødne** (www.rodne.no; 450 kr) operates car ferries on the fjord in the summer, traveling from Lauvvik to Lysebotn (Lauvvik/Forsand/Oanes to Lysebotn) and stopping at various places along the way. There is an audio guide on board these boats, providing you with fun facts and information about the fjord and sights along the way. The drive from Stavanger to Lauvvik is around 45 minutes. There are no buses between Stavanger and Lauvvik, so in order to join this fjord cruise you need to travel by car.

TOUR FROM STAVANGER

Additionally, some companies offer private and group boat tours from Stavanger, which is ideal for those visiting the city without a car. The FjordSafari and private boat charter leave from the center of Stavanger, taking you into the fjord and back to the city (page 125).

you will not find restaurants or hotels in this area. Expect simple accommodations aimed at hikers.

HIKING

TOP EXPERIENCE

★ Pulpit Rock

Distance: 8.2 kilometers (5 mi) round-trip
Time: 4-5 hours
Difficulty: Moderate
Trailhead: Preikestolen Basecamp
Information and Services: https://ut.no/turforslag/1111875/preikestolen

Pulpit Rock (Preikestolen) is perhaps one of the most famous attractions in Norway, and can only be reached on foot. This rock plateau is well-known for its (almost completely) flat surface, towering hundreds of meters above the Lysefjord below. The plateau is found at 604 meters (1,980 ft) above

sea level, and the hike to reach it is a little over 4 kilometers (2.5 mi).

This is a very popular hike, and the trail is well marked and clear the entire way to the top. You will pass through both forested and mountainous landscapes, as well as marshlands (where wooden planks have been laid to make it easier to cross). There are also some stone steps to climb, but the hike is not technical. Still, you should have some experience hiking and be dressed properly for a mountain hike. Additionally, it is not ideal for those who are afraid of heights. The final leg of the trail up to the viewpoint is quite "airy," as Norwegians say, with a long drop on one side and no fence or railing. Always tread carefully and take your time.

The hiking season for Pulpit Rock starts in May (as soon as the snow melts) and ends in

1: Pulpit Rock 2: standing atop Kjeragbolten 3: part of the trail to Pulpit Rock

October. The trail is usually very crowded, so if you want to avoid encountering too many other hikers, aim to start your hike early (before 9am) or later in the day (after 4pm).

Hiking Pulpit Rock can take anywhere between 1 and 2.5 hours one way, depending on your pace. It is a great hike, where you gain about 330 meters (1,080 ft) of elevation, and are treated to incredible views of the fjord below as a result.

Kjerag and Kjeragbolten

Distance: *9.3 kilometers (5.7 mi) round-trip*
Time: *5-6 hours*
Difficulty: Strenuous
Trailhead: Øygardstølen
Information and Services: https://ut.no/
turforslag/118458905/topptur-til-kjerag-majesteten-i-lysefjorden

Along the Lysefjord you will find another popular hike that is somewhat more demanding than Preikestolen. Kjerag is the name of the mountain, and Kjeragbolten ("the Kjerag bolt") is a famous round rock wedged within a slit in the mountain. Standing on Kjeragbolten with the fjord far below you is a very popular photo op.

The hike starts at the parking lot by Øygårdstølen and includes climbing 761 meters (2,496 ft). This is a strenuous hike, with great views as a reward. The majority of the hike keeps the fjord below in plain view, and the scenery just gets more spectacular as you climb. The trail is clear and well-marked and was given a major overhaul in 2015-2016.

The Flørli Stairs

Distance: *9.7 kilometers (6 mi) round-trip*
Time: *5-6 hours*
Difficulty: Strenuous
Trailhead: Flørli Ferry Dock
Information and Services: https://ut.no/
turforslag/116552/flrli-og-flrlitrappen

Flørli is a small community only reachable by boat. Here, you can challenge yourself by heading up the world's longest wooden staircase—straight up the mountainside from the fjord. As you climb the 4,444 wooden steps to the top, you will ascend 740 meters (2,427 ft). This is a strenuous hike—a proper workout for anyone wanting to try it—that will reward you with great views of the fjord below.

If you find that this is too much of an undertaking for you, there is a spot where you can take a trail back down to the fjord after around 700 steps. You can also take photos of the stairs from the boat as you pass, as they are a sight in and of themselves. If you plan on doing the hike, make sure to travel on the earliest boat departure to Flørli, to give yourself extra time (usually 9am-10am).

FOOD

There are no restaurants along the fjord. Hikers should opt for a light dinner the night before their hike and bring a lunch or arrange for a packed lunch from their accommodation before they head out.

Matsalen på Fjellstua

Preikestolen Basecamp; tel. 51 74 20 74; daily noon-4pm and 5pm-8pm
The dining hall at Preikestolen Basecamp is open for breakfast (for those staying), lunch, and dinner. The warm cabin-style restaurant is large, and the atmosphere at dinner is lively when all the hikers have made it back to the basecamp. On the menu you can expect Norwegian dishes such as komle (a traditional potato dumpling) and meatballs.

ACCOMMODATIONS

Lysebotn B&B

Fv500; tel. 99 49 95 99; www.visitkjerag.no/overnatting; 1,400 kr
Lysebotn B&B is an overnight option for those traveling on the Lysefjord by boat and needing a place to stay on their drive elsewhere in Norway. Fourteen simple rooms are available for rent, with single beds or bunk beds.

Preikestolen Basecamp

Preikestolvegen 521; tel. 51 74 20 74; https://preikestolenbasecamp.com; 1,600 kr

Preikestolen Basecamp is the ideal place to stay overnight for those planning to hike Pulpit Rock. The trailhead starts from the parking lot at the basecamp, and if you intend on getting an early start to your hike, staying here is a must. Their 28 rooms are simple and a little bare; shared rooms and self-service cabins are also available. This is more of a cabin-like basecamp than a hotel, with friendly staff and a very convenient location.

INFORMATION AND SERVICES

The nearest hospital and emergency room to the Lysefjord is in Stavanger.

Reisemål Ryfylke Tourist Information

Rådhusgaten 7; https://ryfylke.com; Mon.-Fri. 10am-2pm

This information center in Jørpeland is the tourist information closest to Pulpit Rock. There, you can get weather updates and hiking information for Pulpit Rock, as well as ask questions relating to the Lysefjord.

GETTING THERE

The Lysefjord is located a little outside of Stavanger, and reaching it is best done by car, unless you are joining one of the fjord cruises that depart from Stavanger center. By car, take E39 and Route 13 east toward Lauvvik, which is the first stop on the Lysefjorden car ferry (www.rodne.no). The 42-kilometer (26-mi) drive takes around 45 minutes. From Lauvvik, the car ferry takes you all the way to Lysebotn at the end of the fjord several times a day in the summer months. There is no road running along the Lysefjord, and so the best way to see it is by boat (or hiking along it).

To reach Jørpeland and the start of the Pulpit Rock hike from Stavanger, you need to follow Route 13 north, across the new Ryfast tunnel. The 40 kilometers (25 mi) to Preikestolen Basecamp is a 45-minute drive.

Øygardstølen (where the Kjerag and Kjeragbolten hikes start) is a 15-minute drive from Lysebotn, so those taking the ferry through the fjord can drive from there. If you are driving from Stavanger, it is a 2.5-hour drive (139 km/40 mi) to get to Øygardstølen.

Bergen and the Western Fjords

The fjords are, to many travelers, the highlight of Norway, and the reason to visit in the first place. The most dramatic Norwegian fjords are located in western Norway, north of Bergen (with the exception of the Lysefjord, which is just outside of Stavanger, south of Bergen). This region of Norway is the place to take in the unique scenery of the country, from cascading waterfalls and steep mountains to the deep fjords themselves and the villages scattered along them. Whether you are driving or traveling via public transportation, you'll find yourself catching your breath at every turn.

In addition to being "the gateway to the fjords," Bergen is packed with history, dating back to its time as the capital of Norway, from its founding in 1070 to around 1300. Through the centuries, due to

Highlights

Look for ★ to find recommended
sights, activities, dining, and lodging.

★ **Bergenhus Fortress:** One of the oldest
fortress complexes in Norway, it is also home to
the Rosenkrantz Tower and Håkonshallen medieval hall (page 144).

★ **KODE Art Museums:** This group of art
museums in the Bergen city center offers an
impressive collection of Norwegian and international art (page 149).

★ **Steinsdalsfossen Waterfall:** There
are several impressive waterfalls worth seeing
around the Hardangerfjord, but here you can
actually walk behind the fall, which is a truly
unique experience (page 170).

★ **Folgefonna National Park:** Folgefonna
is the third-largest glacier in Norway, and in the
national park you can try your hand at glacier
hiking (page 179).

★ **Voss Gondol:** This gondola takes you
from the center of Voss to the top of Mount
Hangurstoppen, where there are plenty of hiking
options (page 183).

★ **Fjord Sauna:** Jump in the fjord and head
into a warm sauna floating on the water where
you can relax while taking in the scenery (page
192).

★ **Stegastein Viewpoint:** This viewpoint
650 meters (2,133 ft) above sea level offers spectacular views of the Aurlandsfjord below (page
198).

★ **The Nærøyfjord:** The UNESCO-listed
Nærøyfjord is the world's most narrow fjord,
with scenery that will truly take your breath away
(page 203).

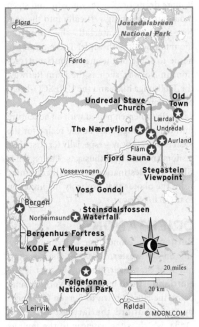

★ **Undredal Stave Church:** The world's
smallest stave church is located in the picturesque village of Undredal, nestled along the
Aurlandsfjord (page 206).

★ **Lærdal Old Town:** Gamle Lærdalsøyri is
the former village center of Lærdal, dating back
to the 1700s. Today it is considered one of the
most important collections of protected buildings in Norway (page 209).

its strategic location on the coast, Bergen was the largest city in Norway, and many say the most important in terms of trade. In the 1800s it was Europe's largest wooden city. Today, Bergen is a lively city that isn't quite as cosmopolitan as Oslo, but is more historic and charming.

Beyond Bergen, the magnificent Hardangerfjord and Sognefjord fjords are simply magnificent, and each has its unique features. In the Hardanger region you will find rounded mountaintops with rolling hills of orchards stretching down to the wide fjord, while the Sognefjord, with its well-known fjord arms Aurlandsfjord and Nærøyfjord, is more dramatic. There, you will find steep mountains dropping vertically into the narrow fjord, with waterfalls sheathing the mountain walls with white. These fjords are home to some of the major tourist attractions in Norway, such as the Flåm Railway, the Trolltunga hike, and the UNESCO-listed Nærøyfjord.

A trip to Bergen paired with an adventure to the fjords might just be the recipe for the ideal trip to Norway—especially for first-time visitors and hiking enthusiasts. The region is filled with destinations you will recognize from the photos that probably inspired you to travel to Norway.

ORIENTATION

Bergen, the second-largest city in Norway, sits on the western coast of the country, north of Stavanger. Just to the east is the **Hardangerfjord** region, with Norheimsund being the closest town to Bergen (1.5 hours by car), Eidfjord the farthest east, and Odda, which is the gateway to the famous **Trolltunga** hike, at the southern end of the fjord.

North of the Hardangerfjord and northeast of Bergen is the inner Sognefjord and its spectacular fjord arms, the **Aurlandsfjord** and the UNESCO-listed **Nærøyfjord.** Flåm,

the transportation hub of the region with its **Flåm Railway,** sits at the southern end of the Aurlandsfjord (3 hours from Bergen by car). The village of **Lærdal,** also on the southern side of the inner Sognefjord, is located northeast of the Aurlandsfjord, while Balestrand and Fjærland, the gateway to the largest glacier in mainland Norway, **Jostedalsbreen,** are located on the northern side of the inner Sognefjord.

Between the Hardangerfjord and the inner Sognefjord is **Voss,** the Extreme Sports Capital of Norway, which is also about midway on the route between Bergen and Flåm.

PLANNING YOUR TIME

You will need at least a week in Bergen and the western fjords region to truly experience what it has to offer. If you have a week, you will be able to explore Bergen itself, and either the Sognefjord or the Hardangerfjord. Spend 2 days in Bergen before heading to the fjord of your choice for the rest of the week. However, if you try to see Bergen and both fjords in just a week you will be much too rushed. A 10- to 14-day trip is recommended to allow plenty of time to explore Bergen and both fjords, and this is especially ideal if you want to spend some time hiking.

How to choose between the Sognefjord and Hardangerfjord? The Sognefjord offers the dramatic, bucket-list scenery of its two arms, the Aurlandsfjord and Nærøyfjord, while the Trolltunga hike, rolling hills, and cider tastings await you in Hardanger, which is closer to Bergen. If you rent a car and head out early (and check in advance for potential roadwork), it is possible to see some of the highlights of Hardanger on a day trip from Bergen. Just allow for extra driving time as the fjord roads are narrow and traffic is heavy.

As for when to travel, all seasons have their charms by the fjords. Of course, the **high season** is in the summer (June-Aug.), with the months of April, May, and September also

BERGEN AND THE WESTERN FJORDS

Bergen and the Western Fjords

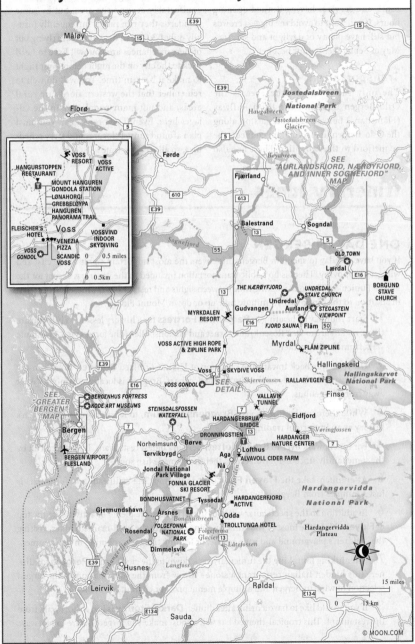

Måløy

Florø

Førde

Jostedalsbreen
National Park

Haugabreen

Jostedalsbreen
Glacier

Bøyabreen

SEE
"AURLANDSFJORD, NÆRØYFJORD,
AND INNER SOGNEFJORD"
MAP

Fjærland

Balestrand

Sogndal

OLD TOWN

Lærdal

BORGUND
STAVE
CHURCH

THE NÆRØYFJORD

UNDREDAL
STAVE CHURCH

Gudvangen

Undredal

Aurland

STEGASTEIN
VIEWPOINT

MYRKDALEN
RESORT

FJORD SAUNA

Flåm

Myrdal

FLÅM ZIPLINE

Hallingskeid

VOSS ACTIVE HIGH ROPE
& ZIPLINE PARK

Voss

SKYDIVE VOSS

Hallingskarvet
National Park

VOSS GONDOL

SEE
DETAIL

Skjervsfossen

RALLARVEGEN

Finse

SEE
GREATER
BERGEN
MAP

BERGENHUS FORTRESS

KODE ART MUSEUMS

VALLAVIK
TUNNEL

STEINSDALSFOSSEN
WATERFALL

HARDANGERBRUA
BRIDGE

Eidfjord

Vøringfossen

Bergen

DRONNINGSTIEN

HARDANGER
NATURE CENTER

BERGEN AIRPORT
FLESLAND

Norheimsund

Børve

Lofthus

Tørvikbygd

Aga

ALVAVOLL CIDER FARM

Nå

Jondal National
Park Village

FONNA GLACIER
SKI RESORT

Hardangervidda
National Park

BONDHUSVATNET

Tyssedal

HARDANGERFJORD
ACTIVE

Gjermundshavn

Årsnes

Bondhusbreen

Odda

Rosendal

FOLGEFONNA
NATIONAL
PARK

Folgefonna
Glacier

TROLLTUNGA HOTEL

Hardangervidda
Plateau

Dimmelsvik

Låtefossen

Husnes

Langfoss

Leirvik

Røldal

Sauda

© MOON.COM

VOSS DETAIL MAP:

VOSS
RESORT

VOSS
ACTIVE

HANGURSTOPPEN
RESTAURANT

MOUNT HANGUREN
GONDOLA STATION

LØNAHORGI
GREBBELØYPA
HANGUREN
PANORAMA TRAIL

FLEISCHER'S
HOTEL

VOSS

VENEZIA
PIZZA

VOSSVIND
INDOOR
SKYDIVING

VOSS
GONDOL

SCANDIC
VOSS

0   0.5 miles

0   0.5km

Sognefjord

Hardangerfjord

Sørfjorden

becoming increasingly busy. The **low season** (Oct.-Mar.) is quiet, with many hotels, restaurants, and services having limited opening hours. If you want to avoid the biggest crowds but still have plenty of daylight and services, May or September is your best bet.

Transportation

The only rail route in the area is the Oslo-Bergen line, and the Flåm Railway (Flåmsbana) between Myrdal (a stop along the Oslo-Bergen line) and Flåm connects the Sognefjord to the two cities. There are also bus services connecting Bergen to most destinations. These regional buses let you travel comfortably around the area, but by some standards they run rather infrequently (usually only 1-3 times a day). If you are flying out of Bergen, chances are you will have to head back to the city on the night before your flight to make it back in time. You will do well to remember that the western fjords are rural areas, and not many people live in the villages here. Even if you rent a car, you must plan around tunnel closures and ferry schedules, so allow extra time.

Itinerary Ideas

ONE DAY IN BERGEN

If you have one day to spend in Bergen, this covers the most important sights of the city, and will get you moving. There is no public transportation included in the itinerary, except for the Fløyen Funicular. The total walking time between sights and restaurants is around 30 minutes, in addition to the (optional) 45-minute hike up or down Mount Fløyen.

1 Start your day by heading to **Bergenhus Fortress** for a history lesson. While you are there, make sure to visit Rosenkrantztårnet and Håkonshallen. The fortress is a 15-minute walk from the city center.

2 On your way back toward the city, stop at UNESCO-listed **Bryggen** to take in the beautiful wooden houses on the city's historic wharf. Bryggen is located a 5-minute walk away from Bergenhus.

3 While there, make sure to visit **Bryggens Museum,** to learn more about Bergen's history as an important trading port.

4 For lunch, walk over to **Bryggeloftet,** Bergen's oldest restaurant. It has been run by the same family since 1910. Don't miss their homemade fish soup.

5 After lunch, take the **Fløyen Funicular** to the top. The trailhead (and funicular) is just 3 minutes from Bryggeloftet.

6 In addition to the spectacular views of the city, there are plenty of activities at the top of **Fløyen.** Make the most of your time by going on one of the (well-marked) hikes, visiting the children's playground and rope course, or feeding the goats roaming in the summer.

7 After hiking (or taking the funicular) back down to the city, head to **Pergola** for dinner. This hidden Italian restaurant a stone's throw from the funicular offers the largest selection of wine in Bergen and a simple menu: pizza or charcuterie boards.

8 If you would like to have a drink after dinner, **Dark & Stormy** is just a short walk from the restaurant. This tropical-themed bar will almost make you forget you are in Norway.

Itinerary Ideas

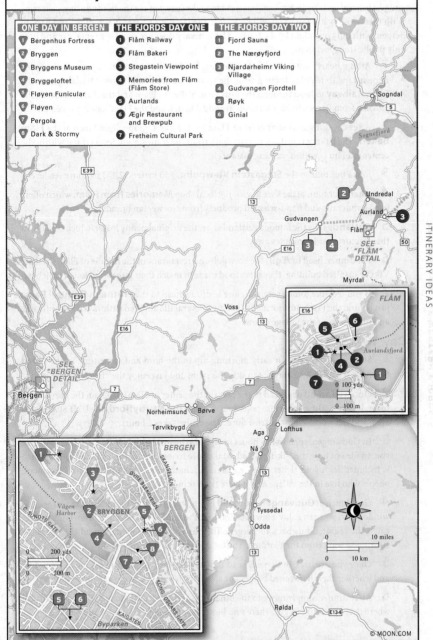

ONE DAY IN BERGEN
1. Bergenhus Fortress
2. Bryggen
3. Bryggens Museum
4. Bryggeloftet
5. Fløyen Funicular
6. Fløyen
7. Pergola
8. Dark & Stormy

THE FJORDS DAY ONE
1. Flåm Railway
2. Flåm Bakeri
3. Stegastein Viewpoint
4. Memories from Flåm (Flåm Store)
5. Aurlands
6. Ægir Restaurant and Brewpub
7. Fretheim Cultural Park

THE FJORDS DAY TWO
1. Fjord Sauna
2. The Nærøyfjord
3. Njardarheimr Viking Village
4. Gudvangen Fjordtell
5. Røyk
6. Ginial

© MOON.COM

THE FJORDS IN TWO DAYS
Day One

Are you limited on time in Norway, but want to make sure you see the fjords during your trip? With this two-day itinerary you will make it to the UNESCO-listed Nærøyfjord and back to Bergen, with only one night by the fjords. The itinerary does not require a rental car and uses only public transportation.

1 After a hearty hotel breakfast in Bergen, head to the train station to catch the Oslo-Bergen Line to Myrdal, leaving with the train at around 8am. From Myrdal, get on the **Flåm Railway** to head through the lush Flåm Valley to Flåm and the Aurlandsfjord. The journey from Bergen to Myrdal takes around 2 hours, and the Flåm Railway takes 1 hour.

2 After checking into your hotel in Flåm for the night, grab a light lunch at the **Flåm Bakeri.** The bakery is just a 2-minute walk from the train station (everything within the center of Flåm is within walking distance).

3 Join a bus tour to the **Stegastein Viewpoint,** 650 meters (2,133 ft) above sea level.

4 After your tour, make sure to visit the local shop **Memories from Flåm,** which offers local handcrafts and hand-selected products from Norwegian brands.

5 **Aurlands** sells the famous Aurland shoe, the original penny loafer, which is made in their factory just 10 minutes away.

6 For dinner, head to **Ægir,** the brewpub and restaurant in the middle of Flåm. In their Viking-inspired building, they serve food made to match their large selection of craft beer.

7 If you feel like some exercise before bedtime, head to the **Fretheim Cultural Park,** just behind the Fretheim Hotel. You will find several illuminated pathways on the hillside, and nice views of the village below.

Day Two

1 Start your day with an early morning dip in the fjord and some time in the **Fjord Sauna.** Of course, you may opt to skip the swim and just enjoy the view from the sauna.

2 Once you are all dry, head to the pier (in the center of Flåm) to get on the fjord cruise to Gudvangen. The fjord cruise takes you through **the Nærøyfjord,** the UNESCO-listed area, and the world's most narrow fjord. The cruise takes 2 hours.

3 In Gudvangen, spend a few hours in **Njardarheimr Viking Village,** which will give you an idea of how the Vikings lived. Make sure to join one of their guided tours, which is included with your ticket. Then you can purchase handcrafts made by the "freemen": people who live in the village as if it were the Viking Age.

4 Grab lunch at **Gudvangen Fjordtell** in Gudvangen. This spacious hall has large glass windows, so you can enjoy a few final looks at the fjord before leaving. From Gudvangen, catch the regional bus back to Bergen. The bus stop is by the main road (E16), a 5- to 10-minute walk from the Fjordtell. The total journey takes 2.5 hours.

5 Once you are back in Bergen, head to **Røyk** for dinner. Their name means "smoke," and whether their barbecued burgers or spareribs tempt you, you won't leave hungry.

6 After dinner, simply move to the other side of the entrance door to their bar, **Ginial,** where they specialize in gin. There's no better place for a gin and tonic in Bergen.

Bergen

Bergen is the second-largest city in Norway, and a popular base and starting point for anyone wanting to explore the fjords. However, the city is also a destination in and of itself. Offering epic hikes within easy reach, a well-established cultural scene, and a growing number of great restaurants and nightlife options, Bergen perfectly complements a visit to the fjords.

Orientation

The city center of Bergen is small and walkable. **Vågen harbor** is the body of water separating **Nordnes** to the south and **Bryggen** to the north, and walking around the harbor will take no more than 5-10 minutes (with no stops). Most of Bergen's sights, restaurants, and bars can be found in this area, with the majority of them being on the Nordnes side. This is considered the **city center** by locals, but as Bryggen is such a main attraction, many tourists use the Bryggen side of the water as their base. In addition to Vågen, there are two other landmarks just a stone's throw away from each other on the south side of the harbor: the small lake **Lille Lungegårdsvann,** and the great open plaza **Torgalmenningen.** Torgalmenningen is considered by locals to be the actual core of the city, and it is usually what they refer to when they say "the city center."

SIGHTS
★ Bergenhus Fortress

Tel. 55 54 63 87; www.forsvarsbygg.no/no/festningene/finn-din-festning/bergenhus-festning; Mon.-Sun. 6am-11pm; free

Bergenhus Fortress is one of the best preserved fortresses in Norway, and one of the oldest. It has a long history as the seat of kings and bishops, as well as being of military importance. Inside the fortress area, you will find **Håkonshallen** and **Rosenkrantztårnet**—both sights in their own right. The building of

Bergenhus started in the early 1500s, around the already existing Håkonshallen (built in the 1200s). The fortress is still an active military site today and has been continuously since 1628.

The fortress area consists of the walled cobblestone streets and squares around Håkonshallen and Rosenkrantztårnet, several large grass lawns (used for concerts and events), and a cluster of white stone buildings used by the military. Additionally, you will find **Sverresborg,** a formerly separate fortress complex, just up the hill behind it. Sverresborg was built by King Sverre sometime after 1184 and before his death in 1202. Today, Sverresborg is considered part of the Bergenhus Fortress complex, and is a park with views overlooking the grass lawn **Koengen,** the city, and the harbor.

The fortress area is open for visitors all day. Entrance is free, though when events such as the annual **Bergenfest Festival** and **Bergen Food Festival** are being held, parts of the fortress grounds are closed for non-ticket holders. The fortress is located just a 5-minute walk from Bryggen.

Håkonshallen

Tel. 55 30 80 30; https://bymuseet.no; daily 10am-4pm June-Aug., daily 11am-2pm Sept.-May; adults 120 kr, children under 17 free

A visit to the hall gives you a glimpse into the history of the building where kings dined over 700 years ago. Built between 1247 and 1261, Håkonshallen ("the hall of Håkon") was the residence and banquet hall of King Håkon Håkonsson. At the time, Bergen was the most important city in Norway, and so several important events have happened within these four walls. For example, there was the creation of Norway's first set of (common) laws, and

---

Previous: 1: Bergen's UNESCO-listed Bryggen **2:** Stegastein Viewpoint **3:** the Fjord Sauna

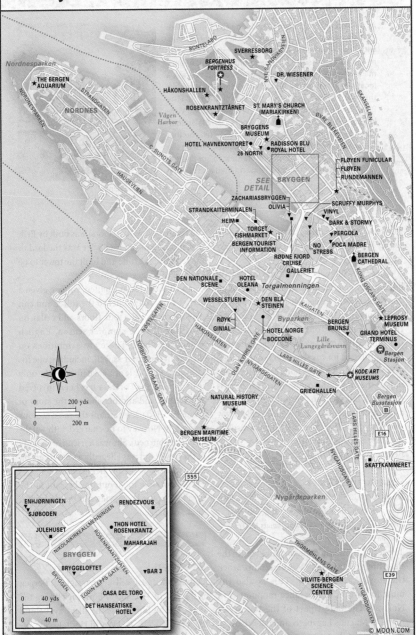

Bergen

Nordnesparken

THE BERGEN AQUARIUM ★

NORDNES

Vågen Harbor

SVERRESBORG

BERGENHUS FORTRESS

DR. WIESENER

HÅKONSHALLEN ★

ROSENKRANTZTÅRNET ★

ST. MARY'S CHURCH (MARIAKIRKEN)

BRYGGENS MUSEUM

HOTEL HAVNEKONTORET ●

26 NORTH

RADISSON BLU ● ROYAL HOTEL

FLØYEN FUNICULAR

FLØYEN

RUNDEMANNEN

SEE DETAIL

BRYGGEN

ZACHARIASBRYGGEN

STRANDKAITERMINALEN

OLIVIA

SCRUFFY MURPHYS

VINYL

HEIM

DARK & STORMY

TORGET FISHMARKET

BERGEN TOURIST INFORMATION

PERGOLA

NO STRESS

POCA MADRE

RØDNE FJORD CRUISE

BERGEN CATHEDRAL

GALLERIET

DEN NATIONALE SCENE

HOTEL OLEANA

Torgalmenningen

WESSELSTUEN ▼

DEN BLÅ STEINEN

KAIGATEN

Byparken

RØYK

GINIAL

HOTEL NORGE

BOCCONE

Lille Lungegårdsvann

BERGEN BRUNSJ

LEPROSY MUSEUM

GRAND HOTEL TERMINUS

Bergen Stasjon

LARS HILLES GATE

KODE ART MUSEUMS

GRIEGHALLEN

Bergen Busstasjon

NATURAL HISTORY MUSEUM

BERGEN MARITIME MUSEUM

E16

SKATTKAMMERET

Nygårdsparken

VILVITE-BERGEN SCIENCE CENTER

E39

0   200 yds

0   200 m

© MOON.COM

555

ENHJØRNINGEN

SJØBODEN

RENDEZVOUS

JULEHUSET

THON HOTEL ROSENKRANTZ

MAHARAJAH

BRYGGEN

BRYGGELOFTET

BAR 3

CASA DEL TORO

DET HANSEATISKE HOTEL

0   40 yds

0   40 m

Den Blå Steinen

At the end of Torgalmenningen in the city center there is a large, flat, blue stone sculpture. It lies on the ground, with one part lifted at an angle. It was gifted to the city in 1993 and has since become a unique Bergen landmark when it comes to giving directions. If you ask a local where something is in the city center, chances are they will explain it in reference to "Den Blå Steinen" (The Blue Stone). This has even become a joke among visiting comedians. So take note of where Den Blå Steinen is, because you are likely to hear someone tell you that the restaurant you are looking for is located "just up the street and to the right from Den Blå Steinen," or that the KODE museum is "straight ahead and then a left at Den Blå Steinen."

Den Blå Steinen

the wedding of Magnus Håkonsson Lagabøte (King Håkon's son) to the Danish Princess Ingeborg in 1261.

There is no signage or exhibits in the hall, but you are given an informative leaflet with your ticket. Read the leaflet as you go through the rooms in Håkonshallen. There are three floors to explore. Tours in English are held daily in the summer season as well. Today the hall is still used for royal banquets and official events, so there is a large banquet table on the dais at the end of the room. This furniture is roped off, but you can get quite close to have a look at where the king and queen of Norway would sit during such events. You can also see the impressive wall textiles woven by Sigrun Berg and Synnøve Anker Aurdal.

Rosenkrantztårnet

Tel. 55 30 80 30; https://bymuseet.no; daily 10am-4pm June-Aug., daily 10am-2pm Sept. and May, Tues. 4pm-7pm, Sat.-Sun. 10am-2pm Oct.-Apr.; adults 120 kr; children under 17 free

The second building of importance within the Bergenhus Fortress walls is Rosenkrantztårnet, the Rosenkrantz Tower. This is also the most important Renaissance monument in Norway. The oldest part of the tower was home to Magnus Lagabøte, and dates back to the 1270s, but the tower we see today (with its square shape and five floors) was built by Erik Rosenkrantz in the 1560s. He was the lord of the region at the time and built the tower to be his own residence.

As with the Håkonshallen, you are given a leaflet with your ticket to the tower and can explore each of the four floors and cellar on your own. In the summer season, English tours are offered. There are exhibitions on display in the tower as well, including one focusing on the Battle of Vågen in 1665 (the only time Bergenhus Fortress has been involved in a battle), and another sharing the story of Anne Pedersdatter, perhaps the most famous woman in Norway to be charged with witchcraft (and burned). She was a friend of the lady of the tower and was allegedly a guest there on many occasions (before her accusal).

It is possible to go out on the roof of the tower for some lovely views of the water and docks of Bergen.

TOP EXPERIENCE

Bryggen

Perhaps the most well-known sight of Bergen is the row of 17 colorful buildings lining the dock. The buildings, and the alleyways behind them, are a UNESCO World Heritage Site, offering visitors a glimpse into the history of

Bergen. The facade is a great photo op, and in the summer the (usually indoor) bars fill the square in front of Bryggen with tables and chairs, so you can enjoy a beer in the sun.

Once you head into the (surprisingly) wooden alleyways of Bryggen, you will find shops, cafés, and a museum. Bryggen can be very crowded in the summer months, especially on days when cruise ships are docked (which is most days from June to August).

The historical significance of Bryggen is simple: This is where the first settlements of Bergen were located, and where the city's importance as a trade port grew. The bay of Vågen is pretty sheltered from the worst of the North Sea weather, and so the area became a natural meeting point for traders and sailors from northern Norway (usually carrying fish, but also cod liver oil and grain) and the rest of Europe.

Bryggens Museum

Dreggsallmenningen 3; tel. 55 30 80 30; https:// bymuseet.no; daily 11am-5pm May-Aug., Mon.-Fri. 10am-3pm, Sat.-Sun. 10am-4pm Sept.-Oct. and Apr.-May, daily 11am-3pm Nov.-Mar.; adults 160 kr, children under 17 free

The modern Bryggens Museum, located a short walk from the Bryggen buildings, takes you through the history of Bryggen (and the region) by showcasing archaeological finds through the ages. Bergen has been a thriving city for almost 1,000 years, and archaeologists have uncovered thousands of treasures from the past centuries. The museum itself is built over what remains of the oldest house in Bergen, dating back to the 1100s. You can see these remnants through a glass floor, which is one of the highlights of the museum. They also showcase findings of Middle Eastern and southern European artifacts, which further illustrates how vast Bergen's trade really was.

St. Mary's Church (Mariakirken)

Dreggsallmenningen 15; Tues. and Fri. noon-2pm Oct.-Apr., Mon.-Fri. 10am-4pm May-Sept., service Sun. 11am and 6pm

Behind Bryggen you will find Mariakirken, Bergen's oldest parish church. Mariakirken is the best kept building in the city. Built between 1130 and 1170, it has been in continuous use since the late Middle Ages. The large church is gray, with two tall white towers on each side of its front entrance. The church is a typical medieval basilica, which means that it has one tall, long hall, with two smaller rooms built on each side. The pulpit is quite unique, as it is the only one in Norway that contains turtle skin, which can imply some exotic origin. It was gifted to the parish in 1676 by a group of wealthy German traders.

Fløyen Funicular (Fløibanen)

Vetrlidsallmenningen 23A; tel. 55 33 68 00; www. floyen.no; Mon.-Fri. 7:30am-11pm, Sat.-Sun. 9am-11pm; return ticket adults 150 kr, children 75 kr

The funicular that takes you up Mount Fløyen is not to be missed when in Bergen. Mount Fløyen is located right in the city center, and locals and visitors alike enjoy making their way to the top to enjoy the view. The funicular opened in 1918 and takes you right up to the mountaintop 320 meters (1,000 ft) above sea level. It leaves every 15 minutes from both the bottom and the top station, and the total one-way travel time is 5-8 minutes. At the top you will find a restaurant, café, ice cream kiosk (summer), playground for children, rope course, and several easy hiking trails to enjoy.

Central Bergen
The Bergen Aquarium

Nordnesbakken 4; tel. 55 55 71 71; www.akvariet.no; daily 10am-6pm; adults 315 kr, children 200 kr

The Bergen Aquarium is located at the tip of Nordnes, just a 15-minute walk from Den Blå Steinen. It is popular among locals, especially on a rainy day. Here, you can see a large selection of aquatic life from all over the world, including octopi, small sharks, and tropical fish like the clown fish and dory. They also have otters, sea lions, and crocodiles. One of the highlights is seeing the penguins, and there's

Every day there are set times for feedings and "shows," where you can watch the aquarium staff feed the animals and teach you more about them. Check the daily schedule for feeding times during your visit.

Torget Fishmarket (Fisketorget)

Torget; Sun.-Thurs. 9am-9pm, Fri.-Sat. 9am-10pm (outdoors May-Sept.)

As with many other coastal towns, Bergen has its own fish market. Right in the middle of Vågen harbor, across the bay from Bryggen, you will find Fisketorget. In addition to seafood, fruit and vegetables are for sale at this charming outdoor market. Locals, traders, and fishermen have been meeting here since the city's origin, and in recent years an indoor market has popped up as well. Mathallen is located in the same building as the Bergen Tourist Information office, just a stone's throw from the original Fisketorget. The market is open year-round, while the outdoor market usually starts around May 1 each year, lasting until late August or early September.

Bergen Cathedral

Domkirkeplassen 1; tel. 55 59 71 75; Fri. noon-2pm, services Sun. 11am and Tues. 9am

The Bergen Cathedral (Domkirken) is a large, white stone church with a big tower at the front. Find it just a few minutes' walk northwest from the train station. The oldest parts of the church date back to around 1150, but it has been severely damaged in several fires through the centuries and then rebuilt in a slightly different form and style. During the Battle of Vågen in 1665, it was hit by a cannonball, which was left in the wall of the church tower. It is quite an interesting sight on the otherwise "clean" facade of the cathedral. You

can see it to the left of the large window on the front wall of the cathedral tower.

Leprosy Museum

Kong Oscarsgate 59; tel. 55 30 80 30; https:// bymuseet.no; Mon.-Thurs. 2pm-6pm, Fri.-Sun. 11am-3pm late May-mid-June, daily 11am-5pm mid-June-mid-Aug., Mon.-Thurs. 2pm-6pm, Fri.-Sun. 11am-3pm mid-Aug.- early Sept., closed rest of the year; adults 120 kr, children under 18 free

A lot of people are surprised to learn about Bergen's significance in the medical field related to leprosy. Between 1850 and 1900, Bergen had three leprosy hospitals and the largest concentration of people living with leprosy in Europe. In addition, the leprosy germ was isolated in Bergen, by Gerhard Armauer Hansen in 1873. This was considered a medical breakthrough.

St. Jørgen's Hospital, where the Leprosy Museum is housed, was in use from the 1400s until the last leprosy patients in Bergen died in 1946. Today, a visit to the museum gives you a glimpse into what it was like to live in the hospital, and what part Bergen has played in leprosy research and treatment. The museum consists of nine protected buildings, and is one of the best preserved leprosy hospitals in Europe.

★ KODE Art Museums (KODE Kunstmuseer)

Rasmus Meyers Allé 9; tel. 55 00 97 00; https:// kodebergen.no; daily Tues.-Sun. 11am-5pm, Thurs. until 8pm; adults 150 kr, children under 18 free

"Kode" is the name of Bergen's art museums, which are housed in the four buildings lining the long side of Lille Lungegårdsvann lake. Each of the buildings, called KODE 1, 2, 3, and 4, houses different exhibitions and has a different focus. While most of the exhibitions in the four buildings change 1-2 times a year, there is a permanent exhibit in KODE 3 worth seeing; there, you will find the world's third-largest collection of Edvard Munch pieces. Although *The Scream* and *Madonna* are in Oslo, you might recognize a few of the paintings here, such as *Evening on Karl*

1: Rosenkrantz Tower at Bergenhus Fortress
2: Bryggen 3: a street in Bergen's city center
4: KODE 1

Johan and *Melancholy*. Other permanent exhibitions (also in KODE 3) include paintings from the Norwegian "Golden Age of Art" (the late 1800s, when most of Norway's most famous art pieces were made) by artists such as Nikolai Astrup and Hans Gude.

Among the rotating and temporary exhibitions of KODE 1, 2, and 4 you will find a variety of Norwegian and international art. In the past, they have shown works by renowned international artists such as Paul McCarthy and Paul Cézanne, in addition to portraits by local artist Arvid Pettersen. You will usually find a mix of names you recognize and ones that are new to you.

The ticket to KODE gives you access to all four buildings, so prepare to spend some time. Start at one end (with KODE 3 and 4 or 1 and 2), and grab some lunch or a light bite before tackling the other two.

Natural History Museum

Muséplassen 3; tel. 55 58 88 00; www. universitetsmuseet.no/nb; Tues.-Sat. 10am-4pm, Sun. 11am-5pm; adults 150 kr, children under 18 free

The University of Bergen's Natural History Museum consists of several interesting collections covering botany, zoology, and geology. One of their permanent exhibits focuses on the depths of the ocean, what is yet to be explored in the deep sea, and what we have managed to explore so far. One of the highlights here, and perhaps the best-known part of the museum, is Hvalsalen ("the whale hall"), where the skeletons of massive whales hang from the ceiling. The museum has a café, Christie, where you can enjoy a coffee and some baked goods from Norwegian bakery Godt Brød overlooking the museum gardens.

Bergen Maritime Museum

Haakon Sheteligs plass 15; tel. 55 54 96 00; https:// sjofartsmuseum.museumvest.no; Mon.-Fri. 10am-4pm, Sat.-Sun. 11am-4pm; adults 120 kr, children under 18 free

At the Bergen Maritime Museum, you will be presented with the history of Norwegian seafaring through the centuries. Varied displays of items showcase archaeological findings, and full-scale as well as smaller boat models to illustrate the importance of the ocean to Norwegians. Their collections include models of ships dating all the way back to year 200 BC. Among the museum highlights is the 22-minute film *The Burnt Ship*, about the discovery of a burial ship from the Viking Age. The movie is in Norwegian, with English subtitles.

VilVite - Bergen Science Center

Thormøhlens Gate 51; tel. 55 59 45 00; www.vilvite.no; Tues.-Fri. 9am-3pm, Sat.-Sun. 10am-5pm; adults 190 kr, children under 15 165 kr

VilVite is fun for adults, but perhaps best enjoyed as a family. If you and your children are interested in science and technology, spending half a day at VilVite is right up your alley. The science center is packed with activities made to encourage learning, and you can explore several phenomena you might not have previously understood. Here, you can stand in a house during a hurricane, and learn how underwater earthquakes create waves. The main attraction is the 360-degree bicycle, where you can try your hand at cycling around a wheel and feel the effects of gravity. There is a daily science show that is very popular with the younger crowd, so make sure to check the schedule during your visit if you are there with children.

Greater Bergen
Gamle Bergen Museum

Nyhavnsveien 4; tel. 55 30 80 30; https://bymuseet.no; daily 11am-4pm June-Aug., 11am-3pm Sept. and May; adults 140 kr, children under 17 free

If you truly want to immerse yourself in the history of Bergen and get a feel for what life was like here during 18th, 19th, and early 20th century, a visit to Gamle Bergen ("Old Bergen") is a must. Here, you can relive history alongside actors and hosts from the museum, and walk cobbled streets lined with historic buildings. The outdoor museum consists of 55 wooden buildings, most of which were moved there from the city center. The

Greater Bergen

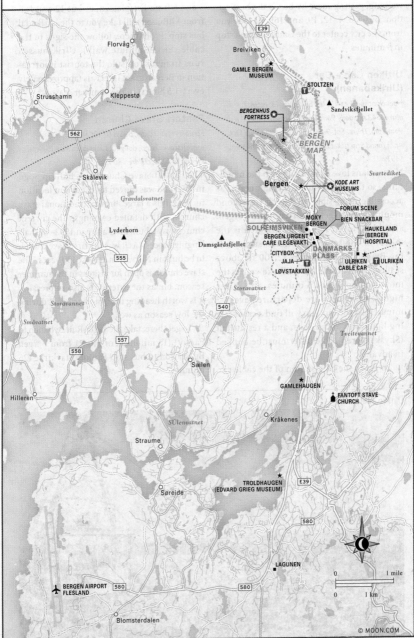

Florvåg

Breiviken

E39

GAMLE BERGEN MUSEUM

STOLTZEN

Strusshamn

Kleppestø

Sandviksfjellet

562

BERGENHUS FORTRESS

SEE "BERGEN" MAP

Skålevik

Gravdalsvatnet

Svartediket

Bergen

KODE ART MUSEUMS

Lyderhorn

SOLHEIMSVIKEN

FORUM SCENE

MOXY BERGEN

BIEN SNACKBAR

HAUKELAND (BERGEN HOSPITAL)

Damsgårdsfjellet

BERGEN URGENT CARE (LEGEVAKT)

555

CITYBOX

JAJA

LØVSTAKKEN

DANMARKS PLASS

ULRIKEN CABLE CAR

ULRIKEN

Storavatnet

Storavannet

540

Småvatnet

Tveitevannet

558

557

Sælen

Hilleren

SUlenvatnet

GAMLEHAUGEN

FANTOFT STAVE CHURCH

Straume

Kråkenes

Søreide

TROLDHAUGEN (EDVARD GRIEG MUSEUM)

E39

580

LAGUNEN

BERGEN AIRPORT FLESLAND

580

580

0   1 mile

0   1 km

Blomsterdalen

© MOON.COM

museum is located a 40-minute walk from Bryggen and the harbor. If you don't feel like walking, getting there by bus is the best option. Buses 3, 4, 12, 19, and 16E all take you from the city center to the Gamle Bergen stop in 8 minutes.

Ulriken Cable Car (Ulriksbanen)

Haukelandsbakken 40; tel. 53 64 36 43; https:// ulriken643.no; daily 9am-11pm May-Sept., Tues.-Wed. 9am-7pm, Thurs.-Sat. 9am-11pm, Sun. 9am-7pm Oct.- Apr.; round-trip ticket adults 345 kr adults, children 145 kr

Norwegians love heading up into the mountains, so they try to make the mountains as accessible as possible. Ulriken is the second mountaintop to get a shortcut from Bergen, after the Fløyen Funicular. Ulriken is the tallest of the seven mountains surrounding Bergen, at 643 meters (2,100 ft) above sea level. This cable car will take you to the mountaintop in just 5 minutes, and in the high season there are departures every 7 minutes. At the top, you will find a café serving light bites and snacks, and a restaurant (Skyskraperen). The latter must be booked in advance.

To get to the base station of the cable car, you can either travel by public transportation, or take Ulriksbussen (100 kr return). Buses 5 and 6 from Festplassen, or bus 12 and 16E from Xhibition will take you to the Ulriksdal bus stop. From there, follow the signs to the cable car (10-minute walk). Ulriksbussen runs from just outside the tourist information in Bergen at set intervals (approximately every 1.5 hours) in the summer season.

Fantoft Stave Church

Fantoftvegen 38; tel. 55 28 07 10; https:// fantoftstavkirke.no; daily 10:30am-6pm May 15-Sept. 15; adults 70 kr, children 30 kr

The Fantoft Stave Church was built in Sogn in 1170 and was moved to its current location in 1883. It is a large, brown, traditional stave church, with detailed carvings. The current church was rebuilt after a fire in 1992—a challenging process, as it was the first stave church to be built in Norway in almost 400 years. The stave church is open for visitors in the summer season, but as the exterior is also impressive, it is worth heading to Fantoft to see it during the low season as well.

To get there, take the Light Rail Bybanen to Fantoft (18 minutes), or bus 21 from Bergen Busstasjon to bus stop Fantoft Stavkirke (25 minutes).

Ulriken cable car

Gamlehaugen

Gamlehaugvegen 10; tel. 91 91 22 91; www.kongehuset.
no/artikkel.html?tid=27638; daily tours Mon.-Fri. in
summer

Gamlehaugen is the official residence of the Norwegian royal family in Bergen. The large white building with its round tower makes it the most "castle-like" royal residence in Norway. It was designed in 1899 for the prime minister at the time, Christian Michelsen. Surrounding the castle is a large park with a lot of greenery. The park and beach just below it are open for visitors year-round, so even if you aren't able to join a tour, you can enjoy the area. Tours take approximately one hour.

To get there, take a bus from the city center (bus stop Bergen Busstasjon) and get off at Fjøsangerkrysset; the ride will take about 9 minutes. From there, Gamlehaugen is just a 5-10-minute walk. Several buses operate on this route, including 67, 25, 51, and 600.

Troldhaugen (Edvard Grieg Museum)

Troldhaugvegen 65; tel. 55 92 29 92; https://
griegmuseum.no; daily 10am-5pm June-Sept., Tues.-Fri.
11am-4pm, Sat.-Sun. 11am-5pm Oct.-May; adults 90 kr,
children free

Best known for musical pieces such as *In The Hall of the Mountain King* and *Morning Mood,* Edvard Grieg was a pianist and composer from Bergen. He lived from 1843 to 1907, and for 22 years lived in a house he named Troldhaugen ("the troll hill"). Today, Troldhaugen is a museum dedicated to Grieg and his life, and the interior in the living room is just how Grieg left it in 1907. Edvard and his wife Nina are both buried in a cliff by the lake on the property.

Tuesday to Sunday in summer, there are daily lunch concerts at Troldhaugen at 1pm, and the ticket includes a half-hour piano concert, providing an introduction to Grieg's music, as well as entrance to the museum and villa. The ticket price is 200 kr per adult, which is great value.

To get to Troldhaugen, take the Light Rail ByBanen to Hop (22 minutes from ByParken). From there, take a right toward the road crossing, heading north, and follow Troldhaugsveien to the left. From there, the way is signposted (25-minute walk). Alternatively, take bus 53 and 57 from Bergen Busstasjon to Hop Sjølinjen (14 minutes) and walk 20 minutes following the signs.

SPORTS AND RECREATION

Bergen provides easy access to nature, with several hikes and mountaintops being accessible from anywhere in the city center. Additionally, there are several parks, giving the city a small-town charm you might not expect. As the self-proclaimed "gateway to the fjords," Bergen also offers tour options that take you out of the city and into the fjords without the need of a rental car.

Parks

In the center of Bergen you'll find three parks worth visiting: Nygårdsparken, Byparken, and Nordnesparken. All three are popular with locals and are quite busy on warm summer days. They are open 24/7.

Nygårdsparken

Parkveien 28; www.facebook.com/Nygardsparken

Bordering the University of Bergen and the Natural History Museum, Nygårdsparken starts at the top of the hill and follows the hill down to a small lake at the edge of the park. The downhill slope of the park makes it a great place for events, and from time to time the park offers free concerts by the Bergen Philharmonic and others. Check the park Facebook page to see if any events will happen during your visit. At the top of the hill is a children's playground and a café, open 11am-4pm on weekends year-round, and 11am-4pm on weekdays in the high season.

Byparken

Christies Gate 3A

Byparken is the name of the park at the end of the city lake Lille Lungegårdsvann. This park is small but lovely with beautiful

The Seven Mountains of Bergen

In addition to being called "the gateway to the fjords," Bergen has another nickname that is perhaps more familiar to Norwegians than to tourists. It is called "byen mellom de syv fjell," which translates to "the city between the seven mountains."

The seven mountains surrounding Bergen are Sandviksfjellet, Fløyfjellet (Fløyen), Rundemanen, Ulriken, Løvstakken, Damsgårdsfjellet, and Lyderhorn. All of these are great places to hike, and most of them are accessible without needing to have a car or to travel far on public transportation. Fløyen is perhaps the one that the most tourists know about, as it is very close to Bryggen.

Ulriken, Stoltzen (the most popular hike up Sandviksfjellet), and Løvstakken can also be reached by walking from the city center. Alternatively, if you prefer to start your hike at one of the trailheads, they are easily reached via public transportation.

Rundemanen is a little farther behind Fløyen, so this peak can also be reached by hiking up to Fløyen (or taking the funicular) and then following the signs. This is a great way to make the Fløyen hike a little longer, as the trip to Rundemanen will add about 45 minutes to your hike (one way).

flower beds and symmetrical pathways. The flowers are especially nice in the springtime, and garden lovers will enjoy a (short) walk through the park. The main attraction of the park is the gazebo, Musikkpaviljongen ("the music pavilion"). It was gifted to the city of Bergen in 1888 by businessman F. G. Gade (1830-1904). Today, it is used for small concerts, weddings, and photography; there is usually a line of people waiting to take their photos in the beautiful pavilion. There is a small sign at the entrance to the pavilion indicating whether any concerts are planned.

Nordnesparken

Nordnesparken 1

Nordnesparken is located at the tip of Nordnes, the body of land shaped like a fingertip, with Vågen harbor and the Puddefjord on each side. The result is a beautiful, half-moon-shaped park, with great views looking out to the ocean and the islands of Askøy and Sotra. If you have an hour to spend, a walk from the city center (Torgallmenningen or Den Blå Steinen), around the tip of Nordnes and back, will take you around 1 hour. The park is right next to the Bergen Aquarium, so you could pair a stroll in the park with a visit there.

Hiking

Ulriken

Distance: *1.8 kilometers (1.1 mi, Sherpa steps route),*
3.3 kilometers (2 mi, alternative route)
Time: *2-3 hours round-trip*
Difficulty: Strenuous
Trailhead: *End of Johan Blytts Vei*
Information and Maps: *www.fjordsandbeaches.com/mount-ulriken-bergen*

Ulriken is the highest of Bergen's seven mountains and offers spectacular views of the city, surrounding islands, and the ocean. It is 643 meters (2,100 ft) above sea level, and at the top you will find a café and restaurant (advance bookings only).

The hike to Ulriken is quite strenuous but worth it in the end. The majority of the hike is climbing Sherpa steps. It starts on a nice gravel path for about 1 kilometer (0.6 mi), that gets steeper until you reach the base of the steps (a spot called Steinen). From there, you can opt to hike the 2.4-kilometer (1.5-mi) route that goes around the backside of the mountain, or brave the Sherpa steps (800 m/2,600 ft).

If you want to try both, I recommend the Sherpa steps up, and the longer route back down. This is easier on your knees than hiking down the Sherpa steps.

The large (and at times, uneven) steps take

you 800 meters (2,600 ft) straight up to the top of Mount Ulriken. You'll get a good workout as you gain around 300 meters (1,000 ft) of elevation. To take the "back way" down, follow the trail toward Årstadhytten and Djervhytten. Stay on the left of Lægdetjernet lake and follow the path to the right as you pass the cabins. The trail is well-marked.

The hike to the top can take anywhere from 1 to 2 hours, depending on your pace. Some run up the steps in just 40 minutes, whereas families with younger children who want to take their time should set aside 2 hours for the hike. To be on the safe side, plan for it to take 3-4 hours in total, depending on which way you take back down (the longer way back down takes almost as long as hiking the steps up). This will also give you plenty of time to enjoy the view at the top.

To get to the trailhead, either walk from the city center (1 hour), or take bus 12 to Montana (21 minutes). Then, head toward Montana Hostel and walk to the end of Johan Blytts Vei, where you'll find the trailhead (you will pass the hostel, and a power station). There are signs to the trailhead from the bus stop.

Stoltzen
Distance: 0.9 kilometers (0.5 mi)
Time: 25-45 minutes one-way
Difficulty: Strenuous
Trailhead: Stoltzekleiven
Information and Maps: https://ut.no/turforslag/117019/treningstur-opp-stoltzekleiven

For an intense hike that offers pretty great views of Bergen (from the opposite direction of Ulriken), you'll want to hike the steps known as Stoltzen up Sandviksfjellet. The 908 steps have an incline of 36 percent, and although it is perhaps the hardest of the seven mountains to hike, it is the easiest in terms of finding the way. There is no way to go wrong here, as you simply start at the bottom of the steps and start climbing.

When you are at the top, you can opt to hike back down the stairs, or take a slightly more leisurely route. Hiking back down the stairs is very hard on your knees, and not very

popular among those hiking up, as the steps are quite narrow in some places.

Some walk from the top of Stoltzen along the lakes to Fløyen, and either hike or take the funicular down from there (after a well-deserved ice cream at the top). Or, you can hike down via Skredderdalen, which is what most people do. At the top of the mountain, walk toward Storevatnet lake and take a right when you get to it (this is the same route as hiking to Fløyen). Follow the flat gravel path for 10-15 minutes, before you get to another lake (Nedrediket). There, you will see signs on the right of the path pointing you to Skredderdalen (the valley you follow to get down) and a narrow trail. Skredderdalen is actually the valley separating Fløyen and Sandviksfjellet.

The trailhead for Stoltzen is located along Fjellveien in Sandviken, past Bryggen. To get there, there are several options. You can take bus 10 from Torget to Prahls Vei (9 minutes), or bus 18 from Torget to Formanns Vei (9 minutes). Additionally, buses 3, 4, 12, and 16E from Torget to Munkebotn (6 minutes) bring you close to the trailhead. From each bus stop, you have to walk for 5-10 minutes to get to the trailhead (follow signs to Fjellveien and Stoltzen).

Løvstakken
Distance: 2.5 kilometers (1.4 mi)
Time: 1.5-2 hours total
Difficulty: Moderate
Trailhead: Løvstakkveien 51
Information and Maps: https://en.visitbergen.com/things-to-do/hike-up-mount-lovstakken-one-of-bergens-seven-mountains-p5609103

At 477 meters (1,500 ft) above sea level, Løvstakken is another hike that gives you quite an impressive view of the city and its surroundings. There are many routes to go up this mountain, but the favored one starts near Danmarks Plass. To get there, take bus 10 from Festplassen to Blekenberg (10 minutes). From there, follow the signs to Løvstakken (5-6 minutes).

The first part of the hike is steep, on a

gravel road, but after just 15 minutes this turns into a mountain hike. The path is rocky, so it is important to keep your focus. In turn, this is a really good workout for your knees and ankles. You will hike through some forested areas, and once the forest clears, the view of the city just gets better and better.

It can be quite windy at the top, so make sure to dress warm. Hike back down the same way as you came. Make sure to take note of your trail on the way up, as there are many paths to take and it can be easy to follow the wrong one back down if you don't pay attention.

Fløyen

Distance: 3 kilometers (1.9 mi)
Time: 45 minutes one-way
Difficulty: Moderate
Trailhead: Vetrlidsallmenningen 23A (Fløibanen funicular bottom station)
Information and Maps: www.floyen.no

The hike up Fløyen is perhaps the most well-known of the hikes surrounding Bergen, and there are several trail options to get to the top of this mountain (400 m/1,300 ft above sea level). From the bottom station of the funicular, follow the winding stairs and roads going uphill just behind it. You will reach a playground and small park with benches where you can take a break to enjoy the view. Then, take a right onto a pathway called Fløysvingene (the Fløyen turns). This path winds its way up the mountain, and after about 35 or so minutes you will reach the top. Alternatively, you can continue to follow the paved road, and walk the road as it winds along the funicular to the top. The length and hike time are about the same, and the Fløysvingene path will make you feel a little closer to nature.

At the top of Fløyen, you will find a café, restaurant, ice cream kiosk (summer), and lots of activities for children, such as a rope course and another playground.

Rundemannen

Distance: 4 kilometers (2.5 mi) from Fløyen

Time: 1 hour from Fløyen one-way
Difficulty: Easy
Trailhead: The Fløibanen top station
Information and Maps: www.floyen.no

Rundemanen (568 meters/1,800 ft above sea level) can be reached by continuing the hike once you have reached the top of Mount Fløyen. Therefore, this hike can be considered a continuation of the Fløyen hike, or you can take the Fløyen funicular and start it without having to hike both segments.

From the Fløyen playground and restaurant area, follow signs toward Brushytten. The gravel road toward Brushytten is nice and relatively flat (with some uphill in the beginning), and you will walk past a couple of mountain lakes on the way. Once you get to Brushytten, continue along the gravel road on the left side of the small kiosk. Keep following the road until you reach Rundemanen and get some pretty epic views of Bergen and the ocean. This hike is relatively easy and follows a well-kept gravel road the whole way.

Tours
Norway in a Nutshell (FjordTours)
Tel. 55 55 76 60; www.norwaynutshell.com

Norway in a Nutshell (often abreviated to NIN) is perhaps the most popular tour in Norway. It takes you from Bergen to Flåm, via the UNESCO-listed Nærøyfjord, the Oslo-Bergen Line, and the Flåm Railway—and then back to Bergen. It combines bus, train, and boat travel to really give you a snapshot of some of Norway's most beautiful scenery. However, this is more of a package deal than a tour. When you book the NIN tour, you are traveling on the same public transportation as those who booked it on their own, and there is no guide.

The route can be taken in either direction. One way is that from Bergen, you first travel to Myrdal by train on the Oslo-Bergen line, then Myrdal to Flåm by train on the Flåm Railway, Flåm to Gudvangen by boat on the Nærøyfjord cruise, and then Gudvangen to Bergen by bus. Alternately, you can travel

Fjord Tours from Bergen

If you want to see the fjords from Bergen in a day, the fjord cruise to **Mostraumen** is a great option (page 157). There are ways to see other fjords in a short amount of time as well.

HARDANGERFJORD

Rødne (tel. 51 89 52 70; https://rodne.no/fjordcruise/fjordcruise-til-hardanger/) also offers a boat trip to **Rosendal** in the Hardangerfjord. This cruise takes around 2 hours each way, with two daily departures in the summer months (so you can spend a day in Rosendal and the Hardangerfjord area before returning to Bergen on a later departure). During the winter, there is only one daily deparute on the weekends. In the low season departures don't always align, so you may have to spend a night in Rosendal before returning to Bergen.

NÆRØYFJORD AND AURLANDSFJORD

on the waters of the Hardangerfjord

To see the more spectacular Nærøyfjord and Aurlandsfjord in a day, you have to start your day early in Bergen and travel by bus to Gudvangen. This journey is operated by **Nor-Way Bussekspress** (www.nor-way.no) and takes around 2.5 hours. From Gudvangen, you can take a fjord cruise (www.norwaysbest.com) through the Nærøyfjord to Flåm, before returning to Bergen from Flåm by bus (3-hour journey). It is advised to book the bus and fjord cruise tickets in advance for this, so you are guaranteed a space on board, and have your schedule set before you go. It is possible to do this journey year-round.

these segments in reverse order. Another option: the last leg from Gudvangen to Bergen can be split between a bus to Voss and then a train (the Oslo-Bergen line) to Bergen. You also have some flexibility in the length of your trip, as this can all be done in a day, or in 2-3 days with an overnight stay in Flåm.

Rødne Fjord Cruise to Mostraumen

Zachariasbryggen; tel. 51 89 52 70; https://rodne.no/fjordcruise/fjordcruise-til-mostraumen

Rødne offers a 3.5-hour fjord cruise from Bergen to Mostraumen. This small-vessel excursion leaves from Zachariasbryggen, right by the Bergen Fish Market. You will travel along the Osterfjord, one of the lesser-known fjords of Norway, just north of the city. There is a small kiosk on board, serving baked goods and drinks. In addition to seeing beautiful scenery on this trip, you might also get to see

some wildlife along the coast, such as seals and eagles.

Bergen Walking Tour

www.freetourbergen.com

This free English walking tour of Bergen starts at Torgallmenningen and takes you on a 1.5- to 2-hour walk around the main sights of the city. The length of the tour depends on the weather, as well as the time spent answering people's questions. You can expect to see highlights such as Bryggen, Bergenhus Fortress, the Fish Market, and the National Theater along this tour.

Winter Sports

Bergen isn't huge on winter sports; as opposed to Oslo, it doesn't quite get cold enough for the snow to set for very long. Due to its location on the coast, Bergen is more likely to have a layer of slush in the streets, as the snow usually melts within 2-3 days, even in the winter. There are some cross-country ski trails in the surrounding mountains (Fløyen has a few, for example), but most ski enthusiasts are more likely to take the train to Voss, a haven of winter sports just an hour away.

Cross-Country Skiing

At Fløyen, there is a 500-meter (1,640-ft) trail that's lit with artificial lights until 10pm every evening. To get there, simply take the Fløyen funicular to the top (you are likely to meet locals with their skis on board as well) and follow Blåmansveien (a road) until it crosses Halvdan Griegs Vei. From there, follow Halvdan Griegs Vei to the trail; there are signs the whole way.

There are limited ski rentals in Bergen. **Skattkammeret** (Kong Oscars Gate 62; https://kirkensbymisjon.no/skattkammeret/bergen; tel. 55 60 31 10; Mon. 11am-2pm, Wed. 3pm-6pm, Fri. 11am-2pm; adults are asked to pay a "token fee," children free) has a small selection of skis for rent on a first-come, first-served basis.

ENTERTAINMENT AND EVENTS

The Arts

Den Nationale Scene

Engen 1; tel. 55 60 70 80; https://dns.no

Den Nationale Scene is the main theater in Bergen. This grand and majestic venue at the top of a small hill in the city center was founded in 1850 as Det Norske Theater (the Norwegian Theatre), with the goal of showcasing Norwegian arts (as opposed to Danish productions, which were more prevalent due to Norway's longstanding union with Denmark 1380-1814). Henrik Ibsen worked at the theater from 1851 to 1858.

In 1906, the foundation was laid for the current building, and it opened just 3 years later. Since then, the theater has seen several expansions, a major fire, and the bombing of Bergen in 1940. Den Nationale Scene puts on modern, classical, and children's plays, mainly in Norwegian.

Grieghallen

Edvard Griegs Plass 1; tel. 55 21 61 00; www.grieghallen.no

Grieghallen's large, gray concrete building sticks out from the charming wooden houses of Lille Lungegårdsvann nearby like a sore thumb. Locals have had a love-hate relationship with this venue's design—which was inspired by the brutalist concrete architecture of Japan—since it was finished in 1978. However, this important soundstage has possibly the best acoustics of any venue in Norway. In Grieghallen, Norwegian and international artists and academies have put on concerts, operas, and ballets. The Eurovision Song Contest was held there in 1986.

Forum Scene

Fjøsangerveien 28; tel. 92 98 28 00; www.forumscene.no

Forum Scene is a newcomer in the Bergen art world, having opened its doors in 2019. The building itself is a lot older than that, however. Forum used to be a cinema, and when it opened in 1946 it was the largest independent cinema in Norway with its 1,140 seats. Headliners at this protected historic venue have included comedians, bands, and solo artists. Forum is located near Danmarks Plass, just 8-10 minutes on the Light Rail ByBanen from the city center.

Festivals and Events

Bergenfest

Bergenhus Fortress; tel. 55 21 50 60; www.bergenfest.no; June; day pass 1,200 kr

Bergenfest started as an intimate blues and Americana festival spread across the city, and is now the largest festival in town, drawing names such as Zara Larsson, Bon Iver, Ellie Goulding, Queens of the Stone Age, and Bastille. The festival has relocated to Koengen, inside Bergenhus Fortress. So, in addition to showcasing a large selection of Scandinavian and international artists,

Bergenhus has a uniquely appealing location. The 2-3 festival stages are built in various areas of Bergenhus Fortress, so you are in historic surroundings while you enjoy the music.

Bergen Food Festival

Festplassen; https://matfest.no; Sept.; free entry
Farmers and producers from all over Vestland county come together for a weekend in December during Bergen Matfestival. The whole festival is a homage to local producers of cheese, meat, honey, seafood, and even beer (more on the Bergen Beer Festival below). You can browse each stand and speak directly with the farmers.

Bergen Beer Festival

Kulturhuset; www.olfestival.no; Sept.; 200 kr
Bergen Ølfestival is, you guessed it, a celebration of local beer and breweries from all around Norway. Tickets to this indoor market must be bought in advance, and are valid for specific time intervals of 3 hours each. To save yourself time and hassle at the festival, get one of their ticket packages, which includes the entrance fee and a set number of vouchers that can be exchanged for samples at the festival. That way, you don't have to get your credit card out for every beer you'd like to taste.

BIFF (Bergen International Film Festival)

Bergen Kino; tel. 55 30 08 40; www.biff.no; Oct.; 100 kr per movie, or 700 kr for 10 movies
Every year, more than 150 films are displayed in Bergen for the weeklong BIFF (the Bergen International Film Festival). This is the largest film festival in Norway, and it's perfect for any movie fanatic. From Norwegian and Scandinavian indie films to documentaries and major international movies, there is a large to be seen on the big screen here. The films are usually shown at Bergen Cinema, with its two buildings both located in the city center.

Pepperkakebyen (Gingerbread City)

Småstrandgaten 3; www.pepperkakebyen.org; Dec.; adults 150 kr, children 100 kr, children under 12 free
Every year, the world's largest gingerbread town is built in the center of Bergen. Schools, businesses, and families from all over the city bake and build various gingerbread houses that they contribute, and then the city is put together. This has been a tradition since 1991, and each year the city gets bigger.

SHOPPING

As Bergen is quite a weather-prone city, with an average of 231 days of rain a year, it's no surprise to find that most of the shopping in the city happens inside malls, even in the city center. The rectangular main square of the city, Torgallmenningen, actually has two large shopping malls (**Galleriet** and **Sundt**; the latter is closed for complete refurbishment until 2024) on one side, and cafés and a few individual shops on the other side. Along Bryggen you will find mainly souvenir stores, with the exception of the well-known Julehuset.

Bryggen
Julehuset

Holmedalsgården 1; tel. 55 21 51 04; www. julehusetbergen.no; Mon.-Fri. 9am-9pm, Sat. 10am-8pm, Sun. 10am-6pm
Julehuset has been a staple on Bryggen since it opened in 1993. This Christmas store is open year-round and sells everything you might need or want for Christmas. Expect to find wrapping paper, cards, ornaments, Christmas lights, and much more.

Rendezvous

Øvregaten 13; tel. 91 15 15 72; www.bergensentrum.no/ bedrift/rendezvous; Mon.-Sat. 11am-6pm
Rendezvous sells home decor, with a specific focus on exclusive design and vintage treasures you might not be able to find anywhere else. Their main goal was to provide something unique and new to Bergen, and as a

result, almost all the brands they have selected are sold exclusively at Rendezvous.

Central Bergen

Heim

Strandgaten 25; tel. 97 33 10 79; https://heimbryggen. no; Mon.-Wed. 10am-6pm, Thurs. 10am-7pm, Fri.-Sat. 10am-6pm

Heim is nynorsk (the lesser used of the two Norwegian written languages) for Home, and this quirky home decor shop has everything you need to fill your home with color. Expect an array of colors as you walk into the store, and products such as bright, oddly shaped candles, stylish coffee-table books, and chocolate truffles in containers so pretty you'll never want to open them. Heim also has a small store at Bryggen (Bredsgården 18), selling a smaller selection of their products.

Galleriet (Shopping Center)

Torgallmenningen 8; tel. 91 54 98 21; https://galleriet. com; Mon.-Fri. 9am-9pm, Sat. 9am-6pm

Perhaps the go-to shopping center for locals, Galleriet has been a staple along Torgallmenningen since it opened in 1988. It is the largest shopping center in Bergen, and with an open floorplan this shopping center makes the indoor shopping experience feel a little less "indoors." The seven floors of shops all line the perimeter of the building, with just a walking bridge crossing the large open space in the middle. Galleriet has more than 70 stores and restaurants. The stores are primarily well-known Norwegian or international brands, such as H&M (clothing) Kremmerhuset (interiors), Newbie (baby and toddler clothes), and Norli (books).

Greater Bergen

Lagunen (Shopping Center)

Laguneveien 1; tel. 55 11 74 00; www.lagunen.no; Mon.-Fri. 10am-9pm, Sat. 10am-6pm

Lagunen opened in 1985 and is the largest shopping center in Bergen, with more than 200 shops, restaurants, and cafés. It is located 30 minutes from the city center via the Light Rail and is usually the choice for those who are planning on a full day of shopping without wanting to walk all around the city center. There is also a cinema and a gym at Lagunen, and it has become the preferred shopping and entertainment destination for those who live outside of the city center.

FOOD

Bergenhus Fortress

Dr. Wiesener

Nye Sandviksveien 17A; tel. 98 12 77 32; www. drwiesener.no; daily 1pm-1am; 219-299 kr

Dr. Wiesener is housed in the former Dr. Wieseners Folkebad, the public bath that was founded in 1889 to improve the health of the Bergen locals. This charming pub and restaurant is located behind Bergenhus Fortress, right near Oscarsborg. Their menu changes seasonally, offering dishes such as shrimp sandwiches and vegetable soup. The menu is rather seafood-focused, so if you don't eat seafood, you will find that the already small menu is quite limited. The outdoor seating area around the restaurant is busy on sunny days, and you'll find lots of locals who have been going here for years.

Bryggen

Maharajah

Rosenkrantzgaten 5; tel. 55 31 25 55; www.maharajas. no; Mon.-Thurs. 3pm-11pm, Fri.-Sat. 3pm-midnight, Sun. 2pm-10pm; 251-305 kr

Maharajah is a small restaurant up the hill just behind Bryggen. Here you'll be greeted with a warm and welcoming atmosphere, and the interior is decorated with beautifully carved chairs and patterned tablecloths from India. On the menu are classics, such as lamb and chicken tikka, as well as a selection of Indian street food, which is a welcome variation. On this section of the menu, you can find dishes such as Aloo Tikki (Indian potato cakes with herbs and spices) and Kathi Rolls (grilled chicken or lamb mixed with spices and vegetables, wrapped in roti).

Casa Del Toro

Rosenkrantzgaten 6; tel. 55 55 03 10; www.casadeltoro.
no; Tues.-Sat. 4pm-10pm; 229-349 kr

Bergen's only Tex-Mex restaurant serves fajitas, enchiladas, and burritos prepared using fresh ingredients. Tortilla chips are made in house. The small restaurant is simply decorated with wooden tables, leather chairs, and Aztec-style patterns on the benches. They also serve great margaritas.

Olivia

Torget 2; tel. 55 90 25 00; https://oliviarestauranter.no/
restaurant/zachariasbryggen; Mon.-Sat. 11am-midnight,
Sun. noon-midnight; 165-389 kr

Olivia is perhaps the only Norwegian chain restaurant worth mentioning. They only have one restaurant in Bergen, and it is located on the docks in the large white building named Zachariasbryggen, right where Vågen Harbor ends. Olivia is a large restaurant that still manages to create an intimate and cozy atmosphere; you will feel as if you have walked into an Italian home or backyard. Decorations include empty wine bottles and olive trees, and even though it can get loud at times, the noise level rarely feels bothersome under the high ceiling of this two-story restaurant. Expect a large wine selection and Italian classics such as pasta di manzo (pasta with beef) and quattro formaggi (four-cheese) pizza.

Enhjørningen

Enhjørningsgården 29; tel. 55 30 69 50; www.
enhjorningen.no; Mon.-Sat. 4pm-11pm; 375-425 kr

Enhjørningen is located in one of the houses lining the front of Bryggen, and some people visit simply for the historic locale and restored interior. However, the food at this seafood restaurant has left its own mark on the Bergen restaurant map, and some say it is one of the best seafood places in town. On the menu you will find not only classics like homemade fish soup and bacalao, but also innovative dishes such as whale carpaccio and steamed halibut.

★ Bryggeloftet

Bryggen 11; tel. 55 30 20 70; www.bryggeloftet.no;
Mon.-Sun. 4pm-11pm; 325-495 kr

For truly authentic Norwegian food, a trip to Bryggeloftet is a must. The restaurant has been run by the same family since 1910, and here you will get to enjoy your food in truly historic surrounding. The restaurant is warm and traditional, with dark leather couches, dark wood paneling, and exposed brick. Among their signature dishes are their reindeer steak served with a wild game sauce, and the fish soup starter.

Bryggeloftet is on the second floor of the building, while Bryggestuene (often just called Stuene) is on the first floor. Both are owned and run by the same family and serve a similar menu. If you are looking for a nice lunch spot, Bryggestuene on the ground floor opens earlier than Bryggeloftet upstairs (daily noon-11pm). Their Bergen Fish Soup is also available as a lunch option.

Central Bergen
★ Pergola

Nedre Korskirkeallmenningen 9B; tel. 55 01 86 73;
Mon.-Fri. 4pm-midnight, Sat. 2pm-midnight

Down an alleyway along one of Bergen's many cobbled streets you will find the entrance to Pergola. Once you find the alleyway, you will notice that it has been decorated with clothes hanging out to dry—almost like a Roman street. This small restaurant can remind you a little of a cellar, and that's exactly the point. They have Bergen's largest selection of wine, and this is the main attraction of this place. In addition, they have a simple menu consisting of charcuterie boards and pizza (available ingredients are listed instead of pre-set pizzas). Enjoy an evening of wine tasting and snacking on home-made pizza and cheese with friends. Because the space is rather small, you should book a table in advance.

Bergen Brunsj

Kaigaten 16; tel. 48 51 69 97; Sun.-Wed. 11am-6pm,
Thurs.-Sat. 11am-11pm; 179-249 kr

This is the place to be for meals between 11am

and 4pm. Bergen Brunsj was the first local restaurant to focus solely on a lunch/brunch concept, and while they are open late, this is still what they are known for. Their dishes are inspired by cities from all over the world that start with the letter "B" and are served on wooden boards. The menu changes often, and the only dish that seems never to change is their staple Bergen Brunsj board, which includes freshly made bread, cheese from Fana, smoked salmon, scambled eggs, and a salad. Past favorites have included Brooklyn Brunsj (pastrami sandwich, french fries, tomatoes, and American pancakes) and the Beauvais Brunsj (croque monsieur, french fries, salad, and an apple crumble).

Poca Madre

Skostredet 14; tel. 94 07 05 00; www.pocamadre.no; Tues.-Thurs. 4pm-11pm, Fri. 4pm-2:30am, Sat. 1pm-2:30am, Sun. 4pm-11pm; 253-360 Kr

Poca Madre opened in Skostredet during the pandemic and has quickly become a popular dining spot. This is an authentic Mexican restaurant decorated with dark leather sofas, Aztec patterns, and lots of greenery. You won't find the American version of Mexican food here, as the Mexican chefs focus on "cooking the way mama did it." Instead, expect dishes such as Lamb Birria (marinated lamb legs with homemade adobo sauce, a dish originating from Jalisco) and slow-cooked beef tongue (their signature dish). Their cocktails are especially nice, and when the outdoor seating area is open in the summer, it's the perfect place for a drink.

Wesselstuen

Øvre Ole Bulls Plass 6; tel. 55 55 49 49; https:// wesselstuen.no; Mon.-Sat. noon-11pm; 215-375 kr

Wesselstuen is a traditional restaurant located just a stone's throw from Den Blå Steinen, with old-school furnishings and a nostalgic atmosphere. A favorite of the older generations, this place has been welcoming guests since 1957. They serve a mean fish soup, and their Skagen Toast (prawns on toast) starter is a classic that should not be missed. Mains

include Norwegian reindeer, steamed mussels, and beef tenderloin from Jæren.

Røyk

Vaskerelven 6; tel. 91 92 90 79; https://roykbbq.no; Mon.-Thurs. 4pm-10pm, Fri.-Sat. 4pm-11pm, Sun. 4pm-9pm; 179-444 kr

Røyk ("Smoke") is a haven for meat lovers. This is the place to go for the best barbecue in town. Expect American barbecue and street food, such as brisket, short ribs, and pork neck. All the meat is smoked on-site daily. If you are having a hard time choosing, try their BBQ-Meny for 444 kr per person (minimum 2 people), which includes a selection of their meats and sides. The restaurant is dimly lit and decorated with dark undertones, creating a gentle and informal atmosphere.

Boccone

Nedre Ole Bulls Plass 4; tel. 53 01 44 88; https:// boccone.no; Sun.-Thurs. 3pm-10pm, Fri.-Sat. 3pm-11pm; 229-449 kr

Boccone is one of the more recent additions to the Bergen food scene and has quickly become a local favorite for Italian food. Their stylish, upscale interior transports you to some fancy hotel on Lake Como in an instant. The restaurant feels intimate yet covers two floors and seats quite a few people. They offer personal pizzas featuring specialty ingredients such as n'duja sausage and buffalo burrata, and if you like garlic, their creamy ravioli is a must.

Greater Bergen

Bien Snackbar

Fjøsangerveien 30; tel. 55 59 11 00; www.bienbar. no/snackbar; Mon.-Sat. 4pm-11pm, Sun. 1pm-9pm; 164-169 kr

In Danmarks Plass you will find the best hamburger in the city. Bien has a restaurant in the city center as well (Bien Centro; Nordahl Bruns Gate 9; tel. 55 59 11 00; Mon.-Fri. 4pm-9pm, Sat.-Sun. 1pm-9pm), but it is only at their Snackbar you can get their famed burgers. The main attractions on the menu are those juicy burgers, served with various condiments and sauces (such as blue cheese, homemade chili and jalapenos, or halloumi). Their parmesan- and parsley-topped fries are also a must. The small restaurant space gives off a casual and low-key vibe. They have a large selection of beer to complement the burgers.

JAJA

Danmarks Plass 23; tel. 91 31 42 35; www.jajabergen. no; Tues.-Fri. 11:30am-midnight, Sat. 1pm-midnight, Sun. 1pm-10:30pm; 99-199 kr (sharing plates)

Located at Danmarks Plass, just a short Light Rail ride from the city (8-9 minutes), JAJA is worth the trip. The menu here is all about international street food and changes every 3-4 months with new inspiration. All dishes are made to share, and it is recommended to order 1.5-2 dishes per person. This informal restaurant is simply decorated, and the large glass windows make it a great place to people-watch. On the menu you will find dishes inspired by food trucks from all over the world, such as steamed buns (Asia), birria tacos (Mexico), sliders (USA), and chaat (India).

BARS AND NIGHTLIFE

Bryggen

26 North

Dreggsallmenningen 1; tel. 47 71 04 67; https://26north. no; Mon.-Thurs. 4pm-midnight, Fri.-Sat. 11:30am-1am, Sun. 4pm-10pm

This bar (and restaurant) is located right near Bryggen, in one of the front-facing buildings. You'll find the restaurant inside Hotel Radisson, while the bar is right at the front toward the water. Their small outdoor seating area is popular in summer. With white tablecloths and dark chairs, the bar is modern and chic, and the atmosphere slightly formal.

Sjøboden

Bryggen 29; tel. 41 42 22 22; www.sjoboden-bergen.no; Tues.-Sat. 7pm-3am

Sjøboden, right in the middle of Bryggen, is named for the fact that the building it is located in was the last working sjøbod (boathouse/storage for fishermen) in Bergen. It was in use up until 2002. Sjøboden today is a darkly lit, traditionally decorated bar with

live music most nights of the week. They have more than 60 types of beer on their menu. In the summer they open a large outdoor seating area in front of the Bryggen houses, which is the perfect spot to enjoy a beer in the sun.

Bar 3

Rosenkrantzgaten 3; tel. 48 88 92 00; www.bar3.no; Sun.-Thurs. 4pm-1am, Fri.-Sat. 4pm-2:30am

The large Bar 3 is located in a basement behind Bryggen. Here, you will find lots of fun activities for the whole friend group, including pool, shuffleboard, foosball, and darts. There's lots of seating areas, and a dance floor that gets busy after 11pm. On weekends, the age limit to enter is 23, so you'll find that this place doesn't get packed with the typical young crowd that frequents some nightclubs. The vibe is relaxed and informal.

Central Bergen

Zachariasbryggen

Torget 2; tel. 55 55 31 55; www.bergensentrum.no/ bedrift/zachariasbryggen; daily noon-midnight

Zachariasbryggen, often just called Zachen by locals, is a large bar and social club encompassing several themed bars and pubs. Inside this big white building, right at the end of the Vågen Harbor, you will find Olivia Restaurant, a saloon-themed country bar, a piano bar (especially lively on weekends), a nightclub (on the top floor), and an English-style pub with large outdoor seating on the dock. The last is especially popular on summer nights and regularly puts on live music.

Scruffy Murphys

Torget 15; tel. 55 30 09 20; https://scruffymurphys.no; Sun.-Thurs. 3pm-1:30am, Fri.-Sat. 1pm-3am

This spot calls itself the only true Irish pub in Bergen, so you might already know what to expect here. This traditional pub covers two floors, and has a small stage for live music and a dance floor on the ground floor. There is live music regularly, and it can get quite packed with limited seating on those nights. In the summer, there is live music most weekends.

No Stress

Hollendergaten 11; www.nostressbar.no; Mon.-Thurs.

5pm-1:30am, Fri.-Sat. 3pm-2:30am, Sun. 5pm-1am

No Stress is a small cocktail bar with retro furnishings often frequented by locals. Their large cocktail menu is impressive, and if you manage to snag one of their (very few) outdoor seats you will be good for the night. They also have board games and an old Nintendo 64 that is usually already taken—but Mario Kart enthusiasts might find that it is worth the wait.

Vinyl

Kong Oscars Gate 8; www.vinylbar.no; Sun.-Mon 5pm-midnight, Tues.-Thurs. 5pm-1am, Fri.-Sat. 4pm-2:30am

If you want great music and beer, this is the place to go. Vinyl was built to resemble a recording studio, and they only play music from real vinyl discs. They have a large selection of beer on tap (almost 30), and even more in bottles. It is a small and intimate place, often busy with friends gathering around the tables lining the walls.

Dark & Stormy

Kong Oscars Gate 12; www.darkandstormy.no; Tues.-Thurs. 5pm-1am, Fri.-Sat. 4pm-2:30am

This tropical cocktail bar will make you completely forget you are in Bergen. Their interior hints at a much warmer climate than you can find in Norway, with palm trees, coconuts, and bright colors throughout. They have a large selection of cocktails, and an even bigger patio in the back (complete with heat lamps and large umbrellas, making it possible to sit there almost year-round). You will recognize Dark & Stormy as soon as you walk around the corner, due to their bright turquoise facade.

Ginial

Vaskerelven 6; tel. 91 92 90 79; Mon.-Thurs. 4pm-10pm, Fri.-Sat. 4pm-11pm, Sun. 4pm-9pm

Ginial is the gin bar belonging to Røyk BBQ. The name is a pun on the Norwegian word for genius ("genial"), and they truly are geniuses when it comes to gin. In this stylish and dimly lit bar you will find a number of variations on a gin and tonic, in addition to American whiskeys.

ACCOMMODATIONS

Most hotels in Bergen are centered on Bryggen, Torgallmenningen, and the main train station. If you stay in one of these locations, you will have access to most sights and restaurants in the city within walking distance. The price points of the central hotels are all pretty similar, especially in the summer season when demand is high. To make your stay a little more budget-friendly, venture just beyond the city center to Solheimsviken and Danmarks Plass (15-minute walk, 8-9 minutes on the Light Rail), where you will find **Moxy Bergen** and **Citybox** (Solheimsgaten 23; tel. 53 01 99 90; https://citybox.no/danmarksplass; 1100 kr). As in Oslo, the chains Thon, Clarion, and Scandic dominate the hotel scene in Bergen.

Bryggen

Radisson Blu Royal Hotel

Dreggsallmenningen 1; tel. 55 54 30 00; www.radissonhotels.com/no-no/hoteller/radisson-blu-bergen; 1,600 kr

The Radisson Blu Royal Hotel can be found in historic surroundings on Bryggen. The hotel is modern, and the bright rooms are classically furnished with turquoise and light wooden details. This is a large hotel with over 300 rooms, some of which have views of the back of Bryggen.

Hotel Havnekontoret

Slottsgaten 1; tel. 55 60 11 00; www.nordicchoicehotels.no/hotell/norge/bergen/clarion-collection-hotel-havnekontoret; 1,900 kr

With a sleek and stylish interior, the large, fashionable Hotel Havnekontoret offers 113 rooms in one of the front-facing buildings along Vågen, just past Bryggen when walking away from the city center. They serve a simple buffet evening meal for their guests each night (6pm-8pm), which is great for those who have just arrived from a long flight. Most guests opt to head out to dine at a restaurant, but if you are trying to save money on your trip, this will surely help. Don't miss a trip to the top of their tower, where you can get a 360-degree view of the city.

Thon Hotel Rosenkrantz

Rosenkrantzgaten 7; tel. 55 30 14 00; www.thonhotels. no/hoteller/norge/bergen/thon-hotel-rosenkrantz-bergen; 2,100 kr

With the colorful interior typical to Thon, the completely refurbished Rosenkrantz is a modern hotel right behind Bryggen. From the bright pink chairs in the lobby to the lime green curtains in the 157 rooms, you'll find that no detail is ignored. The blue and gold wallpaper gives the rooms an extra air of elegance, and each room is equipped with Bose speakers you can connect to. They serve an evening meal (buffet) 6pm-9pm.

Det Hanseatiske Hotel

Finnegården 2A; tel. 55 30 48 00; www. dethanseatiskehotel.no; 2,400 kr

This charming, historic hotel takes you back in time with 37 uniquely decorated rooms. The style here ranges from light, upscale elegance to old-fashioned cottage. The original wooden walls of the building—visible in each room—are 300 years old, and the owners have done their best to preserve them.

Central Bergen
Grand Hotel Terminus

Zander Kaaes Gate 6; tel. 55 21 25 00; www. grandterminus.no; 1,800 kr

A classic hotel right by the train station with 131 rooms, Grand Hotel Terminus is a great choice for those arriving late on the Oslo-Bergen line. The hotel and its interior are grand and stately, with dark wood paneling and stone floors across the lobby and communal areas. The hotel originally opened its doors in 1928, and recent refurbishments were designed to preserve its former flair. The rooms are sleek, with green and lime details throughout. Worth mentioning is their Bar Amundsen, named for the polar explorer Roald Amundsen. The bar is in the room

where he held his last press conference before heading out on an expedition to find his lost rival, Umberto Nobile. Sadly, Amundsen disappeared somewhere in the Arctic Ocean on this journey.

Hotel Oleana

Øvre Ole Bulls Plass 5; tel. 55 21 58 70; www. hoteloleana.com; 2,000 kr

Hotel Oleana is a unique hotel inspired by Bergen's first celebrity, Ole Bull (1810-1880). He was a composer and violinist, and found huge success in both Europe and the US. He even tried to found his own Norwegian settlement in Pennsylvania, called Oleana. Today, the area is part of the Ole Bull State Park. Hotel Oleana is named after this settlement, and across the hotel you will find violin- and Ole Bull-inspired art. Their 97 rooms are intimate and almost sensual, with purple details and exposed showers, while the atmosphere in the rest of the hotel is sleek and modern.

★ Hotel Norge

Nedre Ole Bulls Plass 4; tel. 55 55 40 00; www. scandichotels.no/hotell/norge/bergen/hotel-norge-by-scandic; 2,000 kr

Hotel Norge originally opened in 1885 and has since been one of Bergen's most popular hotels due to its central location along Torgallmenningen. From the east-facing rooms you can enjoy views over Lille Lungegårdsvann Lake. This property underwent major renovations in 2018, and is now stylish and sleek, with an impressive lobby area reached via escalators from the entrance. While the lobby area is stylish and almost 1920s-like, the 415 rooms are more Nordic, with gray wood paneling and dark accents. Hotel Norge also has a spa and pool available to guests for a fee.

Greater Bergen
Moxy Bergen

Solheimsgaten 3; tel. 90 71 75 23; www.marriott.com/ en-us/hotels/bgoox-moxy-bergen/overview; 1,300 kr

Just outside the city center you will find one

of the newest hotels in Bergen. Moxy's location at the end of Solheimsviken bay affords beautiful views of the Puddefjord from most guest rooms and the breakfast room. Moxy has a young and modern feel to it, with street art from local artists and bare concrete walls lining the lobby. The rooms are modern and somewhat basic, with no extra amenities such as a minibar or kettle. However, this is the point, as Moxy is a no-nonsense hotel made for those who just want a good night's sleep in one of their 199 rooms and a great breakfast before heading out to explore. Restaurants **JAJA** and **Bien Snackbar** are within walking distance.

INFORMATION AND SERVICES
Bergen Tourist Information
Strandkaien 3; tel. 55 55 20 00; www.visitbergen.com/praktisk-informasjon/turistinformasjonen

The tourist information in Bergen is located in the same building as the indoor Fish Market, right on the docks of Vågen harbor. The offices and reception area are on the second floor, so take the stairs or elevator up. In addition to helping you with advice on things to do and how to get around Bergen, the staff here can help you book tours and concert tickets.

Health and Safety
Bergen Urgent Care (Legevakt)
Solheimsgaten 9; tel. 116117; www.bergen.kommune.no/omkommunen/avdelinger/bergen-legevakt

The Bergen Urgent Care is located in Solheimsviken, right by the Moxy Hotel. To get there, take the Light Rail ByBanen to Danmarks Plass, walk under the main road (E39) and then down the slope toward the water (3 minutes). It is necessary to call (116117) before showing up, a change added in 2022 to avoid unnecessary long waits and to make it easier for the staff to determine the urgency of an accident. The Legevakt is open 24/7. If you have an emergency and/or are in need of an ambulance, the number for this is 113.

Haukeland (Bergen Hospital)
Jonas Lies Vei 65; tel. 55 97 50 00; https://helse-bergen.no

Haukeland is the largest hospital in Bergen, offering surgeries and treatments for most illnesses and diseases. For major health issues, patients from the Urgent Care may be sent here for checkups and treatment. However, the first stop if anything happens during your travels should be the Urgent Care. If you call 113 (Norway's equivalent of 911), the ambulance may elect to bring you to the hospital instead of the Urgent Care.

GETTING THERE
Air
Bergen Airport Flesland
Flyplassvegen 555; tel. 67 03 15 55; https://avinor.no/bergen-lufthavn

Bergen has an international airport 18 kilometers (11 mi) outside of the city center. Although most international flights to Norway are routed to Oslo, Bergen is growing as a major international hub. The Bergen Light Rail **ByBanen** services the airport as its end stop, and so you can easily travel between the airport and the city center cheaply in around 40 minutes. Alternatively, the Airport Express Bus **FlyBussen** (tel. 05505; www.flybussen.no) has been running for years. There are direct flights to Flesland from European destinations such as Paris, Frankfurt, and Amsterdam. Travelers from Asia or America usually connect in Oslo, Copenhagen, or Stockholm before reaching Bergen.

Train
Bergen Stasjon
Strømgaten 4; www.banenor.no

The main (and only) train station in Bergen is the end stop of the well-known Oslo-Bergen Line **Bergensbanen**. From here, you can reach Oslo and stations in between, including Voss, Gol, and Geilo. The train also connects with the Flåm Railway at Myrdal, taking you to Flåm and the Sognefjord. This is the only rail line from Bergen, which might seem limited when compared to the rest of Europe.

The Bergen Line

Bergensbanen, or the Bergen Line, is a famous railway journey in Norway, known for its scenic route. It connects Oslo and Bergen, Norway's two largest cities. During the almost 7-hour trip, the train crosses Hardangervidda National Park and the Hardangervidda plateau, offering beautiful views of Europe's largest mountain plateau. The Oslo-Bergen Line opened in 1909, and is Northern Europe's highest railroad, with its highest point being the stop at Finse, 1,222 meters (4,000 ft) above sea level.

SCENERY

As you leave Oslo, the train takes you through the landscape of eastern Norway, with its cities and rivers (such as Drammen and Drammenselva), lakes (such as Tyrifjorden and Krøderfjorden), and forests (at Flå there is a bear habitat). As you reach **Geilo,** you have climbed to 794 meters (2,600 ft) above sea level. From there, you will cross **Hardangervidda,** and get a glimpse at some spectacular scenery (and sometimes the extreme weather). Expect mountain lakes, peaks, and vast flats. In the winter, you might want to wear sunglasses, as the entire area is bright white with snow, and it can be quite glaring. (Those traveling in the winter may recognize the scenery around **Finse** station. Scenes from *Star Wars Episode V: The Empire Strikes Back* were filmed there.) Both in winter and summer you might catch a glimpse of **reindeer** on the plateau, as there are more than 9,000 of them living there.

Once you reach **Voss,** the Hardangervidda plateau is behind you, and you will start noticing the famous landscape of the western fjords take shape. From Voss, Bergen is just an hour away. Take note of the **tunnels** along the way. Many were carved and blown out by hand, such as the 5.3-kilometer-long (3.3-mi) Gravhalstunnelen between Myrdal and Voss, which took 10 years to build.

FREQUENCY AND PRICE

There are four daily departures of Bergensbanen, with one being an overnight train. The price varies, as the cheapest tickets are few and often sell out quickly, but it is possible to travel from Oslo to Bergen (or vice-versa) for as little as 349 kr. Most likely you will be paying around 700-900 kr, however, and in peak season with few tickets left they can cost as much as 1,050 kr.

The station is serviced by Norway's national rail company **Vy** (tel. 61 05 19 10; www.vy.no).

The station is located at Nonneseter, which is also a stop on the Bergen Light Rail. It is just a short walk from the city center (around 5 minutes), and about a 15-minute walk from Bryggen.

Bus

Bergen is serviced by two main bus companies, **Vy Buss** (tel. 61 05 19 10; www.vy.no) and **Nor-Way** (tel. 22 31 31 50; www.nor-way. no). Nor-Way's Kystbussen connects Bergen with Stavanger in as little as 4.5 hours. They have several daily departures, with some making more stops, lengthening the journey time

to 5.5 hours, so make sure to check the total journey time to book the faster one. Their route Sognefjordekspressen connects Bergen with the Sognefjord, heading to Sogndal via Voss, Flåm, and Lærdal. Vy operates on the 9.5-hour bus journey between Bergen and Ålesund, with one daily departure.

Bergen Busstasjon (Bergen Bus Station)

Also called Bystasjonen ("the city station"), the bus terminal in Bergen is located just a stone's throw from the train station and is operated by the Bystasjonen Light Rail stop. It is a 5-minute walk from Den Blå Steinen, and 15 minutes from Bryggen.

Car

Bergen can be reached by car via E16 from Oslo and eastern Norway. The drive from Oslo to Bergen is long (463 km/288 mi) and takes around 7 hours. Allow 1-2 extra hours in the high season, when the roads are busy with tourist drivers (who are often a lot slower than the locals, even on the wide main roads). As you reach Voss driving from Oslo, the road gets increasingly more winding and narrow and this is a pain point for commuters between Voss and Bergen.

From Stavanger and the cities along southern Norway, take E39 to reach Bergen. This route includes two ferries, so make sure to allow for extra time. The drive is a little less than 5 hours.

Car Rental

There are a few car rental agencies available in central Bergen, and a couple more at the airport. **Hertz** (www.hertz.no) has a self-service location in in the city center (Fjøsangerveien 4; tel. 55 29 25 00) and a location at the airport (Flyplassvegen 555; tel. 55 22 60 75). **Avis** (www.avis.no) and **Budget** (www.budget.no) share a car rental address (Solheimsgaten 15; tel. 55 55 39 55) near the Danmarks Plass Light Rail stop, just a 7-minute commute from the city center. Avis is also available at the airport (Flyplassvegen; 55 11 64 30).

GETTING AROUND

As mentioned, Bergen is an extremely walkable city, and if you are staying at a hotel in the small city center, you might not need to rely on public transportation at all. Still, the city has a great public transportation system with light rail and buses, run by **Skyss** (tel. 55 55 90 70; www.skyss.no). The apps Skyss Billett (for tickets) and Skyss Reise (for schedules and travel planning) are all you need to travel around Bergen and the surrounding regions (such as Askøy and parts of Hardanger). A one-way ticket costs 40 kr, and a 24-hour pass is 105 kr. All tickets are valid on both the bus and light rail.

Light Rail

The Bergen Light Rail **Bybanen** is the city's pride. Line 1 travels between the city center (stop ByParken) and the airport from around 5am until 3am, with 6-, 10-, or 15-minute intervals. The total journey time is 43 minutes. Line 2 is the most recent addition, traveling from the city center through the Løvstakken mountain to Fyllingsdalen via a long-awaited stop at Haukeland hospital. Both lines go to the Kronstad stop, where you can transfer to the other line. The Light Rail does not go to Bryggen but stops in the city center by Torgallmenningen.

Bus

The buses in Bergen cover every area of the city in an impressive web of routes. Most of them stop at either the main bus station, Bergen Busstasjon, or in the city center (Festplassen or Lars Hilles Gate). Most buses run all day, but some offer limited service on Sundays and holidays, and between midnight and 6am.

Taxi

Both Uber and taxis are available in Bergen, and the city's major taxi company is **Bergen Taxi** (tel. 07000; www.bergentaxi.no). Their app "07000 Taxi" is worth downloading before your visit, as you can book a taxi to your location in minutes. Additionally, taxis can be flagged down wherever you see them, and they follow the international taxi lights system (light on means available, light off means unavailable). In the city center, there is a taxi stop right by Den Blå Steinen, where you will usually find several taxis waiting.

Walking

Bergen is a pedestrian-friendly city, and you can get to all sights and places around the city center and Bryggen on foot. As with the rest of Norway, all streets have sidewalks, and both Torgallmenningen and Bryggen are pedestrian-only zones. There is a road passing in front of Bryggen that is closed to private cars in the summer months as well, making the city center very pleasant for walking.

The Hardangerfjord

The Hardangerfjord Region, just east of Bergen, is a popular destination for those who want to explore the fjords without straying too far from the city. There are bus services leaving Bergen regularly, taking you to destinations in Hardanger in just 1.5 hours. The 179-kilometer-long (111-mi) Hardangerfjord offers less dramatic scenery than the more famous Geirangerfjord and Nærøyfjord, but it is beautiful and worth visiting nonetheless.

The scenery of Hardanger has inspired many painters and is frequently seen in the art from the height of Norway's Romantic period (during the 1800s). Perhaps the most famous example is the painting *Brudeferd i Hardanger* (1848) by Norwegian artists Adolph Tidemand and Hans Gude. The painting depicts a wedding party all dressed up in their national costumes rowing across the Hardangerfjord.

Some significant sights can be found in Hardanger. The region is home to several epic waterfalls—10 out of the 30 highest waterfalls in the world are found in Norway, and five of these are in Hardanger—and to the famous Trolltunga rock formation. The latter is a bucket-list hike for many avid hikers. Additionally, you will find Folgefonna Glacier and National Park in Hardanger. This is Norway's third-largest glacier and one of the southernmost glaciers in the country.

Hardanger is slightly less busy than other tourist destinations in Norway, and it is still mainly a summer destination. Some sights and attractions close in the low season (such as Baroniet Rosendal), and some of the waterfalls freeze over or have very limited water flows (such as Låtefossen) during the winter months. Therefore, visiting from June to August is ideal, to get the most out of your visit.

Orientation

Most sights and attractions in Hardanger are centered on the towns of Odda (at the southern end of the fjord), Norheimsund, and Eidfjord, all located along the Hardangerfjord.

Hardanger is easiest to reach from Bergen or Voss. When arriving from the east (Oslo), you will come down from the mountain plateaus in **Eidfjord,** so this is a good starting base for your trip to Hardanger. From Voss, either Eidfjord or **Odda** will be within reach, and you get to cross the Hardangerbrua Bridge along the way. Travelers visiting from Bergen should aim to travel to **Norheimsund,** and then explore the region from there.

The Folgefonna Glacier and National Park covers the mountain plateau west of Odda and stretches across the mountains of the Hardangerfjord, with the fjord surrounding it on three sides (west, east, and north). Odda and Bondhus are both good bases to stay for those wanting to explore the park.

Getting There and Around

Bus

You can reach Hardanger by bus from Bergen and Voss. All routes in the area are operated by **Skyss** (tel. 55 55 90 70; www.skyss.no). Around Hardanger, there are several bus routes taking you through the region. With routes between Nordheimsund and Odda, and Odda and Eidfjord, you can travel between the main destinations of Eidfjord, Odda, and Norheimsund. However, there are many more places to see, so make sure to check the Skyss websites or their app (Skyss Reise) for up-to-date schedules and route options.

Car

Driving to Hardanger is very popular. The only problem is the crazy amount of traffic on the narrow roads along the fjord in the summer months. Trailers, campervans, and rental cars back up the roads for miles on end, so make sure you bring a lot of patience with you if you plan on driving, and expect all travel times to be longer in the summer. There are several gas stations along the fjord, though most towns will have only one.

There are very few car rental agencies along the Hardangerfjord. If you want to drive yourself, the best option is to rent your car at your starting point, such as Bergen or Oslo.

NORHEIMSUND AND ØYSTESE

These two towns are located on the western shore of the Hardangerfjord and are ideal to visit if you are based in Bergen and have limited time. Travel time to either one of these destinations takes only about 1.5 hours by bus.

Sights

★ Steinsdalsfossen Waterfall

Mo ved Steinsdalen, 5600 Norheimsund; free

This is one of the most popular waterfalls to visit in the region (and in Norway). Steinsdalsfossen is quite unique because you can walk behind it without getting wet! The spectacular waterfall has a 50-meter (164-ft) drop, and the short pathway to the waterfall viewpoint goes right behind it. The walk to the viewpoint gives you an up-close look at the waterfall, and from the viewpoint you can also enjoy a great view of Steinsdalen

valley and the town of Norheimsund below it. The waterfall is located in Norheimsund, and the trail to the viewpoint starts just by the road.

Hardanger Skyspace

Hardangerfjordvegen 626, Øystese; tel. 47 47 99 87; https://kabuso.no/hardanger-skyspace; Thurs.-Fri. 11am-3pm, Sat.-Sun. 11am-4pm; adults 150 kr, children 75 kr

Hardanger Skyspace is a permanent art installation by American artist James Turrell. The Skyspace is meant to be a window to the sky, and the artist has created several of these across the globe. This one is in Øystese along the Hardangerfjord. The small, black building is shaped like an octagon and seats 18 people at the same time. There is an opening in the ceiling, and during dusk and dawn the room is filled with a colored light to match the mood of the sky outside. Each visit is completely unique, as the time of year and weather affect the experience.

Tickets must be booked in advance, and there are two daily time slots available for the experience. Dress warm, as if you were going to be outside. If it is cold, you can pick up blankets from the reception of Hardangerfjord Hotel (this is also where you pick up the key to the installation).

Steinsdalsfossen

Spildegarden

Nedre Vik 78, Øystese; tel. 97 11 92 12; www.

spildegarden.no; hours vary; cider-tasting tour 490 kr

One of Hardanger's many orchards and cider makers, Spildegarden is located right in the middle of Øystese village. It is family owned and run, and they make both cider and juice. Their tour and cider tasting lasts 1-1.5 hours, during which you will learn all about the family history (Spildegarden has been run by several generations of the same family), and how they make juice and cider. Of course, you will also get to try several varieties of their cider (Spildesider), while children can enjoy their different juices (Spildemost). They also have a (very) small shop where you can buy the ciders and juices. Check tour and tasting times online (there is usually one tasting a day in the summer season) and book in advance by reaching out via email to jane@spildegarden.no, or with your hotel reception (they can usually contact them for you).

Fjord Cruises

There are two main ways to explore the Hardangerfjord by boat: either by the faster, smaller RIB (Rigid Inflatable Boat) or on a slower, more relaxed fjord cruise (on board the award-winning hybrid vessel *Vision of the Fjords* out of Odda). Leaving from Øystese, the RIB tour gets you the closest to nature.

Hardangerfjord Adventure

Hardangerfjordvegen 613, Øystese; tel. 93 20 44 17;

https://hardangerfjord-adventure.no; Basic FjordSafari

990 kr

This company offers several tour choices, depending on the time you have available and if you have a specific focus in mind. For example, their fjord and landscape safari (900 kr; 2.5 hours) takes you to the end of Fyksesundet, an arm of the Hardangerfjord, to the village of Botnen. No roads lead here, and the only way to reach this village is by boat. On this trip you will learn a lot about life along the fjord, especially before cars came. Their 45-minute Short FjordSafari (625 kr) is perfect if you would rather zoom through the

fjord than get off the boat, and especially if you are a little short on time.

Food

Restaurant Sandven

Kaien 28, Norheimsund; tel. 56 55 20 88; www.

thonhotels.no/hoteller/norge/norheimsund/thon-hotel-

sandven; daily noon-9pm

Restaurant Sandven can be found inside the historic Thon Hotel Sandven. Here, you will enjoy your meal in a beautiful large dining room, decorated with several chandeliers and large oil paintings on the wall. The atmosphere is regal and grand, and even though it is not expected, you might feel like dressing up a little. Expect classic dishes such as chicken Caesar salad, beef tenderloin, and salmon. On Saturdays 1pm-5pm they serve afternoon tea, which has become a popular event.

Kafe Krus

Sjusetevegen 3, Øystese; tel. 45 08 52 31; Mon.-Sat.

8am-7pm; 109-249 kr

This small café in Øystese is a local favourite, serving traditional Norwegian dishes such as komle/raspeball (a Norwegian potato dumpling) and meatballs, as well as international dishes such as hamburgers and ribs. This café is popular for lunch, with open sandwiches and freshly made baguettes available for both takeaway and dining in.

Accommodations

Staying in Norheimsund is ideal for anyone wanting to visit the Hardangerfjord from Bergen, as it is just a short bus ride from the city, with several daily connections to both Øystese and back to Bergen. In Norheimsund you will find grocery stores and the area's Vinmonopol (wine store), and the historic hotel in the town center is worth visiting.

(Thon) Hotel Sandven

Kaien 28, Norheimsund; tel. 56 55 20 88; www.

thonhotels.no/hoteller/norge/norheimsund/thon-hotel-

sandven; 1,900 kr

Hotel Sandven first opened its doors in 1857 and is located right by the fjord in

Norheimsund. This is a Thon hotel, but while most of the newer rooms in the hotel have the typical Thon style of bright colors and fun wallpaper, the original section of this hotel has kept its classic style. Out of of the hotel's 102 rooms, 32 are in the original wing, and there, you can expect luxurious headboards and flowered wallpaper. In the lobby and bar area, the original wood paneling has been preserved.

Information and Services
Norheimsund Tourist Information
Tel. 56 55 31 84; https://hardangerfjord.com; Mon.-Sun. 10am-6pm

Overseen by Visit Hardangerfjord, the regional destination company, Norheimsund's visitors center along the western shore of the fjord might be your first stop if you are traveling from Bergen. They can assist you in booking tours and fjord cruises.

Getting There and Around
Bus
All bus routes in the area are operated by **Skyss** (tel. 55 55 90 70; www.skyss.no). From Bergen, Route 925 takes you to Norheimsund in 1.5 hours, with departures approximately every second hour 6:30am-9pm. A one-way ticket costs 61 kr, and the bus drops you off right in the center of Norheimsund, in front of Thon Hotel Sandven. Route 930 travels between Odda and Norheimsund. A one-way ticket with this route costs 40 kr, and the bus travels between Odda and Norheimsund up to 3 times daily (less frequently on weekends). The journey takes a little less than 1.5 hours.

Car
From Bergen, the 78-kilometer (48 mi) drive to Norheimsund along Routes 49 and 7 takes around 1.5 hours. From Voss, Norheimsund is about the same distance (75 km/46 mi) along Route 13 and then you will follow the Hardangerfjord, passing Øystese on the way. The car ride between Øystese and Norheimsund is 8 minutes (6 km/4 mi) along the fjord.

EIDFJORD
Eidfjord is a small village along the Hardangerfjord, close to Voss. Those wanting to see the Vøringfossen waterfall and visit the Hardanger Nature Center should consider Eidfjord as a day trip from either Voss (1-hour drive) or Odda (1.5-hour drive), or on the way between the two.

Sights
Hardangerbrua Bridge
Vallavik-Bu

Hardangerbrua is quite a sight. This 1,380-meter-long (4,500-ft) bridge crosses the fjord from Vallavik in Ulvik to Bu in Ullensvang. It opened in 2013, lessening the need for ferries in order to cross the fjord. It is one of the 10 longest suspension bridges in the world. On the south side of the bridge (at Bu), there is a small parking spot with toilet facilities and a viewpoint where you can admire the bridge in all its glory. There is a sidewalk along the entire bridge, so it is possible to cross on foot. The bridge is just 20 minutes from Eidfjord, and around 1 hour from Norheimsund.

Hardanger Nature Center
Sæbøtunet 11, Øvre Eidfjord; tel. 53 67 40 00; https://norsknatursenter.no; daily noon-6pm Apr.-Oct.

The Hardanger Nature Center (Norsk Natursenter) is the official visitors center for the Hardangervidda National Park, a mountain plateau found just east of the Hardanger fjord. It is a modern activity and exploration center, with three floors of displays and exhibitions focusing on Norwegian nature, climate, and environment. The exhibits—which illustrate how Norway's fjords and mountains developed over 2.9 million years into what you see today—are interactive, making this an enjoyable visit for children as well as adults.

The absolute highlight is a 225-degree panorama cinema screen, showing the spectacular movie *Fjord Fjell Foss (Fjord, Mountain, Waterfall)*. Produced by Norwegian filmmaker Ivo Caprino, it takes you on an epic journey across Hardangervidda and through

Ring of Waterfalls

If you plot the most popular waterfalls in the Hardanger region on a map, they will form a ring, starting and ending in Bergen (via Voss and Hardanger). Driving the Ring of Waterfalls route from Bergen will show you a lot of the Hardanger region. The below route can be taken in either direction (but do go in order, from 1 to 10 or 10 to 1, to avoid unnecessary driving). The total driving time is around 10 hours, so it is recommended to either start very early in the day or add an overnight stop (for example in Odda) to make it a little less strenuous.

The waterfalls can all be entered into your navigation/GPS. All of the waterfalls are beautiful, but if you can't stop at every one, be sure to stop at Vøringfossen, Låtefossen, and Steinsdalsfossen.

1. From Bergen, head to **Hesjedalsfossen** by following E16 toward Voss, and taking a little detour off Route 569 at Dale. This drive is 1 hour and 20 minutes.

2. Drive back onto E16 and continue on the 1-hour drive to Voss. Just 10 minutes past Voss you will get to **Tvindefossen.**

3. Turn back around, and when you get to Voss take Route 13, driving toward Hardanger. On the way you will get to **Skjervsfossen.**

4. Keep following Route 13, through the **Vallavik tunnel** and over the impressive Hardangerbrua Bridge. Head onto Route 7 after crossing the bridge to drive through Eidfjord and up to the beautiful **Vøringfossen** waterfall and viewpoint (page 173).

5. Head back past Eidfjord and to where you left Route 13. Continue on Route 13 along the fjord. Pass Odda and follow Route 13 until you get to **Låtefossen,** right by the side of the road (page 176).

6. Keep going along Route 13 and take a right when you get to E134. Follow it to see the stunning **Langfoss,** Norway's fifth-highest waterfall with a 612-meter (2,008-ft) descent.

7. It's time to turn around again and drive back to Odda. In the town center, take a left to continue along Route 49, and eventually Route 500 toward the beautiful village of Rosendal and the **Hattebergsfossen** waterfall.

8. Turn back around again, and on the drive back along Route 500, stop at **Furebergfossen.**

9. Take a left when you hit Route 49 again, following the road to Norheimsund and **Steinsdalsfossen,** where you can walk behind the waterfall (page 170).

10. The final waterfall is found just a little farther along the road from Norheimsund (along Route 49) and is called **Fossen Bratte.** From here, Bergen is just a 55-kilometer (35-mi) drive (1 hour).

the Hardangerfjord. The center is located a 15-minute drive along the valley from the center of Eidfjord. Bus 991 travels through Eidfjord and Øvre Eidfjord (the stop for the Nature Center) several times daily (www.skyss.no).

Vøringfossen
Eidfjord; free
Vøringfossen is perhaps Norway's most famous waterfall. The 182-meter (597-ft) fall from the Hardangervidda plateau down into Måbødalen Valley is a sight to behold, as this large waterfall (although regulated) always has massive amounts of water flooding through it.

There is a **viewpoint** built in front of Fossli Hotel (Fosslivegen 252; June-mid-Sept.). To get really close to the waterfall, you can park in a small lot by the entrance to Måbøtunellen Tunnel along Rv 7 to take the 45-minute hike along the river, starting right by the lot. The waterfall is located a 20-minute drive from central Eidfjord.

Food
Sjel og Gane
Eidfjordvegen 300, Eidfjord; tel. 93 25 73 70; 185-330 kr; daily 1pm-10pm May-Aug., reservation only in low season
For lunch in Eidfjord, head to Sjel og Gane,

located in a beautiful white house in the town center. The house (the oldest in town at 300 years) and restaurant were fully renovated in 2016. You can expect to find seasonal ingredients and house-caught seafood on the menu, as well as fresh produce from their own garden (in season). Dishes include home-smoked salmon and pan-fried halibut, moules frites, and hamburgers.

Information and Services
Eidfjord Tourist Information

Ostangvegen 23; tel. 53 67 34 00; https:// hardangerfjord.com; Mon.-Fri. 9am-4pm

Overseen by Visit Hardangerfjord, the regional destination company, this visitors center will be helpful for anyone visiting the northern part of the Hardangerfjord and planning a visit to Vøringfossen waterfall. Drop by to pick up brochures, and get driving directions and assistance in booking tours.

Getting There and Around
Bus

All routes in the area are operated by **Skyss** (tel. 55 55 90 70; www.skyss.no). Buses 990 and 991 operate along the fjord between Eidfjord and Odda (Route 990 from Odda to Bu, and then 991 from Bu to Eidfjord). The journey time takes 1.5 hours. The bus stops in the middle of the village in Eidfjord. To get to Eidfjord from Bergen, take bus Route 930 to Odda (around 3 hours), and change to 990/991 there.

Car

Eidfjord is probably easiest to visit with a car, on a day trip from Voss or Odda. Alternatively, stop in Eidfjord on the way from Oslo to the Hardanger region. From Oslo, reach Eidfjord via Route 7 (334 km/208 mi via Geilo). The journey time is 4.5-5.5 hours. From Bergen, follow E16 and Route 13 to make the 2.5-hour drive via Voss. From Voss, the drive to Eidfjord is a little less than 1 hour. There are no car rentals available in Eidfjord.

LOFTHUS

On the eastern shore of Sørfjorden, an arm of the Hardangerfjord, you will find Lofthus, between Eidfjord and Odda. Hardangerfjord is known for its many apple orchards, and you'll get a good look at them on the surrounding banks. Here, the orchards stretch all the way down to the fjord, on rolling hills and mountains.

Cider Tasting
Alvavoll Cider Farm

Oppedalsvegen 39, Lofthus; tel. 93 83 41 69; www. alvavoll.no; Mon.-Sat. 10am-6pm; 435 kr

At Alvavoll, in the center of Lofthus, you can enjoy a 90-minute local cider tasting. Tastings are available year-round, and in the summer season a walk through the orchards is included. During the tour, you will also learn about the farm's history and the culture of cider making in the Hardanger region. The tour may be canceled if too few people are booked on it, so it is recommended to book in advance (so they know you are coming).

Hiking
Dronningstien

Distance: *16 kilometers (10 mi)*
Time: *6-9 hours*
Difficulty: *Strenuous due to length*
Trailhead: *Røte, Kinsarvik*
Information and Maps: *https://hardangerfjord. com/en/attractions/hm-queen-sonjas-panoramic-hiking-trail-1038523*

Dronningstien is the shortened name for Her Majesty Queen Sonja's Panoramic Hike. It is one of the most popular hikes in Norway, and you will quickly understand why this is the queen's favorite hike. The trail takes you across the mountains along Sørfjorden, with quite spectacular views of the fjord below.

When starting at Røte, the first part of the hike takes you up to 750 meters (2,460 ft) above sea level on a gravel path. From there, the trail crosses mountains, heading toward Lofthus. The hike goes one way from

Kinsarvik to Lofthus and is well marked the whole way with blue D's (for *Dronning*, the Norwegian word for queen).

Since this is a one-way hike, you can take advantage of **Shuttlebus Hardanger's** (tel. 91 17 43 49; https://shuttlebushardanger.no) services. During the hiking season (mid-May-mid-Oct.), they run a daily shuttle between Lofthus and Kinsarvik, the two end points of the hike. There are departures in the morning, and then again in the late afternoon to match the morning hikers. Tickets to the shuttle must be booked in advance, and they can give advice on which shuttle to book. The drive time in between the two is 15-25 minutes, depending on traffic.

Kayaking and Canoeing
Hardangerfjord Active
Lutro (3km north of Lofthus); www.hardangerfjordactive.com; kayak 550 kr per day, rowboat 750 kr per day
Hardangerfjord Active has kayaks available for rent by the day. You need to have some kayaking experience to qualify for a rental. This is a truly unique way to explore the fjord and get close to nature. Paddle along the edge of the fjord to take in the scenery. Make sure that you are aware of boats if you cross the fjord. Rowboats are also available.

Food
Spisesalen Restaurant
Ullensvangvegen 865, Lofthus; tel. 53 67 00 00; www.hotel-ullensvang.no; 2,200 kr
At the main restaurant of Hotel Ullensvang, you can enjoy dishes prepared using Norwegian produce and seasonal ingredients. They regularly change out their three-course set menu, and you can expect dishes such as beet carpaccio and tenderloin of local lamb. The large restaurant seats 300 guests and offers a buffet dinner on selected nights.

Accommodations
Visitors often opt to spend a night in Lofthus at the historic Hotel Ullensvang in order to sample some of the best cider in the region, and to go hiking. Norwegians also enjoy staying for a weekend at this large spa hotel, coupled with hiking Dronningstien.

Hotel Ullensvang
Ullensvangvegen 865, Lofthus; tel. 53 67 00 00; www.hotel-ullensvang.no; 2,200 kr
Dating back to 1846, Hotel Ullensvang is a large resort hotel along the Hardangerfjord. The hotel has 170 rooms, each with a great view of either the fjord or the orchards stretching toward the mountain behind it. Most of the rooms have a balcony, and all are wheelchair-accessible. Rooms are plainly decorated, with blue, beige, and deep red accents. The hotel has a tennis court, and an indoor and an outdoor pool, with free access to the pools and sauna for staying guests.

Getting There and Around
Boat
The **Fjord Cruise Hardangerfjord** (tel. 57 63 14 00; www.norwaysbest.com/no/ting-a-gjore/fjorder/fjord-cruise-hardanger; daily departures June-Sept.; 540 kr round-trip) doubles as a mode of transportation, connecting Odda and Lofthus three times a day (1.5 hours). The return ticket allows you to hop on and off as you please for one day. It also stops in Tyssedal, Nå, Børve, and Aga.

Bus
All routes in the area are operated by **Skyss** (tel. 55 55 90 70; www.skyss.no). The bus between Odda and Eidfjord (990/991) stops at Lofthus.

Car
Lofthus is located between Eidfjord and Odda and is about a 40-minute drive from either, along Route 13. If you are traveling from Bergen, the total drive time is around 2 hours and 45 minutes via Voss (following E16 and Route 13). Those visiting Norheimsund first can reach Odda in 1.5 hours. There is no car rental in Lofthus.

ODDA

Odda is first and foremost the chosen overnight stop for those hiking Trolltunga. As one of the larger towns in Hardanger (but still with only 5,000 inhabitants), it is a natural place to stay if you are traveling between one area of the Hardangerfjord, such as Norheimsund and Øystese on the western side, and the inner areas of Lofthus and Eidfjord. It is a convenient place to stop, as you will find grocery stores and gas/charging stations here. Odda is also a great place to get information about the Folgefonna Glacier and National Park, due to its close proximity to the glacier.

Sights
Låtefossen

Låtefossbrua; free

Låtefossen is a twin waterfall (meaning there are two waterfalls close enough to have been given one name) with a 165-meter (541-ft) drop. It is conveniently located right by the main road, and when you drive across the stone bridge spanning the river below the waterfall, your car will get a nice wash during snow-melting time (Apr.-July). The waterfalls are illuminated in the evenings, which makes for a fairy-tale atmosphere. The bridge was completed in 1859 and expanded in 1940. There is a pull-off point right by the bridge where you can stop to walk closer to the waterfall.

Fjord Cruises

If you want to explore the fjord at a leisurely pace, opt for the **Fjord Cruise Hardangerfjord** (tel. 57 63 14 00; www.norwaysbest.com/no/ting-a-gjore/fjorder/fjord-cruise-hardanger; daily departures June-Sept.; 540 kr round-trip). The cruise departs Odda 2-3 times a day and travels to Lofthus making stops along the way. The first departure from Odda is usually around noon, and the last arrival back is at 5:15pm, leaving just a handful of hours to go cider tasting if Odda is your base. For a leisurely fjord cruise through the Sørfjorden arm

of the Hardanger fjord, however, this is perfect.

The total journey time from Odda to Lofthus is 1.5 hours, with stops in Tyssedal, Nå, Børve, and Aga. The vessel used is called *Vision of the Fjords*, the first ever hybrid vessel of its kind, making this a more environmentally friendly option than some other boats. Onboard there are toilets and a small café where you can get snacks (and even cider). The vessel was built for ultimate views, so wherever you are on the boat, you'll see the beautiful landscape. You can even walk outside on the roof.

Hiking

TOP EXPERIENCE

Trolltunga

Distance: *20 kilometers (12.5 mi)*
Time: *7-10 hours round-trip*
Difficulty: *Strenuous*
Trailhead: *P3 Mågelitopp, 13 kilometers (8 mi) from Odda*
Information and Maps: *https://hardangerfjord.com/en/attractions/trolltunga-958013*

The hike to Trolltunga, along with Pulpit Rock, is probably the most famous hike in Norway. The flat rock formation at 1,180 meters (3,870 ft) above sea leavel is a popular photo op as it stretches out around 700 meters (2,300 ft) above Ringedalsvatnet lake. The hike is considered extra demanding, and only experienced hikers in good shape should attempt it. As it is a long hike, an early start is recommended.

The trail is clearly marked the whole way, with signs telling you how far you have left to walk. However, you should not attempt the hike on your own unless you are confident in your abilities. You can also join a guided hike led by **Trolltunga Active** (tel. 99 11 21 21; www.trolltunga-active.com). The season for hiking Trolltunga is June (after the snow has melted) to September. Hikes during off season should only be attempted with a guide.

The trailhead is around 13 kilometers

(8 mi) from Odda. Take Route 13 north to Tyssedal, and then follow the signs toward Skjeggedal. There are three sets of parking spaces and starting points for the hike, P1 (the longest), P2, and P3 (the shortest). During the season, there is a public shuttle taking you up to the Trolltunga Active Base, leaving from the Trolltunga Hotel just down the road.

Given the length of the Trolltunga hike, a lot of people opt to camp at the top before heading back down. Due to Norway's freedom/right to roam, you can set up camp anywhere at the top.

Food
Smeltehuset
Almerket 23, Odda; tel. 45 90 88 33; www.smeltehuset. no; daily noon-9pm; 264-339 Kr

Smeltehuset is located along the docks of Odda. This charming little restaurant and café serves a a variety of casual dishes, from their hamburger with jalapeños and manchego cheese sauce to American- and Italian-style pizzas. Their outdoor seating, recognizable by its big orange umbrella, is popular with both locals and travelers in the summer season. Indoors you will find that the interior reminds you more of a diner than a restaurant, with a glass display of sandwiches next to the bar and a screen advertising the specials.

Fjoren
Røldalsvegen 29, Odda; tel. 97 33 57 90; www.fjoren. no; Wed.-Sat. 5pm-10pm; 265-445 kr

Fjoren is the only fine dining establishment in town, offering 3- or 5-course set menus with matching wine pairings, in addition to an a la carte menu. This is a small and intimate restaurant, with only 32 indoor seats (and 24 outside), so booking in advance is recommended. Their menu changes frequently, but local meat and fish can usually be expected, such as entrecote, tempura, and lamb.

Trolltunga Lille Bakeri
Eitrheimsvegen 32, Odda; tel. 53 64 44 33; www. trolltungalillebakeri.no; Mon.-Wed. 9am-4pm, Thurs.- Fri. 9am-5pm, Sat. 9am-4pm; 35-75 kr

The local bakery, with its charming name "Trolltunga Small Bakery," is the ideal place to drop by for breakfast or stock up on baked goods for your Trolltunga hike. They bake daily, so you can always expect fresh bread, pastries, and snacks, such as the Norwegian kanelsnurr (cinnamon twist), homemade ciabatta with cheese and ham, or even hand-tossed salads.

atop Trolltunga

Accommodations

The main reason people stay in Odda is to hike Trolltunga, but for some travelers it is also a convenient stopover, as it is located at the end of the fjord where three roads meet: Route 13 from Lofthus, Eidfjord, and Voss, which also continues east; and Route 550/55, which takes you toward Norheimsund and Bergen. There are only two hotels in town, mostly aimed at hikers.

Trolltunga Hotel

Vasstun 1, Odda; tel. 40 00 44 86; www. trolltungahotel.no; 1,700 kr

Trolltunga Hotel is where most people opt to stay before hiking Trolltunga. The hotel offers a daily shuttle bus to and from the starting point of the hike, and even has a rental service for outdoor/hiking clothes. The hotel building dates from 1928 but went through a complete refurbishment in 2017. The newest rooms are from 2021. Rooms are basic, with modern furnishings and little "fluff." This is first and foremost an overnight stay before heading out on a long day of activities the next day. Not all rooms have en suite bathrooms. Trolltunga Hotel is closed in the winter months.

Hardanger Hotel

Etrheimsvegen 13, Odda; tel. 53 64 64 64; www. hardangerhotel.no; 1,700 kr

Hardanger Hotel offers 50 rooms for travelers staying in Odda, right in the town center. They have single and double rooms, and all are simply furnished with the amenities you need for a good night's sleep. Breakfast in their on-site restaurant is included. The staff are knowledgeable about the Trolltunga hike and can give you any advice you may need.

Information and Services
Odda Tourist Information

Torget 2; tel. 48 07 07 77; https://hardangerfjord.com; Mon.-Sun. 9am-7pm mid-June-Aug., Mon.-Fri. 9am-4pm Apr. and Sept., Mon.-Fri. 9am-3pm Sept.-May

The staff here can assist you with questions about the Hardanger region and the Folgefonna National Park. They are also knowledgeable about hiking Trolltunga, since Odda is the closest town to the hike. This center is overseen by Visit Hardangerfjord, the regional destination company.

Getting There and Around
Boat

The **Fjord Cruise Hardangerfjord** (tel. 57 63 14 00; www.norwaysbest.com/no/ting-a-gjore/fjorder/fjord-cruise-hardanger; daily departures June-Sept.; 540 kr return) is not just a great way to see the beautiful fjord landscape, but also it doubles as a mode of transportation. So, if you want to get around the villages and explore the region in a day, get a return ticket (valid all day) and hop on and off as you please. There are six stops in total along the cruise: Odda, Tyssedal, Nå, Børve, Aga, and Lofthus.

Bus

All routes in the area are operated by **Skyss** (tel. 55 55 90 70; www.skyss.no). From Voss, Route 990 takes you to Odda in 2 hours, also with departures every 2 hours between 9am and 6pm. The **Odda Bus station** (Almerket 8) is located by the fjord, right in the center of town. Bus 990/991 operates along the fjord between Eidfjord and Odda, while Route 930 travels between Odda and Norheimsund. The price to travel one way in the Hardanger region is 40 kr. The journey to both Norheimsund and Eidfjord takes 1.5 hours, with up to three daily departures.

Car

From Voss to Odda, the drive along Route 13 (over the Hardanger Bridge) is 93 kilometers (58 mi) and will take you around 1.5 hours. From Bergen, you drive via Norheimsund in less than 3 hours (135 km/84 mi), and from Oslo the total drive time is 5.5 hours along E134 (346 km/215 mi). The drive between Odda and Lofthus is 40 minutes.

If you need to rent a car in Odda, there is a **Hertz (Partner)** (Smelteverkstomta; tel. 53 65 04 10; www.hertz.no/p/leiebil/norge/odda; Mon.-Fri. 8am-4pm).

★ FOLGEFONNA NATIONAL PARK

Ullensvang, Etne, and Kvinnherad; https://folgefonna.
info

Established in 2005, Folgefonna National Park is one of 42 national parks in Norway. The core of the park is the Folgefonna Glacier, Norway's third-largest and southernmost glacier. The national park offers a varying Norwegian landscape, from lush valleys with green glacial rivers around the edges, to (mainly) bared mountains and expansive arctic vistas of the glacier. There are lots of activities available in and around the national park, such as hiking, glacier walking, ice climbing, and skiing. However, you should only head out onto the ice with a qualified guide and proper gear.

Folgefonna is not a park you should explore on your own; you should join a tour or have a guide with you. You can also stay around the edges of the park, which will allow you to explore the beautiful fjord villages nestled around it—no guide needed. The towns of Rosendal and Jondal are ideal for this, but Odda can also be a base for your national park adventure.

Orientation

Folgefonna National Park is large, and there are several access points where you can start exploring. In each of these places you can also get information about the park and nearby activities. The most popular is the **Folgefonna Center** (Skålafjæro 17, Rosendal). Other access points include **Odda Tourist Information** (Torget 2), at the end of Sørfjorden; the **Juklafjord** visitors center (Jonavegen 20) in **Jondal National Park Village,** just 19 kilometers (12 mi) west of the national park; and **Agatunet** (Aga 104; tel. 47 47 99 02), the northeastern access point to the park.

Folgefonna Glacier

Folgefonna Glacier is the third-largest glacier in Norway, consisting of three larger glacier levels (Nordfonna, Midtfonna, and Sørfonna). In total, these three make up Folgefonna and cover an area of 207 square kilometers (129 sq mi). Of course, you won't be able to see the entire glacier unless you are in a helicopter or airplane, but it is possible to see one of the "glacial tongues" or outflow arms, the spots where the glacier stretches from the mountain plateau above and down into the valleys

Bondhusvatnet Lake in Folgefonna National Park

toward the fjord. The two outflow arms that are easiest to reach for visitors are **Buarbreen** and **Bondhusbreen.**

Buarbreen and Bondhusbreen can both be reached on a hike. For the former, staying in Jondal is the best place to base yourself. For the latter, pair your hike with a stay in **Rosendal** and include a visit to the beautiful stately home Baroniet Rosendal (see below). The access point to the hike is a 40-minute drive.

It is not possible to explore the rest of the glacier yourself, but you can do so on a blue ice tour with a guide.

Glacier Tours
Folgefonni Breførerlag
Jonavegen 20, Jondal; tel. 95 11 77 92; www.folgefonni. no; daily tours June-Oct.; 1,040 kr

Folgefonni Breførerlag are specialists when it comes to glacier hiking. Their guided blue ice hike starts at Fonna Glacier Ski Resort and takes you across Juklavassbreen, one of the most accessible parts of Folgefonna glacier. The guides will adapt the tour according to your experience and fitness level, and the trip includes both flat, easy terrain, and more demanding areas with crevasses. Along the way, the guides will share information about the area, and its history and culture. The tour takes 5-6 hours total and includes a lunch break with great views of the mountains and the North Sea. You need a car to be able to get to the Fonna Glacier Ski Resort to meet the team.

Baroniet Rosendal
Baronivegen 50, Rosendal; tel. 53 48 29 99; www. baroniet.no; tours hourly 11am-4pm, Tues.-Sun. May-Aug.; adults 190 kr, children 50 kr

Baroniet Rosendal is a stately home dating back to 1665. The grand house may not seem much like a typical castle from the outside (it is a large, white, and square), but inside you will see what Baroniet would have looked like through the ages, from 1665 until the last owners left it in 1927. Statthaldarkammeret, one of the rooms in the castle, is the only fully

preserved room from the 1600s in Norway. In the main hall of the building, called Riddersalen, concerts are held regularly, featuring performers such as Minor Majority, Susanne Sundfør, and Vamp. On the walls, you will find original paintings by Norwegian artists such as H. F. Gude, A. Askevold, and J. C. Dahl. In addition, the 300-year-old gardens are absolutely beautiful in the summer, with lots of roses and an herb garden. Baroniet Rosendal, and the village of Rosendal, is located outside of the national park. Bondhus, where you may start the Bondhusvatnet hike to see the glacier outflow, is a 40-minute drive away.

Hiking
Bondhusvatnet
Distance: *4.6 kilometers (2.8 mi)*
Time: *2 hours round-trip*
Difficulty: *Moderate*
Trailhead: *Sunndal*
Information and Maps: *https://hardangerfjord. com/en/attractions/lake-bondhusvatnet-5175833*

Bondhusvatnet is a glacier lake near Bondhusbreen glacier arm. The picturesque lake with its surrounding peaks can be reached after a relatively easy 2.3-kilometer (1.4-mi) hike along a mostly gravel road. Along the way you will climb from 60 to 190 meters (195 to 625 ft) above sea level. As the hike takes 2 hours round-trip, I recommend bringing some snacks to enjoy by the lake as you take in the scenery.

The gravel road up to the lake has an interesting history. It was built in 1863 by ship owner Johan Martin Dahl, with the goal of transporting ice for sale from Bondhusbreen (before the refrigerator was invented, ice was used to keep food cold). They rowed the ice across Bondhusvatnet Lake and then transported it by horse and carriage down the gravel road—aptly named Isvegen (the Ice Road). The ice was taken all the way down to the docks in Sunndal and loaded onto ships. Unfortunately, this whole ordeal was slow, and too much of the ice melted by the time they reached the ships. Additionally, the ice would melt during the crossings and in turn affect the balance of the boat. So, while "the Ice Road" failed at its purpose, it is now a popular road for hikers and tourists.

From Rosendal, follow Route 551 along the fjord to Bondhus. It is best to have a car for this, so you can take your time with the hike and at the lake, and not be reliant on bus schedules. However, if you are traveling by bus (www.skyss.no), Route 760 travels between Rosendal dock and Bondhus in 30 minutes, with six daily departures on weekdays (four on weekends). The bus stop in Bondhus is called Leite.

Buarbreen

Distance: 2.4 kilometers (1.5 mi) each way
Time: 1.5 hour one-way
Difficulty: Strenuous
Trailhead: Buer Farm (20-minute drive from Odda)
Information and Maps: https://ut.no/turforslag/1114635/buarbreen-folgefonna-nasjonalpark

The hike to see the Buarbreen glacial tongue is beautiful, with lush scenery all around as you follow the glacial river up the valley to the outflow arm (tongue). The incline on this hike gains 436 meters (1,430 ft) of elevation, making it rather strenuous in such a short distance. You will start by the Buer Farm and follow a farm trail on a slight incline. The trail is well marked, but even if you lose the markings (red T's), you know that you are headed upward through the valley.

During the hike, you will cross a hanging bridge over the glacial river, giving you views of the glacier ahead of you and the valley behind you. The trail gets steeper as you go, and toward the end there are ropes along the mountain walls that you can use for support as you climb some of the rocky parts. It is recommended to use these, even if you feel like you don't need to. If you linger at the end, to have lunch for example, you may be lucky enough to see parts of the glacial arms fall into the lake, especially on warm days.

Skiing
Fonna Glacier Ski Resort
5629 Jondal; tel. 94 10 00 00; www.folgefonn.no; daily in summer

Fonna is located on the Folgefonna glacier at 1,200 meters (3,930 ft) above sea level and is one of the leading summer ski resorts in Europe. And yes, you actually ski on the glacier. If you want to ski during your trip to Hardanger, you'll be excited to find that they have three downhill slopes and one cross-country trail at the resort. The ski lift takes you up to 1,470 meters (4,820 ft) above sea level, and from the top you can enjoy panoramic views of the glacier, Hardangerfjord, and the North Sea. The season is usually May-September. The ski resort is about a 25-minute drive from Jondal.

Food and Accommodations

There is only one restaurant inside the actual national park, located at the Fonna Glacier Ski Resort. There are also few hotels in this rural region, so those looking to stay close to the glacier should book as early as possible (or they might prefer staying in Odda or even Lofthus). Odda is just a 20-minute drive from the trailhead to Buarbreen, so this hike could be paired with a hike to Trolltunga during your stay there (though not on the same day).

The area around Jondal is a good home base for seeing the glacier, as both the ski resort and blue ice hike are a short drive from there. Additionally, Rosendal is a good spot for those wanting to hike along Bondhusvatnet.

Fonna1199
5629 Jondal; tel. 94 10 00 00; www.fonna1199.no; daily 9am-6pm in summer; 149-239 kr

Fonna1199 is the restaurant at Fonna Glacier Ski Resort, and the only spot to grab lunch during your day of skiing. However, it is also worth visiting for a meal if you are staying nearby, for their unique location at 1,199 meters (3,933 ft) above sea level. The restaurant is warm and cozy, giving off a chalet-style vibe, and on the menu, you will find a large selection of international and local dishes, ranging from sandwiches to a hearty stew.

Rosendal Fjordhotel & Restaurant

Rosendalsvegen 46, Rosendal; 53 48 80 00; www. rosendal-fjordhotel.no; 2,300 kr

Located right by the fjord in Rosendal, Rosendal Fjordhotel is a charming home-away-from-home in Hardanger. It's just a short walk from Baroniet Rosendal, and a 30-minute drive or bus ride from Bondhus and the Bondhusvatnet hike. The hotel has a total of 94 rooms, and it is possible to request a fjord view (at a cost). The rooms are classic and Nordic, with light wood details and a splash of color.

The hotel's restaurant seats up to 260 guests with a lovely view of the Hardanger fjord. They cook Nordic and international dishes using local ingredients, and on their a la carte menu you can expect dishes such as entrecote, lamb, and chicken salad.

Hardanger House (Hotel and Restaurant)

Nordbøen 6, Jondal; tel. 40 43 34 01; www. hardangerhouse.no; 3,300 kr

The unique design of this hotel will catch your eye the second you arrive. The modern building stands out from the charming wooden houses of the village, and each of its (only) 9 rooms is individually furnished with hand-selected objects and modern furniture.

The on-site restaurant serves a gourmet dinner using local produce, aiming to give you the perfect taste of Hardanger. The restaurant works with local farms when it comes to both food and drink, and you can expect great value from their three-course menu (695 kr per person). They also have a large selection of wine and local cider. The intimate restaurant at Hardanger House seats 40 people.

Information and Services

The closest towns and villages to the national park are Odda, Rosendal, and Jondal.

In addition to Folgefonna Center, there are several places to get information about the park and the nearby activities, such as **Odda Tourist Information** (Torget 2), at the end of Sørfjorden; the **Juklafjord** visitors center (Jonavegen 20) in **Jondal National Park Village,** located just 19 kilometers (12 mi) west of the national park; and **Agatunet** (Aga 104; tel. 47 47 99 02), which is the northeastern access point to the park.

Folgefonna Center (Folgefonnsenteret)

Skålafjæro 17, Rosendal; tel. 53 48 42 80; https:// folgefonna.info; daily 10am-6pm May-Sept., Mon.-Fri. 10:30am-2:30pm, Sat.-Sun. 12:30pm-4:30pm Sept. and Apr.-May, Mon.-Fri. 10:30am-2:30pm Oct.-Mar.

Before heading out to discover Folgefonna, learning more about the park and its surroundings is recommended. At Folgefonnsenteret you can learn more about the biodiversity of the park, and about how the glacier has developed (and retreated) through time. The topics covered in the exhibits here include information about the villages surrounding Folgefonna and what life is like there, the importance of water and how it travels around the earth, and the geology of the national park. The Folgefonna Center is one of the access points to the national park, and a great place to get information before you venture into the wilderness.

Getting There and Around

There are no formal entrances to the park. The two main tongues of the glacier that can be accessed from "fjord level" are Buarbreen and Bondhusbreen, located close to Odda and Rosendal, respectively. If you aim to go skiing at the Glacier Ski Resort, Jondal is your best access point.

Boat

The only way to reach Hardanger by boat is to travel on **Hardangerfjordekspressen** (tel. 51 89 52 70; https://rodne.no; 2 daily departures summer, 2 daily departures Mon.-Fri., 1 daily Sat.-Sun. winter; 633 kr). The boat leaves from **Strandkaiterminalen** in Bergen, and travels to Rosendal in Hardanger, on the west side of Folgefonna National Park. This mode of transportation is perfect for those who want to hike to Bondhusvatnet Lake, and to explore Baroniet Rosendal. The boat from Bergen to Hardanger takes 2 hours. The Rosendal dock is right in the center of the village. It is not a car ferry.

Bus
From Rosendal, there is a bus to Odda meant to correspond with the boat. It is organized by **Skyss** (tel. 55 55 90 70; www.skyss.no) and takes you to Odda in around 50 minutes. If you are visiting Jondal, Route 930 from Bergen will take you to Jondal in 2 hours and 15 minutes.

Car
Although it is possible to visit the villages around the glacier on public transportation, it is easiest to explore the area by car. If you want to ski or hike, it is preferable not to be dependent on bus schedules, and with the heavy traffic on these narrow roads in the summer months, it is easier to calculate time for delays when driving on your own.

From Bergen to Jondal, the 95-kilometer (59-mi) drive will take you just over 2 hours, traveling via Norheimsund and including a ferry between Tørvikbygd and Jondal (www.fjord1.no). Rosendal is a 2.5-hour drive (119 km/74 mi), also including a ferry (between Gjermundshavn and Årsnes). There is a gas station in both Jondal and near Rosendal (in Dimmelsvik, a 5-minute drive from Rosendal).

Voss

Voss, just a 1.5-hour drive from Bergen, is the last large town before you reach the inner Sognefjord and the Aurlandsfjord, and the Nærøyfjord is less than an hour away. Though it is not necessary to stop there when heading to the fjords, it is the perfect destination for adrenaline junkies and adventure sports lovers. Known as the Extreme Sports Capital of Norway, Voss is a haven for skydiving, BASE jumping, river rafting, and paragliding.

However, not all of the activities here are terrifying; you can also enjoy hiking, kayaking, and SUP, and the (perhaps safer) indoor skydive center lets you feel weightless without jumping out of a plane. The Voss Gondol cable car opened in 2019, making the many hikes and pathways of Mount Hangur more accessible than ever. Throw in a historic hotel located right by the railroad tracks, and Voss becomes a great destination for a short stay and some hiking in Norwegian nature.

SIGHTS
★ Voss Gondol
Evangervegen 5; tel. 47 00 47 00; www.vossresort.no; daily 10am-8pm; return ticket 425 kr, 2-day pass 875 kr
Northern Europe's largest gondola, Voss Gondol, opened in 2019. This gondola takes you from the center of Voss to the top of Mount Hanguren, traveling from 0 to 818 meters (2,680 ft) above sea level in just 9 minutes. The journey up is breathtaking, and you will find lots of hiking opportunities and a restaurant at the top. If you are planning on traveling with the gondola over a couple of days (perhaps for dinner one evening and hiking the next day), the best value is to get the two-day pass.

SPORTS AND RECREATION
One of the biggest reasons people visit Voss is for the easy access to recreational and outdoor activities.

Hiking

Hiking is a beloved activity in Voss, and several hikes are within easy reach of the town. Most of these are reached by traveling up to Mount Hanguren with the gondola and starting your hike there. There is a selection of trails and hikes available, suitable for various skill levels.

Hanguren Panorama Trail

Distance: *1 kilometer (0.6 mi)*
Time: *30 minutes*
Difficulty: *Easy*
Trailhead: *Mount Hanguren Gondola Station*
Information and Maps: *www.vossresort.no/opplev/fotturar*

At the top of Mount Hanguren you can follow the Hanguren Panorama Trail that goes in a loop at the top of the mountain. The trail follows a well-kept gravel path and is wheelchair- and stroller-accessible. On this hike, you will get a panoramic view of the town of Voss and mountains surrounding it. It is perfect as an easy stroll before dinner.

Grebbeløypa

Distance: *3.2 kilometers (2 mi)*
Time: *1.5 hour*
Difficulty: *Moderate*
Trailhead: *Mount Hanguren Gondola Station*
Information and Maps: *www.vossresort.no/opplev/fotturar*

Grebbeløypa is another loop but is a little longer and slightly more strenuous than the panoramic trail. Also located at Mount Hanguren, it starts in the same spot, heading the opposite direction. The hike follows a well-marked trail, and there is elevation gain. However, it is still a nice hike that won't leave you too exhausted. You'll be walking through the mountainous terrain, passing mountain lakes, rocky areas, and mountain farms, getting scenic views of the surrounding mountaintops. If you bring your swimming clothes, a swim in one of the lakes is refreshing on a hot day. The trail is narrow and uneven, so good shoes are essential, and this hike offers a great sample of typical Norwegian mountain terrain.

Lønahorgi

Distance: *16 kilometers (10 mi)*
Time: *6-8 hours*
Difficulty: *Strenuous*
Trailhead: *Mount Hanguren Gondola Station*
Information and Maps: *www.vossresort.no/opplev/fotturar*

For those wanting a more strenuous hike,

view from the Voss Gondol

Lønahorgi is a good one. The trail starts at Mount Hanguren, and there are signs and red T's marking the trail the whole way. This hiking trail first goes to a Red Cross cabin in the mountains, and then crosses the path of the ski lift on Slettafjellet mountain. Eventually, you will follow the mountain ridge toward a place called Horgaletten, before heading to Lønahorgi via another cabin (Kvilehytta). During this part of the hike, you will ascend around 800 meters (2,600 ft), so make sure to pack enough water.

Lønahorgi mountain peak is at 1,410 meters (4,620 ft) above sea level and offers spectacular views of the mountain ranges. On a clear day, you can see up to four glaciers from the peak: Fresvikbreen, Hardangerjøkulen, Vossaskavlen, and Folgefonna.

Skiing

Skiing has been a popular activity in Voss for decades, and people travel from all over western Norway to go skiing at one of their two main ski resorts: Myrkdalen and Voss Resort.

Myrkdalen Resort

Klypeteigane; tel. 47 47 16 00; www.myrkdalen.no; ski season mid-Nov.-May; day pass 485 kr

Myrkdalen Resort has a large selection of downhill ski slopes and cross-country ski trails around their hotel and cabin complex. The cross-country trails are suitable for all types of skiers, and their main trail, Lysløypa, is lit in the evenings, so you can keep skiing even after dark. Downhill skiers will find 22 slopes with varying difficulty, so there is something for everyone here. The resort is located in the Myrkdalen valley, approximately half an hour from Voss (32 km/20 mi). They have a free shuttle bus taking you from the Voss train station to Myrkdalen, perfect for those traveling by train from Oslo or Bergen. At the resort you can also rent skis and equipment.

Voss Resort

Bavallsvegen 227; tel. 47 00 47 00; www.vossresort.no; ski season Nov.-Apr.; day pass 565 kr

Voss Resort in the center of Voss offers 24 downhill slopes and over 20 kilometers (13 mi) of cross-country trails. Included in the ticket price is traveling with the gondola, which also takes you to the top of the ski center where you will find most of the cross-country trails. Their slopes are varied, so anyone can find a suitable downhill ski slope. This resort hosted the World Cup in 1970, and their slope Utforløypa is one of Norway's longest at 3.6 kilometers (2.2 mi).

Climbing

There are a few options for climbing in Voss, whether you want to try your hand at outdoor rock climbing or just have a great day outdoors.

Wild Voss Climbing Experience

Skjerpestunet 5; tel. 93 48 40 41; www.wildvoss.no/ klatreoppleving; daily late May-late Oct.; 1,790 kr

The Wild Voss Climbing Experience is perfect for first-time climbers or those who are more experienced. Here, you can try climbing in a safe environment or challenge yourself at a rock wall that is 30 meters (100 ft) high. You will also get to try your hand at rappelling during this experience. This is a full-day activity, starting at 9:30am and returning to Voss by 4pm. However, if the group is on the smaller side, the experience might take less time, as activities are adapted to the individuals in each group.

Voss Active High Rope & Zipline Park

Vossestrandvegen; tel. 56 51 05 25; www.vossactive.no/ high-rope-zipline-park; daily 10am-3pm (last check-in) mid-June-Aug., weekends 10am-3pm (last check-in) May-mid-Oct.; 796 kr

This outdoor climbing park and zipline park is a fun day for the whole family. You will spend the day climbing around their tree-top course, and zooming through the forest and across rivers in their zipline park. They have seven different ziplines and 27 different obstacles/elements in their climbing course. The longest zipline is 160 meters (520 ft) long.

Extreme Sports

As Voss is the Extreme Sports Capital of Norway, it is no surprise that there are a few high-octane options here. Whether you want to try your hand at skydiving (indoors or outdoors) or white-water rafting, or perhaps feel the thrill of the indoor wind tube at VossVind, there's something exciting for you here.

VossVind Indoor Skydiving

Oberst Bulls Veg 28; tel. 40 10 59 99; https://vossvind. no; Tues.-Sat. noon-8pm, Sun. noon-6pm; 4 flights 1,399 kr

At VossVind Indoor Skydiving, you can soar inside their wind tunnel, and it is a great introduction to skydiving. Their flights last 1.5 minutes—the equivalent of two skydive jumps from 3,660 meters (12,000 ft).

Skydive Voss

Flyplassvegen 135; tel. 56 51 10 00; www.skydivevoss. no; daily Apr.-Sept.; 4,890 kr per jump

For the real deal, Skydive Voss offers tandem jumps with their experienced skydivers in the summer half of the year. The free fall during the jump lasts for around 45 seconds, and the Skydive Voss team will have one of their members join you to film your entire experience. The total jump time is 5-7 minutes, and it is truly exhilarating.

Voss Hangliding and Paragliding

Flyplassvegen 135; www.vosshpk.no; hours vary; 2,400 kr per flight

If you want a slower pace as you fly through the air, paragliding might be for you. At Voss Hangliding and Paragliding Club you can join them for a tandem paragliding experience. An experienced paraglider will take you along in a tandem paraglider with room for two, and you can even try steering a little during the flight. The flights are mainly from Mount Hanguren, and you take the gondola up to the top (not included in the flight price). You can even take photos during the flight, so pack your camera!

Voss Active

Nedkvitnesvegen 25; tel. 56 51 05 25; www.vossactive. no; 2 daily departures at 9:30am and 2:30pm May-mid-Oct.; Class 4 1,390 kr per person, Class 2 790 kr per person

If water sports are more your jam, you'll be happy to find that Voss Active offers white-water rafting on the Stranda or Raundal Rivers in Voss (depending on the water levels in the rivers). The rafting is classified as Class 4, which means it will be quite action-packed. The rafting experience has a medium difficulty and lasts around 4 hours, with 1.5-2 hours being on the river. They also offer a Class 2 family rafting experience (790 kr per person).

FESTIVALS AND EVENTS

Ekstremsportveko

www.ekstremsportveko.com; June-July

The establishment of Ekstremsportveko (Extreme Sports Week) is one of the reasons Voss is known as Norway's capital for extreme sports. Every summer, people from all over Norway and the world gather in Voss to get their adrenaline pumping (and to watch others do it). It is a great time to visit Voss, as there is lots happening all around the town (and in the surrounding areas). From long boarding and skateboarding to BMX and speed flying, there are events to catch wherever you go.

In addition to being a gathering place for athletes and extreme sports enthusiasts, Ekstremsportveko is also a music festival. Throughout the week, (mainly Norwegian) artists put on performances, and past names have included Kjartan Lauritzen, Turbonegro, and Sidebrok.

FOOD

★ Nuten Fondue

Klypeteigane; tel. 47 47 16 00; www.myrkdalen.no/nb/ mat-og-drikke/restauranter/restaurant-nuten-fondue; daily 6pm-10pm; 435 kr set price for meat and cheese fondue

Nuten Fondue is the fondue restaurant at

Myrkdalen Resort. For a set price, you get a selection of meats, bread, potatoes, vegetables, and fruits, along with a cheese and meat (oil) fondue. The fondue restaurant is in a smaller side room from the Nuten main restaurant, with mirrors with gold details on the walls and warm red accent colors. The atmosphere is warm and cozy, as if you have just come in for a day of skiing, and less loud than in the main dining room. They share a wine list with the Nuten Restaurant, and the selection is great.

Hangurstoppen Restaurant

Hangurstoppen; tel. 47 00 47 00; www.vossresort. no/restaurant/hangurstoppen-restaurant; Sun.-Thurs. 10am-4pm, Fri. 10am-9pm, Sat. 10am-8pm; 149-269 kr

At the top of Voss Gondol, at 818 meters (2,680 ft) above sea level, you will find Hangurstoppen Restaurant. This restaurant covers two floors and has large windows offering great views of the mountains outside. The menu is seasonal and based on fresh (and available) ingredients and Norwegian produce. Expect dishes such as beef hamburgers, Norwegian salmon, and tomato soup with homemade bread. The interior reminds you of a mountain cabin, creating a warm and welcoming atmosphere.

Venezia Pizza

Vangsgata 10, Voss; tel. 56 51 82 51; daily 10am-11pm; 199-299 kr

This pizza restaurant near Voss station serves authentic Italian pizza and other international dishes, such as hamburgers and kebabs. Their pizza menu is the preference of most visitors, however, and they have most classic varieties such as pizza Margherita and calzones. The atmosphere at this small restaurant is informal, and you'll often find local youth hanging out here.

Haik Grill og Bar

Evangervegen 1a; tel. 56 52 82 01; www.scandichotels. com; 259-395 kr

Haik is located in the new Scandic Voss hotel and is a modern restaurant with a welcoming atmosphere. The dishes focus on Norwegian traditions and local produce, including reindeer and leg of lamb, as well as halibut from Glitne (along the Sognefjord). The interior here is Nordic and warm, with bare concrete floors and bar furniture, and red details.

ACCOMMODATIONS

Voss is a small town, so most of the limited accommodation options are within walking distance of each other and the train station. The only exception is Myrkdalen Hotel, which is a part of Myrkdalen Resort, 30-40 minutes from Voss.

Fleischer's Hotel

Evangervegen 13; tel. 56 52 05 00; www.fleischers.no; 2,000 kr

Fleischer's is the large, Swiss-style wooden building located along the train tracks of Voss station. It was completed in 1889 and has been welcoming guests ever since. Historically, it was favored by wealthier travelers, but today its guests are travelers with all kinds of budgets. The 110 rooms in the hotel are traditionally decorated with historic elegance, featuring dark red carpeted floors and wooden headboards. For guests, use of the large indoor pool and spa facilities is included in the room rate.

Scandic Voss

Evangervegen 1A; tel. 56 52 82 00; www.visitvoss.no/ scandic-voss; 2,000 kr

This new and modern hotel opened the doors to its 215 rooms in 2020. The rooms are simple, with light wood and little detail, similar to other Scandic hotels found around Norway. The hotel restaurant, Haik, has outdoor seating in the summer months. There is a modern gym and sauna at the hotel, and the hotel bar has games such as chess and shuffleboard.

Myrkdalen Hotel

Klypeteigane; tel. 47 47 16 00; www.myrkdalen.no/nb/ myrkdalen-hotel; 2,300 kr

Myrkdalen Hotel is the hotel at Myrkdalen Resort, and usually the main option for those visiting the area to go skiing. The 112 rooms at the hotel are basic, with simple furnishings. If you are lucky, you will get a slope-facing room so you can watch the skiers zoom down the hills. The hotel restaurant Nuten serves a great breakfast and even better dinner (the tenderloin steak is not to be missed), and they also have a fondue restaurant on-site. This large hotel is busy on weekends in the winter, and their after-ski bar starts to fill up with staying (and visiting) guests at about 4pm (as soon as the lifts close).

INFORMATION AND SERVICES

Voss Tourist Information

Evangervegen 3; www.visitvoss.no; Sun.-Mon. 9am-4pm, Tues. 9am-7pm, Wed.-Thurs. 9am-4pm, Fri.-Sat. 9am-6:30pm

At the tourist information you can get advice on the current condition of nearby hikes or ski slopes, and get hiking maps for your trip. They can also help you book activities and experiences in the area. Find it right by the train station and Voss Gondol.

GETTING THERE AND AROUND

Train

Voss is located along the Oslo-Bergen line, so traveling there by train is ideal. The **main train station** (Stasjonsvegen 5) is located right by the Voss Gondol bottom station and the tourist information. Most activities and excursions will leave from near here, and shops and restaurants are within walking distance. Travel time to Voss via train from Bergen is around 1 hour and 15 minutes, with Vy operating several departures (approximately) every hour. Travel time from Oslo is 5.5 hours, and there are 4 daily departures.

Bus

From Bergen you can also reach Voss by bus. **Nor-Way Bussekspress** (tel. 22 31 31 50;

www.nor-way.no) has three daily departures from Bergen Bus Station, and the travel time is 1.5-2 hours (traffic dependent). The buses stop outside Voss Train Station. There are few local buses operating around the small town of Voss. The bus from Bergen to Voss costs around 310 kr.

It is also possible to travel between Voss, Flåm, and Gudvangen by bus, all on the same route (www.nor-way.no). The travel time is around 1 hour and 10 minutes from Flåm, and less than an hour from Gudvangen. The price is 150-200 kr.

Local buses in and around Voss are operated by Skyss (www.skyss.no). Route 950 travels from the center of Voss to both Voss Active and the High Rope Park.

Car

If you are driving, you can reach Voss from Bergen in 1.5 hours by following main road E16. Voss is 102 kilometers (63 mi) from Bergen. From Oslo, Voss is a 7-hour drive via Route 7 (crossing Hardangervidda toward Eidfjord and then over the Hardangerbrua Bridge). The distance is 464 kilometers (288 mi).

Voss is located a 1-hour drive from Flåm (66 km/41 mi) and around 45 minutes from Gudvangen (46 km/29 mi), both along E16 toward Bergen.

Most places in the center of Voss are within walking distance of each other (Scandic Hotel, Haik Restaurant, Voss Gondol, and the train station, for example). However, if you are headed to Myrkdalen, or to the High Rope Park, you will have to follow E16 toward Flåm and Gudvangen.

Car Rental

- **Hertz Voss:** Storrviki 2; 46 50 02 20; www. hertz.no
- **Avis Leiebil-Voss:** Øvre Langhaugen 11; 91 63 22 55; www.avis.no

The Aurlandsfjord and Nærøyfjord

The Aurlandsfjord and the Nærøyfjord are both fjord arms of the Sognefjord. The municipality of Aurland covers both fjords, and the four villages Aurland, Flåm, Gudvangen, and Undredal are all popular destinations; this is not only for their picturesque location at the end of the world's longest fjord, but also for their charm, and sights and attractions.

In Aurland, you can enjoy the view of the fjord below from the Stegastein Viewpoint at 650 meters (2,100 ft) above sea level. Flåm is not only the starting point of the fjord cruise through the Nærøyfjord, but also where you will find the Flåm Railway, which is said to be one of the most scenic railways in the world. Gudvangen, located at the end of the UNESCO World Heritage-listed Nærøyfjord, is home to the Njardarheimr Viking Village. Undredal is the smallest of the four villages, and it is where you will find the world's smallest stave church.

When planning a trip, opt to spend at least 2-3 nights in this area in order to enjoy key sights ad activities, namely the Flåm Railway, the Nærøyfjord, and the Stegastein Viewpoint. If you want to do one of the hikes in the area (such as the Aurlandsdalen Valley or Flåm Valley), set aside a day for this too.

Orientation

The Nærøyfjord and Aurlandsfjord are two arms of the Sognefjord, creating fingers stretching south from the main "arm" of the Sognefjord. On the map seen from above, these two fjords look like a two-pointed fork. Nestled along the "U"-shape of the fjords are the villages of Gudvangen, Undredal, Flåm, and Aurland (in that order). At the end of each fjord are Gudvangen (at the end of the Nærøyfjord) and Flåm (at the end of the Aurlandsfjord), with Undredal lining the shore where the fjords meet and Aurland just a 10-minute drive along the Aurlandsfjord from Flåm.

Getting There

The Aurlandsfjord and Nærøyfjord are reachable by train, bus, car, and boat. Of the four main villages along the fjords— Flåm, Aurland, Gudvangen, and Undredal— Aurland and Flåm are the largest, so they are the most accessible. Flåm is the main transportation hub, since it is the only one of the villages reachable by train.

Train

The only train station in the region is located in **Flåm** (Flåm Stasjon; A-Feltvegen 11; tel. 57 63 14 00). To travel to Flåm via train, book the Oslo-Bergen Line from either Oslo or Bergen, and change to the Flåm Railway at Myrdal. All one-way train tickets can be purchased via **Vy** (tel. 61 05 19 10; www.vy.no). Travel time from Bergen is 3-4 hours, depending on the wait at Myrdal. From Oslo, the travel time is 6.5-7 hours. The journey from Myrdal to Flåm takes around 1 hour.

Bus

If you are traveling via bus, you can reach Gudvangen, Flåm, and Aurland from both Bergen and Oslo. **Nor-way** (tel. 22 31 31 50; www.nor-way.no) has 2-3 daily departures from Bergen to the Aurlandsfjord, via Voss. Their bus route takes approximately 3 hours to reach Gudvangen, another 20 minutes to reach Flåm, and then 10 more minutes before stopping in Aurland. From Oslo, there is one daily departure in the morning, which includes swapping at Fagernes Station. Due to the swap, most people prefer taking the train from Oslo to Flåm. The bus takes 7 hours.

Boat

In the summer months, an express boat from Bergen services the villages of Aurland and Flåm. The **Norled** boat (tel. 51 86 87 00; www.norled.no) leaves Bergen every day

Aurlandsfjord, Nærøyfjord, and Inner Sognefjord

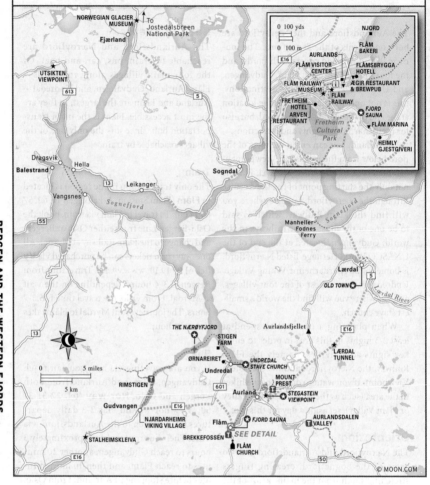

in the morning, heading for Flåm and the fjords. The total journey time from Bergen to Flåm is 5.5 hours (a little less if you get off in Aurland).

Car

By car, the villages are reached via main road E16 from both Oslo and Bergen. The drive from Bergen takes around 3 hours, and from Oslo it will take you around 5 hours to drive (via Route 7 and E16).

Getting Around

All four of the villages are walkable, as they are all very small. There are no local buses or modes of transportation running within them. There is a shuttle bus between Flåm and Gudvangen (tel. 57 63 14 00; www.norwaysbest.com/things-to-do/bus-services/shuttlebus), and the journey between the two villages takes 20 minutes. Additionally, the three regional Nor-Way buses from Bergen go through the villages, so it is also possible to travel between Gudvangen, Flåm, and Aurland on these. Undredal is only reachable by car or boat.

Aurland Taxi (tel. 90 13 08 08; www.aurlandtaxi.no) operates in the entire area, but as they have a limited number of cars, the scheduled buses are sometimes more reliable. It is also possible to use the Nærøyfjord fjord cruise (tel. 57 63 14 00; www.norwaysbest.com) as a hop-on, hop-off service, as it stops in all of the villages. So, if you are planning on visiting several of the villages in a day, you can travel by boat.

Gudvangen, Flåm, and Aurland are all connected via E16, with Undredal being just 10 minutes off the main road on a side road between Gudvangen and Flåm. The total drive time from Gudvangen to Aurland is 20 minutes (21 km/13 mi), and Flåm is about halfway between the two.

FLÅM

Flåm is a small village of around 300 inhabitants, located at the very end of the Aurlandsfjord. It is a popular destination, and most travelers opt to spend a night or two here during their trip to the fjord. It is perhaps most well-known for the famous Flåm Railway, one of the most beautiful train journeys in Europe, but also for its proximity to the UNESCO-listed Nærøyfjord.

Sights
The Flåm Railway
A-Feltvegen 11; tel. 57 63 14 00; www.norwaysbest.com/no/flamsbana; daily departures; 500 kr

One of the main attractions of the region, the Flåm Railway has been named one of the world's most scenic train journeys. The railway connects **Myrdal Mountain station** (along the Oslo-Bergen line) with the village of Flåm and the Aurlandsfjord. The journey from Flåm to Myrdal takes around 1 hour, and there are several daily departures (up to 10 in the high season, and as few as 4 in the winter). Along this beautiful journey, you will travel through the lush Flåm Valley, as the train climbs up along mountainsides, across

rivers, and through tunnels. The entire journey is beautiful, and along the way you will see steep waterfalls, the powerful Flåm River, and even people flying down the Flåm Zipline (if you are lucky).

In addition to being an incredibly beautiful journey, the trip showcases the impressive engineering skills and hard work that went into building the railway. Along the 20-kilometer (12-mi) journey, the train passes through 20 tunnels, 18 of which were built by hand.

There are no hotels in Myrdal, and the only dining option is the café in the train station. Therefore, travelers arriving from Oslo or Bergen by train opt to hike or take the train down to Flåm immediately.

Flåm Railway Museum
Stasjonsvegen 8; tel. 57 63 14 00; www.norwaysbest.com/no/inspirasjon/the-flam-railway-museum; daily; free

While the Flåm Railway today is one of the most visited tourist attractions in Norway, it is so much more than that. The building of the railway was incredibly important for the villagers of Flåm and nearby, as it connected them with the major cities of Oslo and Bergen via train. Before this, roads crossing the mountains in the winter would be closed due to snow, and the inner parts of the fjord (where Flåm is located) would freeze over, making boat travel impossible. To learn more about life in the village and how the railway affected it, as well as how the railway was built, visit the free Flåm Railway Museum. It is located right next to the train tracks in Flåm and offers a glimpse into what life was like for the workers on the railway, and the history of the train. Their gift shop, Memories from Flåmsbana, sells exclusive Flåm Railway merchandise.

The Aurlandsfjord
The Aurlandsfjord is not on the UNESCO World Heritage List like the neighboring Nærøyfjord, but it is still well worth seeing, and a reason people visit Flåm and the area. The fjord can be seen from most places in the

village center, so make sure to stop and take note of it at some point during your trip. A great spot to gaze over the fjord is at the end of the cruise port, next to where the Flåm river meets the fjord.

★ Fjord Sauna

Vikjavegen 4; tel. 90 93 41 59; www.fjordsauna.no; daily 10am-8pm May-Sept., weekends and selected weekdays Oct.-Apr.; 325 kr for 1.5 hours

In the bay of Flåm you will find a floating sauna called Fjord Sauna. Here, you can warm up and relax while gazing out at the fjord from their large window. Inside the sauna is a hole in the floor with a ladder you can climb down for a refreshing dip, or you can just jump in the fjord from the dock surrounding it. Those who want a little adrenaline rush can also jump off from the roof of the sauna! This is the perfect way to spend some time, whether you just want to relax in the hot sauna or go for a swim in the fjord first.

You can either join their communal sauna time slots or book a private sauna session. The sauna seats up to 12 people, and there is a small changing area outside where you can change in and out of swimming clothes. There is also a fridge available where guests can stow a beverage of choice to enhance the experience.

Fretheim Cultural Park

Fretheimshaugane 82; tel. 57 63 14 00; daily; free

Just behind the Fretheim Hotel in the center of Flåm you will find Fretheim Cultural Park. This hillside park consists of a web of trails, suitable for most ages and fitness levels, and offers a lovely view of the village with very little effort. Around the trails you will find benches where you can sit and enjoy the view, and sculptures such as a crown and a large piece of candy. Finding all the sculptures is a fun activity for children, who might not be so enamored of the scenery.

Flåm Church

Ryavegen 5; daily in summer, hours vary; free

The small, brown wooden church is located in the former center of the village, a 10-minute walk from the current village center. The church dates back to 1670 and has one tower and spire. The inside of the church is quite beautiful, with hand-painted decorations all over the walls depicting roses, patterns, and animal figures such as lions, deer, and foxes.

Flåm Zipline

Flåmsdalsvegen; tel. 97 74 43 18; www.flaamzipline.no; daily 10am-5pm May-Oct.; 750 kr

Flåm Zipline is the longest zipline in Northern Europe, and the fastest. It zooms through the Flåm Valley, starting at Vatnahalsen (one of the stops along the Flåm Railway). The experience is 100 percent sure to get your adrenaline pumping, as you will gather speeds up to 100 kilometers (60 mi) per hour! To reach the zipline, take the Flåm Railway to Vatnahalsen. The top zipline station is right by the train tracks. The zipline ends in Kårdalen in the Flåm Valley, and from there, you can rent bikes and cycle down to Flåm in around 1 hour or enjoy the 3-4-hour-long (downhill) hike through the valley. Simply follow the road/trail all the way down the valley, following the river. There is only one road, so you don't have to worry about taking the wrong one. The bicycle return is located right by the train tracks in Flåm.

TOP EXPERIENCE

Fjord Tours

The Nærøyfjord has been on the UNESCO World Heritage List since 2005 and is one of the most dramatic fjord landscapes you will come across in Norway. There are two main ways to discover it during your visit: either by taking a slow and relaxing fjord cruise from

---

1: the Aurlandsfjord 2: boat tour on the Aurlandsfjord 3: Fjord Sauna's view 4: a dip in the water at Fjord Sauna

Flåm to Gudvangen (or vice versa), or by jetting off on a (much quicker) FjordSafari.

Nærøyfjord Fjord Cruise

Pier 1-3; tel. 57 63 14 00; www.norwaysbest.com/no/ting-a-gjore/fjorder/fjord-cruise-naeroyfjord; daily departures year-round, 9:30am and 3pm Nov.-Apr., 9:30am, 11:30am, 3pm, 4:35pm May-Oct.; 540 kr

The Nærøyfjord Fjord Cruise sails through the Aurlandsfjord and the Nærøyfjord from Flåm to Gudvangen. The total journey time is 2 hours each way, and you will sail past the villages of Aurland and Undredal, mountain farms (like Stigen Farm), steep mountains, and roaring waterfalls. On board the boat there is a small kiosk selling coffee, snacks, and drinks. Because the return trip is exactly the same, there are shuttle buses ready to take you back to your starting point, corresponding with the boat arrival. The cruise also stops in Aurland and Undredal.

FjordSafari

Inner Harbour; tel. 99 09 08 60; www.fjordsafari.no; daily departures 11:45am Nov.-Apr., 9:50am and 2:45pm May-Oct.; 890 kr

Going on a FjordSafari from Flåm is a much quicker and more exhilarating experience than taking the cruise. Onboard one of their RIBs (Rigid Inflatable Boat), you will really get close to nature, and on the way, you might see eagles, porpoises, and seals. Your driver is also a very knowledgeable guide who can tell you about the area and its history, and answer any questions you may have about the fjords and living there.

Hiking
Brekkefossen

Distance: 0.6 kilometers (0.4 mi)
Time: 30 minutes one-way
Difficulty: Moderate
Trailhead: Lundaåkeren 17
Information and Maps: www.visitnorway.com/listings/brekkefossen-waterfall-hike/221093

Brekkefossen is a waterfall in the Flåm Valley, and the trailhead can be found about 15 minutes' walk from the station and center of the village. Simply follow the Flåm River up the valley on the right-hand side for 15-20 minutes, and you will see the waterfall on your right. From the trailhead (there is a small parking lot there), this steep hike is intense, but short. You will hike up 528 stone steps to get to a viewpoint called Raokjen, overlooking the village of Flåm and the beautiful Brekke waterfall.

Cycling
Rallarvegen

Distance: 53 kilometers (33 mi)
Time: 6 hours
Trailhead: Finse
Information and Maps: www.norwaysbest.com/no/inspirasjon/sykle-rallarvegen-fra-finse-til-flam

Rallarvegen is one of the most famous cycling routes in Norway and goes from Finse (along the Oslo-Bergen line) to Flåm, via the Flåm Valley. The cycling season starts in July, and lasts until September, and the route is especially popular among Norwegians looking for an active holiday. Along the route you will see the mountainous terrain of Hardangervidda, the lush valley from Myrdal to Flåm, and the fjord landscape as you reach Flåm.

Those who want to experience the route, but are a little shorter on time, usually cycle from Vatnahalsen to Flåm. The route down the Flåm Valley is 17 kilometers (10.5 mi) and takes around 1.5 hours. This part of the route includes the 21 hairpin turns below Myrdal station, and a lot of cyclists get off their bikes and walk down these steep hills. If you want to pair the cycling with the Flåm Zipline (starting at Vatnahalsen), the zipline crewmembers are happy to send your bicycle down the zipline as well.

Fjordsplorer Electric Bike Rental

A-Feltvegen; www.fjordsplorer.no; daily; from 150 kr/hour

Opened in 2022, Fjordsplorer is an electric bicycle rental company with stations in both Flåm and Aurland. It is powered through an app, and once you have unlocked your bicycle you are free to roam the area as you please! This is perfect for those who want to explore

Flåm and the Flåm Valley in an efficient and sustainable way.

Kayaking and Canoeing
Njord
Flåm Beach; tel. 91 32 66 28; www.seakayaknorway. com; daily tours 8:30am, 10am, noon, 3pm June-Aug., 10am and 3pm May and Sept.; 990 kr

Njord offers both longer and shorter kayaking adventures on the fjord. Experienced kayakers who want to travel deep into the fjord landscape might want to join their 3-day kayaking excursion, while most travelers opt for their 3-hour trip. You do not need any previous experience to participate, and children as young as 5 years can participate. On this trip, you will paddle along the Aurlandsfjord and then back to Flåm. The guides will point out interesting things to spot along the way, such as the Viking graves by Fronneset on the side of the fjord.

Shopping
Memories from Flåm (Flåm Store)
A-Feltvegen 11; www.memoriesfromnorway.com; daily 10am-5pm

In the train station building you will find Memories from Flåm, a concept store selling high-quality Norwegian and other Scandinavian brands. Amongst their products you'll find souvenirs, hiking gear, clothes, wool blankets, and home décor.

Aurlands
A-Feltvegen; www.aurlands.com; daily 10am-5pm summer

The brand behind the Aurland Shoe (the original penny loafer) has an outlet in Flåm, and here you can browse several designs and versions of the shoe, as well as the other high-quality leather products they produce, such as tote bags, wallets, and belts.

Food
Arven Restaurant
Nedre Fretheim; tel. 57 63 14 00; www.norwaysbest. com/no/overnatting-og-restauranter/arven-restaurant; daily 7pm-9pm; 190-320 kr

Arven, meaning "the Heritage" is the restaurant found at historic Fretheim Hotel. Here, you can enjoy Norwegian and international dishes in a formal atmosphere. The restaurant is found on the second floor of the hotel, just above the lobby, and through the large glass façade of the hotel you have views of the village and fjord outside. Depending on the season and how busy the hotel is, they might serve a continental dinner buffet (local cheeses, smoked salmon, lots of cured meats, and warm dishes such as Norwegian salmon, risotto, and vegetable soup). On their a la carte menu, you will find dishes such as barley risotto (vegetarian), beef tenderloin, and goat. The menu changes with the season and primarily includes local produce.

Flåm Marina
Vikjavegen 4; tel. 57 63 35 55; www.flammarina.no; daily 2pm-8pm; 160-360 kr

Just around the bend of the bay of Flåm you will find Flåm Marina, a dock restaurant serving international dishes for lunch and dinner. The main event here is the view, so try to get a table outside if you can. This modern restaurant is informal and relaxed, and on the menu, you will find dishes such as Caesar salad, beef burgers, and chicken sandwiches.

★ Ægir Restaurant and Brewpub
A-Feltvegen 23; tel. 57 63 20 50; www.aegirbryggeri. no; daily 6pm-9pm year-round, opens 1pm in June-Aug.; 190-665 kr

Ægir is the local brewery, making award-winning beer sold all over Norway. They also have a pub and restaurant, located in a stave church-looking building right on the docks of Flåm. Inside, the interior is dark with lots of wood and a large fireplace in the middle of the room, surrounded by benches covered in reindeer pelts. The atmosphere is rustic and warm, and from the second floor you can look through a large glass window to see the brewing process happening.

On the menu they have a selection of Viking-themed dishes, such as smoked cod (named after the Viking god Njord) and the

Ragnarok Ribs. The main event on this menu is their Ægir Viking Plank, a five-part tasting menu giving you a little bit of everything. It is meant to be paired with their beer tasting plank, as each dish was created especially with the beer in mind. In fact, at Ægir they believe that beer should be in the food as much as next to it, so most of their recipes incorporate beer in some way.

Flåm Bakeri

Stasjonsvegen; tel. 99 20 26 04; daily 8am-5pm
The local bakery is open year-round, and sells pastries and bread baked fresh daily. This is the ideal place to drop by if you want to bring some lunch on your excursions for the day. The bakery is small and charming, with limited outside seating. They supply baked goods to some local restaurants and concessions, such as Arven Restaurant and the kiosk on board the fjord cruise. Their white chocolate brioche and cinnamon rolls are particularly yummy.

Accommodations

Most people spend a night in Flåm, in order to check the two main attractions in the area off their list: the Flåm Railway and the Nærøyfjord. However, staying another night lets you explore the nearby villages and sights as well, such as the Njardarheimr Viking Village in Gudvangen, Stegastein Viewpoint in Aurland, or even Borgund Stave Church in Lærdal.

Heimly Gjestgiveri

Vikjavegen 15; tel. 57 63 23 00; www.norwaysbest.com/ no/overnatting-og-restauranter/heimly-pensjonat; May-Sept.; 2,000 kr
Heimly Gjestgiveri is a small inn with just 22 rooms open in the summer months. This charming place offers accommodation on a half-board basis, with breakfast and dinner included in the price. The rooms are basic, with comfortable beds and few details. In their large garden there are plenty of seats so you can enjoy the Norwegian summer and the

views of the fjord (some of the rooms also have a lovely fjord view).

Flåmsbrygga Hotell

A-Feltvegen 25; tel. 57 63 20 50; www.flamsbrygga. no; 2,800 kr
What's perhaps most exciting about the 41 rooms at Flåmsbrygga is that all the balconies are built at an angle, so they all have a fjord view! There's nothing better than enjoying your morning coffee while overlooking the fjord. In addition, the cabin-inspired interior of the hotel will make you feel right at home. Think checked blankets and dark-wood furniture. The rooms and lobby are warm and welcoming, so you will get a real taste of hygge during your stay here.

★ Fretheim Hotel

Nedre Fretheim; tel. 56 63 63 00; www.norwaysbest. com/no/fretheim-hotel; 3,200 kr
The history of Fretheim Hotel started way back in the 1870, when local Martha Fretheim opened her farmhouse to rich salmon fishers arriving from England. Since then, the hotel has been expanded and refurbished, but the historic wing from the 1800s still stands. The hotel has 122 rooms in total. The 17 historic rooms are all uniquely decorated, with old-fashioned furniture and a grand atmosphere. In their America wing, their stylish "America Rooms" are inspired by the Norwegian national costume, with rich colors and beautiful details. The rooms in their new wings are also richly decorated, with burgundy, gold, and red details and wood furniture. There are daily tours of the historic part of the hotel available free of charge for hotel guests, and it is worth doing if you have the time. Inquire in the lobby for the schedule.

Information and Services
Flåm Visitor Center

A-feltvegen 11; tel. 57 63 14 00; www.norwaysbest.com; daily 8:30am-5pm low season, 8am-7pm summer

1: Ægir Restaurant and Brewpub 2: the Viking Plank at Ægir

The visitors center in Flåm is located inside the station building, a stone's throw from all the sights, hotels, and restaurants in the village. Here you can pick up hiking maps and brochures, get advice on local activities, and book your tour tickets.

Getting There and Around

Most people arrive in Flåm via the Flåm Railway from Myrdal, a stop on the Oslo-Bergen line. Flåm can also be reached by either boat (from Bergen), bus (from Bergen), or car (from Bergen or Oslo). The driving time from Oslo to Flåm is around 5 hours (312 km/194 mi), via E16 and Route 7, crossing the Hemsedal mountain and passing through Lærdal and Aurland. From Bergen, Flåm is about a 3-hour drive (167 km/104 mi) along the E16. The route passes through Voss, which is around 1 hour from Flåm.

There is a small car rental company in Flåm, **Flåm Bilutleie** (Nedre Fretheim 15; tel. 93 08 56 45; www.flamcarrental.com), with a handful of cars available.

If you are not driving or planning on renting a car, it is best to get around by using a mix of the regional buses, taxis, and tours. The Nor-way bus between Bergen and the fjords goes through Gudvangen, Flåm, and Aurland (in that order). The route can also be used to travel between the villages by bus. **Aurland Taxi** (tel. 90 13 08 08; www.aurlandtaxi.no) operates in the entire area, including Flåm.

AURLAND

Aurland is the administrative center for the municipality, and the largest village in the area, with around 700 inhabitants. While many tourists prefer staying in Flåm to see its more well-known sights, Aurland gives off a more local feel, as many inhabitants work here (unless they work in the tourism industry), at the village hall, in social services, or at the hydro-energy company found a little farther up the Aurland Valley in the area called Vassbygdi.

Those wanting to stay a little away from the masses, but still be close to all the sights along the fjord, might prefer Aurland as their base. There are several great hikes here, in addition to the famous Stegastein viewpoint.

Sights
★ Stegastein Viewpoint
Bjørgavegen 83; free
The Stegastein Viewpoint is a viewing platform at 650 meters (2,130 ft) above sea level. This wooden structure has a glass fence and gives the illusion that it "drops off" at the end, due to the rounded shape of the front of the platform. It offers one of the most spectacular views in the area. From the center of Aurland, the platform is a 20-minute drive up the winding roads of Aurlandsfjellet mountain.

The narrow road gets very congested in the summer months, so going with a bus tour is recommended. There are several daily departures from Aurland and Flåm (tel. 57 63 14 00; www.norwaysbest.com/no/ting-a-gjore/bussruter/stegastein-utsiktpunkt/; daily departures; 360 kr). The bus tour gives you 30 minutes to gaze at the view and take your photos at the top.

Vangen Church
Vangen 9; daily, hours vary; free
The local church is the largest in the municipality and dates back over 800 years to 1202. This massive, white stone church overlooks the square in the village center as it has for centuries. Emanuel Vigeland, brother of the more famous Gustav Vigeland (the sculptor behind the Vigeland Park in Oslo), made the stained-glass windows of the church. It is believed that in 1926 Emanuel said that the church was one of the most interesting churches in the country.

Aurland Shoe Factory and Outlet
Odden 13; www.aurlands.com; Mon.-Fri. 10am-4pm year-round, also on weekends in summer; free
The Aurland Shoe Factory is the only working shoe factory left in Norway, but that is not the only reason it is famous. The Aurland Shoe is believed to be the original penny loafer, worn by celebrities such as James Dean and

Michael Jackson. The penny loafer became popular in the US, and for a long time the shoe was nicknamed "weejuns," a word deriving from "Norwegians." The shoe factory includes a small museum dedicated to the history of the shoe and its importance for the village of Aurland. In addition, you can see the makers working on their craft, and shop for shoes in the outlet.

Merete Rein Glass

Vangen 12; www.mereterein.no; hours vary, usually daily 10am-3pm; free

Merete Rein is a glassblower whose workshop is located right by the village main square. Here, you can see her hard at work through the glass windows between her studio and small shop. In the shop, you can browse her creations and pick up some new decorations for your home. Her style is colorful and quirky, and in addition to glasses and vases you will find colorful glass fish and chickens, which have become popular decorations among locals.

Hiking
Aurlandsdalen Valley

Distance: *20 kilometers (12.5 mi)*
Time: *6-8 hours one way*
Difficulty: *Strenuous (due to length)*
Trailhead: *Østerbø Fjellstove*
Information and Maps: *https://flamtravelguide. com/aurlandsdalen-valley*

The Aurland Valley (Aurlandsdalen) is known as Norway's Grand Canyon. This lush and beautiful hike starts at Østerbø, at the top of the valley, and takes you all the way down to Vassbygdi (a neighbourhood/village in Aurland). Østerbø is about a 1-hour drive from the center of Aurland. On this hike you will come across abandoned mountain farms, beautiful waterfalls, and mountain lakes.

The hiking season is from June (depending on when the snow melts) until September. The best time to hike is August-September. This hike is mainly downhill but is still considered rather strenuous due to the rocky trail and the

length of the hike. The trail is well-marked the whole way with red T's. There are hiking buses running in the summer months, taking you from Aurland and Flåm to Østerbø (the trailhead), and back from Vassbygdi at the end of the day.

Dagsturhytta

Distance: *1 kilometer (0.6 mi)*
Time: *30-40 minutes one-way*
Difficulty: *Strenuous*
Trailhead: *Vinjavegen 18-12*
Information and Maps: *https://ut.no/ hytte/101337/vinjeasenhytta-dagsturhytta-i-aurland*

Dagsturhytta (Day Trip Cabin) is one of many such cabins found all over western Norway. The cabins were built as a way to encourage more people to take small hikes in nature, and this one not only provides a beautiful viewpoint and resting place, but also contains a small library of books to read while you are there. The cabin is located a short hike away from town and is the perfect place to enjoy your lunch (or read a book).

The Dagsturhytte in Aurland is called Vinjaåsenhytta, and it can be found at approximately 300 meters (985 ft) above sea level. It affords great views of the Aurlandsfjord and the village of Aurland after just a short (but intense) climb. The hike itself usually takes no more than 30-40 minutes (although you are free to take as long as you need, as it is very steep). Locals use the hike as an exercise route, and some will run up the trail in as little as 15 minutes. Follow the same trail back down and expect that it will take just as long as hiking up. It is a narrow trail, and since it is so steep you need to tread carefully.

Stegastein

Distance: *2.6 kilometers (1.6 mi)*
Time: *2 hours one-way*
Difficulty: *Strenuous*
Trailhead: *Vinjavegen 18-12*
Information and Maps: *www.fjordsandbeaches. com/stegastein-viewpoint*

Once you have made it to Dagsturhytta, you are about one-third of the way to the

Stegastein Viewpoint. The hike is steep the whole way, as you are literally hiking up the mountain to 650 meters (2,130 ft) above sea level, straight to the viewpoint from the fjord. Experienced hikers will find that the view from the Stegastein platform is even better after 2 hours of hard work. To get back down, either hike the same way or stroll down the main road at a leisurely pace. If you head down the main road, be careful of cars, as there is no sidewalk on this narrow stretch.

Mount Prest (Røyrgrind)
Distance: 3 kilometers (1.9 mi)
Time: 3 hours round-trip
Difficulty: Strenuous
Trailhead: Bjørgavegen (2 km/1.2 mi past the Stegastein Viewpoint)
Information and Maps: www.visitnorway.com/listings/hike-to-prest-aurland/233794

Røyrgrind is technically the name of the destination for this hike, but locals just call it Prest. Prest is the name of the mountain, and once you have reached Røyrgrind it is possible to keep hiking to reach the top of Prest Mountain (but people usually don't bother, as the main part of the hike goes to Røyrgrind, and this destination offers an epic fjord view). This hike is strenuous, but the whole way you have spectacular views of the Aurlandsfjord below, as you hike up the ridge of the mountain.

There is a parking lot at the trailhead, approximately 4-5 minutes' drive from the Stegastein Viewpoint. Hiking season is May-October, but it is best to wait until June, as there is often a lot of snow left in May. Norway's Best (www.norwaysbest.com/things-to-do/bus-services/bus-prest; daily departures June-Oct.; 180 kr) have arranged for a shuttle bus from Flåm and Aurland to the trailhead, which is convenient for anyone visiting without a car.

Festivals and Events
The Aurland Festival (Aurlandsmarknaden)
www.aurlandsmarknaden.no; first weekend of July

Every year since 1997, with the exception of two years during the pandemic, locals and anyone with a connection to Aurland have come together in the first weekend of July for a large event. Aurlandsmarknaden (technically, the Aurland Market) is a two-day festival and market that sees sellers and artisans from all over the country gather in the day to sell their handcrafts and souvenirs. In the evening, there is a concert on the dock, drawing big national names such as Hellbillies, Rotlaus, and Keiino. In recent years, the Friday event has been deemed a family event, with no alcohol being served on the grounds. Saturday is a more traditional festival, with the sale of alcohol, dancing, and high spirits until late.

Food
Marianne Bakeri
Onstadvegen 2A; tel. 90 51 29 78; Mon.-Sat. 8am-4pm

Marianne is both the name of the owner and her bakery, located just by the river in Aurland. Here, you will find freshly baked bread and sweet and savory pastries that you can either bring with you on a day of exploring the fjords, or enjoy on her large outdoor terrace. Don't miss the cream cheese-stuffed focaccia—it is a local favorite.

Vangsgaarden Gastropub
Nedstagata 1; tel. 57 63 35 80; www.vangsgaarden.com; hours vary; 160-340 kr

At Vangsgaarden Gastropub you are treated to lovely views of the fjord in historic surroundings. The former bakery and telegraph facility is now a restaurant, but traces of the building's history remain. Behind the bar you will find the old telephones, and the old baker's oven can also still be seen there. The atmosphere inside is relaxing and informal, while their large outdoor pergola (terrace with a roof and walls that can be taken down on a sunny day) is lively and friendly. On the menu you will find international dishes such as beef burgers, carbonara pasta, and tenderloin steak.

1: Aurland 2: Stegastein Viewpoint 3: Dagsturhytta
4: view from the hike to Prest

Hotel Aurlandsfjord Restaurant

Bjørgavegen 1; tel. 94 86 21 00; daily 3pm-8pm May-Sept.; 190-340 kr

The stylish restaurant at Hotel Aurlandsfjord serves Norwegian and international dishes using local produce and ingredients. The atmosphere is informal and intimate, with a livelier outdoor seating area. The interior is reminiscent of the lavish 1920s era, with tiled floors, velour details, and dark green accents. On the menu, you can expect to find classic dishes like chicken salad, local halibut, and duck confit.

Accommodations

★ Vangsgaarden Hotel

Nedstagata 1; tel. 57 63 35 80; www.vangsgaarden.com; 1,900 kr

Vangsgaarden dates back to the 1700s, and the breakfast at this historic hotel is served in the oldest building on the property: Aabelheim, a former minister's residence (Vangsgaarden is just across the road from the church) from the late 1700s. The rooms in the main building of this charming hotel are all fully refurbished, and the modern bathrooms meet the old-fashioned furniture and style of the 34 rooms in a perfect blend.

The main attractions at this family-owned hotel are their nine self-catering fishermen's cabins (rorbuer), located right on the fjord. Each cabin has a small kitchen and sleeps up to four people. Staying in one of these is as close to the fjord as you can get.

Hotel Aurlandsfjord

Bjørgavegen 1; tel. 94 86 21 00; www.norwaysbest.com/no/overnatting-og-restauranter/hotel-aurlandsfjord; May-Oct.; 2,100 kr

Hotel Aurlandsfjord is a seasonal hotel where you can enjoy lovely views of the fjord from some of their balcony rooms. Regardless of your view, their renovated modern rooms are all stylish. They have 30 rooms in total, each with beautiful photos from the fjord region decorating the walls. In their informal bar you will find TVs showing European soccer matches, and a shuffleboard table.

Getting There and Around

Most people arrive in Aurland by bus or car. It is just a little farther along E16 from Flåm. From Bergen and Voss, the Nor-Way regional bus will take you to Aurland; from Bergen the journey is 168 kilometers (104 mi) and takes 3 hours, and from Voss it's 67 kilometers (42 mi) and takes 1 hour—about the same as if you were arriving by car. Road E16 goes the whole way from Bergen to Aurland, via Voss.

From Oslo, the drive to Aurland takes around 5 hours (312 km/194 mi) via E16 and Route 7, crossing the Hemsedal mountain.

To get around without a car, a mix of tours, boat, and bus is ideal. **Aurland taxi** (tel. 90 13 08 08; www.aurlandtaxi.no) operates in Aurland, but you can use public transportation to get between the villages as long as you check schedules in advance.

GUDVANGEN

Gudvangen is very small, even smaller than Flåm, and is beautifully nestled at the very end of the UNESCO-listed Nærøyfjord. For decades people have visited this village to see the fjord, or to travel through the fjord. The landscape in and around Gudvangen is all part of a World Heritage Site, and you can expect to see steep, dramatic mountains, cascading waterfalls, and lush greenery surrounding the fjord at sea level.

In recent years, Gudvangen's Viking attraction has increased interest in the area, and people now come to experience the Njardarheimr Viking Village, as well as to see the fjord.

Sights

TOP EXPERIENCE

Njardarheimr Viking Village

Njardarheimr; tel. 46 24 54 62; www.vikingvalley.no; daily 10am-6pm June-Aug., daily 10:30am-2pm low season; adults 205 kr, children 98 kr

Located in the village of Gudvangen, which has strong ties to the Viking Age (800-1066 AD), the Viking Village Njardarheimr opened in

2017 and delivers on its promise to offer an authentic Viking experience. This is a living village, where Vikings (actually Viking reenactors) eat, sleep, work, and play, and it looks just like what you would imagine, with wooden buildings topped by grass-covered roofs, dirt roads, and chickens roaming free. This isn't the place to find plastic horn helmets, but rather to learn more about the real history of Vikings in Norway and how they lived.

It turns out that the Vikings were not as barbaric as you may think. In fact, in each village only a small group of people were considered actual Vikings; Viking, in the old Norse language, was actually the name given to those who went raiding and seafaring. The rest were mainly farmers, and it's easy to see why they would have settled in a place like Gudvangen: The village sits at the end of the Nærøyfjord, protected by the mountains, making it impossible for anyone to arrive by boat without being spotted.

After paying the entrance fee, visitors are free to roam the village and meet the "Vikings." The chieftain, Georg, has lived there since it opened, and if you have any questions about the Viking Age, he's your man. The reenactors wear authentic dresses, capes, and tunics—clothes that would have been easy to come by in the Viking Age, made from wool, leather, and fur. Many of these Vikings have studied traditional trades and display handicrafts, including fabrics, yarn, and items made in the armory, which can be purchased on-site.

Walking tours are given several times a day (included in the ticket), and are especially recommended for Viking history buffs. With Viking reenactors hosting each tour, it's truly a one-of-a-kind experience for those looking for a more authentic, immersive way to understand Norway's Viking period.

★ **The Nærøyfjord**

The UNESCO World Heritage-listed Nærøyfjord is a fjord arm that stretches from the Aurlandsfjord all the way to Gudvangen at its end. Along the fjord, you will pass by abandoned farms, quaint villages (such as Bakka and Dyrdal, where no one lives anymore), steep mountains, and cascading waterfalls. At its narrowest, the distance from one side of the fjord to the other is just 250 meters (820 ft), making it the world's most narrow fjord. The total length of the Nærøyfjord is around 17 kilometers (10.5 mi).

The dramatic landscape of the Nærøyfjord put it on the World Heritage List, and famously inspired the scenery in Disney's movie *Frozen*. See it on a **fjord cruise** (www.norwaysbest.com/no/ting-a-gjore/fjorder/fjord-cruise-naeroyfjord) between Flåm and Gudvangen, or on a **FjordSafari** (www.fjordsafari.no) from Flåm. On land, the **docks of Gudvangen** give a scenic vantage point for the fjord, and the **Old Postal Road hike** takes you deep into the fjord landscape along the Nærøyfjord.

Stalheimskleiva (Stalheim Hairpin Turns)

Stalheim Hotel, 5715 Stalheim; tel. 56 52 01 22; www.stalheim.com

The hairpin turns at Stalheim were for years a popular tourist route, as the narrow road winds its way back and forth up the steep Stalheim valley, with two large mountain falls on each side. The road has been closed to traffic since 2021, as it can no longer handle any traffic. However, it is still possible to enjoy the view of the hairpin turns and the valley from the viewpoint at the **Stalheim Hotel** (Stalheimsvegen 131; tel. 56 52 01 22; www.stalheim.com; 2,500 kr). Stop at the hotel for a coffee or a waffle on your way between the Sognefjord and Bergen, and marvel at the dramatic view below. The hotel is located a little farther up the valley, about a 15-minute drive from Gudvangen (13 km/8 mi). Follow E16 for almost the whole drive, before taking Stalheimsvegen (the Stalheim road) for the final 2 minutes to reach the hotel.

Hiking
Rimstigen
Distance: *1.5 kilometers (1 mi)*

Time: *3-4 hours round-trip*
Difficulty: *Strenuous*
Trailhead: *Tufto*
Information and Maps: *https://ut.no/ turforslag/1114631/rimstigen-opp*

This beautiful hike offers some of the best views of the Nærøyfjord. It is a steep hike from beginning to end, as it ascends from the fjord at sea level to 724 meters (2,375 ft) high. You are quickly rewarded on this hike, as the view just gets better and better every time the shrubbery and trees give you an opening to see the fjord. The hike is strenuous, and it is especially important that you have good knees as it goes down the same way as up. Though this is a steep hike, it is often preferred by visitors over Bakkanosi, which takes a lot longer. As long as your knees can handle hiking back down the (sometimes) rocky trail, you can take all the time you need to make it to the top.

Bakkanosi

Distance: *20 kilometers (12 mi)*
Time: *7-8 hours round-trip*
Difficulty: *Strenuous*
Trailhead: *Jordalen (by the old schoolhouse)*
Information and Maps: *www.visitnorway.no/ listings/bakkanosi-1398-moh/222653*

Bakkanosi is another lovely hike, offering great views of the narrow fjord below. Bakkanosi mountaintop is at 1,398 meters (4,580 ft) above sea level. The hike starts at 560 meters (1,830 ft), so you do not have to hike the entire way. This hike is less steep than Rimstigen but is still considered strenuous due to its length. You should be in relatively good shape to do it. The hike follows the backside of the Bakkanosi mountain, through a lush valley, along a river, and eventually onto rocky, mountainous terrain. Be very careful at the top and the viewpoint, as there is a steep drop off the mountain cliff.

The Old Postal Road (Styvi-Bleiklindi)

Distance: *5.5 kilometers (3.5 mi)*
Time: *1 hour one-way*

Difficulty: *Easy*
Trailhead: *Styvi or Blekilindi, in the Nærøyfjord*
Information and Maps: *www.norwaysbest.com/ packages/historical-hike-in-naroyfjord*

The Old Postal Road along the Nærøyfjord is a hidden gem not many travelers are aware of. The remnant of this former road goes from Styvi to Bleiklindi, through the lush greenery along the Nærøyfjord. This is where the postmen would carry mail during the winter when the fjord would freeze over. From Styvi the mail would be carried by boat, as the outer parts of the fjord would not be covered in ice. During this easy hike you follow the fjord as you cross waterfalls and rivers, and explore the fjord landscape on foot.

Both Styvi and Bleiklindi must be reached by boat. Norway's Best and FjordSafari (tel. 57 63 14 00; www.norwaysbest.com/packages/ historical-hike-in-naroyfjord; daily June-Aug.; 1,190 kr) have created a hiking package that will take you from Flåm to Bleiklindi on board one of the small FjordSafari boats, and then pick you up in Styvi with the Fjord Cruise 3 hours later. This gives you 3 hours to hike the postal route slowly, stop for lunch wherever you'd like, and truly take in the scenery. Perhaps you'll pack a swimming suit for a refreshing dip in the fjord?

Festivals and Events
The Viking Market

Njardarheimr; www.facebook.com/ GudvangenVikingMarket; Oct.

The Gudvangen Viking Market takes place every year inside the walls of Njardarheimr. Viking artisans and handcraftsmen from all over Scandinavia (and the world) come together to display their products and sell their services. During the festival you can browse the stalls, have your runes read, try your hand at a game of Hnefatafl (some call it "Viking chess"), and purchase handcrafted products straight from the makers.

1: Njardarheimr Viking Village 2: view of the Nærøyfjord from the Rimstigen hike 3: Undredal Stave Church

Food and Accommodations
Viking Diner

Njardarheimr; daily 11am-11pm; 189-259 kr

This Viking-style diner is situated by the Njardarheimr Viking Village, and you do not need a ticket to Njardarheimr to stop and eat here. On the menu you will find classic diner dishes with a Norwegian twist, such as a grilled cheese sandwich made with locally smoked cheese from Voss, and more traditional Norwegian dishes such as komle (also known as raspeballer, a Norwegian version of potato dumplings).

Gudvangen Fjordtell

Fetagata 43; tel. 48 07 55 55; www.gudvangen.com; 2,700 kr

Gudvangen Fjordtell is the large, rounded building with the grass roof and glass facade that you will find in the center of Gudvangen. The glass side of the hotel faces the fjord, giving you lovely views from their restaurant and lobby area. The 37 basic rooms are modern and simply furnished, while their Viking-themed rooms have lots of wood details, complete with reindeer fur on the beds. The hotel has a cafeteria that is open for lunch and a restaurant (Kongshallen) open in the evenings, serving a la carte meals with views of the fjord. Dishes at Kongshallen include lamb shank, wild mushroom soup, and deer tenderloin.

Getting There

Along E16, Gudvange is 2 hours and 45 minutes' drive from Bergen, and a little less than an hour from Voss. If you are driving from Oslo, it will take a little over 5 hours along E16 and Route 7.

The regional Nor-way buses stop in Gudvangen on their way to Aurland and Flåm from Bergen/Voss. If you are catching a train in Flåm, taking a bus there is the best option. **Aurland Taxi** (tel. 90 13 08 08; www.aurland-taxi.no) also serves Gudvangen.

UNDREDAL

Undredal is the smallest of the fjord villages in the area, and is often visited for a day trip. Those who decide to stay here overnight do so to unplug and slow down for a day or two. With just around 80 inhabitants, this sleepy place is perfect for a quiet stroll or for relaxing on the docks and taking in the beauty of the fjord. The location and layout of the village inspired the Disney movie *Frozen*, something which has really put Undredal on the map.

Sights
★ Undredal Stave Church

Kyrkjevegen 9; tel. 95 13 74 03; www.undredal-stavkyrkje.com; daily guided tours upon request; 150 kr

Undredal Stave Church is the smallest stave church in Scandinavia (some say the world) that is still in use. This small, one-room church has a small tower and spire and does not look like what you'd expect a stave church to look like due to its color. Most stave churches are dark brown, but the church in Undredal is painted white. The church is believed to have been built in 1147, as the year is carved into one of the beams in the ceiling of the church. The church seats only 40 people.

Guided tours of the church are available on request, and it is not possible to enter the church without a guide. You can book a tour by calling the number above or reaching out via email to booking@visitundredal.no.

Stigen Farm

The Aurlandsfjord; https://stigengard.no

Stigen Farm is a mountain farm that can be seen from the fjord cruise between Flåm and Gudvangen, located just a couple of kilometers from Undredal along the fjord. It is quite impressive to see this farm, perched on a small mountain plateau high above the fjord (at 360 m/1,180 ft above sea level). In the olden days, the only way to get up there was on a rope ladder! Old folk tales say that this was the wealthiest farm in the area, much because the rope ladder was never let down when the tax man came rowing across the fjord. Since then, a small pathway has been made in the mountainside, so it is possible to walk up to the farm once you get there.

It is unclear how old the farm is, but the farm is mentioned in tales of when the bubonic plague came to the area for the first time (1349), so there is believed to have been a settlement there since then. Today, it is possible to stay overnight at Stigen, or join one of the nature camps and yoga weekends that are arranged there (https://stigengard.no). During these camps, you get to help run the farm, do lots of hiking, and get to know new people who are interested in a natural and sustainable farm life. These weeklong camps and overnight stays are the only ways to stay at the farm, but it is also possible to visit by hiking 20-30 minutes up the trail along the fjord. However, most visitors stop at marveling at the sight of the farm from the fjord, as it is the place's history and unique location that make it special.

Eldhuset Goat Cheese Center
On the dock; tel. 57 63 31 00; www.visitnorway.no/listings/eldhuset-undredal/221177; daily 11am-8pm summer, hours vary in winter; cheese tasting 175 kr

On the docks of Undredal you will find Eldhuset, a building dedicated to teaching you the old goat's cheese traditions of the village. Undredal is known for its goat's cheese, and at Eldhuset you can sample some of the cheese made in the village and browse the display of old tools and equipment used in cheese making.

Hiking
Hovdungo
Distance: *8.2 kilometers (5 mi)*
Time: *1.5 hours one-way*
Difficulty: *Strenuous*
Trailhead: *Hjødna*
Information and Maps: *https://ut.no/turforslag/1114291/stlen-hovdungo-i-undredal*

Hovdungo is a former mountain farm, located around 740 meters (2,430 ft) above the village of Undredal. The farm has not been

in use since 1947 but is still a popular hike among locals and visitors alike. The trail to Hovdungo is well-marked and very steep. Therefore, the hike is considered strenuous, and you need to be in good shape to attempt it. The view from the top is great, giving you a glimpse of the Aurlandsfjord as it becomes the Sognefjord and stretches out to sea. A little farther above the farm you will find a small hut called Ørnareiret, where it is possible to stay overnight.

Stokko
Distance: *2.8 kilometers (1.7 mi)*
Time: *3 hours round-trip*
Difficulty: *Easy*
Trailhead: *Pottefot (parking lot just outside of the village center)*
Information and Maps: *https://ut.no/turforslag/1112155070/stokko*

The hike from Undredal to Stokko is absolutely lovely, and similar to the Old Postal Road in Gudvangen it traces the fjord as you go. The trail follows an old tractor road, a narrow trail, and a rather rocky stone patch along the fjord. The total elevation is 231 meters (760 ft) as the trail ascends and descends along the fjord. On a sunny day this is a particularly lovely hike. Bring some snacks with you and stop at Stokko for lunch before returning the same way you came.

Festivals and Events
Dock Dance (Bryggedans)
www.facebook.com/visitundredal; selected weekends June-Aug.

On selected Fridays and Saturdays through the summer the small village of Undredal comes alive with music and dancing. The dock dances draw people from all over the neighboring villages, most of them arriving (and leaving) by boat. The live music usually consists of local bands and artists playing everything from country to pop covers, and the village gets quite crowded as people dance on the docks in front of the stage set up there. If you are visiting during one of these weekends, make sure to join in.

Food and Accommodations
Osteklokka Café

Tel. 57 63 31 00; www.facebook.com/visitundredal; daily 11am-8pm summer, hours vary in winter

Osteklokka Café is on the docks of Undredal, serving light meals and coffee all day in the summer months. Here, you can enjoy a freshly made waffle, sample local goat's cheese, or dig in to a locally made goat-based dinner, such as a kjebab, a kebab made with goat's meat, called "kje" in Norwegian. The seating is all outside on the docks.

Ørnareiret

Above Hovdungo; tel. 91 30 90 21; www.inatur.no/hytte; 900 kr

Farther up the mountain from the Hovdungo mountain farm you will find what might be the most unique accommodation in the area. Ørnareiret is a tiny hut at around 1,000 meters (3,280 ft) above sea level, overlooking the spectacular landscape below. To get there, you have to hike to the top. Follow the hike to Hovdungo, and then continue up the trail for another 1.5 hours. This hike is tough, but it will be worth it when you wake up the next day to enjoy the view. Included in the overnight stay is camping kitchen equipment, a first aid kit, toilet paper (for outside use), and a radio. You have to bring your own sleeping bag. The hut sleeps up to 6-8 people.

Visit Undredal Apartments

Undredalsvegen 127; tel. 95 03 98 81; www.facebook.com/visitundredal; 2,700 kr

In the middle of Undredal you will find four self-catering apartments of varying sizes. The largest apartments have three bedrooms and sleep up to six people, and the smaller ones have two bedrooms (sleeping up to four people). The apartments are basic, with simple and homey furniture. Each of the apartments comes with a fully equipped kitchen, a laundry machine, free parking, and a private terrace or outdoor area.

Getting There

Undredal is a bit of an outlier from the other villages, as it is not directly along E16. Road 601 is a 10-minute drive and connects the village with E16 between Flåm and Gudvangen. The total drive time to both Flåm and Gudvangen is 20 minutes. Aurland is another 10 minutes along E16 past Flåm.

There are no bus connections to Undredal, so arriving via the **Nærøyfjord cruise** (www.norwaysbest.com) or with **Aurland Taxi** (tel. 90 13 08 08; www.aurlandtaxi.no) is the best bet for those without a car.

The village itself is tiny, and you can walk everywhere.

Inner Sognefjord

The Aurlandsfjord and Nærøyfjord are fjord arms of the Sognefjord and are technically part of the "Inner Sognefjord" as well. The rest of the Sognefjord also stretches inland, and you will find several charming towns and picturesque villages around it. The villages of Lærdal, Balestrand, and Fjærland are all worth seeing, as they have lots to offer visitors who want to venture away from the more popular areas along the Aurlandsfjord.

Both Fjærland and Balestrand are located in Sogndal municipality, and Lærdal is its own municipality (neighboring Aurland). You might find that there is not enough time in your fjord adventure to cover all of these villages in addition to those along the Aurlandsfjord and the Nærøyfjord, so plan your time carefully. If you would like to see the famous Borgund Stave Church, a trip to Lærdal can easily be paired with a few days in Flåm. If you want to experience the picturesque village of Balestrand or get close to the glacier Bøyabreen in Fjærland, you might want to prioritize these two on the north side of the Sognefjord before crossing south to see the Nærøyfjord. Each of these villages can be explored in a day or two, but with some travel time in between you need to plan accordingly.

LÆRDAL

Just through the world's longest tunnel from Aurland you will find the village of Lærdal. Previously these two villages were only connected by a mountain road that is closed for larger parts of the year (due to snow), but with the opening of the **Lærdal tunnel** in 2000 it is now possible to drive straight through this mountain year-round. This makes Lærdal ideal to visit while in the Aurlandsfjord and Nærøyfjord area, even though it is technically not on either of these fjords (it is located along the Sognefjord). The main reasons for visiting Lærdal are to visit the UNESCO-listed old town (Gamle Lærdalsøyri) and to see the famous Borgund Stave Church. Through the Lærdal tunnel, the village of Lærdal is just a 30-minute drive from Aurland. Lærdal, and the sights there, are therefore often visited as a day trip from this area.

When researching and looking at maps before your trip, you may get confused that the name Lærdalsøyri appears frequently. This simply means "Lærdal center," and is the name of the village center, similar to Vossevangen (Voss center) and Aurlandsvangen (Aurland center).

Sights
★ **Old Town**
(Gamle Lærdalsøyri)
Gamlegata
Lærdalsøyri, also known as Lærdal Old Town, is one of the best kept neighborhoods of wooden houses in Norway. The historical center of Lærdal comprises about 170 protected buildings dating back to the 18th and 19th centuries. These charming timber buildings include homes, farmhouses, shops, storage buildings, and fishermen's cottages. A stroll through the old village center is a great afternoon activity, as you will find that the buildings today include a few small shops

and cafés. In 2014, four of the buildings were lost in a large fire that spread throughout the village due to high winds. A total of 40 houses were destroyed in the fire. The whole area is quaint and perfect for a nice stroll. It is a small area that can be covered in less than 30 minutes (unless you stop to look at shops or at the café).

Norwegian Wild Salmon Center
Øyraplassen 14; tel. 45 56 22 03; daily June-Aug.; 50 kr
The Lærdal River has for a long time been a popular destination for salmon fishing, and at the Norwegian Wild Salmon Center you can learn more about the river's history, the importance of salmon fishing in the region, and the history and current situation of the wild salmon. The center has a café (Laksen) and an observatory where you can see live wild salmon and trout up close.

Borgund Stave Church
Vindhellavegen 606; tel. 57 66 81 09; daily 9:30am-5:30pm mid-Apr.-mid-Oct.; adults 100 kr, children 80 kr
The beautiful Borgund Stave Church is the best-preserved stave church in Norway, and it is what most people will have in mind when thinking of stave churches. It was built around 1180 and is located approximately 27 kilometers (16.8 mi) from the village center. The brown wooden church is one of the major attractions of the area. Included in your entry ticket is access to a permanent exhibition on findings from the Viking Age. Another exhibit covers the importance of stave churches in the Middle Ages, ideal for anyone wanting to learn more about these unique Norwegian buildings.

The stave church is a 30-minute drive (27 km/17 mi) from the center of Lærdal. In the summer months there is a **shuttle bus** (www.visitkongevegen.no; June-Aug.; 100 kr) that leaves from the village center in the morning, and returns a little over an hour later. The local taxi company, **Solheim Taxi** (41 51 01 00), can also take you to the church.

Hiking

Mjølkeflathytta

Distance: 0.9 kilometer (0.5 mi)

Time: 30 minutes one-way

Difficulty: Moderate

Trailhead: Route 5, by the tunnel entrance

Information and Maps: https://ut.no/hytte/101303/mjlkeflathytta-dagsturhytta-i-lrdal

Mjølkeflathytta is the day trip cabin (dagsturhytte) of Lærdal municipality. If you hike to the day trip cabin in both Aurland (the neighboring municipality) and Lærdal, you will find that they are of almost the exact same design. The cabin was placed there to be a short hike away for anyone wanting somewhere to relax and unwind with a lovely view of the village below. There is also a collection of books you can read during your visit to the cabin. This hike is not too strenuous, and the trail is well-marked the whole way.

The hike starts by the tunnel entrance along Route 5 just north of the village center. There is parking just before the bridge.

Salmon Fishing

The Lærdal River is one of Norway's best (and most famous) rivers for salmon fishing. The king of Norway himself travels to Lærdal for his holidays to go salmon fishing, and has been quoted as saying that he has two great loves in his life: "Her Majesty the Queen and the Lærdal River." This is also, perhaps, why the river has been nicknamed "the queen among salmon rivers." The king first fished here when he was 14 years old.

Salmon fishing in the river is constantly regulated, with the main season being summer. The fishing rights are rented out by the owners of the river, via **Lærdal Elveeigarlag** (tel. 91 19 06 34; https://lakseelver.no/nb/elver/laerdalselva). At the time of writing, salmon fishing in the Lærdal river is not permitted, in an attempt to increase the salmon population in the river. The Lærdal Elveeigarlag website is the best place to get information about the current regulations.

Shopping

Fredag

Monsemarki 4; https://heifredag.no; Tues.-Fri. 8am-4:30pm, Sat.-Sun. 10am-4pm

"Fredag" means Friday, and in this colorful concept store each product was selected to help give you that weekend feeling that only comes on a Friday. Products here include creative bullet journals and notebooks with prompts, luxurious scented candles, fun board games, and clever travel gear. The shop is situated in one of the charming timber houses in the Old Town.

Food

Laksen Bakeri & Café

Øyraplassen 14; tel. 99 20 26 14; www.norwaysbest.com/no/overnatting-og-restauranter/laksen-bakeri--kafe; noon-8pm June-Aug.

Laksen Bakeri & Cafe is located in the same building as the Norwegian Wild Salmon Center. The name Laksen translates to "the salmon," which is fitting. Here, you can enjoy a large selection of freshly made pastries and savory baked goods, in addition to ready-made sandwiches (perfect for lunch). They also have takeaway pizza available, and there is a large outdoor seating area.

Kort og Godt

Øyraplassen 6; tel. 94 25 22 22; daily 11am-5pm; 59-199 kr

Kort og Godt is a small café right on the main street in Lærdal. This is a relaxed place where you can grab a sandwich or bite for lunch, or try some more traditional Scandinavian dishes (such as smoked salmon or rømmegrøt—sour cream porridge).

Accommodations

Lærdalsøren Hotel

Øyragata 15; tel. 93 87 45 82; www.lardalsorenhotel.no; 1,000 kr

Lærdalsøren Hotel is a traditional hotel located in one of the old wooden houses of

---

1: Lærdalsøyri 2: view from the hike to Mjølkeflathytta

downtown Lærdal. The streets surrounding the hotel make you feel like you've traveled back in time, and the hotel itself aims to do the same. The 11 guest rooms of the hotel are all decorated in a classic style, inspired by the 1800s. Only one of the rooms has an en suite bathroom. The other 10 rooms share four bathrooms, reminiscent of how one would have lived there 200 years ago.

Lindstrøm Hotel
Øyraplassen 3; tel. 57 66 69 00; www.lindstromhotel. no; 1,600 kr

Lindstrøm Hotel is located in the center of Lærdal. The hotel has a newer main building from the 1960s, and a Swiss-style wooden villa from 1899. In the newer building and annex, the modern Scandinavian rooms are bright and stylish, while old meets new in the Swiss building "Nybu," where some of the furniture is original and some has been swapped out for more modern pieces. The hotel has 86 rooms in total.

Information and Services
Lærdal Tourist Information
Øyraplassen 14; tel. 48 27 75 26; daily 11am-7pm June-Dec.

For hiking maps, brochures, and information about the surrounding area, visit the tourist information in Lærdal.

Getting There and Around
From Flåm and Aurland, Lærdal is located through Norway's longest road tunnel, the Lærdal Tunnel. The tunnel goes through the mountain Aurlandsfjellet. It is 24.5 kilometers (15.2 mi) long, which is quite impressive, and it takes around 20 minutes to drive through.

The drive from Flåm to Lærdal takes around 40 minutes, and it is 30 minutes from Aurland. The tunnel makes up the majority of the drive. In the summer, Lærdal can also be reached by driving across Aurlandsfjellet on the road called The Snow Road (part of Norway's National Tourist Routes, and technically Route 243). The Snow Road (Snøvegen) is usually open from May to

October (snow-dependent). The drive across the mountain between Aurland and Lærdal takes around 1.5 hours.

The regional Nor-way buses that pass-through Gudvangen, Flåm, and Aurland along E16 also pass through Lærdal. They offer the best (and most popular) way to travel between the Aurlandsfjord and Lærdal by bus.

Driving from Oslo to Lærdal will take you around 4.5 hours, along E16 and Route 7 (284 km/177 mi). This is the same as the drive for the Aurlandsfjord area.

From Oslo, Vy (tel. 40 70 50 70; www.vy-buss.no) has daily departures, and the journey time is around 6 hours. The Nor-Way (tel. 22 31 31 50; www.nor-way.no) bus from Bergen also stops in Lærdal, with a journey time of 3.5 hours.

Get around Lærdal by walking. The village is small, and all of the sights in the village center are within walking distance.

FJÆRLAND AND JOSTEDALSBREEN

The main reason to visit the town of Fjærland is its proximity to the Jostedalsbreen glacier. The largest glacier in (mainland) Norway is worth seeing, and those visiting Fjærland are able to experience it with just a 5-minute walk from the road. This is the reason Fjærland became a tourist destination in the first place, as 100 years ago wealthy travelers would arrive to the village by boat (it is nestled along the Sognefjord, and thus reachable from the ocean), and be transported up the valley to the glacier arm Bøyabreen by horse and carriage.

Today, the glacier itself is a cool sight, but you can also learn a lot at the Norwegian Glacier Museum in the town center. Therefore, Fjærland is the ideal stop for travelers with a fascination for glaciers.

Sights
Jostedalsbreen Glacier
https://jostedalsbreen.no

Jostedalsbreen is the largest glacier in (continental) Europe and covers 487 square meters (1,600 sq ft) across the municipalities of Sogndal, Luster, Jølster, and Stryn. When looking at a map of Norway, Jostedalsbreen is the largest white "dot" you see on the map, so it is quite easy to spot. The glacier is young, no more than 2,000 years old, which means it is not a remnant from the last ice age in Norway (some 7,000 years ago), as many people assume. Jostedalsbreen National Park was founded in 1991, and today the glacier makes up about half of the park. The rest of the national park consists of narrow, lush valleys, rushing rivers, and cascading waterfalls.

In Fjærland you will find one of the three main gateways to the glacier, with the other two being in Jostedalen 8 (1 hour and 45 minutes away), and Stryn (a 2-hour drive from Fjærland), both north of Fjærland. One benefit of seeing the glacier arm Bøyabreen in Fjærland is how easy it is to get to. Another reason for Fjærland being a popular choice is that it is closer to other tourist destinations, such as the Nærøyfjord and the Borgund Stave Church, making it easier to plan around.

Bøyabreen

Bøyabreen is the arm of the Jostedalsbreen glacier that is visible from Fjærland, just a short walk from the road (it is even visible from the road). In recent years the glacier arm has retracted significantly but is still visible. Walk up to the base of the mountain to see the beautiful glacial lake below Bøyabreen, and see the glacier arm itself up close. To get to it, drive north along Route 5 for 15 minutes, and you will see it on your right. There is a dirt road and parking area just before you enter the Fjærland tunnel where you can park. From there, the walk to the glacier lake just below Bøyabreen is an easy 5-minute stroll.

Norwegian Glacier Museum

Fjærlandsfjorden 13; www.bre.museum.no; daily Apr.-Oct.; adults 140 kr, children 70 kr

The Glacier Museum in Fjærland opened in 1991 and is an interactive museum meant to share the knowledge we have of glaciers and how they affect the landscape below and around them. Viewing the exhibitions here,

you will learn more about how glaciers form, how they shape the landscape, and how they can help us learn more about past civilizations and cultures. Part of the museum is the Ulltveit-Moe Climate Center, where you are taken on an interactive journey through the ages, from the earth's creation to the year 2100. It is worth noting that the Norwegian Glacier Museum in Fjærland is an authorized national park center for Jostedalsbreen National Park.

Book Town

Fjærlandsfjorden 308; https://bokbyen.no; daily May-Sept.; free

In Mundal, the village center of Fjærland, you will find the Norwegian Book Town, which opened in 1996. Across the town you will find lots of miniature libraries, built as small huts, roofed bookshelves, and inside actual buildings. In the collection they have more than 150,000 used books for sale in all categories, and it truly is a haven for literature lovers. The several outlets that are part of the Book Town are open from May to Sepbember, with some "honesty outlets" being open all year.

Glacier Tours
Fjærland Guiding

Tel. 95 82 91 71; https://fjaerlandguiding.com; daily tours July-Sept.; 950 kr

Fjærland Guiding offers a wide range of guided tours. If you want to try glacier hiking, they have a 6-7-hour excursion and hike to Haugabreen, one of Jostedalsbreen's glacier arms. The experience includes 2-3 hours spent on the ice. For those who want to remain a little closer to the fjord, Fjærland Guiding also offers a shorter family hike along the fjord on a 12-kilometer (7.5-mi) trail (https://fjaerlandguiding.com/mundalvalleyhike; May-Oct.; 300 kr).

Food and Accommodations
Fjærland Fjordstove
Hotel & Restaurant

Fjærlandsfjorden 258; tel. 48 23 78 44; https:// fjaerlandhotel.com; 2,500 kr

This charming place is part of the Historic Hotels of Norway. The guesthouse dates back to 1937, and the small hotel, although fully renovated, is all about keeping that old-school charm. There are only 14 rooms, each individually decorated with basic furniture and charming details, such as wooden poufs or built-in bookshelves beside the bed. They all also have en suite bathrooms and views of either the fjord or the mountains behind. The restaurant is open for lunch and dinner daily from May to October, and hotel guests get a discounted price off their three-course set menu (620 kr). The menu changes frequently, depending on the season and ingredients available. Expect New Nordic dishes, such as wild salmon in lemon and thyme, and vegetable soup with cinnamon butter.

Information and Services
Fjærland Tourist Information
FvI52 41; tel. 94 79 80 36; www.fjaerland.org; daily 11am-5pm June-Aug.

The tourist information in Fjærland is open in the summer months to answer any questions you may have about the small town and its center (Mundal), or the Jostedalsbreen glacier.

Getting There and Around
The best way to reach Fjærland is by car, so making this a stop on a western Norway road trip is ideal. Fjærland is a 4.5-hour drive from Bergen (248 km/155 mi) via E39 and a 6-hour drive from Oslo (352 km/219 mi) via Route 52. The nearest regional bus station is Sogndal Skysstasjon (6856 Sogndal), a half-hour drive from Fjærland. There are direct buses to Sogndal from both Bergen (www.nor-way.no) and Oslo (www.vybuss.no). From Sogndal, local buses (2-3 departures a day) head to a bus stop called Fjærland Kryss, right by the Glacier Museum. To reach Fjærland from Voss, the villages along the Aurlandsfjord, and Lærdal, take the regional bus to Sogndal before changing to the local bus.

To reach Fjærland from Voss, simply follow E16 past Gudvangen, Flåm, Aurland, and Lærdal (through the Lærdal tunnel). In Lærdal, continue along Route 5, crossing the Sognefjord on the Manheller-Fodnes ferry (www.fjord1.no). The distance is 172 kilometers (107 mi) and will take you around 3 hours. From Lærdal, the drive is a little less than 1.5 hours (67 km/42 mi).

BALESTRAND
Balestrand is a very picturesque fjord village, mostly visited by those wanting to spend a quiet weekend (or night) at the historic Kviknes Hotel while taking in the serenity of the village and area. The sights here are not significant or numerous enough to fill a full day, but the sight of the fjord and the quiet of the place is reason enough to visit. This is a destination, similar to Undredal, for those wanting to get away from it all.

Sights
The English Church (St. Olaf's Church)
Kong Beles Veg 35; tel. 57 69 15 48; hours vary

The small wooden church in Balestrand, correctly named St. Olaf's Church but nicknamed the English Church, is one of the main sights of this beautiful village. It is owned and run by the Church of England, which explains the nickname. The red and yellow church is not a stave church, but was built to look just like one, which is why a lot of people mistake it for one. It was opened in 1897 and seats 95 people.

The reason why there is an English church in Balestrand is, one of the locals married an Englishwoman, Margaret Sophie Green Kvikne. The story goes that she never felt quite at home with the Lutheran ways of the Norwegian church, and that her last wish was for an Anglican church to be built in the village. Her widowed husband, Knut Kvikne, arranged for the building of the church after her passing. Services are held in English in the summer, by visiting ministers who spend summer by the fjord.

1: the English Church in Balestrand 2: Kviknes Hotel

Norwegian Museum of Travel and Tourism

Holmen 12; tel. 47 45 30 53; http://reiselivsmuseum.no; Tues.-Sun. 10am-3pm May-Sept., Thurs. 10am-3pm only in low season; adults 100 kr, children under 18 50 kr

The Norwegian Museum of Travel and Tourism displays exhibits relating to the history and importance of tourism in Norway through the years. From the salmon lords visiting the rivers of Norway to modern travelers taking epic hikes around the fjord, visitors have been coming here for ages. One of the exhibits is all about the National Tourist Routes of Norway, with Gaularfjellet being the nearest one to Balestrand.

Utsikten Viewpoint (Gaularfjellet)

www.nasjonaleturistveger.no/no/turistvegene/gaularfjellet

Gaularfjellet is a National Tourist Route (Norwegian Scenic Routes), starting in Balestrand and ending in Sande or Moskog, on the other side of the Gaularfjellet mountain. Not everyone drives across the entire mountain, but if you have some time in Balestrand, a drive up to the viewpoint Utsikten will be worth your time. This concrete viewpoint is built in pointed "peaks" from which you can enjoy the dramatic view of the valley below, and the hairpin turns of Route 13 as it climbs up the mountainside. From early May to the end of October there are public restrooms open at the viewpoint.

The viewpoint is a 40-minute (37 km/23 mi) drive from the Balestrand village center, along Routes 55 and 13.

Fjord Cruises
Balestrand Fjord Sightseeing

Holmen 3; tel. 47 85 53 23; www.balestrandfjordadventures.no; 1-2 departures daily mid-Apr.-mid-Oct.; 880 kr

The Sognefjord is at your feet when you join one of the RIB tours leaving the village with Balestrand Fjord Adventures. During this trip you will travel into the Esefjord and view the 120-meter-high (390-ft) waterfall Kvinnafossen. On the way back to the village you will learn about the Viking history of the area as you pass the statue of Fridtjof the Bold, a Viking who fell in love with a local princess. The duration of the tour is around 1 hour and 20 minutes.

Food and Accommodations
Balholm Bar & Bistro

Kviknevegen 8; tel. 57 69 42 00; www.kviknes.no; daily 1pm-7pm

Balholm is the a la carte restaurant at Kviknes Hotel. Here you can expect local and international dishes with seasonal and fresh ingredients. Dishes include a Caesar salad with trout from the fjord, and the Sognefjord sandwich: crayfish and smoked salmon on sourdough bread. Balholm is more casual than the hotel's main dining room, with beautiful blue accents across the restaurant.

Kviknes Hotel

Kviknevegen 8; tel. 57 69 42 00; www.kviknes.no; 2,800 kr

Kviknes Hotel is the first building you will notice when visiting Balestrand. This grand Swiss-style hotel has 190 rooms and dates back to 1752. Through the years it has hosted several notable guests, such as Emperor Wilhelm II of Germany and other royalty, movie stars, and presidents. The rooms are renovated and modern, but with a quaint, historic charm. With pastel colors and delicate details, they will make you feel right at home.

Information and Services
Balestrand Tourist Information

Holmen 3; tel. 94 87 75 01; www.visitbalestrand.com; open daily in summer, hours follow Balestrand Adventure's departure times

Balestrand Adventure functions as the tourist information of Balestrand, and can be found on the docks of the village. Here you can pick up maps of the area and information about nearby sights.

Getting There and Around

The best way to reach Balestrand from Bergen in the summer months is by boat. Travel along the fjord with the express **Norled** boat (tel. 51 86 87 00; www.norled.no) from Bergen. The boat leaves Bergen every morning between mid-May and end of September and gets you to Balestrand (or back) in 4 hours. The boat ride is quite scenic, though it is an express boat and travels fast through the fjord. You will get to experience the Sognefjord as it grows more dramatic (i.e., steeper mountains and narrower in parts) as you travel into the country.

From Oslo, Balestrand is a 6.5-hour drive along Route 52. From Bergen, the drive will take you 3 hours and 40 minutes via Voss (196 km/121 mi). Follow E16 to Voss and a little farther, before taking Route 13 toward Vik (and crossing the Vikafjellet mountain). The drive from Voss to Balestrand takes a little more than 2 hours.

If you travel by bus, there are express buses to Sogndal from both Oslo and Bergen (www.vybuss.no and www.nor-way.no). Local Route 516 (tel. 177; www.skyss.no) leaves Sogndal for Balestrand three times a day, with a journey time of 1 hour and 15 minutes. In the summer, the best way to reach Balestrand from the Aurlandsfjord (Flåm, Aurland, Gudvangen, Undredal) area is by boat; the same express boat company that goes from Bergen also operates from Flåm once a day in the summer. For the rest of the year, traveling by regional bus to Sogndal (www.nor-way.no) and then taking local bus 820 (www.skyss.no) will get you from Flåm to Balestrand in 3.5 hours.

Ålesund and the Northwestern Fjords

North of Bergen and the Sognefjord you will

find more fjords cutting into the coastline, and the Geirangerfjord and Nordfjord offer more of the dramatic scenery that is synonymous with Norway. The Sognefjord might be Norway's longest, but the Geirangerfjord is probably the most photographed fjord in Norway. With sheer vertical mountain drops, tiny farms nestled on mountain plateaus, and impressive waterfalls, the Geirangerfjord was added to the UNESCO World Heritage List in 2005 along with the Nærøyfjord. Together, these two fjords epitomize the Norwegian landscape, and if you manage to see both during your trip (they are located almost 5.5 hours apart), you can really say you have seen the World Heritage fjords of Norway.

Highlights

Look for ★ to find recommended sights, activities, dining, and lodging.

★ **Aksla Viewpoint:** The city mountain of Ålesund is accessible via a short hike or by car, and offers the most famous view of the city (page 226).

★ **Seven Sisters and Suitor Waterfalls:** During the Geiranger fjord cruise you will see two of the most famous waterfalls in Norway: the Seven Sisters and the Suitor (page 238).

★ **Geiranger Fjord Cruises:** Going on a fjord cruise through the Geiranger fjord is a bucket-list experience (page 240).

★ **Loen Skylift:** The new cable car takes you from the fjord to the top of Mount Hoven in just a few minutes, where you'll find spectacular views and a restaurant (page 244).

★ **The Atlantic Road:** This impressive piece of road, connecting several small islands by bridges is a destination in itself (page 251).

Nordfjord is 106 kilometers (65 mi) long, stretching into the country and ending in the tourist towns of Stryn, Loen, and Olden. Here, you will find historic hotels, picturesque villages, glacier lakes, and several access points to the Jostedalsbreen Glacier and National Park. The towns along Nordfjord are natural stopping points on the drive between the Nærøyfjord and Geirangerfjord, and should not be missed. Whether you are looking for a bit of technical hiking on the Via Ferrata in Loen, or just want to explore the epic views from Mount Hoven (made accessible by the Loen Skylift cable car), you'll do well to spend a few days here.

At the top of this region, you will find Norway's art nouveau city of Ålesund. This charming city, with its turrets, towers, and fairy-tale buildings, is different from the wooden fishing towns that are typically found along Norway's coastline; Ålesund actually looks nothing like Bergen or Stavanger. This is because the majority of the city burned down in a fire in 1904, which led to the city being rebuilt in the current art nouveau style. The city is worth visiting for its architectural style alone but is also a great base for anyone wanting to explore the fjords from the north.

ORIENTATION

Ålesund, Åndalsnes, and the village of Geiranger on the Geirangerfjord form a triangle in this region of western Norway. Ålesund is the farthest west, with Åndalsnes lying almost directly east of it. Geiranger is south of Åndalsnes. The county Møre og Romsdal covers the region around Ålesund, Åndalsnes, and Geirangerfjord. The county is split into three geographical regions: Sunnmøre (where you will find Geiranger and Ålesund), Romsdal (which includes Molde and Åndalsnes), and Nordmøre (where you will find Kristiansund).

The Nordfjord region is south of the Geirangerfjord.

PLANNING YOUR TIME

A week is an ideal amount of time to explore this part of Norway. If you intend on getting between the different areas using public transport, spend 2-3 nights in Ålesund, 1-2 in Geiranger, and 2-3 in the Nordfjord area. The rural areas covered in this chapter are not heavily serviced by public transportation, so you will need to plan around the limited departures. If you have a car, you can spend a week with a lot more freedom, but you could also get away with spending as little as 3-4 days in the region. The scenery around Ålesund and the northwestern fjords is beautiful, and you'll want to set aside plenty of time to take in the views.

However, note that many experiences and sights, such as going glacier hiking or embarking on the Via Ferrata, are full-day activities. Additionally, there are some significant distances between the locations mentioned, which means that you will need to plan an itinerary that includes moving from town to town. Western Norway is not a place where you can see the region from one home base for the duration of your trip.

If you have less time, you might find that you have to skip a fjord. If so, consider your point of departure: If you are flying into Ålesund and starting your trip there, focus your time on Ålesund and the Geirangerfjord. If your trip starts in Bergen or around the Sognefjord, it might be best to go no farther north than Nordfjord. Regardless, each of the fjords in this chapter has its own appeal, and each is worth visiting.

The small village of Geiranger is best visited in the summer months, with several restaurants and shops only being open from June to August. The fjord cruise through the Geirangerfjord also only runs in the summer months. As Ålesund is a city, you'll find that most services and activities are available year-round, but even here the opening hours are more limited in the low season. Therefore, this

---

Previous: the picturesque village of Geiranger; Seven Sisters Waterfall; view of Ålesund from Aksla Viewpoint.

Ålesund and the Northwestern Fjords

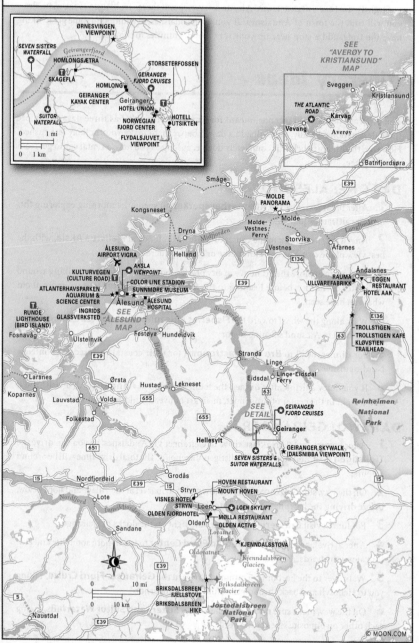

ØRNESVINGEN VIEWPOINT
SEVEN SISTERS WATERFALL
Geirangerfjord
HOMLONGSÆTRA
STORSETERFOSSEN
SKAGEFLÅ
GEIRANGER FJORD CRUISES
HOMLONG
GEIRANGER KAYAK CENTER
Geiranger
HOTEL UNION
SUITOR WATERFALL
NORWEGIAN FJORD CENTER
HOTELL UTSIKTEN
FLYDALSJUVET VIEWPOINT
0   1 mi
0   1 km

SEE "AVERØY TO KRISTIANSUND" MAP
Sveggen
Kristiansund
THE ATLANTIC ROAD
Kårvåg
Vevang
Averøy
Batnfjordsøra

Småge
Kongsneset
Dryna
MOLDE PANORAMA
Molde
Molde-Vestnes Ferry
Storvika
Vestnes
Åfarnes
E39
Midhjorden
Langfjorden
ÅLESUND AIRPORT VIGRA
Helland
E136
Åndalsnes
AKSLA VIEWPOINT
KULTURVEGEN (CULTURE ROAD)
COLOR LINE STADION
ATLANTERHAVSPARKEN AQUARIUM & SCIENCE CENTER
SUNNMØRE MUSEUM
ÅLESUND HOSPITAL
E39
RAUMA ULLVAREFABRIKK
EGGEN RESTAURANT
HOTEL AAK
RUNDE LIGHTHOUSE (BIRD ISLAND)
INGRIDS GLASSVERKSTED
Ålesund
SEE ÅLESUND MAP
E136
Fosnavåg
Festøya
Hundeidvik
Storfjorden
TROLLSTIGEN
TROLLSTIGEN KAFÉ
KLØVSTIEN TRAILHEAD
Ulsteinvik
63
E39
Stranda
Linge
Larsnes
Ørsta
Hustad
Lekneset
Eidsdal
Linge-Eidsdal Ferry
Reinheimen National Park
Koparnes
Lauvstad
Volda
655
63
Folkestad
655
GEIRANGER FJORD CRUISES
651
SEE DETAIL
Geiranger
Hellesylt
GEIRANGER SKYWALK (DALSNIBBA VIEWPOINT)
SEVEN SISTERS & SUITOR WATERFALLS
15
Nordfjordeid
Grodås
15
HOVEN RESTAURANT
MOUNT HOVEN
Nordfjord
E39
Lote
Stryn
VISNES HOTEL STRYN
Loen
LOEN SKYLIFT
Innviksfjorden
OLDEN FJORDHOTEL
Olden
MØLLA RESTAURANT
OLDEN ACTIVE
Sandane
Lovatnet Lake
KJENNDALSSTOVA
Oldevatnet
Kjenndalsbreen Glacier
E39
BRIKSDALSBREEN FJELLSTOVE
Briksdalsbreen Glacier
5
Naustdal
BRIKSDALSBREEN HIKE
Jostedalsbreen National Park
E39
0   10 mi
0   10 km

© MOON.COM

region is best for a summer trip, to ensure you don't miss out on any of the major activities.

Slightly farther inland from Ålesund you will find the town of Åndalsnes. If you have the time, add a stop here on your way to Geiranger, in order to drive the famous Trollstigen mountain pass and stop at the viewpoint there. Trollstigen is the main draw to Åndalsnes, in addition to some great hiking opportunities in the area.

Itinerary Ideas

The itinerary below is a busy one, meant for someone who only has three days to explore these destinations. Ideally, you will add a day in between, to make your holiday less rushed. However, the itinerary below is completely doable, as long as you have a rental car to get from place to place.

DAY ONE: ÅLESUND

1 After breakfast, head to **Atlanterhavsparken** to spend the morning exploring this unique saltwater aquarium.

2 Afterward, head back to the center of Ålesund for lunch at **Fjellstua Aksla,** with the best view of the city. You can either hike or drive up there.

3 It's time to explore the art nouveau city of Ålesund. Spend some time walking around the center of the city, before heading to the **Art Nouveau Center** to learn more about what you have seen.

4 Walk along the wharf toward the **Fisheries Museum,** where you can explore exhibitions related to Ålesund's fishing history.

5 For dinner, head to **Bro Kystgastronomi** for their coastal-inspired take on New Nordic cuisine.

6 If you fancy a drink after dinner, the lounge and bar at **Anno** is worth a visit. You'll find it right in the center of Brosundet, in an art nouveau building from 1907.

DAY TWO: GEIRANGER

1 After an early hotel breakfast, drive to Geiranger via Åndalsnes, so you can drive the **Trollstigen** road, and stop at the Trollstigen Viewpoint. The total drive time will be around 4 hours.

2 On the way, stop at **Ørnesvingen Viewpoint** to marvel at the village and fjord below, before driving the hairpin turns down to the fjord.

3 For lunch, visit **Brasserie Posten** to dine right on the docks of Geiranger.

4 After arrival, head to the **Norwegian Fjord Center** to learn more about life and culture along the fjords.

5 Walk over to the harbor (4-5 minutes) to board the **Geiranger Fjord Cruise,** taking you to Hellesylt and back through the famous Geirangerfjord.

6 On the way, make sure not to miss the **Seven Sisters and Suitor Waterfalls,** facing each other on opposite sides of the fjord.

Itinerary Ideas

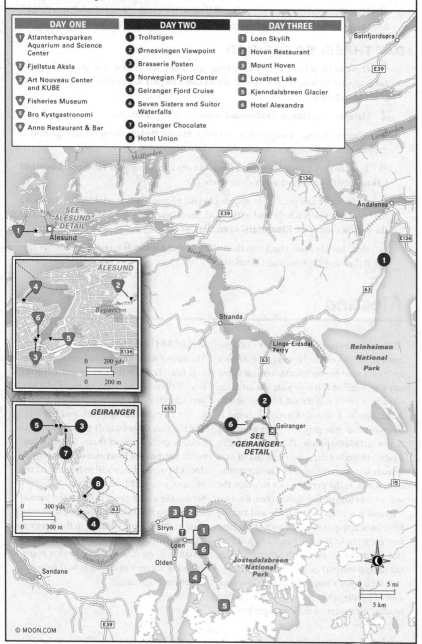

DAY ONE

1. Atlanterhavsparken Aquarium and Science Center
2. Fjellstua Aksla
3. Art Nouveau Center and KUBE
4. Fisheries Museum
5. Bro Kystgastronomi
6. Anno Restaurant & Bar

DAY TWO

1. Trollstigen
2. Ørnesvingen Viewpoint
3. Brasserie Posten
4. Norwegian Fjord Center
5. Geiranger Fjord Cruise
6. Seven Sisters and Suitor Waterfalls
7. Geiranger Chocolate
8. Hotel Union

DAY THREE

1. Loen Skylift
2. Hoven Restaurant
3. Mount Hoven
4. Lovatnet Lake
5. Kjenndalsbreen Glacier
6. Hotel Alexandra

© MOON.COM

7   After your fjord cruise, make sure to visit **Geiranger Chocolate,** a shop located in the center of the village by the docks.

8   Have dinner at the Brasserie at **Hotel Union.** If you are craving after-dinner drinks, head to the lobby bar at Union to sample some wines from their extensive cellar.

DAY THREE: NORDFJORD

1   Drive to Loen immediately after breakfast, along Route 63 and Route 15. The drive takes around 1.5 hours. Upon arrival, get on **Loen Skylift** to enjoy the spectacular views of the fjord below.

2   Have lunch at **Hoven Restaurant** at the top of the mountain.

3   After lunch, enjoy a walk around the top of **Mount Hoven.** There are several trails to explore here, including a zipline for those who dare.

4   Take the skylift back down to the fjord, and drive up to enjoy the views over **Lovatnet Lake.** The drive is 5-10 minutes along Route 723.

5   Once you've had your fill of stopping to take photos of Lovatnet, keep driving along the lake until you reach the end of the road. From here, walk the 5 kilometers (3 mi) up the narrow road to see **Kjenndalsbreen Glacier.**

6   Head back to Loen, check into the historic **Hotel Alexandra,** and enjoy a buffet dinner at their elegant Restaurant Charlotte.

Ålesund

Ålesund is a beautiful city nestled along the coast of northwestern Norway. It is known for its art nouveau architecture (most of the city was rebuilt in this style after a devastating city fire in 1904), and the Atlanterhavsparken Aquarium and Science Center. Ålesund is Norway's ninth-largest city, with a population of just 67,000 people. This makes this city a perfect blend of the urban and quaint as it spreads across several islands. The city mountain, Aksla, is the perfect place to watch the sun set into (or rise from) the ocean. Because Ålesund is a coastal city, trade and fishing have been important to the way of life here for centuries. In the mornings you will find that the docks are alive with fishermen coming in (and leaving) on their boats.

Since it is just a 2-hour drive from Geiranger, a lot of people opt to fly into Ålesund before heading off to explore the Geirangerfjord and surrounding area.

Orientation

The city of Ålesund is spread out across several islands, with the city center covering one of them, in addition to parts of a second island. When you are walking around in the city center, however, you can't really tell that these islands are separated, as bridges cross between them. The city center surrounds the **Brosundet Marina,** the docks between the two islands. Around the Marina you will find plenty of the city's hotels, the art nouveau district, the base of the hike up to Aksla Mountain, and several restaurants. Basing yourself in this area ensures that most sights are within walking distance. Regardless of where you are going, knowing where Brosundet is will help you to get your bearings.

Ålesund

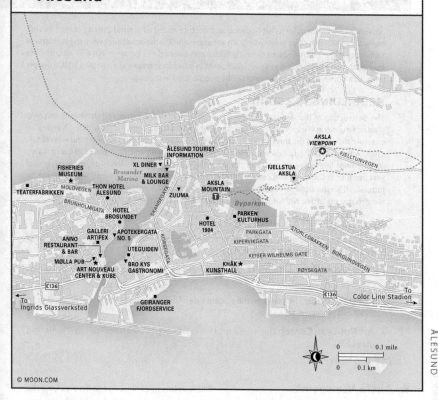

Map labels:
AKSLA VIEWPOINT
ÅLESUND TOURIST INFORMATION
FJELLTUNVEGEN
XL DINER
FISHERIES MUSEUM
Brosundet Marina
MILK BAR & LOUNGE
FJELLSTUA AKSLA
TEATERFABRIKKEN
MOLOVEGEN
THON HOTEL ÅLESUND
AKSLA MOUNTAIN
ZUUMA
Byparken
BRUNHOLMGATA
HOTEL BROSUNDET
SKANSEGATA
PARKEN KULTURHUS
GALLERI ARTIFEX
APOTEKERGATA NO. 5
HOTEL 1904
ANNO RESTAURANT & BAR
UTEGUIDEN
KORSEGATA
PARKGATA
KIPERVIKGATA
STORLEDBAKKEN
BORGUNDVEGEN
MØLLA PUB
ART NOUVEAU CENTER & KUBE
BRO KYS GASTRONOMI
KEISER WILHELMS GATE
KHÅK KUNSTHALL
RØYSEGATA
E136
To Ingrids Glassverksted
GEIRANGER FJORDSERVICE
E136
To Color Line Stadion

© MOON.COM

0   0.1 mile
0   0.1 km

SIGHTS

Art Nouveau Center and KUBE

*Apotekergata 16; tel. 70 10 49 70; www.vitimusea.no/
musea/jugendstilsenteret-kube; Tues.-Fri. noon-6pm,
Sat.-Sun. noon-4pm; adults 110 kr, children free*

In the heart of Ålesund you will find the Art
Nouveau Center and KUBE, an art museum
dedicated to the art nouveau style, as well
as being the main center for arts in the region. You can expect to find everything from
original art nouveau interior pieces to exhibitions of contemporary art. Their collection
comprises pieces dating from the late 1800s
until today, and they have a specific focus on
Nordic artists and art with a connection to the
region surrounding Ålesund.

Fisheries Museum

*Molovegen 10; tel. 70 23 90 00; www.vitimusea.no/
musea/fiskerimuseet; Mon.-Fri. 11am-4pm, Sat.-Sun.
noon-4pm June-Aug.; adults 70 kr, children free*

Trade and fishing have always been important for the coastal city of Ålesund, and at
the Fisheries Museum you can learn more
about this history. Explore how modern fishing came about and how the city was shaped
by it. You will find the museum on one of
the best preserved streets from before the
1904 fire. The building that houses the museum, Holm-bua (also called Jervell-bua by
older locals) is a large, white wooden wharf
building—easily recognizable in the harbor.
It dates back to 1858.

Art Nouveau in Ålesund

Ålesund is well-known for its art nouveau architecture found all around the city center. As with many other wooden cities in Norway (such as Bergen and Kristiansand), fires were the main threat to the city in the 1800s and into the early 1900s, and one night in January 1904 a devastating fire burned through the city, leaving over 800 houses in ashes and rendering more than 10,000 people without a home. At the time, around 12,000 people lived in the city.

REBUILDING ÅLESUND

The destruction of that January night made headlines all over Europe, and donations and help started pouring in—especially from Germany, which had trade agreements with the Norwegian coastal cities. During the three years that followed, between 1904 and 1907, Ålesund was rebuilt. The government passed a new regulation, insisting that Norwegian cities needed to use concrete for buildings in the city centers. The city was rebuilt using concrete and brick, in the style that was popular in Germany and central Europe at the time. However, the term "art nouveau" (or jugendstil) wasn't used to describe the aesthetic choices of the day. The Norwegian architects were more concerned with preventing fires and accidents than with style.

ARCHITECTURAL HIGHLIGHTS

You can find examples of art nouveau architecture all over the city center, and here are a few of the best places to see them:

- **Brosundet Marina:** The buildings surrounding the Marina are a great sampling of the art nouveau style.
- **Kongens Gate:** This street on the eastern side of the Marina was the first in Ålesund to be listed as a protected area.
- **Art Nouveau Center:** This museum is a necessary stop to understand this style in Ålesund (page 225).

★ Aksla Viewpoint

Parkgata 11; open 24/7; free

The most well-known image of Ålesund is taken from the Aksla Viewpoint, which is at the top of the city mountain. Named "the roof of Ålesund," there is no better place to take in the sights of the city, and to get an overview of all the small streets and art nouveau buildings below. In addition, you can see the other mountains surrounding the city, and the ocean just past them. It is possible to hike the 418 steps to the top or drive the whole way (follow Fjelltunvegen to Fjellstua Aksla).

Atlanterhavsparken Aquarium and Science Center

Tueneset; tel. 70 10 70 60; www.atlanterhavsparken.no; daily 9am-5pm in summer, daily 10am-4pm in winter; adults 225 kr, children under 15 100 kr

There is lots to explore in the ocean along the Norwegian coast, and at Atlanterhavsparken Aquarium and Science Center you can get a glimpse of it all. In the Aquarium part of the center, you can view fish and species found in the Atlantic Ocean and along the Norwegian coastline, such as herring, otters, and seals. The Aquarium contains one of Europe's largest saltwater tanks, where you can view some of the massive cold-water fish that live off the coast. Throughout the day there are several experiences to join, such as feeding the fish and penguins. In the Science Center they have several interactive exhibits that teach you about aquatic life and how fishing has affected Norway.

Atlanterhavsparken—which is at the end of Hessa, the western-most island in Ålesund—is a 10-minute drive from the city center, and there is free parking for visitors. Bus route 1 (tel. 71 28 01 00; www.frammr.no) leaves from Apotekertorget in the city center every 20 minutes, and takes you to bus stop Tuenesvegen in less than 5 minutes. From there, the Aquarium is a 10-15-minute walk.

Sunnmøre Museum

Museumsvegen 12; tel. 70 23 90 00; www.vitimusea.no/musea/sunnmoere-museum; Tues.-Fri. noon-6pm, Sat.-Sun noon-4pm; adults 110 kr adults, children free

The Sunnmøre Museum is an outdoor museum consisting of buildings from all around the Sunnmøre region, the southern part of the Norwegian county Møre og Romsdal ("sunn" means south), where Ålesund is located. The region is distinct due to its dramatic fjords and peaked mountains (the mountain ranges in the region are nicknamed "the Sunnmøre Alps" as a result). The museum tells the story of how people lived as farmers in communities all around the area, and what life was like for them. In the summer months, there are costumed actors bringing the museum to life, giving you a truly immersive way to learn.

SPORTS AND RECREATION

Fjord Cruise

Geiranger Fjordservice

www.geirangerfjord.no/fjord-cruise-alesund-geiranger; daily departures June-Sept., select days Mar.-May; 1,410 kr round-trip

If you are visiting the region but don't have time to travel between Ålesund and the fjords, you'll be happy to hear that it is possible to explore the UNESCO-listed Geirangerfjord from the docks of Ålesund. This tour takes you from Ålesund and into the Geirangerfjord, past the famous waterfalls of the Suitor and the Seven Sisters onboard a catamaran vessel. There are refreshments sold onboard, and audio guides are available in English. The trip takes 3 hours each way, and it is possible to book a return for the same day. The tour leaves from Brosundet Marina, the docks in the center of Ålesund.

It is possible to travel one-way on the fjord cruise and spend a night in Geiranger. The one-way cost of the fjord cruise is 830 kr per person, and a night's accommodation in Geiranger costs around 2,100 kr. If you are visiting Ålesund and the area without a car, this is a great mode of transportation to see both the village of Geiranger and the Geiranger fjord.

Kayaking

Uteguiden

Notenesgata 3; tel. 40 55 46 70; https://uteguiden.com/havkajakk/familietur-alesund; 10am and 2pm; 699 kr

Kayaking out of the bay of Ålesund and around the city is a great way to explore. This family kayak trip is a guided tour of around 7 kilometers (4.5 mi), suitable for beginners and families. The excursion starts and ends in the city center and lasts around 2.5 hours. Along the way the guide will tell you about the history of Ålesund and point out interesting things you see while you paddle.

Hiking

Kulturvegen (Culture Road)

Distance: *3 kilometers (1.9 mi)*
Time: *45 minutes one-way*
Difficulty: *Easy*
Trailhead: *Valdervoll sports ground*

The Culture Road is an easy 3-kilometer (1.9-mi) stroll along a well-marked nature trail at Valderøya island. Along the way you might see the majestic sea eagle and can explore several caves and rock formations created by the ocean through the centuries. Follow the trail back the same way as you came. The Culture Road was given its name due to the rock formations and caves, as it is assumed that these were of cultural significance to those living on the islands centuries ago. From the Ålesund Bus Station, bus route 3 (www.frammr.no) leaves once an hour and will take you to bus stop Ytterland on Valderøya island in 15 minutes. From there, the sports ground is a 10-minute walk.

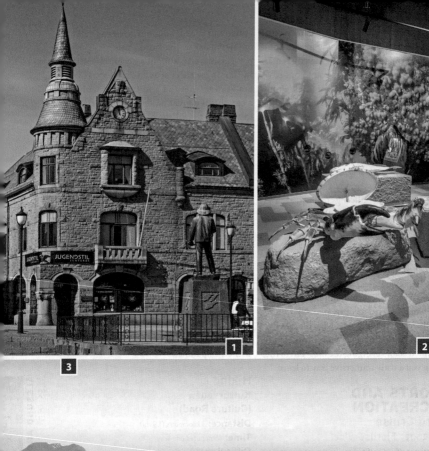

1

2

3

Best Places to See the Sunset

Due to its location all the way out at the coast, and the way the islands scattered in and around Ålesund keep the nearby waters relatively still, you can catch some pretty spectacular sunsets from almost anywhere in the city. The absolute best place to catch the sunset is from **Aksla Viewpoint** (page 226). Either hike or drive up to the top and enjoy the views of the surrounding islands and the ocean as the sun sets. Another great spot is from **Atlanterhavsparken** (page 226). From there, you have almost unobstructed views of the ocean and can watch the sun set on the horizon.

Aksla Mountain

Distance: *418 steps (140 m/460 ft)*
Time: *20 minutes one-way*
Difficulty: *Moderate*
Trailhead: *Kanona*
Information and Maps: *www.visitnorway.no/ listings/aksla-utsiktspunkt/13893*

Taking in the view from the Aksla Viewpoint is a must when in Ålesund, and the relatively short hike up to the top from the city center (just east of Brosundet Marina) has been made easier by the creation of 418 steps. Along the way, turn around from time to time to look at the view of the city; it just gets better and better. Additionally, you will find several benches and break points as you go, so you can climb the stairs at a leisurely pace.

Runde Lighthouse (Bird Island)

Distance: *3.3 kilometers (2 mi)*
Time: *1.5 hours one-way*
Difficulty: *Moderate*
Trailhead: *Kvalneset*

If you have a car, consider driving even farther west, to Runde Island. Runde Lighthouse is located at the tip of the small island of Runde, inhabited by a large variety of birds. This is one of the best places in Norway to see puffins, and Runde is often referred to as a "bird island." Please note that because of the birds' endangered status, it is illegal to hike to the lighthouse from March 15 to August 31.

1: Art Nouveau Center and KUBE
2: Atlanterhavsparken Aquarium and Science Center **3:** view of Ålesund from Aksla Viewpoint

The hike itself starts off very steep (a 200-m/650-ft ascent) before you start following the well-marked path across the islands. Keep your camera ready here, as you will see a lot of birds. Finally, you descend to the lighthouse, which opened in 1767. Runde island is a 2.5-hour drive from Ålesund.

ENTERTAINMENT AND EVENTS

The Arts

Parken Kulturhus

Parkgata 3B; tel. 70 16 24 68; https://parkenkulturhus. no

Parken Kulturhus is a cultural venue in Ålesund seating 500 people in its main hall. Here, you can see mainly national (but also some international) musicians, stand-up comedians, and theater productions.

Teaterfabrikken

Moloveien 22; tel. 70 10 04 10; www.teaterfabrikken.no

Teaterfabrikken is a live venue set in a former tran (cod liver oil) factory. Stand-up shows, comedy nights, and plays are staged here throughout the year.

Festivals and Events

Jugendfest

Color Line Stadion; www.jugendfest.no; Aug.

Jugendfest takes its name from the Norwegian term for art nouveau: jugendstil. This large two-day festival is packed with well-known Scandinavian and international artists within the pop, rap, and hip-hop genres; past performers have included Westlife, G-Eazy, Toto, and Steve Aoki.

Ålesund Live

St Olavs Plass; https://alesundlive.no; year-round

Ålesund Live are hard at work bringing big-name international artists to the city, with concerts being put on year-round. Music-lovers visiting Ålesund will do well to check their page for upcoming events. In the past, they have hosted artists such as Tiësto, Deep Purple, and Brit Floyd.

GALLERIES AND SHOPPING

KHÅK Kunsthall

Keiser Wilhelms Gate 36; www.khaak.no; Tues.-Thurs. 10am-5pm, Fri.-Sat. 11am-4pm, Sun. noon-4pm; free entry

KHÅK Art Hall is a gallery in the center of Ålesund where you can view exhibitions of contemporary art and graphics from a large selction of artists. There is free entry, and through the year they put on 8-10 rotating exhibitions.

Galleri Artifex

Apotekergata 10; www.artifex.no; Tues.-Sat. 11am-4:30pm

One of the largest galleries in the city is Galleri Artifex. They are dedicated to an-tiques, and arts and crafts from all over the world, with a special focus on art nouveau and the Norwegian National Romanticism period (ca. 1840-1860).

Ingrids Glassverksted

Ivar Aasens Gate 19; https://ingridsglassverksted.no; hours vary

Ingrid is a local glassblower with her own workshop in the city center. Here, you can shop home decor and practical gifts she has created, or even watch her work if you are lucky. Her colorful and flower-detailed col-lections are particularly popular.

FOOD

Anno Restaurant & Bar

Apotekergata 9B; tel. 71 70 70 77; www.anno.no; Mon. 11am-3pm, Wed. 11am-3pm, Thurs. 1pm-6pm, Fri.-Sat. 11am-3pm; 165-199 kr

Anno is located in one of the art nouveau houses of Ålesund, dating back to 1907. It is a short walk from the Art Nouveau Center. Their international menu is inspired by both French and Italian cuisine, and the pizza is made in their own wood-fired oven. Their ex-tensive menu includes lobster soup, stockfish, and fried catfish.

Zuuma

Skansegata 20; tel. 70 12 70 70; https://zuuma.no; daily 2pm-9pm; 145-269 kr

Zuuma is a popular Asian restaurant offer-ing a modern menu of Japanese-inspired food. In addition to sushi, they serve a selection of barbecue dishes, mixing Norwegian ingredi-ents with Asian fusion. On the menu you will find halibut dumplings and smoked teriyaki spareribs. The restaurant is bare and informal, with dark leather chairs and dark wood tables.

Apotekergata No. 5

Apotekergata No. 5; tel. 70 11 45 00; www. apotekergata5.no; Mon.-Sat. 11am-2am, Sun. 11am-6pm; 240-400 kr

Apotekergata 5 is simply named after its ad-dress, making it an easy restaurant to find. This relaxed and informal restaurant serves a menu of small dishes you are encouraged to share, such as bolinhos, smoked mackerel, and cheese from their own shop. They also have main courses for one (such as baked cod and marbled tenderloin), but the best value may be to choose their 5-course small-plates option for 775 kr, especially for two people sharing.

Bro Kystgastronomi

Notenesgata 1; tel. 70 30 81 81; http://brobro.no; daily 6pm-10pm; 300-450 kr

Bro Kystgastronomi (coastal gastronomi) focuses on local, seasonal ingredients and high-quality food. They serve dishes inspired by the Norwegian coast in their rustic, charming restaurant with bare concrete walls and light wooden chairs. The menu changes with the seasons, and you may find dishes such as mackerel, halibut, and crayfish.

XL Diner

Skaregata 1B; tel. 70 12 42 53; https://xldiner.no; Tues.-Thurs. 6pm-11pm, Fri.-Sat. 5pm-11:30pm; 178-498 kr

XL Diner might sound like an American truck stop, but this is actually quite an authentic Norwegian diner experience. They are famous for their bacalao, which comes in several different variations. The atmosphere is lively and friendly, and if you are lucky you will get a window table overlooking the harbor. Make sure to book in advance to get a table at this nautical-themed restaurant.

Fjellstua Aksla

Aksla; www.fjellstua.com; daily noon-5pm

At the top of Mount Aksla, Fjellstua Aksla is the perfect place to stop for an ice cream or cold drink after you have hiked the 418 steps to the top. Additionally, this bright, modern café serves dishes inspired by traditional Norwegian food, with a menu that changes daily based on the available ingredients. Expect dishes such as raspeballer (a traditional Norwegian dish made of potato, flower, salt, and water) and kjøttkaker (Norwegian meatballs).

BARS AND NIGHTLIFE

Milk Bar and Lounge

Skateflua, Skaregata 1A; tel. 70 12 42 53; www.milkbar.no; Mon.-Thurs. 6pm-1am, Fri.-Sat. 5pm-2:30am

Modern and stylish Milk Bar is located in old dock buildings right in the middle of the Marina. The name derives from the era when this was the hub for local farms to deliver milk and produce for shipments leaving the dock. The bar is trendy and welcoming, with muted lighting and dark wooden floors—as if you are walking on the dock. On the menu you will find a selection of cocktails, wine, and bottled beer, and enjoy them while looking over the marina.

Mølla Pub

Kirkegata 1; tel. 48 32 11 36; https://mlla.business.site; Sun.-Fri. 1pm-2am, Sat. 10am-2am

Mølla is a traditional pub where you will find pool, darts, and even karaoke on selected nights. It is frequented by locals, and ideal for those who want to enjoy some time in a warm and friendly atmosphere. They have several beers on tap, in addition to bottled beer. The cellar-like exposed brick walls are painted white and covered in slogans and quotes you'll have fun reading. It gets busier and livelier as the night goes on, especially on karaoke nights.

ACCOMMODATIONS

Hotel Brosundet

Apotekergata 1-5; tel. 70 10 33 00; www.brosundet.no; 1,600 kr

This design hotel is named after the neighborhood it is found in: Brosundet. The hotel is modern and stylish, with some traditional details, such as exposed wood beams in the rooms and ceilings, which makes for an interesting contrast to the bright walls and Nordic design found throughout the property. They have 129 rooms in total, including the famous Room 47, located in Molja Lighthouse. The lighthouse is set at the end of the bay in Ålesund, a 5-minute walk from the hotel's main building.

Thon Hotel Ålesund

Molovegen 6; tel. 70 10 20 80; www.thonhotels.no/hoteller/norge/alesund/thon-hotel-alesund; 1,600 kr

This large hotel is centrally located and contains 175 guest rooms, as well as amenities such as a gym and bar. The rooms are bright and colorful, with yellow details and funky wallpaper. Their substantial hotel breakfast focuses on local ingredients and produce, and is a great way to start the day. The hotel also has a guest dock available for those arriving with their own boat.

Hotel 1904

Løvenvoldgata 8; tel. 70 15 78 00; https://1904.no;
1,700 kr

The oldest hotel in Ålesund is Hotel 1904, dating back to (you guessed it) 1904. This historic hotel is modern and bright, with 80 rooms of various sizes. The rooms are decorated in a clean, Nordic style, with natural materials and white walls. The hotel has a popular espresso bar and eatery, Green Garden, where they serve both lunch and dinner Monday through Saturday.

INFORMATION AND SERVICES

Ålesund Tourist Information

Skateflukaia; tel. 70 30 98 00; Mon.-Fri. 10am-4pm
Sept.-May, Mon.-Sun. 10am-4pm June-Aug.

At the tourist information in Ålesund you can pick up a large selection of brochures, as well as purchase a selection of souvenirs and postcards. You can also book excursions and tours for the city and region.

Ålesund Emergency Room and Hospital

Åsesvingen 16; tel. 116 117; open 24/7

The hospital and emergency room in Ålesund are adjacent to each other. Always call ahead to make sure they have capacity and can make time for you for minor accidents and issues, and remember to call 113 for an ambulance in case of emergency.

GETTING THERE

Bus

Route 430 with **Vy** (www.vybuss.no) travels directly from Bergen to Ålesund, a journey that takes 9.5 hours. **FRAM** (tel. 71 28 01 00; www.frammr.no), the local transportation provider, has express buses between Ålesund and Trondheim, Ålesund and Kristiansund, and Ålesund and Åndalsnes (where the nearest train station is). Ålesund Rutebilstasjon (Larsgårdsvegen 2) is the main bus station in Ålesund.

Car

Driving might be the easiest way to reach Ålesund, if you don't opt for a domestic flight. Note that driving times may take longer than planned, due to busy roads (especially in the summer months). From Bergen, follow E39 all the way to Ålesund, allowing at least 7 hours for the 423-kilometer (263-mi) drive.

The drive from Ålesund to Åndalsnes covers a distance of 108 kilometers (67 mi) and will take you around 1.5 hours along main roads E39 and E136. From Ålesund to Geiranger, you can drive via Åndalsnes (in the summer months when Trollstigen is open), which will take around 4 hours (194 km/120 mi). Head straight to Geiranger from Ålesund via E39 and Route 60. This journey will take you 2.5 hours and includes a ferry crossing from Linge to Eidsdal (www.fjord1.no).

From Oslo, drive along E6 and E136 to reach Ålesund. The journey takes 7-8 hours and covers 545 kilometers (338 mi).

Air

Ålesund Airport Vigra

Flyplassvegen; https://avinor.no/en/airport/alesund-airport

The small airport in Ålesund is mainly serviced by domestic flights from Oslo, Bergen, and Trondheim by airlines SAS, Widerøe, and Norwegian. Additionally, it is possible to reach Europe, with Wizzair flying to Gdansk and KLM operating daily flights to Amsterdam. To reach the city center from the airport, the airport bus operated by Vy (www.vy.no/buss/alesund-vigra) leaves twice an hour and will get you into town in 20 minutes. The journey costs 109 kr when purchased in advance.

GETTING AROUND

For the most part, you will get around the city by walking. The exceptions are the Sunnmøre Museum, Atlanterhavsparken, and some hikes (such as Runde) that are outside of the city. For those, if you don't have a rental car, local buses in and around the city are operated by FRAM (tel. 71 28 01 00; www.frammr.no).

Åndalsnes

Åndalsnes is a small town (although it is classified as a city) with around 3,000 inhabitants, located a short drive from Ålesund. The hike Rampestreken is well-known among Norwegians, and paired with Trollstigen being near the city, it is one of the reasons people visit. Also, the Raumabanen train stops (and starts) in Åndalsnes, making it a natural stopping place for those arriving to the area by train. Raumabanen offers one of the most beautiful Norwegian rail journeys, and it is worth booking a ticket if you are spending the night in Åndalsnes.

Most people will simply stop in Åndalsnes on their way between Geiranger and Ålesund in order to drive the famous Trollstigen road in the summer months (the road is usually closed Oct.-May). However, if you want to hike Rampestreken and experience the Raumabanen train line, consider spending a night here.

SIGHTS

Raumabanen

www.sj.no; 4 daily departures; 250-350 kr one-way

Raumabanen (Rauma Railway) is the name of the 1-hour-40-minute train stretch between Åndalsnes and Dombås (east and farther inland from Geiranger and Ålesund). It has been named one of the most beautiful train journeys in Europe, showing you forested valleys, lush scenery, and steep mountains. In Dombås, you can connect to Oslo and Bergen via Lillehammer. Harry Potter fans will love knowing that the only scenes of Harry Potter and the Half-Blood Prince that were filmed outside of the UK were filmed on this train as it passed Bjorli, one of the stops along Raumabanen.

Trollstigen

Route 63, 19 km/12 mi south of Åndalsnes; www. nasjonaleturistveger.no

Trollstigen is a mountain pass that you are bound to have seen photos of when researching Norway. The 11 hairpin turns taking you up the steep mountainside in the Romsdalen Valley connect Åndalsnes with Valldal on the other side. As you drive up (or down), you are surrounded by dramatic mountains, such as Kongen ("the King"; 1,614 m/5,295 ft above sea level) and Dronninga ("the Queen"; 1,544 m/5,065 ft above sea level).

The road opened in 1936. It closes due to snow and weather in the winter months and is usually open from May to October. Always check conditions on the Norwegian Road Directory website (www.vegvesen.no) if you are traveling in the shoulder season. At the top of the hairpin turns there is a viewpoint where you can enjoy pretty epic vistas of the 11 turns, as well as the lush, green valley that stretches back to Åndalsnes and the bare, steep mountains on either side of it.

Romsdalsgondolen

Jernbanegata 1; 45 72 40 60; https://billetter. romsdalen.no; Thurs. 2pm-8:30pm, Fri. 2pm-10pm, Sat.-Sun. noon-8pm; 495 kr return

The Romsdal gondola takes you up to the top of Nesaksla Mountain where you will also find Eggen Restaurant. Even if you are not dining, a trip to the top (and back down) with the gondola is worth it for the views of the surrounding mountains and the fjord below. The gondola leaves approximately every 8 minutes during opening hours. The cars of the gondola offer 360-degree views of the surroundings as you ascend and descend, and it is a pretty spectacular experience.

SPORTS AND RECREATION

Hiking

Rampestreken

Distance: 3.5 kilometers (2 mi)

Time: 2 hours one-way

Difficulty: Strenuous

Trailhead: *Romsdalsvegen 24 (Rampestreken Starting Point)*

Information and Maps: *https://ut.no/ turforslag/1112596/rampestreken*

This popular hike takes you up 607 meters (1,991 ft) of elevation in a relatively short distance. It ends at a viewpoint on the mountainside, looking over Åndalsnes, with the fjord and the mountains surrounding you. A narrow, fenced walking platform has been built into the mountainside, offering a unique opportunity for photos and views for those who aren't afraid of heights. From the parking lot below and a smaller viewpoint called Nebba, the hike goes pretty much straight up the mountainside, so it is hard to get lost, but it is also well-marked all the way. The trail is mostly a dirt path, with some rocky bits, but there are also stone steps built into the terrain to help in some places. The trailhead is right at the bottom of the mountain in the center of Åndalsnes. Simply follow Romsdalsvegen from the train station in the city center toward the mountain to get to the trail.

Kløvstien

Distance: *5 kilometers (3 mi)*
Time: *3 hours one-way*
Difficulty: *Moderate to strenuous*
Trailhead: *Parking lot in Isterdalen (at the bottom of the hairpin turns)*
Information and Maps: *www.fjordnorway.com/ no/se-og-gjore/trollstigen---klovstien-858-moh*

Those who want to reach the viewpoint at the top of the Trollstigen hairpin turns without driving them will be pleased to hear that it is possible to hike up. This trail follows the path that was the main travel vein before the road opened in 1936. So, if you take this hike, you will be walking in the footsteps of farmers, horses, and traders. You can start at the parking lot down in Isterdalen Valley, at the bottom of the hairpin turns. From there, follow the road for about 100 meters (330 ft) before taking a left onto a tractor

road. At the end of this road, you will cross the river Istra over the bridge and follow the trail upward from there. The trail, which is well-marked the whole way, is a mix of dirt/ tractor roads and Sherpa steps, and in some areas (especially the last 150 m/490 ft before the Stigfossbrua Bridge) it gets very steep. In those areas, fencing and railings have been put into place for safety. At one point (after the Stigfoss Bridge), you have to follow the car road for two hairpin turns, before getting back on the trail on the left side of the road. Take caution along the road, as there is no sidewalk.

SHOPPING
Rauma Ullvarefabrikk
Kolstadgata 3; tel. 71 22 05 00; Mon.-Fri. 9am-5pm, Sat. 10am-3pm

Rauma Ullvarefabrikk is a Norwegian wool company dating back to 1927. Their production hails from Rauma and Åndalsnes, and their store in Åndalsnes is worth a visit if you are stopping in town—especially if you are looking for an authentic Norwegian knitted sweater. In addition to sweaters, they have scarves, hats, gloves, and other knitted garments, as well as yarn for those who want to knit something special themselves.

FOOD
Trollstigen Kafe
Trollstigen 1; tel. 94 84 97 55; www.trollstigen.no; daily May-Sept.; 135-259 kr

Trollstigen Kafe is a large café serving snacks and meals to visitors passing by on the road or arriving on foot after having hiked up Kløvstien. Their large cafeteria-like space seats up to 160 people and can get loud when many guests are dining at the same time. The menu focuses on traditional Norwegian cuisine and local produce from the nearby area, and you can expect dishes such as goat cheese salad, traditional rømmegrøt (sour cream porridge), and reindeer meatballs.

1: Trollstigen **2:** Romsdalsgondolen **3:** Åndalsnes **4:** viewpoint on the Rampestreken hike

Piccola Mama Rosa

Vollan 5; tel. 71 22 20 07; www.mamarosaa.no; daily 2pm-10pm; 159-289 kr

This rustic Italian restaurant offers a varied menu that goes beyond just Italian food. In addition to traditional Italian pizza and pasta dishes, you can also order spareribs and hamburgers. Their dark leather furniture and exposed brick interior contribute to a homey and warm atmosphere.

Eggen Restaurant

Nesaksla Mountain; tel. 40 50 40 04; www. eggenrestaurant.no; Wed.-Thurs. 4pm-8:30pm, Fri. 4pm-11pm, Sat.-Sun noon-11pm; 3 courses 695 kr

For a truly unique New Nordic experience, head to Eggen Restaurant at the top of Nesaksla mountain. Located above the Rampestreken viewpoint, their modern building boasts large windows where you can look out at the alpine mountaintops nearby. To get to the top, you can either hike Rampestreken and then walk a little farther, or travel on the Romsdalsgondolen gondola. The opening hours of the gondola are set to match the restaurant. At Eggen, they put together multicourse meals at set prices, with a focus on creating true culinary experiences using regional ingredients. On the menu, you may find dishes such as halibut from Averøy (just north of Molde) and lamb from Bjorli (one of the stops on the Rauma Railway).

ACCOMMODATIONS

Grand Hotel

Åndalgata 5; tel. 71 22 75 00; www.classicnorway.no; 1,500 kr

Grand Hotel by Classic Norway Hotels is the only proper hotel in Åndalsnes. They have 86 rooms, each decorated with stunning photography of the local landscape and clean, bright details. Rooms offer views of either the Romsdal mountains or the fjord outside—both equally beautiful. Their **restaurant La Vue** (Mon.-Sat. 6pm-10pm; 195-335 kr), located on the first floor, is a family-friendly option serving pizza, hamburgers, and the fresh catch of the day.

Hotel Aak

Romsdalsvegen 9842; tel. 71 22 17 00; www.hotelaak. no; 2,800 kr

Hotel Aak is a small boutique hotel with 16 rooms a little farther up the valley from Åndalsnes (5-10 minutes' drive from the town center along E136). This property is one of Norway's Historic Hotels, and dates back to the 1800s, when climbers and hikers would stop here before starting their mountain adventures. Some rooms have en suite bathrooms, and some have shared bathrooms, but all have a feel of being part of something historic, with vintage-style furniture and lovely views of the surrounding forest and mountains.

INFORMATION AND SERVICES

Åndalsnes Tourist Information

Jernbanegata 1; tel. 93 04 97 55; www.visitmr.no; Mon.-Fri. 10am-4pm, Sat.-Sun. 8am-4pm

In the train station you will find the Åndalsnes and Romsdalen tourist information. Here, you can pick up hiking maps for the area or get help booking tickets (such as for the gondola).

GETTING THERE

Train

The Raumabanen train connects Åndalsnes with Dombås, a mountain station. From Dombås, you can connect to trains going north (such as to Trondheim) and south (such as to Lillehammer and Oslo). Trains are operated by **Sj** (www.sj.no) and **Vy** (www.vy.no). The **train station** in Åndalsnes is located right in the town center and houses the tourist information. The train ride from Oslo to Dombås takes around 4 hours, and from Trondheim it is a 2-hour 45-minute train ride. Raumabanen takes around 1 hour and 40 minutes.

It is not possible to reach Åndalsnes by train from Ålesund or Geiranger.

Bus

FRAM (www.frammr.no) is the local transportation provider. From Ålesund, Route 681 takes you from the main bus stop in Ålesund to Åndalsnes train station in 2 hours and 20 minutes. There are no direct buses from Trondheim, but you can take Route 905 with ATB, the transportation provider in and around Trondheim (tel. 47 80 28 20; www.atb.no), to Molde and change there to Route 420 (tel. 71 28 01 00; www.frammr.no), which goes to Åndalsnes. The bus journey from Trondheim to Molde takes a little over 4 hours, and from Molde to Åndalsnes the bus takes 1 hour and 15 minutes. There are no bus connections between Geiranger and Åndalsnes.

Car

The drive from Ålesund to Åndalsnes is 108 kilometers (67 mi) and takes 1.5 hours, following main roads E136 and E39. From Geiranger, the drive is 2 hours and 15 minutes, along Trollstigen mountain pass (87 km/54 mi, summer months only). If you are driving between Åndalsnes and Geiranger in the winter, you can drive along E39 instead, and the journey will take you a little over 2.5 hours (134 km/83 mi). If you are driving from Trondheim, Åndalsnes is a 4.5-hour drive along main roads E6 and E136 (301 km/187 mi).

GETTING AROUND

Åndalsnes is a small town, and everything in the town center is reachable on foot, including the Rampestreken hike, the gondola base station, and train station. The only exception is the Trollstigen mountain pass (and Kløvstien hike). If you want to drive the mountain pass, rent a car from one of the two car rentals in Åndalsnes, both located less than a 5-minute walk from the train station. These are **Avis** (Åndalgata; Aandalsnes Bilverksted; tel. 45 72 64 48; www.avis.no) and **Hertz** (Romsdalsvegen 5; tel. 71 20 14 44; www.hertz.no).

The Geirangerfjord

TOP EXPERIENCE

The small village of Geiranger and the Geirangerfjord are two of the most popular places in Norway. The fjord is listed in the UNESCO World Heritage List together with the Nærøyfjord, and while the two fjords are equally spectacular, they are slightly different. The Geirangerfjord is more rugged, with steep, bare mountainsides (as opposed to the Nærøyfjord's more lush mountain scenery). The fjord can be best seen from the water, as there are no villages along it (as there are along the Nærøyfjord and Aurlandsfjord). The villages of Hellesylt and Geiranger mark the start and end points of the fjord, and the most popular fjord cruise goes between the two. Note that Hellesylt is just a stop on the fjord cruise (the end stop), and not a destination in itself.

The only time you would visit Hellesylt is if you decide to get off the fjord cruise to grab lunch at the small café there.

The village of Geiranger is a small town that comes alive with tourists and seasonal workers in the summer. Here, you will find the **Norwegian Fjord Center,** where you can learn a thing or two about life along the fjords, and several famous viewpoints overlooking the fjord.

SIGHTS
Ørnevegen and Ørnesvingen

Fv63 27, 7 km north of Geiranger; www.
nasjonaleturistveger.no/no/turistvegene/geiranger-
trollstigen/ornesvingen; free
Ørnevegen is the name of the 11 hairpin turns you drive through when heading north from Geiranger (or vice versa). The name directly

translates to "the Eagle's Road," and the road covers just 5 kilometers (3 mi) of incline up the mountainside. Most travelers visiting Geiranger will drive up the hairpin turns from Geiranger, stop at the viewpoint, and then drive back down. It does not matter which direction you are driving. There is a waterfall at the viewpoint at the top, Ørnesvingen, and you can look down to the village of Geiranger, or across the Geirangerfjord toward the Seven Sisters Waterfall. The viewpoint—a wooden platform that offers a 180-degree view of the spectacular Geirangerfjord below—was created by artist May Elin Eikaas-Bjerk and architects 3RW-Sixten Rahlff.

Norwegian Fjord Center

Gjørvahaugen 35, Geiranger; tel. 70 26 38 10; www. fjordsenter.com; daily 10am-3pm; adults 140 kr, children 70 kr

The Norwegian Fjord Center is a visitors center and interactive museum dedicated to the culture and history of the Norwegian fjords. Here, you can learn more about the geography and landscapes in western Norway, and about what life has been like along the fjords through the years. In their cinema room, you can enjoy a video dedicated to the spectacular fjord scenery that will truly take your breath away. Plan to spend at least an hour at the Fjord Center.

Flydalsjuvet Viewpoint

Fv 63 28, 4 km/2.5 mi south of Geiranger

Flydalsjuvet is a rest stop and viewpoint from which you have probably seen a photo or two. The scenery you can see from this spot is the Geirangerfjord between the steep mountains on either side, with the village of Geiranger nestled at the end of it. There are toilet facilities here, built using several-hundred-years-old timber. From Flydalsjuvet you can see across to Ørnesvingen, so the two viewpoints perfectly complement each other. The platform is located at 320 meters (1,050 ft) in height, and offers views in one direction, toward the fjord.

Geiranger Skywalk (Dalsnibba Viewpoint)

End of Nibbevegen, 21 km/13 mi southeast from Geiranger; https://dalsnibba.no

For an even higher and more spectacular view of the village, fjord, and mountaintops of the area than Flydalsjuvet, head to Geiranger Skywalk, located at 1,500 meters (4,920 ft) above sea level. This is the highest fjord view you can get anywhere in Norway without hiking, as you can drive all the way up to the viewpoint. This spot offers the same views as at Flydalsjuvet, but from much higher up, so that you see more of the mountaintops, and the village of Geiranger looks absolutely tiny below you. Since you are on a mountaintop, you get a 360-degree view here, and turning around will let you look inward to the mountaintops and plateaus of inner Norway. The road there (Nibbevegen) is closed in the winter season, so check their website if you are visiting in April-May or September-October to ensure they are open. There is a 5-kilometer (3-mi) toll road to get there, and you can pay the toll in advance online.

★ Seven Sisters and Suitor Waterfalls (De Syv Søstre/Friaren)

The two most famous waterfalls along the Geirangerfjord face each other on opposite sides of the Geirangerfjord. These beautiful falls both have an interesting shape, which has inspired legends about their origins and their names.

Folklore tells the story of a man on one side of the fjord, who wanted to marry one of the beautiful sisters that lived on the other side. Because he wasn't able to reach them, and thus couldn't marry any of them, he ended up "throwing himself on the bottle" (a Norwegian expression for alcoholism). The Suitor Waterfall is therefore shaped like a beer bottle. On the other side of the fjord, you will

1: Ørnesvingen 2: Seven Sisters Waterfall 3: cruising through the Geirangerfjord 4: Geiranger Skywalk

see that the Seven Sisters is a waterfall where the water cascades into seven parts.

You can see the Seven Sisters Waterfall from the Ørnesvingen Viewpoint, or from a boat in the Geirangerfjord. The Suitor can only be seen from a boat in the fjord.

Hellesylt Waterfall

Hellesylt

Right in the middle of Hellesylt you will find Hellesylt Waterfall, one of the most photographed attractions in the area. Most travelers will see it as soon as they get off the Geiranger-Hellesylt ferry. The waterfall is beautiful and dramatic, especially in May and June when the snow is melting. There is no vertical drop, and it comes across more like a very active river (it is only 20 m/66 ft high).

You will see this waterfall when arriving in Hellesylt on the fjord cruise from Geiranger, especially if you get off to spend some time in Hellesylt. It is possible to drive around the fjord and over the mountain passes to get to Hellesylt, but this is not recommended as there is not much to see other than the waterfall—plus you'd miss the journey through the fjord.

SPORTS AND RECREATION

TOP EXPERIENCE

★ Fjord Cruises

Going on a fjord cruise is the best and only way to truly experience the Geiranger fjord.

Geiranger Fjord Cruise

Geiranger Ferry Dock; tel. 57 63 14 00; www. norwaysbest.com/no/ting-a-gjore/fjorder/fjord-cruise-geirangerfjord; daily May-Oct.; 505 kr return

The classic Geiranger Fjord Cruise runs between Geiranger and Hellesylt up to eight times a day in the high season. The slow journey through the fjord takes a little over an hour each way, with an audio guide to describe the sights, farms, and waterfalls en route. There are no stops between Geiranger

and Hellesylt. This is a car ferry, so those wanting to travel one-way across the fjord and bring their car to drive farther south can do so. During this journey you will see the Seven Sisters and the Suitor waterfalls in the first third of the trip when sailing from Geiranger. The ferry has a café and indoor seating, but you'll have a better view if you stay outside on the deck. Most people just take the same ferry back to Geiranger, but it is possible to get off for a couple of hours to have lunch at the café in Hellesylt.

Geiranger FjordSafari

Maråkvegen 49; tel. 70 26 30 07; www.geirangerfjord. no; daily departures, hourly from 10am-4pm; adults from 495 kr

To experience the fjord in a way that's more up-close and thrilling than the fjord cruise, opt for a Geiranger FjordSafari. This 75-minute adventure (around 50 minutes spent on the fjord) takes you closer to the sides of the fjord, with stops for your experienced driver and guide to tell you more about what you see. This is an adventure aboard an RIB (rigid inflatable boat), similar to other fjord safaris. These boats are open, but you will only get wet if it is raining.

Hiking

Storseterfossen

Distance: *2.4 kilometers (1.5 mi)*
Time: *1 hour one-way*
Difficulty: *Strenuous*
Trailhead: *Westerås Farm*
Information and Maps: *https://ut.no/ turforslag/1114284*

If you want to experience walking behind a waterfall, consider the hike to Storseterfossen. This hike is strenuous due to its (mainly) uphill route, but the waterfall is spectacular. The hike follows well-marked Sherpa steps all the way to the top and can get a little slippery if it has been raining. Even though it is steep, most people can do it by simply taking their time up the steps. The total climb to the top is 440 meters (1,440 ft). The trailhead at Westerås farm can be reached via a 40-minute hike from just behind Hotel Union, or by driving to Westerås farm (a 10-minute drive from the fjord).

the Seven Sisters Waterfall costs 1,250 kr per person and lasts 3-5 hours.

Skageflå (and Homlong)
Distance: *0.7 kilometers (0.4 mi) to Skageflå; 6.4 kilometers (4 mi) to Geiranger via Homlong and Homlongsætra*
Time: *1 hour one-way to Skageflå, 4-5 hours one-way to Geiranger via Homlong and Homlongsætra*
Difficulty: *Moderate to Strenuous*
Trailhead: *Skagehola*
Information and Maps: *www.skagefla.no*
Skageflå is a farm that can be seen from the fjord cruise on the Geirangerfjord. The farm is located on a mountain shelf 250 meters (820 ft) above the fjord, and from the top you can enjoy great views of the fjord below and waterfalls on the other side. To get to the start of the hike you have to take a boat, offered by **FjordGuiding** (www.skagefla.no). The hike is steep but short, at only 45-60 minutes one-way.

If you want to keep hiking, as opposed to going back down and getting picked up by boat, you can follow signs to Homlong and **Homlongsætra,** which are farms along the fjord. As you hike along the Geirangerfjord back to the village, you will see the dramatic fjord landscape, mountains, and waterfalls. From there, you can keep walking until you reach the village of Geiranger. The total length of this hike (including the hike to Skageflå from the fjord) is 6.5 kilometers (4 mi) and will take around 4-5 hours.

Kayaking and Canoeing
Geiranger Kayak Center
Gjørvahaugane 35, Geiranger; tel. 70 26 30 07; daily 9am-5pm mid-May-mid-Oct.; 1-3 hour rental 500 kr
For those wanting to explore the fjord a little closer to sea level, going on a kayaking excursion will be a good choice. At Geiranger Kayak Center you can rent kayaks and canoes, or join one of their guided tours to the waterfalls of the Geirangerfjord. Experience is not necessary, as they will tailor the tours to each group. They offer different tours of varying length and prices. A guided kayaking tour to

SHOPPING
Geiranger Chocolate
Maroksveien 29, Geiranger; tel. 96 72 52 05; https://geirangersjokolade.no; hours vary May-Oct.
In a small wooden hut near the harbor you will find Geiranger Chocolate, a local chocolate factory and café serving homemade treats. They have been making chocolate since 2010.

FOOD
Geiranger
Naustkroa Restaurant
Maråkvegen 31; tel. 70 26 32 30; daily noon-10pm; 179-229 kr
This rustic and informal spot is great for lunch, with their classic international dishes focusing on cheeseburgers and homemade pizza. The dark timber interior in this historic restaurant is what makes the atmosphere of this small restaurant.

Brasserie Posten
Geirangervegen 4; tel. 70 26 13 06; www.brasserieposten.no; daily noon-9pm in summer, 7pm-9pm in low season, closed in winter; 225-369 kr
Near the harbor of Geiranger you will find the small restaurant Brasserie Posten, with just 35 indoor seats. There is also a popular outdoor seating area facing the fjord, and snagging one of those tables is worth it for the view alone. They serve Scandinavian dishes such as fish soup and grilled veal prepared with local ingredients.

Restaurant Olebuda
Maråkvegen 19; tel. 70 26 32 30; www.facebook.com/olebuda; daily noon-8pm June-Aug.; 250-399 kr
Olebuda is a traditional restaurant in a charming white, wooden house in the center of Geiranger. On the second floor you will find their welcoming and relaxed restaurant serving a blend of classic Norwegian dishes and international meals, such as cheeseburgers, halibut, and mussels. They have an outdoor patio on the second floor, which is lovely

on a summer day and takes you away from the crowd in the street below.

Restaurant Julie

Hotel Union, Geirangervegen 100, Geiranger; tel. 70 26 83 00; www.hotelunion.no; 215-435 kr

Restaurant Julie is the main restaurant at Hotel Union, offering a wide selection of a la carte options in a welcoming and slightly upscale atmosphere. The large restaurant is frequented by groups, but dividers are set up throughout the room to break up the space, so it feels less busy. A wall of windows faces the fjord, offering great views of the rest of the village and the fjord outside. On their a la carte menu you will find pizza, as well as baked rack of lamb, cod, and burgers. They also serve a buffet daily in the summer months.

Hellesylt
Hellesylt Boutique & Bar

Gata 29, Hellesylt; tel. 40 51 65 35; daily noon-5pm June-Aug., weekends noon-5pm year-round

Hellesylt Boutique & Bar is not only a café serving great coffee and freshly baked goods, but also the only bookstore in Hellesylt, with a large selection of new and used books. Whether you borrow one while drinking your coffee or purchase one to take home is up to you. If you are stopping in Hellesylt on the fjord cruise, this is the spot to grab a light lunch before returning to Geiranger on the ferry.

ACCOMMODATIONS

Staying in Geiranger is the best option for those wanting to explore the Geirangerfjord. Between the two small villages of Geiranger and Hellesylt, this is where you will find the most options for lodging and restaurants (although even in Geiranger there are only a handful of options).

Hotell Utsikten

Geirangervegen 348, Geiranger; tel. 70 26 96 60; www. classicnorway.no; May-Oct.; 1,900 kr

This small, seasonal hotel from 1893 is perched on a hill overlooking the village, a short drive from the Flydalsjuvet viewpoint (or a 45-minute walk). The 29 rooms in the hotel are small, comfortable, and bright, with heavy curtains to block out the long daylight hours of the Norwegian summer. The hotel is 4 kilometers (2.5 mi) up the road from the village, and they have a restaurant on-site.

the view from Hotel Union

Havila Hotel Geiranger

*Geirangerveien 22, Geiranger; tel. 70 26 30 05; https://
havilahotelgeiranger.no; 2,190 kr*

This modern and stylish hotel is found right on the waterfront of the Geirangerfjord. There are 151 rooms, some more modern than others. Rooms range from the most basic, with carpeted floors and simple furnishings, to newly renovated ones with hardwood floors and balconies overlooking the fjord.

★ Hotel Union

*Geirangervegen 100, Geiranger; tel. 70 26 83 00; www.
hotelunion.no; 2,200 kr*

Hotel Union is perhaps the best-known hotel in Geiranger, and one of the Historic Hotels in Norway. This property is perhaps most famous for affording beautiful views of Geiranger and the fjord, but this luxurious hotel also boasts a memorable pool, spa, and restaurant. The 197 rooms here are classic and timeless, with dark timber details and traditional Nordic furnishings. Splurge on a room with a balcony to enjoy your morning coffee with one of the best views in town.

The hotel was originally built in 1891, but it has been refurbished and expanded several times since then. In the cellar there is a museum dedicated to classic cars dating back to the 1920s—quite unique for a hotel!

INFORMATION AND SERVICES
Tourist Information
Geiranger Tourist Information
*Geirangervegen 2; tel. 70 26 30 07; daily 10am-4pm
May-Sept.*

The tourist information in Geiranger can help you with booking excursions and travel in the area. It is also a great place to pick up brochures or hiking maps.

Emergencies

Geiranger shares an emergency room service with nearby villages, and the doctor visits once a week for scheduled appointments (tel. 70 26 59 70; Wed. 9:45am-1pm). If you need to visit the emergency room, call 116117 to find

out where to go. For urgent emergencies, call an ambulance at 113. Note that there is only an ambulance stationed in Geiranger during the summer months.

GETTING THERE
Boat
Geiranger Fjordservice (www.geiranger-fjord.no/fjord-cruise-alesund-geiranger; 1 daily departure June-Sept., select days Mar.-May; 830 kr one-way, 1,410 kr return) offers a way to reach Geiranger from Ålesund without a car. Leaving from Brosundet Marina, the catamaran passes through the Geirangerfjord and its waterfalls on its way to Geiranger (3 hours one-way).

Car
Geiranger is most easily reached by car, and it is best to visit in the summer months. In the summer, the National Tourist Route via Trollstigen (Route 63) is an attraction on its own, and many travelers elect to add it to their route (even if they aren't coming from the Åndalsnes area). It's tricky to reach Geiranger in the winter, when the tourist ferry is not running and several nearby mountain passes are closed. Trollstigen usually closes around October and will stay closed until May. Route 15 to Otta also closes in the winter. The best place to stay up to date on road closures is via the **Statens Vegvesen website** (www.vegvesen.no), where there is an interactive map of the Norwegian roads, indicating which are open and which aren't.

The drive from Ålesund to Geiranger either goes via Åndalsnes (in the summer months when the Trollstigen road is open) and takes around 4 hours (194 km/120 mi) or goes straight to Geiranger via E39 and Route 60. If you drive directly from Ålesund, the trip will take you 2.5 hours and includes a ferry crossing from Linge to Eidsdal (www.fjord1.no).

From Åndalsnes, the drive via Trollstigen is 2 hours and 15 minutes (87 km/54 mi, summer only). If you are driving from Åndalsnes in the winter, follow E39 instead, which will take you a little over 2.5 hours (134 km/83 mi).

Getting Around

Geiranger itself is a very small village with limited to no public transport. For sights in the village center, such as the chocolate store and the restaurants along the fjord, you can get around on foot. But if you want to see any of the viewpoints of the fjord, such as Flydalsjuvet or Ørnesvingen, you need a car. There is a small taxi company in the village (Geiranger Taxi; tel. 40 00 37 41; www.geirangerturbuss.no).

The Nordfjord

Nordfjord is often overlooked by travelers not visiting Norway on a cruise, but it makes for a natural stopping point for anyone planning to explore the western fjords from Bergen to Ålesund on their trip to Norway. The fjord itself is less dramatic than the Geirangerfjord and Sognefjord, but anyone who decides to stay overnight will be glad they did. The towns of Loen and Olden have plenty to offer travelers, from the main event Loen Skylift to easy access to two Jostedalsbreen Glacier arms: Kjenndalsbreen and Briksdalsbreen. Those hoping to go on a glacier hike (or just to see a glacier) during their trip to Norway will find that Nordfjord is the perfect place to include in their itinerary.

Orientation

The villages and towns along the fjord are laid out similarly to the villages along the Aurlandsfjord: a little spread out from each other, all along the fjord. Stryn, Loen, and Olden are all a 10-minute drive from each other, with Stryn and Olden marking the ends of the drive (20 minutes in between) and Loen in the middle. From both Loen and Olden, valleys stretch up from the fjord toward arms of the Jostedalsbreen Glacier. Basing yourself in any of these towns will work to explore the area, with Loen perhaps being the best spot because it's in the middle.

SIGHTS

Loen

★ Loen Skylift

Fjordvegen 1011, Loen; tel. 57 87 59 00; www.loenskylift. no; daily 9am-10pm June-Aug., daily 10am-7pm Sept.- May; 450 kr return

Mount Hoven is one of the tall mountains surrounding the Nordfjord and the town of Loen. It is recognizable due to a large, round indentation in the mountain. The Loen Skylift cable car will have you at the top of Mount Hoven in just a few minutes. The cable car has become one of the most popular attractions in the area, and at the top you can enjoy views of the fjord and Lovatnet Lake below. In addition to the view from 1,011 meters (3,316 ft) above sea level, there are several hikes and walks at the top of Mount Hoven, and a restaurant serving lunch and dinner. The gondolas have been named after Norse god Odin's two ravens: Hugin and Munin. From the top of Mount Hoven, you can see the fjord stretching out toward the sea (but you can't quite see the sea) with its nooks and crannies and small villages along it, the nearby mountaintops, and parts of the Kjenndalsbreen glacier.

Lovatnet Lake (Lake Loen)

Fv723, Loen

Lovatnet in Loen is one of the most shared images in Norway, due to its clear, green color and calm waters. This glacier lake is made up of water melting from Jostedalsbreen and

The Legend of Mount Hoven

The Norwegian word "hoven" means the hoof. An old Norse legend says that Mount Hoven (The Hoof Mountain) gets its name from Odin's horse Sleipner's hoof. On a ride across the mountains of Nordfjord, Sleipner (with its eight feet) made the jump across the fjord from Mount Auflem on the other side to the top of Mount Hoven. It was a stormy day, and Odin and Sleipner were caught in a powerful gust of wind on the way across.

As a result, one of Sleipner's hooves kicked a large piece of the mountain down into the fjord, and this imprint can still be seen today as a large white indentation in the mountainside of Mount Hoven. Loen Skylift takes you up the mountain just in front of this indentation.

Kjenndalsbreen, and all along the lake you will find beautiful photo ops and relaxing views. Bringing a packed lunch to eat along the edge of the lake is a great way to spend an afternoon. (Make sure to visit a grocery store in the village center before you head up to the lake.) Alternatively, head to **Kjenndalsstova** (tel. 90 53 40 87; www.kjenndalsstova.no; open in the summer months, hours vary) at the very southern end of the lake for lunch or to rent rowboats. The drive from the center of Loen to Kjenndalsstova will take half an hour, but the drive to the northern end of the lake is just 7 minutes. As you can probably tell, this is a very large lake, and it is not possible to walk around it.

Kjenndalsbreen Glacier
At the end of Fv273, Loen
At the southern end of Lovatnet you will find one of the arms of Jostedalsbreen: Kjenndalsbreen Glacier. This arm is perhaps one of the easiest to reach and see, as the road goes almost all the way up to the glacier. The road is narrow and heavily trafficked in summer, so if you want to avoid long waits and frustration, park at Kjenndalsstova and walk the 5 kilometers (3 mi) to the end of the road. The drive from the center of Loen up to the parking lot by the glacier takes around 40 minutes—often longer with traffic. It is a narrow road, with just one lane in places, so make sure you are comfortable with driving and that you bring along your patience. Allow for 1 hour of driving each way in the summer months. To avoid crowds, go very early in the

morning (it stays light almost all day, so you could even go before breakfast).

Olden Valley
Briksdalsbreen Glacier
Oldedalsvegen 2211, Olden; www.briksdal.no
At the end of the Olden Valley you will find Briksdalsbreen, another arm of **Jostedalsbreen.** This glacier arm stretches from 1,200 meters' (3,937 ft) height and down into the valley below. From **Briksdalsbreen Fjellstove** (Oldedalsvegen 2211), a small café, the walk up to the glacier is 2.5 kilometers (1.5 mi) and will take 45-60 minutes. The path up to the glacier includes crossing the **Kleivafossen** waterfall by bridge. In the top melting season (May-June), you may get wet during the crossing. Briksdalsbreen Fjellstove also offers lifts in its small "troll cars," which can be booked in advance on their website if you prefer not to walk. The glacier is only accessible by foot or troll car. On the drive up to Briksdalsbreen Fjellstove, you will pass Oldevatnet (Olden Lake), the large glacial lake with melted water from the Briksdalsbreen Glacier. This beautiful green lake gets its color from the particles of the glacier (like Loen Lake).

HIKING AND GLACIER HIKING
Loen
Mount Hoven
Distance: *2.2-6.3 kilometers (1.4-4 mi)*
Time: *0.5-1.5 hours*
Difficulty: *Easy*

Trailhead: *At the top of Loen Skylift*
Information and Maps: *www.loenskylift.no*
At Mount Hoven, the destination at the top of Loen Skylift, there are several hikes available for all fitness levels. The short trail **Gjølrunden** (2.2 km/1.4 mi) takes you in a loop around the mountaintop, with lovely views of the valleys below, starting with a 170-meter (550-ft) incline before you follow a rather leisurely loop back to the start. Those who are after a more strenuous hike can try their hand at hiking **Årheimsfjellet** (6.3 km/4 mi one-way), where you will follow the ridge of the mountain for the majority of the hike to the top of Mount Årheim (total incline on this hike: 340 meters/1,115 ft).

Via Ferrata Loen

Loen Active; www.loenskylift.no/viaferrataloen; daily guided tours May-Oct.; 1,585 kr
Those looking for a more technical hike and climb will be intrigued by the Via Ferrata. This climbing and hiking course takes you to the top of Mount Hoven and includes crossing Europe's largest Via Ferrata bridge at 750 meters (2,460 ft) above sea level. This is not for the faint of heart or those with a fear of heights. The Via Ferrata is only available with an instructor (unless you are a very experienced climber), and there are daily departures from Loen Active in the high season. At the end of the climb, you will take Loen Skylift back down (included in the price).

Olden Valley
Briksdalsbreen Hike

Distance: *5.9 kilometers (3.7 mi)*
Time: *2 hours round-trip*
Difficulty: *Moderate*
Trailhead: *Briksdalsbre Fjellstove*
Information and Maps: *https://ut.no/ turforslag/1112155413/briksdalsbreen-lett-fottur*
The gravel trail up to Briksdalsbreen is well-marked and has been split in two in order to make a nice loop for anyone planning

on hiking there. This ensures that the trails aren't too crowded in the summer. Start at Briksdalsbreen Fjellstove and walk toward the Kleivafossen waterfall. Here, you can decide to cross the bridge by the waterfall, or take a shorter route on the north side of the waterfall called Emperor Wilhelm's Path. This is a shortcut and not one of the paths that was created to make a loop. This path choice comes after the waterfall, and it is recommended that you take different paths going up and down. Both trails lead to the glacier and small glacier lake at the top. During the melting season you may get wet on this hike.

Stryn
Olden Active

Gamle Strynefjellsvegen 800, Stryn; tel. 90 13 83 08; www.oldenactive.com; weekends mid-June-mid-Aug.; 1,240 kr
Olden Active guides take you on a blue ice hike on the **Tystigbreen glacier,** 40 kilometers (25 mi) east of Stryn. The experience will last 5-7 hours, and the experienced guides will tailor each hike to the group. The time spent on the glacier is 2-4 hours. You do not need any glacier hiking experience, and children as young as 12 can participate. Bring your own lunch for the lunch break or book a lunch when you book the experience.

ENTERTAINMENT AND EVENTS
Stryn
Oktoberfest Stryn

www.oktoberfeststryn.no; Oct.
Not many people associate the German Oktoberfest with Norway, but in Stryn every year there is a huge Oktoberfest party that draws people from all around the country. This is the largest Oktoberfest in Norway, and it is worth attending if you are in the area. The 2-day celebration includes a house band playing oompah music and lots of different beers available for purchase.

1: Loen Skylift **2:** view from Mount Hoven

1

2

FOOD
Loen
Hoven Restaurant

Fjordvegen 1002; tel. 57 87 59 00; https://loenskylift. no; daily noon-9pm June-Aug., daily noon-6pm in low season (select weekends noon-9pm); 270-440 kr

The restaurant on top of Mount Hoven offers a 210-degree view of the fjord below. The large restaurant is bright and modern, with picture windows ensuring you get to take in as much of the view as possible. Their menu is inspired by local ingredients, and there is a separate pizza menu. Local Norwegian dishes include reindeer stew, codfish, and deer.

Restaurant Andrine

Lodalsvegen 22; tel. 57 87 50 00; www.alexandra.no; 385-545 kr

Restaurant Andrine at Hotel Alexandra offers several a la carte options, whether you prefer three or five courses. While the small dining room is elegant and rather upscale, they still manage a relaxed and friendly atmosphere. The menu changes often, depending on fresh and seasonal ingredients, and may include dishes such as filet of veal, entrecote, and halibut.

Fiskekroken Restaurant

Fjordvegen 1047; tel. 57 87 57 00; www.loenfjord.no; daily June-Sept.

This is the a la carte restaurant of Hotel Loenfjord. They serve traditional Norwegian dishes such as fish soup and salmon, but the menu also has some international dishes, such as moules frites and fish and chips. The indoor seating area is simple and welcoming, and the smaller outdoor patio is a great spot to grab dinner on long summer nights.

Olden Valley
Mølla Restaurant

Fjordvegen 1567; tel. 901 38 308; daily 11am-9pm; 149-289 kr

Along the fjord in Olden, you will find Mølla, serving a mix of Norwegian and international dishes using local ingredients. The menu changes according to the produce and ingredients that are available, and dishes may include halibut, fish and chips, and hamburgers. The large restaurant is popular with tourists and covers three floors in a former millhouse ("Mølla" translates to "the mill") from 1920. The atmosphere here is informal and relaxed. You might want to avoid it on cruise days, as the cruise ships dock just outside the restaurant, making it very busy and partially obstructing the view.

ACCOMMODATIONS
Loen
Hotel Loenfjord

Fjordvegen 1047; tel. 57 87 57 00; www.loenfjord.no; Apr.-Sept.; 2,300 kr

Hotel Loenfjord is a cozy and informal family-run hotel located right by the river in Loen. It is only open in the summer months, offering 137 rooms with bright details and en suite bathrooms.

Hotel Alexandra

Lodalsvegen 22; tel. 57 87 50 00; www.alexandra.no; 4,200 kr

The prestigious Hotel Alexandra is for some a reason to visit Nordfjord on its own. The traditional hotel is family-run, and their spa and pool overlooking the fjord have made the hotel a weekend getaway destination for many Norwegians. The hotel is large, with 343 rooms, but still has a welcoming and personal atmosphere. The rooms are modern and stylish, with individual furnishings and Nordic details.

Olden Valley
Olden Fjordhotel

Solstrandvegen 1; tel. 57 87 04 00; https:// oldenfjordhotel.no; 1,600 kr

The small traditional hotel is located right near the docks in Olden. All 60 rooms have beautiful views of the fjord, and the majority of them have a private balcony. The rooms are simply furnished in a slightly outdated style, with carpeted floors and striped furniture. For extra space, opt for the Standard Plus room category.

Stryn

Visnes Hotel Stryn

Prestestegen 1; tel. 57 87 10 87; www.visneshotel.no;
mid-Apr.-mid-Oct.; 2,600 kr

This wooden hotel on the waterfront dates back to 1850 and has kept history alive in its communal areas and rooms. The historic Swiss-style hotel is furnished to make you feel like you have stepped back in time to 1930. Each room is individually decorated in the same historic style as the rest of the hotel.

INFORMATION AND SERVICES

The villages along the fjord all have their own tourist information, where you can pick up hiking maps and brochures, and get help with booking tickets and excursions in the area. The **Stryn Tourist Information** (Perhusvegen 24; tel. 57 87 40 54; www.nordfjord.no/turistinformasjon; daily 9am-4pm July, Mon.-Fri. 9am-4pm Aug.) can be of help with questions relating to activities nearby, such as the Blue Ice Hike and Oktoberfest. At **Olden Tourist Information** (tel. 57 87 40 54; www.nordfjord.no/turistinformasjon; open June-Aug.) you can ask questions relating to activities in Olden and Loen.

If you are in need of medical attention, the **emergency room** for the area is in Stryn at Stryn Legekontor (Setrevegen 4; tel. 57 87 69 80; daily 8am-4pm). If you are in need of medical services outside of their opening hours, call 116117 or 113 (for urgent emergencies requiring an ambulance).

GETTING THERE AND AROUND

Traveling between the towns along the Nordfjord is best done by car, but you can also get around the region via local transportation (www.skyss.no) and taxis **Stryn Taxi** (tel. 57 87 23 50; www.stryntaxi.no). The short drive from Olden to Loen is 5-10 minutes (6.7 km/4 mi) and from Loen to Stryn it's 10-15 minutes (10.2 km/6 mi).

Bus

Express bus route 431 (www.nor-way.no) travels daily from Bergen to Olden, Loen, and Stryn. A one-way ticket for the 6-hour drive starts at 600 kr, depending on how early you book. Vy Express Route 146 (www.vybuss.no) travels direct from Oslo to Stryn in a little under 8 hours. This route has one daily and one nightly departure, and the nightly departure utilizes a double decker sleeper bus for extra comfort. To reach Ålesund from the area, local bus 110 from Stryn Rutebilstasjon/Bus station (Hegrevegen; www.skyss.no) takes you the whole way in 3.5 hours.

Car

The drive to Stryn from Bergen via E39 is the fastest route, covering a distance of 294 kilometers (182 mi) in 5 hours. This route includes the Brekke-Lavik ferry, which has three hourly departures and takes around 20 minutes (www.norled.no). Note that the ferry has limited departures at night and on national holidays. The alternative, but more picturesque, route from Bergen to Stryn via Flåm and Fjærland will take a little over 6 hours along E16, Route 5, and E39 (375 km/233 mi), but will allow you to see more of the Sognefjord as you drive along it. This, too, will include a ferry, as the vast Sognefjord has to be crossed at some point (Manheller-Fodnes, also 3 hourly departures).

If you are continuing north toward Ålesund (or starting there and traveling south), the drive between Stryn and Ålesund covers 128 kilometers (80 mi) and will take you 2.5 hours along E39.

From Oslo, the drive to Nordfjord via Otta and Lom follows E6 and Route 15 for just over 6 hours. The 473-kilometer (293 mi) drive travels north and eventually west to reach Stryn, from where you can continue on to reach Loen and Olden (10 and 20 minutes, respectively).

If you are arriving from Bergen, you will pass through both Olden and Loen.

North of Ålesund

Those spending time in Ålesund usually want to head north to drive the famous Atlantic Road. En route from Ålesund, you will come across a few sights and towns worth noting before you reach the Atlantic Road. Below you will find these in the order you reach them, in case you want to make your road trip a little more interesting. The journey up to the Atlantic Road can be done in a day trip from Ålesund, or take your time and spend a night in Kristiansund (30 minutes north of the Atlantic Road).

Getting There and Around

The area north of Ålesund is best explored by car. Kristiansund can be reached in 3 hours along E39 and Route 70 (151 km/94 mi). However, if you want to travel via the Atlantic Road, plan for at least 3.5 hours (and that's without stopping for photos). E39 crosses the Midfjord via the Molde-Vestnes ferry (tel. 91 55 58 88; www.boreal.no). The crossing takes around 45 minutes, and there are departures three times an hour on weekdays between 6am and 7pm (2 hourly departures on weekends).

MOLDE

Sights

Romsdalsmuseet

Per Amdams Veg 4; tel. 71 20 24 60; Tues.-Sun. noon-4pm; 150 kr

There is a large outdoor museum in the center of Molde. It consists of around 40 houses from the Romsdal region, giving you a glimpse into the lives of the locals here from the 1600s through the early 1900s.

In the summer months there are daily tours at quarter past noon, included in the ticket price. Tours last around 60 minutes. In addition, you will find guides stationed in several of the open buildings around the museum, ready to answer any questions you may have.

The new museum building Krona is where you will find the museum shop and a permanent exhibit dedicated to the regional culture and history of Romsdal.

Molde Panorama

Vardevegen, Molde

The Molde Panorama is a nickname given to all the mountain peaks you can see on the south of the Romsdals fjord. From the viewpoint Varden you can actually see 222 mountaintops, most of which are over 1,000 meters (3,280 ft) high. The Varden viewpoint itself is at 407 meters (1,335 ft) above sea level and can be reached by car just 10 minutes from the center of Molde. There is a small café there that is open from May to October.

Food

Køl Bar og Bistro

Torget 1; 915 67 325; https://kølmolde.no; daily from 2pm; 185-315 kr

Along the seafront of Molde is Køl Bar og Bistro, a modern restaurant serving Nordic and French dishes that are prepared using local ingredients. They also have an impressive wine list, hand-selected to complement their menu, which changes every second month and may include dishes such as beef tartar and moules frites.

Glass Restaurant og Bar

Moldetorget, Torget 1; 904 13 089; https://glassmolde.no; Tues.-Sat. 4pm-10:30pm; 225-425 kr

Glass is an Italian-Norwegian restaurant serving a selection of dishes from pizza bianca and pasta Bolognese to local beef tenderloin and clipfish (dried, salted cod). From June to August their rooftop terrace is open, with a beach club atmosphere and view over the rooftops of Molde. The interior of the restaurant is dark, friendly, and informal, perfect for after-work drinks or a family dinner.

Averøy to Kristiansund

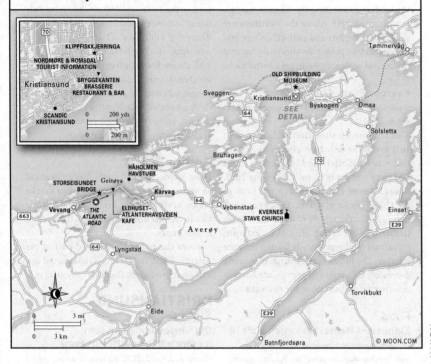

© MOON.COM

Getting There

Molde can be reached along E39 after around 2 hours of driving from Ålesund (81 km/50 mi). The route ends with the Molde-Vestnes ferry (www.fjord1.no), which drops off right in the center of Molde.

AVERØY

Averøy is the large island between Kristiansund (on the mainland on the north side) and Molde (on the mainland on the south side). You will cross Averøy on your drive between Molde and Kristiansund, and reach it after you have crossed the bridges of the Atlantic Road from Molde.

Sights
★ The Atlantic Road

The Atlantic Road links the island of Averøy with the mainland. It is a part of Route 64 and

the 8.3-kilometer (5-mi) stretch of road is also known as the Atlantic Ocean Road. Although there are several roads like this across Norway, this one is the most well-known. Through the years it has been made famous by several movies, such as the James Bond film *No Time to Die,* and in international car ads, and people will gladly drive almost 3 hours from Ålesund to see it. There are 8 bridges along the Atlantic Road, the most famous being **Storseisundet** simply because it is the most photographed, and there are stopping bays along the islands to allow visitors to pull over safely and take pictures. It won't take you more than 10 minutes to drive across the most popular bridges.

The Atlantic Road starts around the village of Vevang on the mainland and ends at a place called Karvag on Averøy. From Molde, Vevang is a 45-minute drive along Route 64 (46 km/29 mi). When you reach Vevang, simply keep going on Route 64 to the Atlantic Road. There is no sign indicating the start of the road, and the bridges connecting the islands start almost immediately. Along the way there are signed parking lots and pull-offs where you can stop to take photos. As always, do not stop in the road or slow down to get a better view.

Kvernes Stave Church

Stavkirkeveien 46, Averøy; daily 11am-5pm mid-June-mid-Aug.; 100 kr

This red wooden stave church dates back to 1631 and is the only stave church in Norway that was built after the Middle Ages. This discovery was made recently, as before 2020, it was believed that the church was built in the 1300s. The long, square church has a bell tower right in the middle of its roof, and large timber logs are set up around its exterior, presumably to keep it steady during extreme weather. The inside of the church is ornately decorated, with gold and gray painted details covering a large portion of the red walls.

Food
Eldhuset-Atlanterhavsveien Kafe

Atlanterhavsveien Eldhusøya; tel. 916 18 346; daily 11am-5pm June-Aug., weekends 11am-5pm low season

When driving up to the Atlantic Road you'll find Eldhuset on the Lyngholmen island. This small café serves ice cream, light bites such as sandwiches and waffles, and coffee for travelers, and is a natural stopping point for information (there is an information plaque nearby with facts about the Atlantic Road). A small hiking trail behind it gives you a great view of the bridges nearby.

Accommodations
Håholmen Havstuer

Håholmen 1; tel. 71 51 72 50; www.classicnorway.no; May-Sept.; 2,000 kr

On Håholmen island, not too far from the Atlantic Road, you can immerse yourself in the fresh ocean air and spend some time away from modern society. Services on the small island consist of 47 hotel rooms, a small café,

and a museum. Some of the rooms are found across the island, in small houses dating back to the 1700s and 1800s, while others are found in newer structures. Each is uniquely decorated and gives off an atmosphere of nostalgia. You reach Håholmen island via a 7-10-minute boat ride from Geitøya (105 kr return) on Averøy. Geitøya is one of the islands connected along the Atlantic Road. There are daily scheduled boat departures from June to August, and in the low season the transfer is arranged when you book your stay.

Getting There

From Molde, you will reach Averøy in about 55 minutes (or more if you stop often to take photos as you cross the bridges of the Atlantic Road), and the drive onward to Kristiansund is 30 minutes.

From the end of the bridged part of the Atlantic Road, in Karvag, Kristiansund is a half-hour drive along Route 64 (30 km/18 mi).

KRISTIANSUND
Sights
Old Shipbuilding Museum (Levende Skipsverftsmuseum)

Kranaveien 22; tel. 71 58 70 00; www.nordmore. museum.no; daily noon-5pm; 70 kr

To dive into the fishing industry of Kristiansund and the area surrounding it, visit this museum found on a former ship-building wharf dating back to 1856. It is still in use today, and on a visit to the museum you can learn more about shipbuilding, and see some of the veteran ships docked nearby.

Klippfiskkjerringa

Kirkelandet, Kristiansund

This statue is the icon of Kristiansund and was unveiled by Queen Sonja in 1992. This bronze statue shows a woman working with clipfish, drying and salting it to preserve it in a similar way to the Lofoten stockfish. The statue serves as a tribute to the area's fishing history.

1: the Atlantic Road **2:** Molde Panorama

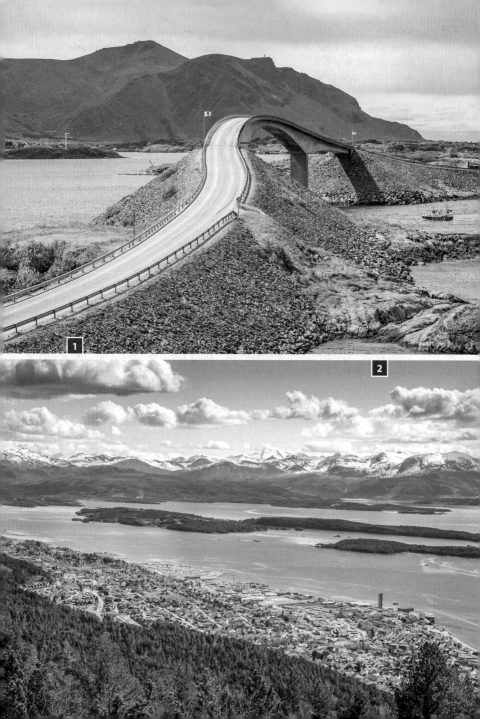

Food
Bryggekanten Brasserie Restaurant and Bar

Storkaia 1; tel. 71 67 61 60; www.fireb.no; Mon.-Thurs. 11:30am-11pm, Fri.-Sat 11am-2:30am; 675 kr for 3 courses

On the docks in Kristiansund you will find Bryggekanten, a large, welcoming restaurant with views of the harbor and waters beyond. The restaurant has a patio with glass walls, a glass roof, and heating lamps, allowing you to sit "outside" year-round. Bryggekanten focuses heavily on using locally sourced produce, and the menu changes with the season. This restaurant offers both a la carte and a set menu, and you can expect dishes such as cod, salmon, and deer.

Accommodations
Scandic Kristiansund

Storkaia 41; tel. 71 57 12 00; www.scandichotels.no; 1,200 kr

Scandic Kristiansund is one of many chain hotels in the city (they also have a Thon and a Comfort Hotel). The modern hotel offers bright, comfortable rooms (they have 102 in total), and a lavish breakfast buffet. As with all hotels in the Scandic chain, rooms are simply decorated with modern furnishings and basic amenities.

Information and Services
Nordmøre & Romsdal Tourist Information

Kongens Plass 1, Kristiansund; tel. 70 23 88 00; Mon.-Wed. 9am-5pm

In the center of Kristiansund you will find the tourist information for the region, where you can pick up maps and brochures, as well as get help with tickets and excursions.

Getting There

Kristiansund is a 30-minute drive from Averøy along Route 64, and around 1.5 hours from Molde (also along Route 64, via the Atlantic Road). If you are driving south from Trondheim, Kristiansund is a 3.5-hour drive along E39 (198 km/123 mi), including the Halsa-Kanestraum ferry.

Trondheim and Inland Norway

Often overlooked by travelers, Trondheim and the areas surrounding it have lots to offer for anyone looking to learn more about Norway's past and its culture. The city of Trondheim has just around 200,000 inhabitants, yet it offers a wealth of rich history, great food experiences, and one of the best hotels in the country. The reason there is so much history to explore here is that the city used to be Norway's capital, and as a result, it is home to Norway's crown jewels, the famous Nidaros Cathedral, and a current royal residence.

Central Norway is also where you will find the UNESCO World Heritage Town of Røros, a thriving destination ideal for anyone who wants the full experience of visiting Norway in the winter but does not have the time to travel as far north as Tromsø or Alta.

Highlights

Look for ★ to find recommended sights, activities, dining, and lodging.

★ **Maihaugen:** At this outdoor museum, you can explore Norwegian culture at its finest (page 261).

★ **Lillehammer Olympic Park:** Learn more about Norway's Olympic history and the history of ski jumping (page 261).

★ **Lom Stave Church:** This beautiful stave church found right by the road is perhaps one of the most accessible in Norway (page 267).

★ **Røros Bergstad:** The UNESCO World Heritage List has included all of this mining town since 1980 (page 271).

★ **Nidaros Cathedral:** This Gothic cathedral is one of the most famous in Norway, and a must when visiting Trondheim (page 276).

★ **Stiftsgården:** This is one of the few current royal residences in Norway you can visit year-round (page 278).

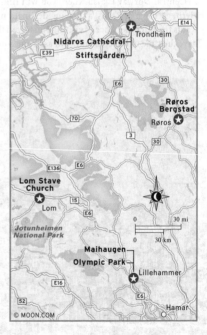

Trondheim and Inland Norway

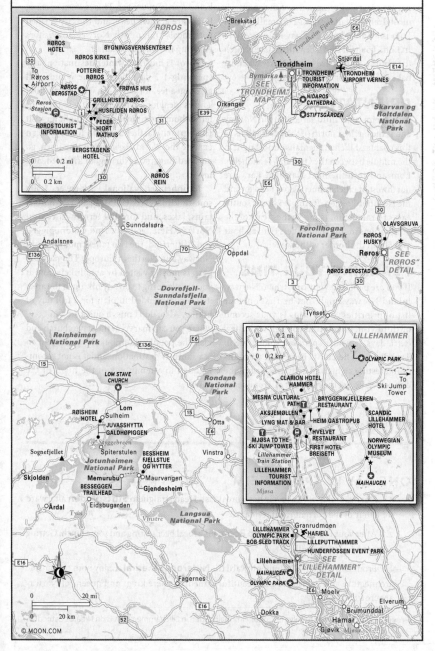

RØROS

RØROS HOTEL
BYGNINGSVERNSENTERET
RØROS KIRKE
POTTERIET RØROS
To Røros Airport
30
RØROS BERGSTAD
FRØYAS HUS
Røros Stasjon
i
GRILLHUSET RØROS
HUSFLIDEN RØROS
RØROS TOURIST INFORMATION
PEDER HIORT MATHUS
31
BERGSTADENS HOTEL
0   0.2 mi
0   0.2 km
30
RØROS REIN

Brekstad
Trondheim Fjord
E6
Trondheim
Stjørdal
E14
Bymarka
i TRONDHEIM TOURIST INFORMATION
TRONDHEIM AIRPORT VÆRNES
SEE "TRONDHEIM MAP"
NIDAROS CATHEDRAL
STIFTSGÅRDEN
Orkanger
Skarvan og Roltdalen National Park
E39
30
E6
30

Sunndalsøra
Forollhogna National Park
OLAVSGRUVA
RØROS HUSKY
Åndalsnes
E136
Oppdal
70
Røros
SEE "RØROS" DETAIL
RØROS BERGSTAD
Dovrefjell-Sunndalsfjella National Park
3
30
Tynset

Reinheimen National Park
E136
E6
Rondane National Park
LILLEHAMMER
OLYMPIC PARK
To Ski Jump Tower
CLARION HOTEL HAMMER
MESNA CULTURAL PATH
BRYGGERIKJELLEREN RESTAURANT
AKSJEMØLLEN
LYNG MAT & BAR
HEIM GASTROPUB
SCANDIC LILLEHAMMER HOTEL
MJØSA TO THE SKI JUMP TOWER
HVELVET RESTAURANT
FIRST HOTEL BREISETH
NORWEGIAN OLYMPIC MUSEUM
Lillehammer Train Station
LILLEHAMMER TOURIST INFORMATION
MAIHAUGEN
Mjøsa
0   0.2 mi
0   0.2 km
15
LOM STAVE CHURCH
Lom
RØISHEIM HOTEL
Sulheim
JUVASSHYTTA
GALDHØPIGGEN
Styggebreen
Otta
E6
Spiterstulen
Sognefjellet
Jotunheimen National Park
BESSHEIM FJELLSTUE OG HYTTER
Vinstra
Skjolden
Memurubu
BESSEGGEN TRAILHEAD
Maurvangen
Gjendesheim
Årdal
Eidsbugarden
Tyin
Langsua National Park
Vinstre
GRANrudmoen
LILLEHAMMER OLYMPIC PARK BOB SLED TRACK
HAFJELL
LILLEPUTTHAMMER
HUNDERFOSSEN EVENT PARK
SEE "LILLEHAMMER" DETAIL
Fagernes
E16
Lillehammer
MAIHAUGEN
OLYMPIC PARK
E6
Moelv
Elverum
Dokka
52
Hamar
Brumunddal
Gjøvik
Mjøsa
0   20 mi
0   20 km
E16

© MOON.COM

The Jotunheimen National Park, with Norway's tallest mountains, is a haven for nature-lovers, offering some of the country's most dramatic landscapes. The small town of Lom is a natural place to stay in this region. In Lom, you will find a beautiful stave church (one of the 28 that are left in Norway) and a bakery famous for cinnamon buns.

ORIENTATION

Trondheim is the third-largest city in Norway and is the farthest north of the destinations in this chapter. Lillehammer falls almost right in the middle between the Oslo and Trondheim. Lom and Jotunheimen National Park are northwest of Lillehammer as you head toward the Nordfjord region. Røros, 2.5 hours southeast of Trondheim, is the farthest east of the destinations in this chapter, less than an hour away from the border with Sweden.

PLANNING YOUR TIME

If you are planning your first trip to Norway, inland Norway might not be first on your list of priorities. But, if this is your second or third visit, or you find yourself with a few extra days, consider spending some time in Trondheim. The city is beautiful, with lots of interesting sights and activities within the city center. To get the most out of Trondheim,

set aside at least 2 days. The city comes alive in the summer, with the best months to visit being April-September. This is when opening hours are at their peak, and the city is filled with locals and (mostly Norwegian) visitors enjoying the warmer weather.

Røros is mostly a winter destination, and spending 1-2 days here in the winter will give you a feel for Norway's winter activities. This is ideal for anyone traveling in the winter without the time to catch a flight (or visit Hurtigruten) farther north. In Røros you can explore the World Heritage mining town, go dog sledding, try a Norwegian kick sled, and more!

Jotunheimen National Park covers 3,500 square kilometers (1,351 sq mi) of mountains, lakes, and forested terrain in central Norway. Here, you will find Galdhøpiggen and Glittertind, the two tallest mountains in Norway and Northern Europe. The national park is mostly visited by avid hikers, and if you are planning to do any hiking in the area, it is recommended to plan for a full day of hiking. Also, don't miss a quick stop in Lom, where you can marvel at the stave church and visit the popular Lom Bakery. Jotunheimen is a summer destination, and it is not recommended to attempt any of the hikes in the winter.

Itinerary Ideas

ONE DAY IN TRONDHEIM

1 Start your day with a lovely hotel breakfast. Head straight to **Stiftsgården** afterward for a tour of the current royal residence.

2 After your tour, head to **ØX Tap Room** for a local beer tasting and some lunch. Getting there is a 5-minute walk.

3 From ØX, walk 5-10 minutes toward the **Nidaros Cathedral.** Enjoy both the outside architecture and interior of this beautiful cathedral where kings and queens of Norway are crowned.

Previous: buildings along Nidelva in Trondheim; Maihaugen in Lillehammer; details on Nidaros Cathedral.

Itinerary Ideas

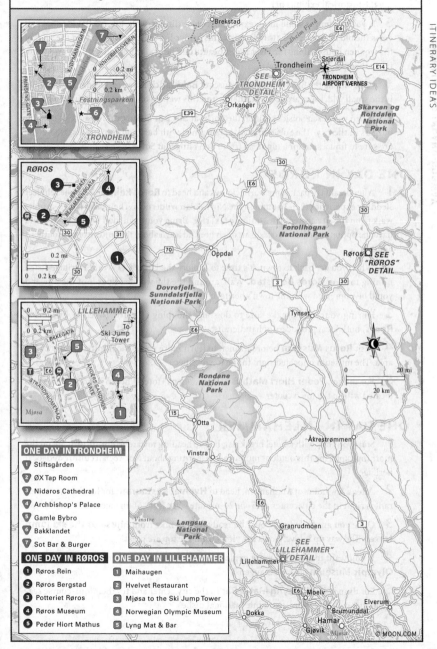

ONE DAY IN TRONDHEIM
1. Stiftsgården
2. ØX Tap Room
3. Nidaros Cathedral
4. Archbishop's Palace
5. Gamle Bybro
6. Bakklandet
7. Sot Bar & Burger

ONE DAY IN RØROS
1. Røros Rein
2. Røros Bergstad
3. Potteriet Røros
4. Røros Museum
5. Peder Hiort Mathus

ONE DAY IN LILLEHAMMER
1. Maihaugen
2. Hvelvet Restaurant
3. Mjøsa to the Ski Jump Tower
4. Norwegian Olympic Museum
5. Lyng Mat & Bar

© MOON.COM

4 From the cathedral, head next door to the **Archbishop's Palace,** where 27 archbishops of Norway have lived. Take your time looking at the Norwegian crown jewels and exploring the historical exhibits here.

5 If you are up for some more exploring before dinner, walk toward Bakklandet and cross the old city bridge, **Gamle Bybro.** This bridge is a famed photo op, and the view of the wooden houses along the river is just beautiful. The bridge is a 5-10 minute walk from the cathedral.

6 Walk among the historic wooden houses of **Bakklandet** toward Solsiden. Bakklandet is the small Old Town area of Trondheim, and this walk takes about 10 minutes.

7 When you reach Solsiden, sit on the docks at **Sot Bar & Burger,** for some of the best burgers in the city. The Solsiden dock area is lined with bars and restaurants, where you are sure to find a spot for a nightcap if you don't linger at Sot.

ONE DAY IN RØROS

1 After breakfast, pack some warm clothes and head to **Røros Rein** for a unique reindeer sledding experience (2.5-3 hours) in the Norwegian wilderness. Their farm is a 15-minute walk from the city center, or a 2-minute taxi ride. Bring your own food for lunch. You will have the option to grill hot dogs on an open fire and learn about the culture of the southern Samis.

2 When you get back to town, it's time to explore the UNESCO World Heritage-listed mining town of **Røros Bergstad.** Walk around the the wooden houses of the city and you'll be impressed with the town's heritage.

3 During your stroll, make sure to do some shopping at Røros Tweed or **Potteriet Røros,** both local producers of handicrafts.

4 Visit **Røros Museum** before dinner, to learn more about the mining history of the area. The museum is located right in the town center.

5 For dinner, **Peder Hiort Mathus** at Bergstadens Hotel is not to be missed. It's also located within the town center.

ONE DAY IN LILLEHAMMER

1 Start your day with a hotel breakfast, before heading toward **Maihaugen.** Spend the morning exploring this outdoor museum and learning about Norwegian culture and local heritage.

2 After a few hours at Maihaugen, head to **Hvelvet Restaurant** for lunch. The restaurant is right in the city center, a 15- or 20-minute walk from Maihaugen.

3 Once you are fueled up, you'll be ready for the hike from **Mjøsa to the ski jump tower.** The way up is lovely, and the views from the top are great.

4 If you want to do some more exploring before dinner, don't miss the **Norwegian Olympic Museum** near Maihaugen.

5 For dinner, head to **Lyng Mat & Bar** in the city center and try their four-course seasonal menu of New Nordic and international dishes.

Lillehammer

If you don't have the time to travel too far out of Oslo, and especially if you are on a family trip, Lillehammer might be the ideal destination. The city is known for being full of family-friendly experiences, and for being the home of the 1994 Winter Olympics. There are several Olympics-related sights and experiences, such as the Norwegian Olympic Museum and the Olympic Park itself. Lillehammer is a fun destination for a day trip from Oslo, or as a one-night stop for those traveling from Oslo to Trondheim.

Orientation

The city center of Lillehammer covers just a small area, and you'll find that most shops, restaurants, and sights are within walking distance from the main street, Storgata. The Olympic Park and Maihaugen are both just east of the city center, and no longer than a 20-minute walk (however, both are up a hill, so prepare for that).

SIGHTS
South of City Center
★ Maihaugen

Maihaugvegen 1; tel. 61 28 89 00; https://maihaugen. no; Tues.-Fri. 11am-3pm, Sat.-Sun. 11am-4pm; adults 140 kr, ages under 25 65 kr

Maihaugen is an outdoor museum with a history dating back to 1885, when dentist Anders Sandvig moved to Lillehammer. He collected local artifacts of cultural importance, and eventually this collection turned into the outdoor museum we see today. Many of the artifacts here are old tools and items used for needlework. Today, this outdoor museum consists of over 200 buildings from the area that have all been moved to the museum, with some dating back to the 1700s. Among the newer additions is the childhood home of HRH Queen Sonja of Norway. You will also find a stave church, a school, and an old police station in the area called "bygda"—the village.

The area is large, so expect to spend at least 2-3 hours walking around. There is a gift shop and café at the visitors center (where you enter), where you can grab a snack when you get hungry. Some of the buildings now have QR codes you can scan to get more information, and some will have a guide to answer questions.

Norwegian Olympic Museum

Maihaugvegen 1; tel. 61 28 89 00; https://ol.museum.no; Tues.-Fri. 11am-3pm, Sat.-Sun. 11am-4pm; adults 140 kr, ages under 25 65 kr

The Norwegian Olympic Museum is almost like an homage to the Olympic Games through the ages, and especially the Winter Olympics hosted in Norway in 1952 and 1994. During your visit you will learn about the history of the Olympic Games, through fun and interactive exhibits, including touch screens with games and stories to dive into. The museum opened in 1997 and is popular with travelers of all ages. One of the highlights of the museum is the round theater (included in the entrance fee) showing various movies related to the Olympics on a 180-degree screen.

★ Olympic Park

Nordsetervegen 45; tel. 61 05 42 00; https:// olympiaparken.no; hours vary; prices vary

The Olympiaparken Olympic Park in Lillehammer consists of the arenas used during the 1994 Olympic Games: Håkon's Hall (a sports hall), Lysgårdsbakkene ski jumping facility, the Lillehammer Snow Park, and the Olympic bobsleigh and toboggan run. Across the park, you can join activities and try different sports year-round. In the summer the wheel bob (a bob sled on wheels) is the most popular activity. Each bob seats 2-3 people and costs 1,200 kr per ride, and you can experience speeds of up to 97 kilometers per hour (60 mph) as you zoom around the track. In the winter, you can try bob sledding on the same

World Class Winter Olympians

Perhaps to no surprise, some of the best Olympic athletes have been Norwegian. In fact, Norway is the country with the most Winter Olympic medals in the world. Since the 1924 Winter Olympics in Chamonix, Norwegians have been collecting medals left and right, including a record 37 medals during the 2022 Beijing Olympics.

SKI CULTURE

There is a saying in Norway that "Norwegians are born with skis on," and it couldn't be more true. It is not uncommon to start skiing shortly after you learn to walk in Norway, and this is perhaps what makes for such strong contenders in the Winter Olympics. Norway is the leading nation in cross-country skiing (129 Olympic medals), the biathlon (55 medals), Nordic combined (35 medals), and ski jumping (36 medals). Cross-country skiing, dowhill skiing, and even ski jumping are popular hobbies among Norwegians.

FAMOUS MEDALISTS

Famous Norwegian Olympic winners include cross-country skier Marit Bjørgen (15 Olympic medals 2002-2018), biathlon athlete Ole Einar Bjørndalen (13 medals 1994-2014), and Bjørn Dæhlie, who is perhaps Norway's most famous cross-country skier (12 medals 1992-1998, including 8 gold medals).

track. The top of the ski jump is also a popular hiking/walking destination.

The Olympic park is a 15-20 minute walk east of the city center.

North of Lillehammer
Lilleputthammer

Hundervegen 41; www.lilleputthammer.no; daily June-Aug.; 369 kr

Lilleputthammer is a summer amusement park, where kids can enjoy various activities and rides, as well as meet Norwegian cartoon and fairy-tale characters. Rides such as small bumper cars, a Ferris wheel, and carousels can be found here, as well as trampolines and playgrounds. Throughout the day, actors put on short shows and make appearances around the park, so you can catch different characters in action.

To get there, drive along E6 northbound for a little less than 20 minutes (17 km/10.5 mi). Alternatively, bus routes 141 and 142 (tel. 91 50 20 40; www.innlandstrafikk.no) will take you from Lillehammer bus station to Øyer Sentrum, and Lilleputthammer is a 3-minute walk from there.

Hunderfossen Event Park

Fossekrovegen 22; tel. 61 27 55 30; https:// hunderfossen.no; daily 10am-5pm June-Aug., select weekends 10am-5pm May-Sept.; from 435 kr

The Hunderfossen park is an amusement and fairy-tale park dedicated to Norwegian folklore. With a large focus on trolls and the popular Norwegian tales of Espen Askeladd (a main character of many Norwegian fairy tales), the park portrays a very Norwegian world, with forests, rivers, and waterfalls, and the world's largest seated troll (14 m/46 ft high, to be exact). Beneath the trolls are caves that can be explored, to learn more about the fairy-tale world of Espen Askeladd and the trolls. The park is open in the summer months and is a popular destination for Norwegian families.

The drive here goes north via E6 and takes 30 minutes. Additionally, Hunderfossen has its own train stop, with Vy (www.vy.no) and Sj (www.sj.no) trains going north toward Trondheim.

1: Lillehammer Olympic Park 2: buildings at Maihaugen

Norwegian Fairy Tales

Norwegian fairy tales and folklore can be a little dark, as they often have grim endings (for the bad guys). Similar to the Brothers Grimm, who collected folklore from all over Germany, two men also traveled around Norway to collect and write down fairy tales found across the country. Their names were Peter Christen Asbjørnsen and Jørgen Moe, and they are usually just referred to as **Asbjørnsen and Moe.** If you are looking for a book to bring home from Norway, consider their collection, titled *Asbjørnsen and Moe's Collection of Fairy Tales.*

ESPEN ASKELADD

Norwegian folk tales usually depict beautiful, rural landscapes and farm life, and are rarely set in urban areas. Espen Askeladd (the inspiration for the theme of Hunderfossen Fairytale Park) is a typical protagonist in these tales: a kind, simple soul who just wants to do well and make his family proud. Espen also doesn't see the bad in others, and while his brothers often mistreat and bully him, he only thinks the best of them.

TROLLS

The villains in the tales of Espen Askeladd, as well as in most other fairy tales, are trolls. These large, terrifying creatures are usually big enough to pull trees out of the ground and would ravage and menace farms and villages. The grim ending for the bad guy usually comes when Espen Askeladd outmaneuvers the troll in the story, leaving the troll to die a gruesome death.

HIKING
Mesna Cultural Path
Distance: 3 kilometers (1.8 mi)
Time: 30 minutes one-way
Difficulty: Easy
Trailhead: By CC Strandtorget, Strandpromenaden 85
Information and Maps: www.visitnorway.no/listings/mesna-kultursti-%7C-lillehammer/237624

Along the Mesna river in Lillehammer you will find a lovely trail with a focus on the history of the city and river. You will see factories, bridges, and mills that are all of historic importance to the city.

Mjøsa to the Ski Jump Tower
Distance: 4 kilometers (2.5 mi)
Time: 60 minutes one-way
Difficulty: Moderate
Trailhead: CC Strandtorget, Strandpromenaden 85
Information and Maps: www.lillehammer.com/opplevelser/helt-til-topps-med-byens-beste-utsikt-for-den-spreke-p5534773

This option is for those who want to take that walk along the river to the next level. Start by the river, or anywhere along the lake Mjøsa, and follow the river until you reach the Olympic Park. From here, head to the ski jumping facility and make your way up the 936 steps to the top! This is a popular exercise activity among locals and will give you the best view in town.

WINTER SPORTS
Skiing
Hafjell
Hundervegen 122; tel. 61 24 90 00; www.hafjell.no; Nov.-Apr.; day pass 530 kr

Hafjell is one of the most popular ski resorts in eastern Norway, particularly among people from Oslo in the winter months. The tallest peak at this ski destination is 1,089 meters (3,582 ft) above sea level, and from there you can enjoy a large selection of slopes as you come down the mountain. In total they have 29 slopes of varying difficulty, from children's slopes to black diamond. They have 18 ski lifts. Find them just across the river from Hunderfossen, a 30-minute drive from the center of Lillehammer. Take bus route 142 or 141 to Hafjell Alpinsenter if you are traveling on public transport.

Bob Sledding
Lillehammer Olympic Park Bob Sled Track

*Nordsetervegen 45; tel. 61 05 42 00; https://
olympiaparken.no/aktiviteter/taxibob; weekends noon-
4pm Nov.-Mar.; 1,000 kr*

With a drop of 1,710 meters (5,610 feet), the bob sled track at the Lillehammer Olympic Park is a must for thrill seekers. It is actually the only bob sled track in the Nordics, and in one of their bob sleds (seating up to 4 people) you can reach speeds of over 96 km/ph (60 mph), feeling 3G pressure in some of the turns.

FOOD
City Center
Hvelvet Restaurant

*Stortorget 1; tel. 907 29 100; https://hvelvet.no; Mon.-
Thurs. 4pm-10pm, Fri.-Sat. 4pm-11pm; 349-359 kr*

Hvelvet ("the vault") is located in a former Bank of Norway building, which was the inspiration for the restaurant name. The menu changes monthly and the best value is to opt for the set menu of 3 or 4 courses with an optional wine pairing (3 courses with wine pairing 1,025 kr). The cuisine can best be called French-Norwegian fusion, and the menu includes moules frites, duck confit, and oven-baked char.

Heim Gastropub

*Storgata 84; tel. 61 10 00 82; www.heim.no; Mon.-
Thurs. noon-midnight, Fri.-Sat. noon-3am, Sun. 3pm-
10pm; 169-369 kr*

Heim is the Norwegian word for home, and their goal is to welcome you with their unpretentious atmosphere, homemade "no fluff" burgers, and large beer selection. The burgers are popular, and the sharing menu consisting of local cured meats and cheese (295 kr) is not to be missed as a starter. Each dish has a suggested beer pairing.

Lyng Mat & Bar

*Nymosvingen 2; tel. 906 17 774; https://lyngmatogbar.
no; Mon.-Thurs. 4pm-10pm, Fri.-Sat. 4pm-midnight,
Sun. 4pm-9pm; 335-395 kr*

At Lyng Mat & Bar in the center of Lillehammer you are served seasonal dishes in a dark, stylish restaurant. Some consider this the best restaurant in town. Purple details and hardwood floors make the atmosphere here intimate and cozy, and on the menu you can expect to find dishes such as baked trout, veal tenderloin, and local cheeses.

Bryggerikjelleren Restaurant

*Elvegata 19; tel. 61 27 06 60; www.bblillehammer.
no; Tues.-Thurs. 6pm-11pm, Fri.-Sat. 6pm-midnight;
349-649 kr*

Meat and seafood lovers will also love Bryggerikjelleren. The name literally translates to "the brewery cellar," as this establishment is in a brewery cellar from 1855. Bryggerikjelleren is particularly known for steaks, and for good reason. In addition to their great beef tenderloin (served with pepper sauce, vegetables, and your choice of potatoes), they have an extensive selection of over 190 wines. The atmosphere here is intimate and relaxed.

ACCOMMODATIONS
City Center
First Hotel Breiseth

*Jernbanegata 1-5; tel. 61 24 77 77; www.firsthotels.no;
1,000 kr*

First Hotel Breiseth is located right by the train station in Lillehammer and exudes historic charm. The 89 rooms are decorated with old-style furniture and gold-framed paintings, taking you a few decades back in time. The paintings and artworks around the hotel were gifts from local artists who stayed in the hotel in the early 1900s and paid for their lodging with their art.

Clarion Hotel Hammer

Storgata 108; tel. 61 26 73 73; www.nordicchoicehotels.
no; 1,600 kr

Hotel Hammer by Clarion has 142 rooms, each simply furnished with light colors and a Nordic style. In addition to a large breakfast, the hotel serves fika (a Swedish concept of having a little bite with coffee in the afternoon) and an evening meal for guests, making this a great option for travelers who want to save money on food during their trip.

Aksjemøllen

Elvegata 12; tel. 61 05 70 80; www.classicnorway.no;
1,600 kr

In the city center you will find Aksjemøllen, a boutique hotel along the Mesna river. This small, luxurious hotel has 58 rooms in various sizes, all with satin details and lavish decor, in addition to beds from Wonderland. On the 11th floor, the hotel has a popular rooftop bar called Toppen ("the top").

Near Olympic Park
Scandic Lillehammer Hotel

Turisthotellvegen 6; tel. 61 28 60 00; www.
scandichotels.no; 1,200 kr

Scandic Lillehammer is a beautiful white hotel located in a private park near the city center. The hotel has 303 rooms, all designed and decorated in the classic Scandic style, with blue and wood details and imagery from winter sports (as is only appropriate in Lillehammer). The hotel has a wellness center with a pool, spa, and fitness room, in addition to two restaurants, one for buffets and one for a la carte dinner.

INFORMATION AND SERVICES
Lillehammer Tourist Information

Jernbanetorget 2; tel. 61 28 98 00; www.lillehammer.
com; Mon.-Fri. 8am-4pm

At the Lillehammer tourist information, you can pick up city maps or hiking maps, and book tickets for nearby excursions and activities. They can also help you plan your itinerary during your stay.

GETTING THERE

Lillehammer is easily reached from Oslo or Trondheim; it falls almost right in the middle between the two cities along main road E6. The distance between Lillehammer and Oslo is 180 kilometers (112 mi) and takes 2.5 hours to drive. From Lillehammer to Trondheim is 350 kilometers (217 mi), a 5-hour drive.

Regional trains operate between Lillehammer and Oslo (and even Oslo Airport) up to 18 times a day year-round, making it easy to reach this city from the capital. Regional Route R10 ends in Lillehammer and services both Oslo and the airport. Headed north from Lillehammer, the regional route Dovrebanen departs for Trondheim 1-3 times a day.

GETTING AROUND

Lillehammer is a small and walkable city, but a handful of local **Innlandstrafikk** buses (tel. 02040; www.innlandstrafikk.no) service the city as well. A one-way ticket costs 43 kr when bought on the bus, but is much cheaper when purchased through the Innlandstrafikk Billett app (26 kr).

Lom and Jotunheimen National Park

The Jotunheimen National Park covers the Jotunheimen mountain range, which includes the two tallest mountains in Norway: Galdhøpiggen and Glittertind. Here, hikers from all over the country gather to climb Besseggen, a mountain ridge, and Galdhøpiggen. The mountain range is named after the large trolls known as Jotuns in Norse mythology, as the majestic mountains of the range seemed to be the only place where these trolls could hide in plain sight.

Lom, a small town in the center of Norway, is known as the gateway to the Jotunheimen National Park. When traveling between the east and northwest, you are likely to cross through Lom. Norwegians even have a saying that "All roads lead to Lom" because so many travel routes are likely to lead you through the town.

Orientation

The Jotunheimen National Park covers the large mountain ranges between the towns of Årdal and Skjolden (along the Sognefjord) in the southwest, Lom in the north, and Otta in the east. The town of Lom is to the north of the park, where Routes 15 and 55 meet. The two most popular hikes, Galdhøpiggen and Besseggen, are on opposites sides of the park, with Galdhøpiggen to the west and Besseggen to the west. To reach the trailheads for these, you have to drive around the outside of the park, as the roads do not go through it.

SIGHTS
Lom
★ **Lom Stave Church**
Bergomsvegen 1; https://lomstavechurch.no; daily 10am-4pm in summer; adults 100 kr, children under 15 free
One of only 28 stave churches remaining in Norway, the Lom Stave Church is a sight worth seeing when in Lom, whether you are staying for the night or traveling through. The

church structure dates back to 1160 through the 1200s and is one of the largest remaining stave churches in the country. In the surrounding area and in the graveyard, several interesting archeological discoveries have been made, and have shown that there was a church in the same spot even before the current stave church was built. Findings include coins from the 1200s, a proposal letter written in runes from the 1300s, and a roll of parchment with music from the 1200s.

HIKING

The hikes in Jotunheimen are long, full-day hikes, and quite strenuous. You do not need any technical hiking knowledge, but you should have some basic experience in order to do these. Also, as with all strenuous hikes in Norway, these should not be attempted unless you truly enjoy hiking.

Jotunheimen National Park
Besseggen
Distance: *13.3 kilometers (8 mi)*
Time: *7-9 hours one-way*
Difficulty: *Very strenuous*
Trailhead: *Memurubu, reached via the ferry from Gjendesheim*
Information and Maps: *https://besseggen.net*
Besseggen has been rated one of the 20 best hikes in the world by National Geographic, and it is one of the most popular hikes in Norway. Besseggen itself is a narrow ridge, with beautiful views of the Gjende Alps. The highest point of the hike is at 1,743 meters (5,718 feet) above sea level. It is best to start your hike by taking the **Gjende ferry** from the dock at Gjendesheim (Gjendevegen 244; www.gjende.no/en) across the lake to **Memurubu** where the trail starts. The Gjende lake is large, and walking along it is not recommended.

The hike, which takes you along the ridge above the lake back to Gjendesheim, is considered very strenuous, not only because it is steep, but also because you will need to set aside the whole day for it. The entire hike is noteworthy, as you follow the edge/ridge of the mountain along the lake. The final climb across the Besseggen ridge is the most famous part of the hike, as this is when you are actually scaling the Besseggen mountain ridge, and it is not for those with a fear of heights. Because this is a narrow hike along a mountain ridge, everyone hikes it in the same direction.

Gjendesheim, where you take the ferry, is a 1-hour drive from Lom along Routes 15 and 51 (76 km/47 mi). From Oslo, Gjendesheim is 344 kilometers (213 mi), and the drive along E6 and Route 51 takes 4.5 hours.

Galdhøpiggen

Distance: *11.4 kilometers (7 mi)*
Time: *7 hours round-trip*
Difficulty: *Strenuous*
Trailhead: *Juvasshytta*
Information and Maps: *www.juvasshytta.no*

Hiking the highest mountain in Norway is worth bragging about, and luckily this isn't one of the hardest hikes in the country. It is still considered strenuous, as you will climb the final 648 meters (2,125 feet) from the starting point at Juvasshytta to the top. The trail is clearly marked the whole way, and the majority of the hike is over rocky terrain. After a little less than 3 kilometers (1.8 mi) you get to the edge of the glacier Styggebreen. To continue on from here to reach the top, you have to go with a glacier guide. This can be reserved through the Juvasshytta lodge (www.juvasshytta.no). The hiking season here is from the end of May to mid-September.

From Lom, follow Route 55 and Galdhøpiggvegen to get to Juvasshytta in 40 minutes (34 km/21 mi). The drive from Oslo to Juvasshytta is 381 kilometers (236 mi) and will take around 5 hours.

FOOD AND ACCOMMODATIONS

The options for both restaurants and places to stay are limited in the area, with most people staying in Lom doing so to break up long travel days. Additionally, the standard of the accommodation is usually simple, as these are mostly used by hikers as a place to rest before they head out to hike Galdhøpiggen or Besseggen the next day. People staying in the area primarily eat at their accommodation.

Lom
Bakeriet i Lom
Sognefjellsvegen 7; tel. 907 85 999; www.bakerietilom.no; daily 9am-5pm

The bakery in Lom is famous for their kanelsnurr (cinnamon rolls) and other baked goods, all made in their wood-fired stone oven. Travelers have been stopping at the bakery for lunch and travel snacks since it opened in 2004, and it grows in popularity every year. Don't miss their cinnamon rolls or homemade foccacia during your visit, baked fresh every morning.

Fossheim Hotel and Restaurant
Bergomsvegen 32, Lom; tel. 61 21 95 00; www.fossheimhotel.no; 1,400 kr

Fossheim Hotel in Lom dates back to 1897 and is still run by the same family today. The hotel is one of the Historic Hotels of Norway, and the decor in the common areas reflects the traditional simplicity of the early 1900s. Each room is simply furnished and decorated, with birch furniture and muted colors. The **restaurant** (Mon.-Sat. 6pm-9:30pm; 3-course meal 560 kr) serves traditional Scandinavian dishes such as baked halibut and meatballs. Reservations are required.

Jotunheimen National Park
Bessheim Fjellstue og Hytter
Sjodalsvegen 2977, Tessanden; tel. 61 23 89 13; www.bessheim.no; June-Oct.; 1,600 kr

Those who are planning to hike Besseggen

1: Lom Stave Church 2: view of Galdhøpiggen

usually stay at one of the tourist cabins run by the Norwegian Trekking Association (www.dnt.no) or at Bessheim Fjellstue (Mountain Lodge), just an 8-minute drive from the ferry dock at Gjende. They are not a traditional hotel, but rather a simple hikers' lodge, with 27 cabins, several camp spots for those bringing their own tent, and 27 rooms in the main building. They serve both breakfast and a la carte dinner in their restaurant, and at breakfast you can make your lunch for the day (and fill up your thermos for the hike).

Røisheim Hotel
Sognefjellvegen, Bøverdalen; tel. 61 21 20 31; https://roisheim.no; May-Sept.; 2,600 kr

North of the Jotunheimen National Park you will find Røisheim Hotel, in a former coach/carriage station where travelers have been staying since the 1800s. This cozy hotel is located closer to Galdhøpiggen than Lom and has 24 rooms, all refurbished with modern amenities. The common areas and rooms all have an old-Norwegian charm, and each guest room is individually decorated and furnished with vintage furniture and details. The rooms are spread across old farmhouse buildings dating back to the 1700s, creating a truly authentic atmosphere.

Juvasshytta
Galdhøpiggvegen; tel. 61 21 15 50; https://juvasshytta.no; May-Sept.; 2,650 kr

Most hikers opt to stay at Juvasshytta, either before or after hiking Galdhøpiggen. The simple lodgings started as a cabin for travelers that opened in 1884 and has since been upgraded and expanded as the hike increased in popularity. The lodge is family-owned and -run, and offers basic amenities and assistance to those planning on hiking Norway's highest mountain. From booking the Galdhøpiggen glacier hike to making your lunch box, they specialize in the Galdhøpiggen hike.

INFORMATION AND SERVICES

The best place to get information about hiking Galdhøpiggen is at **Juvasshytta** (www.juvasshytta.no) lodge, and that's also where you can book the glacier guiding necessary to get across to the top of the mountain. There is also a **tourist information** in Lom (Bergomsvegen 17; www.visitjotunheimen.no; daily 10am-2pm July-Aug., Mon.-Fri. 10am-3pm rest of the year) where they can assist you with how to best explore the nearby national park. You can also pick up hiking maps there.

GETTING THERE AND AROUND

Lom is the best place to stay before entering the Jotunheimen National Park, and the town can be reached easily from Oslo, Trondheim, or Bergen by bus or car. Norwegians like to say that all roads lead to Lom, and you'll find that this is true if you are driving. If you are planning to hike Galdhøpiggen or Besseggen during your stay, consider booking the night before your hike at either Bessheim (for Besseggen) or Juvasshytta (for Galdhøpiggen), so that you can just get up and go in the morning.

From Oslo (around 350 km/217 mi), follow E6 north to Otta before following Route 15 all the way to Lom. The drive time from Oslo is approximately 4.5 hours. Those driving from Bergen (also 350 km/217 mi) will find that while the distance to Lom is the same, the western roads and mountain crossings make driving times a little longer (6 hours). Follow E16 via Flåm and Aurland toward Lom, and then cross the Sognefjellet mountain along Route 55. From Trondheim, Lom is a 4-hour drive along E6, Route 438, and Route 15 (280 km/173 mi).

If you are arriving from the northwestern fjord, you will find that Lom is a 2-hour drive along Route 15 from Stryn in the Nordfjord (124 km/77 mi), and the drive from Geiranger along Routes 63 and 15 will also take you around 2 hours, even though it is shorter (96 km/59 mi). The road leaving Geiranger

(Route 63) includes a lot of winding curves before joining Route 15. Lom can be reached from Lillehammer in 2.5 hours along E6 and Route 15 (169 km/105 mi).

There are daily bus routes from Oslo, Bergen, and Trondheim to Lom with **Norway** (www.nor-way.no) and **Vy** (www.vybuss. no).

Røros

The mining town of Rorøs dates back to the 1600s, including 300 years of mining history, and it feels almost like a living museum. The town center itself consists of old wooden buildings, and a large part of the town has been on UNESCO's World Heritage List since 1980. The World Heritage area consists of not only the town itself, but also the surrounding area, out to 45 kilometers (28 mi) around Røros. This area offers the opportunity for you to enjoy Norwegian winter activities without having to travel too far north. Røros is a great place to try your hand at dog sledding, learn about the Sami, and try a Norwegian kick sled for the first time!

SIGHTS
★ Røros Bergstad
(Røros Mining Town)

Røros was founded in 1646. It eventually became a mining community, as well as a farming town, and most of the historic buildings are still intact. The whole town center itself feels like a living museum, as you walk between these old, colorful timber buildings. Here you'll get a glimpse into what life was like for the miners back in the day. Most of the buildings are still occupied today, which gives the site a very authentic feel.

It is free to enter the town and walk around at your own pace. The Røros Museum offers a guided tour around the town (150 kr per person), which is not to be missed. The tours will share more about the town history and point out interesting sights as you walk through the streets. The tours start at the museum building called Smelthytta and last about 1 hour and 20 minutes.

Røros Museum

Lorentz Lossius Gata 45; tel. 72 40 61 70; https:// rorosmuseet.no; Smelthytta daily 10am-3pm Sept.-May; entrance to Smelthytta 130 kr, tour of Olavsgruva 180 kr

To learn even more about the Røros mining town and UNESCO World Heritage Site, the Røros Museum should be on your list. The museum runs several of the buildings in and around town, each with a selection of exhibitions inside: **Smelthytta** (where the guided town tours start), **Olavsgruva** (a 15-minute drive north of town, or take daily shuttle bus), and **Bygningsvernsenteret** (a center for the preservation of the buildings within the mining town). At Smelthytta you can view one of the main exhibitions dedicated to the copper mines, while at Olavsgruva the focus is on what conditions for the workers were like through the ages.

Røros Kirke (Bergstadens Ziir)

Kjerkgata 39; tel. 72 41 98 11; www.roroskirke.no; Mon.-Sat. 11am-1pm Jun.-Aug.; free

During the mining ages, a church and tower were built and nicknamed the "cathedral of the mountain." Today, it is mostly just known as Røros Church, and this white stone building with black accents towers above the timber buildings of the mining town. The church is shaped like an octagon. Completed in 1784, it is Norway's fifth-largest church. The interior of the church is decorated with beautiful light-blue details and paintings, and the church tower bears the emblem of Røros: two mining tools crossing each other under the mark of Venus (also the symbol for copper).

WINTER SPORTS

Røros is a great destination for winter activities, one reason being that it allows you to have experiences such as going on a reindeer sleigh ride and trying out dog sledding without traveling too far north. It is easy to reach from the rest of southern Norway, as opposed to Tromsø or Alta, both of which are very far north. This means you can easily pair a trip to Røros for winter activities with a visit to the western fjords.

Spark (Norwegian Kick Sled) Rental

Peder Hiorts Gate 2; tel. 72 41 00 00; www.roros.no; winter; 100 kr per day

The spark, or Norwegian kick sled, is a common mode of transportation in towns such as Røros, where snow covers the ground for most of the winter season. This small sled consists of a seat mounted on metal "skis," each with a designated spot where you can put your feet. The sled is propelled forward by someone standing on it (behind the seat) and kicking it forward. Sparks are used all over Scandinavia, and in the winter months you can rent one at the Røros tourist information. It is a great way to explore the town, and a fun ride for two people. You do not need any previous experience to try a kick sled, and while it might seem a little unsteady at first, you will find that it is much easier than skiing.

Reindeer Experiences
Røros Rein

Hagaveien 17; tel. 98 01 32 68; www.rorosrein.no; Nov.-Mar.; 1,700 kr

Sami-run Røros Rein offers several reindeer experiences year-round, with reindeer sledding in the wintertime being the most popular. From November to March, you can join a longer sleigh ride through the forests around Røros, and it is a lovely experience. During the excursion you will make a stop where you light a fire to stay warm and enjoy some hot coffee. You'll also get to check out some of their homemade products (such as key chains and jewelry) and learn about the South Sami and their lifestyle. If you'd like, you can bring your own food to barbecue over the fire. The experience lasts up to 3 hours.

Dog Sledding
Røros Husky

Ormhaugen Gård; tel. 91 51 52 28; www.roroshusky.no; late Nov.-late Apr.; from 1,500 kr

There's nothing better to do in the winter than to try dog sledding! During one of the excursions with Røros Husky, you can try steering the sled, with 4-6 dogs eagerly pulling you through the snowy landscapes. If you have a buddy with you, you can take turns sitting in the seat and steering. Their knowledgeable guides are in the lead, and constantly in control of what's going on. This is the perfect way to get an introduction to dog sledding. Trips last 1.5-6 hours.

FESTIVALS AND EVENTS
Christmas Market

Tel. 72 41 00 00; https://julemarkedroros.no; early Dec.

For a few days every December, Røros comes alive with Christmas spirit, as the annual Christmas market kicks off. This 4-day market has been a tradition for over 13 years, and the streets between the old timber houses are lined with vendors offering local produce, Christmas snacks and foods, and of course winter themed activities. From caroling and sleigh rides to meeting Santa, visiting the Christmas market is guaranteed to put you in a festive mood.

SHOPPING
Røros Tweed at Husfliden Røros

Bergmannsgata 6; tel. 72 41 11 97; www.rorostweed.no; Mon.-Fri. 9am-4:30pm, Sat. 10am-3pm

Røros Tweed has been producing high-quality Norwegian wool products since 1940 and is perhaps best known for making beautiful (and warm) blankets, found in most Norwegian homes today. Røros Tweed does not have its own storefront, but at Husfliden (a knitting/

1: Røros Bergstad 2: riding Norwegian kick sleds

274

TRONDHEIM AND INLAND NORWAY
RØROS
274

TRONDHEIM AND INLAND NORWAY
RØROS

Christmas in Norway

Christmas is a quiet time of year in Norway, and usually not the best time for visiting because opening hours of attractions and services are limited during the holidays, and grocery stores and other shops are closed on the 25th and 26th of December (in addition to many closing on Christmas Eve, when Norwegians celebrate Christmas). However, the weeks leading up to Christmas are a charming time of year, especially in towns such as Røros, where there is almost a guarantee of snow, and there's a cozy Christmas market in early December.

CHRISTMAS FESTIVITIES

Christmas in Norway is celebrated slightly differently from the English-speaking world in that most celebrations happen on the 24th of December, Christmas Eve. As in the rest of the world, Christmas is a very family-focused holiday, when Norwegians gather with their families to enjoy hearty traditional foods, open presents, sing carols, and be merry. Ribbe and pinnekjøt are two dishes that are most commonly served for Christmas in Norway (along with lutefisk, a type of dried fish that is highly popular in the north). Ribbe is pork ribs, while pinnekjøtt is a dish based on lamb ribs. Presents are opened in the evening, usually after dinner, so young children have to spend all day anticipating their gifts.

SANTA

Another tradition that makes a Norwegian Christmas unique is that Santa doesn't deliver presents out of sight overnight, but instead he shows up during the evening, often while presents are already being opened. Santa will knock on the door and enter the house with a bag of presents. Traditionally, the family will then sing a carol for him (usually a Christmas song about Santa himself), before he hands out the presents and leaves.

home crafts shop) you will find a large selection of the blankets and other wool products.

Potteriet Røros

Fargarveien 4; tel. 98 69 06 79; https://potteriet-roros. no; Mon.-Fri. noon-4:30pm, Sat. noon-3pm

Potteriet Røros is a well-known pottery workshop making traditional Norwegian dishware and ceramics. Here you'll find copies of Norwegian ceramic pieces dating back to the 1800s, from bowls and trays to drinking mugs and cups. These rustic clay collections are very popular with visitors.

FOOD

Peder Hiort Mathus

Osloveien 2; tel. 72 40 60 20; https://bergstadenshotel. no; daily 5pm-10pm; 165-345 kr

At Peder Hiort Mathus you can enjoy Nordic and international dishes in an intimate and welcoming atmosphere. There is a heavy focus on local, fresh ingredients, and on the menu,

you can expect to find dishes such as reindeer burger, cuttlefish, local reindeer steak, and a variety of pizzas.

Grillhuset Røros

Kjerkgata 8; tel. 406 06 700; https://grillhuset.no; Wed.-Sat. 5pm-11pm; 795 kr for 3 courses

Grillhuset literally translates to "the barbecue house," but you'll find more than hot dogs and burgers here. Their 3-course set menu was created to showcase some of the best local produce. Dishes change with the season, and may include wagyu carpaccio, moose culotte, and a rhubarb tiramisu. They have set times for seating, usually 3 times a day during their opening hours.

Frøyas Hus

Mørkstugata 4; tel. 72 41 10 10; www.froyashus.no; hours vary; 89-189 kr

Frøyas Hus (Freya's House) is a charming, wooden building near the center of Røros, and it's a great spot for lunch. This rustic little café offers snacks to go with your coffee, such as Norwegian waffles, pai, and baguettes, in addition to more filling dishes such as sour cream porridge (rømmegrøt) and game stew.

ACCOMMODATIONS

Bergstadens Hotel

Osloveien 2; tel. 72 40 60 80; https://bergstadenshotel. no; 1,400 kr

In the center of Røros you will find the traditional Bergstadens hotel. The 90 rooms in this rustic hotel have all been renovated between the years of 2007 and 2014, and each has its own distinct charm, layout, and design. The rooms feature Nordic decor, with wood details and splashes of color, and the common areas are warm and welcoming, decorated in a cabin-like style.

Røros Hotel

An-Magrittveien 48; tel. 72 40 80 00; www.roroshotell. no; 1,400 kr

This historic hotel is located a short walk out of the city center and offers a relaxing retreat for staying guests. The rooms have a distinct Scandinavian interior style, with bright colors and clean lines, and local design elements scattered in (such as Røros Tweed blankets). They have a spa that consists of both an indoor and outdoor pool, a jacuzzi, and a sauna—perfect for relaxing after a day of exploring the historic town.

INFORMATION AND SERVICES

Røros Tourist Information

Peder Hiortgata 2; tel. 72 41 00 00; www.roros.no; Mon.-Fri. 9am-4pm, Sat. 10am-4pm

At Røros tourist information you can pick up maps of the historic town center, and book some of your activities. This is also where you can rent the spark (Norwegian kick sled).

GETTING THERE

You can reach Røros by train, plane, or car.

Train

If you take the train from Oslo, you have to change at Hamar, and the journey takes around 5 hours. From Trondheim, the **SJ train** (www.sj.no) takes 2.5 hours. **Røros Stasjon,** the train station in Røros, is located right in the town center, just a short walk from Bergstadens Hotel.

Car

If you are driving yourself, you can reach Røros in 5 hours from Oslo, by following main road E6 north. At Elverum, head onto Route 3. The distance is 392 kilometers (244 mi). The drive from Trondheim is shorter and will take you a little less than 2.5 hours along Route 30 (154 km/96 mi).

Air

Røros Airport

Grind-olaveien 50; tel. 67 03 24 60; https://avinor.no/ flyplass/roros

Widerøe (www.wideroe.no) has two daily departures between Oslo and Røros and will get you to Røros in less than an hour (the flight time is 55 minutes). The airport is located just outside the city center, and a taxi will cost around 100 kr each way (Drosjesentralen Røros; 72 41 12 58).

GETTING AROUND

Røros town is very walkable, and you can get around to most sights by walking or renting a kick sled (in the winter). The Røros Museum offers scheduled shuttle buses to take you to the sights that are outside of the town center, such as the Olavsgruva mine.

Trondheim

As Norway's third-largest city, Trondheim might be on your radar already. The city is filled with historic sites and attractions that have been of importance since it was Norway's capital 1,000 years ago. If you are interested in history, architecture, and stately homes, you will love visiting Trondheim. Highlights of the city include the Nidaros Cathedral, where kings and queens of Norway have been crowned and married for centuries, and Stiftsgården, which is still a royal residence.

There is also a thriving cultural and food scene in Trondheim that has emerged in recent years. The restaurants found in the city offer a blend of New Nordic cuisine and international dishes. If you have some extra time on your travels through Norway, consider spending a few days in Trondheim.

Orientation

The city center of Trondheim is rather compact and found on a small (almost) island created by the river Nidelva that runs in a loop around the city center. In the city center, you will find sights such as Stiftsgården and the cathedral, as well as restaurants and hotels. To the east, across the river, is Bakklandet (the city's Old Town) and Solsidan, just to the north of Bakklandet, where there are restaurants and shops lining the lovely docks along the river. No two sights in Trondheim are more than 15-20 minutes' walk from each other.

SIGHTS
City Center

TOP EXPERIENCE

★ Nidaros Cathedral (Nidarosdomen)

*Kongsgårdsgata 2; tel. 73 89 08 00; www.
nidarosdomen.no; Mon.-Fri. 9am-2pm, Sat. 9am-3pm,
Sun. 1pm-4pm; adults 120 kr, children 60 kr*

The breathtaking Nidarosdomen (Nidaros Cathedral) towers over the city center of Trondheim, and its main spire can be seen from quite far away. This gothic cathedral can remind you of Notre Dame in Paris, as it has a similar Gothic style and design. The exterior of the church features numerous sculptures of saints and gargoyles. The large, round stained-glass window on the front of the church is particularly beautiful seen from the inside in the summer, when the long summer days let the sun shine through it for hours. The building of the cathedral started in 1070, and it was fully completed around the year 1300. This makes the Nidaros Cathedral the northernmost Gothic cathedral from the Middle Ages. The cathedral is open daily, with opening hours depending on the season (and sermons and events). You'll want to spend at least an hour taking in the details on both the outside and inside of this beautiful cathedral.

Archbishop's Palace (Erkebispegården)

*Kongsgårdsgata 1B; tel. 73 89 08 00; www.
nidarosdomen.no; Mon.-Fri. 10am-5pm, Sat. 11am-3pm,
Sun. noon-4pm; adults 120 kr, children 60 kr*

A stone's throw from the Nidaros Cathedral you will find the Archbishop's Palace, where 27 archbishops of Norway have resided for 800 years. Today, there are three museums inside. One focuses on archaeological findings from the palace and cathedral grounds, as well as important sculptures and pieces highlighted through the cathedral's renovation. There is also a defense museum on the grounds, highlighting the role of the Norwegian armed forces. Finally, and perhaps the most popular of the museums/exhibits, are the Royal Crown Regalia, including the crown of King Harald of Norway. You can buy your ticket for both the cathedral and the Archbishop's Palace together, and head straight there after visiting the Nidaros Cathedral.

Trondheim

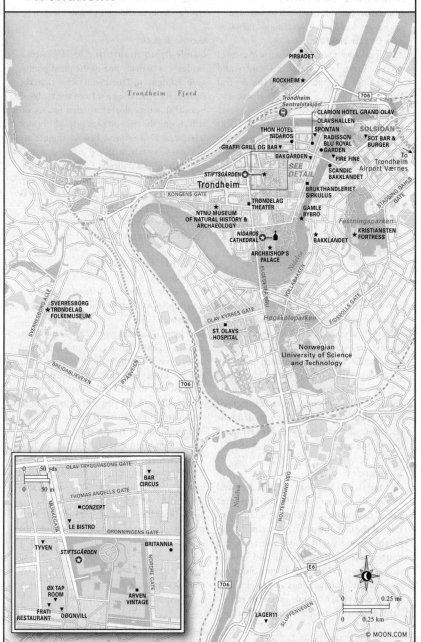

Trondheim Fjord

PIRBADET

ROCKHEIM ★

Trondheim Sentralstasjon

706

CLARION HOTEL GRAND OLAV

OLAVSHALLEN

THON HOTEL
NIDAROS

SPONTAN

RADISSON
BLU ROYAL
GARDEN

SOLSIDAN

SOT BAR &
BURGER

To
Trondheim
Airport Værnes

GRAFFI GRILL OG BAR ▼

FIRE FINE

BAKGÅRDEN

SCANDIC
BAKKLANDET

SEE
DETAIL

STIFTSGÅRDEN ✿ ★

Trondheim

KONGENS GATE

★
NTNU MUSEUM
OF NATURAL HISTORY &
ARCHAEOLOGY

TRØNDELAG
THEATER

BRUKTHANDLERIET
SIRKULUS

GAMLE
BYBRO

NIDAROS
CATHEDRAL

★ BAKKLANDET

★ KRISTIANSTEN
FORTRESS

Festningsparken

STADSING DAHLS
GATE

ARCHBISHOP'S
PALACE

Nidelva

ELGESETER BRU

VOLLABAKKEN

EIDSVOLLS GATE

SVERRESBORG
★ TRØNDELAG
FOLKEMUSEUM

SVERRESBORG ALLE

OLAV KYRRES GATE

Høgskoleparken

ST. OLAVS
HOSPITAL

Norwegian
University of Science
and Technology

BREIDABLIKVEIEN

BYÅSVEIEN

706

HOLTERMANNS VEG

Nidelva

E6

706

SLUPPENVEGEN

LAGER11
▼

0   0.25 mi

0   0.25 km

© MOON.COM

Detail inset

0   50 yds

0   50 m

OLAV TRYGGVASONS GATE

BAR
CIRCUS ▼

THOMAS ANGELLS GATE

■ CONCEPT

MUNKEGATA

LE BISTRO ▼

DRONNINGENS GATE

NORDRE GATE

TYVEN ▼

STIFTSGÅRDEN ✿

BRITANNIA
●

ØX TAP
ROOM ▼

ARVEN
VINTAGE ▼

FRATI
RESTAURANT ▼

DØGNVILL ▼

NTNU Museum of Natural History and Archaeology

Erling Skakkes Gate 47B; tel. 73 59 21 60; www.ntnu. edu/museum; Tues.-Fri. 10am-4pm, Sat.-Sun. 11am-4pm; adults 120 kr, children 70 kr

At Vitenskapsmuseet (The Science Museum) you can learn more about the history and archaeological importance of the central Norway region through a variety of artifacts. Pieces here date back to the Stone Age and Iron Age (such as Viking swords and buckles), and there are changing exhibitions put on to keep things interesting for the younger generation. Temporary exhibits include one focusing on the Norwegian wolf, and another one about a skeleton found in the Sverresborg castle ruins.

★ Stiftsgården

Munkegata 23; tel. 73 84 28 80; https://nkim.no/ stiftsgarden; daily tours June-Aug.; adults 120 kr, children 70 kr

Stiftsgården is the largest wooden palace in Europe, built in the late 1700s. This is the current royal residence of the Royal Family of Norway when they visit Trondheim. In the summer months, parts of the palace are open to the public, and joining a guided tour is the only way to visit this beautiful building. This yellow wooden palace was built in a classic baroque style, with some elements inspired by the rococo movement. Each guided tour lasts around 45 minutes, with time for questions at the end.

Bakklandet

Not far from the Nidaros Cathedral and Stiftsgården you will find the charming area called Bakklandet, which is by many considered the Old Town of Trondheim. In this neighborhood you'll find slanted wooden houses, narrow passageways, and cobblestoned streets. Within these cute buildings you will find vintage shops and cafés, and it is the perfect place to grab a coffee or enjoy a light lunch while people-watching. The area

is found just east of the city center, across the bridge Gamle Bybro, and stretches along the river both north and south from there.

Gamle Bybro

Gamle Bybro (translating to "Old Town Bridge") is perhaps one of the most photographed sights in Trondheim (other than the cathedral). First, the view from the bridge is beautiful, with colorful wooden houses on stilts lining the river on each side. The bridge itself can also remind you of something out of a fairy tale, with red detailed "gates" functioning as a doorway into the old town, Bakklandet. The original bridge was completed in 1685, and the current bridge was built in 1861. The bridge has been pedestrian- (and cyclist) only since 2014, so there is ample opportunity to get your photo here.

Outside City Center
Rockheim

Brattørkaia 14; tel. 73 60 50 70; https://rockheim.no; Tues.-Fri. 10am-4pm, Sat.-Sun. 11am-5pm; adults 160 kr, children under 15 free

Rockheim is a contemporary music museum, and it's an experience every music fan will enjoy. Travel through an interactive "time tunnel" through the history of music, from the 1950s up until today's modern jams. In their Hall of Fame, you will be introduced to Norwegian artists and bands who have had an important role in shaping Norway's music scene into what it is today, such as A-ha (perhaps most famous for their '80s hit "Take on Me"), popular Norwegian rock band Dumdum Boys, and Alf Prøysen, who wrote many well-known Norwegian children's songs. Rockheim is about a 20-minute walk from the center of Trondheim (around the cathedral).

Kristiansten Fortress

Kristianstensbakken 60; tel. 46 87 04 00; www. forsvarsbygg.no/no/festningene/finn-din-festning/

1: Nidaros Cathedral 2: Archbishop's Palace
3: Stiftsgården 4: Gamle Bybro

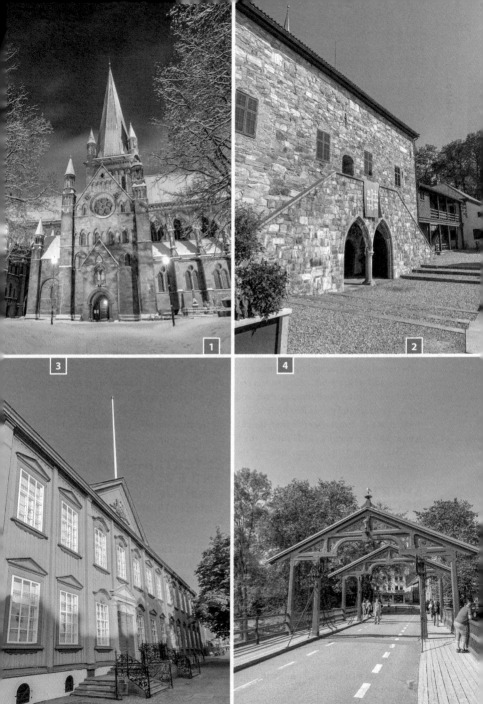

kristiansten-festning; daily 9am-9pm in summer, 9am-sunset in winter; free

Looking down on the city of Trondheim from a hill east of the city, Kristiansten Fortress is among the best-preserved tower fortresses in Norway. It contributed greatly to the safety of the city and held its ground against the Swedish when they attacked during the Great Northern War in 1718. There are trails you can follow around the fortress grounds, offering a lovely view of the city center below. The tower itself is an impressive and imposing white building, and you can enter it to explore on days when it is staffed.

Sverresborg Trøndelag Folkemuseum

Sverresborg Alle 13; tel. 73 89 01 00; https://sverresborg.no; daily 10am-5pm June-Sept., Tues.-Fri. 10am-3pm, Sat.-Sun. 11am-3pm winter; adults 180 kr, children under 15 free

Sverresborg is an outdoor museum with over 60 buildings dating back to the 18th and 19th centuries. In the summer months, events and activities take place throughout the museum grounds, such as live actors telling stories and fairy tales to bring the buildings alive, and animal feedings and games for children. The museum is a 10-minute bus ride from the city center. The Sverresborg castle ruins, which date back to the Middle Ages, make up the center of the museum.

SPORTS AND RECREATION
Parks
Høgskoleparken

Høgskoleveien 2; daily; free

Just across the river from the cathedral and Archbishop's Palace you will find Høgskoleparken, a popular hangout for students and locals alike. On a sunny day you will find the flat lawns busy with people, and it is a great spot for a picnic after a day of sightseeing. In the winter, the park is the ideal spot to play in the snow and it slowly but surely fills up with snowmen built by families through the colder months.

Bymarka

Skistua or Fjellsetra; daily; free

Just a short bus ride west of Trondheim's city center you will find Bymarka. This forested area offers a plethora of walks, trails, and hikes for all ages and capabilities. Bus 26 takes you straight from the city center (stop Kongens Gate) to Skistua (a cabin) or Fjellsetra (a former mountain farm) in 19 minutes; both Skistua and Fjellsetra are good places to start your walk. From either, you can walk around one of the small lakes, Kobberdammen or Vintervatnet (short, easy routes), or try hiking up some of the small mountains in the area (such as Geitfjellet or Herbernheia). Pick up a hiking map at the Trondheim tourist information before you go.

Swimming
Pirbadet

Havnegata 12; tel. 73 83 18 00; www.pirbadet.no; Mon., Wed., Fri. 6:30am-9pm, Tues., Thurs. noon-9pm, Sat.-Sun. 10am-7pm; adults 195 kr, teens 170 kr, children 130 kr

Norway's largest indoor aquatic center, Pirbadet, is the ideal place to spend a rainy day. With two fun water slides, diving boards, a sauna, wave pool, and several pools to choose from, families especially love this indoor water park.

ENTERTAINMENT AND EVENTS
Performing Arts
Trøndelag Theater

Prinsens Gate 20; tel. 73 80 51 00; www.trondelag-teater.no

Trøndelag Theater is one of the longest-running theaters in Scandinavia, dating back to 1816. Here, you can see plays and musicals, usually in Norwegian. Make sure to check the language before booking, as even international plays are sometimes translated into Norwegian.

Olavshallen

Kjøpmannsgata 48; tel. 73 99 40 50; www.olavshallen.no

Olavshallen is the largest cultural venue in

Trondheim, offering a variety of concerts, plays, musicals, and stand-up comedy shows throughout the year. International performers such as Adam Douglas and Ed Byrne have been onstage here, in addition to Norwegian children's plays and Christmas concerts during November and December.

Festivals and Events

Olavsfest

Nidaros Cathedral, citywide; tel. 73 84 14 50; https://olavsfest.no; July

Olavsfest is the local nickname for St. Olav's Festival, the largest festival in Trondheim. Over several days (sometimes more than 10), concerts, entertainment, seminars, and even a medieval fair are put on throughout the city and near the Nidaros Cathedral. St. Olav is also known as Olav den Hellige (Olav the holy), and he is the patron saint of Norway. He was also king of Norway 1015-1028, and is believed to be buried in Trondheim below the Nidaros Cathedral.

SHOPPING

Trondheim has a large population of students, which over the years has led to the establishment of a good number of vintage and secondhand shops. For students, or anyone else who enjoys thrifting, Trondheim is definitely the place to go for secondhand and vintage treasures.

Conzept

Thomas Angells Gate 21; tel. 46 74 74 13; https://conzeptstore.no; Mon.-Sat. 10am-6pm

Conzept is a clothing store with hand-selected items for men and women. If you are interested in discovering new Scandinavian brands, make sure to drop by their store in the center of Trondheim.

Arven Vintage

Nordre Gate 4; https://arvenvintage.no; Mon.-Sat. 10am-5pm

For vintage shopping, head to Arven Vintage where there are many treasures to be found.

They have an especially large collection of vintage jeans from brands such as Levi's, Lee, and Wrangler. The focus at Arven Vintage is on timeless classics, and you will find a lot of high-quality clothing that is made to last.

Brukthandleriet Sirkulus

Kjøpmannsgata 33; tel. 73 84 23 60; www.sirkulus.no; Mon.-Thurs. 10am-5pm, Fri. 10am-4pm, Sat. 11am-3pm

At Sirkulus you will find all sorts of secondhand items, including clothing and shoes to kitchen utensils, books, jewelry, and home decor finds. Sirkulus is a haven for anyone who likes a good bargain. The store also has a charitable mission; it opened in 1999, primarily to offer work training for individuals who have been out of the workforce due to mental health issues.

FOOD

City Center

Bakgården

Kjøpmannsgata 40; tel. 452 22 488; www.bakgaarden.com; daily 3pm-10pm; tapas 59-145 kr

This spot is called Bakgården ("backyard") because it is hidden away through a formal archway along Kjøpmannsgata. Here, you'll enjoy tapas dishes in a friendly and unpretentious restaurant, with sharp black and white decor. The menu is inspired by Spanish cuisine, but they use primarily local ingredients and produce. It is possible to order a la carte, but the best value is to opt for their menu combinations (455-635 kr per person) to try a range of tapas dishes.

Sot Bar & Burger

Solsiden, Tmv-kaia 3; tel. 45 83 15 24; www.sotbar.no; Mon. 11am-1am, Tues.-Wed. 11am-midnight, Thurs. 11am-1am, Fri.-Sat. 11am-2am, Sun. 1pm-midnight; 120-165 kr

Sot Bar & Burger is a busy bar and club on Solsiden by night, and a great spot for delicious burgers by day. Their menu includes patties made with ground beef, chicken, beetroot, or plant-based meat substitutes, catering to carnivores and vegans alike.

Døgnvill

Munkegata 26; tel. 73 80 86 00; https://dognvillburger. no; daily 11:30am-10:30pm; 169-199 kr

With a retro-looking neon sign above the door, Døgnvill is known to have some of the best burgers in town. In this modern diner-style restaurant, you will find a burgers to suit every meat-eater's taste. Døgnvill's meat is supplied by a local butcher, and the chicken burgers are from a farm outside of Trondheim. A special "burger of the week" is updated every Tuesday.

Frati Restaurant

Kongens Gate 20; tel. 73 52 57 33; www.frati.no; Mon.-Thurs. 11am-10pm, Fri.-Sat. 11am-11pm, Sun. 2pm-9pm; 169-219 kr

Frati is a friendly, charming Italian restaurant in the city center of Trondheim, offering traditional Italian dishes such as linguine with seafood and capricciosa pizza (with ham, mushroom, artichoke, and tomato). The dinner menu becomes available from 3pm (204-354 kr), but the affordable lunch dishes are also available all day.

ØX Tap Room

Munkegata 26; tel. 458 48 480; www.oxtap.no; daily 3pm-2am; 175-335 kr

Beer-lovers should head down into the cellar bar and restaurant at ØX Tap Room. The owners brew their own beers, and offer a selection of other local beers—all on tap. Choices on the Italian food menu include spaghetti Bolognese, seafood pasta, and a selection of pizzas.

Le Bistro

Munkegata 25; tel. 73 60 60 24; https:// lebistrotrondheim.no; daily 4pm-10pm; 265-465 kr

For fancy French food in an informal atmosphere, head to Le Bistro. On the menu you will find classic dishes such as escargot, duck confit, and frog's legs, as well as an extensive selection of French wines. The small outside seating area is especially lovely for lunch on a sunny day, and if you are visiting for dinner, their three-course fixed-price menu (595 kr) is a nice option.

Graffi Grill og Bar

Olav Tryggvasons gate 24; tel. 46 46 70 00; www. graffigrill.no; Mon.-Sat. 11am-11pm, Sun. noon-11pm; 89-429 kr

This modern, informal restaurant is the ideal spot to grab lunch, and the menu features an international assortment of choices, such as a grilled halloumi sandwich, chicken salad with avocado, and sliders. There are a few seats outside that are usually full on a sunny day. The interior is stylish, with black and white floors and low lighting.

Outside City Center

Lager11

Sluppenvegen 11; tel. 948 38 447; https://lager11.no; hours vary

Lager is a funky food court-style restaurant, offering several different street food stalls and a stage where there are concerts on selected weekends. Vendors include Morro Fino (Spanish pintxos and tapas), Bui Bui (subs and sandwiches), and Mat fra Midtøsten (Middle Eastern dishes). This is the ideal place to go with a large group of friends when everyone is in the mood for something different.

BARS AND NIGHTLIFE

City Center

Tyven

Dronningens gate 11; tel. 400 06 620; www. tyventrondheim.no; daily 6pm-2:30am

Tyven ("Thief") is a popular bar and club in the center of Trondheim, with live DJs most weekends (including Sundays). They have a large and ever-changing wine list, and the interior decor is sort of basement meets jungle (think green plants and bare brick walls).

Spontan

Fjordgata 1; tel. 919 14 912; www.spontanvinbar.no; daily 5pm-1am

Spontan is the perfect place to relax after a long day of exploring, with a large, international wine selection and charcuterie boards available to snack on. This 35-seat bar works closely with small wine producers, and favors biodynamic and organic wines.

Bar Circus

Olav Tryggvasons gt. 27; tel. 934 61 100; www. barcircus.no; Tues.-Sun. 8pm-2:30am

Bar Circus has been a city staple for more than 17 years, offering its own creative concoctions and cocktails. This funky and relaxed bar plays rock music all night, and on their website you can submit your favorite song in the hopes that they will play it. The homey and welcoming atmosphere makes this place feel like your favorite pub back home.

Fire Fine

Verftsgata 2B; tel. 466 27 205; www.firefine.no; Thurs.- Sun. 8pm-2am

Across the river from the city center, just between the historic Bakklandet and Solsiden, you will find Fire Fine bar and nightclub. The place comes alive on weekends, with live DJs and locals flocking to the dance floor. There is no official dress code, but people get dressed up for their night out at this loud and lively club.

ACCOMMODATIONS
City Center
Radisson Blu Royal Garden

Kjøpmannsgata 73; tel. 73 80 30 00; www. radissonhotels.com; 1,500 kr

Right along the river Nidelva, the glass facade of the Radisson is easily recognizable. Inside the brick-and-glass building you will find a modern hotel with brightly colored details. The 298 rooms have a very Nordic feel to them, with brown leather and light wood details, crisp white bedding, and tiled bathrooms. The hotel is particularly popular for conferences, with their business center and 12 conference rooms.

Scandic Bakklandet

Nedre Bakklandet 60; tel. 72 90 20 00; www. scandichotels.no; 1,600 Kr

At Scandic Bakklandet you can stay right in the center of the historic Bakklandet, the old town of Trondheim. The breakfast (served in the on-site restaurant, Brasseri Bakklandet) is well-known among locals and travelers and has won several awards. The large hotel has 169 rooms and a 24/7 gym available for guests. Rooms are traditionally furnished, with dark wood, leather details, and funky wall art (think photos of a deer playing the cello).

Thon Hotel Nidaros

Søndre gate 22B; tel. 73 87 01 30; www.thonhotels.no; 1,700 kr

Thon Hotel Nidaros mixes the old and traditional with the bright, colorful style of the Thon chain. Here, velour and leather furniture in bright yellow and green meet brocade wallpaper and photos of historic local buildings. The 163 rooms are elegant and colorful as well, in true Thon style. In addition to a lavish breakfast, the hotel serves an evening meal for all guests, and offers free coffee in the reception area.

Clarion Hotel Grand Olav

Kjøpmannsgata 48; tel. 73 80 80 80; www. nordicchoicehotels.no; 2,500 kr

In the same building as the Olavshallen concert hall, the Grand Olav has been given the nickname "backstage," and many artists stay here. The rooms are bright and spacious, with white walls and deep red and blue details. They serve snacks during the day and an evening meal from 6pm to 8pm—perfect if you're heading to a concert. The hotel is also within walking distance of most sights in the city center.

★ Britannia

Dronningens gate 5; tel. 73 80 08 00; https://britannia. no; 3,500 kr

One of the most famous accommodations in Norway, Britannia is worth the splurge. Marble details, muted tones, and plush fabrics create a luxury aesthetic, but the elegant service at this hotel is what really sets it apart. The staff are always ready and eager to help. After a day of exploring Trondheim, a warming visit to the spa (complimentary for guests) is a must. Rooms start at 23 square meters (248 sq ft), and all have a minibar, robe and slippers, an in-room safe, and luxurious cotton bedding.

INFORMATION AND SERVICES

Trondheim Tourist Information

Kongens Gate 11; tel. 73 53 69 94; https:// visittrondheim.no; Mon.-Sat. 10am-6pm

At the tourist information office, located right in the city center, you can find general information about things to do in the city, and use their free Wi-Fi to book tickets yourself. There is also a tourist information office in Olavshallen (where you will also find the Grand Olav hotel).

St. Olavs Hospital

Prinsesse Kristinas Gate 3; tel. 72 57 30 00 (tel. 116 117); daily

St. Olavs Hospital in Trondheim is one of the larger hospitals in Norway. The emergency room (Trondheim Legevakt; tel. 73 96 95 80) is located right by the hospital at Mauritz Hansens Gate 4.

GETTING THERE

Train

The **Trondheim Sentralstasjon** (Central Station; Fosenkaia) links Trondheim to destinations as far north as Bodø (Nordlansbanen; www.vy.no; 9.5 hours) to the south, including Oslo (Dovrebanen; www.sj.no; 7 hours).

Car

Trondheim is a 534-kilometer (332 mi) drive from Oslo along main road E6. This journey will take you around 6.5 hours. If you are starting your adventure in Bergen, the 662-kilometer (411-mi) drive will take you up to 10 hours.

From Ålesund, follow E39 north to reach Trondheim in a little less than 6 hours (299 km/186 mi). If you are starting in Kristiansund, the 197-kilometer (122-mi) stretch along E39 will take you around 3.5 hours.

Air

Trondheim Airport Værnes

Lufthavnsveien; www.avinor.no

Perhaps the easiest and best way to reach Trondheim is to fly from Oslo or Bergen (there are several daily departures between the cities, operated by SAS, Widerøe, or Norwegian). There are also some international flights going in and out of Trondheim Airport, with KLM flying to Amsterdam, SAS flying between Trondheim and Stockholm, and Norwegian operating a daily route to London (Gatwick).

The airport is located 33 kilometers (20 mi) east of the city center, and the airport bus **Værnes-ekspressen** (www.vaernesekspressen.no/) travels directly between the airport and the city center in 25 minutes, stopping at major hotels along the way.

GETTING AROUND

Most major sights—such as Stiftsgården, the Nidaros Cathedral, and Bakklandet—are located in the small city center and can be reached by walking. The public transportation system consists of buses and a tram operated by AtB (tel. 47 80 28 20; www.atb.no). Download the app to get your tickets in advance, as AtB no longer allows for tickets to be purchased on board. A one-way ticket costs 42 kr, and 24-hour pass costs 126 kr.

The tram Gråkallbanen is the northernmost tram in the world. It takes you from the city center to Bymarka (a forest area outside of the city that is popular with hikers and skiers). If you want to go on a hike or a walk around Bymarka, take the 25-minute tram line to Lian.

Lofoten and the North

Dreams of Norway that begin with the magnifi-
cent fjords and mountains of the west soon turn to the wonders of the
North. The jaw-dropping scenery of Lofoten, for example, is enough to
make even a well-traveled Norwegian gasp, and the snowy mountains
of Tromsø and Alta are popular destinations for many reasons. In the
north, it is all about nature, a landscape like nowhere else.

From epic hikes in Lofoten to chasing the northern lights outside
of Tromsø, northern Norway offers once-in-a-lifetime experiences.
Around the Lofoten isles you'll see steep mountains dropping down
to meet almost tropical-looking beaches and crystal-clear water. The
roads here bridge the islands, taking you from one amazing landscape
to the next, similar to the Atlantic Road farther south.

Highlights

Look for ★ to find recommended sights, activities, dining, and lodging.

★ **Arctic Surfers:** The Arctic Surfers on Unstad Beach in Lofoten have become a popular subject for photographers (page 301).

★ **Unique Overnight Experiences:** Sleep in a glass dome under the dancing northern lights or in a traditional Lofoten fishing cabin (page 307).

★ **Å:** Quite literally at the end of the road, Å is a picturesque fishing village and museum (page 308).

★ **Tromsø University Museum:** Learn more about the northern lights and the history of the Sami (page 313).

★ **Learning about Sami Culture:** There is no better place than Tromsø to learn about the Indigenous people of Norway (page 314).

★ **Dog Sledding in Alta:** Learn how to set up your sled before zooming through the forest (page 324).

★ **Wildlife-Watching on Svalbard:** Svalbard is home to the polar bear, and you'll be able to go on whale-watching and bird-watching excursions starting in Longyearbyen (page 334).

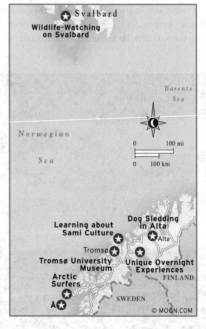

© MOON.COM

Lofoten and the North

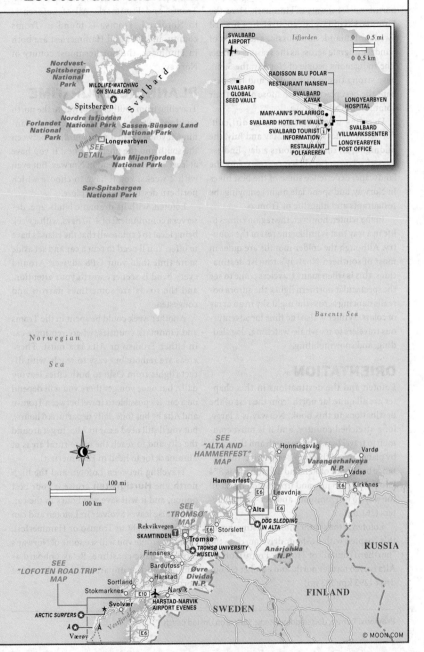

Nordvest-Spitsbergen National Park
WILDLIFE-WATCHING ON SVALBARD
Spitsbergen
Nordre Isfjorden National Park
Forlandet National Park
Sassen-Bünsow Land National Park
Longyearbyen
SEE DETAIL
Van Mijenfjorden National Park
Sør-Spitsbergen National Park

SVALBARD AIRPORT
Isfjorden
0   0.5 mi
0   0.5 km
RADISSON BLU POLAR
RESTAURANT NANSEN
SVALBARD GLOBAL SEED VAULT
SVALBARD KAYAK
LONGYEARBYEN HOSPITAL
MARY-ANN'S POLARRIGG
SVALBARD HOTEL THE VAULT
SVALBARD TOURIST INFORMATION
SVALBARD VILLMARKSSENTER
RESTAURANT POLFAREREN
LONGYEARBYEN POST OFFICE

Barents Sea

Norwegian Sea

0   100 mi
0   100 km

SEE "ALTA AND HAMMERFEST" MAP
Honningsvåg
Vardø
Varangerhalvøya N.P.
Vadsø
Hammerfest
Leavdnja
Kirkenes
SEE "TROMSØ" MAP
Alta
DOG SLEDDING IN ALTA
RUSSIA
Rekvikvegen
Storslett
SKAMTINDEN
Tromsø
TROMSØ UNIVERSITY MUSEUM
Anárjohka N.P.
Finnsnes
SEE "LOFOTEN ROAD TRIP" MAP
Bardufoss
Øvre Dividal N.P.
Sortland
Harstad
FINLAND
Stokmarknes
Narvik
Svolvær
HARSTAD-NARVIK AIRPORT EVENES
SWEDEN
ARCTIC SURFERS
Å
Værøy
Vestfjorden
E6
E10
© MOON.COM

Farther north, you will find Alta, Tromsø, and Hammerfest in Norway's largest and northernmost county of Finnmark. Here, the Finnmarksvidda plateau stretches toward Sweden, Finland, and Russia, and herds of reindeer migrate across as the seasons change. The Indigenous people of Norway, the Sami, have strong ties to this region, and it is perhaps the best place to learn more about their communities and culture.

Deciding when to visit can be difficult. For about 76 days between May and July, the midnight sun shines 24 hours a day. Endless days give you optimal chances to explore the landscape, experience some of the best hikes in Norway, and spend late nights enjoying the restaurants and nightlife of Tromsø.

In the winter, however, the region comes to life in a way that is unlike the rest of the country. Although the colder months are quiet in most of southern Norway's tourist destinations, this is when many travelers come to see the spectacular northern lights, the aurora borealis dancing across the night sky in an array of colors. Winter is also the time for adventurous travelers to try whale-watching, dog sledding, and snowmobiling.

ORIENTATION

Lofoten and the destinations in this chapter are all quite far north from the rest of the destinations in this book. Norway is a large, long-stretched country, and it is most common to travel between the north and the south by plane. To put this into perspective, the distance between Lofoten and Trondheim is 874 kilometers (543 mi), and from Lofoten and all the way up to Tromsø it's another 421 kilometers (261 mi).

Lofoten is the southernmost destination in this chapter, with a 6-hour drive north to the "northern capital" of Tromsø. From Tromsø, Alta is even farther north, and another 6-hour drive (295 km/183 mi).

The counties that comprise northern Norway, from south to north, are Nordland, Troms, and Finnmark. All of Loforen is in Nordland, Tromsø is found in Troms county, and Alta and Hammerfest are both in Finnmark, the northernmost county of Norway.

PLANNING YOUR TIME

Traveling from southern Norway to the north requires air travel and requires careful planning. If you want to divide your time between the south and the north, it's best if you have at least 2 weeks to spend in Norway. But even with 2 weeks, you'll have to choose which northern destinations to explore.

Lofoten, with its dramatic landscape, deserves a commitment of 4-10 days, with a week being ideal to explore all that the islands have to offer. You'll need to rent a car and set aside more time than your GPS advises: Around every bend is scenery worth your attention, and the roads are sometimes narrow and congested.

Another week could be spent in the Troms and Finnmark counties, where renting a car in either Tromsø or Alta is a must. These areas are remote but easy to reach, with direct flights from Oslo to both cities leaving daily, but once you get there you will depend on a car. It's possible to travel between Tromsø and Alta by bus (one daily departure; 6 hours), but you'll still need a car in Alta, to get around the city and to reach the more rural areas of Finnmark (or to head to Hammerfest).

Traveling between Lofoten and the high north, the **Hurtigruten** cruise is your best option, and it will save you hours in the car. The cruise leaves Svolvær in Lofoten and can take you straight to Tromsø or Hammerfest. Along the route you will see some of Norway's most dramatic coastline. Relax onboard as you take in the unparalleled landscape of northern Norway.

Previous: Tromsø; dog sledding; Arctic Surfers on Unstad Beach.

Seasons and Hours

Northern Norway is a winter destination through and through. Winter is the time to enjoy outdoor activities such as dog sledding and snowmobiling. Also, if you are hoping to go whale-watching or to see the northern lights, you'll want to do this in the winter months. Winter weather up north is cold and harsh, with the mean temperature in Tromsø reaching -4°C (24°F). However, freezing temperatures come with beautiful snowy scenery, and as long as you bundle up (layers are a must), the cold won't hinder you. Many providers offering winter excursions will also give you thermal suits and extra layers when needed.

In the summer, the weather is milder but still not warm. The mean temperature in July is around 12°C (54°F). Summer also brings the midnight sun and increased hiking opportunities, thanks to the snow melting and longer days. The hiking season in Lofoten is usually May to October, depending on the snowfall and conditions. Make sure you know the current conditions before heading out on a hike.

In general, crowds are rarely a problem in northern Norway, even during busy times such as festivals. Tours may book up early, but the area never feels crowded like some of the cruise ports in southern Norway. The high season, and the busiest time of year here, is in the winter months, mainly December-March.

In rural areas, especially in Lofoten, opening hours vary depending on tourist flow and staff availability. Many of the galleries and businesses in the area are family-run and might only have one person working. Therefore, check opening hours before you go by calling or checking their Facebook page (where many Norwegian small businesses update their opening hours).

Itinerary Ideas

ONE DAY IN SVOLVÆR

1 After breakfast at your hotel, head to the trailhead for **Fløya,** for a 3-hour hike that gives you spectacular views of Svolvær below.

2 Head to **Nordis Restaurant** for a well-deserved outdoor lunch on the docks.

3 Visit the **Lofoten War Memorial Museum** after lunch to see Norway's largest collection of war memorabilia, and learn more about how World War II affected the country (and especially the north).

4 Svolvær is home to several artists' galleries. Before dinner, do some gallery-hopping, stopping first at **Gallery Dagfinn Bakke** to view his art and that of other local artists. A few blocks away is Gallery Stig Tobiassen, known for his paintings of the landscape around Lofoten.

5 For dinner, head to **Børsen Spiseri** for a lovely meal in a historic setting. This restaurant is inside one of the commercial docks of Svolvær, dating back to 1828.

6 After dinner, head to **Magic Ice** for drinks in a bar made entirely out of ice.

ONE DAY IN TROMSØ

1 Start your day by taking bus 26 from Sjøgata to **Fjellheisen.** Travel up the mountainside in the gondola for some epic views of the city from Storsteinen.

Itinerary Ideas

ONE DAY IN SVOLVÆR
1. Fløya
2. Nordis Restaurant Svolvær
3. Lofoten War Memorial Museum
4. Gallery Dagfinn Bakke
5. Børsen Spiseri
6. Magic Ice

ONE DAY IN TROMSØ
1. Fjellheisen
2. Fjellstua Kafe
3. The Arctic Cathedral
4. Smørtorget
5. Tromsø University Museum
6. Polaria
7. La Famiglia
8. Rooftop Bar at The Edge Hotel

ONE DAY IN ALTA
1. Alta Museum
2. Sami Siida
3. Trasti og Trine
4. Maku
5. Sorrisniva Arctic Wilderness Lodge

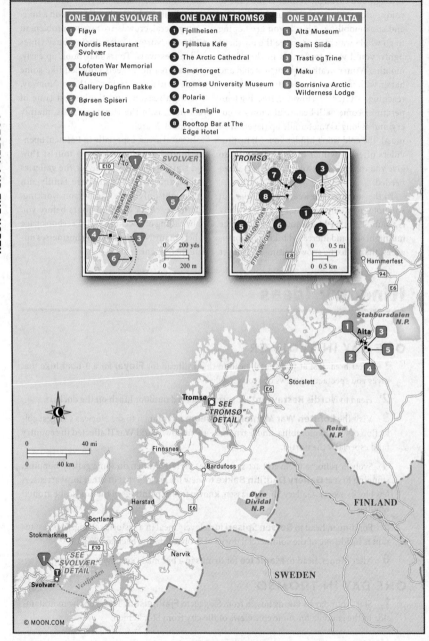

© MOON.COM

2 While you are up there, grab a coffee with a view at **Fjellstua Kafe.**

3 Once you've taken the cable car back down, follow Anton Jakobsens Veg north until you hit Turistvegen, and follow that west to **the Arctic Cathedral.** The walk to the spectacular cathedral is about 10 minutes.

4 After you have visited the cathedral, either take the bus across the bridge (several routes available; 5-10 minutes to Tromsø city center), or walk (15-20 minutes) to grab lunch at **Smørtorget,** which is also a vintage shop. After lunch, consider buying the chair you were sitting in or have a look at the unique vintage items on sale around the room.

5 After lunch, head to the **Tromsø University Museum.** This is either a 40-minute walk along the coastal path of Tromsø, or an 8-minute bus ride (bus 40 from Bankgata toward Tromsø Museum).

6 The **Polaria** aquarium is a fun place to spend time before dinner. Take the bus back to the city center, or walk along the coast.

7 For dinner, head to **La Famiglia** for an Italian dinner in a homey atmosphere.

8 If you are in the mood for some after-dinner drinks, the **Rooftop Bar at The Edge Hotel** offers great views of the city and, if you time it right, is a great place to see the northern lights.

ONE DAY IN ALTA

You'll need a car for this itinerary. The drives between experiences are short, however, and the total drive time today is 30-40 minutes.

1 After breakfast, head to the **Alta Museum** to learn more about the UNSECO-listed rock carvings that have been found on-site. The Alta Museum is a 5-minute drive from the town center.

2 **Sami Siida** is the place to go next. Make the 5-8 minute drive to visit this siida (meaning collective or community) and learn about Sami culture and heritage, and reindeer herding. Enjoy lunch at the Sami Siida restaurant. Here, you can try the traditional Sami stew of biđus, in addition to reindeer meatballs and salmon.

3 Head to **Trasti og Trine** for a real dog sledding adventure! During this experience you will get to meet and harness your own dogs, and learn how to dog sled through the woods nearby. The drive here is around 7-10 minutes.

4 You'll be hungry after your excursion, so head to Sorrisniva for a great meal. Drive 8 minutes farther up the valley and enjoy a three-course meal with a great wine pairing at **Maku.**

5 After dinner, head to the **Sorrisniva Arctic Wilderness Lodge.** If it is a clear night, check with reception about the northern lights activity. Alta is a rural area with minimal light pollution, so if there is a chance to see them, simply head outside of the hotel. Know that seeing the northern lights is a waiting game, so grab a coffee or hot chocolate from the Sorrisniva bar to keep you warm.

Lofoten

The Lofoten archipelago, often referred to as the Lofoten isles or just Lofoten, stretch across the islands of (east to west) Austvågøy, Gimsøy, Vestvågøy, Flakstadøy, and Moskenesøy. In addition, there are some smaller islands that are considered part of Lofoten, such as Henningsvær, Værøy, and Skrova.

Lofoten offers a wealth of dramatic landscapes, with clear waters, jagged mountaintops, and white-sand beaches. You will come across charming fishing villages and cozy fishing cabins, usually painted red or yellow. Each town or village is small, and even Svolvær, the largest town, has fewer than 5,000 inhabitants.

So, prepare yourself for long drives and slow days. Lofoten is a place to slow down and take in your surroundings; enjoy a mountain hike, have your slow morning coffee overlooking the ocean, and marvel at the views as you drive across the islands.

SVOLVÆR

Svolvær is located on the island of Austvågøy, which is the first (closest to the mainland) of the Lofoten islands. It is the largest town in the area, and a natural starting point for your road trip. A lot of people rent their cars here, if they hadn't already at the airport. Svolvær is a natural center for the area, and being the largest town (with around 5,000 inhabitants), it offers several restaurants, shops, a shopping mall, a cinema, and several hotels.

Sights
Lofoten War Memorial Museum
Fiskergata 3; tel. 91 73 03 28; www.museumnord.no/ vare-museer/lofoten-krigsminnemuseum; daily 6:30pm-10pm year-round, Mon.-Fri. 10am-4pm, Sat.-Sun. 11am-3pm June-Sept.; adults 100 kr, children 50 kr

For the largest collection of war artifacts and memorabilia in Norway, head to the Lofoten War Memorial Museum. Here, you can learn more about the Second World War in Norway, the occupation, and how it affected the country. The museum places a special emphasis on northern Norway and Lofoten. The Gestapo had their local headquarters in Svolvær, and the wreckage of a ship, the MS *Hamburg*, can be seen in the Svolvær bay.

Galleries and Shopping
Gallery Stig Tobiassen
Kirkegata 9; tel. 47 60 27 22; Mon.-Fri. 11am-4pm, Sat. 11am-2pm

Stig is a third-generation artist who has been painting since the age of 10. His first gallery, Galleri Konrad, was named for his grandfather. At Gallery Stig Tobiassen, you can view his dramatic paintings (oils, aquarelles, and acrylics) of the sea, mountains, and ships around Lofoten.

Nordnorsk Kunstnersenter
Torget 20; tel. 40 08 95 95; https://nnks.no; Tues.-Sun. 10am-4pm

With so many artists and painters located in Lofoten, it is no wonder that Svolvær is the base and headquarters of the North Norwegian Art Center (Nordnorsk Kunstnersenter). At their gallery, focusing on contemporary visual arts, you can see a rotating selection of exhibitions. Check their website for what will be on display during your visit. Exhibits are usually live for 2-3 months before being changed.

Gallery Dagfinn Bakke
Rich Withs gate 4; tel. 99 59 69 49; www.dagfinnbakke. no; Tues.-Wed. 11am-3pm, Thurs. 11am-7pm, Fri. 11am-3pm, Sat. 11am-2pm

At Gallery Dagfinn Bakke there is actually a variety of local artists' work on display. Exhibits have included paintings by Dagfinn and Dag Fyri, photographs from Kine Hellebust and Kjell Ove Storvik, and sculptures by Skule Waksvik.

Lofoten Road Trip

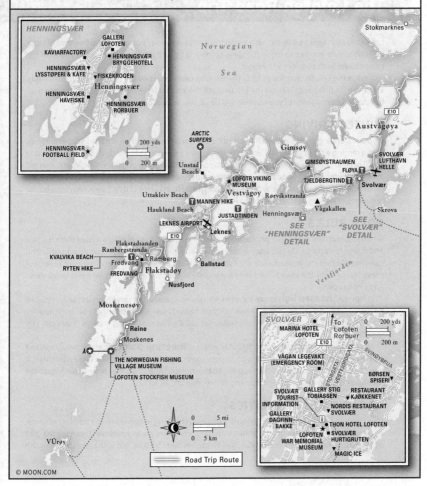

© MOON.COM

Road Trip Route

Hiking

Fløya

Distance: *6 kilometers (3.8 mi)*

Time: *3-4 hours round-trip*

Difficulty: Strenuous

Trailhead: *By the kindergarten in Blåtindveien*

Information and Maps: *https://lofoten.info/ hiking-highlights/floya-and-devils-gate-hike*

The hike to the Fløya mountain is one of the most popular in the area and is considered a must when visiting Svolvær. It is a demanding hike, and after following the trail for a little while (from the parking lot), you'll climb the Sherpa steps that locals call Djeveltrappa (Devil's Stairs). Along the way, you'll find several benches where you can rest and enjoy the view. After the stairs end, the trail splits. Follow the path straight ahead, into the valley between Fløya and the mountain Frosken. Once you have passed over the marshes here, the final part is a steeper climb along the ridge. The hike during this part is airy (a

The Lofoten Road Trip

Lofoten is best explored by car, and a road trip across the islands gives you the freedom of stopping whenever you like to enjoy the view. Lofoten is beautiful year-round, and so this road trip can be done both summer and winter.

Navigating Lofoten is quite easy, as there is only one main road, **E10,** connecting the islands. There are smaller roads leaving the E10 to reach the smaller towns and villages (and some trailheads), but the majority of your driving will be on this main route.

WINTER DRIVING

If you are driving in winter, you'll need to be comfortable driving on icy (and slippery) roads. When renting a car in the winter, winter tires and an ice scraper will be included in the rental, and you'll have to set aside time in the morning to scrape ice and snow off your windows and mirrors. In Norway, you will get fined if you drive without perfect visibility. The roads around Lofoten are open year-round, but always check the **Norwegian Road Directory** (www.vegvesen.no) for any alerts or notices before going on a long drive.

ROAD RULES

When stopping the car to take photos (or to start a hike), only do so in places where there is space and it is safe to do so. Do not stop or slow down in the road, as this will slow down traffic and can cause accidents. Instead, wait until you find a **rest area** to pull over. There are several of these throughout the islands, and they are usually placed strategically to give you good views and photo ops.

In Norway, **hazard lights** are for emergencies only, and other drivers are actually required by law to stop and check on you. Never use your hazards just to indicate that you are stopping. It's quite embarrassing to have a flustered driver ask if you are okay and answer, "I was just taking photos."

Along the narrower roads you will find several car **meeting points** that are clearly marked with signs saying "M." When driving on narrow roads, make a note of these as you pass them. If you see a car coming from a distance, pull into the meeting point. You may have to back up to the meeting if you come across a car coming in the opposite direction.

GAS AND PRACTICALITIES

One thing to be aware of when driving in Lofoten is that bigger towns are few and far between, so pay attention to where the gas stations and grocery stores are as you drive. There are **no gas stations** on the southern-most islands of Moskenes and Flakstad, but with some planning this

term Norwegians use to describe hikes along mountain ridges, where you are high up with dangerous drops and no railing). Once you are at the top you will see all of Svolvær and the surroundings below.

Tjeldbergtind

Distance: *3 km (1.9 mi)*

Time: *2 hours round-trip*

Difficulty: *Moderate*

Trailhead: *Tjeldbergtind Hike Trailhead, just off Kongsvatnveien 26*

Information and Maps: *www.northadviser.com/ no/hjem/fjellturer/fjellturer-lofoten/tjeldbergtinden*

Tjeldbergtind is an easier hike that also offers great views of the area. The trail is good, with clear markings and some steep parts, as you hike your way up to the top at 367 meters (1,200 ft) above sea level. For the first 20 minutes of the hike, you follow a gravel path before you continue on a forest trail. As you

shouldn't be a big problem. There are shops and gas stations in both Svolvær and Leknes, operating on standard opening hours. Leknes is the "last" stop to fill up your tank before heading toward Flakstadøy and Moskenesøy.

There is generally good cell phone coverage all over the Lofoten islands. The only exception is on high mountaintops and remote hikes, but along the road, you will have service.

SUGGESTED ITINERARY

The route below starts at Svolvær and covers towns and sights along the E10 all the way to Å (the literal end of the road). When planning your trip, add time to explore on your own, discover picturesque villages, and to stop and enjoy the views. Use this as a baseline and give yourself plenty of time.

Lofoten scenery

- **Day 1:** Visit Svolvær. This may be your arrival day to the area, or the next day.

- **Day 2:** Drive from Svolvær to Vestvågøy, stopping in Henningsvær on the way. Spend the night in Leknes or Ballstad.

- **Day 3:** Spend a day exploring the island of Vestvågøy. Take your car to some of the beautiful beaches in the area, relax in the sauna at Hattvika Lodge, and visit the Lofotr Viking Museum. Return to your accommodations in Leknes or Ballstad.

- **Day 4:** Make sure to fill up on gas in Leknes. Drive from Leknes/Ballstad to Moskenesøy, stopping at some of the sights in Flakstadøy on the way. Stay at the historic fishermen's cabins in Reine.

- **Day 5:** Explore Moskenesøy's hikes and museums, and make sure to visit Å at the end of the road. Spend the night back in Reine.

- **Day 6:** Make your way back to Svolvær, stopping at whatever sights or viewpoints you missed along the way. The total drive time from Reine to Svolvær is just under 2.5 hours.

exit the forest, you can see the mountaintop ahead of you, just across the marshes (trails have been laid out so you can cross with dry shoes). From the top you can look over to Fløya, on the other side of town.

Nightlife
Magic Ice

*Fiskergata 36; tel. 45 41 85 35; www.magicice.no/
listings/svolvaer-lofoten; daily 6pm-10pm; 250 kr per
person*

Magic Ice is more than just a bar made out of ice. It is also a gallery filled with ice sculptures and art pieces that illustrate the story of Lofoten, its fishing history, and the Vikings that lived here. When you arrive, you will be equipped with thermal gloves and a poncho made to withstand the cold, so you can enjoy your visit without freezing. Their signature drink is served in a glass made entirely out of ice. The entrance fee includes the signature drink.

Tørrfisk

Lofoten's tørrfisk (stockfish in English) is considered a Norwegian delicacy, and has been important to trade and export in northern Norway for centuries. In short, tørrfisk is cod that has been caught in the ocean outside the Lofoten islands and then hung to dry and mature in the wild. When visiting Lofoten, you will notice that many of the villages have a very strong (and not great) smell; that's coming from the codfish hanging to dry in the breeze along the ocean.

The fish is hung to preserve it, and it has to stay on the racks for several months (Feb.-June). Afterwards, it is placed in a temperature-controlled storage facility, where it is sorted according to size and quality. It is then exported for both domestic and international markets. Lofoten stockfish has received the EU's Protected Geographical Indication status, similar to Champagne and Roquefort cheese. To learn more about Lofoten stockfish and how important it has been for the local culture and trade, visit the **Lofoten Stockfish Museum** in Å, on Moskenesøy island (page 308).

WHERE TO TRY IT

You'll be able to try the rich, pungent-tasting tørrfisk in many of the restaurants along the island. Most places are proud to serve this local delicacy.

- **Børsen Spiseri:** Tørrfisk is a specialty at this historic Svolvær restaurant (page 296).

- **Makalus:** This restaurant in Leknes includes tørrfisk on the dinner menu (page 303).

- **Restaurant Karoline:** This Nusfjord restaurant makes its own stockfish (page 304).

Food

Nordis Restaurant Svolvær

Torget 15; tel. 41 29 20 00; www.nordisrestaurant.no/svolvar; daily 11am-10pm; 185-295 kr

For a more modern restaurant serving a mix of international and Scandinavian food, head to Nordis. There, you can find a varied menu consisting of hamburgers, Italian pizza, fish and chips, and homemade fish soup. This large restaurant covers two floors and has a lively and relaxed atmosphere. For an even less formal experience, head outside to their large patio.

Restaurant Kjøkkenet

Lamholmen; tel. 76 06 64 80; https://anker-brygge.no/en/restaurant; Tues.-Sat. 4pm-11pm; 295-410 kr

In the center of Svolvær, the building housing Restaurant Kjøkkenet dates back to around 1880, and the name translates to "The Kitchen Restaurant." This is because the large dining room used to be the kitchen of a century home in a complex that also includes lodging and the Seaside Bar. The interior tells the building's history, with artifacts from traditional Norwegian kitchens decorating the walls. The atmosphere is rustic yet formal, as white tablecloths and fancy table settings contrast with the dark timber walls. The menu changes with the seasons and focuses on traditional local dishes, stockfish, and roasted tongue of cod.

Børsen Spiseri

Gunnar Bergs vei 2; tel. 76 06 99 31; seatings daily 6pm-9pm; 295-425 kr

On a former trade dock that dates back to 1828, you will find a fine dining establishment specializing in local food and tørrfisk (stockfish/dried fish). Their stockfish is served with carrot stew, egg butter, and locally cured ham, and is a favorite amongst travelers and locals. The interior of this restaurant is traditional, as they have done their best to preserve the prestige of this historic building, but the atmosphere is lively and friendly. The restaurant was awarded Kulturminnefondet's (the Norwegian

Cultural Memory Fund) award for great preservation work in 2021, one of only three awards handed out that year.

Accommodations
Lofoten Rorbuer
Jektveien 10; tel. 91 59 54 50; www.lofoten-rorbuer. no; 1,200 kr

In one of the oldest dock houses in Svolvær, dating back to 1828, you will find Lofoten Rorbuer. The dock was originally built by Børsen Spiseri and moved to its current location in 1928. Since then, the building served as a fisherman's cabin and storage unit before becoming the quaint hotel it is today. They have eight regular rooms, with en suite or shared bathrooms, and eight rorbu (cabin) rooms with kitchen facilities. The decor of all rooms is traditional Scandinavian, with white timber walls and checkered curtains.

Marina Hotel Lofoten
Repslagergata 30; tel. 41 51 83 00; https://marina-hotel-lofoten.no; 1,500 kr

The newly renovated Marina Hotel in Svolvær is a modern hotel that is also completely contactless. They have no traditional reception area, and the check-in experience is mobile (you receive a code to open your room). The hotel is centrally located within a short walking distance of most sights and restaurants in Svolvær. It offers 76 rooms, all simply furnished with muted colors and wood accents.

Thon Hotel Lofoten
Torget; tel. 76 04 90 00; www.thonhotels.no/hoteller/ norge/lofoten/thon-hotel-lofoten; 2,500 kr

On the docks of Svolvær, right by the Hurtigruten terminal, you will find a 190-room Thon Hotel. The harbor-facing rooms have great views of the bay and ocean beyond it, and each room is stylishly decorated with bright colors and fun wallpaper. Their award-winning breakfast is reason enough to stay here, as it is considered one of Norway's best hotel breakfasts.

Information and Services
Svolvær Tourist Information
Torget 18; tel. 76 07 05 75; www.visitlofoten.com; Mon.-Fri. 9am-4pm

The tourist information in Svolvær works as the main tourist center for the entire Lofoten archipelago. This is a great place to stop before embarking on your road trip, to pick up maps and check current driving and hiking conditions.

Vågan Legevakt (Emergency Room)
Kong Øysteins Gate 9; tel. 116117; Mon.-Fri. 8am-3:30pm

The doctor's office and emergency room in Svolvær is Vågan Legevakt, and they operate during business hours. However, the emergency room (tel. 116117) is open 24/7, and if you need to see a doctor outside of these hours it will be arranged. The ambulance number for urgent emergencies is 113.

Getting There
Travelers to Svolvær usually arrive by plane or boat.

Boat
Those arriving by boat will travel from ports all along the Norwegian coast via **Hurtigruten** (tel. 81 00 30 30; www.hurtigruten.no; 3 weekly departures; from 4,000 kr). Hurtigruten starts in Bergen and stops in Ålesund, Trondheim, Bodø, and some smaller towns before docking in Svolvær after 4 days at sea. Hurtigruten docks right in the center of the city, a short walk from the Scandic and Thon hotels.

Air
The local airport is **Svolvær Lufthavn Helle** (Helle; tel. 67 03 39 50; https://avinor.no/svolvaer), less than a 10-minute drive from the city center, just northeast of the town. There are 4-5 daily direct flights between Svolvær and Bodø (a little farther south), operated by Widerøe. There are no flights between Svolvær and Oslo or Bergen.

Flying into **Harstad-Narvik Airport**

Evenes (tel. 67 03 41 00; https://avinor.no/fly-plass/harstad), a 2.5-hour drive from Svolvær along E10, might be preferable, especially if you're arriving from Oslo or Bergen. There are daily direct flights from both cities, including 5-6 daily flights to and from Oslo.

Car

The drive time from Tromsø to Svolvær is around 6 hours, driving south along E6 and E10.

Getting Around

There are plenty of car rentals available at both airports. At Svolvær you will find major rental agencies such as **Avis** (tel. 76 07 11 40; www.avis.no), **Europcar** (tel. 95 45 06 20; www.europcar.no), **Hertz** (tel. 95 13 85 00; www.hertz.no), and **Sixt** (tel. 76 70 60 00; www.sixt.no), in addition to the smaller **Rent A Car Lofoten** (tel. 47 64 35 60; www.rentacar-lofoten.com).

At Harstad-Narvik Airport, you will find **Avis** (tel. 76 98 21 33; www.avis.no), **Budget** (tel. 76 98 21 33; www.budget.no), **Europcar** (tel. 76 98 21 20; www.europcar.no), **Hertz** (tel. 41 58 22 28; www.hertz.no), and **Sixt** (tel. 76 98 23 00; www.sixt.no).

RØRVIKSTRANDA

For those heading to Henningsvær from Svolvær, Rørvikstranda, located just where you turn off from E10 to reach Henningsvær, makes a good place to stop, take in the view, and even go for a swim. The backdrop of the steep mountains behind the beach is quite beautiful, and the small sandy beach is shallow, making it appropriate for families. There are no services or facilities here.

HENNINGSVÆR

Henningsvær is a tiny village that is worth visiting mainly for its unique location across a few small islands right on the ocean. The islands are connected by bridges, and the Vågakallen mountain creates a dramatic backdrop. The road there is also one of the more spectacular and unique of the routes

on this road trip, as narrow and winding Route 816 takes you right along the coast, with steep mountain cliffs on the other side. There are several meeting points (marked with a clear "M" sign) along the road, so keep your focus on the road and pull off when it's safe.

Sights

Henningsvær Football Field

Løktveien 25; www.henningsvaril.no

The football (soccer) field in Henningsvær might seem like an odd sight to suggest, but this little fishing village is known for this sports field, or more accurately, its spectacular location. The village of Henningsvær itself is scattered across several islands, and the football field takes up the majority of one of them. The edge of the green field is within just a few feet of cliffs and the ocean. Used by the local sports club for practices and local matches, it is used mostly by youth and kids' teams, and from time to time, weekend cups are put on for the teams. Information about events can be found on the Henningsvær Sports' Club website.

Sea Fishing

Henningsvær is one of the oldest fishing villages in Lofoten (and in Norway), and sea fishing remains a popular activity.

Henningsvær Havfiske

Heimgårdsbrygga; https://henningsvaerhavfiske.no; tours twice daily June-Aug.; adults 995 kr, children under 12 650 kr

To try your hand at sea fishing, join one of the tours from Henningsvær Havfiske. In the summer they offer a 3-hour fishing excursion daily, where you'll get to try a few different tools for fishing.

Art Galleries

Galleri Lofoten

Misværveien 18; www.galleri-lofoten.no/nb; daily 10am-9pm May-Aug., Wed.-Sun. 11am-4pm low season

Galleri Lofoten contains Norway's largest collection of northern Norwegian paintings from the turn of the 20th century—considered by many to be the Golden Age of northern Norwegian art. The gallery's permanent collection includes *Lofotmalerne* (Lofoten Painters), an exhibit focused on paintings from famous local artists, such as Even Ulving, Ole Juul, and Einar Berger.

Kaviarfactory

Henningsværveien 13; tel. 90 80 33 63; www. kaviarfactory.com; hours vary

The Kaviarfactory is a modern venue filled with contemporary and alternative art. The building used to house the local caviar factory, a workplace for many locals for over 40 years. Exhibitions here rotate, but all are curated in a similar way, using various artforms to display the theme, from paintings and photographs to sculptures and ceramics. You will find mainly local and Norwegian artists displayed here.

Food
Henningsvær Lysstøperi & Kafe

Gammelveien 2; tel. 90 55 18 77; www.henningsvarlys. no; daily 10am-4pm; 25-119 kr

This cozy café serves a selection of homemade cakes and lunch dishes, in addition to pizza and Fairtrade coffee. They also make wax candles for sale here. The interior is fun, with colorful candles lining the walls, and the atmosphere is homey and welcoming.

Fiskekrogen

Dreyersgate 29; tel. 76 07 46 52; www.fiskekrogen.no; Mon.-Fri. 2pm-9pm, Sat. noon-10pm, Sun. noon-8pm; 295-340 kr

At Fiskekrogen (Fishing Hook), you can enjoy the view of Henningsvær harbor and a nice selection of seafood. Expect to find local classics like fish stew and cod tongue, as well as creative dishes such as cod cheeks and smoked whale carpaccio. Their kitchen is open, making for a lively and fun atmosphere in this unpretentious yet classy restaurant. The wall is lined with aerial photos of Henningsvær.

Accommodations
Henningsvær Bryggehotell

Hjelleskjæret; tel. 76 07 47 50; www.classicnorway.no/ hotell/henningsvar-bryggehotell; 2,600 kr

One of the Classic Hotels of Norway, this hotel on the docks of Henningsvær has 30 charming double rooms. Each has modern amenities but all have purposely been decorated in a simple style to fit in a fishing village. Yet, standards are high and the beds luxurious. Some of the rooms have a small loft with extra space, ideal for families. One charming side to this hotel is that coffee, tea, and waffles are available all day for staying guests.

Henningsvær Rorbuer

Banhammaren 53; tel. 76 06 60 00; www.henningsvar-rorbuer.no; 2,600 kr

The traditional fishermen's cabins at Henningsvær are all painted bright red, as is common in the area. They are situated on docks, and each cabin is unique, simple, and traditional, with dark timber walls and homey furniture. When making your booking, simply choose a property on the map that accommodates your group. There is also a wood-fired sauna on property, and two hot tubs filled with sea water, making for a truly traditional "spa" experience.

Getting There and Around

Find Henningsvær 25 kilometers (15.5 mi) from Svolvær, approximately a half-hour drive. However, the road there (E10 at first, and then the smaller Route 816/Henningsværveien for the last 15 minutes) is narrow and busy in the summer, so add some extra time to your itinerary for this scenic drive. If you fancy a swim, you will drive past **Rørvikstranda** beach on the way.

VESTVÅGOY

Vestvågøy is one of the islands in the Lofoten archipelago, with **Leknes** as its administrative center. Leknes is the second-largest city in Lofoten, and it is located right in the middle of the island. Consider spending a night or two in either Leknes or **Ballstad** (a little farther

south) during your Lofoten trip, to have easy access to the beautiful beaches and sights on Vestvågøy. The hour-long drive from Svolvær to either place is beautiful, but keep your eyes on the road. Only pull over where it is safe to do so, and take your time. One place worth stopping is by the massive **Gimsøystraumen bridge** (840 m/2,755 ft). There is a rest stop on the Svolvær side of the bridge and a bus stop on the Leknes side.

Sights
Lofotr Viking Museum
Vikingveien 539, Bøstad; tel. 76 08 49 00; www.lofotr. no/nb; Tues.-Sat. 11am-4pm; 225 adults kr, children 150 kr

One of the major attractions in the area is the outdoor Lofotr Viking Museum. Here you can meet Viking reenactors who demonstrate what life was like here in the Viking Age. You can see what the living and working quarters would have looked like during this era, and learn more about Viking culture. The location of the museum is not random, as it has been built on high ground, believed to have been strategically important to the Vikings. Artifacts that were found here indicate that the chieftain's house is built on the site of an actual chieftain's house.

Buksnes Church
Buksnesveien 450, Gravdal; Tues.-Fri. 10am-3pm; free

This beautiful, large wooden church is close to the road in Gravdal. The church is red, with white and green details and a large front tower, making it a popular photo subject. Built in 1905, Buksnes Church seats 600 people. It remains an active parish, so opening hours vary. However, the highlight of this church is its beautiful exterior and the view, as it is perched on a hill overlooking the Lofoten landscape.

1: Henningsvær 2: Buksnes Church 3: Lofoten scenery 4: Arctic Surfers on Unstad Beach

Möller's Tran Tasting Depot
Hattvikveien, Ballstad; https://hattvikalodge.no/ activity/mollers-cod-liver-oil; hours vary; free

For centuries, Norwegians have believed that cod liver oil (tran) is a source of health, and a tablespoon of it used to be served to school children every morning as the school bell rang. Möller's is perhaps the most famous Norwegian producer of tran, and their factory is located in Ballstad. There, you can also find the world's only tran tasting depot, where you can sample various versions of tran. (Don't be fooled by the fancy flavors, though; it tastes exactly as it sounds.) The depot is run by Hattvika Lodge, and so hours vary depending on their availability. The Tasting Depot overlooks the bay with the factory on the other side. It is not possible to visit the working factory.

★ Surfing
Surfing might not spring to mind when you think of Lofoten, but there is a beach up here that is famous for its waves and the Arctic Surfers who brave the frigid temperatures.

The Arctic Surfers
Unstadveien 105; www.unstadarcticsurf.com; daily 10am-6pm; surfboard rental from 300 kr per hour

Some visitors come just to photograph the Arctic Surfers on Unstad Beach, but if you want to brave the waves yourself, you can rent surfboards or take surf lessons from highly trained professionals. During a 3-hour beginner lesson, you will learn surf theory and water safety, as well as how to start surfing yourself. An on-site sauna is available for you after the lesson. The Arctic Surfers also host surf retreats for more experienced surfers with accommodation included. They are only able to accommodate 55 people at a time, so advance booking is recommended.

Hiking
Mannen Hike
Distance: *4 kilometers (2.4 mi)*
Time: *2-3 hours round-trip*
Difficulty: *Moderate*

Swimming in the North

Although Lofoten is far north, it has some beautiful beaches, rendering the cold water rather tempting to many people. In the summer, you'll find people sunbathing and even taking a refreshing dip in the sea, which approaches temperatures of 10-12ºC (50-54ºF). Some people even swim year-round. As long as you are prepared (with towels, warm clothes, and ideally a warm car, to heat you back up shortly after), it is possible to get in the water during the colder months, when the water temperature dips to around 5ºC (41ºF).

Most of the beaches in Lofoten are unserviced; lifeguards and changing facilities are practically nonexistent. In general, you can swim anywhere you'd like, unless there are signs prohibiting it along the beach or rocks. However, as with hiking and skiing, swimmers should avoid taking any unnecessary risks, watch the weather, and never attempt something outside of your capabilities.

Trailhead: *Uttakleivveien 200*
Information and Maps: www.visitnorway.
no/listings/fjelltur-til-mannen-i-lofoten-(400-
moh-)/225289

This short but steep hike takes you up to 400 meters (1,310 ft) above sea level with some great views of the mountains and beaches below. The hike is easy (no climbing) but can be scary for people who are afraid of heights. It gets quite airy (with a long sheer drop and no railing) in some areas, especially toward the end. The final part of the hike follows the ridge of the mountain, and the view just gets better and better. As the hike is quite exposed during this part, do not attempt it if the weather conditions are bad.

Justadtinden

Distance: *6 kilometers (3.7 mi)*
Time: *4-5 hours round-trip*
Difficulty: *Strenuous*
Trailhead: *Hagskaret*

Justadtinden gives you great views, particularly toward the fishing village of Henningsvær. The trail is marked for most parts, but this is a strenuous hike and you should be in decent shape before attempting it. You start at Hagskaret, at 131 meters (430 ft) above sea level and make your way up to the top (tind) of the mountain at 738 meters (2,420 ft). During the long and steady climb you will pass several small mountain lakes

and enjoy some views of the mountains, and eventually the surrounding archipelago when you reach the top.

Beaches
Haukland Beach
Uttakleivveien; www.hauklandbeach.no

Haukland is the beach you see from the Mannen hike. This popular, sandy beach might just have the bluest water in the Lofoten isles, and has several times been on lists of the most beautiful beaches in the country. This spot is great for swimming, and in the high season there are toilet facilities and a small café open (daily 11am-5pm June-Sept.).

Uttakleiv Beach
End of Uttakleivveien

From Haukland Beach you can drive through the tunnel, under the mountain Mannen, and get to one of the most popular photo ops in Lofoten. This sandy beach is scattered with rocks and rocky terrain, shaped by the ocean through the centuries. This makes for a beautiful sight as the waves roll in and pour back out, and you'll often see photographers gathered toward the south end to catch a shot of the water with long exposure (creating a "blurry" effect). It is possible to swim here, but note that there are no facilities available. Most people just change in their car and use nature's toilet.

Unstad Beach
Unstadveien

Known for its waves and resident Arctic Surfers, Unstad Beach is not ideal for swimming, but it is perfect for a long stroll between the high mountains perched on each side of it. It's an even better place to sit and watch the surfers. At **Arctic Surfers** (Unstadveien 105; www.unstadarcticsurf.com; daily 10am-6pm; from 300 kr) you can rent wetsuits and stand-up paddleboards.

Food
Makalaus
Storgata 27, Leknes; tel. 92 50 96 80; www.makalaus. as; Mon.-Thurs. 11am-9pm, Fri. 11am-midnight, Sat. 11am-1am; 185-225 kr

For a relaxed and informal lunch or dinner, visit Makalaus. During the daytime, simple lunch items include sandwiches and hamburgers, while the menu gets slightly more sophisticated at night with the addition of dishes such as the local staple stockfish (tørrfisk) and pepper steak.

Restaurant Bevares
Lillevollveien 15, Leknes; tel. 76 05 44 30; www. scandichotels.no; Mon.-Sat. 6pm-10pm; 195-350 kr

This informal and relaxed restaurant serves traditional Norwegian dishes as well as international cuisine, so there's something for everyone. Their a la carte menu changes monthly and is based on what's available from local suppliers and producers. Highlights include homemade burgers on fresh brioche buns, and slow-roasted lamb shank with local vegetables.

Fangst
Hattvikveien 14, Ballstad; tel. 93 02 88 87; www. hattvikalodge.no; daily seatings 6pm, 7pm, and 8pm in summer, Wed.-Sat. in winter; 350-425 kr

Fangst is an oceanfront fine dining restaurant that mixes New Nordic with the traditional rustic design found across Lofoten. On their seasonal menu you can expect find locally sourced seafood and other ingredients. Dishes change several times a year (and at least once a season), and may include smoked arctic char (from nearby Sigerfjord) and bacalao made with local salted cod.

Lofoten Food Studio
Jacob Jentofts Vei 29, Ballstad; tel. 94 13 57 40; www. lofotenfoodstudio.no; Wed.-Sat. at 7pm by reservation only; set menu 1,695 kr

Roy is the award-winning chef behind the Lofoten Food Studio, an intimate dining experience where he creates high-quality dishes inspired by the ocean, mountains, and nature of Lofoten. This is a "chef's table" experience, with just 12 available seats per evening. The menu changes with the season and available ingredients, and reservations open for two months at a time on the first of each month.

Accommodations
Scandic Leknes
Lillevollveien 15, Leknes; tel. 76 05 44 30; www. scandichotels.no/hotell/norge/lofoten/lekneslofoten; 1,600 kr

Scandic Leknes is a modern hotel in the center of Leknes. Their 60 rooms are clean and stylish, with blue details and dark wood accents. Leknes is the second-largest town in Lofoten (after Svolvær), so this might be a good base for a stay due to its location in the middle of Lofoten. All their rooms have blackout curtains, which is an appreciated touch during Lofoten summers.

★ Hattvika Lodge
Hattvikveien 14, Ballstad; https://hattvikalodge.no; 2,300 kr

Hattvika Lodge is a collection of cabins and rooms in the former fishermen's cabins at Ballstad. Their rorbuer (cabins) date back to 1880, but have all been fully refurbished, creating modern and comfortable rooms with a historic twist. Each rorby comes in a different size, and most have fully equipped kitchens. In some rooms, you can enjoy cold (and long) winter nights in front of a fireplace, as Hattvika will provide you with all the firewood you need.

There are two saunas available on property,

one with a traditional wooden hot tub right next to it, and one on the docks, next to the ocean. The owners have a hands-on approach, and make sure you feel taken care of at all times. Don't be surprised when they knock on your door with more firewood or just to make sure you have everything you need.

Information and Services
Vestvågøy Tourist Information
Storgata 8, Leknes; tel. 90 02 03 29; https://tourist-information-vestvagoy.mailchimpsites.com; Mon.-Fri. 10am-7pm, Sat. 10am-4pm

In the main shopping center of Leknes (Lofotsenteret; www.lofotsenteret.no) you will find the local tourist information, where the staff can help answer questions and provide hiking maps for the entire Vestvågøy island.

Getting There and Around
Route E10 goes straight through the middle of Vestvågøy. The travel time from Svolvær, where you may have started your trip, to Leknes (the administrative center and largest city on Vestvågøy) is a little over an hour (69 km/43 mi). Several smaller roads lead off of E10 to some of the more popular sights in the area. The most beautiful beaches in Lofoten can be found on the north side of the island, and Ballstad (where you will find the Möller's Tran Depot and Hattvika Lodge) is a 15-minute drive along Route 818 south of Leknes.

Leknes Airport
Lufthavnveien 30; tel. 67 03 39 00; https://avinor.no/flyplass/leknes

The small airport in Leknes can be reached from Bodø, with several daily departures. There is one daily flight from Oslo to Leknes airport. **Widerøe** (tel. 75 53 50 10; www.wideroe.no) operates all flights to and from the airport.

FLAKSTADØY

Flakstadøy is the next island you will reach after Vestvågøy. The highlight here is the beautiful fishing village of Nusfjord.

Sights
Nusfjord
Nusfjord is one of the oldest fishing communities in Norway, and I am sure you have seen photos of this fishing village when looking up Lofoten. The (mainly) yellow-painted wooden buildings of this charming village are all nestled on the docks and it will take you anywhere from a half-hour to an hour to stroll around the docks and village. This is still an active haven for fishermen, and you'll find plenty of fish hanging out to dry on the docks. There is a small hill right by the houses, and heading up to the top of it (2-3 minutes' walk) will give you views out to the ocean.

Beaches
Flakstadsanden and Rambergstranda
If you are looking for beaches, both **Flakstadsanden** (8380 Ramberg) and **Rambergstranda** (E10 190) are worth a stop. They are located just a short drive (5 minutes) apart, in the municipality's administrative center of Ramberg and Flakstad. Both of these white-sand beaches face steep, snow-covered mountains—a sight that is rare to see anywhere else in the world. At Rambergstranda there is a viewpoint with parking, and this is where you will find the red hut that is one of Lofoten's most common photo subjects. You can swim at both beaches, but Rambergstranda is calmer as the surf is protected by islands across the bay.

The bay just before you reach Flakstad has especially beautiful views, and a pullout by Djupvika (just before you reach the takeoff towards Nusfjord) is a good place for a photo.

Food
Restaurant Karoline
Nusfjord; tel. 76 09 30 20; www.nusfjordarcticresort.com; daily 5pm-9pm; 205-355 kr

One of very few restaurants on Flakstadøy, Restaurant Karoline is worth visiting for dinner if you are driving through the island in the evening. The focus on local seafood and fresh catches is extra special as you enjoy a view of the ocean where your dinner was caught. On the menu you will find the famous Lofoten codfish and homemade stockfish. If you spend an hour walking around Nusfjord village before your meal, you will see the stockfish used in the restaurant hanging out to dry. Advance reservations are necessary for this small and intimate restaurant.

Getting There and Around
The E10 continues on through Flakstadøy from Vestvågøy, taking you from Leknes on Vestvågøy to Ramberg on Flakstadøy in just 30 minutes. Nusfjord is more rural, and getting there will require exiting the E10 for the smaller Route Fv807. This is a beautiful drive past lakes and mountains, through the inner parts of the island. The drive from Ramberg to Nusfjord takes 20 minutes, but give yourself extra time to travel this narrow road.

MOSKENESØY
Moskenesøy is the last of the islands that are connected by road in Lofoten. Here, you will find some recognizable photo ops, such as the red **Eliassen Rorbuer** in Hamnøy and the town of **Reine,** nestled amongst dramatic mountains. The landscape of Moskenesøy is perhaps the most striking in Lofoten, with jagged mountain peaks rising from the deep blue water. Don't miss the viewpoint of the Fredvang Bridges, where E10 meets Route 808.

Sights
Reine
Reine is the administrative center of the Moskenes municipality, and it is worth taking a stroll around the town. Reine is surrounded by water and incredibly steep mountains, which makes for some spectacular photos, especially when the water is still, reflecting the landscape. Whether or not you're a photographer, you'll enjoy the viewpoint where the small road to the town center connects with the main road (E10).

Galleri Eva Harr
Reine Kultursenter; tel. 76 09 10 10; daily 10am-5pm May-Sept.
Eva Harr is a Norwegian painter and artist who is best known for her landscape paintings of northern Norway. She was born in Harstad, and in 2007, a permanent exhibition dedicated to her career opened in Reine. There is also a small book shop there, where you can buy Eva Harr graphics and prints.

Reine

Hiking
Kvalvika Beach
Distance: *3 kilometers (1.9 mi)*
Time: *1.5 hours one-way*
Difficulty: *Moderate*
Trailhead: *Fv806 7 (Fredvang School), Fv808 (Kvalvika Beach trailhead)*
Information and Maps: *https://ut.no/ turforslag/1112155862/ryten-og-kvalvika*

Kvalvika Beach is a secluded spot on Moskenesøy that can only be reached by hiking. The beach is surrounded by tall mountains, and the trail takes you up and through the valley between them. The first part of the hike is steep; it flattens out as you head through the valley, and eventually takes you back down when you get to the beach. The hike is relatively easy, but the descent at the end is steep, so it is recommended for those with some hiking experience.

The (small) parking lot at the trailhead tends to fill up quickly in the summer months, so parking at the nearby Fredvang School is encouraged. From the school to the trailhead it's a level 20-minute walk.

Ryten Hike
Distance: *3.5 kilometers (2.2 mi)*
Time: *2 hours one-way*
Difficulty: *Strenuous*
Trailhead: *Fv806 7 (parking at Fredvang School is encouraged)*
Information and Maps: *https://ut.no/ turforslag/1112155862/ryten-og-kvalvika*

The hike to Ryten has the same starting point as the hike to Kvalvika Beach, so these two hikes can be done in the same trip. Most people opt to hike Ryten first and then head down to the beach. The trail splits where you can either opt to go down to the beach or continue up the mountain ridge towards Ryten. As you hike along the ridge you will have spectacular views, but take care as it is a steep drop.

There is a rock formation at the top of the mountain (543 m/1,780 ft above sea level), where lots of people take photos. Here, you can pretend to be "hanging" in thin air, with nothing below you. However, this is a bit of an illusion, and completely safe to do. Just angle the camera so the ground is out of the image. This is perhaps the most well-known hiking image in Lofoten.

Reinebringen Hike
Distance: *2.7 kilometers (1.7 mi)*
Time: *2.5 hours one-way*
Difficulty: *Strenuous*
Trailhead: *The center of Reine*
Information and Maps: *www.facebook.com/ reinebringen*

Reinebringen is one of the most popular hikes in Norway, offering spectacular views of the town of Reine, just below the mountain, and the jagged mountain ranges of Moskenesøy. At 448 meters (1,470 ft) above sea level, this is not the highest of hikes, but it is still considered relatively difficult because you will be climbing steep Sherpa steps most of the way. From the center of Reine (start anywhere) follow the main road (E10) until you get to the old main road heading south. Follow this on the outside of the tunnel (E10 goes through the tunnel), until you get to the Sherpa steps. From here, the steps go straight up the mountainside, almost all the way to the top. At the time of writing, the steps were not completed for the final leg of the hike, and there are a lot of loose rocks at the very end, so step carefully as you reach the top.

The hike is not recommended for children, and the trail is not recommended for anyone to undertake in the wintertime. Check the Reinebringen Facebook page for up-to-date information on whether the hike is accessible or not during your visit, and as always, ask locals for advice.

Food
Restaurant Gammelbua
Reineveien 165; tel. 76 09 22 22; www.classicnorway. no/hotell/reine-rorbuer/restaurant/a-la-carte; daily 6pm-9pm

Fresh a la carte dishes are served in historic surroundings at Gammelbua, which dates back to 1790. Here, you dine in an old fisherman's cabin (rorbu), with dark timber walls

☆ Unique Overnight Experiences

Northern Norway is the place to be if you are looking for unique places to stay, from the famous fishermen's cabins right on the waterfront in the Lofoten isles (called rorbuer) to a hotel made entirely out of snow and ice in Alta. These exceptional accommodations book out early and are often pricier than a traditional hotel, but they offer truly memorable experiences.

- **Eliassen Rorbuer,** Lofoten: The red or yellow traditional fishermen's cabins can be found all over the Lofoten islands, a testament to the area's strong fishing history and culture (page 307).

- **Sorrisniva Igloo Hotel,** Alta: This temporary hotel is rebuilt each year from snow and ice. You can warm up in the sauna available for guests from 7am (page 327).

- **Aurora Canvas Dome,** Alta: With a glass ceiling, these "igloos" give you the feeling of sleeping under the stars (and the northern lights if you are lucky) in the middle of a forest, while still providing you with the comfort of a warm bed and toilet facilities (page 328).

the chapel in Sorrisniva Igloo Hotel

and lots of wood details (wood beams, wood chairs, wood tables, and a wood bar). The menu is based on local ingredients and fresh fish. Expect dishes such as seared scallops, tenderloin of reindeer, and roasted halibut.

Tapperiet Bistro

Reineveien 164; tel. 90 19 73 35; www.tapperiet.com; Mon.-Tues. 12:30pm-9:30pm, Wed. 12:30pm-midnight, Thurs. noon-9:30pm, Fri.-Sat. 12:30pm-midnight, Sun. 12:30pm-6pm; 199-295 kr

Tapperiet is a small and welcoming bistro serving a selection of home-made pizza, meat dishes, and fresh seafood. The interior is charming, with candle-lit dark wooden tables and an almost nautical feel. In the summer, their outdoor seating area is busy. On the menu you can expect classic dishes such as homemade fish soup and bacalao.

Accommodations
★ Eliassen Rorbuer

Hamnøy; tel. 45 81 48 45; https://rorbuer.no; 2,500 kr

Eliassen Rorbuer is the oldest fishing cabin resort in the Lofoten archipelago. Accommodations consist of 105 traditional rorbuer (fishermen's cabins), varying in size. The location by the pointed mountain peaks in Hamnøy has also made this a stopping point for many travelers, even those who aren't staying at the resort. The bridge between Hamnøy and Reine, with a nice view of the cabins, is also a popular place to watch the northern lights.

Each of the cabins at Eliassen is traditionally decorated, with timber walls, checkered curtains, and wooden bunk beds. The cabins are all different, with varying sizes, views, and rooms. Some are located right on the docks, while others are a little inland on the tiny island. This makes for a charming cluster of houses across the island, all belonging to Eliassen.

Reine Rorbuer

Reineveien 165; tel. 76 09 22 22; www.classicnorway.no/ hotell/reine-rorbuer; 4,500 kr

In Reine there are 39 traditional rorbuer

available, most of them with a small kitchen and coffee maker. These cabins are of varying standard, from very simple and traditional, to newly refurbished and modern. When booking, you can select exactly the rorbu you'd like, depending on your preference and the size of your travel party.

Getting There and Around

As it is the final one of the connected islands in Lofoten, getting to Moskenesøy is literally quite straightforward. Simply keep driving along the E10 main road to get there. The administrative center here is Reine, a half-hour drive from Ramberg. There aren't really any side roads on the island, so you can't take a wrong turn.

The Ryten hike and Kvalvika Beach are popular destinations on the island. To get there from Reine, follow E10 back toward Flakstadøy, but take a left onto Route 808 before reaching Ramberg. Before taking this turn, consider stopping at the viewpoint to look out at the impressive Fredvang bridges that connect the small islands, before you drive over them. The total drive time is 35-40 minutes. From Ramberg, you approach along E10 from the other direction, so take a right onto Route 808 and across the Fredvang

bridges after just 5 minutes. The drive to the parking lot takes 10 minutes.

You can also reach Moskenes by car ferry from Bodø, operated by Torghatten Nord (www.torghatten-nord.no). The ferry has 1-2 daily departures in the winter, and up to 8 daily in the summer months. The crossing takes a little over 3 hours, and is an option for those who want to do the road trip from Å and Moskenes to Svolvær.

★ Å

Å is not only the last letter of the Norwegian alphabet, but also it is the last town you get to along E10—literally the end of the road. This town is like a living museum dedicated to the fishing history of Lofoten.

Sights
Lofoten Stockfish Museum

Moskenesveien 1270; tel. 76 09 12 11; daily mid-June-mid-Aug.; 100 kr

You will have noticed cod hanging up to dry all around Lofoten by the time you reach Å. Lofoten stockfish (dried fish) is actually a protected brand in the EU, and the Lofoten Stockfish Museum is dedicated to sharing information about the process of drying fish. Visitors watch a 30-minute movie (with

Å

English subtitles), stroll around the landing station, and try a selection of tørrfisk snacks.

The Norwegian Fishing Village Museum

Å Vegen 21; tel. 76 09 14 88; www.museumnord.no/ vare-museer/norsk-fiskevaersmuseum; daily 11am-6pm June-Aug., Mon.-Fri. 11am-3pm Sept.-May; 100 kr adults, 70 kr children

Here you will find one of the best preserved and most complete traditional fishing villages in Norway, including several buildings of importance. You can visit a working bakery from the 1800s, which still uses its oven from 1878 (open daily in the summer; make sure to get one of their cinnamon buns), as well as the old post office. Signs around the outdoor museum explain what living in a fishing village like this would have been like in the 19th and early 20th centuries.

Å Viewpoint

End of the road

As you drive through the E10 tunnel in Å, you will reach the literal end of the road. There is a large parking lot there (just outside the tunnel). Park your car and walk up the pathway (starting where the road would have continued) for about 5 minutes. When you reach the point where the land ends, you'll enjoy wide open ocean views from the end of the Lofoten isles.

Getting There and Around

Å is located at the end of the E10 main road. The drive from Reine is around 15 minutes. From Svolvær, it takes 2 hours to reach Å.

Tromsø

Tromsø is a small city with a surprisingly urban feel. With just over 40,000 inhabitants in the city center, it is Norway's 15th-largest city but is by far the largest city north of Lofoten. Tromsø has been named the Paris of the North for its busy nightlife and many events, such as the Midnight Sun Marathon and Nordlysfestivalen.

Tromsø is also a popular city for tours. From whale-watching to authentic Sami experiences, there is always a bus or boat leaving to explore the surroundings and wildlife. In the city center, you'll find interesting museums, such as the Tromsø University Museum and the Polar Museum, as well as the famous Arctic Cathedral and Fjellheisen Cable Car.

When planning your visit to Tromsø, allow one day for each tour you'd like to take, and then add 1-2 days to explore the city sights. For example, to get a proper feel for Tromsø and be able to go on a whale-watching tour and Sami experience, set aside 5 days for your visit.

Orientation

Tromsø is a fairly easy city to get around and find your way. Most sights are in the city center (on the island of Tromsø: Tromsøya), and most tours start in the center as well. This makes it a very walkable city. The Arctic Cathedral and Fjellheisen are both across the water, on the other side of the Tromsø bridge, and the Tromsø University Museum is also a short walk from the center, on the southernmost tip of the island. Walking across the Tromsø bridge will take you 5-10 minutes, and from the top of it you will have great views of the city center.

SIGHTS
The Arctic Cathedral

Hans Nilsens vei 41; daily 1pm-5pm Jan.-May, daily 9am-6pm June-Aug., daily 2pm-5pm Sept.-Dec., exceptions apply during services, weddings, and funerals; 55 kr per person

Designed by Norwegian architect Jan Inge Hovig, the Arctic Cathedral is one of the most famous sights of Tromsø. The large glass

Tromsø

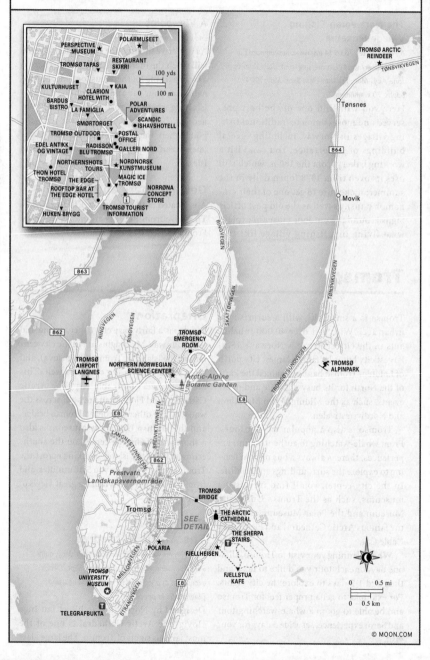

© MOON.COM

facade of the modern church lets in a whole lot of natural light, including the midnight sun in the summer, while the A-frame structure that shapes the church is composed of overlapping triangles arranged to resemble the tip of an iceberg in the ocean.

The cathedral opened in 1965 and the facade of the east end was covered in glass mosaics in 1972; the west end is covered with a massive cross. While the outside of the church is most spectacular, it is worth going inside to see the light shine through the mosaics into the vast, modern interior.

Nordnorsk Kunstmuseum

Sjøgata 1; tel. 77 64 70 20; www.nnkm.no; daily 10am-5pm; adults 80 kr, children 50 kr

In the former telegraph and post office of Tromsø you will find a center for Northern Norwegian art, Nordnorsk Kunstmuseum. Their exhibits change regularly, and previous exhibits include the arts of Sean Snyder in Tromsø and Longyearbyen (on Svalbard), and their recurring (but changing) project Stimuli. Stimuli is a project designed to stimulate the art world during and after the COVID-19 pandemic, and each of the exhibitions (named Stimuli 1, Stimuli 2, Stimuli 3, and so on) display a selection of art, crafts, and designs from northern Norway that are meant to stimulate the senses and our creativity.

Polarmuseet

Søndre Tollbodgate 11B; tel. 77 62 33 60; https://uit.no/tmu/polarmuseet; daily 11am-5pm; adults 100 kr, children free

Since the 1850s, Tromsø has been seen as the gateway to the arctic sea for fishermen, adventurers, scientists, and travelers, and the Polar Museum is dedicated to the history of these pursuits. Through their permanent exhibits, you will learn about seal hunting, the cultural history of Svalbard, and the expeditions of Roald Amundsen and Fridtjof Nansen (Norwegian adventurers from the early 1900s). Polarmuseet is located on an old fisherman's wharf, in a large red building built on stilts.

Perspective Museum

Storgata 95; tel. 77 60 19 10; www.perspektivet.no; Tues.-Fri. 10am-4pm, Sat.-Sun. 10am-5pm; adults 50 kr, children free

The Perspective Museum foundation was established in 1996 by the Tromsø municipality to focus on tolerance, cultural diversity, and alternative perspectives on culture and society. Exhibits are developed to reflect this mission and, as the name suggests, offer perspective. Previous exhibitions have included *Veiled Rebellion,* a study of women in Afghanistan, and *Min Drakt—Min Historie,* translating to "My (National) Costume—My Story," displaying women's national costumes and the story each woman has to tell. Another former exhibit, *Fjellet og Havets Folk* ("The People of the Mountain and Sea"), focused on sharing the story of the Kven people, an ethnic and Indigenous minority in Scandinavia who are often mistaken for Sami.

Polaria

Hjalmar Johansens gate 12; tel. 77 75 01 00; https://polaria.no; daily 10am-4pm; adults 210 kr, children 105 kr

Polaria is an experience center with exhibits dedicated to the study of our environment and climate, and how the land and sea are interdependent. There is also a small aquarium where you can meet arctic species of fish and animals, including king crabs, catfish, bearded seals, and harbor seals. This is actually one of only two places in Europe where you can see bearded seals up close, the other one being Océanopolis in Brest, France. Polaria also has a 21-meter-wide (69-ft) screen showing specially made films throughout the day. One of these films focuses on Svalbard and the arctic wilderness, including a close look into the whale's habitat.

★ Tromsø University Museum

Lars Thørings Veg 10; tel. 77 64 50 01; https://en.uit. no/tmu; Mon.-Fri. 10am-4:30pm, Sat. noon-3pm, Sun. 11am-4pm; adults 100 kr, children free

Tromsø University Museum offers a geological exhibition and a natural history exhibition, but the main reason to visit is to check out permanent exhibits that focus on the Sami people. The Sami Culture exhibit will teach you more about the Sami people's culture, heritage, and history. Meanwhile, the exhibit called *Sápmi—Becoming a Nation* explores a darker side of Norwegian history: the ways that the Sami were long oppressed by Norwegian authorities, eventually leading to the formation of Sápmi, the Sami nation. It does not take long to visit the museum, but set aside at least 30-40 minutes for the Sami exhibits.

Fjellheisen

Sollivegen 12; tel. 77 63 87 37; https://fjellheisen.no; daily 10am-11pm; 260 kr return

The Fjellheisen Cable Car makes the mountains of Tromsø accessible for anyone. Ride up to Storsteinen, at 421 meters (1,380 ft) above sea level, in just a few minutes; each of the two cable cars (named Selen/The Seal, and Bjørnen/The Bear) carries 28 passengers. At the top, you can enjoy panoramic views of Tromsø city and the islands and mountains surrounding it. There are also several hiking trails to follow around the mountaintop. Both Steinbøhytta and Fløya are moderate 1-hour hikes starting from the top station. There is also a café at the top (Fjellstua; https://fjellheisen.no; daily 11am-10pm) serving coffee, light snacks, sandwiches, and ice cream. Their indoor seating area has large windows, so you can marvel at the view while enjoying your lunch.

Tromsø Arctic Reindeer

Fv53 1570; tel. 40 61 14 48; https:// no.tromsoarcticreindeer.com; daily Nov.-Apr.; 1,640 kr

1: the Arctic Cathedral 2: Tromsø 3: view of Tromsø from Fjellheisen 4: Tromsø Arctic Reindeer experience

Tromsø Arctic Reindeer is a Sami family-run company offering authentic experiences where you can learn more about Sami culture and history. This family has worked with reindeer for generations, and welcomes visitors in their camp just outside of Tromsø. Their experiences include meeting some (or all) of their 300 reindeer, joining a reindeer sled ride around the camp, helping with reindeer feeding (they are very friendly!), and enjoying an authentic Sami lunch. A highlight of any day at this camp is gathering around the fire to listen to the Sami hosts share their culture and way of life. Your experience includes transportation to the camp from their pick-up spot in the center of Tromsø, in front of the Radisson and Scandic hotels.

Arctic-Alpine Botanic Garden

Stakkevollvegen 200; https://uit.no/tmu/botanisk; daily; free

The Arctic-Alpine Botanical Garden of Tromsø are probably not what you envision. Instead, these gardens stretch across a rocky, mountainous landscape covered in various kinds of moss and small, colorful alpine plants and flowers from across the world. Some examples are the Siberian fawn lily and the Dianthus superbus (found in Norway). In the gardens there is also a house from 1850 with a small café (Hansine Hansens Kafé; https://uit.no/tmu/botanisk; daily). The flowers usually bloom from early May.

Northern Norwegian Science Center

Hansine Hansens Veg 17; tel. 77 62 09 45; https:// nordnorsk.vitensenter.no; daily 11am-4pm; adults 130 kr, children 70 kr

At this activity center you can explore almost 100 science-based interactive exhibits across three floors. The focus is on four topics: heaven and the universe (Himmelen over oss), the climate and weather (Klima og vær), energy and the environment in the north (Energi og miljø i nord), and the

Sami Culture

The Sami are native people who mainly reside across Norway, Sweden, Finland, and Russia. The oldest scriptures referring to the Sami date back to AD 98. It is estimated that there are around 50,000 to 80,000 Sami today, with the majority of them residing in Norway (40,000). The majority of the Sami people live in Tromsø municipality, followed by Kautokeino, Alta, and Karasjok.

Traditionally, the Sami have lived off the land, with fishing and herding as their main livelihood. They are perhaps best known for their reindeer herding, although not all Sami consider themselves "reindeer" Sami. Today, fewer than 3,000 Sami are still actively involved in full-time reindeer herding in Norway, and the animals provide them with fur, meat, and transportation. The reindeer herding Sami were traditionally nomadic and would follow their herd depending on the season. To this day, only Sami people are allowed to own reindeer in Norway.

traditional Sami bags mde of reindeer hide

The Sami have their own flag, languages, and parliament in Norway. Sami is considered an official language of Norway, and their flag is considered equal to that of the Norwegian flag. However, this is after several decades of being forced to assimilate and conform to Norwegian culture. The Sami were put into Norwegian schools and actively discouraged from using their own language and showing their own culture. This "Norwegianization" was especially prominent around the occupation during World War II, when Norwegian nationalism was strong.

Thankfully, Sami culture and rights have since been acknowledged, with the Sami Parliament of Norway being elected in 1989. The Finnmark Act of 2005 also granted the land rights to large areas of Finnmark to the Sami people. Still, this does not erase this dark chapter of Norway's history.

★ LEARNING ABOUT SAMI CULTURE

When visiting Tromsø and northern Norway, there are several ways to learn about Sami culture. By seeking out these activities you are not only exploring an integral part of the cultural landscape in Norway, but also preventing further ignorance about the Sami.

- **Tromsø University Museum:** A visit here will show you more about how the Sami fought for their rights after World War II (page 313).

- **Tromsø Arctic Reindeer:** This company offers authentic experiences to learn more about Sami culture and history, including reindeer herding (page 313).

- **Sami Siida:** Visitors are welcome at this Sami community, where you can take part in a number of activities, such as reindeer sledding and feeding (page 324).

CUISINE

Traditional Sami cuisine heavily features reindeer meat, which has been an integral part of their lives for centuries. As the Sami would always make use of the whole animal, you will find that many Sami dishes are based on broth from reindeer meat. **Biđus** (the Sami national dish, a stew of reindeer meat and vegetables) and **reindeer meatballs** are worth trying if you get the chance, with the former being served at both Sami Siida and Tromsø Arctic Reindeer.

body and brain (Kropp og hjerne). Amongst their interactive experiences is a climbing wall, the chance to use puffs of air to move items through rings in the air, and a space-pod where you can "travel" around the earth. The Science Center is especially popular with families, as it offers lots of fun activities for kids.

SPORTS AND RECREATION

Hiking

The Sherpa Stairs

Distance: *1.1 kilometers (0.7 mi)*
Time: *2 hours round-trip*
Difficulty: *Moderate*
Trailhead: *Fløyvegen*
Information and Maps: *https://fjellheisen.no/ aktiviteter/fotturer-pa-fjellet/*

The Fjellheisen Cable Car is a popular sight and attraction in Tromsø, but those who enjoy a rewarding hike can reach the mountaintop via Sherpatrappa (the Sherpa Stairs). As with many other popular hikes in Norway, Sherpas from Nepal came to build these 1,200 steps to the top. Along the way you will enjoy a view that just gets better and better, and at the top you will have the same view as those who ride up on the Fjellheisen gondola. Many hikers take Fjellheisen back down to avoid too much strain on their knees.

Along the way there are several landings where you can take a break and enjoy the view. On sunny days, especially Sundays when locals are off work, the hike gets busier. However, the stairs are wide enough for slower hikers to stick to one side, so faster hikers can pass them.

Telegrafbukta

Distance: *6.5 kilometers (4 mi)*
Time: *1.5 hours round-trip*
Difficulty: *Easy*
Trailhead: *Prostneset, Downtown Tromsø*
Information and Maps: *https://ut.no/ turforslag/116822/tur-til-telegrafbukta-fra-sentrum*

Start this hike anywhere in the center of Tromsø. Telegrafbukta (Telegraph Bay) is a park on the south tip of the Tromsø island, and it's a good destination for a lovely afternoon walk that isn't too strenuous. Head south through the city center, staying as close to the waterfront as you can, and as you leave the city center follow the coast. Eventually you will reach a gravel footpath along the water, and walk past parks, beaches, and forested areas. This path is extra busy on Sundays, when you will see families, friends, and dog owners out enjoying their day.

Skamtinden

Distance: *4 km (2.5 mi)*
Time: *2 hours round-trip*
Trailhead: *Rekvikvegen (end of the road)*
Information and Maps: *https://kugo. no/2012/10/skamtinden-884-moh*

On Kvaløya, the island "next to" Tromsø, you will find Skamtinden mountaintop. This peak at 884 meters (2,900 ft) above sea level offers views of the landscape surrounding Tromsø, the nearby islands, and the sea. The first 200-meter (650-ft) climb of this hike goes through a forested area, and the trail is clear the whole way. Once you get through the forest, you will find that the view starts to open up as you climb. The hike follows the ridge of the mountain all the way to the top, and eventually the trail changes to rocks and stone. From there, it is clearly marked with cairns (small piles of stones). Do not remove stones from these or make your own, as it can confuse other hikers. The final stretch includes a very short climbing section; look for evidence of where other people have walked, which will make it easier to climb.

To get to the trailhead, follow Route 862 west, leaving Tromsø island. The road will take you all the way to the village of Tromvik. When you get there, take a left onto Rekvikvegen and drive to the end of the road for the trailhead. The drive takes around 1 hour.

Chase the Northern Lights

The northern lights (aurora borealis) draw a lot of people to Norway. This phenomenon appears year-round but can only be seen when it is sufficiently dark. Therefore, it is mainly during the winter months that you will be able to see them. In wintertime, the northern lights can be seen from most places with little light pollution; in the north, this is practically everywhere.

To chase the northern lights on your own, you should have a car and seek out rural areas. If you are staying in Tromsø, however, a walk out of the city center (for example, to the park around Telegrafbukta) will also make it easier to see them. Check the northern lights forecast each day (the tourist information can help you with this), and hope for a cloudless sky.

Once you have checked the forecast and the weather, and chosen a location, be patient. If you are lucky, intense northern lights will shine in the sky for hours, but you may also see weaker ones in a shorter burst. Bundle up and bring some entertainment, like a deck of cards. It's worth the wait.

PLACES TO GO

Of course, seeing the northern lights is never guaranteed, and you need both the weather (clouds) and aurora activity to be on your side. Additionally, you need to get as far away from light pollution as possible.

- **Telegrafbukta:** a 20-minute walk out of the city will take you to this small park on the southern tip of Tromsø island. It's a great place to see the northern lights without being too far away from the city (page 315).

- **Aurora Canvas Domes, Alta:** Sleep "under the sky" in one of these domes with a glass ceiling—the perfect place to lie warm and cozy while watching the lights dance across the sky (page 328).

- **Fjellheisen:** Head to the top of the mountain on the cable car to get high above the city and lights (page 313).

- **Svalbard:** With Svalbard being so far north, the chances of seeing the northern lights are big. However, with restrictions on being alone outside (due to polar bears), you won't be able to go see them on your own (page 333).

Skiing
Tromsø Alpinpark

Jadevegen 129; https://tromsoalpinpark.no; Mon.-Fri. 4pm-8:30pm, Sat.-Sun. 10am-5pm; 1-day lift ticket 350 kr, 1-day ski rental 200 kr

Tromsø Aplinpark is a ski park just 10 minutes outside of the city center. There are five slopes with varying degrees of difficulty, plus a sledding slope for young children and families. Ski rental is also available.

Snowshoeing
Tromsø Outdoor

Sjøgata 14; tel. 97 57 58 75; www.tromsooutdoor.no; daily Nov.-Mar.; from 1,195 kr

Tromsø Outdoor offers several snowshoe hiking experiences throughout the winter, with outings to suit different skill levels. Their easiest hike, which involves guided easy snowshoeing and a visit to a local café, runs Mondays, Wednesdays, and Fridays December-February; this 4.5-hour experience is suitable for beginners. The hike will take you to Kvaløya (transportation included), and ends with a visit to a quaint dock café, before bringing you back to the city center of Tromsø.

TOURS

Below is a selection of northern lights chase tours, operated from Tromsø. Going with an experienced guide is often a good idea, as they will follow the (lack of) clouds and the forecast, and take you wherever the chances are greatest each night. The season for northern lights tours is usually September to late March or early April.

- **Arctic Guide Service** (tel. 92 20 79 01; www. arcticguideservice.com; 6-7-hour tour; 995 kr): This classic tour takes you out chasing the northern lights onboard a minibus.

- **Arctic Breeze** (tel. 90 98 09 19; www.arcticbreeze. no; 4-8 hour tour, varying depending on Aurora activity; 1,180 kr): Another classic minibus northern lights tour.

- **Tromsø Accessible Tours** (tel. 93 96 29 92; www. tromsoaccessibletours.com; 6-8 hour tour; 1,490 kr): This accessible tour is ideal for wheelchair users, and it includes heated blankets to keep you warm.

the northern lights

- **Rødne Fjord Cruise** (tel. 51 89 52 70; www.rodne.no; 2.5 hours; 850 kr): If you'd like to head out on the water for your northern lights chase, this is a northern lights fjord cruise.

- **NorthernShots Tours** (Roald Amundsens Plass 1; www.northernshotstours.com; daily Oct.-Mar., 6-7 hours; 990 kr): On this northern lights tour, your guides are also professional photographers. They offer a mini workshop for nighttime and northern lights photography, to help you get the perfect shot.

Dog Sledding
Northern Light Dog Adventure
Tel. 93 02 38 19; www.northernlightdogadventure.com; Dec.-Mar.; 2,450 kr

There is nothing quite like the feeling of zooming through the forest on a sled being pulled by a team of overly excited huskies. The starting point for this tour is a 60-minute drive from Tromsø, and the booking includes transportation to and from the city center. At the basecamp you can get to know the friendly huskies while you listen to the important safety instructions. During this tour you will spend 1-2 hours on the sled, either driving or as a passenger (2 guests manage 1

sled and team of dogs together). It is recommended to wear a wool base layer, and to pack a lunch. The total length of the experience is up to 7 hours.

Whale-Watching
Rødne Fjord Cruise
Tel. 51 89 52 70; https://rodne.no; Nov.-Feb.; adults 1,550 kr, children 725 kr

During the 8-hour whale watching tour offered by Rødne Fjord Cruise, they say you are almost guaranteed to see a whale. However, if you don't, they will let you join the next available tour free of charge (once). You leave Tromsø early in the morning in search of killer whales and humpback whales. Onboard the MS *Rygerdronningen* you have plenty of space to move around both indoors and outdoors, and there is a small kiosk onboard where you can purchase snacks and drinks.

Fishing
Polar Adventures
Killengreens gate 7-11; tel. 90 98 99 95; www. polaradventures.no; daily mid-Apr.-Oct.; 1,400 kr
In the summer you can join Polar Adventures for a 3-hour fishing adventure from Tromsø aboard the boat *Capella*. No prior fishing experience is needed to join, and during the trip you will learn about the wildlife and fishing culture of the area. The staff on board are helpful and informative, and will answer any questions you may have. Tea, coffee, and light snacks are served from the small kitchen onboard. Insulated jackets are available for all passengers, but dress warmly regardless.

ENTERTAINMENT AND EVENTS
The Arts
Galleri Nord
Sjøgata 7; tel. 46 80 04 62; www.galleri-nord.no; Mon.-Fri. 10am-5pm, Sat. 10am-4pm, Sun. noon-4pm
Galleri Nord (Gallery North) is an art gallery with a rotating collection and temporary exhibits by Norwegian artists. Among the artists on display here are Elenor Martinsen, Elin Rossing, and Geir Wold. Through the years they have also hosted exhibits and pop-up events with artists such as Vebjørn Sand, Anne Gundersen, and Lisa Aisato.

Kulturhuset
Erling Bangsunds Plass 1; tel. 95 02 32 22; https://kulturhuset.tr.no
Kulturhuset is a venue for the arts in the heart of Tromsø. On their three stages they put on musicals, plays, concerts, and stand-up acts. Most of the shows are in Norwegian, but visiting international acts appear from time to time. Adam Douglas, the Bellamy Brothers, and Jimmy Carr are among the shows that have graced the main venue in Tromsø.

Festivals and Events
Sami Week
Jan.-Feb.
Every winter, Sami Week is celebrated in Tromsø and the city comes alive with seminars and workshops, concerts, and even reindeer racing. The Norwegian Championship of Reindeer Racing is usually held during Sami Week, and it goes through Storgata in the city center. You can expect to see lots of Sami wearing their national costumes, and this is the perfect time to try some bidus (traditional Sami reindeer stew).

Midnight Sun Marathon
Tel. 77 67 33 63; www.msm.no; June
Every year the Midnight Sun Marathon takes place in Tromsø. Runners can participate in the full marathon, half marathon, a 10k, or a mini-marathon. One thing that's unique about this race is that it doesn't start in the early morning like most marathons. Instead, it starts around 9pm, ensuring that you run through the night and through the midnight sun. The half marathon can start as late as 10:30pm.

Nordlysfestivalen
www.nordlysfestivalen.no
Nordlysfestivalen is the major music event in Tromsø. Since 1988 it has grown from a small, traditional music festival, to the large spectacle it is today. The festival lasts 10 whole days, and features a wide variety of artists and bands performing different types of music, from jazz to pop. Previous artists have included Cecilie Norby, Tromsø Storband, and New Religion.

SHOPPING
Edel Antikk og Vintage
Storgata 62; tel. 97 09 79 05; Mon.-Fri. 11am-5pm, Sat. 11am-4pm
This antique and vintage store in the center of Tromsø offers lots of hidden gems and fun finds. From vintage clothing and kitchenware to formerly loved furniture and art, you'll find it in this charming store.

Norrøna Concept Store

Samuel Arnesens Gate 5; tel. 48 89 86 10; www.
norrona.com; Mon.-Fri. 10am-6pm, Sat. 10am-5pm

Norrøna is a Norwegian brand that is well
known for comfortable and sturdy outdoor
clothing. At their concept store in Tromsø you
can explore their collections and get advice on
the best activewear for your needs.

FOOD

The food scene in Tromsø is inspired by the
arctic, with local seafood and other ingredients taking pride of place on many menus. The
arctic also inspires the decor and atmosphere
in many of the restaurants, as they are all designed to be welcoming, warm, and homey—
the perfect refuge from the cold outside. The
word "koselig" (cozy) might be the best way
to describe the feel of these restaurants. Fresh
seafood and local meat (such as reindeer and
moose) are found on most menus, so Tromsø
is the ideal destination to try something new.

New Nordic and Traditional Norwegian
Kaia

Stortorget 2; tel. 40 64 03 33; Mon.-Thurs. 11am-10pm,
Fri.-Sat. 11am-3am, Sun. noon-10pm; 195-295 kr

Kaia literally translates to "The Dock,"
and that's where you will find this charming, nautical-looking restaurant and bar.
Hamburgers, fish soup, and more are served.
The outdoor seating area on the dock is lovely
in the summer. In the evening there is often
live music, and the place gets quite lively and
busy.

Restaurant Skirri

Stortorget 1; tel. 94 82 08 25; www.kystensmathus.no;
Mon. 11am-6pm, Tues.-Sat. 11am-11pm; 235-365 kr

With beautiful views of the harbor of Tromsø,
the large and modern restaurant Skirri is popular for both lunch and dinner. The menu
changes with the season, but the main events
all year are cod and reindeer—both dishes of
local importance. Expect also to find dishes
such as whale steak, fresh fish soup, and tenderloin of reindeer.

Bardus Bistro

Cora Sandels Gate 4; tel. 92 67 48 88; https://bardus.
no; Tues.-Fri. 11am-10pm, Sat. noon-10pm, Sun. 3pm-
9pm; 279-389 kr

Bardus Bistro creates internationally inspired
menus based on fresh, local ingredients. The
menu often includes whale, moose, reindeer,
and king crab. The atmosphere is cozy and
friendly, with bookshelves lining the walls and
large windows facing the street.

International
Tromsø Tapas

Stortorget 5; tel. 77 68 27 27; https://tromsotapas.no;
Mon.-Thurs. 3pm-10pm, Fri.-Sat. 3pm-11pm; 130-250 kr
(small dishes)

Spanish meets Norwegian at Tromsø Tapas,
where you will find both garlic-soaked king
crab and Spanish meatballs on the menu.
The large restaurant is dark and industrial
looking, which gives it a low-key and relaxed atmosphere. There is an open kitchen,
so you can watch the chefs do their magic
as you eat.

La Famiglia

Sjøgata 12; tel. 93 05 09 99; daily 11am-midnight;
195-345 kr

This restaurant offers great Italian dishes in a
friendly and relaxed atmosphere. The interior
is stylish, with gold and green details throughout. Choose from white and red based pizzas,
a selection of pasta dishes, and classic entrées
such as entrecote.

Cafés
Fjellstua Kafe

Top of mount Storsteinen; www.fjellheisen.no/fjellstua-
cafe; daily 10am-10pm

At the top of Fjellheisen, you will find
Fjellstua Kafe, serving light snacks, drinks,
and warm dishes all day. Their opening hours
correspond with the cable car. The main event
in this large, modern restaurant is the view,
with a wall of windows facing the city. On the
menu you will find international and local
dishes, such as hamburgers, reindeer steak,
bacalao, and sandwiches.

★ Smørtorget

Fredrik Langes Gate 9; tel. 95 70 09 30; Mon.-Fri. 8am-6pm, Sat. 10am-6pm, Sun. 11am-6pm

Smørtorget is a café and vintage store in the center of Tromsø, where you will find lots of mismatched furniture, vintage clothes, and decorative pieces waiting for you to take them home. The furniture you sit on while you eat is for sale, and you will find lots more treasures here. Choose between the soup of the day, a selection of sandwiches, chicken quesadillas, and wraps. This is the ideal spot for a late breakfast or lunch, and you'll find lots of locals here.

BARS AND NIGHTLIFE

Rooftop Bar at the Edge Hotel

Kaigata 6; tel. 77 66 84 00; www.nordicchoicehotels. no; Thurs. 5pm-midnight, Fri.-Sat. 5pm-1am

The rooftop of The Edge is the only sky bar in the city, with beautiful views of the island of Tromsø, the bay, and the surrounding islands and mountains. On a clear night, you can even watch the northern lights from here (even though they will be brighter outside of the city where there are no lights). The bar is open to the public (you do not have to be a guest of the hotel), and you will find it on the 11th floor. There is space to hang out indoors and outdoors, though the outdoor area is only tempting for a few months of the year. There is often a DJ on weekends, playing funky hits.

Magic Ice Tromsø

Kaigata 4; tel. 41 30 10 50; www.magicice.no/listings/ tromso-norway; daily 2pm-11pm mid-May-mid-Sept., daily 4pm-9pm Sept.-Oct., daily 11am-11pm Nov.-May

At the northernmost ice art gallery in Norway, you can enjoy a (freezing) cold drink while marveling at impressive sculptures made entirely out of ice. You will be equipped with warm gloves and an even warmer poncho when you arrive, and treated to one of their specialty drinks, served in a glass made of ice. This is a fun, and cold, experience suitable for all ages (not all drinks are alcoholic).

Huken Brygg

Storgata 39; tel. 90 47 43 47; Sun.-Thurs. 3pm-2am, Fri.-Sat. 3pm-3:30am

Huken Brygg is a cozy pub focusing on craft beer and cocktails. Their funky, two-floor bar is equipped with mismatched vintage (and new) furniture, and their bartenders have a large repertoire of cocktails at the ready. Light bites and snacks ranging from sliders to tacos are also available. This is a nice homey place to grab lunch and a beer.

ACCOMMODATIONS

As in many of Norway's other cities, accommodation options in Tromsø are dominated by the major Norwegian chains: Thon, Radisson, Scandic, and Clarion. All the lodgings included here are high-quality properties located in the city center.

Thon Hotel Tromsø

Grønnegata 50; tel. 77 69 80 50; www.thonhotels.no/ hoteller/norge/tromso/thon-hotel-tromso; 1,200 kr

The colorful Thon Hotel Tromsø is a new and modern hotel, with all the amenities needed for your trip. With their orange, yellow, and blue color scheme, their lobby is bright and welcoming. Their 152 rooms are spacious and bright, with blue and lime-green details and lovely flowered wallpaper. They serve an evening meal daily from 6pm to 9pm, and the breakfast buffet in the morning includes lots of local produce.

The Edge

Kaigata 6; tel. 77 66 84 00; www.nordicchoicehotels. com/hotels/norway/tromso/clarion-hotel-the-edge; 1,500 kr

The Edge, which gets its name from its pointed shape, is a large, modern hotel on the docks of Tromsø. It is a Clarion hotel, so you can expect the level of service and comfort that you'd find in any of their other hotels. This property's 290 rooms are simple and welcoming, with a white, gray, and orange color scheme. Even if you are not staying at The Edge, the rooftop bar overlooking the city can be a fun spot for a drink.

Scandic Ishavshotell

Fredrik Langes Gate 2; tel. 77 66 64 01; www.
scandichotels.no/hotell/norge/tromso/scandic-
ishavshotel; 1,600 kr

Scandic, just across the road from the Radisson, is also a great location for visitors who are planning to join any excursions during their trip, because tours depart from just outside the hotel. The 214 rooms at the Scandic are comfortable and warmly decorated, and some showers are equipped with windows overlooking the harbor.

Clarion Hotel With

Sjøgata; tel. 77 66 42 00; www.nordicchoicehotels.
no/hotell/norge/tromso/clarion-collection-hotel-with;
1,600 kr

This 76-room maritime hotel faces Fjellheisen and the Arctic Cathedral, and overlooks the Tromsø harbor. The rooms are comfortable and furnished to a high standard, with white and purple-brown details. The main drawing point for this hotel is that they serve an evening meal every day, included in the price of the room. This is convenient and affordable for anyone returning from a tour and wanting to grab a simple dinner before going to bed.

Radisson Blu Tromsø

Sjøgata 7; tel. 77 60 00 00; www.radissonhotels.com/
en-us/hotels/radisson-blu-tromso; 1,700 kr

At the 269-room Radisson, the water-facing rooms afford views across to Fjellheisen and the cathedral. This hotel also provides a great breakfast and excellent service. Many tours leaving the city depart from just outside. The rooms are traditional, with a clean design featuring light colors and beige wood. There is a gym with a sauna overlooking the harbor on the top floor—the perfect place to warm up after a day of exploring Tromsø.

INFORMATION AND SERVICES

Tromsø Tourist Information

Samuel Arnesens Gate 5; tel. 77 61 00 00; www.
visittromso.no/no/turistinformasjon; Mon.-Fri. 9am-
4pm, Sat. 9am-3pm

The tourist information in Tromsø is the place to go for hiking maps and advice, and to book tickets for activities and tours in the area. They can also help you plan your northern lights chase by advising you on where to go and how to check the forecast.

Tromsø Emergency Room

Sykehusvegen 30; tel. 116117; open 24/7

The Legevakt (Emergency Room) in Tromsø is open 24 hours for all minor accidents and emergencies. It is possible to just show up, but if you need immediate help, calling in advance is recommended. For urgent emergencies requiring an ambulance, call 113.

Tromsø Postal Office

Sjøgata 7; tel. 22 03 00 00; Mon.-Fri. 8am-6pm, Sat.
10am-3pm

At the Tromsø post office you can mail packages and letters and buy stamps for postcards. Stamped postcards can be sent here, or from the red post box outside the office.

GETTING THERE

Tromsø is located far north in Norway, so reaching it by car or bus is not very practical; the total drive time from Oslo to Tromsø is 22 hours. The most efficient way of getting there is on a direct flight from Oslo or Bergen, and there are several each day. Another popular (and much more scenic) way is by boat, as the Hurtigruten ferry travels up the entire coastline of Norway, stopping in Tromsø.

Boat

Hurtigruten (tel. 81 00 30 30; www.hurtigruten.no; from 7300 kr per person from Bergen to Tromsø) leaves Bergen three times a week and stops over in several cities and towns before arriving in Tromsø 4 days later. During the voyage you get to see almost the entire Norwegian coastline; it's a wonderful way to travel for those who have time. Hurtigruten operates year-round, and the **dock** in Tromsø is right in the city center, just a short walk from all central hotels, such as the Clarion, The Edge, and Scandic..

Air

Tromsø Airport Langnes

Flyplassvegen 31; https://avinor.no/en/airport/tromso-airport

Travelers arriving by air will fly into Tromsø Airport Langnes, located just 10 minutes by car from the center of Tromsø. Although this is an international airport, with flights to and from Helsinki and Gdansk, most people heading to Tromsø stop first in Oslo, Bergen, or Trondheim. There are several daily departures via SAS, Norwegian, and Widerøe to those three cities, in addition to other Norwegian cities (such as Harstad, Hammerfest, and Alta).

The approximate flight time from Oslo or Bergen is 2 hours, and from Trondheim it takes around 1.5 hours. The airport bus **FlyBussen** (www.bussring.no) departs 3-4 times an hour and takes you into the city center in around 10-15 minutes, stopping by most city hotels.

GETTING AROUND

Tromsø is a very walkable city, with most sights, hotels, and restaurants located right in the city center. Across the 1-kilometer (0.6-mi) bridge connecting the city to the mainland, you will find Fjellheisen and the Arctic Cathedral. The bridge has a sidewalk, so all Tromsø's sights can be reached on foot. The city is not very large, and in fact the distance from the southernmost tip of the island (where the University Museum is) to the city center (where most sights, hotels, and restaurants are) is just over 3 kilometers (1.8 mi). The distance from the city center to Fjellheisen (at the other "edge" of the city) is just under 4 kilometers (2.5 mi).

If you prefer to travel by public transportation, going by bus is the main way to get around in the city. The buses are operated by **Troms Fylkestrafikk** (tel. 77 78 87 77; https://fylkestrafikk.no; daily 5:30am-1am; one-way ticket 37 kr, 24-hour pass 100 kr). If you travel outside of rush hours (Mon.-Fri. 9am-2pm and 5pm-1am) the one-way ticket is discounted to 20 kr. It is cheaper to buy your ticket in advance than on the bus, so download the **Troms Billett app** before you go. As in Oslo and Bergen, Tromsø buses operate on an honor system, but there are occasional ticket controls onboard. Most buses run 2-4 times an hour, depending on the route.

Alta

Alta is a destination that will blow you away, especially in the winter. Life above the polar circle offers multiple bucket-list experiences for travelers, such as sleeping in a hotel made entirely out of snow and going snowmobiling on the vast mountain plateau Finnmarksvidda. Alta's motto stating "This is Arctic living" is based on a desire to show visitors from all over the world that these seemingly amazing activities are part of daily life in Alta. Here, the Sami and the Norwegians live side by side, sharing their cultures and influences under the northern lights in the winter, and the midnight sun in the summer. Dog sledding, snowmobiling, and reindeer are integral to life up north.

Alta is the ideal destination for those who truly want to experience the essence of northern Norway, learn about Sami culture, and explore what arctic living is truly like. Set aside at least three days to spend in Alta to get the most out of your trip.

Orientation

Alta is a small city with a dense city center. You'll want to rent a car for your stay, as most sights are outside of the center (with the exception of the cathedral). In the center of the city you will find a mall with several shops and restaurants, the Northern Lights Cathedral, and the Scandic Alta Hotel. All other sights, restaurants, and

Alta and Hammerfest

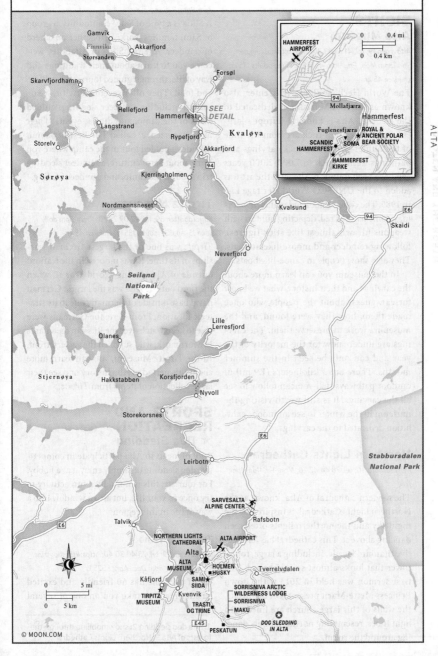

Map labels:

Gamvik
Finnvika
Akkarfjord
Storsanden
Skarvfjordhamn
Forsøl
Hellefjord
Hammerfest
SEE DETAIL
Kvaløya
Langstrand
Rypefjord
Storelv
Akkarfjord
94
Sørøya
Kjerringholmen
Nordmannsneset
Kvalsund
E6
94
Skaidi
E6
Neverfjord
Seiland National Park
Lille Lerresfjord
Olanes
Stjernøya
Hakkstabben
Korsfjorden
Nyvoll
Storekorsnes
E6
Stabbursdalen National Park
Leirbotn
SARVESALTA ALPINE CENTER
Talvik
Rafsbotn
E6
NORTHERN LIGHTS CATHEDRAL
ALTA AIRPORT
Alta
ALTA MUSEUM
HOLMEN HUSKY
Tverrelvdalen
Kåfjord
SAMI SIIDA
SORRISNIVA ARCTIC WILDERNESS LODGE
SORRISNIVA
MAKU
TIRPITZ MUSEUM
Kvenvik
TRASTI OG TRINE
DOG SLEDDING IN ALTA
E45
PESKATUN

0   5 mi
0   5 km

Inset (detail) map labels:

HAMMERFEST AIRPORT
0   0.4 mi
0   0.4 km
94
Mollafjæra
Hammerfest
Fuglenesfjæra
ROYAL & ANCIENT POLAR BEAR SOCIETY
SCANDIC HAMMERFEST
SOMA
HAMMERFEST KIRKE

© MOON.COM

hotels are a 5- to 15-minute drive from the city center.

SIGHTS
Alta Museum

Altavegen 19; tel. 41 75 63 30; www.altamuseum.no; 9am-3pm Mon.-Fri., 11am-4pm Sat.-Sun.; adults 135 kr, children 45 kr

The World Heritage Rock Art Center, also known as the Alta Museum, is dedicated to the fact that Alta is home to Europe's largest concentration of rock art from the time of the hunter-gatherers. Rock carvings and paintings dating back to 7,000-2,000 years ago have been found in Alta, and the art was added to the UNESCO World Heritage List in 1985. The collection includes ancient carvings, some painted red, depicting hunters with weapons (drawn almost like stick figures), following reindeer and moose-like animals. They also show people in canoe-like boats.

In the museum you can learn more about the carvings and their history, what we know (or can guess) about the people who once made them, how they were found, and the museum's work to preserve them. The carvings are under snow for the majority of the year and can only be seen in the summer months. There are 3 kilometers (1.9 mi) of outdoor pathways that you can follow to see all the carvings. It is still worth visiting the museum in the winter to see an indoor exhibition dedicated to the carvings.

Northern Lights Cathedral

Markedsgata 30; tel. 78 44 42 70; Mon.-Fri. 11am-1pm; free

The modern cathedral of Alta, known as the Northern Lights Cathedral, is inspired by the night sky and the northern lights often seen dancing above it. This cathedral has a reflective titanium façade, including a large, round tower that looks almost spiral-shaped. The first sermon was held in 2013 with Crown Princess Mette-Marit present. On the inside, the walls of this large church are lined with light tubes, resembling northern lights dancing around the room.

Sami Siida

Øytunveien 4; tel. 46 83 86 45; www.samisiida.no; daily 3pm-9pm; 975 kr

A Siida is a type of Sami community, a group of Sami families working together on a herd of reindeer. At Sami Siida in Alta, they welcome you to learn about their traditions and way of life, through guided tours, storytelling, and food. They offer several activities year-round, including reindeer sledding, guided tours of the camp, and dinner events. Their main experience, called The Best of Sápmi, includes a guided tour of the camp where you learn about Sami culture, a reindeer sledding trip around the camp, and reindeer feeding.

Tirpitz Museum

Kåfjordbotten 59; tel. 92 09 23 70; 10am-5pm daily June 15-Aug. 31; adults 135 kr, children 45 kr

Tirpitz was one of the largest German warships of its time. It was moored in the Kåfjord outside of Alta during World War II, when the fjord outside Alta was the largest German naval base outside of Germany due to its strategic location. From here, the Germans were able to keep watch over the Russian merchants in Murmansk, who supplied the eastern front. At the Tirpitz Museum, you can learn more about this period of Alta history and see their large collection of items from *Tirpitz*.

SPORTS AND RECREATION
★ Dog Sledding

A lot of locals in Alta participate in competitive dog sledding or simply enjoy it as a hobby. For tourists, this is not only a fun activity to try once in your life, but also a window into a way of life in this region.

Trasti og Trine

Gargiaveien 29; tel. 78 40 30 40; https://trastiogtrine. no; daily noon-8pm Dec.-Apr.; 1,525 kr

Trasti og Trine has 60 friendly and excited huskies ready to take you on one of several

---

1: Alta dog sledding 2: snowmobiling through the forests of Alta 3: Northern Lights Cathedral

dog sledding experiences. The trips last up to five days, but the most popular is their 3-hour experience, "A Taste of Dog Sledding." After a safety briefing, you are given a note with the names of "your" dogs for the day, before you get to enter their enclosure and find your new friends. You will learn how to put their harness on correctly and how to prepare your sled and dog team (with the help of your guide when needed).

The dogs are incredibly excited to set off, and on this experience, you will get to try driving a sled on your own (two people per sled). You zoom through the forests outside Trasti og Trine's camp and along the Alta River. The guide is always ahead of you leading the way, and you'll be surprised at how relaxing this is once you get over the initial adrenaline rush. After about an hour on the sled (either standing and driving or sitting in the seat), you head back to the camp to put the dogs back in their enclosure. Afterwards, you are treated to a hot drink and stories around the fire; the experienced guides have lots to tell and are open to all kinds of questions about their dogs and dog sledding. One of their guides is actually the youngest ever winner of Finnmarksløpet dog sledding race!

Trasti og Trine is located about a 15-minute drive from the center of Alta, and transportation to and from the city center is included in this experience.

Holmen Husky

Holmen 100; tel. 91 76 48 66; www.holmenhusky.no; daily Dec.-Apr.; 1,290 kr

Holmen Husky's 2.5-hour dog sledding excursion takes you along parts of the actual trail followed by Finnmarksløpet every year, which is not something everyone can say they have tried. During this experience, you are picked up outside the tourist information in Alta and taken to the Holmen Husky camp (10-minute drive). The time spent out on the sled is approximately 1 hour, and you can try your hand at both driving and being a passenger. Afterward,

enjoy snacks and hot drinks in their Lacco, listening to the guide's stories about life with the huskies.

Snowmobile Tour
Sorrisniva

Sorrisniva 20; www.sorrisniva.no/experiences/ snowmobile-experiences; daily Dec.-Mar.; 1,800- 2,300 kr

Snowmobiles are often used as a mode of transportation in the snowy areas around Alta, especially on the Finnmarksvidda plateau. During one of the snowmobile excursions from Sorrisniva, you get to learn how to drive one, and go on a guided adventure around the forests and plains of the north. You can opt to drive on your own, or share with a companion. Regardless, this is great fun. You leave Sorrisniva and head into the forested area below Finnmarksvidda before you head out onto the plateau itself for an exhilarating adventure. Experienced guides will also teach you about the area. The tours last 2.5-4 hours and depart from Sorrisniva hotel, about a 20-minute drive from the center of Alta.

Northern Lights Chase
Peskatun

Peskaveien 24; tel. 97 06 04 89; https://peskatun.no/ no/opplevelser/nordlys; Nov.-Mar.; 1,580 kr

You'll be picked up at your hotel by bus at around 7pm, driving out of the city and away from the lights. The whole time, the guides will be checking the weather, locations, and northern lights forecast to figure out the absolute best spot to see the northern lights. You never know how much driving is involved, but during the chase, you will learn about the science behind the northern lights and their cultural significance in the north. In addition, the guides are happy to share their knowledge about photographing the northern lights, which is not always an easy feat. They are also happy to take photos of you under the lights and email them to you after the chase. The tour lasts about 5 hours.

Skiing
Sarvesalta Alpine Center
Nordelvdalen 170; https://sarvesalta.no/alpinsenter; Wed.-Fri. 5pm-9pm, Sat.-Sun. 11am-5pm Nov.-Apr.; 1-day lift ticket 400 kr

With lovely views of the Alta fjord, the Sarvesalta Alpine Center is a family-oriented ski center with several slopes that range from the easiest kids' slope to the hardest Eksperten (Expert) run. Adults and children can rent skis, snowboards, and other gear here.

ENTERTAINMENT AND EVENTS
Finnmarksløpet (Dog Sled Race)
www.finnmarkslopet.no; Mar.

Finnmarksløpet (the Finnmark Race) is Europe's longest dog sled race and it has taken place every year since 1981. The race travels 1,200 kilometers (745 mi) of forested areas, as well as the mountain plateau Finnmarksvidda and more mountainous areas. This is Europe's longest and toughest dog sledding race, with the fastest contestants completing the course in less than 7 days. The race starts and ends in the center of Alta, and seeing them take off (or cross the finish line) is worth your time.

Alta Live
www.altalive.no; Aug.

Alta Live is a large music festival established in 2019, bringing Norwegian and international artists to Alta every year. The festival stage is found right in the middle of the city. Previous performers have included Astrid S, Kjartan Lauritzen, Mari Boine (a Sami artist), and All We Are. This is a two-day festival focusing on a variety of music genres, but the main headliners are usually pop singers.

FOOD
Alattio
Markedsgata 14; tel. 46 28 65 32; www.alattio.no; Mon.-Thurs. 4pm-10pm, Fri.-Sat. 4pm-11pm; 190-279 kr

This Italian restaurant in the center of Alta serves stone-oven pizza and pasta dishes with a Norwegian twist; you'll find reindeer ravioli and pasta with pesto and smoked lard on the menu. The interior is rustic and the atmosphere is lively and friendly.

Erica Food & Wine Bar
Amfi Alta; tel. 40 44 74 00; www.ericarestaurant.no; Mon.-Sat. 10am-midnight, Sun. noon-11pm; 185-295 kr

Erica is a cozy café and wine bar. The informal restaurant serves international dishes such as tapas, pizza, and hamburgers. They have an extensive wine menu, and the staff is friendly and helpful. The neat and Nordic interior features wood-paneled walls, black details, and reindeer photos.

Maku
Sorrisniva 20; tel. 78 43 33 78; www.sorrisniva.no; daily 5pm-8pm; 3-course menu 750 kr

From the restaurant at Sorrisniva you can enjoy panoramic views of the Alta River, and a delicious meal based on fresh, local ingredients. Sorrisniva collaborated with the Norwegian National Chef Team to develop their menu, and you can expect a decadent culinary experience. Dishes include tenderloin of reindeer (from Kautokeino), grilled salmon (from Alta), and a chocolate mousse with black currants from the manager's own garden.

ACCOMMODATIONS
Scandic Alta
Løkkeveien 61; tel. 78 48 27 00; www.scandichotels.no/hotell/norge/alta/scandic-alta; 1,200 kr

Scandic Alta is right in the center of the city, within walking distance of the Northern Lights Cathedral and the main shopping street. Here, you will find 241 modern, bright rooms with simple details and comfortable beds. The rooms are decorated with images of the northern lights, and you can expect the same great service found at all Scandic hotels across Norway.

★ Sorrisniva Igloo Hotel
Sorrisniva 20; tel. 78 43 33 78; www.sorrisniva.no; 2,400 kr

Sorrisniva is a hotel that also builds an igloo hotel every winter, in addition to offering some excursions and experiences to visitors. Around November every year, local contractors get to work on the main event at Sorrisniva: The Igloo Hotel. This temporary hotel is made entirely out of ice and snow and is the northernmost igloo hotel in the world. Inside you will find incredibly detailed works of (ice) art, a bar serving (ice) cold drinks, and a chapel made entirely out of ice (yes, it is possible to get married there). In the daytime, the hotel is open and free for all to visit, including the rooms.

If you stay here, there are a few things you need to know first. The rooms are available to guests from 9pm (when they close to the public), and you are advised to avoid too many drinks before bed, to avoid having to get up to use the toilet at night. The temperature in the hotel hovers between -4 and -7°C (24-19°F), so ideally you won't leave your warm bed until morning.

You will pick up two thermal sleeping bags in the Sorrisniva main building before entering the ice hotel at night, and you are advised to bring only what you absolutely need inside. If you bring your phone, keep it inside your sleeping bag, as the cold will drain the battery. In the main building there are lockers and luggage storage for you to use overnight, and the reception there is always manned.

After a truly refreshing night's sleep in the cold hotel, you can treat yourself to the sauna that opens for Igloo Hotel guests at 7am. Following a nice, warm sauna and a shower, breakfast is served in the main building.

★ Aurora Canvas Domes (Glød Explorer)

Jordfallet 3; tel. 99 79 42 56; www.glodexplorer.no/ nb; 3,000 kr

The Aurora Canvas Domes by Glød Explorer are igloo-shaped tent structures with a glass side and ceiling. Each of these small domes has just one room (and a small bathroom), and the large, plush bed is placed right under the glass ceiling and side of the dome, facing the forest of Alta in a way that feels incredibly secluded and private. Inside, the domes are homey, with wool blankets, leather chairs, and a fireplace. Outside of the dome there is plenty of firewood for you to use. There is no running water, except for in the toilet, so shower facilities are in the main building, where there is also a sauna available for guests.

The glass parts of the dome make you feel incredibly close to nature, and the only

The Sorrisniva Igloo Hotel is made entirely of snow.

thing that can top the view of the snowy forest outside is to see the northern lights dancing high above your bed at night. You'll fall asleep to the sound of the forest outside and the fire crackling inside. The whole experience is rustic and charming, while the warm dome and comfortable bed ensure a good night's sleep. There are only a handful of domes available, so book as early as possible.

Sorrisniva Arctic Wilderness Lodge

Sorrisniva 20; tel. 78 43 33 78; www.sorrisniva.no; 3,000 kr

For a warmer, more luxurious stay at Sorrisniva, their Arctic Wilderness Lodge faces the Alta River and offers more traditional accommodation. There are 24 rooms available for guests, all beautifully decorated with a cabin-like, homey feel. The hotel is new, so each room or suite is state-of-the-art, with blackout shades and heated bathroom floors. Room decor is inspired by the salmon fishing in the Alta River, as you'll see in the artworks along the hallways.

INFORMATION AND SERVICES

Alta Tourist Information

Markvegen 38b; https://visitalta.no; Mon.-Fri. 10am-2pm

The staff at the Alta tourist information are more than happy to help you plan your trip and figure out how to get around the area. You can also drop by to pick up some brochures and information about nearby attractions.

Alta Emergency Room

Dr. Kvammes Vei 21; tel. 116117; open 24/7

The Emergency Room in Alta is located in the city center, just a short walk from the shopping mall and Scandic Alta. Call ahead to notify them of your arrival if you can.

GETTING THERE AND AROUND

Alta is located in Finnmark, the northernmost county of Norway, around 381 kilometers (236 mi) from Tromsø. You can reach Alta from Tromsø by bus or car, but flying directly into Alta airport is the best way to get there. Once in Alta, the best and easiest way to get around is by car. Additionally, several of the tour providers (such as Trasti og Trine and Peskatun) are able to pick you up from your hotel if needed.

Bus

Troms Fylkestrafikk (tel. 77 78 87 77; https://fylkestrafikk.no; one daily departure) operates a bus between Alta and Tromsø. Bus route 150 travels daily between the two northern cities, and the journey takes 6.5 hours.

Car

The drive between Tromsø and Alta takes around 6 hours, and it is a scenic journey through the northern landscape. The roads are narrow and prone to sudden weather changes, so make sure to plan for extra time in case of closures and re-routes.

There are several car rental agencies in Alta. Many of them are located at the airport, such as **Alta Bilutleie** (tel. 90 82 48 93; http://altabilutleie.no), **Avis** (tel. 90 74 90 00; www.avis.no), **Budget** (tel. 90 74 90 00; www.budget.no), **Europcar** (tel. 45 46 77 99; www.europcar.no), **Hertz** (tel. 91 13 87 53; www.hertz.no), and **Sixt** (tel. 99 30 01 10; www.sixt.no).

Air

The best way to reach Alta is via a direct flight from Oslo or Tromsø.

Alta Airport

Altagårdskogen 32; tel. 67 03 49 00; https://avinor.no/en/airport/alta-airport

Alta Airport receives flights from Tromsø and Oslo. Widerøe operates direct flights between Tromsø and Alta, and both Norwegian and SAS fly directly between Alta and Oslo. The airport bus, operated by **Snelandia** (tel. 75 77 18 88; www.snelandia.no), takes you to the city center in 10 minutes.

Hammerfest

Hammerfest is surrounded by beautiful beaches, mountains, and a jagged coastline. This small city of 8,000 inhabitants can be found just 140 kilometers (87 mi) north of Alta. Home to the peculiar Polar Bear Society (the city's coat of arms includes a polar bear), this is a nice day trip for anyone with some extra time to spend during their journey north. The small, beautiful city is nestled along a bay and adds a splash of color to the usually white (or green) landscape. And 2.5 hours north of Hammerfest you will find Havøysund, where several exciting boat excursions are offered for visitors.

SIGHTS
Hammerfest Kirke
Kirkegata 29; tel. 78 40 29 20; www.kirken.hammerfest. no; Mon.-Fri. 8am-3pm, Sun. 11am-1pm; free

The church in Hammerfest is an interesting sight, with its triangle shaped, massive tower in white and brick towering above you. The church was designed by Hans Magnus and built in 1961. The church seats 350 people, and from the inside the ceiling looks like an upside-down wooden boat. The large glass mosaic above the altar was created by artist Jardar Lunde, and includes references to the traditional drying gills of stockfish.

Royal and Ancient Polar Bear Society
Hamnegata 3; tel. 78 41 21 85; www.isbjornklubben.no; Mon.-Fri. 10am-2pm; free

In 1963 the Polar Bear Society was founded in Hammerfest, and since then this has become one of the most well-known attractions in the city. At the Polar Bear Society, you'll find an exhibit explaining the local traditions and history of fishing and hunting in arctic conditions. You will learn about the culture of Hammerfest in particular, with a focus on arctic fishing, hunting, and polar expeditions. There is also a small gift shop where you can buy polar bear-themed souvenirs.

The Society has more than 250,000 members globally, and anyone can join by paying a small membership fee (220 kr). The membership and club don't really mean

Hammerfest Kirke

much, other than to prove you visited Hammerfest, as you can only join the society in person. The membership pin and certificate you'll receive make fun and unique souvenirs.

BEACHES

Fuglenesfjæra and Mollafjæra

Route 94

For those wanting to swim in the cold water of Hammerfest, there are the two city beaches of Fuglenesfjæra and Mollafjæra (both along Route 94, just a short walk apart). Being right in the city center, it's just a short walk to the nearest gas station or grocery store to buy some snacks for your beach day. As with most Norwegian beaches, there are no lifeguards or changing facilities. Beware of the water temperature, as even in the summer it doesn't rise above an average of about 9°C (48°F).

Storsanden

Those hiking to Finnvika can stop off at Storsanden, a beautiful white sandy beach with shallow slopes, almost making you believe you were somewhere tropical.

SPORTS AND RECREATION

Hiking

Breidablikkvannet

Distance: 1.3 kilometers (1 mile)
Time: 1 hour round-trip
Difficulty: Easy
Trailhead: Rypefjord Skole, Fjordtun 1, Rypefjord
Information and Maps: https://ut.no/ turforslag/1111512926/breidablikkvannet-rundt

This easy hike follows a trail around the Breidablikkvannet lake in Hammerfest. Head to the Rypefjord area and walk up toward Rypefjord skole (you can also drive straight there and park at the school). There is a clearly marked path around the water, perfect for a Sunday stroll. The scenery is mountainous all around the water, with some small mountains surrounding you as you walk, though the path itself is flat. There is some forest, but mostly moss, around the lake.

Finnvika

Distance: 8 km (5 mi)
Time: 3 hours round-trip, not including ferry crossing
Difficulty: Easy
Trailhead: Akkarfjord Dock
Information and Maps: https://ut.no/ turforslag/1112155416/finnvika

This hike starts in Akkarfjord, which can be reached by boat from Hammerfest. Take SørøysundXpressen, operated by Snelandia (https://snelandia.no), across the water to Akkarfjord. The crossing takes 30 minutes. From there, follow the road to Storsanden and continue along the path until you reach the bay. Keep following the path until it ends or turn around whenever you feel like it. Along the path you will see windswept grass and moss over small mountain plateaus. Finnvika is a relatively easy hike without too much elevation gain, taking you to the beautiful coastal bay of Finnvika.

Boat Trips

Bonaventure

Havøysund Havn; tel. 48 29 51 71; https://bonaventure. no; prices vary

Bonaventure provides several exciting boating adventures from Havøysund, a 2.5-hour drive north of Hammerfest. Whether you are an animal lover or a nature enthusiast, you will find an excursion that suits you. There are bird safari trips and king crab safari trips from June to September, with the latter including a lovely king crab dinner afterwards. For those who want to experience Nordkapp, the northernmost point of Norway, a 7-hour boat adventure will take you there and back, showcasing the beautiful coastline along the way. You can also choose a midnight sun excursion to experience this phenomenon from the ocean.

FOOD

Soma

Sjøgata 8; tel. 94 79 28 40; Mon.-Fri. 10am-6pm, Sat. 10am-4pm; 145-285 kr

SOMA is a charming restaurant in the center of Hammerfest. This informal restaurant is located inside the Nissen Center, making it feel somewhat like a café. Lunch and dinner are served, including pizza with reindeer, a chipotle burger, and chicken fajitas.

Du Verden

Strandgata 32; tel. 45 25 07 00; www.duverden-hammerfest.no; Mon.-Sat. 5pm-10pm; 190-410 kr

On the promenade in the center of Hammerfest you will find Du Verden. This modern and elegant restaurant serves a selection of international and Norwegian dishes with an extra focus on fresh seafood. On the menu you can expect to find grilled stockfish, scampi pasta, and hamburgers.

ACCOMMODATIONS

Scandic Hammerfest

Sørøygata 15; tel. 78 42 57 00; www.scandichotels.no/hotell/norge/hammerfest/scandic-hammerfest; 1,400 kr

Scandic is located in the center of Hammerfest, with rooms facing either the ocean or the city. The 85 rooms at this hotel are modern and simple, with stylish beige and black details, and photos from the surrounding area decorating the walls. The hotel breakfast is, as at all Scandic hotels, great.

Arctic Sea Hotel

Rossmollgata 26; tel. 91 56 80 62; https://arcticseahotel.no; 1,900 kr

At the Arctic Sea Hotel you'll stay in one of the Sea Lodge apartments, all facing the water. These 16 modern apartments were completed in 2020 and each sleep 1 to 5 people. Apartments also come with a fully equipped kitchen, and the wraparound terrace offers great views of the water.

GETTING THERE AND AROUND

Hammerfest is located by the sea, and can be reached by car, bus, boat, and plane. The town is small, so you can get anywhere by walking.

Having a car is helpful if you want to get out of the city to hike or explore.

Bus

Direct buses operate between Hammerfest and Alta (2.5 hours), Honningsvåg (3.5 hours), and Skaidi (1 hour). All are operated by **Snelandia** (https://snelandia.no).

Boat

Hurtigruten (www.hurtigruten.no) stops in Alta on its journey from the south of Norway. From Tromsø you can reach Hammerfest in less than a day.

From Alta, the express boat **VargsundXpressen** (https://snelandia.no) travels to Hammerfest in less than 2 hours, with two daily departures from Alta Hurtigbåtterminal.

Air

Hammerfest Airport

Finnmarksveien 70; https://avinor.no/flyplass/hammerfest

The regional airport of Hammerfest connects the city to Alta, Tromsø, Honningsvåg, and other destinations in Finnmark County. **Widerøe** (www.wideroe.no) operates all flights to and from Hammerfest. The airport is located just north of the city center, less than a 10-minute drive.

Car

The 140-kilometer (87-mi) drive between Alta and Hammerfest will take you a little over 2 hours. Follow main route E6 north, before continuing onto Route 94 toward the coast and the city of Hammerfest.

There are car rentals available in Hammerfest, mainly from **Avis** (tel. 78 40 78 28; www.avis.no), **Europcar** (tel. 78 42 95 49; www.europcar.no), and **Hertz** (tel. 90 06 18 22; www.hertz.no).

Svalbard

Svalbard is an island of contrasts, and the time of year will decide the type of trip you have. This group of islands north of Norway is perhaps best known for polar bears and the Global Seed Vault, but there's more to it. Visitors to Norway with at least 2 weeks to explore the country should consider making a 3-4-day trip to Svalbard, depending on the time of year.

Svalbard is very remote—as far north as you can get in terms of finding civilization. This is also as far north as you can go in Norway, and the only place in the country where polar bears exist. Around 3,000 people live on Svalbard, and almost all of them in Longyearbyen.

There are three main seasons in Svalbard: the dark winter, light winter, and polar summer. The time of year you visit will determine the available activities and the experience you can have on Svalbard. In the dark winter, from October to February, the sun doesn't rise, and the northern lights dance above you in the daytime as well as the nighttime. Come March-May, the sun makes its appearance

and the light winter starts. Now, you can enjoy winter activities during daylight. Then, June-September, you have the polar summer, when the sun never sets. This is the perfect time of year for hiking in Svalbard.

Orientation

You will be spending the entirety of your time on the one island where people live: Spitsbergen. Longyearbyen is located in the center of the island, in the bay of Isfjorden. This is where all hotels and restaurants are located, and the departure point for all tours.

SPORTS AND RECREATION

Northern Lights Chase

Hurtigruten Svalbard

Tel. 79 02 61 00; https://hurtigrutensvalbard.com; Nov.-Mar.; prices vary

From November to March, you have a chance of seeing the northern lights at any time of day in Svalbard. Hurtigruten Svalbard offers two main ways of chasing the northern lights, depending on the activity level you prefer.

walrus near Svalbard

The Svalbard Global Seed Vault

www.regjeringen.no/en/topics/food-fisheries-and-agriculture/svalbard-global-seed-vault
A building that is vital to the global food system is located in Svalbard. In February 2008, the Norwegian government opened the Svalbard Global Seed Vault. This is the world's largest secure seed storage, and seeds from all over the world are sent here for safekeeping. Tens of thousands of seeds are kept here, meaning we have a safe storage of important food groups such as wheat, rice, and beans.

The vault is located inside the mountain Platåfjellet. The only thing visible to the eye is the entrance, and it is not possible to tour the vault. Inside, the vault keeps an area of 1,000 square meters (10,764 sq ft) in constant permafrost (-3-4°C/24-26°F). The vault is built to withstand the test of time, 130 meters (427 ft) into the mountain and 130 meters above sea level. This means that it should be able to survive the effects of climate change and potential natural disasters.

For those wanting a bit of speed, the 3-hour northern lights chase on a snowmobile will give you a mix of adrenaline and relaxation, as you drive on your own snowmobile. If you don't want to drive yourself, choose a northern lights excursion in a beltevogn, a tracked vehicle with space for the entire family to sit and relax. This tour is suitable for anyone, and does not require any physical activity.

★ Wildlife-Watching

Wildlife-watching in Svalbard mainly focuses on arctic animals, such as whales and walrus. There are 12 species of whales that frequent the waters around the island, including the narwhal and the beluga whale. In addition, you are likely to see several species of seal, such as the bearded seal and the harbor seal.

You might expect to find polar bears on the list of animals to see in Svalbard. However, it is actually illegal to seek out polar bears. In addition to being endangered, the polar bear is extremely dangerous to humans, so this law protects both. If you do end up seeing one on a tour (it is possible, just not the purpose of the tour), listen to your guides and get your camera out if you can.

Walrus Safari

Tel. 79 02 61 00; https://hurtigrutensvalbard.com; May-Sept.; 2,490 kr
The walrus safari takes you across Isfjorden in a hybrid boat. Thanks to the hybrid engine

you can approach the area where the walruses often rest and relax without making a sound. This increases your chances of seeing them. The walrus became a protected species in Svalbard in 1952, when there were just a few hundred of them left. As a result, the walrus population on the island has grown significantly, and they are now quite a common sight in some of the fjord areas.

Polar Charter Whale-Watching

Tel. 48 05 57 00; www.polarcharter.no; Nov.-Feb.; 1,400 kr
From November to February there is a chance of seeing several species of whales in Svalbard. Isfjorden has become a frequent feeding spot for belugas, humpback whales, fin whales, and even blue whales. The captain and guides on board are experienced in looking for whales and will take you to different spots where the odds are high of seeing them. Of course, there is no guarantee, but the chase is half the fun.

Hiking

Hiking in Svalbard is best experienced with a guide, as not only can they provide a lot of extra insight about the environment and areas you see, but also they know where it is safe to explore. Due to the risk of meeting polar bears, do not go off alone to areas you are not familiar with. The main season for hiking in Svalbard is May-September.

Spitzbergen Adventures

Tel. 45 88 63 83; www.spitzbergen-adventures.com

This tour company offers a hike that is suitable for most people: **Bjørndalen** (1,450 kr), which translates to "the bear valley," and the hike goes mainly through the valley. The whole excursion lasts 6 hours and includes a barbecue at the end.

Poli Arctici

Tel. 48 28 03 67; www.poliarctici.com

For those who are after a more strenuous hike, the guided hike from Poli Arctici to **Nordenskiöldtoppen** (1,390 kr) might be for you. This is a challenging hike and a local favorite, lasting 8 hours total. This hike takes you to the top of the highest mountain near Longyearbyen (1,051 m/3,440 ft above sea level), where you'll enjoy great views of the island and ocean beyond on a clear day.

Kayaking and Canoeing
Svalbard Kayak

Tel. 99 33 95 41; www.svalbardkayak.no; 500 kr per day

Svalbard Kayak offers both kayaks for rent and guided tours. In addition to the rental price, you can pay an additional 500 kr per day to rent all the equipment needed for a dry and warm kayak trip. Alternatively, those who really want to dive into kayaking can opt for a 3-day trip in the Ekman fjord. The Ekman fjord is an 18-kilometer (11-mi) long fjord arm of the Nordfjord (which, in turn, is an arm of Isfjorden), across the bay from Longyearbyen.

Dog Sledding
Svalbard Villmarkssenter

Tel. 79 02 17 00; www.svalbardvillmarkssenter.no; 990-2,490 kr

Svalbard Villmarkssenter has lots of friendly dogs waiting to greet you and take you out on an adventure. Several dog sledding tours are offered year-round (on wheels in the summer). If you just want a taste of sledding, the 3-hour tour is ideal (990 kr). If you want to spend some more time behind the "wheel," book a full-day expedition (5 hours; 2,190 kr) or an overnight trip (2,490 kr).

Arctic Husky Travellers

Tel. 99 29 39 43; https://huskytravellers.com; 1,750-2,990 kr

Arctic Husky Travellers and their 45 huskies offer several tour options for those who want to try dog sledding in Svalbard. In the summer, most of their tours happen on wheels. Their 3-hour daytime excursion during the polar night (1,750 kr) includes 1.5 hours on the sled and makes an ideal introduction to dog sledding. If you want a longer experience, opt for the 7-hour Explore the Arctic experience (2,990 kr), which will let you spend 5.5 hours on the sled as you explore Svalbard.

ENTERTAINMENT AND EVENTS
Arctic Chamber Music Festival

https://acmf.no; Feb.

Head to the 4-day Arctic Chamber Music Festival, when classical musicians from all over the world come to Svalbard. This is the world's northernmost festival of classical music. Previous performers have included the Arctic Philharmonic (who are the hosts), Espen Langvik (baritone vocalist), and Truls Mørk (cello).

Dark Season Blues

www.svalbardblues.com; Oct.

The Dark Season Blues festival takes place during the darkest season in Svalbard. Every October, the world's northernmost blues festival celebrates the long nights with performances by Norwegian and Scandinavian acts such as Bergen Blues Band, Bjørn Berge, and Dalegaarden Blues Company.

FOOD
Restaurant Nansen

Vei 229-3; tel. 79 02 34 50; https://hurtigrutensvalbard.com/en/restaurants/restaurant-nansen; daily 6pm-10pm; 295-340 kr

At Restaurant Nansen you can enjoy their take on New Nordic right in the center of Longyearbyen. The interior is upscale, yet the atmosphere is informal and relaxed. In fact, they say that the dress code is "snowmobile gear," so you'll be welcome after a long day of excursions. On the menu you will find dishes such as reindeer tenderloin and arctic char.

Restaurant Polfareren

Vei 223-2; tel. 79 02 50 00; https://svalbardadventures.com/en/food-and-drinks/restaurant-polfareren; daily 6pm-11pm; 225-375 kr

This Nordic cuisine restaurant offers a new selection of dishes each month, all based on the fresh ingredients available to the chef. Located inside the Svalbard Hotel Polfareren, the interior is cozy and the atmosphere warm and welcoming. On the menu you may find dishes such as king crab with tahini mayonnaise and salmon with Okinawan sweet potato puree.

ACCOMMODATIONS

Mary-Ann's Polarrigg

Longyearbyen; tel. 94 00 77 80; www.polarriggen.com; 2,100 kr

This charming hotel has 39 unique and practical rooms, each of them simple, yet warm and cozy. The three buildings of the hotel were originally built to house mine workers on Svalbard, but the property was turned into a hotel by Mary-Ann Dahle in 1999. Dahle passed away in 2020, but her spirit lives on in this quaint hotel. Throughout the hotel you will find artifacts from the old coal mines on Svalbard.

Svalbard Hotel The Vault

Vei 507-1; tel. 79 02 50 04; https://svalbardadventures.com/en/accommodation/the-vault; 2,700 kr

The Vault is a boutique hotel with 35 rooms. This new and modern hotel focuses on functionality and simplicity, inspired by the Svalbard Global Seed Vault. The rooms are minimalistic and comfortable, with a gray color scheme and mustard details.

Radisson Blu Polar

Vei 229-3; tel. 79 02 34 50; www.radissonhotels.com/no-no/hoteller/radisson-blu-spitsbergen-polar; 2,800 kr

The Radisson in Longyearbyen has 128 modern and cozy rooms, all decorated in a stylish and Nordic way, with muted gray and beige details. Rooms are comfortable, and most of all, warm.

INFORMATION AND SERVICES

Svalbard Tourist Information

Vei 221-1; www.visitsvalbard.com; Mon.-Fri. 10am-4pm, Sat.-Sun. midnight-4pm

At the Svalbard Tourist Information in Longyearbyen you can get help with planning your adventures on the island, book your excursions, and pick up brochures about the various offerings nearby. In the summer months you can also rent bicycles.

Longyearbyen Hospital

Vei 227-3; tel. 79 02 42 00

The hospital in Longyearbyen is the main provider of healthcare and emergency care for the island of Svalbard. Ambulances are dispatched from here. As in the rest of Norway, call 113 for emergencies.

Longyearbyen Post Office

Vei 227-2; Mon.-Fri. 10am-5pm

For stamps and shipments, the post office in Longyearbyen is open 5 days a week. The post box outside of the post office is open 7 days a week from 7am to 9pm for those who just need to drop off letters and postcards.

Internet and Cell Service

Svalbard is connected to the mainland by two undersea optical fiber cables, providing the island with strong Wi-Fi. Wi-Fi is readily available and free of charge in all hotels and most restaurants and cafés (unless they have elected to force their customers to speak to each other instead).

The cell service around Svalbard is surprisingly good, considering how remote it is. There is 4G signal in all inhabited and frequently visited areas, such as Longyearbyen and the airport, as well as in some of the mines on the island. You may find that you occasionally lose signal on some excursions that take you far away from the city, but generally the entirety of the Isfjorden bay has strong signal. 5G is available in Longyearbyen as well.

GETTING THERE

There is only one way to get to Svalbard: by plane.

Svalbard Airport

Longyearbyen; tel. 67 03 54 00; https://avinor.no/en/ airport/svalbard-airport

Svalbard Airport is located just a little more than 5 kilometers (3 mi) from Longyearbyen. The airport is serviced by daily departures to and from Tromsø and Oslo 6 days a week. The direct flight time from Tromsø is 1 hour and 40 minutes, while a flight from Oslo is 3 hours direct. The airport bus (www.svalbardbuss. no/gallery; departure 30-40 minutes after each arrived flight; 100 kr) takes you from the airport to Longyearbyen, stopping by several of the main hotels in the city. Departures to the airport are also timed for each flight. Check your hotel reception for the updated schedule.

GETTING AROUND

When it comes to getting around, you'll be surprised to find that there are only 40 kilometers (25 mi) of road on the island, so traveling between the settlements is usually done by boat or snowmobile. However, the airport, hotels, restaurants, and excursion departures are all in Longyearbyen. Longyearbyen, your best home base on Svalbard, is quite a walkable city, except that the two main parts of town, downtown and NyByen, are 2.5 kilometers (1.5 mi) apart. **Longyearbyen Taxi** (tel. 79 02 13 75) and **Svalbard Buss og Taxi** (tel. 79 02 10 52; www.svalbardbuss.no) can help you travel between these two neighborhoods.

Background

The Landscape

From the famous fjords in the west to the peaceful archipelago in the south, and all the way up to the arctic tundra of the north, Norway's landscape will take your breath away. Thousands of years ago, glaciers carved all these varied fjords, inlets, islands, and valleys and created the dramatic mountain peaks you see today.

GEOGRAPHY

Mainland Norway is a long, surprisingly large body of land, stretching 1,748 kilometers (1,086 mi) from 58 degrees longitude north to 71

degrees (81 if you include Svalbard). To put this into context, the northernmost city of Alaska (Barrow) also sits at 71 degrees, while the southernmost latitude of Norway can be equated to the northern parts of Manitoba, Saskatchewan, Alberta, and British Columbia in Canada. The widest part of the country is 432 kilometers (268 mi), but the narrowest is just 1.6 km (1 mi). It is at its widest from the Sognefjord straight across to the east, and the narrowest point is measured in the north, between Bøkfjord and the Russian border. It is said that if you flip Norway around, with the southernmost point staying in the same place, you can reach Rome; this gives you an idea of the country's size.

Less than 2 percent of the country is inhabited, and this will become clear when you travel here. Almost 40 percent of the country is forested, and up to 45 percent of the land is found above the tree line (at around 1,000 m). So, the natural beauty of Norway truly is largely untouched.

Fjords

Thousands of years ago, glaciers carved their way into the mountains, creating large valleys and cuts in the land. The glaciers continued to dig until these valleys reached far below sea level. Eventually, as the glaciers melted and retreated, ocean water started to fill the valleys, and the fjords were complete. One rule of thumb is that a fjord is longer than it is wide (as opposed to a bay or sound, which might also have been carved by a glacier, but is wider than it is long).

Visually, the fjords look like long lakes (where you don't see the end), with either steep cliff-like mountains, or tall, rolling hills surrounding them. The popular Sognefjord and the Geirangerfjord both have steep, massive mountains towering over them on either side.

There are more than 1,700 fjords in Norway, stretching all along the Norwegian coastline.

Mountains

Through the middle of the country, you will find long mountain ranges that almost always must be crossed in order to travel from east to west; Hallingskarvet is the mountain range you are most likely to cross when traveling between Oslo and Bergen. The mountainous terrain of Norway covers almost 60 percent of the country. However, don't worry that you'll suffer from elevation sickness when you visit; most towns and villages in the country are found at sea level, and the mountains of Norway are not actually that tall. The tallest mountains of Norway, Galdhøpiggen and Glittertind (both found in the Jotunheimen mountain range), are 2,469 and 2,452 meters high (8,100 and 8,044 ft), respectively.

Glaciers

Norway is home to many large glaciers, both on Svalbard and on the mainland, though they are shrinking as the climate warms. The glaciers are easily recognizable from the air, as large white patches of snow and ice covering the terrain. From the ground, you can usually spot some of the glacial "tongues" peeking down the valleys from the top of the mountain. The largest glaciers in Norway are Jostedalsbreen, Svartisen (located in northern Norway, in the narrow strip between Trondheim and Tromsø), and Folgefonna.

CLIMATE

The Norwegian coast, especially in the south and west of the country, benefits from the warming heat of the Gulf Stream. This means that the temperature around the entire southern coastline of Norway stays surprisingly mild in the winter, and gets nice and hot in the summer. Farther inland (and north, of course), it gets much colder in the winter, with the mean temperature in Røros in February being -10.4°C (13.3°F).

The temperature and weather trends across the country vary a lot; though as a rule it is

---

colder in the north than in the south, you will also find regional differences within these areas. Norway is such a large country that you will need to check the temperature and climate for each destination on your itinerary, not the country as a whole.

- Oslo—summer average: 16.4°C (61.5°F); winter average: -4.3°C (24°F). Rainiest month: August

- Kristiansand—summer average: 16°C (61°F), winter average: 1°C (34°F). Rainiest month: October

- Stavanger—summer average: 15°C (59°F); winter average: 2°C (35.6°F). Rainiest month: October

- Bergen—summer average: 17°C (62.6°F); winter average: 2°C (35.6°F). Rainiest month: December

- Flåm—summer average: 16 degrees, winter average: -2 degrees. Rainiest month: November

- Geiranger—summer average: 16°C (61°F); winter average: 1°C (34°F). Rainiest month: December

- Tromsø—summer average: 12°C (53.6°F); winter average: -3°C (26.6°F). Rainiest month: October

In the winter months it can snow anywhere in Norway, with the risk increasing the farther north you go. Traveling to northern Norway during December-February will guarantee you a winter wonderland-like backdrop.

Destinations away from the coast also have a higher chance of snow in the colder months. Coastal cities such as Bergen and Stavanger also get snow, but it is rare that it sticks, because the winter temperature rarely drops below freezing. In December-January, winter storms along the coast are not uncommon and can lead to closed mountain passes and sometimes damage to property.

ENVIRONMENTAL ISSUES

The biggest debate in recent years has concerned oil and drilling in the arctic. Oil has been a major source of Norwegian wealth, and those in favor of looking for more of it in the arctic argue that Norway has a more sustainable production process than other oil nations. However, environmentalists point to the arctic being an important ecosystem for many endangered species.

Another debate that has been going on for a while regards cruise ships. Cruise tourism has seen a large increase in Norway over recent years, and small villages such as Flåm and Geiranger are packed with thousands of cruise travelers on most days during the summer. In addition to the "people pollution" on those days, emissions from cruise ships negatively impact the natural fjord landscape. Norway is currently working to lower (and eventually eliminate) emissions from cruise ships in and around the World Heritage fjords.

Plants and Animals

TREES AND PLANTS

All across Norway you will find thick forests of birch trees. Birch wood is used for firewood, and also as timber for construction. Spruce, pine, and oak are also common around the country, and forests of these trees cover large areas. In the woodland and mountainous areas you will find arctic plants and berries, such as lingonberry, cloudberry, and

arctic cranberry. Norway is not particularly known for its flowers, but some arctic plants are worth noticing when spring comes along, such as the arctic poppy, snow buttercup, and sedum (stonecrop).

Norway doesn't have a distinct fall foliage season, as the temperature drops quickly. This means that there is only a short period when the leaves are bright and colorful on the trees

Norway's UNESCO World Heritage Sites

In 1979, the first areas of Norway were added to the UNESCO World Heritage List, both on the basis of cultural importance. These were the Bryggen area in Bergen, and Urnes Stave Church (one of just 28 remaining in Norway). Since then, more listings have been added, and today, Norway has eight places on the World Heritage List of Cultural and Natural Significance. All of these are considered to be of cultural importance; the West Norwegian Fjords is the only place in Norway that is listed because of its natural importance. These are Norway's eight UNESCO sites.

- Bryggen in Bergen (1979), page 146

- Urnes Stave Church (1979), located a 1-hour and 45-minute drive (50 km/31 mi) from Lærdal

- Røros Mining Town (1980), page 271, and the Circumference (2010)

- The Rock Art of Alta (1985), page 324

- The Vega Archipelago (2004), located along Norway's central coast

- The Struve Geodetic Arc (2005), a scientific entry on the UNESCO World Heritage List, is a chain of survey triangulations stretching from Hammerfest through 10 different countries to the Black Sea

- The West Norwegian Fjords—Nærøyfjord and Geirangerfjord (2005), pages 203 and 237

- Rjukan-Notodden Industrial Heritage Site (2015), located in Rjukan, a 3-hour drive (178 km/110 mi) from Oslo

before they fall off. But generally, during the end of September and early October, you have a good chance of seeing the beautiful orange and yellow birch leaves.

BIRDS
Puffins and Other Seabirds

Puffins are perhaps the most well-known of the seabirds that nest in Norway, with the islands of Runde (near Ålesund) and Røst (in Lofoten) being famous as prime puffin-watching territory. In addition to the puffins, seabirds such as gannets, guillemots, and kittiwakes nest on these islands and along Norway's rugged coastline. The nesting season is from February to September, and during this time hiking and traveling around Runde and Røst are limited to protect the birds.

Birds of Prey

The sea eagle (also known as the white-tailed eagle) is the largest bird of prey in Europe,

with a potential wingspan of over 2 meters (6.5 ft). They nest all along the Norwegian coastline, and can even be found hunting in the fjords, miles and miles from the coast. Hawks, snowy owls, and golden eagles are also found around the country.

MAMMALS
Polar Bears

Perhaps the most famous of the Norwegian mammals, the polar bear is not as common around the country as you think. It is only found in Svalbard, and in very limited numbers. Polar bears are an actual danger to those living in and visiting Svalbard, and it is illegal to try and seek them out. Tour operators are heavily fined for trying to find polar bears for their groups to gawk at, and it is necessary to carry a firearm in some of the more rural areas. The average size of a polar bear when standing on its hind legs is 1.8-2.4 m (6-8 ft). An adult male polar bear weighs 350-700 kilograms (770-1,540 lbs).

Musk Oxen

The musk ox lives mainly across Dovre National Park. This type of ox is large and odd-looking, resembling a very small mammoth. They originally hail from Alaska, Canada, and Greenland, and came to Norway around 100 years ago. Their average weight is 180-410 kilograms (397-904 lbs) and their height is 1.1-1.5 meters (3.5-5 ft). They mainly live in Dovrefjell-Sunndasfjella National Park (https://dovrefjell-sunndalsfjella.no), which can help arrange guided safaris. The park staff have developed a code of conduct for those wanting to see musk oxen, stating that visitors must always keep 200 meters (656 ft) away, and not make any unexpected movements.

Moose

The massive Norwegian moose is an impressive sight and can be spotted in the forested regions all over the country. A typical souvenir to bring home is a fridge magnet of a moose danger road sign, like the ones that can be seen on highways all across the country. The warning signs are necessary because these are very large animals that can kill a driver if hit at a high speed. A moose can weigh up to 635 kilograms (1,400 lbs) and is usually almost 2 meters (6 ft) tall. Therefore, it is important to stay vigilant.

Reindeer

Herds of reindeer are easily spotted when crossing the mountains in southern Norway. Reindeer are still herded by the Sami, but in the south, they roam with little to no human contact. In the central and western areas, reindeer hunting is a popular activity. Reindeer are usually found in the mountain ranges, so when driving across mountainous regions, you may encounter them. Look out for reindeer danger signs and be extra vigilant when driving in those areas. A large reindeer can weigh up to 250 kilograms (550 lbs).

SEALIFE
Whales

Off the coast of Svalbard and northern Norway, whale-watching is popular during the winter months, when these massive creatures can be spotted. Fin whales, humpback whales, white whales, and even blue whales can all be seen off the coast of Norway. Orcas (killer whales) have in recent years made their way into the fjords in the wintertime, killing and chasing away some of the local wildlife (mainly porpoises and harbor seals).

Otters

Otters are found all over Norway, but mostly along the central and north coast. These small creatures are often seen playing in rocky coastal areas.

Salmon

Norwegian salmon is one of the world's favorite types of fish to eat, and it has been exported from Norway for decades, primarily to the EU. Most of it is farmed, and salmon fishing is mostly considered a sport these days, popularized by wealthy Englishmen and the king of Norway.

History

EARLY HISTORY

Rock art shows that people living in Norway between 4000 and 1800 BC were primarily hunter-gatherers, moving around and following the food and weather. From about 1800 BC to around year AD 500, permanent dwellings and farms started to take shape, and it is believed that the Roman Empire was a cultural influence on the country during the first century. Norwegians developed an alphabet, and the earliest runes (an old alphabet) that have been found in Norway date back to the year AD 200.

THE VIKING AGE

It is commonly thought that the Viking Age officially began with the attack on Lindisfarne in the UK, in AD 793, and most people will say that it lasted until 1066, when the Norwegian king (Harald Hardråde) died in the Battle of Stamford Bridge in England. The battle marked the end of the Viking invasions on England. Vikings are well-known all around the world, and this is probably the most famous period in Scandinavia.

One thing worth noting is that "Viking" isn't the name of a society; it was more like a profession at the time. Thus, not everyone who lived in Norway during the Viking Age were Vikings. People living during the Viking Age were mainly farmers, and even though only a few of them would have been referred to as Vikings at the time, today the term is commonly used regarding whole communities of people who lived during the Viking Age. People lived across Scandinavia, mainly along the coast, and spoke a language called Old Norse. Old Norse eventually developed into the modern languages spoken across the Nordics today, such as Norwegian, Icelandic, Danish, and Swedish.

The Viking Age resulted in a considerable amount of expansion into regions beyond Scandinavia, as the Vikings would travel from Norway to areas such as England, Scotland, Iceland, and even France, to gain riches and capture people to be enslaved. Viking settlements have also been found in North America, such as the L'Anse Aux Meadows in Newfoundland, Canada. The most famous Vikings were those who ventured out and made a name for themselves abroad, such as Rollo (who was the first ruler of Normandy), Leif Eriksson (who encountered the Americas 500 years before Christopher Columbus), and Erik the Red (who founded the first Norse settlement on Greenland).

Vikings are commonly portrayed as bloodthirsty men with animal horns on their helmets, but this is inaccurate. Vikings were not necessarily motivated by blood spill and torture, but more likely by material gains. Also, Vikings weren't all men; women could own property and fight in wars alongside men at the time. Last but not least, Vikings didn't actually wear helmets with animal horns on them.

MIDDLE AGES

Norway moved into the Middle Ages as a Christian farming country, with the church and crown claiming a large amount of tax from landowners and (subsequent) farmers. In the 1300s, a seat of the Hanseatic League—a commercial alliance of cities, towns, and merchants across Europe—was established in Bergen, increasing the development and riches of the city, and (in turn) of the country as a whole. The important trade with European merchants allowed settlements to thrive even in northern Norway, a region that was traditionally challenging for merchant vessels from central Europe to reach (due to cold, ice, and harsh weather). In 1349, a ship arriving in Bergen brought the bubonic plague to Norway, and one third of the population were killed within a year.

Historical Timeline

9500 BC	The oldest confirmed traces of human life in Norway.
9000-8000 BC	A "new" glacier covers most of the land.
4200-3600 BC	The rock carvings in Alta (UNESCO-listed) date back to this period.
500 BC	The oldest findings of Sami settlements.
600-800	Pre-Viking Age. The Viking ship is developed.
793	Vikings invade the English island of Lindisfarne, and the Viking Age begins.
872	Harald Hårfagre (Fairhair) becomes the first king of Norway.
995	Olav Tryggvason becomes king, and founds the first Christian church in Norway.
1015	Olav Haraldsson (later Saint Olav) becomes king. He later unifies Norway in the Christian faith and bans belief in the Norse gods.
1066	The Middle Ages start.
1349	The bubonic plague (Black Death) arrives in Bergen by ship and kills a third of the Norwegian population.
1380	Norway enters into a union with Denmark, which will last until 1814.

DENMARK-NORWAY AND UNION WITH SWEDEN

In 1380, Norway entered into a union with Denmark, as a result of Olav Haakonsson inheriting both thrones. His father was King Håkon Magnusson of Norway, and his mother Queen Margrete Valdemarsdotter of Denmark. Norway was practically a Danish county for hundreds of years, and this was further strengthened in 1536 when the Norwegian national council disbanded. During this time, the Protestant Reformation also made its way to Norway, and Catholicism had to give way to the Lutheran branch of Protestantism in Denmark and Norway. During this time, Bergen was the largest city in Norway, and in the 1800s it was the largest wooden city in Europe. Oslo was named Christiania (after the Danish king Christian the 4th).

In 1814 Norway peacefully left the union with Denmark and signed its own constitution on the 17th of May. This date is still celebrated across the country each year. Still, Norway left one Scandinavian country and entered into a union with another: Sweden. This union lasted until 1905, and while Norway remained under the rule of the same king, this was a period of growth, with many important buildings being raised in Christiania during the 1800s (such as the Royal Palace, the University of Oslo, and the Norwegian parliament Stortinget). During this period of Norway's union with Sweden, more than 750,000 Norwegians emigrated to the US, around half the population! This was

345

1536-1537	The reformation. Norway-Denmark's religion changes from Catholicism to Lutheranism.
1814	Norway's constitution is signed on the 17th of May. Norway enters into a union with Sweden.
1905	Norway leaves the union with Sweden, and King Håkon VII is crowned.
1940	Norway is under German occupation for 5 years.
1969	The first bit of oil is found on Norwegian territory, catapulting Norway toward the wealth it has today.
1990	The Norwegian Sovereign Wealth Fund ("the oil fund") is established and becomes one of the best managed Sovereign Wealth Funds in the world.
1994	Norway hosts the Winter Olympics in Lillehammer. In the same year, the majority of the country votes "No" to joining the EU in a referendum.
2001	Norway joins the Schengen area, making travel between many European countries passport-free.
2011	The far-right terror attack on Utøya and Oslo, killing 77 people, shakes the Norwegian population.

because Norway was generally a poor farming country, while in America everyone who emigrated from Europe were given land to farm. Numbers especially increased after the American Civil War ended.

INDEPENDENCE

In 1905, Norway left the union with Sweden on friendly terms, and crowned its first independent king, Håkon the 7th. In the years to come, Norway stayed neutral during the World War I (although Norwegian ships assisted on the British side of the war, and 2,000 Norwegian sailors were killed during the war years). On April 9, 1940, German troops marched into Norway and began an occupation that would last until the end of the war. During the Nazi occupation of Norway, Norwegians' freedoms were curtailed; they were given a curfew, and a ban on radios and strict food rations were in place.

There was some resistance by the Norwegian population. The country's military built an underground army, ready to pounce at the first sign of liberation. In the final year of the war, they also actively sabotaged the Nazis. In daily life, civilians showed resistance through protests, hiding and listening to radios, and doing their best to keep people's spirits raised.

After the war, Norway was one of the founding members of NATO (the North Atlantic Treaty Organization), a defense alliance consisting of 30 European and North American countries, including the US and UK. Hosting the 1952 Winter Olympics in

Vikings in Popular Culture

If you want to immerse yourself in the world of the Vikings, don't miss these three popular screen adaptations.

- *Vikings* **(2013-2020):** The story of Ragnar Lothbrok and his family, portrayed through the early years of the Viking Age, offers semi-historically accurate entertainment.

- *The Northman* **(2022):** This movie stars Swede Alexander Skarsgård as a Viking prince set on avenging his father's murder.

- *The Last Kingdom* **(2015-2022):** Put yourself in the shoes of the English in this story about English-born Uhtred, who was raised in Denmark.

Oslo gave the country an economic boost, and farming and fishing became increasingly automated during the time after the war.

MODERN TIMES AND THE OIL ERA

In the late 1960s, oil was discovered in the Ekofisk area outside the Norwegian mainland, and the Norwegian "oil fairy tale" officially began. Several companies were founded as a result, in order to meet the demand of the growing oil industry, and this also created a large number of new jobs. Working in oil remains lucrative in Norway today. The oil fund (the Norwegian Sovereign Wealth Fund) was established in 1990 and is considered the world's best managed Sovereign Wealth Fund. The fund is mainly left alone, to grow and work as a safety net for generations to come. When it is used, it is to run the welfare state of Norway, funding any gaps that are not covered by taxes.

Government and Economy

POLITICS

Norway is a constitutional monarchy. The current king of Norway is Harald V, with Crown Prince Haakon being next in line. The monarch is mostly a figurehead, and all political power lies within the Parliament (Stortinget) and prime minister. Elections are held every 4 years. The current prime minister of Norway is Jonas Gahr Støre (elected in 2021). Election turnout is relatively high in Norway, and Norwegians have a high level of trust in their government. This is one of the reasons the country made it through the COVID-19 pandemic with very little conflict; people listened to the government and believed that government decisions were the correct and best decision for all.

There are many political parties in Norway, and each party sends a number of representatives to Parliament equivalent to the party's percentage of the vote (with some exceptions for extremely small parties). In theory, if a party gets 22 percent of the votes in a national election, that party is given 22 percent of the representatives in Stortinget. The high number of political parties usually result in a coalition government.

Power tends to shift back and forth between the liberal and "conservative" coalitions, but in general, both sides can be considered quite liberal; Norwegian conservatives are practically left-wing when compared to the British Conservative Party and the American Republican Party. For example, even the most right-wing parties in Norway do not oppose abortions or same-sex marriage (which have been legal in Norway since 1978 and 2009, respectively). The right-wing parties in Norway do not oppose the welfare state but they do have a different view from the left wing as to how taxation and fees should work.

AGRICULTURE

Only 3 percent of Norway's land mass is farmed land, and so agriculture is a heavily subsidized industry. Most farms and farmed land is found along the coast, fjords (even though you wouldn't first think it was possible to farm the land along the steep mountains), and in the flat, central areas. Most farms in Norway are small, and many farmers do not farm full time (in fact, only one third of farmers are able to make a living from it). Most farmers have animals (with cows being the most common), while around 30 percent of Norwegian farms are primarily plant farms (wheat, vegetables, and potatoes).

INDUSTRY

Norwegian industry is heavily focused on raw material, with the oil industry being a major business. The farming and export of fish are not only important for the country, but also globally leading, especially with regards to salmon, which yields an annual profit of over 80 billion kr. Norway is one of the top three countries worldwide when it comes to seafood export. Other industries in Norway include hydro energy and natural gas, with the former supplying most of the country's power.

TOURISM

Tourism is an up-and-coming income source for the Norwegian economy, with many towns and cities relying heavily on tourists during the high season in order to live there during the low season. The travel industry contributes about 4 percent of Norway's gross domestic income and provides jobs for around 150,000 people. The industry is especially important in rural Norway, where villages and towns are struggling with declining populations. Year-round jobs as a result of the travel industry has helped prevent many rural villages from being abandoned in the long term.

INCOME EQUALITY

Generally speaking, Norway is a country with a fairly equitable distribution of income, with the average monthly salary being around 49,000 kr (around 588,000 kr yearly), and the mean being around 44,000 kr (528,000 kr yearly). About 42 percent of the population earn between 300,000 and 600,000 kr per year; 25 percent earn more than this, and 32 percent earn less.

Due to the state of the welfare system, which provides the Norwegian population with free healthcare, education, and other benefits, income disparity is never as pronounced as it is elsewhere. It is only when people reach an extreme level of wealth or poverty that differences become noticeable. Luckily, the system is set up to take care of those who are unable to make a living wage.

People and Culture

DEMOGRAPHY AND DIVERSITY

Norway has a population of 5.4 million. Norwegians consist primarily of people of north Germanic descent, and ethnic Norwegians are closely related to the Danes and Swedes. Immigrants make up 19 percent of the Norwegian population, and you'll find that Norway is at its most diverse in Oslo, where many economic refugees have settled (24 percent of Oslo's population are immigrants). Norway's immigrant population mainly comes from Poland, Lithuania, Sweden, Somalia, and Germany.

Most of the country's population is spread around the southern coast, especially the southeast area around Oslo. There are many cities and large towns surrounding Oslo, with the majority of Norway's 12 largest towns surrounding the Oslofjord, such as Drammen, Skien, Tønsberg, and Sandefjord.

INDIGENOUS PEOPLE

The Indigenous Sami people settled across Scandinavia around 8,000 years ago, and live in Norway, Sweden, Finland, and Russia. Sápmi is the name of their land, which crosses the northern borders of these four countries. Amongst the 11 Sami languages, five of them are spoken in Norway, with North Sami being the largest. The language is of Uralic descent and has no connection with Norwegian. Historically, the Sami people were nomadic reindeer herders, and would follow the reindeer throughout the year and settle temporarily near the herds. Reindeer were their main source of support, providing them with meat, clothing, and transportation. Today, only a few thousand still herd reindeer, and most of the Sami that have settled in Norway live in the cities.

RELIGION

The Church of Norway is a Lutheran church and has been since the Reformation started in 1537. In 2012 Norway started the process of separating the state and church, and Norway today has no formal state religion. A little less than 70 percent of Norwegians are registered members of the Norwegian Church, with many of them being non-practicing Christians. Fewer than 200,000 Norwegians are registered members of the Islamic faith, and most mosques in Norway are found in and around Oslo.

LANGUAGE

The Scandinavian languages are north Germanic languages that are closely related and very similar to each other. Norwegians, Danes, and Swedes can all understand each other to some extent and can usually read each other's languages. In northern Norway, Sami is commonly spoken, and you will find that street signs and names are listed in both languages.

Understanding English is very common in Norway, and most Norwegians you encounter will be able to understand and hold a conversation in English. As a general rule, the younger the person you speak to, the better their English will be, with Millenials and Gen Z being practically fluent in English from a young age.

Written Languages

There are two official written Norwegian languages: Nynorsk and Bokmål. Bokmål derives from Danish and came about during the union with Denmark. Nynorsk was created as a collection of Norwegian words used in rural Norway, where Danish rule wasn't as prominent. Therefore, Nynorsk is seen as the more traditional language, and is used mostly in rural areas (especially along the western Norwegian fjords). Over 85 percent of the population writes Bokmål, and even though both written languages are taught in schools, Nynorsk is slowly dying. The main way these written languages differ is that they use different spellings. For example, Norway is spelled "Norge" in Bokmål and "Noreg" in Nynorsk.

Dialects

The spoken Norwegian language is complex and difficult to learn due to its many dialects. There are hundreds of dialects in Norway, and no one knows the exact number. There is no "official" spoken dialect, as opposed to the two official written languages. Dialects differ across Norway, not only in pronunciation but also in how words are spoken. The dialect spoken in and around Oslo (Østlandsk) is the most commonly taught in language schools and is closest to the written Bokmål.

Once you travel out to the towns and villages of rural Norway, you'll find that people speak differently from each other. From one town to the next, even if they are just a 30-minute drive apart, words can be completely different and have large variations in pronunciation. This is because many of the towns along the fjords were completely isolated from each other until as recently as 30

Greeting a Norwegian

Norwegians are friendly enough, but don't expect to be blown away by their hospitality when meeting them on the street. In fact, a Norwegian will go out of his way to avoid sitting next to you on the bus or making eye contact with you while waiting in line. Perhaps it's the years of fighting the cold, bitter climate and the long, dark winters, but regardless, Norwegians may come across as quite rude toward strangers on the street—especially in the cities (though in smaller villages you may notice people greeting their neighbors).

There is one exception to this rule though, and it is an important one. Norwegians will always greet each other when they are out hiking or skiing. You won't meet a friendlier Norwegian than the one you meet in the mountains or forests of Norway, and you'll be surprised to find that they may even stop to ask how your hike is going so far, or offer you helpful directions.

years ago, before roads and tunnels connected them.

LITERATURE

Norway's claim to literary fame is Henrik Ibsen (1828-1906), who is considered one of the world's greatest playwrights after William Shakespeare. His critically acclaimed works *Hedda Gabler, Peer Gynt,* and *A Doll's House* are still produced around the world today.

Crime fiction is the number one literary export from Norway and Scandinavia. The term "Nordic Noir" has been used since the 1990s to describe Nordic crime novels and TV shows, and has increased in popularity in the past 20 years. Authors such as Jo Nesbø, Unni Lindell, and Anne Holt have all written noteworthy novels that will send chills down your spine. Their works share a simple, clear writing style, with little to no descriptive language. Some books to check out include *The Consorts of Death* (Gunnar Staalesen), *The Snowman* and *The Redbreast* (Jo Nesbø), *Death Deserved* (Jørn Lier Horst), and *Death in Oslo* (Anne Holt). Fun fact: Anne Holt is actually Norway's former Minister of Justice.

VISUAL ARTS

The most famous artist of Norway is Edvard Munch (1863-1944), whose well-known paintings include *The Scream, Madonna,* and *The Ladies on the Bridge.* His expressionistic works can be seen at the Munch Museum in

Oslo, and some of his works are also on display at the KODE museum in Bergen.

The National Romanticism period (1830-1970) in Norway came about during Danish rule and Swedish partnership, when Norwegians started longing for a country to call their own. Landscape pieces showing the true natural beauty of Norway became the new standard, and painters such as Johan Christian Dahl (1788-1857), Nikolai Astrup (1880-1928), Amaldus Nielsen (1838-1932), and Adolph Tidemand (1814-1876) created artworks that are still admired today. Their notable works include *Vinter ved Sognefjorden* (*Winter by the Sognefjord,* Dahl), *Brudeferda i Hardanger* (*Bridal Procession on the Hardangerfjord,* Tidemand and Gude), and *Fra Fjorden* (*From the Fjord,* Nielsen).

FILM

The Norwegian government offers tax breaks to make Norway an attractive destination for movie makers, which has resulted in several international blockbusters being filmed in Norway in recent years. The majestic and unparalleled scenery helps too, and rock formations such as Pulpit Rock and the fjord landscape of western Norway have been seen on the big screen.

Norway has a small film industry with (what seems like) only a handful of actors and actresses being given roles, and a big focus in recent years has been on war movies and disaster movies. The Norwegian home-front

Norwegian Disaster Movies

The success of the movie *Bølgen* (*The Wave*) in 2015 spurred a number of other Norwegian disaster movies. In addition to the suspenseful action, these movies are worth watching for their settings showcasing Norwegian landscapes and cities. The general plot buildup is that viewers get to know a main character and his or her loved ones, before noticing omens that something bad is about to happen. Then, disaster strikes and for the majority of the movie we follow our protagonist's struggle to save their loved ones. Here is an essential watch list:

- **Bølgen** (*The Wave*, 2015): The movie that started the Norwegian disaster movie. *The Wave* depicts an imminent tsunami heading straight for Geiranger, caused by a large piece of the mountain Åkerneset falling into the fjord below. (This is an unsteady part of the mountain that is currently being closely monitored, as scientists and geologists await its fall.) The movie follows a geologist, Kristian, as he assists in the evacuation of the village while trying to keep his family safe.

- **Skjelvet** (*The Quake*, 2018): This sequel to *Bølgen* follows the same geologist and his family as a giant earthquake threatens Oslo.

- **The Tunnel** (2019): This movie is about a tunnel fire that turns fatal and was loosely based on two tunnel fires that happened in western Norway's Gudvangatunnel, one of Norway's longest tunnels.

- **The North Sea** (2021): A serious accident at an oil platform in the North Sea, where the entire rig is in danger of crumbling into the ocean, is the disaster at the center of this movie.

movement, and their sabotage of the German occupying forces, have been depicted in movies such as *Max Manus* (2008), *The King's No* (2016), and *The Battle of Narvik* (2022).

MUSIC

Norwegians are very proud of the music that has been made and produced in Norway, and when listening to the radio with a Norwegian, you'll often hear them say, "This is a Norwegian song!" on the rare occasion that such a song is played. Modern Norwegian artists who are currently being played abroad include Kygo, Astrid S, and Alan Walker. Here are some Norwegian songs you should know about.

- **"In the Hall of the Mountain King"** (Edvard Grieg, 1875): This dramatic and dark piece was originally written for Henrik Ibsen's play *Peer Gynt*, but has since been used in countless movies.

- **"Take on Me"** (A-Ha, 1985): Perhaps one of the most famous songs to leave Norway, this '80s pop song was a hit all around the world.

- **"Hymn to the Sea"** (James Horner, 1997): This is one of the most familiar sounds from the movie *Titanic*, but most people don't know that the mystical humming in the soundtrack was recorded by Norwegian singer Sissel Kyrkjebø.

- **"Barbie Girl"** (Aqua, 1997): Three of Aqua's four members were Danish, but the fourth and arguably most important band member was Norwegian lead singer Lene Nystrøm.

- **"The Fox"** (Ylvis, 2013): This song was named a "plague" in Norway before making its way up the charts across the pond in both the US and the UK. To this day, Norwegians do not know what the fox says.

Essentials

Transportation

GETTING THERE
By Air

Most international travelers will arrive in Norway via one of the two main international airports: **Oslo Airport Gardermoen** (OSL) or **Bergen Airport Flesland** (BGO). From either of these airports, you can connect to most domestic destinations, so if you are starting your adventure in a city such as Tromsø, Ålesund, or Kristiansand, you will most likely stop in either Oslo or Bergen before continuing on to your destination. Both of these main airports are located just outside their

respective cities, with easy and efficient transportation options to the city center.

From North America

A few airlines operate flights to Norway from the east coast of the United States. Schedules have been slightly limited since the COVID-19 pandemic, but **Scandinavian Airlines** (www.flysas.com) and **United Airlines** (www.unitedairlines.com) are back up and running, in addition to newcomer **Norse Atlantic** (www.flynorse.com), which flies from New York and Orlando to Oslo. United operates direct flights from New York to Bergen. There are no direct flights from Canada to either Oslo or Bergen.

From Europe

The two main airlines operating between Norway and the rest of Europe are **Scandinavian Airlines** (www.flysas.com) and **Norwegian Airlines** (www.norwegian.com). In recent years, **Widerøe** (www.wideroe.no) has also added European flights. These three carriers serve most major airports across Europe.

From Australia and New Zealand

If you are traveling from Oceania, you will have to plan for at least one stopover, and most likely two. If you want to arrive from Australia with just one stopover, both **Emirates Airlines** (www.emirates.com) and **Qatar Airways** (www.qatarairways.com) can help you do that with a stop in the Middle East.

From South Africa

Lufthansa (www.lufthansa.com), **Swiss Airlines** (www.swiss.com), and **Turkish Airlines** (www.turkishairlines.com) operate flights between Cape Town and Oslo via Frankfurt, Zürich, and Istanbul respectively, making it surprisingly easy to travel between Norway and South Africa.

By Train

All trains to Norway run via Sweden, due to the long border between the two countries. From both Stockholm and Gothenburg you can book **Sj** trains (www.sj.no) that take you directly to **Oslo Central Station (Oslo S)**. The train from Stockholm to Oslo takes 5.5 hours, and the journey to Oslo from Gothenburg takes 3 hours and 45 minutes. If you are flying to Copenhagen in Denmark, the 3.5-hour train journey onboard Öresundståget (the Øresund train) will take you to Gothenburg, where you can connect to the train to Oslo.

By Bus

International bus lines arrive at **Oslo Bussterminal** (Oslo Bus Terminal), and you can connect to Norway from most European destinations via Sweden. **Vybuss** (www.vybuss.no) and **Flixbus** (www.flixbus.com) operate routes between Oslo and major cities in Sweden.

By Boat

Oslo can be reached via car ferry from Copenhagen, Denmark, on **DFDS** (www.dfds.com; overnight crossing; approx. 990 kr per person in an inside cabin) and from Kiel, Germany, on **Color Line** (www.colorline.com; overnight crossing; approx. 500 kr per person in a standard inside cabin). Both are considered "booze cruises," and you will find many Norwegian friend groups on their bachelor/bachelorette parties or weekends away partying on these boats. The Oslo-Copenhagen crossing departs in the afternoon (around 3-4pm) and arrives in the late morning the next day (around 10am). The Oslo-Kiel crossing also leaves Oslo in the afternoon (2pm), and arrives at 10am the next day.

By Car

If you want to arrive in Norway by car, you can take advantage of the fact that Sweden,

Norway by Cruise Ship

A large number of travelers have been visiting Norway via cruise ship, and while cruises to Norway paused during the pandemic, post-pandemic levels are practically back to normal. Several cruise operators have routes going around the southern coast of Norway and/or into the fjords. The most popular cruise ports in Norway are Oslo, Bergen, and Flåm, with many cruise ships also stopping in Stavanger, Olden, and Geiranger.

These cruise ships differ from fjord cruises in that they are package holidays where the cruise ship is your "hotel" for the duration of your trip. Cruises in the Norwegian fjords usually last 5-8 days, and will stop at several destinations along the way. Some of the major companies offering cruises to Norway are Viking Cruises, P&O Cruises, Costa Cruise Lines, and MSC.

PROS

Seeing Norway on a cruise ship can be a great way to explore the fjords for those who may not be up to traveling independently. Waking up and looking at the majestic mountains float by as you cruise into the Sognefjord or the Nordfjord is a sight you will never forget, and it allows you to visit several destinations in Norway during your short trip.

CONS

As in other destinations, cruise ships are a topic for serious debate in Norway, and they are often unpopular with locals. So, the price you pay for the beautiful views might be some nasty looks or comments from residents of the towns you visit.

There is, naturally, an environmental issue to consider when opting for a cruise, and measures are being put in place to decrease the impact these vessels have on the surroundings. The current aim is for the World Heritage fjords to become zero-emission destinations by 2026. Additionally, there is also the aspect of "people pollution" to consider. When villages of 200-300 people are filled with 5,000 cruise passengers for a day, you may find that you don't get the picturesque trip to Norway you had hoped for. The towns (and activities) fill up completely with the passengers from the ship, and a normally sleepy Norwegian village turns into mayhem when everyone is trying to get a ticket for the same attraction.

Denmark, and Germany are within the Schengen zone. Regardless of which country you arrive from, you can simply drive on through. If you arrive from Denmark or Germany, you will be arriving via car ferry, and there are several places to cross into Norway directly along the Swedish border. The border crossings are open, with the occasional customs control to make sure people aren't bringing illegal goods into the country.

GETTING AROUND

The smaller airports around Norway (Tromsø, Trondheim, and Kristiansand, for example) all connect to Oslo and Bergen. Most likely, unless you are traveling up north, you will arrive by air and then stay on the ground for the duration of your visit.

Train

Train travel in Norway is easily managed in the east, so if your trip centers around Oslo, you'll find that traveling by rail is pretty straightforward. However, in the west (and all the way north), trains aren't as well connected. The two companies operating trains around Norway (mainly in the east, but also up north to Trondheim and beyond) are **Vy** (www.vy.no) and **Sj** (www.sj.no).

The most famous, and scenic, rail journeys are the **Oslo-Bergen Railway** (crossing the country from east to west connecting the two cities), the **Flåm Railway** (an hourlong train journey from Myrdal to Flåm), and **Raumabanen** (a 1 hour and 40 minute journey connecting the main line Dombåsbanen with Åndalsnes).

Traveling Norway Without a Car

My number one recommendation for travelers to Norway is to try to do it without a car. Unless you are visiting the Lofoten isles (where a car is recommended to make the most of your trip), you can get by using buses and trains. Even in rural western Norway, traveling by bus is a great way to see the country, and you can relax on board while enjoying the beautiful scenery. The main issue when traveling Norway without a car is that in rural areas, buses and trains don't run as often. However, as long as you check schedules in advance, you'll enjoy your trip, and you can feel confident that you've chosen the most sustainable way to travel.

RECOMMENDED ROUTE

My most recommended route for traveling Norway without a car will take you all the way into the UNESCO World Heritage-listed **Nærøyfjord** from either Oslo or Bergen, and back again! The Oslo-Bergen railway connects with the Flåm Railway to take you to Flåm, which is at the end of the Sognefjord. From there, you can travel by bus to Aurland, Gudvangen (also accessible by fjord cruise), Voss, Bergen, and even Ålesund if you'd like.

The destinations in this book that can be reached by train include most towns in eastern and southern Norway, as well as Bergen, Flåm, Åndalsnes, and Trondheim.

To save money, purchase train tickets as early as possible, because the cheapest tickets are sold first, and then the prices increase as the train fills up.

Car

A lot of travelers opt to rent a car (or bring their own) when traveling around Norway. This is easily the most convenient way to explore the country but is not without hassle. Norway is a beautiful country with lots to see out the car window, which causes a lot of travelers to lose focus on the road. This can (and has) created a lot of potentially dangerous situations, so do not rent a car unless you are 100 percent confident in your skills on driving narrow, winding roads, and that you won't be distracted by the scenery around you.

Rules and Documentation

In Norway, cars drive on the right side of the road. Speed limits in Norway are generally low for safety reasons, given that many roads are winding and narrow. You will need a valid driver's license when driving in Norway, and if it originates from outside of the European

Economic Area or European Union, you can use it for up to 3 months (the length of a Schengen tourist visit). If you have a valid driver's license from the EEA/EU area, you can use it without limitation. The car registration papers need to be with you in the car during your trip and must be shown (together with your license) if you get pulled over by the police. When renting a car, you will automatically sign up for basic liability insurance, which is required by law in Norway.

Car Rental

Norway's major cities (Oslo, Bergen, Stavanger, Trondheim) all have several options for car rentals, both at the airports and in the city center. Smaller areas have limited options for car rental. The major rental companies in Norway are **Europcar** (www.europcar.com), **Hertz** (www.hertz.com), **Avis** (www.avis.com), and **Budget** (www.budget.com). One-way rental fees are quite high, and most travelers opt to pick up and deliver their rental car in the same spot. It is possible to take rental cars on car ferries.

Driving Warning and Recommendations

Try to avoid driving a car in Norway if you can. However, if you do drive, make sure to stick to the speed limit, and never stop anywhere that could be unsafe (such as the side of the road or the road shoulder). Always pull into a pullout or rest stop if you want to stop. Also, do not drive excessively slowly. If you are feeling insecure or unsafe, and you wish to drive much more slowly than the speed limit indicates, pull over often to let other drivers overtake you. Following all of this advice will help you to avoid potentially dangerous situations.

In general, you need to be a very confident driver, whether you're going backwards or forwards. On all the narrow roads, you risk meeting cars coming the other direction and you will have to know how to back up to the nearest meeting point, often with a steep hill on one side of your car and sometimes with limited (or no) barrier. On narrow roads, **meeting points** are marked with a blue sign with a white "M" on it. This is a spot where the road has been widened enough for one car to stop to let another to drive past.

It is also worth noting that **hazard lights** are only to be used for emergencies. Drivers in Norway are legally required to stop at the scene of any emergency, yet many tourist drivers use these lights just to stop and take photos anywhere along the road. Please don't do this, as it creates a very dangerous situation for vehicles trying to pass, and locals will further complicate the situation when they stop to ask if you are okay.

Bus

Traveling by bus is a great way to explore Norway, and several bus companies operate across the country. For regional and long-distance buses, **Nor-Way** (www.nor-way. no) and **Vy Buss** (formerly Nettbuss, www. vybuss.no) are the main operators. In and around Bergen, **Skyss** (www.skyss.no) operates both local and regional buses. As with train tickets, purchase bus tickets as early as possible to save money.

Boat

A staple of Norwegian travel is the **Hurtigruten ferry** (www.hurtigruten.no), which follows all along the coast of Norway, from the south to the north. It is a popular way to explore the country but is also a great mode of transportation for those who have the time and money. The entirety of the trip from Bergen to Kirkenes in far northern Norway takes 7 days and starts at 9,500 kr. Along the way, it makes several stops, including Ålesund, Kristiansund, Svolvær, Tromsø, and Hammerfest.

When traveling around Norway, you will come across several ferries. These are essentially a part of Norway's road system, especially in western Norway, and serve the same purpose as bridges and tunnels. Depending on the body of water you are crossing (usually a fjord), the journey can take anywhere from 10 to 45 minutes. When reaching a ferry, you will simply drive onto it, as if it was a continuation of the road, and drive off when you get to the other side. The ferries are open at both ends, so you usually do not have to turn around or reverse off (unless there are technical issues). Onboard there are trash cans, toilets, and a small café where you can get snacks for the drive.

Taxi

In the major cities, taxis are easy to come by, but will set you back at least 150 kr, even for the shortest of distances. In smaller areas, even those frequented by tourists such as Flåm and Geiranger, you will find that there are usually only one taxi company in the area, with a handful of cars; in Geiranger, for example, the local taxi company has four cars. Taxis are an expensive, but sometimes necessary, means to get to where you need to be.

Visas and Officialdom

PASSPORTS AND TOURIST VISAS

As Norway is a part of the European Schengen Agreement, travelers from any other Schengen country may enter Norway without a passport (26 countries at the time of writing). If you arrive from any other country within the Schengen area (even if you are a citizen of a non-Schengen country), you will find that there are no passport checks at the airport or border.

However, to enter the Schengen area you need to show your passport. So, if Norway is the first stop on your trip, you will go through passport control upon arrival. If another Schengen country is your first visit, you will show your passport there, and will not need to produce it again upon entering Norway from that country.

When visiting Norway as a tourist you may stay in the country for up to 90 days without a visa. This goes for travelers from the United States, Canada, the UK, and Australia. Travelers from certain countries need to apply for a tourist visa to visit Norway, also for up to 90 days. This visa is valid in the entire Schengen region, and once it is obtained, you can travel passport-free between the countries. Travelers from South Africa, for example, need to apply for a tourist visa in order to enter. The application is digital.

CUSTOMS

Norway is not part of the European Union and so it has slightly different customs rules from some neighboring countries. To the frustration of many Norwegians, bringing goods into the country is not always straightforward, and especially alcohol and tobacco have a straight quota. For visitors, there are no restrictions on the amount of luggage and personal items you can bring into the country, if you take it with you when you leave. If you intend to leave anything in Norway, this is considered importing goods. Cash valued at over 25,000 kr (or a foreign equivalent) must be declared upon arrival, and it is forbidden to import any meat or dairy products from outside the European Economic Area (EEA).

If you want to bring alcohol into Norway (probably a good idea, considering how expensive it is there), knowing your allowed duty-free limit is important. There are many variations on the rules, depending on the type of alcohol you bring, so it is best to check the KvoteAppen app, where you can enter the amount of alcohol (beer, wine, hard liquor) you intend to bring to see if you are within the limit. You can also pay the customs fee directly in the app if you plan to bring more than the duty-free allotment.

Recreation

BEACHES

Norway mostly practices what some call "free swimming," which basically means that you are free to swim or bathe at any beach. Most beaches are sandy, with some variations on the color of the sand. In the far north and all the way along the south coast, you will find white, almost tropical beaches.

On Norwegian beaches, there are usually no services, such as toilets or changing rooms. When Norwegians go swimming, they simply change under their towel or behind a bush. Equally, there are no signs or lifeguards on duty.

HIKING

Hiking is the unofficial national sport of Norway, and Norwegians flock to the mountains on their days off. There are hikes of all difficulties to be found all over the country, and regardless of whether you are visiting the fjords or the cities, you'll find treks and trails close by. Locals will happily share their top recommendations for where to go, and whether you prefer a steep hike with spectacular views or an easier forest trek, you'll find it in Norway.

Keeping the weather in mind when hiking in Norway is important. The weather can change suddenly, and is often different higher up in the mountains than down by the fjord. Always check the weather forecast before heading out on a hike, and ask locals about current conditions.

The Norwegian Trekking Association (Den Norske Turistforening; www.dnt.no) is responsible for the upkeep of hundreds of cabins scattered around the country, where you can stay if you are embarking on a longer, multiday hike. A great resource provided by the Norwegian Trekking Association is Ut.no (www.ut.no). Although the website is only in Norwegian, it is packed with hiking maps and recommendations, most of which

will be helpful even if you are using a translator app or service. This site invites individuals and organizations to add their suggestions, and you will find a range of hikes suitable for all skill levels.

SKIING

Both downhill and cross-country skiing are popular sports in Norway. So popular, in fact, that there is a common saying in Norway that "Norwegians are born with skis on." On weekends and evenings in the winter, people head to nearby ski resorts for a day or a weekend filled with downhill skiing (or snowboarding) and the ever popular apres-ski party. Cross-country trails are prepped and managed by hundreds of volunteers around the country, and many areas have lysløyper (lit trails), where you can ski even on the dark evenings of the Norwegian winter months.

KAYAKING AND CANOEING

In the summer months, Norwegians like to get out on the water, and whether they live along the coast or by the fjord, they enjoy kayaking and canoeing. Along the fjords, you will see groups of kayakers gliding past, and a lot of people like to spend several days going on kayak trips, camping along the way. In some fjord destinations, such as Gudvangen, it is possible to join guided tours by kayak. As the fjords are usually calm, kayaking is accessible for people of all experience levels. However, as always, check the current conditions and the weather forecast, and don't embark on a longer kayaking trip than you think you can handle.

HUNTING AND FISHING

Norwegians enjoy the great outdoors, and during hunting season (in the fall), many of them spend every weekend in the mountains hunting for deer and reindeer (and moose, in some areas). Hunting rights are regulated by local hunting groups (Jaktlag). The hunting season starts in late August/early September, and only overlaps with the hiking season by a few weeks. Hunters usually stay far away from hiking routes, as animals don't tend to frequent those areas.

Mountain fishing is also popular, with mountain trout being the most common fish. Anyone can fish in the mountain lakes around Norway. August and September are the best months for hiking and trout fishing in the mountains.

EXTREME SPORTS

Extreme sports such as skydiving, BASE jumping, and paragliding are popular in certain circles around Norway. In western Norway, the town of Voss has been a destination for extreme sports for several years, but people go skydiving and BASE jumping all over the country these days.

Festivals and Events

The majority of Norway's festivals and events take place during the summer months, when the weather is at its nicest. Annual festivals are common around the major cities, so if you are visiting Oslo or Bergen, check to see if anything is on during your trip. In addition to music festivals (such as Findings and Øya in Oslo, and Bergenfest in Bergen), there are farmers markets, food festivals, beer festivals, and even cheese festivals held throughout the country, usually on weekends.

SPRING
The 17th of May
May

Norway's Constitution Day is simply called 17 Mai, and regardless of where you are in Norway, there will be festivities on this day, including a parade, a marching band, and games for children. That said, Oslo is perhaps the best place to be on this day: The parade up Karl Johans Gate is massive, and the royal family looks on from the balcony of the palace.

SUMMER
Bergenfest
Bergen; 55 21 50 60; www.bergenfest.no; June

Bergenfest started as an intimate blues and Americana festival spread across Bergen, and is now the largest festival in town, drawing names such as Zara Larsson, Bon Iver, Ellie Goulding, Queens of the Stone Age, and Bastille. The 2-3-day festival stages are built in various areas of Bergenhus Fortress, so you are in historic surroundings while you enjoy the music.

Midnight Sun Marathon
Tromsø; www.msm.no; June

During this summer race in Tromsø, runners can participate in the marathon, half marathon, a 10k, or a mini-marathon under the midnight sun—quite a unique experience. Unlike most marathons, it starts late in the evening (around 9pm), and the half marathon can start as late as 10:30pm.

American Fesitival
Vanse; www.americanfestival.no; June

During this 4-day festival, usually held on the last weekend of June, the small town of Vanse in southern Norway comes alive with a street parade of American cars, food and souvenir stands, and of course several concerts.

Ekstremsportveko
Voss; www.ekstremsportveko.com; June-July

The establishment of Ekstremsportveko (Extreme Sports Week) is one of the reasons Voss is known as Norway's capital for extreme sports. From long boarding and skateboarding to BMX and speed flying, there are events to catch wherever you go.

Palmesus

Kristiansand; www.palmesus.com; first weekend of July

Palmesus is perhaps the most famous festival in Kristiansand, selling out months and months in advance. This beach festival features club, DJ, pop, and hip-hop music, and will make you forget you are in a (usually) cold country.

The Aurland Festival (Aurlandsmarknaden)

Aurland; www.aurlandsmarknaden.no; first weekend of July

Since 1997, the 2-day Aurlandsmarknaden (technically, the Aurland Market) draws sellers and artisans from all over the country to sell their handcrafts and souvenirs.

Sørlandets Matfestival

Kristiansand; www.sorlandetsmatfestival.no; second weekend of July

The Southern Norway Food Festival takes place every year in July, with street food vendors and local producers displaying their goods in the city center. There is even a chili competition to determine southern Norway's "Chili Master."

Olavsfest

Trondheim; 73 84 14 50; https://olavsfest.no; July

Olavsfest is the local nickname given to St. Olav's Festival, the largest festival in Trondheim. Over the span of several days (sometimes more than 10), concerts, entertainment, seminars, and even a medieval fair are put on throughout the city and near the Nidaros Cathedral.

Øyafestivalen

Oslo; www.oyafestivalen.no; Aug.

Traditionally a rock-focused festival, the four-day Øyafestivalen (known to locals as simply Øya) has expanded to include a variety of music genres and artists over the years. Tickets usually sell out months in advance, as this is one of the biggest happenings in Oslo.

Utopia Music Festival

Stavanger; www.utopiafest.no; Aug.

Utopia is Stavanger's "city festival," as it takes place in a park in the middle of the city. The 2-day music festival has a lineup consisting of pop, rock, hip-hop, and rap.

FALL

by:Larm

Oslo; https://bylarm.no; Sept.

The perfect event for anyone wanting to discover new Scandinavian musicians, by:Larm spreads across four days and several venues in Oslo.

Matstreif

Oslo; www.innovasjonnorge.no/matstreif; Sept.

Matstreif is a national food festival, where producers from all over Norway gather to display (and sell) their food. From popular Norwegian cheese (from Ostegården cheesery, among others) to cider from Hardanger, everything is represented at this festival.

Bergen Food Festival

Bergen; https://matfest.no; Sept.

Farmers and producers from all over Vestland county come together for a weekend in December during Bergen Matfestival. The whole festival is devoted to local producers of cheese, meat, honey, seafood, and even beer.

Bergen Beer Festival

Bergen; www.olfestival.no; Sept.; 200 kr

Bergen Ølfestival celebrates local beer and breweries from all around Norway. Tickets to this indoor market must be bought in advance.

BIFF (Bergen International Film Festival)

Bergen; 55 30 08 40; www.biff.no; Oct.

Showing more than 150 documentaries and fiction movies every year, BIFF (the Bergen International Film Festival) is the largest film festival in Norway; it's perfect for any movie fans who happen to be visiting during the weeklong festival.

The Viking Market

Gudvangen; www.facebook.com/ GudvangenVikingMarket; Oct.

Viking artisans and craftspeople from all over Scandinavia (and the world) come together inside the walls of Njardarheimr to display their products and sell their services.

Dark Season Blues

Svalbard; www.svalbardblues.com; Oct.

Every October, the world's northernmost blues festival takes place on the island of Svalbard, lighting up the dark days with great music.

WINTER

Christmas Market

Røros; https://julemarkedroros.no; early Dec.

For a few days every December, the charming town of Røros comes alive with Christmas spirit, and the streets between the old timber houses are lined with vendors selling local produce, Christmas snacks and foods, and winter-themed activities.

Pepperkakebyen (Gingerbread City)

Bergen; www.pepperkakebyen.org; Dec.

Every year, the world's largest gingerbread town is built in the center of Bergen. Schools, kindergartens, businesses, and families from all over the city bake and build various gingerbread houses to contribute.

Sami Week

Tromsø; Jan.-Feb.

During this weeklong event, Tromsø comes alive with all things Sami, from seminars and workshops to concerts and even reindeer racing. The Norwegian Championship of Reindeer Racing is usually held during Sami Week, and it passes through Storgata in the city center.

Finnmarksløpet (Dogsled Race)

Alta; www.finnmarkslopet.no; Mar.

Finnmarksløpet (the Finnmark Race) is Europe's longest and toughest dog sled race. It travels 1,200 kilometers (745 mi) of forested areas, the mountain plateau Finnmarksvidda, and more mountainous areas. The race starts and ends in the center of Alta.

Nordlysfestivalen

Tromsø; www.nordlysfestivalen.no; Jan.

Nordlysfestivalen is the major music event in Tromsø. Since it began in 1988, it has gone from being a small, traditional music festival to the large spectacle it is today. The 10-day festival features a wide variety of artists and bands performing music. There is also a wide selection of different music from jazz to pop. Previous artists include Cecilie Norby, Tromsø Storband, and New Religion.

Food

MEALTIMES

Norwegians eat their meals earlier than people do in many other European countries. You'll find that your Norwegian friends often will head home for dinner at 4pm-5pm. Lunch is eaten around 11am-noon and is surprisingly similar to the Norwegian breakfast, consisting of brødskive med pålegg (a slice of bread with a spread or other topping, such as ham, cheese, jam, or pâte). Most Norwegian lunch boxes (matpakke) will contain a few slices of bread with a selected topping, and you'll find that people bring their matpakke on hikes as well as into the workplace. Because most Norwegians eat an early dinner, beware that some restaurants close their kitchen as early as 9pm.

The major grocery store chains in Norway are Meny (pricy, but with a large selection of international brands), Coop Extra, Spar, Kiwi, and Rema 1000 (the last two are more affordable grocery stores).

TRADITIONAL NORWEGIAN CUISINE

Norwegian food traditionally consists of meat or fish served with boiled potatoes and a vegetable (usually carrots—you'll find potatoes and carrots next to most meats at a Norwegian dinner table). Restaurants serving Scandinavian dishes tend to spice them up a little by changing out the vegetables and preparing the potatoes in other ways. Norwegian dishes have historically had a reason and purpose behind them, such as betasuppe, a brothy meat and vegetable soup that is made from the week's leftovers, and fish that is dried and salted to preserve it.

Meat

Traditional meats found in Norwegian cuisine include mutton, lamb, goat, reindeer, and pork. One of Norway's national dishes is **fårikål,** a stew made of mutton and cabbage. Perhaps even more common is **kjøttkaker** (meat cakes), served with gravy, carrots, and boiled potatoes.

Cheese

Norwegians love their cheese, and it comes in two main varieties: brown cheese (brunost) and yellow cheese (gulost). **Brown cheese** is considered a Norwegian delicacy and can be made from either goat's milk or cow's milk. The former has a much more intense flavor, while brown cheese made from cow's milk is often quite mild. Brown cheese is just as common as yellow/white cheese in Norway, and you'll find it at breakfast buffets all around the country; it is traditionally eaten in a thin slice on top of a slice of bread. **Yellow cheese** is just the Norwegian term for all white/yellow cheeses, such as gouda, Swiss, American, and Norvegia, a Norwegian white cheese that tastes like a very mild gouda.

Fish and Seafood

Fish dominates Norwegian cuisine, and you'll find salmon, cod, and trout on most restaurant menus. Many restaurants and cafés also offer a traditional creamy fish soup (usually made with salmon, cod, and vegetables), and

take special pride in their fish soup recipe. **Lutefisk** is a traditional Norwegian type of dried, salted cod that is preserved in lye; it is usually eaten around Christmas.

Stockfish from northern Norway is also a popular export, and although it is not as common on the dinner table as it once was, it is still considered somewhat of a delicacy. Stockfish is cod that has been hung outside to dry.

Norwegian Delicacies

Both lutefisk and brown goat's cheese are considered Norwegian delicacies. Additionally, steak of **whale meat** is served in fancier restaurants around the country. If you get the chance, don't miss the chance to say you've tried **smalahove,** roasted sheep's head, usually cut in half after roasting and served while staring at you from your plate. Not many places prepare and serve smalahove these days.

MODERN NORWEGIAN CUISINE

Nowadays, the Norwegian kitchen is much more international than before. Gone are the days of simple mutton or pork with potatoes; now you are more likely to find pizza, pasta, and Mexican food around the country. Mexican food has become especially popular among Norwegians, and taco Fredag (taco Friday) is a national tradition.

BEVERAGES

Norwegians are devoted coffee drinkers, and more than 80 percent of the population drink coffee on a daily basis. Coffee in Norway is usually served black with no sugar, and Norwegians may frown at you for requesting milk or sugar in your coffee.

Alcohol in Norway is very expensive, due to the high taxation on alcoholic beverages. Still, beer, wine, and the traditional spirit akevitt (aquavit, a spirit distilled from potatoes and often flavored with dill or caraway) are consumed all around the country. Beer, cider, and alcopops (sweet, low-alcoholic sparkling drinks such as Smirnoff Ice) can be purchased in grocery stores. The Norwegian wine store (vinmonopolet), where you can purchase wine and hard liquors, is government-regulated and must follow strict laws for sales and opening hours. The over-the-counter sale of alcohol is prohibited on Sundays, and after certain times on weekdays (8pm) and Saturdays (6pm). Therefore, Norwegians know to plan their alcohol purchases accordingly.

EATING OUT
Tipping
Norwegian servers earn a living wage, so while tipping is never frowned upon, it is also never necessary. Some patrons may round up their bill to the nearest 100 kr, but visitors can rest assured that they are not expected to leave a tip.

Accommodations

HOTELS
Hotels in the Norwegian cities are dominated by chains, such as Thon, Clarion, and Scandic. When staying at any of these, you can expect the same standard and level of service across the board. In more rural areas, you will find charming, historic hotels; look for signs indicating that a hotel is a member of De Historiske (The Historic), which is a highly regarded stamp of approval. Hotels in rural Norway will be a little more rustic than the city hotels. In the high season (the summer months especially), hotels fill up quickly, so it is always advised to book your hotel early.

HOSTELS
Hostels are not extremely common in Norway, but you will find them in the larger cities. Staying in a hostel is a good way to save some money on your Norwegian adventure, and a great way to meet other travelers.

CAMPING
There are great camping sites all over the country, usually in very scenic areas. Campsites in Norway fill up almost as quickly as the hotels, so make sure to book early. If you are hoping to camp in the wild, this is also an option in Norway, as the Right to Roam (Allemannsretten) gives avid campers the legal right to stay wherever they'd like (in theory).

It is not very common to rent tents or camping gear in Norway, but a new website called Hygglo (www.hygglo.no) allows individuals to rent out their tents and gear to others. In all major cities you will find XXL (www.xxl.no), a sporting goods store that sells a wide range of camping gear and equipment.

the historic Britannia Hotel in Trondheim

Allemannsretten: The Legal Right to Roam

The Norwegian concept of Allemannsretten is the legal right to roam anywhere in nature, and stay overnight wherever you'd like, with minor restrictions. The main rule to be aware of is that you have to be at least 150 meters (around 500 ft) away from private houses or cabins when putting up a tent or hammock. Other than that, you can sleep practically anywhere that isn't fenced in, cultivated land, or clearly seen as private. It is expected that you leave no trace of your stay and take your rubbish with you when you leave.

Conduct and Customs

ETIQUETTE

There is not a lot you need to know about Norwegian etiquette before visiting, except to be aware of the abruptness of the Norwegian language. Norwegian can come across as rude when directly translated to English, and many Norwegians (especially the older generations) are not aware of this. Therefore, sentences such as "What do you want?" and "Huh?" are common when speaking with locals, but are in no way intended to be (or considered) rude or impolite.

SUNDAYS

Though Norway is no longer considered a religious country, and doesn't have a state religion anymore, some Christian rules and customs are still in effect. This is mainly obvious on Sundays, which Norwegians spend relaxing, meeting friends, and being in nature. All commercial stores, including grocery stores (except very small ones, such as Joker or Bunnpris) are closed, and streets are nearly empty. Legally, you can still get fined if you "disturb the peace" on Sundays, so this is not the day to throw a party or listen to loud music.

SMOKING AND DRINKING

Norway was the first country in the world to bring forth an action plan against smoking hazards, and among the earliest to prohibit tobacco advertisements (1975) and indoor smoking at restaurants and establishments (in 2004). As a result, the country today is virtually smoke-free, and you'll find very few locals smoking. If you wish to smoke, you will have to stay clear of indoor spaces, and stick to designated areas.

Drinking is prominent in Norway, and it's common for Norwegians to enjoy a glass of wine or beer when dining out (though it's not so common at the dinner table in private homes). Norwegians tend to go out late when they go drinking, and it is not uncommon for bars and pubs to be completely empty at 11pm, and then completely packed by midnight.

CLOTHING

Norwegians wear rather sporty clothing, favoring breathable, water-resistant fabrics. Locals on the street may look like they are ready to go hiking. The Norwegian saying goes, "There is no such thing as bad weather, only bad clothing."

Health and Safety

VACCINATIONS

There are no vaccinations required to visit Norway. During, and in the months immediately after, the COVID-19 pandemic, visitors were required to be fully vaccinated (two doses) to enter the country, but this restriction has been lifted across Europe.

EMERGENCY NUMBERS

- Ambulance – 113

- Police – 112

- Fire – 110

- Emergency Room (less urgent) – 116117

MEDICAL SERVICES

Most Norwegian hospitals are public hospitals, funded and operated by the state. Health care in Norway is generally of a very high level, and free for Norwegians through their taxes and the welfare state. Visitors are advised to have travel insurance, and to make sure it covers extreme sports or activities such as hiking, skiing, or snowmobiling before your trip.

Hospitals and emergency rooms are very far apart in rural Norway (around the western fjords and northern Norway especially), and so it is always smart to pick up any medicines or medical supplies you anticipate needing from a pharmacy before leaving the major cities. Painkillers such as paracetamol and ibuprofen are sold in all grocery stores.

The major pharmacy chains in Norway are Apotek 1 and Vitusapotek. Apotek means pharmacy in Norwegian and has the same roots as the English word "apothecary."

CRIME

Norway is a very safe country for both travelers and locals. However, visitors should remain aware of their surroundings and take commonsense precautions, especially in the busier areas of Oslo, around the central station and Karl Johan's Gate.

ILLICIT DRUGS

All drugs are illegal in Norway. They are known to be sold in the busiest areas around Oslo S (Oslo Central Station), but this should not affect visitors, as they are not openly solicited to travelers.

OUTDOOR AND WINTER SAFETY

Staying safe when hiking and doing winter activities should be of prime concern while in Norway. Norwegians take safety very seriously, teaching their young children the nine Fjellvettreglene (Mountain Rules) of Norway. These rules can be literal lifesavers for anyone enjoying Norway's great outdoors.

- Always tell someone where you are going.

- Always adapt the trip to your abilities and the circumstances.

- Always be prepared to turn around (there's no shame in that).

- Always check and be aware of the current weather forecast (and/or avalanche risk level).

- Be prepared for sudden weather changes, even on shorter hikes.

- Bring the necessary equipment to help yourself and others.

- Make safe road choices.

- Use your map and compass—always know where you are.

- Save your energy and seek shelter if needed.

Practical Details

WHAT TO PACK

Regardless of what time of year you are traveling in Norway, layers should be your top priority. As it states in the Fjellvettregler (Mountain Rules, above), you should always be prepared for sudden weather changes, including the ability to add or remove layers as you go through your day's activities. If you are traveling in the winter, wool is a must, and a wool base layer will be your key to staying warm on long days spent outside.

Opt for 2-3 thin layers year-round, plus a final layer that reflects the weather and your activity for the day (such as a waterproof shell or warmer down jacket). Your shoes should be rugged and waterproof, and ideally you won't mind them getting a little muddy, especially if you are planning to hike.

BUDGETING

Norway is an expensive country, and being aware of this before you go is an important part of your trip planning. Advance research can help you save a little money elsewhere as well: A taxi from the airport to the city center will set you back at least 600 kr, so you might want to look into other transportation options. Booking overnight stays early, as well as train and bus tickets (cheaper tickets are sold first, and then prices increase) can also result in savings. However, don't expect to be able to travel Norway on a budget. In general, you can expect to pay a lot more for things in Norway than anywhere else. Below are some typical prices for common purchases, in kroner and US dollars:

- Coffee (latte or similar): 55 kr ($5.50)
- Coffee (black, filter): 35 kr ($3.50)
- Lunch (without alcohol): 200 kr ($20)
- Dinner (without alcohol): 300-450 kr ($30-45)
- Glass of wine: 130 kr ($13)
- Beer (on tap, 0.4l): 110 kr ($11)
- Public transport ticket (in a city): 40 kr ($4)

MONEY
Currency and Exchange Rate

The Norwegian currency is the kroner, indicated by a NOK, kr, or ,- sign, for example 100,- og 49,-. When calculating from US dollars or euros, 1 USD or 1 EUR is approximately 10 kr. Actually, 1 dollar is actually a little bit less than 10 kr, while 1 euro is a little bit more, but thinking 1 = 10 is an easy way to calculate costs when traveling in Norway.

Banks and ATMs

Banks in Norway have limited opening hours (usually Mon.-Fri. 9am-3pm), while ATMs are open 24/7. Most cities will have several ATMs around the center, and even small villages will have one, but in remote areas you run the risk that the one ATM in the village is broken, so you should always be prepared to use your card instead.

Debit and Credit Cards

As Norway is moving toward becoming more of a cashless society, you'll find that credit cards are accepted everywhere. Some places (even hotels) are completely cashless and will have signs at the door saying that they only accept cards.

OPENING HOURS

Shops are usually closed on Sundays, except for small grocery stores (there is a size limit as to how large a store can be and still stay open), gas stations, and kiosks (like 7-Eleven). Opening hours are usually limited on Saturdays, as indicated by brackets on the opening hour signs. For example:

8-21 (18): The store is open 8am-8pm Monday-Friday, and 8am-6pm on Saturdays. These are common opening hours for a city grocery store.

10-18 (16): The store is open 10am-6pm on weekdays, and 10am-4pm on Saturdays. These are common opening hours for a clothes shop or other commercial stores.

Restaurants usually open in the afternoon (around 3pm-5pm) and stay open until the evening (usually 9pm-11pm). If they also serve lunch, they usually open as early as 11am.

Public Holidays

National holidays in Norway are called "red days" by Norwegians, as they are marked in red on national calendars. Businesses that are closed on Sundays are also closed on red days.

Red days include the 17th of May (Norway's national day), most of the Easter days (Maundy Thursday, Good Friday, Easter Eve, Easter Sunday, and the second day of Easter), Christmas (Dec. 26-28), and New Year's Day. Christmas Eve and New Year's Eve follow typical Saturday opening hours, as they are considered holidays after noon.

COMMUNICATIONS
Phones and Cell Phones

Phone service in Norway is very good, which is impressive considering how rural Norway is. Ninety-nine percent of the population has access to 4G and 5G, and you will have no trouble getting signal anywhere in Norway. Visitors from Europe can use their plans in Norway as if they were in their home country.

The country code for Norway is +47. All phone numbers in Norway are registered to their owners, and it is not common (or easy) to buy a SIM card for travel purposes. If you are arriving from outside of Europe, check your cell phone coverage when traveling, and consider purchasing a travel plan before you go.

Internet Access

Wi-Fi is usually free in airports, hotels, malls, cafés, and restaurants in Norway. It is usually fast, and generally considered safe to use. Some tourist villages, such as in Flåm, offer public Wi-Fi at the visitors center.

Postal Service

Posten (www.posten.no), the Norwegian post office, offers some digital services. You can order shipping online, and simply bring your package or letter to a postal counter to ship it. In 2001, Posten introduced a service called Post-i-Butikk (roughly translating to "Mail in Grocery Stores"), where they opened small service counters in grocery stores across the country. Today, most postal services in Norway are offered through these counters. This means that travelers don't have to look for a post office; instead, they can purchase stamps or send postcards from many grocery stores nationwide.

The cost of a stamp for a postcard or letter intended to the US is 35 kr, and it's 29 kr within Europe.

WEIGHTS AND MEASUREMENTS

Norway uses the metric system for weights and measurements. Hiking signs and road signs all display distance in kilometers. Temperatures are given in Celsius.

TOURIST INFORMATION
Tourist Offices

You will find tourist information offices, indicated with a white and green *i*, in all major cities and tourist destinations. In areas where the tourist season is limited to a few months, the opening hours are very limited, but in those cases, maps and brochures can often be found in a nearby hotel or café. Everyone working in tourist information offices in Norway speaks English, and most maps and brochures are available in English as well.

Maps

Hiking maps can be picked up in the tourist information offices, and at many ticket offices, hotels, and cafés. Additionally, many destinations that are frequented by tourists will have information boards centrally located in the town or village with maps of the area and surrounding attractions.

Traveler Advice

ACCESS FOR TRAVELERS WITH DISABILITIES

Public transportation in the major cities, as well as all trains across the country, have all been adapted for complete accessibility. In Oslo, buses, trams, and the underground are also fully accessible. Several of the attractions in the major cities and in the main tourist destinations (such as Flåm and Geiranger) are wheelchair-friendly, and so are most of the museums and indoor attractions around the country. Still, some attractions are not fully accessible, such as fortresses and historic places. Norges Handikapforbund (www.nhf.no) is the Norwegian Association of Disabled, advocating for the rights of disabled persons around the country.

WOMEN TRAVELERS

Female travelers, including those traveling solo, will feel safe and find that Norway is easy to navigate. Of course, you should always use a certain level of vigilance in the major cities, especially at night, and let someone at home know where you are going. Simply take the same precautions that are advisable in any urban destination.

SENIOR TRAVELERS

Norway is a very popular country among retirees and older travelers, and as it offers a high level of accessibility to nature, it can be enjoyed at any pace. As it is also a very safe country, there should be no crime-related issues for senior travelers visiting Norway. Cruise ship travel, in particular, is a popular way to explore the Norwegian fjords for senior travelers.

LGBTQ+ TRAVELERS

Norway is a fairly liberal country, and in general, LGBTQ+ travelers will not be treated differently from any other visitors to Norway, but may encounter some ignorant questions, especially outside of the cities. In Oslo, there is a welcoming and thriving community with several established bars that welcome all who identify as LGBTQ+, and Oslo Pride is the largest Pride celebration in the country. In Bergen, Trondheim, and Stavanger you will find that the communities are smaller, with just one LGBTQ+ venue.

Norway was one of the first countries in the world to pass antidiscrimination legislation to protect the LGBTQ+ community, and lesbian and gay couples have the same legal rights as heterosexual couples when it comes to marriage, adoption, and assisted pregnancies. Around 7 percent of Norway's population identifies as queer.

For gay or lesbian couples, it is safe to book a hotel room together. In the cities especially, you will also be able to freely hold hands or show your partner affection outdoors without getting angry stares or cruel comments.

On June 25, 2022, during Oslo's Pride celebrations, two LGBTQ+ persons were killed in a shooting against a gay bar in the city center. The attack was executed by a single assailant, acting alone. The entire country was devastated, and Pride flags were waving all over the country in the weeks to follow. As a result of the attack, the Norwegian government pledged to strengthen efforts to combat discrimination against LGBTQ+ people, and started work on a new four-year plan for LGBTQ+ rights.

TRAVELERS OF COLOR

Generally speaking, Norway is a tolerant country where tourists from all over the world (regardless of color) are given a friendly welcome. Travelers of color should be safe from direct racism but may experience microaggressions in more rural areas—usually not malicious, but nonetheless hurtful and ignorant. Outside of the cities, you may find that you are the only person of color, as the majority of Norway's population is white.

Resources

Glossary

In the Norwegian language, the definitive form of a noun is shown by adding "-et" or "-en" at the end of the noun, as opposed to adding "the" in front of it (like in the English language). So, for example, whilst waterfall is "foss," the waterfall is "fossen". Likewise, city is "by," and the city is "byen." When reading and listening to Norwegian, this will help you determine whether something is spoken of in a general or specific way.

Akevitt: aquavit, a Scandinavian hard liquor distilled from potatoes

Allmenning: street or avenue, mostly used on older street names in Bergen

Åpen, åpent: open

Bidos: reindeer stew, a traditional Sami dish

Bil: car

Brunost: brown cheese

Buss: bus

Bygd: village, mostly used in place of town, especially in rural Norway

Damer: women/ladies (often indicates women's toilets, sometimes just with the letter D)

Ferge: ferry

Gate: street

Herrer: men/gentlemen (indicated on men's toilets, sometimes with just an H)

Holdeplass: stop, usually used for trams or buses (bussholdeplass = bus stop, trikkeholdeplass = tram stop)

Hytte: cabin

Kommune: municipality

Lege: doctor

Legekontor: doctor's office

Legevakt: A&E, emergency room

Plass: place, usually used for "square" in a city or town

Stasjon: station (togstasjon = train station)

Stengt: closed

Svele: a traditional Norwegian pancake, often served on ferries

Tannlege: dentist

Tannlegekontor: dentist's office

Tog: train

Tilbake: back, often used on signs to indicate that staff will be back soon (straks tilbake, snart tilbake)

Norwegian Phrasebook

Norwegians speak English well, and love to practice it. Some Norwegians may even be slightly offended if you ask them if they speak English, so it is always best to assume that they do. You will definitely put a smile on their face if you attempt to speak to them in Norwegian, but chances are they'll steer the conversation over to English quickly. With the hundreds of dialects spoken throughout Norway, you'll find that it is much easier to understand people in Oslo and the surrounding area, and that it gets increasingly harder the farther away from the capital you get.

PRONUNCIATION

As mentioned, there are hundreds of different dialects that make up the Norwegian language, and pronunciations differ greatly from town to town not only in terms how whole words are pronounced, but also in terms of specific letters. For example, in southern and southwestern Norway (including Stavanger, Kristiansand, and Bergen) locals don't roll their R's like in the rest of Norway but make almost a gargling sound, almost like the French r. Similarly, in southern Norway, T's are pronounced like D's, and P's like B's (these are called "soft consonants" in Norwegian). The pronunciation covered below, and what is usually taught in language lessons, is most similar to the eastern Norwegian dialect (Østlandsdialekt) spoken in Oslo and surrounding areas.

Vowels

The Norwegian alphabet contains three extra letters that are not found in the English alphabet: æ, ø, and å. In addition to these, "y" is considered a vowel in Norwegian.

a similar to the a in "hard"
e similar to the e in "elf"
i similar to the i in "ignorance"
o similar to the o in "oar"
u similar to the ue in "glue"
y similar to the y in "syrup," like an ee sound with pursed lips
æ similar to the a in "sad"
ø similar to the u in "burn"
å similar to the o in "born"

Consonants

b like in English
c like in English (very rare in the Norwegian language)
d like in English
f like in English
g usually a hard letter, like in "gown" (when used in front of i or j it is silent, resembling the y in "yawn")
h like in English
j usually a soft letter, like the y in "yes"
k usually a hard letter, except when used in front of j (then, it makes a "ch" sound, like in "cherry")
l like in English
m like in English
n like in English
p like in English
q like in English (very rare in the Norwegian language)
r a hard letter, and rolled like in Spanish across most of the country (some areas roll it at the back of their throat, like a gargling sound)
s like in English
t like in English
v like in English
w like in English (very rare in the Norwegian language)
x like in English (very rare in the Norwegian language)
z like in English (very rare in the Norwegian language)

General

The Norwegian language can seem quite rude and abrupt to an English-speaking person when translated directly. There is no direct translation to "please" (and "vær så snill" is very rarely used in day-to-day conversations), so if you want to add a layer of politeness, you can add "takk" at the end of your sentence, meaning thank you.

Hello Hei
Good-bye Ha det
Thank you Takk
Thank you very much Tusen Takk
Have a nice day Ha en fin dag
Do you speak English? Snakker du engelsk?
Please Vær så snill (very rarely used)
Thank you Tusen takk
Excuse me Unnskyld meg
Yes Ja
No Nei
How are you? Hvordan går det?
I would like... Jeg vil ha...
I'm sorry Unnskyld
I'm looking for ...? Jeg ser etter...?
Where is the restroom? Hvor er toalettet?
I don't understand. Jeg forstår ikke.
Please speak more slowly. Vennligst snakk saktere.
I'm just visiting. Jeg er bare på besøk.
I Jeg
you Du
he/him han
she/her hun
they/them de

Directions and Transportation

I'd like one/two tickets to... Jeg vil ha en/to billett/billetter til...
Where do I board? Hvor går jeg ombord?
How do I get to...? Hvordan kommer jeg meg til...?
Does this train/bus/ferry go to...? Går dette toget/denne bussen/denne fergen til...?
downtown sentrum
airport flyplass
train station togstasjon
bus station busstopp
plane fly
train tog

bus buss
ferry ferge
car bil
bicycle sykkel
taxi taxi/drosje
tickets billetter
one-way en vei
round-trip rundtur, tur-retur
north nord
south sør
east øst
west vest
left venstre
right høyre
straight ahead rett fram
driver's license førerkort
passport pass
insurance forsikring
luggage storage baggasjeoppbevaring

Money and Shopping

How much is it? Hvor mye koster det?
To pay Å betale
May I try this on? Kan jeg prøve denne?
market marked
shop butikk
bank bank
currency exchange valutaveksler
cash penger
credit card kredittkort

Food and Drink

As mentioned, the Norwegian language is a lot more direct than the English. When ordering at a restaurant, sentences such as "May I please have" will seem superfluous and foreign to a Norwegian waiter, and a Norwegian person would simply say "I want the steak/salad/soup" with a smile. This may make you feel incredibly rude, so feel free to add "takk" to the end of your order—"Jeg vil ha salat, takk"—while pointing to your menu item.

I want the... Jeg vil ha...
I'd like to make a reservation Jeg vil gjerne reservere et bord
A table for two/three/four... et bord til to/tre/fire...

Do you have a menu in English? Har dere en meny på engelsk?
I'm/We're ready to order. Jeg er klar/vi er klare til å bestille.
the check regningen
I'm a vegetarian. Jeg er vegetarianer
I cannot eat... Jeg kan ikke spise...
nuts nøtter
shellfish skalldyr
meat kjøtt
fish fisk
vegetables grønnsaker
salad salat
gluten-free glutenfritt
water vann
tea te
coffee kaffe
juice juice
beer øl
wine vin
breakfast frokost
lunch lunsj
dinner middag
dessert dessert
snack snacks

Accommodations
hotel hotell
hostel vandrerhjem
camping campingplass
cabin hytte
room rom
private/shared bathroom privat/delt bad

Health and Emergencies
Please help me. Vennligst hjelp meg.
drugstore apotek
pain smerte
fever feber
headache hodepine
stomachache magesmerter
toothache tannpine
cramp kramper
nausea kvalme
vomiting oppkast
medicine medisin
antibiotic antibiotika

pill/tablet pille/tablett
aspirin aspirin
I need to see a doctor. Jeg må til legen.
I need to go to the hospital. Jeg må på sykehus.
I have a pain here... Jeg har smerter her...
She/he has been stung/bitten. Hun/han har blitt stukket/bitt.
I am diabetic/pregnant. Jeg er diabetiker/gravid.
I am allergic to penicillin/cortisone. Jeg er allergisk mot penicillin/kortison.
My blood group is...positive/negative. Min blodtype er ... positiv/negativ.

Numbers
0 null
1 en
2 to
3 tre
4 fire
5 fem
6 seks
7 syv
8 åtte
9 ni
10 ti
11 elleve
12 tolv
13 tretten
14 fjorten
15 femten
16 seksten
17 sytten
18 atten
19 nitten
20 tjue
21 tjueen
30 tretti
40 førti
50 femti
60 seksti
70 sytti
80 åtti
90 nitti
100 hundre

101 hundre-og-en
200 tohundre
500 femhundre
1,000 tusen
10,000 titusen
100,000 hundretusen
1,000,000 en million

Time

What time is it? Hvor mye er klokka?
It's one/three o'clock. Klokka er ett/tre.
It's 5:15. Den er kvart over fem.
It's 5:30. Den er halv seks.

hour time
minute minutt
midday middag
midnight midnatt
morning morgen
afternoon ettermiddag
evening kveld
night natt
yesterday I går
today I dag
tomorrow I morgen

Days and Months

Weekdays and months of the year are not capitalized in Norwegian as in the English language.

day dag
week uke
month måned
Monday mandag
Tuesday tirsdag
Wednesday onsdag
Thursday torsdag
Friday fredag
Saturday lørdag
Sunday søndag
January januar
February februar
March mars
April april
May mai
June juni
July juli
August august
September september
October oktober
November november
December desember

Suggested Reading

HISTORY AND CULTURE

Jenny K. Blake. *The Norway Way*. Schibsted, 2011. This small, illustrated book calls itself "the essential guide to Norway & the Norwegians." It's a funny, tongue-in-cheek portrayal of Norwegian culture. From cabins to brown cheese, this book covers it all in a charming, fun way. Blake has published similar books for those who enjoy learning about Norwegian culture with a sense of humor: *The Norwegian Hytte* (Schibsted, 2013) and *Brown Cheese, Please* (Schibsted, 2003).

Neil Kent. *The Sàmi Peoples of the North: A Social and Cultural History*. Hurst, 2019. This deep dive into the history of the Indigenous people of Scandinavia, the Sàmi, will leave you wanting to book a flight to northern Norway immediately. The book explains how the Sàmi have been impacted through the years, up to the ways tourism and other industries have affected their culture and livelihood in recent years.

Lars Mytting. *Norwegian Wood: Chopping, Stacking and Drying Wood the Scandinavian Way*. MacLehose Press, 2015. A book about firewood may sound like a dud, but once you start reading you'll be fascinated by Norwegian and Scandinavian customs when it comes to wood. From building ships and houses for centuries to keeping family homes warm, Norwegians take their timber seriously.

Simon Vincent. *Kingdom of Vikings: The Rise and Fall of Norway.* PaperTrue, 2021. This book covers the impact of 12 kings on the country of Norway, and tells the story of how the country became what it is today. This is a great read for anyone wanting to dive deeper into Norway's Viking Age and beyond.

FICTION

Henrik Ibsen. *Hedda Gabler.* 1891. Perhaps the most famous play Ibsen wrote, after *A Doll's House, Hedda Gabler* is still critically acclaimed to this day. It is the story of a young woman feeling stuck in a life that seems perfect from the outside. Ibsen is considered one of the greatest playwrights since Shakespeare, and Hedda Gabler has been called the female counterpart to Hamlet.

Lise Lunge-Larsen. *The Troll With No Heart in His Body and Other Tales of Trolls from Norway.* University of Minnesota Press, 2013. Trolls figure prominently in Norwegian folklore, and all over the country you will find different tales and stories involving trolls. This collection of troll stories will give you a glimpse into Norwegian culture, and the stories Norwegian children still grow up hearing today.

Jo Nesbø. *The Snowman.* Knopf Publishing Group, 2011. Jo Nesbø has written several crime novels about police investigator Harry Hole, and *The Snowman* is perhaps the most bone-chilling and the most famous; it was adapted for an (English-language) movie starring Michael Fassbender and Rebecca Ferguson in 2017. In Oslo after the first snowfall of the year, Harry Hole has to solve a series of murders and disappearances where the only clues left relate to snowmen built by the killer.

Esther Sandström. *Nora: Huldra from the Fjords.* Norway's Best, 2019. The children's book is by a local writer from Flåm and edited (and translated) by the writer of this guidebook. It was inspired by the many tales in the fjord region about huldra, a mythological creature. The huldra is portrayed as a beautiful woman, and the only way to tell that she is not human is to notice that she has a cow's tail.

Film and TV

Norway's landscapes have often been the backdrop for Hollywood movies through the years, including scenes in *Star Wars: The Empire Strikes Back* (1980), *James Bond: No Time to Die* (2021), *Black Widow* (2021), *Mission Impossible: Fallout* (2018), and *Tenet* (2020). Norwegians are quite proud of this, and if you are ever at the movies with a Norwegian sitting somewhere in the audience, you might hear a gasp and excited whisper of, "That's in Norway!"

Additionally, the movies below are either Norwegian, or relevant for Norwegian history and culture. All are worth watching if you want to get a feel for the country through the screen before you go.

HISTORICAL

Veiviseren / Sàmi: Ofelas (1987). *Veiviseren (The Path Finder)* was the first Sàmi full-length movie ever to have been made and was nominated for an Oscar for best foreign film. It was inspired by Sàmi folklore and portrays how a young Sàmi man has to work with an enemy tribe as their pathfinder.

The Kautokeino Rebellion (2008). This movie is based on true events, and tells the story of the Kautokeino Rebellion in 1852, when a group of Sàmi people attacked representatives of the Norwegian government after years of oppression and abuse.

Max Manus (2008). *Max Manus* was a Norwegian activist during the Second World War. The movie is based on two of his (semibiographical) books, and depicts his work to actively sabotage the German occupying forces in Norway.

Kon-Tiki (2012). This is the Oscar-nominated story of Norwegian explorer Thor Heyerdahl and his crossing of the Pacific Ocean onboard the *Kon-Tiki* vessel in 1947.

Atlantic Crossing (2020). Set during World War II and the occupation of Norway, this is the tale of the royal family's escape across the Atlantic to the United States, and the influence of Crown Princess Märtha on President Roosevelt during the war.

POP CULTURE

Lilyhammer (2012). This is a funny, heartwarming television show starring Steven Van Zandt as a New York gangster who is sent to Lillehammer, Norway, as a part of the witness-protection program. The show depicts his misadventures around the city as he tries to adapt to Norwegian culture (and leave behind his criminal ways).

Bølgen / The Wave (2015). Norway's first disaster movie was based on events that could happen eventually: A large rockslide sends boulders tumbling into the Geirangerfjord, causing a massive tsunami to threaten the village of Geiranger. The movie was so popular that it inspired two disaster sequels: *The Quake* (2018) and *The Tunnel* (2019). They're all great movies, but it might be best to wait until after your trip to watch them.

Home for Christmas (2019). This is the first ever Norwegian Netflix Original Series and plays out as a typical romcom. Thirty-year-old Johanne is going home for the holidays and is tired of being single. So, she embarks on a 24-day journey to find a boyfriend by Christmas Eve.

Exit (2019). Produced by NRK (Norway's national broadcasting channel), *Exit* shocked the entire country when it was released in 2019. The series follows a group of disgustingly wealthy men working in the finance industry of Oslo and was created after a series of anonymous interviews in which people in the industry revealed the (somewhat appalling) behavior that goes on behind the scenes of the filthy rich. If you enjoyed *The Wolf of Wall Street,* you are sure to appreciate *Exit.* Just be warned: None of the main characters are likeable, and knowing that they are based on real people makes it an even harder pill to swallow.

Internet Resources

NEWS AND MEDIA
Norway Today
https://norwaytoday.com
Here you'll find news articles and updates relating to Norway and Scandinavia, all published in English.

The Local
www.thelocal.no
This popular news website in English publishes most of Norway's news from major outlets.

TRAVEL INFORMATION
Vegvesenet (The Norwegian Road Directory)
www.vegvesen.no
Visit this website before any road trip to check for potential road closures or roadwork that could affect your trip.

Visit Norway
www.visitnorway.no
The official tourism board of Norway offers a wealth of articles and inspiration for visiting Norway.

WEATHER
Pent
https://pent.no
Although it is in Norwegian, Pent should be an easy enough website to understand for English-speaking people as well. Enter your destination (Oslo, Bergen, Tromsø, Flåm, etc.) in the search bar on the site, and it will show you the weather forecasted by the two major (and rivaling) weather sites in Norway: Yr and Storm. With this website, you don't have to check the two separately; you can compare the two forecasts on one page (Storm is on the right, Yr is on the left). The actual weather usually ends up somewhere in the middle.

Index

List of Maps

Photo Credits

Get inspired for your next adventure

Follow @**moonguides** on Instagram or
subscribe to our newsletter at **moon.com**

#TravelWithMoon

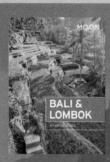
BALI & LOMBOK
CHANTAE REDEN

MOON
Tahiti
& FRENCH POLYNESIA
Chantae Reden

MOON
Japan
Jonathan DeHart

MOON
NEW ZEALAND
JAMIE CHRISTIAN DESPLACES

MOON
Baja
TIJUANA TO LOS CABOS
Jennifer Kramer

MOON
BELIZE
LEBAWIT LILY GIRMA

MOON
CARTAGENA
& COLOMBIA'S CARIBBEAN COAST

MOON
CHILE
STEPH DYSON

MOON
Costa Rica

MOON
Galápagos Islands
Elza Cho

MOON
ECUADOR
& THE GALÁPAGOS ISLANDS
BETHANY PITTS

MOON
TRIP OF A LIFETIME
MACHU PICCHU
With Lima, Cusco & the Sacred Valley
RYAN DUBE

MOON
OAXACA

MOON
TRIP OF A LIFETIME
PATAGONIA
Including the Falkland Islands
WAYNE BERNHARDSON

MOON
Puerto Vallarta
WITH SAYULITA, THE RIVIERA NAYARIT & COSTALEGRE

MOON
YUCATÁN PENINSULA

DOMINICAN
REPUBLIC

BAHAMAS

JAMAICA

MOON
Puerto
Rico

AMALFI
COAST

AMSTERDAM
BRUSSELS & BRUGES

EGYPT

Greek Islands
& ATHENS

Iceland

Morocco

NORMANDY
& BRITTANY

Portugal
WITH MADEIRA & THE AZORES

Croatia &
Slovenia
WITH MONTENEGRO

ROME,
FLORENCE
& VENICE

Scotland

SOUTHERN
ITALY

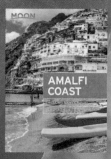
AMALFI COAST

AMSTERDAM
BRUSSELS & BRUGES

AZORES
CARRIE-MARIE BRATLEY

BARCELONA & MADRID
JESSICA JONES

Croatia & Slovenia
WITH MONTENEGRO
Shann Fountain Alguire

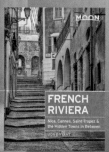
FRENCH RIVIERA
Nice, Cannes, Saint-Tropez & the Hidden Towns in Between

Greek Islands & ATHENS

Iceland
WITH A ROAD TRIP ON THE RING ROAD

More European Travel Guides from Moon

IRELAND
CAMILLE DE ANGELIS

NORMANDY & BRITTANY
CHRIS NEWENS
WITH MONT-SAINT-MICHEL

NORWAY
Lisa Stentvedt

Portugal
WITH MADEIRA & THE AZORES

PRAGUE, VIENNA & BUDAPEST
JENNIFER D. WALKER & AUBURN C. SCALLON

ROME, FLORENCE & VENICE

Scotland

SOUTHERN ITALY
LINDA SARRIS & LAURA THAYER
SICILY, PUGLIA, NAPLES & THE AMALFI COAST

MAP SYMBOLS

═══ Expressway	○ City/Town	ⓘ Information Center	▲ Park
═══ Primary Road	◉ State Capital		⅃ Golf Course
═══ Secondary Road	⊛ National Capital	�ｐ Parking Area	✛ Unique Feature
----- Unpaved Road		♦ Church	
--------- Trail	✪ Highlight	🍇 Winery/Vineyard	⍋ Waterfall
········· Ferry	★ Point of Interest	🚩 Trailhead	◭ Camping
━━━━ Railroad	• Accommodation	🚉 Train Station	▲ Mountain
▒▒▒ Pedestrian Walkway	▾ Restaurant/Bar	✈ Airport	⛷ Ski Area
▨▨▨ Stairs	■ Other Location	✕ Airfield	◌ Glacier

CONVERSION TABLES

°C = (°F - 32) / 1.8
°F = (°C x 1.8) + 32
1 inch = 2.54 centimeters (cm)
1 foot = 0.304 meters (m)
1 yard = 0.914 meters
1 mile = 1.6093 kilometers (km)
1 km = 0.6214 miles
1 fathom = 1.8288 m
1 chain = 20.1168 m
1 furlong = 201.168 m
1 acre = 0.4047 hectares
1 sq km = 100 hectares
1 sq mile = 2.59 square km
1 ounce = 28.35 grams
1 pound = 0.4536 kilograms
1 short ton = 0.90718 metric ton
1 short ton = 2,000 pounds
1 long ton = 1.016 metric tons
1 long ton = 2,240 pounds
1 metric ton = 1,000 kilograms
1 quart = 0.94635 liters
1 US gallon = 3.7854 liters
1 Imperial gallon = 4.5459 liters
1 nautical mile = 1.852 km

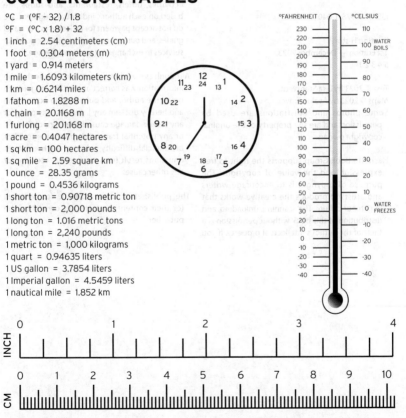

MOON NORWAY

Avalon Travel
Hachette Book Group
1700 Fourth Street
Berkeley, CA 94710, USA
www.moon.com

Editor: Grace Fujimoto
Managing Editor: Hannah Brezack
Copy Editor: Barbara Schultz
Graphics Coordinator: Ravina Schneider
Production Coordinator: Ravina Schneider
Cover Design: Toni Tajima
Interior Design: Domini Dragoone
Map Editor: Albert Angulo
Cartographers: John Culp, Bart Wright (Lohnes +
  Wright)
Proofreader: Brett Keener
Indexer: Rachel Lyon

ISBN-13: 978-1-64049-758-0

Printing History
1st Edition — December 2023
5 4 3 2 1

Front cover photo: northern lights over Hamnoy,
Lofoten Islands. © Boonchet Ch. | Gettyimages.com
Back cover photo: Gamle Bybro, Trondheim. ©
Saiko3p | Dreamstime.com

Printed in China by RR Donnelley